STRATEGY
SYNTHESIS

FOR LEADERS

The first four editions of Strategy Synthesis were co-authored by Bob de Wit and
Ron Meyer. The fifth edition was adapted by Bob de Wit.

CENGAGE
Learning·

Australia • Brazil • Mexico • Singapore • United Kingdom • United States

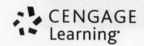

Strategy Synthesis: For Leaders, 5th Edition
Bob de Wit

Publisher: Annabel Ainscow

Commissioning Editor: Jenny Grene

Content Project Manager: Melissa Beavis

Manufacturing Manager: Eyvett Davis

Marketing Manager: Vicky Pavlicic

Typesetter: Lumina Datamatics

Cover design: Jeroen Brinkhuis

Text design: Lumina Datamatics

While the publisher has taken all reasonable care in the preparation of this book, the publisher makes no representation, express or implied, with regard to the accuracy of the information contained in this book and cannot accept any legal responsibility or liability for any errors or omissions from the book or the consequences thereof.

Products and services that are referred to in this book may be either trademarks and/or registered trademarks of their respective owners. The publishers and author/s make no claim to these trademarks. The publisher does not endorse, and accepts no responsibility or liability for, incorrect or defamatory content contained in hyperlinked material.

All the URLs in this book are correct at the time of going to press; however the Publisher accepts no responsibility for the content and continued availability of third party websites.

For product information and technology assistance, contact **emea.info@cengage.com**.

For permission to use material from this text or product, and for permission queries, email **emea.permissions@cengage.com**.

British Library Cataloguing-in-Publication Data
A catalogue record for this book is available from the British Library.

ISBN: 978-1-4737-2518-8

Cengage Learning EMEA
Cheriton House, North Way, Andover, Hampshire, SP10 5BE United Kingdom.

Cengage Learning products are represented in Canada by Nelson Education Ltd.

For your lifelong learning solutions, visit **www.cengage.co.uk**

Purchase your next print book or e-book at
www.cengagebrain.com

Printed in Croatia by Zrinski d.d.
Print Number 01   Print Year 2017

BRIEF CONTENTS

To Pam and Liz
and
Leen and Anneke
Family matters

CONTENTS

SECTION

I

STRATEGY   1

SECTION II

STRATEGY CONTENT

SECTION III

STRATEGY PROCESS

LIST OF EXHIBITS

ACKNOWLEDGEMENTS

The meaning of life is not to be discovered only after death in some hidden, mysterious realm; on the contrary, it can be found by eating the succulent fruit of the Tree of Life and by living in the here and now as fully and creatively as we can.

Paul Winter Kurtz (1925–2012), American skeptic and secular humanist

Only one professor should have been nominated as role model for students; only one colleague as university professor benchmark; only one human as friend exemplar; one man as perfect husband and father. He is the one who understood the meaning of life in full by eating the succulent fruit of the Tree of Life and by living in the here and now. I have worked with him in our early university career, and again many years later. This man has been contributing to the previous edition of this book, with the intention to cooperate in many editions more. Unfortunately, on 15 June 2015, while cycling up the Col du Galibier in the French Alps, enjoying life to the full, my colleague and friend Gep Eisenloeffel had a stroke and passed away in the arms of his wife Nienke. I miss him dearly still, and my thoughts remain with Nienke and their daughter Katrien.

Life went on of course, and apart from an empty heart I also had an empty diary. Summer 2015 was planned to start working with Gep on the next edition of this book, especially on the international perspective paragraphs. Katrien was so kind to donate Gep's library to the one who would take Gep's role in the next edition, and who also contributed to the previous edition: our brilliant student from Leiden University, Wester Wagenaar. He picked up the work, and although not yet as experienced as Gep, Wester did a marvellous job.

As in previous editions, this fifth edition brings together the work of great people in the management field – chiefly from the field of strategy. I thank them for creating new knowledge and insights, for their inspiration and hard work, and for developing the management field to where it is today. Writing this book would not have been possible without the current academic knowledge base and the writers of many phenomenal papers. I also apologize for not including all such excellent contributions in the book. As the architect of this edition, I read many excellent papers, but since there is a limitation to a book's size I could select only a few. It was simply not possible to include all the great papers and, therefore, several tough and (sometimes) personal choices had to be made.

I would like to thank the professors who select the book as the basis of class discussions, to help students develop their strategic mind. As in each revised edition, many improvements in this fifth edition are based on the feedback of professors who have used previous editions in their classrooms. I am grateful for their valuable insights and for sharing their experiences. Many thanks also to other academic colleagues: the anonymous reviewers of the manuscript and particularly Paul Knott, who has been so kind to update his great Fonterra short case again.

I would also like to thank all of my colleagues at Nyenrode Business University, including management, support staff and faculty and, particularly, my strategy department colleagues Jeroen van der Velden for updating the short case on 3M, Claudia Janssen for providing recent insights on the short case on TomTom, and Jeroen Brinkhuis. Jeroen Brinkhuis has helped develop the book's navigation tool *Tree of Strategy*, and has then spent many hours designing the book cover on the basis of the Tree of Strategy.

Developing this edition has also been an enormous effort by my Strategy Works team members, and particularly (in alphabetical order) Adriaan de Bruijn, Alexandra Fulea, Roel Meijers, Christien van Rijs, and Jasper de Vries. Their accomplishments have been significant, yet modest compared to all other contributions to our firm. I am extremely proud and grateful to be a member of this tremendous team. Special thanks to our research associate Sander Wisman. Sander has spent numerous hours – beyond duty and often working throughout the night until sunrise – reading and pre-selecting the growing number of publications and cases in the strategy field, and also co-developing short cases and illustrations. Not only has Sander been very committed, he also proved to be a safe pair of hands and a great brain, which is, in hindsight, not surprising as his main interest and thesis topic of his Leiden University study is cybersecurity.

Leiden University is also Wester Wagenaar's alma mater. While finishing his Japan studies, Wester had already been contributing to the previous edition of this book by co-developing short cases and illustrations, just before he moved to Nagasaki to finish his thesis. Then Wester went to study in Sweden, Germany and Japan for his Master's in Euroculture: Society, Politics and Culture in a Global Context. While in Uppsala, Sweden, our cooperation on this book resumed. This was in itself not surprising as it had been previously planned; however, the timing and magnitude of his contribution to this edition were not anticipated. Gep Eisenloeffel's demise in June 2015 was obviously an unpleasant and not envisioned surprise, but also marked the beginning of an intellectual cooperation with Wester. Although my expectations of Wester's academic talents were already high, he has exceeded even those. His academic performances are at peak professional standards – easily matching those of experienced academics, which, combined with his phenomenal linguistic capabilities, have significantly contributed to what I consider to be the best edition of this book ever. Apart from the already mentioned international perspective paragraphs, Wester has been co-authoring 16 short cases and illustrations.

I would also like to thank the Cengage Learning team I have worked with on this new edition. Particularly, I thank Andrew Ashwin for trusting me to develop the new editions, and Jennifer Grene for doing an incredible job in managing this great project. Also I will not forget the man who got us started over 20 years ago, our first editor, David Godden. Thank you all.

Finally, and most importantly, I would like to thank my family: my wife Pamela, my daughter Liz, my father Leen and his partner Anneke. Thank you so much. I promise that in the immediate future I will be eating the succulent fruit of the Tree of Life and be living in the here and now as fully and creatively as I can.

AUTHOR BIOGRAPHY:

Bob de Wit is Professor of Strategic Leadership at Nyenrode Business University, the Netherlands. He is also founder and director of Strategy Works and Strategy Academy in Rotterdam. Bob is a member of the *Journal of Change Management* Advisory Board, and a reviewer for the Strategic Management Society conference. His mission is to combine academic rigour and practical relevance.

Bob holds a Bachelor's degree in Psychology from Utrecht University, an MBA at the Interdisciplinary Institute Bedrijfskunde in Delft, and a PhD degree in Management Science from Erasmus University Rotterdam. After graduation he became a professor in strategic management at the Rotterdam School of Management, Erasmus University, teaching strategy in MSc programmes and the international MBA programme. In 1996 he started working at the Maastricht School of Management, a market leader in management education in non-Western countries. Since then, Bob has taught in over 40 countries on all continents. Bob has served as the Chairman of the interest group 'The Practice of Strategy' of the Strategic Management Society, and the Dutch Society for Strategic Decision Making (VSB), and has been a member of the Academic Council of the École Nationale des Ponts et Chaussées in Paris.

Bob passionately loves his wife Pamela and daughter Liz.

PREFACE

Not only is there an art in knowing a thing, but also a certain art in teaching it.

Cicero (106–43 BCE), Roman orator and statesman

What is a good strategy for teaching and learning about the topic of strategy? Judging by the similarity of the strategic management textbooks currently available, there seems to be a general consensus among business professors on the best approach to this task. It is not an exaggeration to say that strategic management education is dominated by a strong *industry recipe* (Spender, 1989). Almost all textbooks share the following characteristics:

- *Few differing perspectives.* Only a limited number of perspectives and theories are presented, often as accepted knowledge, from which prescriptions can easily be derived.

- *Step-by-step structure.* A step-by-step strategic planning approach is used as the books' basic structure, to decompose strategy-making into a number of simple sequential activities.

- *No primary material.* The key academic articles and books on strategy are reworked into the textbook authors' own words to create consistent and easily digestible pieces of text.

- *Domestic orientation.* Despite fancy subtitles referring to globalization, the choice of perspectives, theories, examples and cases are heavily biased towards the textbook authors' own domestic context.

It is interesting to speculate on the causes of this isomorphism in the 'strategic management education' industry. Institutionalists would probably point to the need for legitimacy, which leads textbook authors to conform to widely accepted practices and to avoid major innovations (e.g. Abrahamson, 1996; Powell and DiMaggio, 1991). Social psychologists would likely suggest that over the years shared cognitive structures have developed within the strategic management community, which makes the prevailing educational paradigm difficult to challenge (e.g. Smircich and Stubbart, 1985; Walsh, 1995). Theorists taking a new institutional economics perspective would probably interpret the uniformity of strategic management textbooks as a form of lock-in, caused by the large investments already made by publishers and business professors based on a shared educational 'standard' (e.g. Arthur, 1996; David, 1994). Whatever the reason, it is striking that the character of strategic management textbooks has not significantly changed since the founding of the field.

But what would strategy education look like if educational orthodoxy were to be actively challenged and the industry rules broken? How might strategy be taught if the current constraints were thrown aside and the teaching process was boldly reinvented? In short, what would happen if some strategic thinking were applied to the teaching of strategy?

During the last 20 years, we have continuously asked ourselves these questions. Our conclusion is that all four of the above features of current strategic management textbooks greatly inhibit the development of independent strategic thinkers and therefore urgently need to be changed. It is for this reason that we decided to create a book ourselves, with the following characteristics:

- *Multiple strategy perspectives.* A broad range of differing and often opposite perspectives and theories are presented, reflecting the richness of current debate among academics and practitioners in the field of strategic management.

- *Issue-based structure.* An issue-based book structure is used, with each chapter focusing on a key strategic issue, which is discussed from a variety of angles, leaving readers to draw their own conclusions.

- *Original readings.* A large number of original articles and book chapters are included, to offer readers a first-hand account of the ideas and theories of influential strategy thinkers.

- *International orientation.* A strong international orientation is at the core of this book, as reflected in the choice of topics, theories, readings, examples and cases.

In the following paragraphs, the rationale behind the choice for these characteristics is explained. Following this discussion, the structure of the book and the ways in which it can be employed are further clarified.

USING MULTIPLE STRATEGY PERSPECTIVES

Learning without thought is labour lost; thought without learning is perilous.

Confucius (551–479 BCE), Chinese teacher, editor, politician and philosopher

What should students learn in a strategic management or business policy course? It seems an obvious question to start with, especially for professors who teach about objective setting. Yet, in practice, the large majority of strategic management textbooks do not make their teaching objectives explicit. These books implicitly assume that the type of teaching objectives and teaching methods needed for a strategic management course do not radically differ from any other subject – basically, strategy can be taught in the same way as accounting or baking cookies. Their approach is based on the following teaching objectives:

- *Knowledge.* To get the student to clearly understand and memorize all of the major 'ingredients'.

- *Skills.* To develop the student's ability to follow the detailed 'recipes'.

- *Attitude.* To instill a disciplined frame of mind, whereby the student automatically attempts to approach all issues by following established procedures.

This is an important way of teaching – it is how all of us were taught to read and write, do arithmetic and drive a car. This type of teaching can be referred to as *instructional*, because students are told what to know and do. The instructor is the authority who has all of the necessary knowledge and skills, and it is his/her role to transfer these to the students. Thus, the educational emphasis is on communicating know-how and ensuring that students are able to repeat what they have heard. Students are not encouraged to question the knowledge they receive – on the contrary, it is the intention of instructional teaching to get students to absorb an accepted body of knowledge and to follow established recipes. The student should *accept*, *absorb* and *apply*.

However, while instructing students on a subject and programming their behaviour might be useful in such areas as mathematics, cooking and karate, we believe it is not a very good way of teaching strategy. In our opinion, a strategic management professor should have a different set of teaching objectives:

- *Knowledge.* To encourage the understanding of the many, often conflicting, schools of thought and to facilitate developing insight into the assumptions, possibilities and limitations of each set of theories.

- *Skills.* To develop the student's ability to define strategic issues, to critically reflect on existing theories, to creatively combine or develop conceptual models where necessary and to flexibly employ theories where useful.

- *Attitude.* To instill a critical, analytical, flexible and creative mindset that challenges organizational, industry and national paradigms and problem-solving recipes.

In other words, strategy professors should want to achieve the opposite of instructors – not to instill recipes, but rather to encourage students to dissect and challenge recipes. Strategic thinking is in its very essence questioning, challenging, unconventional and innovative. These aspects of strategic thinking cannot be transferred through instruction. A critical, analytical, flexible and creative state of mind must be developed by practising these very qualities. Hence, a learning situation must encourage students to be critical, must challenge them to be analytical, must force them to be mentally flexible and must demand creativity and unconventional thinking. Students cannot be instructed to be strategists, but must learn the art of strategy by thinking and acting themselves – they must *discuss*, *deliberate* and *do*. The role of the professor is to create the circumstances for this learning. We therefore refer to this type of teaching as *facilitative*.

This teaching philosophy has led to a radical departure from traditional textbooks that focus on knowledge transfer and application skills, and that have often been written from the perspective of just one paradigm. In this book, the fundamental differences of opinion within strategic management are not ignored or smoothed over. On the contrary, an important objective of this book is to expose students to the many, often opposite, perspectives in the field of strategy. It is our experience that the challenge of comparing and reconciling rivalling strategy perspectives sharpens the mind of the 'apprentice' strategists. Throwing students into the middle of the central strategy debates, while simultaneously demanding that they apply their thinking to practical strategic problems, is the most likely way to enhance the qualities of creativity, flexibility, independence and analytical depth that students will need to become true strategic thinkers.

FOCUSING ON STRATEGY ISSUES

Some people are so good at learning the tricks of the trade that they never get to learn the trade.

Sam Levenson (1911–1980), American teacher and comedian

While it is the objective of this book to increase students' strategic thinking abilities by exposing them to a wide range of theories and perspectives, it is not the intention to confuse and disorient. Yet in a subject area like strategic management, in which there is a broad spectrum of different views, there is a realistic threat that students might go deaf listening to the cacophony of different opinions. The variety of ideas can easily become overwhelming and difficult to integrate.

For this reason, the many theories, models, approaches and perspectives have been clustered around 11 central strategy issues, each of which is discussed in a separate chapter. These 11 strategy issues represent the key questions with which strategists must deal in practice. Only the theorists whose ideas have a direct bearing on the issue at hand are discussed in each chapter.

The advantage of this issue-based book structure is that it is *decision-oriented* – each chapter is about a key type of strategic decision that needs to be made. Students are challenged to look at a strategic issue holistically, taking various aspects and perspectives into account, and to arrive at a proposed course of action. This type of decision focus closely reflects what strategizing managers need to do in practice. Step-by-step books are much more *tool-oriented*, teaching students how to go through each phase of a strategic planning process and how to use each analysis framework – useful, especially for junior analysts, but unlikely to stimulate real strategic thinking and to provide insight into difficult strategic choices.

Within each chapter, the opposing perspectives on how the strategic issue should be approached are contrasted with one another by staging a virtual 'debate'. Two opposite perspectives are presented to kick off the debate and highlight areas of disagreement, after which the students (and their professors) are invited to further debate the issue and decide on the value and limitations of each point of view.

The advantage of this debate-based chapter structure is that it encourages the students' engagement and provokes critical thinking. As students need to determine the strengths and weaknesses of each strategy perspective, they also become more adept at combining different 'lenses' to gain a fuller understanding of a problem, while becoming more skilled at balancing and mixing prescriptions to find innovative solutions to these problems. Some students will feel ill at ease not being presented with the 'right approach' or the 'best practice', as they are used to getting in many other books. This is all the more reason to avoid giving them one – as strategizing managers, the security of one truth won't get them far, so it is preferable to learn to deal with (and benefit from) a variety of opinions as soon as possible.

While the intention is not to present the 'right answer' or provide a 'grand unifying theory', the chapter offers a third view on the issue that combines elements of both perspectives. Not only leaders take elements of both perspectives into account to manage the issue at hand, increasingly strategy theorists also do. Recent works of thought leaders in the strategy field address a third way of dealing with the issue, not by choosing one of the opposite perspectives, but by providing possible routes on how to deal with opposites. This third view is meant to stimulate students' strategic thinking to find innovative and creative resolutions to the problem, but still students must make up their own minds, depending on the context and based on the arguments placed before them.

TAKING AN INTERNATIONAL PERSPECTIVE

Be bent, and you will remain straight.
Be vacant, and you will remain full.
Be worn, and you will remain new.

Lao Tzu (6th century BCE), philosopher of ancient China

This book has been explicitly developed with an international audience in mind. For students, the international orientation of this book has a number of distinct advantages:

- *Cross-cultural differences.* Although there has been relatively little cross-cultural research in the field of strategy, results so far indicate that there are significant differences in strategy styles between companies from different countries. This calls into question the habit among strategy researchers of presenting universal theories, without indicating the cultural assumptions on which their ideas have been based. It is not unlikely that strategy theories have a strong cultural bias and therefore cannot be simply transferred from one national setting to another. Much of the debate going on between strategy theorists might actually be based on such divergent cultural assumptions. In this book the issue of cross-cultural differences in strategy style is raised in each chapter, to discuss whether strategists need to adapt their theories, perspectives and approaches to the country in which they are operating.

- *International context.* Besides adapting to a specific country, many companies are operating in a variety of countries at the same time. In this international arena they are confronted with a distinct set of issues, ranging from global integration and coordination, to localization and transnationalization. This set of issues presented by the international context is debated in depth in Chapter 12.

CONTACT US

A stand can be made against invasion by an army; no stand can be made against invasion by an idea.

Victor Hugo (1802–1885), French poet, novelist and playwright

Books are old-fashioned, but based on a proven technology that is still the most appropriate under most circumstances. One drawback, however, is that a book is unidirectional, allowing us to send a message to you, but not capable of transmitting your comments, questions and suggestions back to us. This is unfortunate, as we are keen on communicating with our audience and enjoy hearing what works and doesn't work 'in the field'.

Therefore, we would like to encourage both students and professors to establish contact with us. You can do this by visiting our online support resources to check out the extra features we have for you and to leave your comments and suggestions. But you can also contact us directly by email at b.dewit@nyenrode.nl.

REFERENCES

Abrahamson, E. (1996) 'Management fashion', *Academy of Management Review*, 21, pp. 254–285.

Arthur, W.B. (1996) 'Increasing returns and the new world of business', *Harvard Business Review*, July/August, pp. 100–109.

David, P.A. (1994) 'Why are institutions the "carriers of history"?: Path dependence and the evolution of conventions, organizations and institutions', *Structural Change and Economic Dynamics*, pp. 205–220.

Powell, W.W. and DiMaggio, P.P. (eds.) (1991) *The New Institutionalism in Organization Analysis*, Chicago, IL: University of Chicago Press.

Smircich, L. and Stubbart, C. (1985) 'Strategic management in an enacted world', *Academy of Management Review*, 10, pp. 724–736.

Spender, J.C. (1989) *Industry Recipes: The Nature and Sources of Managerial Judgement*, Oxford: Basil Blackwell.

Walsh, J. (1995) 'Managerial and organizational cognition: Notes from a trip down memory lane', *Organization Science*, 6, pp. 280–321.

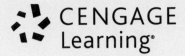

Digital Support Resources

All of our Higher Education textbooks are accompanied by a range of digital support resources. Each title's resources are carefully tailored to the specific needs of the particular book's readers. Examples of the kind of resources provided include:

- A password protected area for instructors with, for example, a testbank, PowerPoint slides and an instructor's manual.

- An open-access area for students including, for example, useful weblinks and multiple choice questions.

Lecturers: to discover the dedicated lecturer digital support resources accompanying this textbook, please register here for access: login.cengage.com.

Students: to discover the dedicated student digital support resources accompanying this textbook, please search for **Strategy Synthesis: For Leaders** on: cengagebrain. co.uk

STRATEGY

1

INTRODUCTION

As conflict – difference – is here in the world, as we cannot avoid it, we should, I think, use it.

Mary Parker Follett (1868–1933), American social worker, management consultant and pioneer in organizational theory and organizational behaviour

THE NATURE OF STRATEGY

In a book entitled *Strategy*, it seems reasonable to expect Chapter 1 to begin with a clear definition of strategy that would be employed with consistency in all subsequent chapters. An early and precise definition would help to avoid conflicting interpretations of what should be considered strategy and, by extension, what should be understood by the term 'strategic management'. However, any such sharp definition of strategy here would actually be misleading. It would suggest that there is widespread agreement among practitioners, researchers and theorists as to what strategy is. The impression would be given that the fundamental concepts in the area of strategy are generally accepted and hardly questioned. Yet, even a quick glance through current strategy literature indicates otherwise. There are strongly differing opinions on most of the key issues, and the disagreements run so deep that even a common definition of the term 'strategy' is illusive.

This is bad news for those who prefer simplicity and certainty. It means that the topic of strategy cannot be explained as a set of straightforward definitions and rules to be memorized and applied. The strongly conflicting views mean that strategy cannot be summarized into broadly agreed-on definitions, rules, matrices and flow diagrams that one must simply absorb and learn to use. If the fundamental differences of opinion are not swept aside, the consequence is that a book on strategy cannot be like an instruction manual that takes you through the steps of how something should be done. On the contrary, a strategy book should acknowledge the disagreements and encourage thinking about the value of each of the different points of view. That is the intention of this book.

The philosophy embraced here is that an understanding of the topic of strategy can only be gained by grappling with the diversity of insights presented by so many prominent thinkers and by coming to terms with the fact that there is no simple answer to the question of what strategy is. Readers who prefer the certainty of reading only one opinion, as opposed to the intellectual stimulation of being confronted with a wide variety, should read no further – there are plenty of alternatives available. Those who wish to proceed should lay aside their 'opinions of habit', and open their minds to the many other opinions presented, for in these pages there is 'knowledge in the making'.

IDENTIFYING THE STRATEGY ISSUES

If the only tool you have is a hammer, you treat everything like a nail.

Abraham Maslow (1908–1970), American psychologist

The approach taken in this book is in line with the moral of Maslow's remark. To avoid hammering strategy issues with only one theory, a variety of ways of viewing strategic questions will be presented. But there are two different ways of presenting a broad spectrum of theoretical lenses. This point can be made clear by extending Maslow's hammer-and-nail analogy. To become a good carpenter, who wisely uses a variety of tools depending on what is being crafted, an apprentice carpenter will need to learn about these different instruments. One way is for the apprentice to study the characteristics and functioning of all tools individually and only then to apply each where appropriate. However, another possibility is for the apprentice to first learn about what must be crafted, getting a feel for the materials and the problems that must be solved and only then to turn to the study of the necessary tools. The first approach to learning can be called 'tools-driven' – understanding each tool comes first, while combining them to solve real problems comes later. The second approach to learning can be termed 'problem-driven' – understanding problems comes first, while searching for the appropriate tools is based on the type of problem.

Both options can also be used for the apprentice strategist. In a tools-driven approach to learning about strategy, all major theories would first be understood separately, to be compared or combined later when using them in practice. A logical structure for a book aiming at this mode of learning would be to allot one chapter to each of the major theories or schools of thought. The advantage of such a theory-based book structure would be that each chapter would focus on giving the reader a clear and cohesive overview of one major theory within the field of strategy. For readers with an interest in grasping the essence of each theory individually, this would probably be the ideal book format. However, the principal disadvantage of a theory-by-theory summary of the field of strategy would be that the reader would not have a clear picture of how the various theories relate to one another. The apprentice strategist would be left with important questions such as: Where do the theories agree and where do they differ? Which strategy phenomena does each theory claim to explain and which phenomena are left unaccounted for? Can various theories be successfully combined or are they based on mutually exclusive assumptions? And which strategy is right, or at least most appropriate under particular circumstances? Not knowing the answers to these questions, how could the apprentice strategist try to apply these new theoretical tools to practice?

This book is based on the assumption that the reader wants to learn to actively resolve strategic problems. Understanding the broad spectrum of theories is not an end in itself, but a means for more effective strategizing. Therefore, the problem-driven approach to learning about strategy has been adopted. In this approach, key strategy issues are first identified and then each is looked at from the perspective of the most appropriate theories. This has resulted in an issue-based book structure, in which each chapter deals with one particular set of strategy issues. In each chapter, only the theories that shed some light on the issues under discussion are brought forward and compared to one another. Of course, some theories are relevant to more than one set of issues and therefore appear in various chapters.

In total, 11 sets of strategy issues have been identified that together largely cover the field of strategic management. These 11 will be the subjects of the remaining chapters of this book. How the various strategy issues have been divided into these 11 sets are explained in the following paragraphs.

Strategizing, missioning and visioning

Section I of this book addresses two important inputs for strategy: the cognitive processes of individual strategists (strategizing) and purpose as the impetus for strategy activities (missioning and visioning).

It is widely presumed that strategists are rational actors who identify, determine, evaluate, choose, translate and carry out, based on rigorous logic and extensive knowledge of all important factors. This belief has been challenged, however. Many authors have criticized the strong emphasis on rationality in these traditional views of the strategizing process. Some writers have even argued that the true nature of strategic thinking is more intuitive and creative than rational. In their opinion, strategizing is about perceiving strengths and weaknesses, envisioning opportunities and threats, and creating the future, for which imagination and judgement are more important than analysis and logic. This constitutes quite a fundamental disagreement about the cognitive processes of the strategizing leader. These issues surrounding the nature of strategic thinking will be discussed in Chapter 2, on strategizing.

Making strategy is not an end in itself, but a means for reaching particular objectives. Organizations exist to fulfil a purpose and strategies are employed to ensure that the organizational mission and vision are realized. Oddly enough, most authors write about missions and visions without any reference to the organizational purpose being pursued. It is generally assumed that all organizations exist for the same basic reasons and that this purpose is self-evident. However, in reality, there is extensive disagreement about what the current purposes of organizations are, and especially about what their purpose should be. Some people argue that it is the business of business to make money. In their view, firms are owned by shareholders and therefore should pursue shareholders' interests. And it is the primary interest of shareholders to see the value of their stocks increase. By way of contrast, others believe that companies exist to serve the interests of multiple stakeholders. In their opinion, having a financial stake in a firm should not give shareholders a dominant position vis-à-vis other groups that also have an interest in what the organization does. Other stakeholders usually include employees, customers, suppliers and bankers, but could also include the local community, the broader industry and even the natural environment. These issues on the organizational purpose will be discussed in Chapter 3, on missioning and visioning.

Strategy dimensions: Content, process and context

The most fundamental distinction made in this book is between strategy content, strategy process and strategy context (see Figure 1.1). These are the three dimensions of strategy that can be recognized in every real-life strategic problem situation. They can be generally defined as follows:

- Strategy content. The combined decisions and choices that lead a company into the future are referred to as the strategy content. Stated in terms of a question, strategy content is concerned with the *what* of strategy: What is, and should be, the strategy for the company and each of its constituent units?

- Strategy process. The manner in which strategies come about is referred to as the strategy process. Stated in terms of a number of questions, strategy process is concerned with the *how*, *who* and *when* of strategy: How is, and should, strategy be made, analysed, dreamt up, formulated, implemented, changed and controlled; who is involved; and when do the necessary activities take place?

- Strategy context. The set of circumstances under which both the strategy content and the strategy process are determined is referred to as the strategy context. Stated in terms of a question, strategy context is concerned with the *where* of strategy: Where (that is in which firm and which environment) are the strategy process and strategy content embedded?

It cannot be emphasized enough that strategy content, process and context are not different parts of strategy, but are distinguishable dimensions. Just as it is silly to speak of the length, width and height parts of a box, one cannot speak of the three parts of strategy either. Each strategic problem situation is by its nature three-dimensional, possessing process, content and context characteristics, and only the understanding of all three dimensions will give the strategist real depth of comprehension. In particular, it must be

FIGURE 1.1   Dimensions of strategy and the organizational purpose

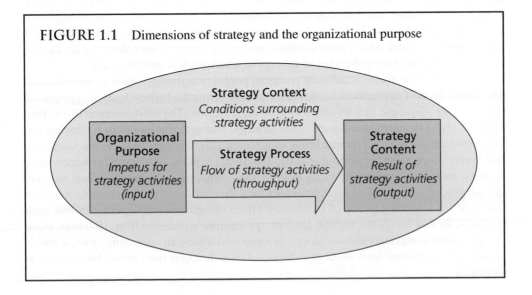

acknowledged that the three dimensions interact (Ketchen, Thomas and McDaniel, 1996; Pettigrew and Whipp, 1991). For instance, the manner in which the strategy process is organized will have a significant impact on the resulting strategy content, while likewise, the content of the current strategy will strongly influence the way in which the strategy process will be conducted in future. If these linkages are ignored, the strategist will have a flat view instead of a three-dimensional view of strategy. A useful analytical distinction for temporarily unravelling a strategic problem situation will have turned into a permanent means for fragmenting reality.

However, it is possible to concentrate on one of the strategy dimensions if the other two are kept in mind. In fact, to have a focused discussion it is even necessary to look at one dimension at a time. The alternative is a debate in which all topics on all three dimensions would be discussed simultaneously: Such a cacophony of opinions would be lively, but most likely less than fruitful. Therefore, the content–process–context distinction is cautiously used as the main structuring principle of this book, splitting the text into three major sections.

Most strategy research, by its very nature, is more atomistic than holistic, focusing on just a few variables at once. Consequently, most writings on strategy, including most of the theories discussed in this book, tend to favour just one, or at most two, strategy dimensions, which is usually complex enough given the need to remain comprehensible. In particular, the divide between strategy content and strategy process has been quite pronounced, to the extent of worrying some scholars about whether the connections between the two are being sufficiently recognized (Pettigrew, 1992). Although sharing this concern, use of the content–process–context–purpose distinction here reflects the reality of the current state of debate within the field of strategic management.

Strategy content: Business, corporate and network levels

Section II of this book will deal with the strategy content. Strategies come in all shapes and sizes, and almost all strategy writers, researchers and practitioners agree that each strategy is essentially unique. There is widespread disagreement, however, about the principles to which strategies should adhere. The debates are numerous, but there are three fundamental sets of issues around which most conflicts generally centre. These three topics can be clarified by distinguishing the level of strategy at which each is most relevant.

Strategies can be made for different groups of people or activities within an organization. The lowest level of aggregation is one person or task, while the highest level of aggregation encompasses all people or activities within an organization. The most common distinction between levels of aggregation made in the strategic management literature is between the functional, business and corporate levels (see Figure 1.2). Strategy issues at the *functional level* refer to questions regarding specific functional aspects of a company (operations strategy, marketing strategy, financial strategy, etc.). Strategy at the *business level* requires the integration of functional level strategies for a distinct set of products and/or services intended for a specific group of customers. Often companies only operate in one such business, so that this is the highest level of aggregation within the firm. However, there are also many companies that are in two or more businesses. In such companies, a multi-business or *corporate level* strategy is required, which aligns the various business level strategies.

FIGURE 1.2   The levels of strategy

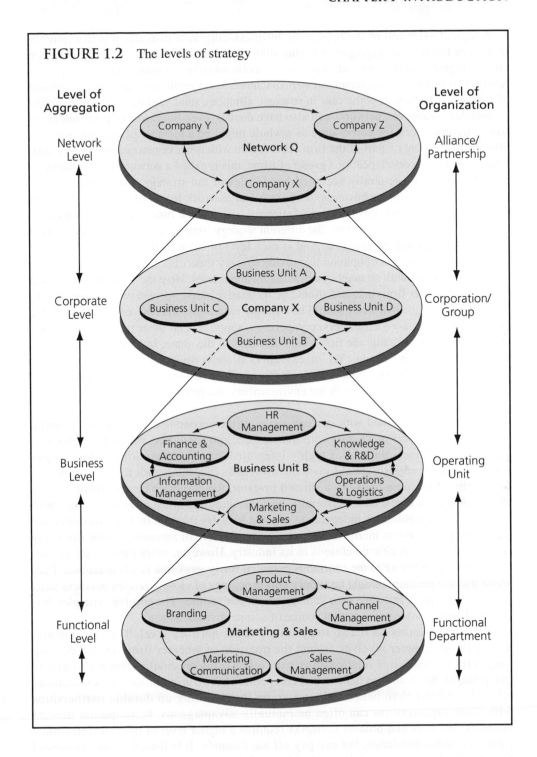

Level of
Aggregation

Level of
Organization

Network
Level

Alliance/
Partnership

Corporate
Level

Corporation/
Group

Business
Level

Operating
Unit

Functional
Level

Functional
Department

Company Y

Company Z

Network Q

Company X

Business Unit A

Business Unit C   Company X   Business Unit D

Business Unit B

HR
Management

Finance &
Accounting

Knowledge
& R&D

Business Unit B

Information
Management

Operations
& Logistics

Marketing
& Sales

Product
Management

Branding

Channel
Management

Marketing & Sales

Marketing
Communication

Sales
Management

A logical extension of the functional–business–corporate distinction is to explicitly recognize the level of aggregation higher than the individual organization. Firms often cluster together into groups of two or more collaborating organizations. This level is referred to as the multi-company or *network level*. Most multi-company groups consist of only a few parties, as is the case in strategic alliances, joint ventures and value-adding partnerships. However, networks can also have dozens, even hundreds, of participants. In some circumstances, the corporation as a whole might be a member of a group, while in other situations only a part of the firm joins forces with other organizations. In all cases, when a strategy is developed for a group of firms, this is called a network level strategy.

In line with the generally accepted boundaries of the strategic management field, this book focuses on the business, corporate and network levels of strategy, although this will often demand consideration of strategy issues at the functional level as well. In Section II, on the strategy content, the different strategy issues encountered at the different levels of strategy will be explored. And at each level of strategy, the focus will be on the fundamental differences of opinion that divide strategy theorists.

Chapter 4 deals with strategy issues at the business level. Here the fundamental debate surrounds whether firms are, and should be, primarily market-driven or resource-driven. Some authors argue that firms should be strongly externally oriented, engaged in a game of positioning vis-à-vis customers, competitors, suppliers and other parties in the environment, and should adapt the firm to the demands of the game. In other words, companies should think 'outside-in'. Yet, other authors strongly disagree, stressing the need for companies to exploit and expand their strengths. They recommend a more 'inside-out' view, whereby companies search for environments and positions that best fit with their resource base.

Chapter 5 is concerned with strategy issues at the corporate level. The fundamental debate in this chapter is whether corporations are, and should be, run as federations of autonomous business units or as highly integrated organizations. Some authors argue that corporate strategists should view themselves as investors, with financial stakes in a portfolio of business units. As a shrewd investor, the corporate centre should buy up cheap companies, divest underperforming business units and invest its business units with the highest profit potential, independent of what industry they are in. Each business unit should be judged on its merits and given a large measure of autonomy, to be optimally responsive to the specific conditions in its industry. However, other authors are at odds with this view, pointing to the enormous potential for synergy that is left untapped. They argue that corporations should be tightly knit groupings of closely related business units that share resources and align their strategies with one another. The ensuing synergies, it is expected, will provide an important source of competitive advantage.

Chapter 6 focuses on the strategy issues at the network level. The fundamental debate in this chapter revolves around the question of whether firms should develop long-term collaborative relationships with other firms or should remain essentially independent. Some authors believe that competition between organizations is sometimes more destructive than beneficial, and argue that building up durable partnerships with other organizations can often be mutually advantageous. Participation in joint ventures, alliances and broader networks requires a higher level of inter-organizational trust and interdependence, but can pay off handsomely. It is therefore recommended to selectively engage in joint – that is, multi-company – strategy development. Other authors, however, are thoroughly sceptical about the virtues of interdependence.

They prefer independence, pointing to the dangers of opportunistic partners and creeping dependence on the other. Therefore, it is recommended to avoid multi-company level strategy development and only to use alliances as a temporary measure.

Again, it must be emphasized that the analytical distinction employed here should not be interpreted as an absolute means for isolating issues. In reality, these three levels of strategy do not exist as tidy categories, but are strongly interrelated and partially overlapping. As a consequence, the three sets of strategy issues identified above are also linked to one another. In Section III, it will become clear that taking a stand in one debate will affect the position that one can take in others.

Strategy process: Forming, changing and innovating

Section III of this book will deal with the strategy process. Traditionally, most textbooks have portrayed the strategy process as a basically linear progression through a number of distinct steps. Usually a split is made between the strategy analysis stage, the strategy formulation stage and the strategy implementation stage. In the analysis stage, strategists identify the opportunities and threats in the environment, as well as the strengths and weaknesses of the organization. Next, in the formulation stage, strategists determine which strategic options are available to them, evaluate each and choose one. Finally, in the implementation stage, the selected strategic option is translated into a number of concrete activities, which are then carried out.

The division of the strategy process into a number of sequential phases has drawn heavy criticism from authors who believe that in reality, no such identifiable stages exist. They dismiss the linear analysis–formulation–implementation distinction as an unwarranted simplification, arguing that the strategy process is messier, with analysis, formulation and implementation activities going on all the time, thoroughly intertwined with one another. In their view, organizations do not first make strategic plans and then execute them as intended. Rather, strategies are usually formed incrementally, as organizations think and act in small iterative steps, letting strategies emerge as they go along. This represents quite a difference of opinion on how strategies are formed within organizations. These issues surrounding the nature of strategy formation are discussed in Chapter 7.

Another major assumption of the traditional view, that strategy is made for the entire organization and everything can be radically changed all at once, has also been challenged. Many authors have pointed out that it is unrealistic to suppose that a company can be boldly redesigned. They argue that it is terribly difficult to orchestrate an overarching strategy for the entire organization that is a significant departure from the current course of action. It is virtually impossible to get various aspects of an organization all lined up to go through a change at the same time, certainly if a radical change is intended. In practice, different aspects of an organization will be under different pressures, on different timetables and have different abilities to change, leading to a differentiated approach to change. Moreover, the rate and direction of change will be seriously limited by the cultural, political and cognitive inheritance of the firm. Hence, it is argued, strategic change is usually more gradual and fragmented than radical and coordinated. The issues surrounding this difference of opinion on the nature of strategic change will be discussed in Chapter 8.

The traditional focus on improving efficiency of current products, services and business models has also been challenged. Many authors argue that companies need constant

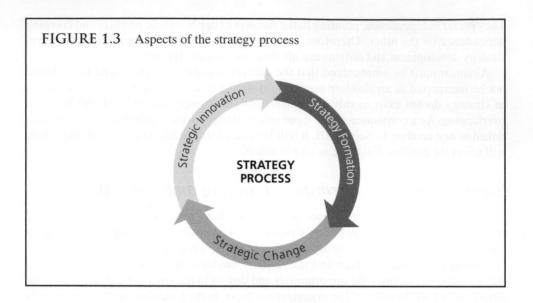

FIGURE 1.3   Aspects of the strategy process

renewal by developing new products, services and business models. Although improved efficiency of the present is important in organizational processes, enhancing effectiveness of innovation processes to secure the future is what managers should be focusing on. Exploring in uncharted waters may be costly and results are not guaranteed, but in order to be able to be efficient in the future, managers need to ensure the company has a future. The issues surrounding this difference of opinion on the nature of strategic innovation are discussed in Chapter 9.

These three chapter topics – strategy formation, strategic change and strategic innovation – do not constitute entirely separate subjects. Let it be clear that they are not phases, stages or elements of the strategy process that can be understood in isolation. Strategy formation, strategic change and strategic innovation are different aspects of the strategy process, which are strongly linked and partially overlapping (see Figure 1.3). They have been selected because they are sets of issues on which there is significant debate within the field of strategy. As will become clear, having a particular opinion on one of these aspects will have a consequence for views held on all other aspects as well.

Strategy context: Industry, organizational and international

Section IV in this book is devoted to the strategy context. Strategy researchers, writers and practitioners largely agree that every strategy context is unique. Moreover, they are almost unanimous that it is usually wise for managers to strive for a fit between the strategy process, strategy content and the specific circumstances prevalent in the strategy context. However, disagreement arises as soon as the discussion turns to the details of the alignments. Does the context determine what the strategizing manager must do, or can the manager actually shape the context? Some people argue or assume that the strategy context has a dynamic all on its own, which strategists can hardly influence, and

FIGURE 1.4   Aspects of the strategy context

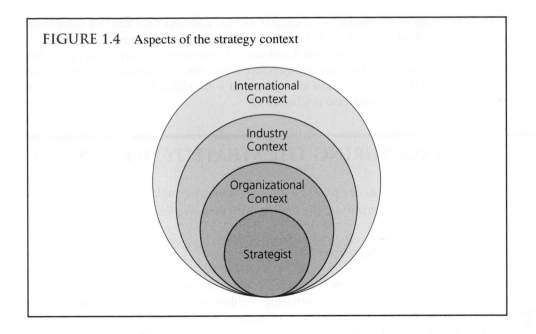

therefore that the strategy context sets strict confines on the freedom to manoeuvre. The context is not malleable and hence the motto for the strategist is 'adapt or die'. Others believe that strategists should not be driven by the context, but have a large measure of freedom to set their own course of action. It is frequently argued that strategizing managers can, and should, create their own circumstances, instead of being enslaved by the circumstances they find. In short, the strategy context can be determined, instead of letting it determine.

In Section IV, the difference of opinion hinges on the power of the context to determine strategy surfaces when discussing the various aspects of the strategy context. The section has been split into three chapters, each focusing on a different aspect of the strategy context. Two distinctions have been used to arrive at the division into three chapters (see Figure 1.4). The first dichotomy employed is that between the organization and its industry environment. The *industry context* is the subject of Chapter 10. In this chapter, the strategic issues revolve around the question of whether the industry circumstances set the rules with which companies must comply, or whether companies have the freedom to choose their own strategy and even change the industry conditions. The *organizational context* is dealt with in Chapter 11. Here, the key strategic issues have to do with the question of whether the organizational circumstances largely determine the strategy process and strategy content followed, or whether the strategist has a significant amount of control over the course of action adopted.

The second dichotomy employed relates to the difference between the domestic and the international strategy context. The domestic context does not raise any additional strategic issues, but the *international context* clearly does. Strategists must deal with the question of whether adaptation to the diversity of the international context is strictly required or whether companies have considerable freedom to choose their strategy process and content irrespective of the international context. The difference of opinion between writers on the international context actually goes one step further. Some authors predict that the diversity of the international context will decline over time and that companies can encourage this process. If global convergence takes place, it is argued, adaptation to the international context will become a non-issue. Other authors, however, disagree that international diversity is declining and therefore argue that the international context will remain an issue that strategists must attempt to deal with. This debate on the future of the international context is conducted in Chapter 12.

STRUCTURING THE STRATEGY DEBATES

Where there is much desire to learn, there of necessity will be much arguing, much writing, many opinions; for opinion in good men is but knowledge in the making.

John Milton (1608–1674), English poet

Every real-life strategic problem is complex. Most of the strategic issues outlined earlier in this chapter are present in every strategic problem, making the prospect of a simple solution an illusion. Yet, even if each set of strategy issues is considered independently, it seems that strategy theorists cannot agree on the right way to approach them. On each of the topics there is widespread disagreement, indicating that no simple solution can be expected here either.

Why is it that theorists cannot agree on how to solve strategic problems? Might it be that some theorists are right, while others are just plain wrong? In that case, it would be wise for problem-solvers to select the valid theory and discard the false ones. While this might be true in some cases, it seems unlikely that false theories would stay around long enough to keep a lively debate going. Eventually, the right (i.e. unfalsified) theory would prevail and disagreements would disappear. Yet, this does not seem to be happening in the field of strategy.

Could it be that each theorist only emphasizes one aspect of an issue – only takes one cut of a multi-faceted reality? In that case, it would be wise for problem-solvers to combine the various theories that approach the problem from a different angle. However, if this were true, one would expect the different theories to be largely complementary. Each theory would simply be a piece in the bigger puzzle of strategic management. Yet, this does not explain why there is so much disagreement, and even contradiction, within the field of strategy.

It could also be that strategy theorists start from divergent assumptions about the nature of each strategy issue and therefore logically arrive at a different perspective on how to solve strategic problems. In that case, it would be wise for problem-solvers to combine the various theories, in order to look at the problem from a number of different angles.

All three possibilities for explaining the existing theoretical disagreements should be kept open. However, entertaining the thought that divergent positions are rooted in fundamentally different assumptions about strategy issues is by far the most fruitful to the strategist confronted with complex problems. It is too simple to hope that one can deal with the contradictory opinions within the field of strategy by discovering which strategy theories are right and which are wrong. But it is also not particularly practical to accept all divergent theories as valid depictions of different aspects of reality – if two theories suggest a different approach to the same problem, the strategist will have to sort out this contradiction. Therefore, in this book the emphasis is on surfacing the basic assumptions underlying the major theoretical perspectives on strategy, and debating whether, or under which circumstances, these assumptions are appropriate.

Assumptions about strategy tensions

At the heart of every set of strategic issues, a fundamental tension between apparent opposites can be identified. For instance, in Chapter 6 on network level strategy, the issues revolve around the fundamental tension between competition and cooperation. In Chapter 10 on the industry context, the fundamental tension between the opposites of compliance and choice lies at the centre of the subject (see Figure 1.5). Each pair of opposites creates a tension, as they seem to be inconsistent, or even incompatible, with one another; it seems as if both elements cannot be fully true at the same time. If firms are competing, they are not cooperating. If firms must comply with the industry context, they have no choice. Yet, although these opposites confront strategizing managers with conflicting pressures, somehow they must be dealt with simultaneously. Strategists are caught in a bind, trying to cope with contradictory forces at the same time.

The challenge of strategists is to wrestle with these tricky strategy tensions. All strategy theories make assumptions, explicitly or implicitly, about the nature of these tensions and devise ways in which to deal with them. However, every theorist's assumptions differ, giving rise to a wide variety of positions. In fact, many of the major disagreements within

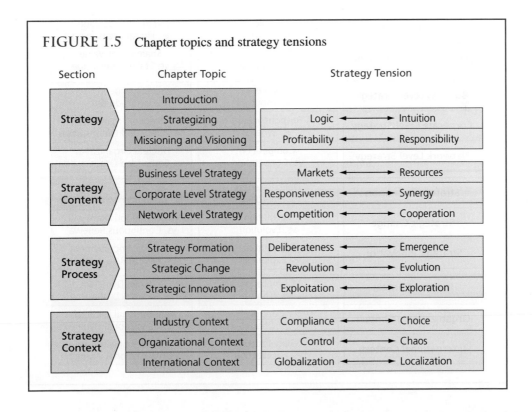

FIGURE 1.5   Chapter topics and strategy tensions

the field of strategic management are rooted in the different assumptions made about coping with these strategy tensions. For this reason, the theoretical debate in each chapter will be centred around the different perspectives on dealing with a particular strategy tension.

Identifying strategy perspectives

The strategy issues in each chapter can be viewed from many perspectives. On each topic there are many different theories and hundreds of books and articles. While very interesting, a comparison or debate between all of these would probably be very chaotic, unfocused and incomprehensible. Therefore, in each chapter, the debate has been condensed into its most powerful form – two diametrically opposed perspectives are confronted with one another. These two poles of each debate are not always the most widely held perspectives on the particular set of strategy issues, but they do expose the major points of contention within the topic area.

In every chapter, the two strategy perspectives selected for the debate both emphasize one side of a strategy tension over the other (see Figure 1.6). For instance, in Chapter 6,

FIGURE 1.6   Strategy topics, paradoxes and perspectives

Strategy Topics	Strategy Paradoxes	Strategy Perspectives
Introduction		
Strategizing	Logic vs. Intuition	Analytic Reasoning vs. Holistic Reasoning
Missioning and Visioning	Profitability vs. Responsibility	Shareholder Value vs. Stakeholder Value
Business Level Strategy	Markets vs. Resources	Outside-in vs. Inside-out
Corporate Level Strategy	Responsiveness vs. Synergy	Portfolio Organization vs. Integrated Organization
Network Level Strategy	Competition vs. Cooperation	Discrete Organization vs. Embedded Organization
Strategy Formation	Deliberateness vs. Emergence	Strategic Planning vs. Strategic Incrementalism
Strategic Change	Revolution vs. Evolution	Discontinuous Renewal vs. Continuous Renewal
Strategic Innovation	Exploitation vs. Exploration	Strategic Improvement vs. Radical Rejuvenation
Industry Context	Compliance vs. Choice	Industry Dynamics vs. Industry Leadership
Organizational Context	Control vs. Chaos	Organizational Leadership vs. Organizational Dynamics
International Context	Globalization vs. Localization	Global Convergence vs. International Diversity

the discrete organization perspective stresses competition over cooperation, while the embedded organization perspective does the opposite. In Chapter 10, the industry dynamics perspective accentuates compliance over choice, while the industry leadership perspective does the opposite. In other words, the two perspectives represent the two extreme ways of dealing with a strategy tension, emphasizing one side or the other.

In the first part of each chapter, the core strategic issue and the underlying strategy tension are explained. Also, the two strategy perspectives are outlined and compared.

Strategy tensions as both/and problems

With both strategy perspectives emphasizing the importance of one side of a strategy tension over the other, how should strategists deal with these opposites? In general, there are two fundamentally different kinds of problem, 'either/or problems' and 'both/and problems', and each should be handled in different ways.

Either/or problems are for example:

- Puzzles. A puzzle is a challenging problem with an optimal solution. Think of a cross-word puzzle as an example. Puzzles can be quite complex and extremely difficult to analyse, but there is a best way of solving them. For example, when facing decreasing margins or market share, managers can solve the puzzle by testing several hypotheses on the root causes of the problem.

- Dilemmas. A dilemma is a vexing problem with two possible solutions, neither of which is logically the best. Think of the famous prisoner's dilemma as an example. Dilemmas confront problem-solvers with difficult either/or choices, each with its own advantages and disadvantages, but neither clearly superior to the other. The un-easy feeling this gives the decision-maker is reflected in the often-used expression 'horns of a dilemma' – neither choice is particularly comfortable. The manager is forced to make a choice in favour of either one or the other. For instance, the man-ager must choose between forming an alliance with firm A or its main competitor firm B, each of which has clear advantages. Which of the two the strategist judges to be the most appropriate will usually depend on the manager's preferences or the specific circumstances.

As opposed to either/or problems that can be solved by analysing and choosing, both/and problems can only be managed. Both/and problems are for example:

- Trade-offs. A trade-off is a problem situation in which there are many possible solu-tions, each striking a different balance between two conflicting pressures. In a trade-off, many different combinations between the two opposites can be found, each with its own pros and contras, but none of the many solutions is inherently superior to the others. Think of the trade-off between work and leisure time as an example – more of one will necessarily mean less of the other. Of course a position on the trade-off line needs to be set, but when circumstances change the position may also change. In other words, the balance is unstable and temporal.

- Paradoxes. A paradox is a situation in which two seemingly contradictory, or even mutually exclusive, factors appear to be true at the same time. A problem that is a paradox has no real solution, as there is no way to logically integrate the two opposites into an internally consistent understanding of the problem. Hence, a paradox presents

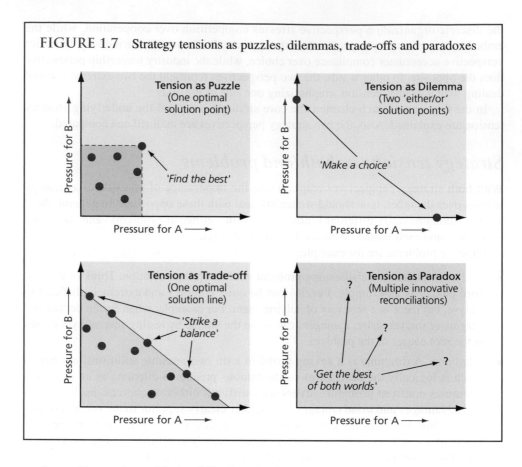

FIGURE 1.7   Strategy tensions as puzzles, dilemmas, trade-offs and paradoxes

the problem-solver with the difficult task of wrestling with the problem, without ever arriving at a definitive solution. For example, companies with more than one business unit need to create synergies between business units but also have to allow the businesses independence to act on market circumstances. Comparable with trade-offs, the problem-solver can find a workable reconciliation to temporarily cope with the unsolvable paradox (see Figure 1.7).

Taking a dialectical approach

Throughout this book, the strategy tensions will be presented as strategy paradoxes. As stated earlier, the virtual debate in each chapter has been condensed into its most powerful form – two diametrically opposed perspectives are confronted with one another, each emphasizing one pole of the paradox. These two opposite positions are, in fact, the thesis and the antithesis of the debate, challenging the reader to search for an appropriate option to manage the two tensions. This form of debate is called 'dialectical enquiry' – by using two opposite points of view, the problem-solver attempts to arrive at a better understanding of the issue and a 'higher level resolution' that integrates elements of both the thesis and the antithesis. This approach has a number of advantages:

- Range of ideas. By presenting the two opposite poles in each debate, readers can quickly acquire an understanding of the full range of ideas on the strategy issue. While these two extreme positions do not represent the most widely held views, they do clarify for the reader how diverse the thinking actually is on each strategy issue. This is the *book-end function* of presenting the two opposite perspectives – they 'frame' the full set of views that exist on the topic.

- Points of contention. Usually there is not across-the-board disagreement between the various approaches to each strategy issue, but opinions tend to diverge on a number of critical points. By presenting the two opposite poles in each debate, readers can rapidly gain insight into these major points of contention. This is the *contrast function* of presenting the two opposite perspectives – they bring the key points of contention into sharper focus.

- Stimulus for bridging. As the two opposite poles in each debate are presented, readers will be struck by the fact that neither position can be easily dismissed. Both extreme strategy perspectives make a strong case for a particular approach and readers will experience difficulty in simply choosing one over the other. With each extreme position offering certain advantages, readers will feel challenged to incorporate aspects of both into a more sophisticated synthesis. This is the *integrative function* of presenting the two opposite perspectives – they stimulate readers to seek a way of getting the best of both worlds.

- Stimulus for creativity. Nothing is more creativity evoking than a challenging paradox whereby two opposites seem to be true at the same time. By presenting the two opposite poles of each debate, which both make a realistic claim to being valid, readers are challenged to creatively deal with this paradoxical situation. This is the *generative function* of presenting the two opposite perspectives – they stimulate readers to generate innovative ways of 'transcending' the strategic paradox.

MANAGING STRATEGY PARADOXES

Conflict is latent. Only by profound and meticulous ordering of aims, in advance, can it be prevented from emerging.

I Ching, *Book of Changes* (3rd to 2nd millennium BCE)

From an academic point of view, a discussion between representatives of opposite perspectives leads to a better and often new understanding of an issue, and so it contributes to the key academic objective: scientific progress. For strategizing managers, however, understanding the problem is a great beginning but not an end in itself. Much more important are the subsequent steps of making better strategic decisions and acting more effectively. And although strategists may prefer the correct academically validated solution, in the case of strategy paradoxes there is no single best answer. After all, either/or puzzles can be solved, while both/and paradoxes can 'only' be managed. So, how then can strategists manage strategy paradoxes? (See Figure 1.8.)

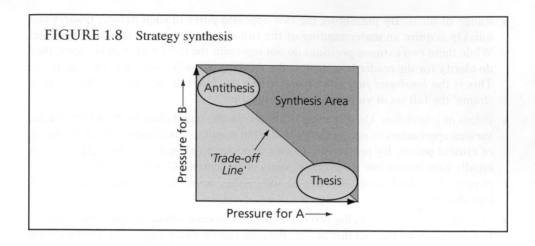

FIGURE 1.8   Strategy synthesis

Dealing with paradoxes

When faced with strategy paradoxes, strategizing managers have a range of options for dealing with the opposite elements of an issue – some of them desirable and others not so much. Not every solution will do – a common misunderstanding when there is no single solution – and there is no fixed number of options. Several options can be considered in some strategy issues, while other possibilities may be thought of in other situations. For example, separating research and development from the company's operations (the paradox of exploration and exploitation) may work, but separating the corporate objective to create multi-business synergies from business unit operations (the paradox of synergy and responsiveness) is no option. To make things worse, the attractiveness of an option is related to the specific company context, such as the industry context and the firm's company culture. In other words, judging which option might work in a particular situation is an important capability for strategists. Yet, the literature indicates that the strategists' option menu is not infinite.

The literature in the strategy field and related disciplines (such as organizational behaviour) suggest that a limited number of options are at the strategist's disposal. In some publications the available options are specifcally related to the strategic issue at hand, e.g. scholars addressing tensions related to strategic innovation, such as Jay (2013), March (1991), Raisch *et al.* (2009), and Tushman and O'Reilly (1996); to missioning and visioning such as Porter and Kramer (2011); and to dynamic capabilities, such as Teece (2007). However, a growing number of publications are also addressing how paradoxes may be dealt with in general, such as Lewis (2000), Poole and Van de Ven (1989), Smith (2009), Smith and Lewis (2011), Smith and Tushman (2005), and Smith, Lewis and Tushman (2016). Taking all suggestions together, the option menu consists of six different options (see the taxonomy in Figure 1.9).

■ Navigating. The first option is to focus on one contrary demand at a time. In this case the paradox is managed over time by a series of contrary initiatives, which leads to a development path comparable with a tacking sailing boat. Hence this option is called 'navigating' (Jay, 2013). In the literature, 'tacking' is also referred to as 'punctuating';

FIGURE 1.9   Managing paradoxes taxonomy

Options:	Alternative terminologies:	Discussed in Chapter:
Navigating	Temporal separation; Punctuated equilibrium	2 (Strategizing) 5 (Corporate level strategy) 6 (Network level strategy) 8 (Strategic change) 9 (Strategic innovation) 12 (International context)
Parallel processing	Spatial separation	2 (Strategizing) 4 (Business level strategy) 6 (Network level strategy) 9 (Strategic innovation)
Balancing	Yin Yang Balancing; Blending; Trade-off; Dilemma; Accepting contradictions	5 (Corporate level strategy) 7 (Strategy formation) 9 (Strategic innovation) 11 (Organizational context) 12 (International context)
Juxtaposing	Manage opposites simultaneously	4 (Business level strategy) 6 (Network level strategy) 7 (Strategy formation) 10 (Industry context) 11 (Organizational context)
Resolving	Synthesis; Resolving the paradox; Beyond trade-off; Best-of-both	3 (Missioning and visioning) 5 (Corporate level strategy) 12 (International context)
Embracing	Dialectic; Combining; Exploit the tension	2 (Strategizing) 11 (Organizational context) 12 (International context)

the phase of sustaining one route is called the state of 'equilibrium'; the combination is called 'punctuated equilibrium' (Burgelman, 2002; Tushman and O'Reilly, 1996). For example, in managing the paradox of multi-business synergy and business responsiveness a company may start a corporate initiative to capture synergies between businesses (such as 'One Firm'), which is then followed by another initiative (such as 'Customer First'), aimed at improving responsiveness of the business units (discussed in Chapter 5 on corporate level strategy).

- Parallel processing. The second option, following Lawrence and Lorsch's (1967) seminal work, is to separate the contrary demands in different internal (departments or business units) or external (alliance partners) organizational units. Often, the differentiated demands are then integrated at a different – usually higher – organizational level (Smith *et al.*, 2016). For example, a company may separate improving existing products and developing a new generation of products in different units, because the drivers such as processes, people and rewards differ (discussed in Chapter 9 on strategic innovation). In this case, managing the paradox of exploitation (improving) and exploration (rejuvenating) takes place at the next organizational level up.

The company may also outsource one side of the paradox to alliance partners (discussed in Chapter 6 on network level strategy) and then import the products or outcomes into the organization (Rothermael, 2001). For example, a firm may outsource production while internally focusing on developing new products – or the reverse. The paradox is then dealt with at higher management levels. This option has also become known as 'spatial separation' (Benner and Tushman, 2003; Duncan, 1976).

■ Balancing. The third option – also referred to as dynamic equilibrium (Smith *et al.*, 2016) – is to manage opposite demands by trading off elements of the opposing demands and blending the most appropriate balance. The strategist is not searching for a (static) synthesis, but instead chooses constituting elements of each demand to create a company-specific balance that can change upon circumstances (dynamic). For example, a manager may choose to comply with some industry rules while changing others (discussed in Chapter 10 on the industry context).

■ Juxtaposing. The fourth option is to simultaneously manage opposite demands on a permanent basis. The conflict between the two opposites is accepted, and the strategist will accommodate both factors at the same time. Juxtaposing requires dynamic capabilities (Teece, Pisano and Shuen, 1997) to manage the paradox on a daily or project basis. For example, companies may cooperate and compete in business networks at the same time, even with the same network partners (discussed in Chapter 6 on network level strategy), or combine client-driven and resource-driven processes in the same units (discussed in Chapter 4 on business level strategy).

■ Resolving. The fifth option is to arrive at a higher level equilibrium, by developing a new synthesis between competing demands or by exploiting the tension. Developing a novel synthesis creates a new balance between contrary elements that will sustain for some time, but will eventually be replaced by a new one. For example, companies may adopt societal demands into their mission statement, and combine the need to create shareholder value with the need to create societal value to arrive at some statement of shared value (discussed in Chapter 3 on missioning and visioning).

■ Embracing. The sixth option is to embrace and actively use the tension as a source of creativity and opportunity (Beech *et al.*, 2004). The conflict between two opposites is not only accepted, but actually exploited to benefit from the innovative power of tensions. For example, a firm may assign two opposite personalities in the leadership team to combine the messy entrepreneurial process with controlled execution (discussed in Chapter 11 on the organizational context).

As organizations are complex and dynamic systems in changing environments, the attractiveness of available options may depend on the specific context (contingencies) and timing. Strategizing managers need to be able to master the variety of alternative options, actively manage strategy paradoxes and change route when needed. In other words, the list of available options as listed above is not a passive checklist of solutions for specific issues, but instead provides a menu of available strategizing options that can be dynamically applied. It should be kept in mind, however, that being able to effectively manage strategy paradoxes is not a *goal* in itself. For strategists, this capability is a necessary *means* to managing paradoxes and creating an advantage over competitors. Ultimately, the desired outcome of managing paradoxes is to outperform competitors.

DEVELOPING AN INTERNATIONAL PERSPECTIVE

Every man takes the limits of his own field of vision for the limits of the world.

Arthur Schopenhauer (1788–1860), German philosopher

In a highly integrated world economy, in which many firms operate across national boundaries, strategy is by nature an international affair. Some theorists ignore the international arena as irrelevant, uninteresting or too complex, but most theorists, particularly those interested in strategy content, acknowledge the importance of the international context and write extensively on international competition and global strategy. In this book, there has been a strong preference to include those authors who explicitly place their arguments within an international setting. Gaining an international perspective is greatly enhanced by reading works that do not take a domestic arena as their default assumption.

To further accentuate the international angle of this book, the international context has been singled out for a closer look in Chapter 12. In this chapter, the conflicting views about developments in the international context will be debated. This, too, should challenge readers to take an international perspective.

However, despite all this attention paid to the international competitive arena, internationalizing companies, cross-border strategies and global products, few authors in the strategy field explicitly question whether their own theories can be globally standardized. Most fail to wonder whether their theories are equally applicable in a variety of national settings. It is seldom asked whether they base themselves on universally valid assumptions, or if they have been severely limited by their domestic 'field of vision'. Yet, there is a very real danger that theories are based on local assumptions that are not true or appropriate in other nations – a threat that could be called 'think local, generalize global'.

Developing an international perspective requires strategists to guard against the indiscriminate export of domestically generated strategy theories across international borders. For international strategists, it is important to question whether theories 'travel' as well as the companies they describe. Unfortunately, at the moment, strategizing managers have little to base themselves on. There has been only a modest amount of international comparative research carried out in the field of strategy. National differences in strategic management practices and preferences have occasionally been identified, but, in general, the topic has received little attention. In practice, the international validity of locally formulated strategy theories has gone largely unquestioned in international journals and forums.

Although there is still so little published material to go on, in this book readers will be encouraged to question the international limitations of strategy theories. Furthermore, they will be challenged to question whether certain strategy perspectives are more popular or appropriate in some countries than in others. To point readers in the right direction, in each chapter, a subsection is presented that places the strategy topic being debated in an international perspective. In these subsections, it will be argued that the strategy paradoxes identified in this book are fundamentally the same around the world, but that there might be international differences in how each paradox is coped with.

Strategy perspectives and theories might be more predominant in particular countries because they are based on certain assumptions about dealing with the strategy paradoxes that are more suitable to the national context. In each 'international perspective' subsection, a number of factors is discussed that might cause national differences in strategy styles.

Using the cases

An additional way of gaining an international perspective is by trying to employ the strategy perspectives in a variety of national settings. It is especially when trying to deal with concrete strategic problems on an international stage that the limitations of each theory will become more apparent. For this reason, a large number of cases have been included in this book, from many different countries. In each case, readers are encouraged to evaluate the specific national circumstances in which the problem situation is embedded, and to question whether the national context will have an influence on the validity or appropriateness of the various strategy theories and perspectives.

The cases have been selected to cover a wide variety of countries and industries. Furthermore, they have been chosen for their fit with a particular chapter. Each of the chapters in this book has two corresponding cases, in which the paradox under discussion is prominently present.

EXHIBIT 1.1   SHORT CASE

DISNEY: IS MAGIC BACK IN THE MOUSE HOUSE?

It is little known that the world's most famous mouse actually used to be a bunny. The main character in Walt Disney's first cartoon was a creature named 'Oswald the Lucky Rabbit', but after Disney was cheated out of his copyrights, he modified the ears and renamed him Mickey Mouse. What is more widely known is that Walt, together with his brother Roy, subsequently captured the attention of audiences around the world with Mickey as *Steamboat Willie* (1928), in the first cartoon with synchronized sound.

After some modest successes with such new characters as Goofy and Donald Duck, the business of Walt Disney Studios really started to accelerate when they moved into full-length animated films, releasing blockbusters like *Snow White and the Seven Dwarfs* (1937), *Pinocchio* (1940) and *Bambi* (1942). Soon Disney discovered the lucrative merchandising business, licensing the use of Disney characters for such things as clothing, pencils and soda cans. On the basis of this success, Disney branched out into TV programmes, film music and live-action movie productions. In 1955, Walt's dream of creating a 'Magical Kingdom' was realized, when Disneyland was opened in Anaheim, California. After Walt's death in 1966, Roy carried on to build Disney World in Orlando, Florida, which was completed just before he passed away in 1971.

While the empire the brothers left behind carried on to entertain billions of children and adults all over the world, the creative pipeline dried up completely. After the release of Walt's last project, *Jungle Book*

(1967), the Disney studios spent the 1970s looking for ways to emulate the founder's magic, but without clear results. By 1983, only 4 per cent of US moviegoers went to a Disney picture, and the 15-year drought of hit movies was being severely felt in the sales of Disney merchandise and licensing income. In the same year, the Disney Channel was launched in the US, but did not get off to a flying start. Making things worse, the hordes that initially swamped the theme parks were getting bored with Disney's dingy image and visitor numbers began to shrink, while at the same time Disney was incurring heavy costs to finish the Epcot Center at Disney World. To stem the tide, a new management team was hired in 1984, consisting of a brash young executive from Paramount Studios, Michael Eisner, who became CEO, and a level-headed operational man from Warner Brothers, Frank Wells, who took on the role of COO.

Together the two worked just like Walt and Roy, with the passionate and outspoken Eisner driving the creative process, and the stable and diplomatic Wells getting things organized. At Paramount, Eisner had produced hit movies such as *Raiders of the Lost Ark* and *Grease*, as well as the successful television shows *Happy Days* and *Cheers*. He was known for his fanatical attention to detail, to the extent of getting involved in reading scripts and selecting costumes. At Disney, he did the same, getting deeply involved in rejuvenating the film business. On the live-action movie side, Eisner and Wells redirected Disney towards lower budget productions, using promising scripts from less established writers and recruiting actors that seemed at the end of their career. Through a new subsidiary, Touchstone Pictures, Disney also entered the attractive market for films for the teen and young adult audience. With hits such as

Good Morning Vietnam and *Down and Out in Beverly Hills*, Disney reached a 19 per cent US box office share by 1988, causing Eisner to comment that 'nearly overnight, Disney went from nerdy outcast to leader of the popular crowd'. Later, Disney was responsible for successes such as *Pretty Woman* (1990) and *Pulp Fiction* (1994) – the latter made by Miramax, an avant-garde movie studio Disney had acquired a year before.

The animation part of the business was also revitalized, with major investments made in new animation technology and new people, in particular a new creative producer, Jeffrey Katzenberg. Eventually, this resulted in a series of very successful films: *The Little Mermaid* (1989), *Beauty and the Beast* (1991), *Aladdin* (1992) and *The Lion King* (1994). To get the new movies back in the limelight, alliances were formed with McDonald's and Coca-Cola to do promotional tie-ins. And to get spin-off merchandise flowing at greater volumes, Eisner moved beyond mere licensing, building up a global chain of Disney stores. Helped by a little luck, Disney also profited from the new home video trend that was sweeping the world. Not only could Disney release its new movies twice – first in the theatres and then on video – but it could also rerelease a steady stream of classic pictures for home audiences.

In the theme park business, the major innovation spearheaded by Eisner and Wells was to make Disneyland and Disney World more appealing to adults. In 1989 the Disney-MGM Studios theme park was opened near Disney World, as well as the Pleasure Island nightlife complex. Based on the success of Tokyo Disneyland, which was opened in 1983, Disney also built a theme park outside of Paris, called Euro Disney in 1992. It turned out that while the Japanese visitors appreciated an almost replica of Disneyland in Tokyo, European tastes were very different, requiring a long period of adaptation to the local market conditions and causing Euro Disney (later renamed Disneyland Resort Paris) to suffer significant losses during a number of years.

Then, in 1994, Frank Wells was killed in a helicopter crash, Eisner had bypass heart surgery, and a period of boardroom infighting commenced, leading to the high profile departure of the studio head, Katzenberg, who later teamed up with Steven Spielberg and David Geffen to found a new independent film company, DreamWorks SKG. Other executives also left, pointing to Eisner's overbearing presence. 'People get tired of being second guessed and beaten down', a former studio executive remarked. 'When people came out of Michael's office wounded, Frank was the emergency room', another Disney insider reported to *Fortune*, but with Wells gone, no one was there to repair damaged egos and soothe hurt feelings. However, Eisner viewed the situation differently: 'I've never had a problem with anybody who was truly talented ... This autonomy crap? That means you're off working alone. If you want autonomy, be a poet.'

In 1996 Eisner made his biggest move yet, acquiring Capital Cities/ABC for $19.6 billion. This deal included the ABC Television Network (distributing to 224 affiliated stations), the ABC Radio Networks (with 3,400 radio outlets) and an 80 per cent share of ESPN, a sports-oriented network, which includes various cable channels and radio stations. Ironically, Eisner had previously worked for ABC as daytime programmer, and felt that he had a lot to add to ABC: 'I would love, every morning, to go over and spend two hours at ABC. Even though my children tell me that I am in the wrong generation and I don't get it any

more, I am totally convinced that I could sit with our guys and make ABC No. 1 in two years.' But the opposite happened, as ABC quickly fell to last place, where it lingered for almost 10 years.

After Katzenberg's departure, Disney's animation track record also took a turn for the worse – movies such as *Pocahontas* (1995) and *Tarzan* (1999) didn't do too badly, although soaring costs made them only mildly profitable. Other features, such as *Atlantis* (2001), *Treasure Island* (2002) and *Home on the Range* (2004), were box office fiascos. Disney's real animation successes came from their deal with Pixar, an independent studio specializing in computer-generated animations, owned by Apple CEO, Steve Jobs. Such co-productions as *Toy Story* (1995), *Monsters Inc.* (2000) and *Finding Nemo* (2003) were hits in the cinemas and on DVD. In the area of live-action films, Katzenberg's replacement Joe Roth scrapped the policy of setting a 'financial box' within which the creatives had to operate, leading to bigger budgets, big names and big special effects – and just a few too many big disasters. Illustrative were *Pearl Harbour* (2001) and *Gangs of New York* (2002), both with immense production budgets, yet unable to live up to their promise. The result was a high market share for Disney films, but profitability hovering just above zero.

Although Eisner had taken Disney from $1.5 billion in revenues in 1984 to $30 billion 20 years later, a revolt broke out among shareholders, led by Walt's nephew Roy Disney and director Stanley Gold. They lambasted Eisner's perceived arrogance and inability to foster creativity, calling for his resignation. Eventually, Eisner decided to step down, upon which, the board appointed Eisner's right-hand man and company president since 2000, Bob Iger, to the position of CEO in 2005. Although Gold called Iger 'a modest man with a lot to be modest about', the new CEO was a popular choice among 'Mouseketeers', because of his calm demeanour and team player mentality.

Iger immediately disbanded the strategic planning department at corporate headquarters in Burbank, California, which was held responsible for blocking many of the divisions' strategic initiatives. Instead, Iger gave the heads of the four divisions – Studio Entertainment (films), Parks & Resorts, Media Networks (TV & radio) and Consumer Products (merchandising) – more autonomy to make decisions, while at the same time keeping Eisner's emphasis on leveraging Disney characters across all activities. Iger also mended relationships with Stanley Gold and Roy Disney, asking the latter to join the board of directors as consultant. A surprised Gold remarked: 'He's got the company working like a team again. It's very impressive.'

Relations with Katzenberg and DreamWorks were also restored, leading to further cooperation, but most importantly Iger was able to defuse the tense relationship with Pixar's owner, Steve Jobs. As the six-year co-production agreement with Pixar was about to end, Iger needed to find some way to continue the partnership, since Pixar's films were responsible for more than half of Disney's studio profits. The solution turned out to be a classic win-win, with Disney purchasing Pixar for $7.4 billion in Disney shares, while bringing in Steve Jobs as board member. Part of the deal was also that Pixar's president, Ed Catmull, and its top creative executive, John Lasseter, would take over Disney's struggling animation studios. Furthermore, Disney would work together more closely with Apple in making premium content available through Apple's iTunes stores.

Disney's financial results were further strengthened by a renaissance at ABC, where hit shows like *Lost, Desperate Housewives, Grey's Anatomy* and *Ugly Betty* helped catapult the network to a leading position. Significant growth was also achieved at the Disney Channel, where the traditional focus on the very young was broadened to include 'tweens', nine to 14-year-olds, offering them shows like *Hannah Montana* and *High School Musical*. Not only did these programmes attract a whole new audience, but they led to a wave of new merchandising opportunities. Although Disney once again proved to possess talent for making money by exploiting its franchises, its portfolio was still lacking those that appealed to the male tween audience.

In order to fill this gap, Disney purchased the comic-book publisher Marvel Entertainment for $4.2 billion. Unfortunately, the barrel of the comic-book publisher was not as full as it could have been; various media competitors already had the most famous characters contracted, with Spider-Man, X-Men and the Hulk bound respectively to Sony, News Corporation and Universal. Although Disney received revenue from projects involving these characters, profiting from highly successful movies such as *Iron Man 2* (2010) and *Thor* (2011), for Disney it was only a matter of time before the contracts would run out and it acquired them exclusively. It seems well worth the wait, with *The Avengers* (2012) accumulating impressive box office results of $1.5 billion, making it the fifth-highest grossing film of all time. In addition, Disney is making good use of the Marvel takeover; television series based on popular Marvel characters debuted on the boy-focused Disney XD channel with the creation of the Marvel Universe block.

Considering *Pirates of the Caribbean* had been the only highly leverageable movie hit Disney had for quite some years, Iger was eagerly looking for new themes around which to build the Disney synergies. He not only found this in Marvel, but also eyeballed Lucasfilm, the company responsible for such hits as *Star Wars* and *Indiana Jones*. Both had a history of collaborating on attractions based on these two franchises for Disney Parks, but the cooperation only went so far. George Lucas, owner of Lucasfilm, considering his retirement, needed someone capable of handling his franchises, while ensuring enduring quality and providing the creators with a certain degree of freedom. He found this in Iger, who had previously handled the acquisition of Pixar well. For a stellar $4.1 billion, Lucasfilm became a subsidiary of Disney. Similar to the Pixar deal, George Lucas was welcomed as a board member and future films would be co-branded with both the Disney and Lucasfilm names. Disney aims to ensure its investment was a solid business decision and *Star Wars VII: The Force Awakens* proved the company right. With box office results of a stellar $207 billion, the seventh iteration in the *Star Wars* series turned into the third-highest grossing film of all time. With five more new *Star Wars* films in the pipeline, the future seems bright.

Yet, peace is not necessarily restored in the Disney galaxy, as Iger has plenty of strategic issues to deal with. One key strategic challenge for him is to continue to reap the synergies between the divisions, by taking movie characters to television, the Internet, theme parks, merchandise and Disney stores. The company now has more than 10 of these 'franchises', ranging from *Mickey Mouse* to *Frozen*, *Disney Fairies* and *Pirates of the Caribbean*, that it tries to leverage, but the question is how this should be managed, without creating a complex organizational structure and reducing each division's freedom to set its own strategy. Throwing in Marvel and Lucasfilm only reinforces the need for Disney to get this right.

Another issue is internationalization, which Iger has set high on his priority list. If Disney wants to break into non-US markets in a big way, can it do so by leveraging its franchises across borders or must Disney go local, developing local movies and characters? With more or less standardized theme parks in Tokyo, Paris and Hong Kong (2005), and resorts in a variety of locations, there is much to be said for sticking to global franchises. Yet, by the same token, emerging markets like China, Russia, India and Brazil might be too diverse to cover successfully with globally standardized wares. Shanghai Disney Resort, which opened on 16 June 2016 and is costumed to serve the taste of China, might be able to indicate what direction is best for Disney.

Disney's future in interactive media is another issue. Disney's gaming division lost $1.4 billion between fiscal year 2008 to 2013. An overhaul was made in 2014, when one-quarter of the employees were fired, fewer games were in development and a shift was made to cater more to the mobile market. Revenues entered the black again, but Disney nevertheless continued to prove overly zealous. Disney Infinity, in which plastic toys of familiar characters can be bought and used in-game, crushed its competitors in terms of sales, but still proved hardly profitable. Higher inventory reserves of the figurines were met with lower unit sales volume. In other words, Disney kept releasing more of the toys that hardly left stores and proved too optimistic at times. It supposedly produced two million figures of the Hulk, while only a million of them left stores.

Probably Iger's biggest challenge, however, is to keep Disney's heart and soul fresh – its film business. With the movie industry suffering from tough times in which people buy fewer physical copies of movies, be it on DVD or Blu-ray Disc, and cinema success is limited to familiar franchises,

Disney places fewer daring bets. Thus far that has proved successful, with for example Marvel's superhero movies consistently raking in hundreds of millions at the box offices worldwide. Meanwhile Pixar also plays the safe card, focusing their resources mostly on sequels, such as the upcoming *Cars 3* and *Toy Story 4*. How many of those can you churn out before it starts to bore audiences, however? By putting only cash cow eggs in one basket, Disney might not be able to guarantee quality can be preserved.

Bob Iger extended his contract to remain CEO through June 2018, making sure that he has enough time to unleash more magic in the Mouse House. He had proved able to do so before, a task the company and shareholders now happily entrust him with. But if Iger fails to make the right strategic decisions, the clock might strike 12 and the magic might be over.

Co-authors: Casper van der Veen and Wester Wagenaar

Sources: www.thewaltdisneycompany.com; www.boxofficemojo.com; Disney Annual Report 2008–2015; *ABC News*, 7 October 2011; *Bloomberg*, 1 September 2009, 1 November 2012 and 16 February 2016; *Business Week*, 5 February 2007, 9 February 2009 and 14 April 2011; *The Economist*, 26 January 2006, 17 April 2008, 3 September 2009 and 3 November 2012; *Fortune*, 23 December 2001; *Kotaku*, 12 May 2016; *Reuters*, 12 June 2014; *Sunday Times*, 20 February 2005 and 2 October 2005.

2

STRATEGIZING

A mind all logic is like a knife all blade. It makes the hand bleed that uses it.

Rabindranath Tagore (1861–1941), Indian philosopher, poet and 1913 Nobel Prize winner in literature

INTRODUCTION

What goes on in the mind of the strategist? A fascinating question that is easy to ask, but difficult to answer. Yet, it is a question that is important in two ways – generally and personally. Generally, knowing what goes on in the minds of managers during strategy processes is essential for understanding their choices and behaviours. Opening up the black box of the strategist's mind to see how decisions are made can help to anticipate or influence this thinking. Grasping how managers shape their strategic views and select their preferred actions can be used to develop more effective strategies. It is due to this importance of strategic thinking that a separate chapter in this book is devoted to the subject. Yet, for each reader personally, the topic of strategizing is also of key importance, as it automatically raises the questions 'what is going on in *my* mind?' and 'how strategic is *my* thinking?' Exploring the subject of strategizing triggers each person to explore their own thought processes and critically reflect on their own strategy preferences. Ideally, wondering about the mind of the strategist should inspire readers to constantly question their own assumptions, thoughts, beliefs and ideas, and to sharpen their strategic thinking as they move through the following chapters. For this reason, it seems only appropriate to start the book with this topic.

So, what goes on in the mind of the strategist? Well, a lot, but if reduced to its bare essentials it can be said that strategists are engaged in the process of dealing with *strategic problems*. Not problems in the negative sense of troublesome conditions that need to be avoided, but in the neutral sense of challenging situations that need to be resolved – a strategic problem is a set of circumstances requiring a reconsideration of the current course of action, either to profit from observed opportunities or to respond to perceived threats. To deal with these strategic problems, managers must not simply think, but they must go through a *strategic reasoning process*, searching for ways to define and resolve the challenges at hand. Managers must structure their individual thinking steps into a reasoning process that will result in effective strategic behaviour. The question is how managers actually go about defining strategic problems (how do they identify and diagnose what is going on?) and how they go about solving strategic problems (how do they generate, evaluate and decide on potential answers?). It is this issue of strategic reasoning, as a string of strategic thinking activities directed at defining and resolving strategic problems, which will be examined in further detail below.

THE ISSUE OF STRATEGIC REASONING

The mind of the strategist is a complex and fascinating apparatus that never fails to astonish and dazzle, on the one hand, and disappoint and frustrate, on the other. We are often surprised by the power of the human mind, but equally often stunned by its limitations. For the discussion here it is not necessary to unravel all of the mysteries surrounding the functioning of the human brain, but a short overview of the capabilities and limitations of the human mind will help us to understand the issue of strategic reasoning.

The human ability to know is referred to as 'cognition'. As strategists want to know about the strategic problems facing their organizations, they need to engage in *cognitive activities*. These cognitive activities (or strategic thinking activities) need to be structured into a strategic reasoning process. Hence, the first step towards a better understanding of what goes on in the mind of the strategist is to examine the various cognitive activities making up a strategic reasoning process. The four main cognitive activities will be discussed in the first subsection below. To be able to perform these cognitive activities, people need to command certain mental faculties. While very sophisticated, the human brain is still physically strictly limited in what it can do. These limitations to people's *cognitive abilities* will be reviewed in the second subsection. To deal with its inherent physical shortcomings, the human brain copes by building simplified models of the world, referred to as *cognitive maps*. The functioning of cognitive maps will be addressed in the third subsection.

In Figure 2.1, the relationship between these three topics is visualized, using the metaphor of a computer. The cognitive abilities of our brains can be seen as a hardware level question – what are the physical limits on our mental faculties? The cognitive maps used by our brains can be seen as an operating system level question – what type of platform/language is 'running' in our brain? The cognitive activities carried out by our brains can be seen as an application level question – what type of programme is strategic reasoning?

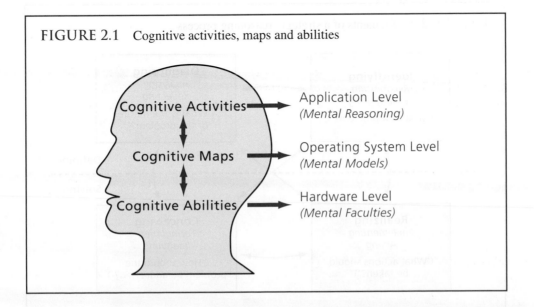

FIGURE 2.1   Cognitive activities, maps and abilities

Cognitive activities

The strategic reasoning process consists of a number of strategic thinking elements or cognitive activities – mental tasks intended to increase the strategist's knowing. A general distinction can be made between cognitive activities directed towards *defining* a strategic problem, and cognitive activities directed at *solving* a strategic problem.

Each of these two major categories can be further split into two (see Figure 2.2), leading to the following general elements of a strategic reasoning process:

- Identifying. Before strategists can benefit from opportunities or to counter threats, they must be aware of these challenges and acknowledge their importance. This part of the reasoning process is also referred to as identifying, recognizing, sense-making or sensing.

- Diagnosing. To come to grips with a problem, strategists must try to understand the structure of the problem and its underlying causes. This part of the reasoning process is also referred to as analysing, reflecting or shaping.

- Conceiving. To deal with a strategic problem, strategists must come up with a potential solution. If more than one solution is available, strategists must select the most promising one. This part of the reasoning process is also referred to as formulating, imagining or seizing.

- Realizing. A strategic problem is only really solved once concrete actions are undertaken that achieve results. Strategists must therefore carry out problem-solving activities and evaluate whether the consequences are positive. This part of the reasoning process is also referred to as implementing, acting or reconfiguring.

A structured approach to these four cognitive activities is to carry them out in the above order, starting with problem identification and then moving through diagnosis to conceiving solutions and finally realizing them (i.e. clockwise movement in Figure 2.2). In this approach, the first step, identifying strategic problems, would require extensive external and internal scanning, thorough sifting of incoming information and the selection of

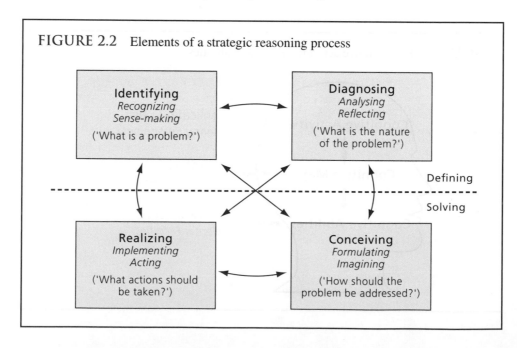

FIGURE 2.2 Elements of a strategic reasoning process

priority issues. In the next reasoning step, the strategic problems recognized would have to be diagnosed by gathering more detailed data, and by further analysing and refining this information. Once the problem has been properly defined, a strategy could be formulated by evaluating the available options and deciding which solution would be best. In the final phase, realization, the strategist would need to ensure execution of the proposed solution by consciously planning and controlling implementation activities. In this case, the four elements of the strategic reasoning process could actually be labelled recognizing, analysing, formulating and implementing.

However, strategists do not always reason in this step-by-step fashion. Their thinking is often less orderly, with identifying, diagnosing, conceiving and realizing intermingled with one another – even going on at the same time. Neither are cognitive activities as straightforward as portrayed above. The identification of strategic problems is often not about objective observation, but rather subjective interpretation – by looking at the world from a particular angle, strategists see and value particular strengths, weaknesses, opportunities and threats. Such sense-making activities (Gioia and Chittipeddi, 1991; Hodgkinson and Healy, 2011; Weick, 1979) lead to attention being paid to some issues, while others do not make the strategic agenda (Dutton, 1988; Ocasio, 1997). Likewise, diagnosing strategic problems is not always a structured analytical process. Gaining a deeper understanding of strategic problems may involve explicit analysis, but also intuitive reflecting – by employing unconscious reasoning rules, strategists often quickly form a general picture of how key aspects of a strategic problem are interrelated.

Conceiving strategic solutions can be equally 'messy' and subjective. Often, strategic options are not chosen from an available repertoire of potential solutions, but they are invented. In other words, new options are often not selected, discovered or figured out, but are envisioned – strategists imagine how things could be done. Such idea generation can involve reasoning by analogy or metaphor, brainstorming or pure fantasizing. New potential solutions may come to the strategist in a flash (Eureka!) or emerge over time, but usually require a period of incubation beforehand and a period of nurturing afterwards. Furthermore, strategists often find it impossible to objectively prove which new idea would be the best solution. Therefore, the process of deciding on the solution to be pursued may involve more judgement than calculation.

Finally, it must be emphasized that action does not always come last, in the form of solution implementation. Often, strategists do not wait for a problem to be precisely defined and for a solution to be fully conceived before starting to act. On the contrary, strategists often feel they must first act – they must have experience with a problem and know that the current strategy will not be able to overcome the problem. To find a suitable solution it is often also necessary to test certain assumptions in practice and to experiment. Hence, acting regularly precedes, or goes hand in hand with, all other cognitive activities.

Cognitive abilities

People are not omniscient – they do not have infinite knowledge. To some extent this is due to the nature of reality – many future events are inherently unpredictable, due to factors that are uncertain or unknowable. Yet, humans are also burdened with rather imperfect cognitive abilities. The human brain is severely limited in what it can know (Simon, 1957). The limitation to humans' cognitive abilities is largely due to three factors:

■ Limited information-sensing ability. Humanity's first 'handicap' is a limited information-sensing ability. While the senses – touch, smell, taste, hearing and seeing – are bombarded with stimuli, much of reality remains unobservable to humans. This is partially due to the physical inability to be everywhere, all the time, noticing everything. However, people's limited ability to register the structure of reality is also due to the inherent superficiality of the senses and the complexity of reality. The human senses cannot directly identify the way the world works and the underlying causal relationships. Only the physical consequences of the complex interactions between elements in reality can be picked up by a person's sensory system. Therefore, the mental representations of the world that individuals build up in their minds are necessarily based on circumstantial evidence.

■ Limited information-processing capacity. Unfortunately, a second drawback is that humans do not have unlimited data-processing abilities. Thinking through problems with many variables, complex relationships and huge amounts of data is a task that people find extremely difficult to perform. Approaching every activity in this way would totally overload a person's brain. For this reason, humans hardly ever think through a problem with full use of all available data, but necessarily make extensive use of mental shortcuts, referred to as 'cognitive heuristics' (Janis, 1989). Cognitive heuristics are mental 'rules of thumb' that simplify a problem, so that it can be more quickly understood and solved. Cognitive heuristics focus a person's attention on a number of key variables that are believed to be most important, and present a number of simple decision rules to rapidly resolve an issue. The set of possible solutions to be considered is also limited in advance.

■ Limited information storage capacity. Another human cognitive shortcoming is poor memory. People have only a limited capacity for storing information. Remembering all individuals, events, dates, places and circumstances is beyond the ability of the human brain. Therefore, people must store information very selectively and organize this information in a way that it can be easily retrieved when necessary. Here again, cognitive heuristics are at play – 'rules of thumb' make the memorization process manageable in the face of severe capacity limitations. Such heuristics help to simplify complex clusters of data into manageable chunks and help to categorize, label and store this information so that it can be recalled at a later time.

To deal with these severe physical limitations, the brain has come up with more than only simple cognitive heuristics. The human mind has come to work with more holistic cognitive maps.

Cognitive maps

Knowledge that people have is stored in their minds in the form of 'cognitive maps' (e.g. McCaskey, 1982; Weick and Bourgnon, 1986), also referred to as 'cognitive schemata' (e.g. Anderson, 1983; Schwenk, 1988), 'mental models' (e.g. Day and Lord, 1992; Knight *et al.*, 1999), 'knowledge structures' (e.g. Lyles and Schwenk, 1992; Walsh, 1995) and 'construed reality' (Finkelstein and Hambrick, 1996). These cognitive maps are representations in a person's mind of how the world works. A cognitive map of a certain situation reflects a person's beliefs about the importance of the issues and about the cause and effect relationships between them.

Cognitive maps are formed over time through education, experience and interaction with others. Based on the inputs of their senses, people will infer causal relationships between phenomena, making guesses about unobservable factors and resolving inconsistencies between the bits of information received. In turn, people's cognitive maps steer their senses; while cognitive maps are built on past sensory data, they will consequently direct which new information will be sought and perceived. A person's cognitive map will focus attention on particular phenomena, while blocking out other data as noise, and will quickly make clear how a situation should be perceived. In this way, a cognitive map provides an interpretive filter or perceptual screen, aiding the senses in selecting and understanding external stimuli (Starbuck and Milliken, 1988). Furthermore, cognitive maps help to direct behaviour by providing an existing repertoire of 'problem-solving' responses (also referred to as 'scripts' or 'recipes') from which an appropriate action can be derived.

In building their cognitive maps, people acquire a lot of their knowledge by means of direct experience. By doing, they learn to communicate, play an instrument, drive a vehicle and solve problems. This knowledge is added to people's cognitive maps without being explicitly articulated. In other words, knowledge gained through experiential learning is usually not codified into formal rules, principles, models or theories, but remains tacit (Nonaka, 1991; Polanyi, 1966). People formulate implicit models and draw conclusions, but do so largely unconsciously. In this way, cognitive maps evolve without people themselves being entirely aware of their own cognitive map. Hence, when people use their intuition, this is not a mystical or irrational way of reasoning, but thinking guided by the tacit knowledge they have acquired in the past (Behling and Eckel, 1991). Intuitive thinking is the opposite of analytical thinking – informal and holistic (Von Winterfeldt and Edwards, 1986). Informal means that the thinking is largely unconscious and based on experiences, variables and causal relationships not explicitly identifiable by those doing the thinking. Holistic means that the thinker does not aim at unravelling phenomena into their constituent parts, but rather maintains a more integrated view of reality.

Yet, people's cognitive maps are not developed independently, but rather in interaction with one another. People tend to construct a shared understanding of the world by interacting with each other within a group over an extended period of time. By exchanging interpretations of what they see, it is said that they *enact* a shared reality (Daft and Weick, 1984; Smircich and Stubbart, 1985). The resulting shared cognitive map is variably referred to as the group's 'dominant logic' (Prahalad and Bettis, 1986), 'common paradigm' (Kuhn, 1970) or 'belief system' (Noorderhaven, 1995). Such a shared worldview can exist within small social units, such as a firm or a family, but also within larger units, such as an industry or a nation.

As individuals can belong to different groups, they can be influenced by different belief systems simultaneously. As members of a national culture, their cognitive maps will to a certain extent be influenced by the beliefs dominant within the nation. As employees of a company, their cognitive maps will be affected by the beliefs common within the firm and the industry as well. In the same manner, people can be impacted by the professional community to which they belong, their religious affiliation, their political party and any other groups in which they interact with others (Hambrick, Geletkanycz and Fredrickson, 1993; Sutcliffe and Huber, 1998). Due to the mutually inclusive nature of group membership, an individual's cognitive map will be a complex combination of elements taken from different group level dominant logics. While these paradigms on which an individual draws can be complementary, or overlapping yet consistent, it is quite possible that inconsistencies arise (Schein, 1985; Trice and Beyer, 1993).

As shared beliefs develop over time through interaction and are passed on through socialization, they remain largely tacit. The shared cognitive map of a group is literally 'common sense' – sense shared by a common group of people. However, where members of different groups come into conflict with one another, or where an individual needs to deal with the inconsistencies brought on by multiple group memberships, beliefs can become more articulated (Glynn, 2000). Different behaviours, based on different cognitive maps, will often lead to the identification and codification of beliefs, either to protect them or to engage in debate with people with other views. As paradigms become more articulated, they also become more mobile, making it possible to transfer ideas to people without direct interaction.

The downside of cognitive maps is that they exhibit a high level of rigidity. People are generally not inclined to change their minds. Once people's cognitive maps have formed and they have a grip on reality, they become resistant to signals that challenge their conceptions. As McCaskey (1982) remarks, the mind 'strives mightily to bring order, simplicity, consistency and stability to the world it encounters', and is therefore reluctant to welcome the ambiguity presented by contradicting data. People tend to significantly overestimate the value of information that confirms their cognitive map, underestimate dis-confirming information, and they actively seek out evidence that supports their current beliefs (Schwenk, 1984). Once an interpretive filter is in place, seeing is not believing, but *believing is seeing*. People might have the impression that they are constantly learning, but they are largely learning within the bounds of a paradigm. When an individual's map is supported by similar beliefs shared within a firm, industry or country, the ability to question key aspects of a paradigm will usually be rather limited. Not only does the individual have no 'intellectual sounding board' for teasing out new ideas, but deviation from the dominant logic might also have adverse social and political ramifications within the group (e.g. Aldrich and Fiol, 1994; DiMaggio and Powell, 1983). Not for nothing the old proverb is: 'Old ideas never change; they eventually die out' (Kuhn, 1970).

For strategists, cognitive rigidity is particularly worrying. Strategists should be at the forefront of market developments, identifying changing circumstances and new opportunities before their competitors do. Strategizing is by its very nature focused on understanding and shaping the future, and therefore strategists must have the ability to challenge current beliefs and to change their own mind. They must be able to come up with innovative, yet feasible new strategies that will fit with the unfolding reality. This places extraordinary cognitive demands on strategists – they must be able to overcome the limitations of their own cognitive maps and develop a new understanding.

THE PARADOX OF LOGIC AND INTUITION

Albert Einstein called the intuitive or metaphoric mind a sacred gift. He added that the rational mind was a faithful servant. It is paradoxical that in the context of modern life we have begun to worship the servant and defile the divine.

Bob Samples (1933–2012), independent scholar, artist and author

Many management theorists have noted that the opposites of logic and intuition create a tension for managers (e.g. Hodgkinson and Healey, 2011; Sadler-Smith, 2004). While some researchers make a strong case for more formal analysis (e.g. Isenberg, 1984; Schoemaker and Russo, 1993; Teece, 2007), there is a broad understanding that managers need to employ both logical and intuitive thinking, even if they are each other's opposites.

The extensive use of intuitive judgement among managers is understood by most as necessary and beneficial. A manager's intuition is built up through years of experience and contains a vast quantity of tacit knowledge that can only superficially be tapped by formal analysis. Intuition, therefore, can give a richer assessment of qualitative information. Moreover, intuitive thinking is faster (Kahneman, 2011) and better at capturing the big picture than logical thinking. And very practically, intuition is needed to cut corners in the large numbers of data and the contradicting information. Management would grind to a halt, overloaded by the sheer complexity of the analyses that would need to be carried out. Such a situation of rationality gone rampant is referred to as 'paralysis by analysis' (Langley, 1995; Lenz and Lyles, 1985).

However, it is equally clear to most that human intuition is efficient, but often also unreliable and imprecise. It helps people to intuitively jump to conclusions without thorough analysis, which increases speed, but also increases the risk of drawing faulty conclusions. The main danger of intuition is that it is inherently biased, as it focuses attention on only a few variables and interprets them in a particular way, even when this is not appropriate (e.g. Bazerman, 1990; Tversky and Kahneman, 1986). For this reason, many academics urge practitioners to bolster their intuitive judgements with more explicit rational analysis. Especially in the case of strategic decisions, more time and energy should be made available to avoid falling prey to common cognitive biases. Otherwise the ultimate result might be a 'corporate gravestone' with the epitaph '*extinct by instinct*' (Langley, 1995).

For strategists a fundamental question is how they can avoid getting stuck with an outdated cognitive map. How can they avoid the danger of building up a flawed picture of their industry, their markets and themselves? As strategists must be acutely aware of the unfolding opportunities and threats in the environment, and the evolving strengths and weaknesses of the organization, they must be able to constantly re-evaluate their views.

On the one hand, this requires rigorous *logical thinking*. All the key assumptions on which a strategist's cognitive map are based need to be reviewed and tested against developments in the firm and its environment. On the other hand, strategists must have the ability to engage in *intuitive thinking*. To be able to 'feel' new opportunities and strengths, strategists must be able to think beyond their current mental models. Both demands on strategists will now be reviewed in more detail.

The demand for logical thinking

It is clear that if the strategizing managers base their strategic decisions only on heavily biased cognitive maps, unconsciously built up through past experiences, this will lead to very poor results. Strategists need to have the ability to critically reflect on the assumptions they hold, to check whether they are based on actual fact or on organizational folklore and industry recipes. They must be capable of making their tacit beliefs more explicit, so that the validity of these mental models can be evaluated and further refined. In short, to be successful strategists, managers need to escape the confines of their own cognitive maps – and those of other stakeholders engaged in the strategy process.

Assessing the validity of a cognitive map requires strong logical thinking. Logical thinking can be characterized as conscious and rigorous, based on formal rules. When employing logic, each step in an argumentation follows from the previous one, based on valid principles. In other words, a logical thinker will draw a conclusion only if it is arrived at by a sound succession of arguments.

Logical thinking can be applied to all four cognitive activities outlined in Figure 2.2. When identifying and diagnosing a strategic problem, logical thinking can help to avoid the emotional interpretations that so often colour people's understanding of environmental opportunities and threats, and organizational strengths and weaknesses. Logical thinking can also expose a person's bullish or bearish bias and can be instrumental in discarding old 'theories' of how the firm and its environment function. By analysing the empirical facts and rigorously testing the hypotheses on which the firm's shared cognitive map has been built, the strategist can prevent building a false model of reality.

When conceiving and realizing a strategic solution, logical thinking can help to avoid the danger of following outdated habits and routines. Routines are programmed courses of action that originally were deliberately conceived, but have been subsequently internalized and are used automatically (March and Simon, 1993). Habits are programmed courses of action that have developed unconsciously. By explicitly formulating strategic options and subjecting them to formal evaluation, the strategist can break away from such established behaviour and develop new approaches to gaining and retaining competitive advantage. Moreover, logical thinking can aid in making a distinction between fantasy and feasibility. Sound logic can serve to weed out strategic options that are flights of fancy, by analysing the factors that will determine success or failure.

The demand for intuitive thinking

Intuitive thinking is the opposite of logical thinking. As described above, when employing logic, a thinker bases each step in a train of thought on the previous steps, following formal rules of valid thinking – also coined 'cold cognition' (Bernheim and Rangel, 2004). However, the intuitive thinker does not follow formal steps in a decision-making process, but instead pursues an informal and holistic judgement process. While judging the situation at hand, the intuitive thinker includes multiple inputs, relates the inputs to the unconsciously stored large quantities of information to detect and understand the inputs, and employs his emotions ('feeling in our marrow') for judging situations – also dubbed 'hot cognition' (Bernheim and Rangel, 2004).

While connecting a diversity of unconsciously stored information, intuitive thinking is quite fast – especially when compared with logical thinking (e.g. Kahneman, 2003). New insights pop up when handling a 'mass of experience or a complex of abstractions in a flash' (Barnard, 1938). And intuitive responses – within seconds or less – are often correct (March and Simon, 1993).

In intuitive thinking a person opens up the unconscious part of the brain – where most of the learnings and experiences are being accumulated. The power of using the unconsciously stored information is that it connects many variables to another into a whole, without a sound explanation of why a correlation is assumed. Without deliberate intent large numbers of inputs are combined and an understanding boils up as a new insight. When this insight appears to 'make sense', the search for supporting evidence gets started. Often logic is used afterwards to justify an understanding that was actually generated by intuitive means.

If a pattern of incidents indicates that there is reason to believe that 'something is going on' which may affect at least some elements of the mental map, common thinking will be challenged. If the intuitive thinker develops a 'gut feeling' in which direction the solution might be, the new idea will be brought forward, even when it challenges orthodoxy and current thinking.

When identifying and diagnosing strategic problems, intuitive thinking is often needed. Old cognitive maps usually have a very compelling logic, locking people into old patterns of thinking. These old cognitive maps are usually tried and tested and have become immune to external signals that they are no longer fitting. Thinking within the boundaries of a shared cognitive map is generally accepted and people tend to proceed rationally – that is, they try to escape from logical inconsistencies by including dissonant signs in the current thinking. Challenging a cognitive map's fundamental assumptions, however, cannot be done in a way that is logically consistent with the map itself. Contradicting a paradigm is illogical from the point of view of those who accept the paradigm. Therefore, changing a rigid and subjective cognitive map, rooted in a shared paradigm, requires strategists that are not captured by common logic and that recognize patterns in a number of seemingly unrelated incidents. Strategic thinkers need to be willing and able to detect signs that may challenge orthodoxy and make leaps of imagination that – although not logically justified – are needed to generate fresh ways of looking at old and new problems.

The same is true when conceiving and realizing strategic solutions. New strategies are not analysed into existence, but need to be generated. Patterns of loosely connected signs need novel solutions that do not follow from the dominant logic, but are the unexpected answers that emerge when the grip of the dominant logic is loosened.

Unfortunately, the conclusion must be that logical thinking and intuitive thinking are not only opposites, but that they are partially incompatible as well. They are based on methods that are at odds with one another. Strategizing managers would probably love to be fully logical and fully intuitive at the same time, but both require such a different mindset and range of cognitive skills that in practice it is very difficult to achieve both simultaneously. The demand for logic and intuition is not only contradictory for each individual, but also within teams, departments and the overall firm: while strategizing groups would like to be fully capable of logical and intuitive thinking, finding ways of incorporating both forms of strategic thinking into a workable strategy process is extremely challenging. Commonly, opposing styles lead to opposing people, and therefore a blend between the two is not that simple. It is for this reason that we speak of the 'paradox of logic and intuition' – the two demands on managers seem to be contradictory, yet both are required at the same time.

EXHIBIT 2.1   SHORT CASE

SAMSUNG: COSMOPOLITANS ON THE HAN RIVER

The South Korean economy expanded from near zero to more than a trillion US dollars between the 1960s and now. This achievement, which became known as the Miracle on the Han River, was made possible with a few national champions. One of these was Samsung.

From its humble beginnings as a small trading firm, Samsung has become the largest of South Korea's chaebols – family business conglomerates – with subsidiaries in electronics, chemicals, insurance, ships, advertising, construction, hospitality, and more. Now the company enjoys recognition and market presence around the globe.

Samsung – literally meaning the 'three stars': large, strong and lasting forever – has strong Japanese roots. South Korea was a Japanese colony when Samsung started, and being educated in Japan, founder Byung-chul Lee was highly influenced by the Japanese way of doing business, with its focus on continuous improvement, a hierarchical labour model, unrelated diversification, dependency on the internal capital market, long-term relationships with stakeholders, seniority-based promotions and limited recruitment.

In the aftermath of ending of Japanese rule in 1945 and the Korean War in 1953, South Korea's economic situation was in terrible shape. Personal conversations with South Korea's first president Syngman Rhee strengthened Byung-chul's belief that he was not just building a company: He was 'engaging in business for national service' – to help create a stronger nation through business prosperity, or 'saeobboguk' in Korean. This is illustrated by Samsung's business philosophy – in 1973 it coined the 'Samsung Spirit' – which refers to 'the principle of engaging in business for national service', 'man and talent first', and 'pursuit of logic and reality'.

When Kun-hee Lee, Byung-chul's son, took over the reins of Samsung in 1987, he was responsible for a decisive moment of Samsung Electronics' success, when the company established a position in the white goods business. Kun-hee Lee had heard of recent developments in semiconductors and decided to personally investigate the situation in Japan. His conclusion after his investigation was that semiconductors were promising enormous opportunities for high-tech products. With a firm position in white goods, the new developments could provide Samsung Electronics with the growth Lee was looking for. He also realized something else: Samsung would be forced to compete in markets dominated by non-Koreans, with new challenges and different competitive rules ahead. Lee was also convinced that Samsung Electronics should not move cautiously, just following the leading Japanese companies Sony and Matsushita. Instead, the company should try to claim a leadership role and become an innovative and entrepreneurial industry shaper. But to achieve this, the company's current slow seniority-based HR and focus on operational excellence was not going to take Samsung to the top. Lee needed a fresh look on things, which he derived from Western thinking.

Lee launched the 'New Management Initiative' in 1993, based on introducing the Western way of doing business into the company. He famously said: 'Change everything except your wife and kids', indicating the far-reaching attempts to reform the organizational culture of the company. For example, employee promotion became merit based instead of seniority based. Lee particularly focused on the Western best practices, such as strategy formation, talent management and innovation. Lee understood that a cold turkey method wouldn't do the job as it would certainly result in heavy resistance. He therefore decided to slowly inject the best practices into the company. But how do you get analysis-based practices into an Eastern firm with holistic DNA? Lee decided to let Western outsiders into his company, equipped with MBAs and a strong know-how of the Western ways of doing business. This slowly but surely opened up the traditional Korean business mentality. In addition, he sent insiders out to the Western world, to personally experience the Western way of doing business and taking Western best practices back into the South Korean context.

These practices were slowly introduced into Samsung. For example, the merit-based compensation system started with a small differential, increasing annually until it reached 50 per cent. Lee also acquired companies that could help him in entering markets. For example, in 1995 Samsung Electronics acquired a 40 per cent stake in AST Research, a United States-based personal computer maker.

Long-term strategic plans were created that would enable Samsung to go beyond supplying simple technology to creating high-tech products, and would finally result in Samsung Electronics becoming a 'three-starred chef' in product and process innovation.

During 1997 and 1998 the industry was hit by a dramatic dip in demand and prices for memory chips. While most competitors became nervous about short-term results, and reduced capital spending and production capacity, Samsung Electronics kept to its strategic long-term planning and continued investing and strengthening its memory chip production operations. When the bust cycle turned into boom again, Samsung was one of the few companies with sufficient manufacturing capacity to reap the benefits. Since 2004 the operating profit of the electronics subsidiary of Samsung has consistently exceeded the sum of Japan's five major electronic firms annual operating profits. Samsung has showcased itself to be the world's largest memory chip manufacturer and the world market leader in LCD screens, monitors, microwave ovens and mobile phones. By 2014 the entire Samsung Electronics had reached an astonishing $196 trillion of revenue, while employing over 319,000 people around the world.

The unique combination of Eastern and Western ways of thinking has made Samsung Electronics the company it is today, but will this combination prove to be as successful in the long term? And how can Lee avoid getting stuck in the middle, being neither a company successful at doing business in an 'Asian way' nor a firm pursuing the 'Western road'? Holistic thinking helped to create the Samsung chaebol. Analytical thinking helped to enter the non-Korean dominated high-tech electronic markets. And the unique Samsung 'holistic analytical thinking combination' has made Samsung Electronics the market leader in many fields and the South Korean champion on the Han River. Employees are not Koreans or Westerners but cosmopolitans who feel at home all over the globe. How can Lee successfully manage logic and intuition to make Samsung Electronics live up to what it stands for: 'large, strong and lasting forever'?

Co-authors: Jeroen Brinkhuis and Wester Wagenaar

Sources: www.samsung.com; Samsung Electronic Annual Report 2014; *Far Eastern Economic Review*, 14 September 2002; *Harvard Business Review*, July–August 2011; Haour and Cho, IMD Business Case, 2000; *The Korea Herald*, 16 January 2009; *The Korean Times*, 2 February 2010.

PERSPECTIVES ON STRATEGIZING

Irrationally held truths may be more harmful than reasoned errors.

T.H. Huxley (1825–1895), English biologist

While the need for both logical and intuitive thinking is clear, this does place strategists in a rather awkward position of needing to bring two partially contradictory thinking systems, also known as System 1 and System 2 (Kahneman, 2011; see also Dane and Pratt, 2007), together in one strategic reasoning process. Logical thinking helps to make the strategic reasoning process rigorous, consistent and precise, instead of haphazard, *ad hoc* and general. Intuitive thinking, contrariwise, helps to make the strategic reasoning process comprehensive, flexible and fast, instead of fragmentary, rigid and slow.

In finding a balance between these opposite forms of thinking, the main question is whether the strategic reasoning process should actually be a predominantly rational affair, or a much more intuitive process. Is strategizing largely a rational activity, requiring logical thinking to be the dominant modus operandi, with occasional bits of gut feeling needed here and there to generate new ideas? Or is strategizing largely an intuitive activity, requiring integrative thinking as the standard operating procedure, with occasional bits of logical analysis needed here and there to weed out unfeasible ideas?

The answer to this question should be found in the strategic management literature. Yet, on closer inspection, the opinions outlined in both the academic and popular literature show that views vary widely among researchers and managers alike. A wide spectrum of differing perspectives can be recognized, each giving its own angle on how strategic thinking should use logic and intuition – sometimes explicitly mentioning the need for both, but more commonly making implicit assumptions about the role of logic and intuition in strategy processes.

As was outlined in Chapter 1, it is not the intention here to summarize all of the 'schools of thought' on the topic of strategic thinking. Instead, only the two opposite points of view will be presented in this section. These two poles in the debate form the input for a good debate – a clear-cut thesis and antithesis in a process of dialectical enquiry.

At one end of the spectrum, there are those who argue – or just assume – that strategizing should be a predominantly conscious analytic process, requiring logic to be the main form of thinking in use. This point of view is referred to as the 'analytic reasoning perspective'. At the other pole, there are those who argue that strategizing is mainly an unconscious holistic process, requiring intuition as the leading thinking style. This point of view will be referred to as the 'holistic reasoning perspective'.

The analytic reasoning perspective

 Strategists employing the analytic reasoning perspective argue that strategic reasoning is predominantly a 'logical activity' (Andrews, 1987; Teece, 2007). To deal with strategic problems the strategist must first consciously and thoroughly analyse the problem situation. Data must be gathered on all developments external to the organization and these data must be processed to pinpoint the opportunities and threats in the organization's environment. Furthermore, the organization itself must be appraised, to uncover its strengths and weaknesses and to establish which resources are available. Once the problem has been defined, a number of alternative strategies can be identified by matching external opportunities to internal strengths. Then, the strategic options must be extensively screened, by evaluating them on a number of criteria, such as internal consistency, external consonance, competitive advantage, organizational feasibility, potential return and risks. The best strategy can be selected by comparing the scores of all options and determining the level of risk the strategist is willing to take. The chosen strategy can subsequently be implemented.

This type of intellectual effort requires well-developed analytical skills. Strategists must be able to rigorously, consistently and objectively comb through huge amounts of data, interpreting and combining findings to arrive at a rich picture of the current problem situation. Possible solutions require critical appraisal and all possible contingencies must be logically thought through. Advocates of the analytic reasoning perspective argue that such reasoning strongly resembles the problem-solving approach of chess grandmasters (Simon, 1987). They also thoroughly assess their competitive position, sift through a variety of options and calculate which course of action brings the best chances of success. Therefore, the reasoning processes of chess grandmasters can be used as an analogy for what goes on in the mind of the strategist.

While depicted here as a purely step-by-step process of recognition, analysis, formulation and implementation, proponents of the analytic reasoning perspective note that in reality strategists often have to backtrack and redo some of these steps, as new information becomes available or chosen strategies do not work out. Strategists attempt to be as comprehensive, consistent and rigorous as possible in their analyses and calculations, but, of course, they cannot know everything and their conclusions are not always perfect: even with the most advanced forecasting techniques, not all developments can be foreseen; even with state-of-the-art market research, some trends can be missed; even with cutting-edge test marketing, scenario analyses, competitive simulations and net present value calculations, some selected strategies can turn out to be failures. Strategists are not all knowing and do make mistakes – their rationality is limited by incomplete information and imperfect cognitive abilities. Yet, strategists try to be as rational as possible. Simon (1957) refers to this as 'bounded rationality' – 'people act intentionally rational, but only limitedly so'.

The (bounded) rational strategist must sometimes improvise to make up for a lack of information, but will try to do this as logically as possible. Inferences and speculation will always be based on the facts as known. By articulating assumptions and explicitly stating the facts and arguments on which conclusions have been based, problem definitions and solutions can be debated within the firm to confirm that they have been arrived at using sound reasoning. This strongly resembles the scientific method, in that hypotheses are formulated and tested as a means for obtaining new knowledge. Only by this consistent alignment of mental models with empirical reality can the strategist avoid the danger of becoming stuck with an outdated cognitive map.

Of course, creativity techniques can be beneficial for escaping from an outdated mental frame. Whether it is by means of brainstorming, six thinking caps or action art, creative thinking can spark some unconventional thoughts. Even a rational scientist like Newton has remarked that 'no great discovery was ever made without a bold guess'. But this is usually where the usefulness of creativity ends and to which it should be limited. To be able to sift the sane from the zany, logic is needed. To make sense of the multitude of new ideas the logical thinker must analyse and evaluate them.

The alternative to this rational approach, it is often pointed out, is to be irrational and illogical, which surely cannot be a desirable alternative for the strategist. Non-rational reasoning comes in a variety of forms. For instance, people's thinking can be guided by their emotions. Feelings such as love, hate, guilt, regret, pride, anxiety, frustration and embarrassment can all cloud the strategist's understanding of a problem situation and the possible solutions. Adherents of the analytic reasoning perspective do not dispute the importance of emotions – the purpose of an organization is often based on 'personal values, aspirations and ideals', while the motivation to implement strategies is also rooted in human emotions. However, the actual determination of the optimal strategy is a 'rational undertaking' *par excellence* (Andrews, 1987).

Neither is intuitive thinking an appealing alternative for strategists. Of course, intuition can often be useful: decision rules based on extensive experience ('frozen knowledge') are often correct (even if they have been arrived at unconsciously) and they save time and effort. For example, Simon argues that even chess grandmasters make many decisions intuitively, based on tacit rules of thumb, formulated through years of experience. Yet, intuitive judgements must be viewed with great suspicion, as they are difficult to verify and infamously unreliable (e.g. Hogarth, 1980; Schwenk, 1984). Where possible, intuitive thinking should be made explicit – the strategist's cognitive map should be captured on paper (e.g. Anthony *et al.*, 1993; Eden, 1989), so that the reasoning of the strategist can be checked for logical inconsistencies.

In conclusion, advocates of the analytic reasoning perspective argue that emotions and intuition have a small place in the strategic reasoning process, and that logical thinking should be the dominant ingredient. It could be said that the analytic reasoning process of the strategist strongly resembles that of the scientist. The scientific methods of research, analysis, theorizing and falsification are all directly applicable to the process of strategic reasoning – so much so, that the scientific method can be used as the benchmark for strategy development processes. Consequently, the best preparation for effective strategic reasoning would be to be trained in the scientific tradition.

EXHIBIT 2.2   THE ANALYTIC REASONING PERSPECTIVE

BERKSHIRE HATHAWAY: NOT OUTSIDE THE BOX

At the peak of the dotcom boom in September 1999, few people were derided as much as Warren Buffett (1930), chairman of the insurance and investment conglomerate Berkshire Hathaway. Buffett – admiringly nicknamed the Sage of Omaha – had gained a phenomenal reputation as an investor during the 1980s and 1990s, but to most it was clear that he hadn't grasped the opportunities presented by the Internet. The grand old man might have been the guru of the old economy, but he simply did not understand the new rules of the information age. He was considered a pitiful example of a once brilliant mind that had not been able to make the leap beyond conventional beliefs and comprehend the 'new paradigm'. The investment strategy of Berkshire Hathaway was deemed hopelessly outdated. When almost all funds were rushing into new economy shares, the investment portfolio of Berkshire consisted of companies like Coca-Cola, Walt Disney, Gillette and the Washington Post. The shares of Berkshire traded at the lowest level in years.

The person least perturbed by this new, dubious status was Buffett himself. In his 1999 annual 'Letter to the Berkshire Hathaway Shareholders', he displayed an untouched faith in the fundamentals that had made him one of the richest people in the world: 'If we have a strength, it is in recognizing when we are operating well within our circle of competence and when we are approaching the perimeter. ... we just stick with what we understand. If we stray, we will have done so inadvertently, not because we got restless and substituted hope for rationality.' He refused to invest in Internet stocks, which he considered 'chain letters', in which early participants get rich at the expense of later ones. As the dotcom bubble eventually burst, Buffett was more than exonerated.

This famous episode was neither Buffet's first provocative stance against lemming behaviour, nor his last. Following his personal mantra that 'when other investors are greedy be fearful, but when other investors are fearful be greedy', Buffett has always stuck to his analysis and gone against the grain. For instance, during the stock market frenzy of 1969 he was widely ridiculed for not participating in the party. To his shareholders he wrote: 'I am out of step with present conditions. When the game is no longer played your way, it is only human to say the new approach is all wrong, bound to lead to trouble, and so on. On one point, however, I am clear. I will not abandon a previous approach whose logic I understand (although I find it difficult to apply) even though it may mean foregoing large, and apparently easy, profits to embrace an approach which I don't fully understand, have not practised successfully, and which possibly could lead to substantial permanent loss of capital.'

Forty years later, during the worst stock market crash since the Great Depression, Warren Buffett was again held to be a fool. With Berkshire Hathaway having lost up to $25 billion of market value within the span of a year, he was arguing that the time was right to boldly buy: 'I don't like to opine on the stock market, and again I emphasize that I have no idea what the market will do in the short term. Nevertheless, I'll follow the lead of a restaurant that opened in an empty bank building and then advertised: "Put your mouth where your money was." Today my money and my mouth both say equities.' True to his words, Buffett invested $5 billion in Goldman Sachs in September 2008, as panic about the American financial system was breaking out all around him. In his 2008 shareholder report, he frankly admitted that he had done 'some dumb things in investments', but that overall he was satisfied with the new additions to his portfolio: 'Whether we're talking about socks or stocks, I like buying quality merchandise when it is marked down.'

When valuing companies, Buffet's approach has always been based on a thorough analysis of company fundamentals, 'to separate investment from speculation'. Ultimately, share prices will reflect these fundamentals and therefore nothing can substitute for a meticulous diagnosis of the sustainability of the competitive advantage of a firm. As Buffet puts it: 'I try to buy stock in businesses that are so wonderful that an idiot can run them. Because sooner or later, one will. 'Following this logic, he stays away from investing in ill-understood businesses and in fast-changing industries, 'in which the long-term winners are hard to identify'. And when he invests, he keeps his shareholdings for years, or even decades. 'Risk', he states, 'comes from not knowing what you're doing.'

His emphasis on rational reasoning and not following the wisdom of crowds ('a public opinion poll is no substitute for thought'), does not mean that he takes a liking to those who pretend to be scientific and rational ('beware of geeks bearing formulas'). He warns of professionals and academicians talking of efficient markets, dynamic hedging and betas: 'Their interest in such matters is understandable, since techniques shrouded in mystery clearly have value to the purveyor of investment advice. After all, what witch doctor has ever achieved fame and fortune by simply advising "Take two aspirins"?'

While still going strong at his advanced age, many commentators have warned that Berkshire Hathaway is vulnerable due to its dependence on its elderly chairman. Buffet's response so far has been totally in character: 'I've reluctantly discarded the notion of my continuing to manage the portfolio after my death – abandoning my hope to give new meaning to the term "thinking outside the box".'

Co-author: Martijn Rademakers

Sources: www.berkshirehathaway.com; *The Economist*, 15 March 2001, 18 December 2008; *Sunday Times*, 1 March 2009; *New York Times*, 16 October 2008, 1 March 2009.

The holistic reasoning perspective

Strategists taking a holistic reasoning perspective are strongly at odds with the unassailable position given to logic in the analytic reasoning perspective. They agree that logic is important, but emphasize the 'wicked' (Mason and Mitroff, 1981; Rittel, 1972), 'ill-defined' (Claxton, 1998; Hayashi, 2001) or 'unstructured' (Shapiro and Spence, 1997) nature of strategic problems. It is argued that strategic problems cannot be rationally and objectively defined, but that they are open to interpretation from a limitless variety of angles. The same is true for the possible solutions – there is no fixed set of problem solutions from which the strategist must select the best one. Defining and solving strategic problems, it is believed, is fundamentally a judgement activity. As such, strategic reasoning has very little in common with the thought processes of the aforementioned chess grandmaster, as was presumed by the rationalists. Playing chess is a 'tame', well-defined and structured problem. The problem definition is clear and all options are known. In the average game of chess, consisting of 40 moves, 10,120 possibilities have to be considered (Simon, 1972). This makes it a difficult game for humans to play, because of their limited computational capacities. Chess grandmasters are better at making these calculations than other people and are particularly good at computational shortcuts – recognizing which things to figure out and which not. However, even the best chess grandmasters have been beaten at the game by IBM's Deep Blue, a highly logical computer with a superior number-crunching capability. For the poor chess grandmaster, the rules of the game are fixed and there is little room for redefining the problem or introducing innovative approaches.

Engaging in business strategy is an entirely different matter. Strategic problems are wicked. Problem definitions are highly subjective and there are no fixed sets of solutions. It is therefore impossible to 'identify' the problem and 'calculate' an optimal solution. Opportunities and threats do not exist, waiting for the analyst to discover them. A strategist understands that a situation can be 'viewed' as an opportunity and 'believes' that certain factors can be threatening if not approached properly. Neither can strengths and weaknesses be objectively determined – a strategist can employ a company characteristic as a strength, but can also turn a unique company quality into a weakness by a lack of vision. Hence, doing a SWOT analysis (strengths, weaknesses, opportunities and threats) actually has little to do with logical analysis, but in reality is nothing less than an interpretation of a problem situation. Likewise, it is a fallacy to believe that strategic options follow more or less logically from the characteristics of the firm and its environment. Strategic options are not 'deduced from the facts' or selected from a 2x2 matrix, but are dreamt up. Strategists must be able to use their intuition to imagine previously unknown solutions. If more than one strategic option emerges from the mind of the strategist, these cannot be simply scored and ranked to choose the optimal one. Some analyses can be done, but as the development of many factors is susceptible to fundamental uncertainty, ultimately, the strategist will have to intuitively judge which vision for the future has the best chance of being created in reality.

Even when a thorough analytic reasoning would be helpful, there is often just not enough time to complete a full analysis. Strategists need to trust the reflexes of the unconscious mind that combines all sort of unrelated signs into a new and comprehending pattern, in order to think and act fast. Holistic thinking is very intense work, as strategists must leave the intellectual safety of analysing and planning processes, guided by little else than their intuition. They must be willing to operate without the security of analysing, testing, arguing, challenging, doubting and living among the rubble of demolished certainties, without having proof and new certainties to give them shelter. To proponents of the holistic reasoning perspective, it is essential for strategists to give leeway to the tacit knowing and feelings of the unconscious mind and arrive at the right judgement.

Proponents of the holistic reasoning perspective stress that logic is often more a hindrance than a help. The heavy emphasis placed on rationality can actually frustrate the main objective of strategic reasoning – to generate a novel understanding, based on intuitive judgement of a multitude of factors and the inputs of all senses (seeing, hearing, feeling) and sources (clients, reports, employees, news channels). Analysis can be a useful tool, but rigidly following formal rules and using logic to redefine deviating signs into confirmations of the common does not tear up outdated cognitive maps. For this reason, proponents of the holistic reasoning perspective argue that strategists should avoid the false certainty projected by rational approaches to strategic reasoning, but should nurture intuition as their primary cognitive asset. To reinvent the future, intuitive thinking should be the driving force, with creativity as a supporting means. As such, strategic reasoning closely resembles the frame-breaking behaviour common in the arts. In fields such as painting, music, motion pictures, dancing and architecture, artists are propelled by the drive to challenge convention and to seek out innovative approaches.

In conclusion, advocates of the holistic reasoning perspective argue that the essence of strategic reasoning is the ability to trust their senses, generate new and unique ways of understanding, and think and act fast. Openness to intuition can be activated by using metaphors, contradictions and paradoxes, and consequently the best preparation for strategic reasoning might actually be to get trained in the artistic tradition of iconoclastic intuition and mental flexibility.

EXHIBIT 2.3   THE HOLISTIC REASONING PERSPECTIVE

Q & A WITH RICHARD BRANSON

He has conquered the most impossible adventure challenges; built over 400 companies by shaking up complacent industries; is on a mission to bring space travel to the man on the street and is committed to building world-class African entrepreneurs. We stalked Richard Branson on a recent trip to the Johannesburg-based Branson Centre of Entrepreneurship and talked intuition vs brainpower and the implausibility of British Airways condoms.

GQ: You and others have said that businesses need to do good in order to stay relevant and in business. Do you think it's easy to get caught out when you are not?

RB: I think the public is no fool and sees through companies that have a corporate-responsibility

office at the back of the building and pretend it's at the front of the building. If you are going to do good, it's got to be absolutely genuine. Having said that, I'd rather people tried something than nothing at all.

GQ: The message from many entrepreneurs is to persevere and everything will work out. You have had both experiences – where you have abandoned certain ventures and in other instances hung in there and eventually made money. Is it a gut thing, knowing which way to go?

RB: It is perhaps one of the reasons having mentors is important – someone who can sit young entrepreneurs down and give them advice when they encounter situations like that. I have in the past been known to go on too long with companies because companies are, in the end, people and you don't want to close a company down and have to lose people. I suspect you really

▶

do know when the chances of being able to pull a plane out of a nosedive sound realistic or if the course is too much. Having one or two people you can trust to go to in those situations [is important] because sometimes you get too close to the situation and the people and cannot make a dispassionate decision.

GQ: Your first business was a magazine. Given the climate we are in, if you were to launch a magazine today, what kind of magazine would it be?

RB: I love physical magazines, but I suspect it would have to be an Internet-based magazine. We recently launched a magazine called *Project on the Internet*, which is quite bold and brave because an Internet-only magazine, or on an iPad, has never really existed before. People have kind of been putting *Wired* magazine on the Internet as well as the bookstores, and therefore the advertising market wasn't there for it. But having said that, *Project* has stuck in there and the advertising is coming. I do think there is a good future for advertisers in that space; it can be so much more imaginative than on a flat page.

GQ: You're pretty much a 'gut' man. Can you identify any brain decisions in your career?

RB: Intuition based on experience is perhaps slightly more useful than pure gut. It is the intuition of flying on other people's airlines and finding that the experience was not that good, feeling you can improve on that, and then starting an airline. It's that kind of intuition that works. The intuition that makes you think that if I want to go into space, there are millions of other people like me who would like to go to space. So if we could get the price down to what was affordable then there would be a market and then therefore, screw it, let's go find an engineer who can build a spaceship company. As far as using brainpower, that comes later: finding someone who can build a spaceship and

maybe finding someone with the brainpower to mop up after you when your intuition was getting ahead of you.

GQ: You have successfully 'Virginized' many industries and brands. If there was a formula for creating successful brand extensions, what would that be?

RB: Most businesses are focused on one sector. I love challenges and have been able to take Virgin forward into a lot of areas. We have been able to build a reputation that makes going to those businesses that much easier. If you were building another brand to do the same thing, you need a name that can work internationally, that works on any product. British Airways condoms wouldn't work particularly well. Anyway, nothing named British Airways would work that well [laughs]. A brand like Apple, you could stretch that brand, but others you wouldn't. So it is worth keeping in mind the international nature of the brand name.

GQ: You are involved in hundreds of businesses and are in partnership with many. How do young empire-building entrepreneurs learn salient things such as how much to take on themselves, when to get partners or when to employ people?

RB: People spend far too long clinging on and not delegating and dealing with the bigger picture. As early on in the business – as soon as you can afford it – as possible, you should find somebody better than yourself to run the business so you can push the company forward and make sure the business survives and thrives. It means you can have more time for your family and your friends and have a more decent life. I could not have grown 400 companies if I hadn't learned the art of delegation at a very young age.

Sources: Siphiwe Mpye, GQ Digital Edition, www. gq.co.za/report/636702.html. Reproduced by permission of Condé Nast Independent Magazines and Siphiwe Mpye.

MANAGING THE PARADOX OF LOGIC AND INTUITION

Men like the opinions to which they have become accustomed from youth; this prevents them from finding the truth, for they cling to the opinions of habit.

Moses Maimonides (1135–1204), Egyptian physician and philosopher

Opinions differ sharply about whether the rational or the intuitive reasoning perspective is more valuable for understanding strategic thinking. Although they are opposites and partially contradictory, both perspectives might reveal crucial aspects of strategic thinking that need to be combined to achieve superior results. Of course, the tension is not so pressing for investment managers and art painters, but most strategizing managers struggle with managing the tension. See Table 2.1 for the main differences.

So, how can strategizing managers manage the paradox of logic and intuition? With the taxonomy of the first chapter in mind (Figure 1.9), the following options have been suggested by scholars in the management sciences.

Navigating

Applying logic and intuition at the same time is complex because it requires different thinking modes and procedures. To deal with these contrasting needs, some authors have suggested 'build in mental time-outs' (e.g. Sadler-Smith, 2010) in daily routines to allow creative ideas to incubate. This kind of 'creativity' is accepted by analytical thinkers as a useful contribution to a largely rational process, while intuitive thinkers categorize creativity as an inherent part of the intuitive and holistic thinking mode. When the leadership team separates formal analytic from informal intuitive processes in time, such teams engage in 'temporal separation' – navigating the paradox.

TABLE 2.1   Analytic reasoning versus holistic reasoning perspective

	Analytic reasoning perspective	*Holistic reasoning perspective*
Emphasis on	Logic over creativity	Intuition over logic
Dominant cognitive style	Analytic	Holistic
Thinking follows	Formal, fixed rules	Informal, variable rules
Nature of thinking	Deductive and computational	Inductive and imaginative
Mode of thinking	Structured	Unstructured
Direction of thinking	Vertical	Lateral
System at work	Conscious, reflective	Unconscious, reflexive
Problem-solving seen as	Analysing activities	Sensemaking activities
Value placed on	Cold cognition	Hot cognition
Assumption about reality	Objective, (partially) knowable	Subjective, (partially) creatable
Thinking hindered by	Incomplete information	Adherence to current cognitive map
Strategizing speed	Slow	Fast
Strategizing based on	Calculation	Judgement
Metaphor	Strategy as science	Strategy as art

Parallel processing

Not all organizational activities need the same levels of logic and intuition, as the nature of the problems differs throughout the firm. For example, increasing production efficiency is a complex yet tame problem that mainly benefits from analytic reasoning, while new business development is more of a wicked problem that leans towards holistic reasoning. By organizing the company's activities in separate units or departments, strategizing managers also allocate people with the required competences and different thinking styles separately. As a consequence, logical and intuitive thinking are processed in parallel throughout the organization.

Embracing

Strategists can deliberately bring analytic and holistic thinkers together in one team, so as to mix 'individuals with analytical and intuitive cognitive styles (Hodgkinson and Clarke, 2007). The intention is not to resolve the tension between logic and intuition, but to capture the advantages of both by bringing together people with different educational backgrounds, thinking styles and also – as in the case of Samsung (Exhibit 2.1) – cultural backgrounds. Of course, applying different thinking styles in one team is likely to create tensions between team members. Such tensions, however, often actually lead to unexpected solutions and innovations. The option is demanding for the strategizing managers in the team and therefore often requires specific capabilities, such as integrative thinking (Martin, 2007) and complexity maturity (as discussed in Chapter 11).

STRATEGIC THINKING IN INTERNATIONAL PERSPECTIVE

Co-authors: Gep Eisenloeffel and Wester Wagenaar

When I look carefully I see the
nazuna blooming
By the hedge.
Matsuo Bashō (松尾 芭蕉 (1644–1694), born Matsuo Kinsaku (松尾 金作), Japanese poet and greatest master of haiku

Flower in the crannied wall, I pluck
you out of the crannies, I hold you
here, root and all, in my hand,
Little flower—but if I could
understand
What you are, root and all, and all
in all,
I should know what God and man is.
Alfred Tennyson, 1st Baron Tennyson, (1809–1892), Poet Laureate of Great Britain and Ireland

The question that must be added to the debate on the mind of the strategist is whether there are discernable international differences in approaches to strategic thinking. Are there specific national or regional preferences between the analytic and the holistic reasoning perspective or are inclinations towards logical or intuitive thinking solely dependent on individual dispositions? Are the differing views spread randomly across the globe or are views on strategic reasoning similar around the world? As a stimulus to the debate, a number of factors will be brought forward that highlight differences in how various regions tackle the paradox between logic and intuition. These are structured into three different levels that influence an inclination towards one of the two sides: the societal, the industry and the personal level.

On the societal level

When it comes to regional preferences to engage in intuitive or analytical reasoning, scholars tend to pit West against East: the US and West European countries favour reason, while China, Korea and Japan emphasize the normative value of intuition over rule-based reasoning (Nisbett *et al.*, 2001; Wonder and Blake, 1992). This is echoed by cross-cultural studies which indicate the preference of Western participants to base decisions on the conscious use of formal, decontextualized rules, more so than do East-Asian participants (Norenzayan *et al.*, 2002). In more practical sense, this difference manifests itself in the way arguments are built up. Where most of the world shapes an argument logically by either putting principles first (France, Spain) or putting applications first (US), Asia is arguably a different case. According to Erin Meyer (2014), Westerners follow a 'specific approach' to build up an argument, while Asians follow a more holistic route.

Historical narratives also emphasize a regional division in preferences. The story usually starts in ancient Greece, taking us through the Age of Reason and on to rationalism and the prestige it enjoyed during the 18th, 19th and 20th centuries. Richard Brooks (2012) argues in his book *The Social Animal* that 'the tradition of rationalism in the West tells the story of human history as the story of the logical, conscious mind. It sees human history as the contest between reason and instinct. In the end, reason triumphs over emotion. Science gradually replaces myth. Logic wins out over passion'.

This is no different in the field of strategy. As Henry Mintzberg *et al.* point out in their book *Strategy Safari* (1998), from its inception, pioneering scholars in the strategy field, such as Ansoff (1965), Chandler (1962) and Porter (1980), were strongly influenced by the rationalist analytic approach. Strategizing was embedded in the tradition of rationality, including the tools and techniques, with problems divided into discrete parts and solved on the basis of reliable facts and figures. Conscious cognition (sensing) was valued over the unconscious (intuition), rational reasoning over holistic reasoning. This general preference of scholars in the field of strategy can also be generalized to managers in the US. Hampden-Turner and Trompenaars (2000) for example, found that over 70 per cent of managers in the US score highest on introvert (versus extrovert), sensing (as opposed to intuition), thinking (instead of feeling), and judging (contrary to perceiving) on the Meyers-Briggs Type Indicator.

Assumptions of the analytic rationalist approach have been criticized by a number of scholars, but there has been a general perception that logic and reason prevail over intuition in the West. Therefore, intuition has traditionally been downplayed or denigrated in Western societies (e.g. Gladwell, 2007; Lieberman, 2000). The Western view was most notably challenged in the 1980s by Japanese alternatives to management practices. For example, Richard T. Pascale, co-author of *The Art of Japanese Management* (1981), criticized the Western perception on strategizing, considering the rational analytic approach to be 'myopic and an oversimplification of reality'. It is only relatively recently that the value of intuition has truly started to enjoy appreciation in English literature on management (e.g. Dane and Pratt, 2007).

On the industry level

While individual dispositions and societies have an influence on an inclination towards either logic or intuition, this is also the case for certain industries. Regardless of where you are, some business sectors tend to demand either one and there are some where a clear preference for one of the two thinking styles can be noticed. In the biotechnology industry, thinking holistically plays a major role. Here strategists tend to encourage scientists to act on promising leads by interpreting data and problems from as many angles as possible – a fine recipe for more than just following formula (Hodgkinson *et al.*, 2009, p. 278). A similar preference can be observed in the creative sector, where designers and developers are often emboldened to think outside of the box. The opposite, where logic is encouraged, can also be true: Accountants generally favour the analytical reasoning perspective over the holistic reasoning perspective. The middle ground is usually occupied by entrepreneurs, people who have been found to adequately balance the intuitive and the deliberate (Groves *et al.*, 2008).

To the strategist

Psychologists tend to agree that the human mind operates through a dual-process structure. Behaviour is jointly influenced by both the slow, deliberately controlled system and the fast, intuitively automatic system (Kahneman, 2011; Mukherjee, 2010; Pachur and Spaar, 2015, p. 303). Every individual has a natural inclination towards either one of them (Nisbett *et al.*, 2001, p. 291) and these differences between individual dispositions are referred to as decision styles. A 'decisional fit' occurs when the way in which a decision is made matches the preferred decision style of the decision-maker. He or she will then perceive the decision as more favourable and will feel less regret in cases of potential negative outcomes (Betsch and Kunz, 2008).

There are a variety of reasons why one style of strategizing might be overly present in one individual and less so in another, with the most prominent being the role played by the environment. When a strategist enters an environment where his preferable thinking style gets penalized, this provides unpleasant experiences. The general result is avoiding situations in which the opposite thinking style is required, which brings about a positive feedback loop of these biases.

Still, individual preferences should not be exaggerated. The wild does not hold two types of strategist, one who relies solely on intuition and the other purely on logic. Instead, we see a continuum of decision-making styles where the two combine. Which of them has the preference is likely to depend on the nature of the problem (Simon, 1987, p. 61). Someone's general tendency does not manifest itself in every decision, because decision styles are not 'chronic'; they are dependent on situations and domains (Pachur and Spaar, 2015). Therefore, the preference for one of the two frameworks depends on the experience and proficiency for a specific problem. For example, expertise in a domain tends to often lead to a desire for intuition (Kahneman, 2011) and a manager's attitude towards risk can vary considerably depending on whether it is a recreational or an investment risk (Hanoch, Johnson and Wilke, 2006).

MISSIONING AND VISIONING

I prefer to be a dreamer among the humblest, with visions to be realized, than lord among those without dreams and desires.

Khalil Gibran (1886–1931), Lebanese-American artist, poet and writer

INTRODUCTION

Corporate mission is a rather elusive concept, often used to refer to the woolly platitudes on the first few pages of annual reports. To many people, mission statements are lists of lofty principles that have potential public relations value, but have little bearing on actual business, let alone impact on the process of strategy formation. Yet, while frequently employed in this superficial manner, a corporate mission can be very concrete and play an important role in determining strategic actions.

A good way to explain the term's meaning is to go back to its etymological roots. 'Mission' comes from the Latin word *mittere*, which means 'to send' (Cummings and Davies, 1994). A mission is some task, duty or purpose that 'sends someone on their way' – a motive or driver propelling someone in a certain direction. Hence, 'corporate mission' can be understood as the basic drivers sending the corporation along its way. The corporate mission consists of the fundamental principles that mobilize and propel the firm in a particular direction.

A concept that is often confused with mission is vision. Individuals or organizations have a vision if they picture a future state of affairs they wish to achieve (from the Latin *videre* – to see; Cummings and Davies, 1994). While the corporate mission outlines the fundamental principles guiding strategic choices, a strategic vision outlines the desired future at which the company hopes to arrive. In other words, vision provides a business ambition while mission provides business principles (see Figure 3.1).

Generally, a strategic vision is a type of aim that is less specific than a short-term target or longer-term objective. Vision is usually defined as a broad conception of a desirable future state, the details of which remain to be determined (e.g. Senge, 1990). As such, strategic vision can play a similar role to corporate mission, pointing the firm in a particular direction and motivating individuals to work together towards a shared end.

The corporate mission and strategic vision contribute to 'sending the firm in a particular direction' by influencing the firm's strategy. To understand how mission and vision impact strategy, three topics require closer attention. First, it is necessary to know what types of 'fundamental principle' actually make up a corporate mission. These elements of corporate mission will be described below. Second, it is important to distinguish between

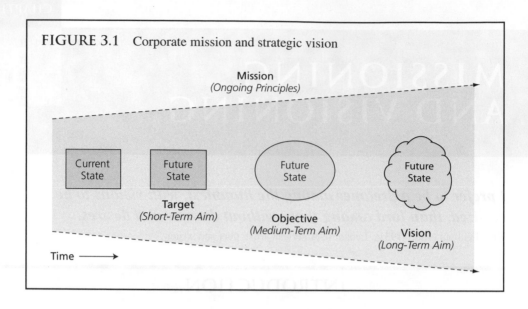

FIGURE 3.1 Corporate mission and strategic vision

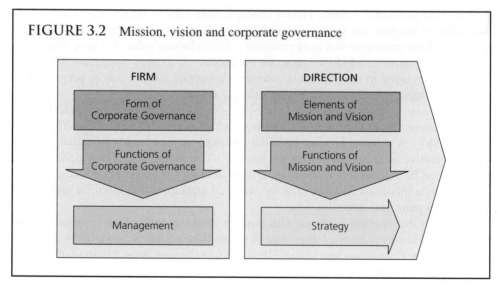

FIGURE 3.2 Mission, vision and corporate governance

different envisioning processes to understand how the vision impacts strategy. Third, it needs to be examined what types of role are played by a corporate mission and strategic vision in the strategy formation process. These functions of corporate mission and strategic vision will also be described (see Figure 3.2).

Besides the 'what' of corporate mission, it is equally important to explore the 'who' – who should determine a corporate mission. The implicit assumption is often that executives are the primary 'strategic actors' responsible for setting the direction of the firm. But, in fact, their actions are formally monitored and controlled by the board of directors. In this way, the direction of the firm must be understood as a result of the interaction between the executives and the board of directors. As the name would imply, directors have an important influence on direction.

The activities of the board of directors are referred to as 'corporate governance' – directors govern the strategic choices and actions of the management of a firm. Due to their importance in setting the corporate mission and strategy, their input will be examined here as well. First, the various functions of corporate governance are reviewed. Then the different forms of corporate governance will be examined, as this can significantly influence the mission, vision and strategy of the organization (see Figure 3.2).

Elements of a corporate mission

A corporate mission is the enduring set of fundamental principles that forms the base of a firm's identity and guides its strategic decision-making. Four components can be distinguished (see Figure 3.3):

- Organizational purpose. At the heart of the corporate mission is the purpose of an organization. Organizational purpose can be defined as the reason for which an organization exists. It can be expected that the perception managers have of their organization's purpose will give direction to the strategy process and influence the strategy content (e.g. Bartlett and Ghoshal, 1994; Campbell and Tawadey, 1990).

- Organizational beliefs. All strategic choices ultimately include important assumptions about the nature of the environment and what the firm needs to do to be successful in its business. If people in a firm do not share the same fundamental strategic beliefs, joint decision-making will be very protracted and tense – opportunities and threats will be interpreted differently and preferred solutions will be very divergent (see Chapter 2). To work swiftly and in unison, a common understanding is needed. The stronger the set of shared beliefs subscribed to by all organizational members, the easier communication

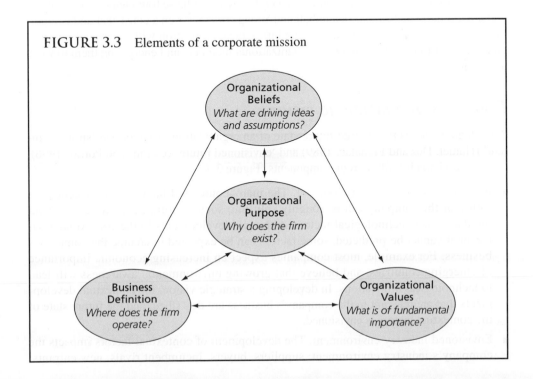

FIGURE 3.3   Elements of a corporate mission

and decision-making will become, and the more confident and driven the group will be. While researchers refer to the organizational ideology ('system of ideas') as their 'collective cognitive map' (Axelrod, 1976), 'dominant logic' (Prahalad and Bettis, 1986) or 'team mental model' (Klimoski and Mohammed, 1994), companies themselves usually simply speak of their beliefs or philosophy.

■ Organizational values. Each person in an organization can have her own set of values, shaping what she believes to be good and just. Yet, when an organization's members share a common set of values, determining what they see as worthwhile activities, ethical behaviour and moral responsibilities, this can have a strong impact on the strategic direction (e.g. Falsey, 1989; Hoffman, 1989). Such widely embraced organizational values also contribute to a clear sense of organizational identity, attracting some individuals, while repelling others. Although it can be useful to explicitly state the values guiding the organization, to be influential they must become embodied in the organization's culture (e.g. Collins and Porras, 1996; McCoy, 1985).

■ Business definitions. For some firms, any business is good business, as long as they can make a reasonable return on investment. Yet, if any business is not fine, the firm will lack a sense of direction. In practice, most firms have a clearer identity, which they derive from being active in a particular line of business. For these firms, having a delimiting definition of the business they wish to be in strongly focuses the direction in which they develop. Their business definition functions as a guiding principle, helping to distinguish opportunities from diversions (e.g. Abell, 1980; Pearce, 1982). Of course, while a clear business definition can focus the organization's attention and efforts, it can likewise lead to short-sightedness and the missing of new business developments (e.g. Ackoff, 1974; Levitt, 1960).

The strength of a corporate mission will depend on whether these four elements fit together and are mutually reinforcing (Campbell and Yeung, 1991). When a consistent and compelling corporate mission is formed, this can infuse the organization with a sense of mission, creating an emotional bond between organizational members and energizing them to work according to the mission.

Elements of a strategic vision

A strategic vision is the desired future state of an organization. Also termed 'strategic intent' (Hamel, Doz and Prahalad, 1989) and 'envisioned future' (Collins and Porras, 1996), a strategic vision is built on four components (Figure 3.4):

■ Envisioned contextual environment. The many contextual factors that influence the future of the company can be roughly split into socio-cultural, economic, political/regulatory and technological factors. Although developments in the contextual environment cannot be predicted, some factors can be expected to change the company's business. For example, most companies expect an increasing economic importance of emerging countries, and believe that growing environmental awareness will lead to technological innovations. In developing a strategic vision, the contextual developments that are relevant to the company's business are described, and the future state of the contextual factors is envisioned.

■ Envisioned industry environment. The development of contextual factors impacts the company's industry environment: suppliers, buyers, incumbent rivals, new entrants,

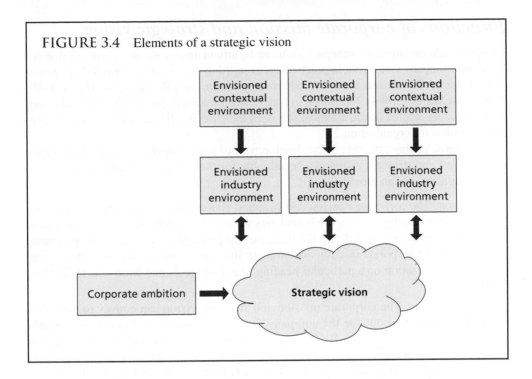

FIGURE 3.4   Elements of a strategic vision

and substitutes and complementors. For example, competitors from emerging countries are expected to enter the industry, and alternative sources of energy are likely to replace fossil fuels in the production process. Some of these developments show up in statistics, strategic intelligence reports, company analyses and other sources of information, while others are based on insider information. In developing a strategic vision, the relevant industry developments are described, and the future state of the industry environment is envisioned.

■ Desired future organizational position. Based on the envisioned contextual and industry environment, the organization describes its desired position in the future. For example, a company may strive for an industry leadership position by forming an alliance with a strong partner in emerging countries and by implementing new sustainable production technologies. The desired position reflects the company's ambitions and is translated into long-term objectives. In a strategic vision, the desired position of the company in the future is described and the long-term objectives are formulated.

■ Time horizon. When developing a strategic vision, leaders must determine how many years ahead the future position will be envisioned. In fact, the time horizon of company visions differs significantly. For some companies 3 years is long term, while others develop visions of 30 years or longer. Many factors determine the time horizon of a company's strategic vision, including industry characteristics. For example, the upstream oil industry requires long-term thinking, as it takes dozens of years between the first exploratory drilling and oil production. Another factor is the cultural context of the company leaders (see the paragraph 'Missioning and visioning in international perspective).

Functions of corporate mission and strategic vision

The corporate mission and strategic vision can be articulated by means of a mission statement and company vision, but in practice not everything that is called a mission statement and company vision meets the above criteria (e.g. Collins and Porras, 1996; David, 1989; Piercy and Morgan, 1994). Firms can, in fact, have a mission and a vision even if it has not been explicitly written down, although this does increase the chance of divergent interpretations within the organization.

In general, paying attention to the development of a consistent and compelling corporate mission and strategic vision can be valuable for three reasons. A corporate mission and strategic vision can provide:

- Direction. The corporate mission and strategic vision can point the organization in a certain direction, by defining the boundaries within which strategic choices and actions must take place. By specifying the fundamental principles on which strategies must be based, the corporate mission and strategy limit the scope of strategic options and set the organization on a particular heading (e.g. Bourgeois and Brodwin, 1983; Hax, 1990).

- Legitimization. The corporate mission and strategic vision can convey to all stakeholders inside and outside the company that the organization is pursuing valuable activities in a proper way. By specifying the business philosophy that will guide the company, the chances can be increased that stakeholders will accept, support and trust the organization (e.g. Freeman and Gilbert, 1988; Klemm, Sanderson and Luffman, 1991).

- Motivation. The corporate mission and strategic vision can go a step further than legitimization, by actually inspiring individuals to work together in a particular way. By specifying the fundamental principles driving organizational actions, an *esprit de corps* can evolve, with the powerful capacity to motivate people over a prolonged period of time (e.g. Campbell and Yeung, 1991; Peters and Waterman, 1982).

These last two functions of a corporate mission and strategic vision, particularly, divide both management theorists and business practitioners. What is seen as a legitimate and motivating organizational purpose is strongly contested. What the main factors of disagreement are is examined in a later section of this chapter.

Functions of corporate governance

The subject of corporate governance, as opposed to corporate management, deals with the issue of governing the strategic choices and actions of top management. Popularly stated, corporate governance is about managing top management – building in checks and balances to ensure that the senior executives pursue strategies that are in accordance with the corporate mission. Corporate governance encompasses all tasks and activities that are intended to supervise and steer the behaviour of top management.

In the common definition, corporate governance 'addresses the issues facing boards of directors' (Tricker, 1994, p. xi). In this view, corporate governance is the task of the directors and therefore attention must be paid to their roles and responsibilities (e.g. Cochran and Wartick, 1994; Keasey, Thompson and Wright, 1997). Others have argued that this definition is too narrow and that, in practice, there are more forces that govern the activities

of top management. In this broader view, boards of directors are only a part of the governance system. For instance, regulation by local and national authorities, as well as pressure
from societal groups, can function as checks and balances, limiting top management's discretion (e.g. Demb and Neubauer, 1992; Mintzberg, 1984). Whether employing a narrow
or broad definition, three important corporate governance functions can be distinguished
(adapted from Tricker, 1994):

- Forming function. The first function of corporate governance is to influence the forming of the corporate mission. The task of corporate governance is shaping, articulating and communicating the fundamental principles that will drive the organization's
  activities. Determining the purpose of the organization and setting priorities among
  claimants are part of the forming function. The board of directors can conduct this task
  by, for example, questioning the basis of strategic choices, influencing the business
  philosophy, and explicitly weighing the advantages and disadvantages of the firm's
  strategies for various constituents (e.g. Freeman and Reed, 1983).

- Performance function. The second function of corporate governance is to contribute
  to the strategy process with the intention of improving the future performance of the
  corporation. The task of corporate governance is to judge strategy initiatives brought
  forward by top management or to actively participate in strategy development. The
  board of directors can conduct this task by, for example, engaging in strategy discussions, acting as a sounding board for top management and networking to secure the
  support of vital stakeholders (e.g. Baysinger and Hoskisson, 1990; Donaldson and
  Davis, 1995; Zahra and Pearce, 1989).

- Conformance function. The third function of corporate governance is to ensure
  corporate conformance to the stated mission and strategy. The task of corporate governance is to monitor whether the organization is undertaking activities as promised and
  whether performance is satisfactory. Where management is found lacking, it is a function of corporate governance to press for changes. The board of directors can conduct
  this task by, for example, auditing the activities of the corporation, questioning and
  supervising top management, determining remuneration and incentive packages, and
  even appointing new managers (e.g. Parkinson, 1993; Spencer, 1983).

These functions give the board of directors considerable influence in determining and realizing the corporate mission. As such, they have the ultimate power to decide on the organizational purpose. Therefore, it is not surprising that the question to whom these functions
should be given is considered extremely important.

Forms of corporate governance

There is considerable disagreement on how boards of directors should be organized and
run. Currently, each country has its own system of corporate governance and the international differences are large. Yet even within many countries, significant disagreements are
discernible. In designing a corporate governance regime, three characteristics of boards of
directors are of particular importance (adapted from Tricker, 1994):

- Board structure. Internationally, there are major differences between countries
  requiring a two-tier board structure (e.g. Austria, China, Germany, the Netherlands and
  Finland), countries with a one-tier board (e.g. Britain, Canada, Finland, Greece, India,

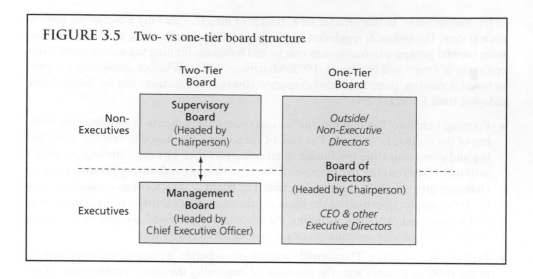

FIGURE 3.5   Two- vs one-tier board structure

Singapore, Spain, Sweden, Turkey, United States), and countries in which companies are free to choose (e.g. Czech Republic, Denmark, Italy, Japan, France, Slovenia and Switzerland). In a two-tier system, there is a formal division of power, with a management board made up of the top executives and a distinct supervisory board made up of non-executives with the task of monitoring and steering the management board. In a one-tier (or unitary) board system, executive and non-executive (outside) directors sit together on one board (see Figure 3.5).

- Board membership. The composition of boards of directors can vary sharply from company to company and from country to country. Some differences are due to legal requirements that are not the same internationally. For instance, in Germany, by law half of the membership of a supervisory board must represent labour, while the other half represents the shareholders. In French companies, labour representatives are given observer status on the board. In China, most of the supervisory board members occupy positions in the Chinese Communist Party. In other countries there are no legal imperatives, yet differences have emerged. In some cases, outside (non-executive) directors from other companies are common, while in other nations, fewer outsiders are involved. Even within countries, differences can be significant, especially with regard to the number, stature and independence of outside (non-executive) directors.

- Board tasks. The tasks and authority of boards of directors also differ quite significantly between companies. In some cases, boards meet infrequently and are merely asked to vote on proposals. Such boards have little formal or informal power to contradict the will of the CEO. In other companies, boards meet regularly and play a more active role in corporate governance, by formulating proposals, proactively selecting new top managers and determining objectives and incentives. Normally, the power of outside (non-executive) directors to monitor and steer a company only partly depends on their formally defined tasks and authority. To a large degree, their impact is determined by how proactive they define their own role.

The question in the context of this chapter is how a board of directors should be run to ensure that the organization's mission is best achieved. What should be the structure, membership and tasks of the board of directors, to realize the ends for which the organization exists?

THE ISSUE OF ORGANIZATIONAL PURPOSE

For many years there has been a lack of attention paid to the subject of organizational purpose in the strategic management literature. This might be due to the widespread assumption that it is obvious why business organizations exist. Some writers might have avoided the topic because it is highly value laden and somehow outside the realm of strategic management. In recent years, however, the subject of organizational purpose has gained increased interest as a result of a number of developments, such as the financial crisis and the increased attention on corporate social responsibility and environmental sustainability.

Managers must constantly make choices and seek solutions based on an understanding of what their organization is intended to achieve. It is hardly possible to avoid taking a stance on what they judge to be the purpose of their organization. They are confronted with many different claimants who believe that the firm exists to serve their interests. Demands are placed on the firm by shareholders, employees, suppliers, customers, governments and communities, forcing managers to weigh whose interests should receive priority over others. Even when explicit demands are not voiced, managers must still determine who will be the main beneficiary of the value-creation activities of the firm.

Determining the organizational purpose is a challenging task, not least because there are so many different views on how it should be done. In this chapter, the issue of organizational purpose will be explored in more detail, with the intention of uncovering the opposite perspectives on the subject of organizational purpose that lie at the heart of the divergent opinions.

THE PARADOX OF PROFITABILITY
AND RESPONSIBILITY

The earth, the air, the land and the water are not an inheritance from our fore fathers, but on loan from our children. So we have to handover to them at least as it was handed over to us.

Mahatma Gandhi (1869–1948), Indian politician and lawyer

Discussions on what firms should strive to achieve are not limited to the field of strategy. Given the influential position of business organizations in society, the purpose they should serve is also discussed by theorists in the fields of economics, political science, sociology, ethics and philosophy. Since the Industrial Revolution and the rise of the modern corporation, the role of business organizations within the 'political economic order' has been a central theme in many of the social sciences. It has been the topic that has filled libraries of books, inspired society-changing theories and stirred deep-rooted controversies.

The enormous impact of corporations on the functioning of society has also attracted political parties, labour unions, community representatives, environmentalists, the media and the general public to the debate. All take a certain position on the role that business organizations should play within society and the duties that they ought to shoulder. Here, too, the disagreements can be heated, often spilling over from the political arena and negotiating tables into the streets.

In countries with a market economy, it is generally agreed that companies should pursue strategies that ensure economic profitability, but that they have certain social responsibilities that must be fulfilled as well. This is, however, where the consensus ends. Opinions differ widely with regard to the relative importance of profitability and responsibility. Some people subscribe to the view that profitability is the very purpose of economic organizations and that the only social responsibility of a firm is to pursue profitability within the boundaries of the law. However, other people argue that business corporations are not only economic entities, but also social institutions, embedded in a social environment, which represents significant social responsibilities. In this view, organizations are morally obliged to behave responsibly towards society and all parties with a stake in the activities of the firm, and profitability is only a means to fulfil this duty.

Most executives accept that both economic profitability and social responsibility are valuable goals to pursue. Yet, as organizational purpose, profitability and responsibility are at least partially contradictory. If managers strive towards profit maximization, shareholders might be enamoured, but this will bring executives into conflict with the optimization of benefits for other stakeholders. In other words, to a certain extent there is a tension between profitability and responsibility (e.g. Cannon, 1992; Demb and Neubauer, 1992; Drucker, 1984; Yoshimori, 1995).

The demand for economic profitability

It is clear that business organizations must be profitable to survive. Yet simple profitability, that is having higher income than costs, is not sufficient. To be an attractive investment, a company must earn a higher return on the shareholders' equity than could be realized if the money were deposited in the bank. Put differently, investors must have a financial incentive to run a commercial risk; otherwise, they could just as well bring their money to the bank or buy low-risk bonds.

Yet, offsetting the risk carried by investors is but a small part of the larger picture. Once a corporation has established a track record of profitability, this inspires trust among financiers. Such trust makes it much easier to raise new capital, either through borrowing (at more attractive rates) or by issuing new shares. And of course, new capital can be used to further the competitive objectives of the organization. Where companies have not been particularly profitable in the past and cannot authoritatively project an attractive level of profitability in the future, they will find it difficult or virtually impossible to find new financing. This can significantly weaken the position of the firm and undermine its long-term competitiveness.

For publicly traded corporations, strong profitability is usually reflected in higher share prices, which is not only beneficial to the shareholders at that moment, but also makes it easier to acquire other firms and to pay with shares. Moreover, a high share price is the best defence against a hostile takeover and the best negotiating chip for a friendly one. In both publicly and privately held companies, retained profits can also be an important source of funds for new investments.

In short, profitability is not only a *result*, but also a *source* of competitive power. Profitability provides a company with the financial leeway to improve its competitive position and pursue its ambitions.

The demand for societal responsibility

As economic entities engaging in formalized arrangements with employees, suppliers, buyers and government agencies, corporations have the legal responsibility to abide by the stipulations outlined in their contracts. Equally, they are bound to stay within the 'letter of the law' in each jurisdiction in which they operate. However, being good corporate citizens entails more than just staying out of court.

Companies are more than just 'economic machines' regulated by legal contracts. They are also networks of people, working together towards a common goal. And as members of a social group, people within a company need to develop a sense of 'community' if they are to function properly. One of the most basic needs is to build a level of trust among people – a feeling of security that each individual's interests will be taken into account. Trust evolves where people feel certain that others will behave in a responsible manner, instead of letting their own self-interest prevail without limitation. Once there is enough trust between people, they can engage in productive teamwork and invest in their mutual relationships.

Hence, societal responsibility – that is, acting in the interest of others, even when there is no legal imperative – lies at the basis of trust. Where there is trust, people are generally willing to commit themselves to the organization, both emotionally and practically. Emotionally, they will become involved with, and can become strongly connected to, the organization, which can lead to a sense of pride and loyalty. Practically, they will be willing to invest years acquiring firm-specific knowledge and skills, and in building a career. Such commitments make people dependent on the organization, as they will be less able and inclined to job hop. It is therefore vital that the organization rewards such commitment by acting responsibly, even where this hurts profitability; otherwise the bond of trust can be seriously damaged.

Acting in the interest of all employees is a limited form of societal responsibility. Just as it is beneficial for trust to evolve within organizations, it is important for trust to develop between the organization and its broader environment of buyers, suppliers, governments, local communities and activist groups. Therefore, it is important that these organizations also come to trust that the organization is willing to act in a societally responsible way, even when this entails sacrificing profitability.

EXHIBIT 3.1 SHORT CASE

FONTERRA: CREAMING THE PROFITS IN DAIRY?

Fonterra is easily one of the world's top six dairy companies – quite an achievement for a firm based in the small, isolated country of New Zealand. An important part of its business is supplying bulk ingredients such as milk powder, butter and cheese to international markets. By 2013, it was the world's largest global processor and trader of milk products. It also owns valuable international brands including Anchor, Anlene and Anmum. Despite an industry downturn in 2014–2017, Fonterra's strategic position still looks attractive given that global

▶

dairy consumption is forecast to continue outstripping supply growth in India, Africa and much of Asia. By way of contrast, size and prominence seldom come without controversy. Fonterra faces conflicting pressures on its strategy, from the farmers who own the business and from other influential stakeholders.

Fonterra, in its present form, was founded in 2001 by a merger of the two largest farmer-owned cooperatives and the Dairy Board, which at that time held a statutory export monopoly. Since then, the dairy industry in New Zealand has continued to expand, growing production volumes from 13 billion litres of milk to 18 billion litres by 2016. This expansion has been possible because New Zealand's climate allows for a highly efficient model of milk production: the cattle graze almost exclusively on natural pasture, eliminating the expense and energy consumption of heated barns and food concentrate. As a result, milk production is not only cost efficient, but also generates lower carbon emissions than other production methods, even after accounting for shipping. The costs of producing a kilogram of milk solids in New Zealand have historically been lower than in almost any other country, although increased land prices and wider international adoption of industrial-scale dairying threaten this lowest cost position.

In common with other dairy businesses around the world, Fonterra is a farmer-owned cooperative, with 10,700 owner-suppliers. The principle of the cooperative is that farmers own shares in proportion to the quantity of milk they supply. Fonterra's shares are not traded on any stock exchange, as non-suppliers cannot buy them and the New Zealand government has no direct involvement with the business. The shares represent a significant financial commitment for the dairy farmers. Many of the farmers are actually highly indebted, due to the cost of land purchases and investment in irrigation,

facilities and stock that many have made during the recent expansion. Indeed, to help them through lean times, in 2015 Fonterra offered its suppliers loans on favourable terms.

Fonterra's governance structure reflects its constitution as a cooperative. Not only do the farmers directly elect nine of the 13 board members, but they also have further oversight of the board via the 35-member elected Shareholders' Council. The Shareholders' Council in turn appoints a Milk Commissioner to mediate in any disputes between Fonterra and individual shareholders. In practice, the farmers indeed have a strong influence on board behaviour. Given the trend towards fewer, larger dairy farms, this influence seems destined to increase.

Another important constraint on Fonterra's strategic freedom to manoeuvre is the reliance many of its shareholders have on dividend payments. This limits the firm's ability to fund growth and investment through retained earnings. When farmers increase the volumes of milk they supply to the cooperative, equity capital flows in and the business can use this capital to fund capacity expansion. However, this dependency on gaining supply volumes biases Fonterra's management towards processing bulk commodity products. In 2012 Fonterra's board introduced a revised capital structure that avoids redemption risk in the event that too many suppliers leave the industry or elect to supply a rival processor. Fonterra suppliers now trade Fonterra shares between them, and can sell economic rights to some of their shares to a separate fund that is open to outside investors. Farmers retain control of the business, as the outside investors do not have voting rights. However, even with the revised capital structure, the firm still has fewer options for raising capital than its larger multinational competitors.

A recurring strategic issue at Fonterra has been how, and to what extent, to build businesses that add value beyond the efficient processing and trading of commodity dairy products. In 2016, its commodity-focused business generated over two-thirds of corporate revenue, despite initiatives to prioritise growth in higher returning products. Although New Zealand's efficient dairy industry means that farmers can profit from the sale of commodities, volatile commodity prices and exchange rates undermine the value of this strategy. So too do trade barriers and farm subsidies in major markets such as the European Union and the United States.

Many of Fonterra's options to develop new sources of value creation draw on its processing and logistics expertise to manage international operations. This often involves partnership agreements with overseas suppliers and customers. The cooperative sources almost 20 per cent of its milk from outside New Zealand. From a shareholder's perspective, this can be problematic because it means that New Zealand farmers' capital helps finance ventures that, by some arguments, compete with their own milk production. The problem is compounded by the fact that many of the opportunities for Fonterra lie in fast-growing but less developed markets such as China and India. This, in turn, increases the risk involved in such ventures and requires more specialist skills at managing politically complex transnational relationships. Commentators have argued that the skills and preferences of Fonterra's farmer-dominated board are not closely aligned with managing multinational ventures. Furthermore, the higher levels of business risk sit uncomfortably with the financial position of many of Fonterra's owners.

One of Fonterra's international ventures was a joint venture agreement with the Sanlu dairy company in China. This arrangement came to an abrupt end in 2008 when Sanlu was struck by a milk contamination scandal that affected thousands of infants and led to the death of at least six. Because it held a 43 per cent equity stake in the business, Fonterra became embroiled in the scandal. It became clear that Fonterra's oversight of this business was weak at both board and operational level to the extent that it either did not know about, or was unable to curtail, the contamination scandal for many months after it first came to the attention of Sanlu's management. When Sanlu went bankrupt, Fonterra had to write off over NZ$200 million of its investment in the venture. In response to these events, Fonterra took more control of its supply chain in China, including investing in several farms and managing them to its own standards. At the same time, dairy businesses in China sought the safety of New Zealand-sourced milk. For example, Bright Dairy took a major stake in Synlait, a rival milk processor to Fonterra. This highlights the importance of New Zealand's reputation as a source of pure product: Some commentators have questioned the wisdom of part-sourcing Fonterra-owned brands from elsewhere.

As well as dealing with pressures from shareholders, Fonterra must manage its relationship with other influential stakeholders. In lobbying for support, during boom times in 2012 it was not shy to point out that it contributed 26 per cent of New Zealand's export revenues. It also makes much of the economic spin-off effects of its activities, which extend beyond dairy farmers to communities, regions and cities. These spin-offs mean that the economic fortunes of the business have a major influence on those of New Zealand as a whole. However, power and importance at this level often do not engender popularity. Fonterra not only controls a very high proportion of the liquid milk supply to the domestic market, but also owns several of the major brands of cheese, butter and yoghurt. When the international commodity milk price is high, dairy prices rise for domestic consumers, which they tend to see as profiteering at their expense.

Another important area of stakeholder interest in Fonterra comes from the environmental impact of its activities. Many of these impacts come from dairy farming itself and hence Fonterra does not directly control them, but stakeholders still consider them to be inextricably linked to Fonterra. Intensive dairying is both a major consumer of water for irrigation and potentially a polluter of water via runoff of effluent and nitrogen fertilizer. The pollution threatens local ecosystems and threatens to undermine the unusually pure municipal water supply enjoyed by domestic consumers. The high water consumption threatens these same water supplies due to over-extraction of this historically lightly regulated resource. Fonterra has initiatives and targets to improve the industry's performance in these areas, but critics say these are still not enough. Even in 2014–2015, the industry acknowledged that almost 6 per cent of the country's dairy farms were in significant breach of standards for effluent runoff.

Perhaps the most crucial long-term stakeholder challenge for Fonterra and the dairy industry is its contribution to New Zealand's emissions of greenhouse gases. The problem arises principally from methane emissions, a by-product of cows' digestion. Methane is an especially potent greenhouse gas, such that in 2014, emissions of methane and nitrous oxide (largely from agriculture) made up 54 per cent of New Zealand's total greenhouse gas output. Because New Zealand has committed to the Kyoto Agreement, it must pay directly for above-quota emissions, triggering the government to consider the possibility that farmers should contribute to this expense.

Despite this apparently daunting set of challenges, Fonterra remains a successful, growing firm that is a leader in its industry. The decision Fonterra's board and management face if it is to sustain its performance is whether and to what degree to take into account the diverse set of stakeholder concerns. If it spends heavily to address these concerns, it risks compromising the immediate interests of its owners, hence losing their support. If it does too little, it risks undermining its operating environment (for example, by stimulating unfavourable legislation), and hence compromising its owners' future interests. The board and management must deal with the latent conflict between competing shareholder interests. They have a delicate path to tread in resolving the tension between respecting the fundamental values perceived by many owners and keeping pace with a dynamic global industry. Quite a few issues to chew over.

Co-author: Paul Knott

Sources: www.fonterra.com; *Sunday Star Times*, 26 September 2008; *The New Zealand Farmers Weekly*, 16 March 2009; Ministry for the Environment (www.mfe.govt.nz), NZ's greenhouse gas inventory 1990–2014; Ministry of Foreign Affairs & Trade (www.mfat.govt.nz), Kyoto Protocol Part II; *New Zealand Herald*, 14 April 2013; *National Business Review*, 10 June 2013; *Brook Asset Management News*, 26 October 2012; Sustainable Dairying Water Accord Two Years On (www.dairynz.co.nz).

PERSPECTIVES ON MISSIONING AND VISIONING

Perfection of means and confusion of goals seems, in my opinion, to characterize our age.

Albert Einstein (1879–1955), German–American physicist

Firms require a certain measure of economic profitability if they want to compete and survive, yet they also need to exhibit a certain amount of social responsibility if they are to retain the trust and support of key stakeholders. In itself, this creates a tension, as the two demands can be at odds with one another. Often, societally responsible behaviour costs money, which can only be partially recouped by the increased 'social dividend' it brings. But if profitability and responsibility are both seen as the ultimate purpose of business firms, the tension becomes even stronger; optimizing the one will be in conflict with maximizing the other. Emphasizing profitability means subjecting all investments to an economic rationale – societally responsible behaviour should only be undertaken if the net present value of such an investment is attractive or there is no legal way of avoiding compliance. Emphasizing responsibility means subjecting all activities to a moral or political rationale – asking who has a legitimate and pressing claim to be included as a beneficiary of the activities being undertaken – which can severely depress profitability.

Hence, it is not surprising to find that the paradox of profitability and responsibility strongly divides people across many walks of life; its relevance reaches far beyond business managers and management theorists. The main point of contention is whether firms should primarily be run for the financial benefit of the legal owners or for the broader benefit of all parties with a significant interest in the joint endeavour. Should it be the purpose of firms to serve the interests of their shareholders or their stakeholders? Should profitability be emphasized because economic organizations belong to the providers of risk capital or should responsibility be emphasized because organizations are joint ventures bringing together various resource providers by means of a social contract?

While there are many points of view on the 'right' organizational purpose in the strategy literature, here the two diametrically opposed positions will be identified and discussed. At the one pole are those who argue that corporations are established to serve the purposes of their owners. Generally, it is in the best interest of a corporation's shareholders to see the value of their stocks increase through the organization's pursuit of profitable business strategies. This point of view is commonly referred to as the 'shareholder value perspective'. At the other end of the spectrum are those who argue that corporations should be seen as joint ventures between shareholders, employees, banks, customers, suppliers, governments and the community. All of these parties hold a stake in the organization and therefore can expect that the corporation will take as its responsibility to develop business strategies that are in accordance with their interests and values. This point of view will be referred to as the 'stakeholder values perspective'.

The shareholder value perspective

To proponents of the shareholder value perspective it is obvious that companies belong to their owners and therefore should act in accordance with the interests of the owners. Corporations are instruments whose purpose it is to create economic value on behalf of those who invest risk-taking capital in the enterprise. This clear purpose should drive companies, regardless of whether they are privately or publicly held. According to Rappaport (1986, p. xiii), 'the idea that business strategies should be judged by the economic value they create for shareholders is well accepted in the business community. After all, to suggest that companies be operated in the best interests of their owners is hardly controversial'.

There is some disagreement between advocates of this perspective with regard to the best way of advancing the interests of the shareholders, particularly in publicly held companies. Many people taking this point of view argue that the well-being of the shareholders is served if the strategy of a company leads to higher share prices and/or higher dividends (e.g. Hart, 1995; Rappaport, 1986). Others are less certain of the stock markets' ability to correctly value long-term investments, such as R&D spending and capital expenditures. In their view, stock markets are excessively concerned with the short term and therefore share prices myopically overemphasize current results and heavily discount investments for the future. To avoid being pressured into short-termism, these people advocate that strategists must keep only one eye on share prices, while the other is focused on the long-term horizon (e.g. Charkham, 1994; Sykes, 1994).

According to supporters of the shareholder value perspective, one of the major challenges in large corporations is to actually get top management to pursue the shareholders' interests. Where ownership and managerial control over a company have become separated, it is often difficult to get the managers to work on behalf of the shareholders, instead of letting managers' self-interest prevail. This is known as the principal-agent problem (e.g. Eisenhardt, 1989; Jensen and Meckling, 1976) – the managers are agents, working to further the interests of their principals, the shareholders, but are tempted to serve their own interests, even when these are to the detriment of the principals. This has led to a widespread debate in the academic and business communities, especially in Britain and the United States, about the best form of corporate governance. The most important players in corporate governance are the outside, or non-executive, members on the board of directors. It is one of the tasks of these outsiders to check whether the executives are truly running the company in a way that maximizes the shareholders' wealth. For this reason, many proponents of the shareholder value perspective call for a majority of independent-minded outside directors on the board, preferably owning significant amounts of the company's stock themselves.

The emphasis placed on profitability as the fundamental purpose of firms does not mean that supporters of the shareholder value perspective are blind to the demands placed on firms by other stakeholders. On the contrary, most exponents of this view argue that it is in the interest of the shareholders to carry out a 'stakeholder analysis' and even to actively manage stakeholder relations. Knowing the force field of stakeholders constraining the freedom of the company is important information for the strategy process. It is never advisable to ignore important external claimants such as labour unions, environmental activists, bankers, governmental agencies and community groups. Few strategists would doubt that proactive engagement is preferable to 'corporate isolationism'. However, recognizing that it is expedient to pay attention to stakeholders does not mean that it is the corporation's purpose to serve them. If parties have a strong bargaining position, a firm might be forced into all types of concession, sacrificing profitability. This has, however, little to do with any moral responsibility of the firm towards these other powers. The only duty of a company is to maximize shareholder value, within the boundaries of what is legally permissible.

The important conclusion is that in this perspective it might be in the interest of shareholders to treat stakeholders well, but that there is no moral obligation to do so. For instance, it might be a good move for a troubled company not to lay off workers if the resulting loyalty and morale improve the chances of recovery and profitability later on. In this case, the decision not to fire workers is based on profit-motivated calculations, not on a sense of moral responsibility towards the employees. Generally, proponents of the shareholder value perspective argue that society is best served by this type of economic rationale. By pursuing enlightened self-interest and maintaining market-based relationships between the firm and all stakeholders, societal wealth will be maximized. Responsibility for employment, local communities, the environment, consumer welfare and social developments are not an organizational matter, but issues for individuals and governments (Friedman, 1970).

EXHIBIT 3.2   THE SHAREHOLDER VALUE PERSPECTIVE

MISSION STATEMENT DEAN FOODS

'The Company's primary objective is to maximize long-term stockholder

value, while adhering to the laws of the jurisdiction in which it operates and at all times observing the highest ethical standards.'

Dated: August, 2011

The stakeholder values perspective

 Advocates of the stakeholder values perspective do not see why the supplier of one ingredient in an economic value-creation process has a stronger moral claim on the organization than the providers of other inputs. They challenge the assumption that individuals with an equity stake in a corporation have the right to demand that the entire organization works on their behalf. In the stakeholder values perspective, a company should not be seen as the instrument of shareholders, but as a coalition between various resource suppliers, with the intention of increasing their common wealth. An organization should be regarded as a joint venture in which the suppliers of equity, loans, labour, management, expertise, parts and service all participate to achieve economic success. As all groups hold a stake in the joint venture and are mutually dependent, it is argued that the purpose of the organization is to serve the interests of all parties involved (e.g. Berle and Means, 1932; Freeman and Reed, 1983).

According to endorsers of the stakeholder values perspective, shareholders have a legitimate interest in the firm's profitability. However, the emphasis shareholders place on stock price appreciation and dividends must be balanced against the legitimate demands of the other partners. These demands are not only financial, as in the case of the shareholders, but also qualitative, reflecting different values held by different groups (e.g. Clarke, 1998; Freeman, 1984). For instance, employees might place a high value on job security, occupational safety, holidays and working conditions, while a supplier of parts might prefer secure demand, joint innovation, shared risk-taking and prompt payment. Of course, balancing these interests is a challenging task, requiring an ongoing process of negotiation and compromise. The outcome will in part depend on the bargaining power of each stakeholder – how essential is its input to the economic success of the organization? However, the extent to which a stakeholder's interests are pursued will depend on the perceived legitimacy of their claim as well. For instance, employees usually have a strong moral claim because they are heavily dependent on the organization and have a relatively low mobility, while most shareholders have a spread portfolio and can 'exit the corporation with a phone call' (Stone, 1975).

In this view of organizational purpose, managers must recognize their responsibility towards all constituents (e.g. Alkhafaji, 1989; Clarkson, 1995). Maximizing shareholder value to the detriment of the other stakeholders would be unjust. Managers in the firm have a moral obligation to consider the interests and values of all joint venture partners. Managing stakeholder demands is not merely a pragmatic means of running a profitable business – serving stakeholders is an end in itself. These two interpretations of stakeholder management are often confused. Where it is primarily viewed as an approach or technique for dealing with the essential participants in the value-adding process, stakeholder management is *instrumental*. But if it is based on the fundamental notion that the organization's purpose is to serve the stakeholders, then stakeholder management is *normative* (e.g. Buono and Nichols, 1985; Donaldson and Preston, 1995).

Most proponents of the stakeholder values perspective argue that, ultimately, pursuing the joint interests of all stakeholders is not only more just, but also more effective for organizations (e.g. Jones, 1995; Solomon, 1992). Few stakeholders are filled with a sense of mission to go out and maximize shareholder value, especially if shareholders bear no responsibility for the other stakeholders' interests (e.g. Campbell and Yeung, 1991; Collins and Porras, 1994). It is difficult to work as a motivated team if it is the purpose of the organization to serve only one group's interests. Furthermore, without a stakeholder values perspective, there will be a deep-rooted lack of trust between all of the parties involved in the enterprise. Each stakeholder will assume that the others are motivated solely by self-interest and are tentatively cooperating in a calculative manner. All parties will perceive a constant risk that the others will use their power to gain a bigger slice of the pie, or even rid themselves of their 'partners'. The consequence is that all stakeholders will vigorously guard their own interests and will interact with one another as adversaries. To advocates of the stakeholder values perspective, this 'every person for themselves' model of organizations is clearly inferior to the partnership model in which sharing, trust and symbiosis are emphasized. Cooperation between stakeholders is much more effective than competition (note the link with the embedded organization perspective in Chapter 6).

Some exponents of the stakeholder values perspective argue that the narrow economic definition of stakeholders given above is too constrictive. In their view, the circle of stakeholders with a legitimate claim on the organization should be drawn more widely. Not only should the organization be responsible to the direct participants in the economic value-creation process (the 'primary stakeholders'), but also to all parties affected by the organization's activities. For example, an organization's behaviour might have an impact on local communities, governments, the environment and society in general, and therefore these groups have a stake in what the organization does as well. Most supporters of the stakeholder values perspective acknowledge that organizations have a moral responsibility towards these 'secondary stakeholders' (e.g. Carroll, 1993; Langtry, 1994). However, opinions differ whether it should actually be a part of business organizations' purpose to serve this broader body of constituents.

The implication of this view for corporate governance is that the board of directors should be able to judge whether the interests of all stakeholders are being justly balanced. This has led some advocates of the stakeholder values perspective to call for representatives of the most important stakeholder groups to be on the board (e.g. Guthrie and Turnbull, 1994). Others argue more narrowly for a stronger influence of employees on the choices made by organizations (e.g. Blair, 1995; Bucholz, 1986). Such co-determination of the corporation's strategy by management and workers can, for instance, be encouraged by establishing work councils (a type of organizational parliament or senate), as is mandatory for larger companies in most countries of the European Union. Yet others emphasize measures to strengthen corporate social responsibility in general. To improve corporate social performance, it is argued, companies should be encouraged to adopt internal policy processes that promote ethical behaviour and responsiveness to societal issues (e.g. Epstein, 1987; Wartick and Wood, 1998). Corporate responsibility should not be, to quote Ambrose Bierce's sarcastic definition, 'a detachable burden easily shifted to the shoulders of God, Fate, Fortune, Luck, or one's neighbour'.

EXHIBIT 3.3 THE STAKEHOLDER VALUES PERSPECTIVE

CREDO JOHNSON & JOHNSON

We believe our first responsibility is to the doctors, nurses and patients, to mothers and fathers and all others who use our products and services. In meeting their needs everything we do must be of high quality. We must constantly strive to reduce our costs in order to maintain reasonable prices. Customers' orders must be serviced promptly and accurately. Our suppliers and distributors must have an opportunity to make a fair profit.

We are responsible to our employees, the men and women who work with us throughout the world. Everyone must be considered as an individual. We must respect their dignity and recognize their merit. They must have a sense of security in their jobs. Compensation must be fair and adequate, and working conditions clean, orderly and safe. We must be mindful of ways to help our employees fulfil their family responsibilities. Employees must feel free to make suggestions and complaints. There must be equal opportunity for employment, development and advancement for those qualified. We must provide competent management, and their actions must be just and ethical.

We are responsible to the communities in which we live and work and to the world community as well. We must be good citizens – support good works and charities and bear our fair share of taxes. We must encourage civic improvements and better health and education. We must maintain in good order the property we are privileged to use, protecting the environment and natural resources.

Our final responsibility is to our stockholders. Business must make a sound profit. We must experiment with new ideas. Research must be carried on, innovative programmes developed and mistakes paid for. New equipment must be purchased, new facilities provided and new products launched. Reserves must be created to provide for adverse times. When we operate according to the principles, the stockholders should realize their fair return.

Source: Johnson & Johnson.

MANAGING THE PARADOX OF PROFITABILITY AND RESPONSIBILITY

A business that makes nothing but money is a poor kind of business.

Henry Ford (1863–1947), American industrialist

So, what should be the purpose of a firm? And how should executives manage the tension between economic profitability and societal responsibility? Should managers strive to maximize shareholder value or stakeholder values? Or should executives search for a way that combines profitability and responsibility? The proponents of the shareholder value perspective are lobbying for more receptiveness to the interests of the shareholders on the part of the board, to increase top management accountability and to curb perceived executive self-enrichment at the expense of shareholders. The advocates of the stakeholder values perspective are vying for a system that would bring more receptiveness to the interests of stakeholders, to ensure that firms do not become more myopically

TABLE 3.1   Shareholder value versus stakeholder values

	Shareholder value perspective	Stakeholder values perspective
Emphasis on	Profitability over responsibility	Responsibility over profitability
Organizations seen as	Instruments	Joint ventures
Organizational purpose	To serve owner	To serve all parties involved
Measure of success	Share price and dividends (shareholder value)	Satisfaction among stakeholders
Major difficulty	Getting agent to pursue principal's interests	Balancing interests of various stakeholders
Corporate governance through	Independent outside directors with shares	Stakeholder representation
Stakeholder management	Means	End
Social responsibility	Individual, not organizational matter	Both individual and organizational
Society best served by	Pursuing self-interest (economic efficiency)	Pursuing joint interests (economic symbiosis)

'bottom-line-oriented' and short-term-driven. While both sides do agree on one or two points (e.g. corporate governance is generally too weak), on the whole, the question remains of how to manage the paradox of profitability and responsibility.

Parallel processing

Managing shareholders involves different processes, departments and people from managing diverse societal stakeholders. Shareholders are managed by executive board members at shareholder conferences and other meetings with owners. In one-tier boards, shareholders are also managed at board meetings – and vice versa, of course. Production departments deal with environmentalists and – when outsourced to low-wage countries – also with non-governmental organizations (NGOs), while finance departments are more in contact with tax authorities and other government representatives. As a consequence, shareholders and diverse stakeholders are managed in parallel – at different levels and organizational departments, by a variety of people. For example, an oil company may deal with environmental issues in a country unit's sustainability department and tax issues in another country, while shareholders are managed by the board.

Balancing

The finance function has always been prominently positioned in the corporate hierarchy of companies, usually at the board level, while diverse societal responsibilities have usually been managed at lower organizational levels. This status difference has had an effect on how societal responsibilities have been dealt with: as more of a tactical and financial issue that needs to be fixed than as a strategic tension that needs to be managed. Parallel processing has, in this case, been sufficient as the preferred means of managing the paradox.

However, this does not apply to all firms, while it can be argued that in recent years the need to manage the paradox of economic profitability and societal responsibility has increased in many industries. After the fall of Lehman Brothers in 2008, which marked the beginning of the credit crisis and an economic slowdown, the societal role of banks has been emphasized. The economic dependency on system banks has become better understood and then reduced, new regulations have been installed and governments have made system changes. Banks could no longer just strive for maximized shareholder value without significant protest of governments, regulators, societal stakeholders and also clients. Also outside the banking sector, societal stakeholders have increased the pressure on companies to take responsibility for the consequences of their behaviour, such as producing in low-wage countries in unsafe working conditions and – often indirectly – using child labour. Oil companies are facing increased pressure from environmental groups, NGOs and governments after a number of accidents and oil spills. The pressure of societal stakeholders on companies has grown further with the accelerated importance of social media and the use of smart phones. Stakeholders are informed better and more quickly and have more means at their disposal to pressure companies if they deem their conduct questionable.

As a result, the tension between economic profitability and societal responsibility has become more prominent and a strategic issue for company directors and sometimes corporate boards. Many companies have decided to not just react on incidents but to balance the opposing needs. Balancing became a prime responsibility of the CEO and, in some cases, a corporate sustainability officer has been appointed in order to be able to balance the tension at the directors' level or the board level.

Resolving the paradox

Balancing the paradox is finding a satisfying position in the trade-off between economic profitability and societal responsibility, resolving aims to combine both demands a higher level. For example, in 2011 the Dutch supermarket company and market leader in the Netherlands, Albert Heijn, had announced a cooperative agreement with the World Wildlife Fund (WWF) with the objective to achieve full sustainability of its assortment of fish – wild caught and farmed. The agreement included packaging and worldwide production of all fish, including mussels, salmon and shrimps. After four years, 90 per cent of all Albert Heijn private-label fish products has been certified by Aquaculture Stewardship Council (ASC) as environmentally responsible 'with minimal negative effects on the environment and strict requirements for use of antibiotics, and respect for the local communities where they operate'. In the long term, the supermarket giant has safeguarded sufficient supply of fish with the initiative and therefore its long-term profitability, while, in the immediate term societal stakeholders are managed.

Resolving the paradox of economic profitability and societal responsibility at a higher level has been named 'shared value' by Michael Porter and Mark Kramer. They argue that 'profits involving a social purpose represent a higher form of capitalism, one that creates a positive cycle of company and community prosperity' and they claim that the shared value concept moves business and society beyond trade-offs. In other words, the authors strive to resolve the paradox at a higher level to achieve a synthesis between firm profitability and societal responsibility.

MISSIONING AND VISIONING IN INTERNATIONAL PERSPECTIVE

Co-authors: Gep Eisenloeffel and Wester Wagenaar

Failure comes only when we forget our ideals and objectives and principles.

Jawaharlal Nehru (1889–1964), first Prime Minister of India

The debate on organizational purpose does not take place in a vacuum: institutional and cultural aspects define its context. Although a strategist can choose his or her own mission, an inclination towards following a shareholder or stakeholder perspective has little to do with individuals and more so with how societies are structured. Companies have to deal with different institutional contexts in host countries while executing their mission, vision and organizational purpose. This becomes even more relevant in today's shifts in the economic power balance. It is clear that the former economic dominance of the traditional countries of the 'triad of economic power' (Ohmae, 1985a) no longer applies and that the institutional context will vary further. As the world is not a level playing field, it is the organizational context which determines how powerful the bargaining power of the stakeholder and shareholders is. It seems this situation will persist: present-day economic reality sees it unlikely a best practice solution will be at hand or that globalization itself will lead to a convergence of perspectives on organizational purpose. It is therefore imperative to analyse similarities and differences in organizational purpose worldwide to better understand the international playing field.

On the societal level

When dealing with organizational purpose, institutional aspects play an import role. Porter pointed out in *The Competitive Advantage of Nations* (1990) that the sustainable competitive advantage of industries and individual companies is to a large extent based on the institutional framework within their countries – and regions – of origin. Institutional forms that have evolved over time in different national contexts have resulted in distinctive models of economic organization. This has not resulted in commonly agreed on categorizations however. Nevertheless, there are some conclusions to be drawn from the scholarly debate.

Albert (1993) concentrates on the differences of what he coined as the Rhineland model in Germany in comparison with the Anglo-Saxon model of the US and (to a large extent) the UK. Peter Hall and David Soskice (2001) elaborate on this point. They stress the differences between what they call coordinated market economies (CMEs), most commonly associated with such countries as Germany, Sweden and Japan, and liberal market economies (LMEs) generally associated with the US and the UK (2001). The main difference between the two can be found in coordination. In CMEs, coordination is achieved through non-market means, investments in specific assets are preferred and banks play a prominent role. In LMEs, by way of contrast, coordination follows market conditions with a preference for transferable assets (Amable, 2003; Cernat, 2004).

Many authors object to this strict dichotomy. Dicken (2015), for instance, identifies four variants of capitalism, based on differing perceptions on the proper role of the government: neo-liberal market capitalism (US, UK), social-market capitalism (Germany, Scandinavia, many other European countries), developmental capitalism (Japan, South Korea, Taiwan, India, Brazil) and authoritarian capitalism (China and Russia). Dicken shows how differences in coordination take various shapes: states operate as regulators, competitors and collaborators at the same time. In this way, states not only create the context for organizational purpose, they also fulfil the roles of shareholders and stakeholders. The more influential the state, the more active its role as shareholder and stakeholder is likely to be. Dicken's model is not the only alternative to the dichotomy of the Rhineland and the Anglo-Saxon model. Another way to categorize the diversity of systems in the world is posited by Amable. He argues for a different categorization of five types of capitalism: the market-based model (US, UK, Canada, Australia), the social-democratic model (Nordic countries), the Continental European model, the Mediterranean model and the Asian model (East Asia) (2003).

As Schneider and Barsoux (1999) point out: Varieties of capitalism are not only defined by the role of governments and legislation. Media, stakeholders' and shareholders' behaviour also play an important role in shaping the context of organizational purpose. For example, concerns over ethics may be due to more aggressive journalism (or, as in the case of the US, libel suits), 'best company' rankings or greater risk of shareholder activism and consumer boycotts. Institutions are also shaped by informal rules and common knowledge acquired through history, by culture in other words.

When it comes to the influences on varieties of capitalism and organizational purpose, culture is not per se the most influential, but it is often the most neglected (Schneider and Barsoux, 1999). Nevertheless, there is a wealth of research findings (Adler and Gundersen, 2007; Hampden-Turner and Trompenaars, 2000; Hofstede, 1980; Schein, 2004; Verluyten, 2010) highlighting how cultural dimensions play an important role not in just who is responsible for formulating organizational purpose and on what grounds accountability is conducted, but on how and for whom the purpose of a company is defined. Hampden-Turner and Trompenaars (2000), for instance, show how in the United States, with its emphasis on individualism and achievement, ethical decisions are considered personal. Likewise moral judgements require individual responsibility and accountability. Universalism is an important by-product of individualism and is deeply rooted in US cultural history (Hampden-Turner and Trompenaars, 2000; Verluyten, 2010). Ethical standards in the US are considered to apply to everyone in the same way. This results in the US legalistic approach to ethics affecting organizational purpose. In more collectivist societies, however, ethical standards are applied either according to specific circumstances, strongly influenced by the nature of one's social status (ascription) like in Brazil, or to social ties (in-group versus out-group) like in China or Japan.

Traditionally, many Western business schools have preached profit maximization as the ultimate goal. This notion reflects underlying cultural assumptions like task orientation (as opposed to relationship orientation) and individualism (contrary to collectivism) (Hampden-Turner & Trompenaars, 2000). Organizations are seen as instrumental and managers as rational economic actors, driven primarily by self-interest. To contrast this approach with defining organizational purpose more to promote the well-being of society and organizations as a system of relationships, consider excerpts from the mission statement of Konosuke Matsushita, founder of Matsushita: 'Profit comes in compensation for contributing to society'. Matsushita did not just want to contribute to society – the end result called for nothing less than the eradication of poverty from the face of the earth (Holden, 2002).

On the industry level

Some industries are expected to have an inclination towards either the stakeholder's or shareholder's perspective on the global playing field. Regardless of where a company operates, when it comes to the financial sector, a preference towards focusing on meeting the demands of shareholders can be expected. Contrariwise, when it comes to service industries, with the health care and education sectors in particular, the demand for adopting a stakeholder perspective is naturally higher. Nonetheless, the global pharmaceutical industry has largely shifted from the belief that improving the lives of patients will naturally lead to generating profits to a state in which companies prioritize satisfying the demands of shareholders (Kessel, 2014).

To the strategist

The institutional and cultural framework is an important context variable in defining company norms and values. Should a strategist impose parent company or home-country norms and values in a host-country environment, or should local customs, rules and regulations be adopted? On the one hand, corporate and head-office efforts to insist on universal ethical principles in foreign subsidiaries are often questioned and considered as cultural imperialism or outright self-righteousness. On the other hand, however, adapting to local rules with a 'when in Rome do as the Romans' approach and presenting the company as a national champion, leads to inconsistently practising corporate norms and values, and tensions with external stakeholders. For example, if company standards are not in line with international rules of conduct, NGOs and home-country customers are likely to protest. In the words of Cor Herkströter, CEO of Shell in the mid-1990s, 'stakeholders hold the *license to operate* of a company'.

Furthermore, the homogeneity of regulations and cultural norms within nations and of the acclaimed uniformity of organizational purpose can also be questioned (Coe, Kelly, and Yeung, 2012). The regulatory and cultural framework often differs from one region to the next and even within regions. In the end, this would mean that the proper unit of analysis is the firm with its specific circumstances.

STRATEGY CONTENT

Every generation laughs at the old fashions but religiously follows the new.
Henry David Thoreau (1817–1862), American philosopher

The strategy content section deals with the question of what the strategy should be. What course of action should the firm follow to achieve its purpose? In determining what the strategy should be, two types of 'fit' are of central concern to managers. First, there needs to be a fit between the firm and its environment. If the two become misaligned, the firm will be unable to meet the demands of the environment and will start to underperform, which can eventually lead to bankruptcy or takeover. This type of fit is also referred to as 'external consonance'. At the same time, managers are also concerned with achieving an internal fit between the various parts of the firm. If various units become misaligned, the organization will suffer from inefficiency, conflict and poor external performance, which can eventually lead to its demise as well. This type of fit is also referred to as 'internal consistency'.

As external consonance and internal consistency are prerequisites for a successful strategy, they need to be achieved for each organizational unit. Most organizations have various levels, making it necessary to ensure internal and external fit at each level of aggregation within the firm. In Figure II.1 all these possible levels within a corporation have been reduced to just three general categories, to which a fourth, supra-organizational level has been added. At each level, the strategy should meet the requirements of external consonance and internal consistency:

- Functional level strategy. For each functional area, such as marketing, operations, finance, logistics, human resources, procurement and R&D, a strategy needs to be developed. At this level, internal consistency means having an overarching functional strategy that integrates various functional sub-strategies (e.g. a marketing strategy that aligns branding, distribution, pricing, product and communication strategies). External consonance is achieved when strategy is aligned with the demands in the relevant external arena (e.g. the logistics or procurement environment).

- Business level strategy. At the business level, an organization can only be effective if it can integrate functional level strategies into an internally consistent whole. To achieve external consonance the business unit must be aligned with the specific demands in the relevant business area.

- Corporate level strategy. When a company operates in two or more business areas, the business level strategies need to be aligned to form an internally consistent corporate level strategy. Between business and corporate levels there can also be divisions, yet for most strategy purposes they can be approached as mini-corporations (both divisional and corporate level strategy are technically speaking 'multi-business level'). Achieving external consonance at this level of aggregation means that a corporation must be able to act as one tightly integrated unit or as many autonomous, differentiated units, depending on the demands of the relevant environment.

- Network level strategy. When various firms work together, it sometimes is deemed necessary to align business and/or corporate level strategies to shape an internally consistent network level strategy. Such a network, or multi-company, level strategy can involve anywhere between two and thousands of companies. Here, too, the group must develop a strategy that fits with the demands in the relevant environment.

As the strategy content issues differ greatly depending on the level of aggregation under discussion, this section has been divided along the following lines. Chapter 4 focuses on business level strategy, Chapter 5 on corporate level strategy and Chapter 6 on network level strategy. The functional level strategies will not be given extensive coverage, as they are usually explored in great detail in functionally oriented books. It must be noted, however, that the aggregation levels used here are an analytical distinction and not an empirical reality that can always be found in practice – where one level stops and the other starts is more a matter of definition than of thick demarcation lines. Hence, when discussing strategy issues at any level, it is important to understand how they fit with higher and lower level strategy questions.

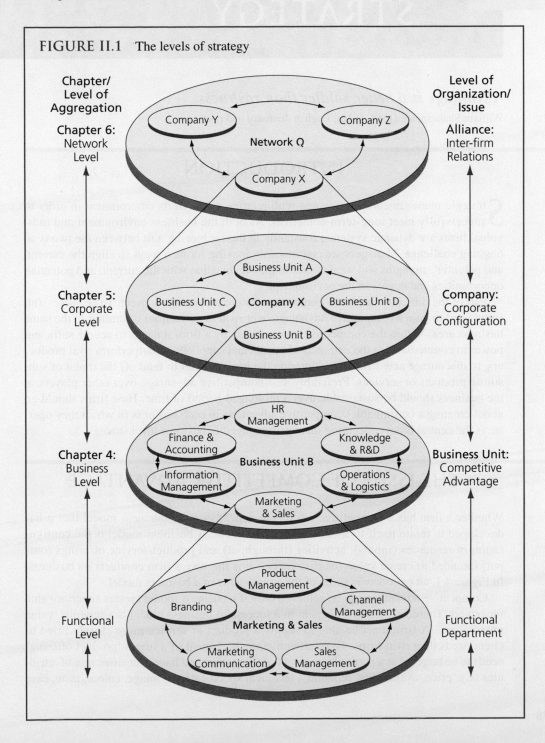

FIGURE II.1 The levels of strategy

BUSINESS LEVEL STRATEGY

Advantage is a better soldier than rashness.
William Shakespeare (1564–1616), English dramatist and poet

INTRODUCTION

Strategic management is concerned with relating a firm to its environment in order to successfully meet long-term objectives. As both the business environment and individual firms are dynamic systems, constantly in flux, achieving a fit between the two is an ongoing challenge. Managers are continuously looking for new ways to align the current, and potential, strengths and weaknesses of the organization with the current, and potential, opportunities and threats in the environment.

Part of the difficulty lies in the competitive nature of the environment. To be successful, firms need to gain a competitive advantage over rival organizations operating in the same business area. Within the competitive arena chosen by a firm, it needs to accrue sufficient power to counterbalance the demands of buyers and suppliers, to outperform rival producers, to discourage new firms from entering the business and to fend off the threat of substitute products or services. Preferably, this competitive advantage over other players in the business should be sustainable over a prolonged period of time. How firms should go about creating a (sustainable) competitive advantage in each business in which they operate is the central issue concerning managers engaged in business level strategy.

THE ISSUE OF COMPETITIVE ADVANTAGE

Whether a firm has a competitive advantage depends on the business model that it has developed to relate itself to its business environment. A business model is the configuration of resources (inputs), activities (throughput) and product/service offerings (output) intended to create value for customers – it is the way a firm conducts its business. In Figure 4.1, an overview is given of the components of a business model.

Competitive advantage can be achieved only if a business model creates superior value for buyers. Therefore, the first element in a successful business model is a superior 'value proposition'. A firm must be able to supply a product or service more closely fitted to client needs than rival firms. To be attractive, each element of a firm's 'product offering' needs to be targeted at a particular segment of the market and have a superior mix of attributes (e.g. price, availability, reliability, technical specifications, image, colour, taste, ease

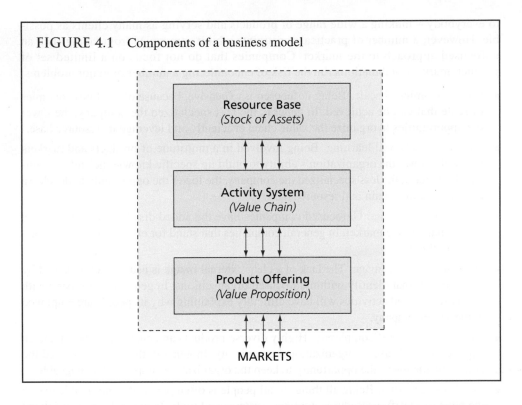

FIGURE 4.1   Components of a business model

of use, etc.). Second, a successful company must also have the ability to actually develop and supply the superior product offering. It needs to have the capability to perform the necessary value-adding activities in an effective and efficient manner.

These value-adding activities, such as R&D, production, logistics, marketing and sales, are jointly referred to as a firm's value chain. The third component of a business model consists of the resource base required to perform the value-adding activities. Resources such as know-how, patents, facilities, money, brands and relationships make up the stock of assets that can be employed to create the product offering. If these firm-specific assets are distinctive and useful, they can form the basis of a superior value proposition. To create a competitive advantage, alignment must be achieved between all three elements of a business model. In the following pages, all three elements will be discussed in more detail.

Product offering

At the intersection between a firm and its environment, transactions take place whereby the firm supplies goods or performs services for clients in the marketplace. It is here that the alignment of the firm and its environment is put to the test. If the products and services offered by the firm are more highly valued by customers than alternatives, a profitable transaction could take place. In other words, for sales to be achieved a firm must have a competitive value proposition – a cluster of physical goods, services or additional attributes with a superior fit to customer needs.

For the strategizing manager the key question is which products should be developed and which markets should be served. In many cases, the temptation is to be everything to everybody – making a wide range of products and serving as many clients as possible. However, a number of practical constraints inhibit companies from taking such an unfocused approach to the market. Companies that do not focus on a limited set of product–market combinations run the risk of encountering a number of major problems:

■ Low economies of scale. Being unfocused is expensive, because of the low economies of scale that can be achieved. In general, the less specialized the company, the lower the opportunities to organize the value chain efficiently and leverage its resource base.

■ Slow organizational learning. Being involved in a multitude of products and markets generally slows the organization's ability to build up specific knowledge and capabilities. In general, the less specialized the company, the lower the opportunity to develop a distinctive value chain and resource base.

■ Unclear brand image. Unfocused companies have the added disadvantage of having a fuzzy image in the market. In general, companies that stand for everything tend to stand out in nothing.

■ Unclear corporate image. The lack of a clear external image is usually compounded by a lack of internal identity within unfocused organizations. In general, a company with highly diversified activities will have difficulty explaining why its people are employed at the same company.

■ High organizational complexity. Highly diverse products and customers also create an exponential increase in organizational complexity. In general, the less specialized the company, the lower the opportunity to keep the organization simple and manageable.

■ Limits to flexibility. Being all things to all people is often physically impossible due to the need to specify procedures, routines, systems and tools. In general, less specialized firms are often forced into certain choices due to operational necessity.

For these reasons, companies need to focus on a limited number of businesses and within each business on a limited group of customers and a limited set of products. This focus should not be arbitrary – the challenge for strategizing managers is to understand which businesses are (or can be made to be) structurally attractive and how their firm can gain a competitive advantage within each business, by offering specific value propositions to selected customer segments.

Determining a focus starts by looking for the 'boundaries' of a business – how can managers draw meaningful delineation lines in the environment, distinguishing one arena of competition from another, so that they can select some and ignore others? Ideally, the environment would be made up of neatly compartmentalized businesses, with clear borders separating them. In reality, however, the picture is much messier. While there are usually certain clusters of buyers and suppliers interacting more intensely with one another, suggesting that they are operating in the same business, there are often numerous exceptions to any neat classification scheme. To explore how a business can be defined, it is first necessary to specify how a business differs from an 'industry' and a 'market'.

Delineating industries.   An industry is defined as a group of firms making a similar type of product or employing a similar set of value-adding processes or resources. In other words, an industry consists of producers that are much alike – there is *supply side similarity* (Kay, 1993). The simplest way to draw an industry boundary is to use product similarity as the delineation criterion. For instance, British Airways can be said to be in the airline industry, along with many other providers of the same product, such as Singapore Airlines and Ryanair. However, an industry can also be defined on the basis of value chain similarity (e.g. consulting industry and mining industry) or resource similarity (e.g. information technology industry and oil industry).

Economic statisticians tend to favour fixed industry categories based on product similarity and therefore most figures available about industries are product-category-based, often making use of Standard Industrial Classification (SIC) codes. Strategists, by way of contrast, like to challenge existing definitions of an industry, for instance by regrouping them on the basis of underlying value-adding activities or resources. Take the example of Swatch – how did it conceptualize which industry it was in? If it had focused on the physical product and the production process, then it would have been inclined to situate Swatch in the watch industry. However, Swatch also viewed its products as fashion accessories, placing emphasis on the key value-adding activities of fashion design and marketing. On this basis, Swatch could just as well be categorized as a member of the fashion industry (Porac, Thomas and Baden-Fuller, 1989). For the strategizing manager, the realization that Swatch can be viewed in both ways is an important insight. As creating a competitive advantage often comes from doing things differently, rethinking the definition of an industry can be a powerful way to develop a unique product offering.

Figure 4.2 gives four examples of traditionally defined 'industry columns', which Porter (1980) draws not top down, but left to right, using the term 'value system'. These columns start with upstream industries, which are involved in the extraction/growing of raw materials and their conversion into inputs for the manufacturing sector. Downstream industries take the output of manufacturing companies and bring them to clients, often adding a variety of services into the product mix. In practice, industry columns are not as simple as depicted in Figure 4.2, as each industry has many different industries as suppliers and usually many different industries as buyers.

A second limitation of the industry columns shown in Figure 4.2 is that they are materials flow oriented – industry boundaries are drawn on the basis of product.

Segmenting markets.   While economists see the market as a place where supply and demand meet, in the business world a market is usually defined as a group of customers with similar needs. In other words, a market consists of buyers whose demands are much alike – *demand side similarity*. For instance, there is a market for air transportation between London and Jamaica, which is a different market from that for air transportation between London and Paris – the customer needs are different and therefore these products cannot be substituted for one another. But customers can substitute a British Airways London–Paris flight for one by Air France, indicating that both companies are serving the same market. Yet, this market definition (London–Paris air transport) might not be the most appropriate, if, in reality, many customers are willing to substitute air travel for rail travel through the Channel Tunnel, or by ferry. In this case, there is a broader London–Paris transportation market, and air transportation is a specific *market segment*. If many customers are willing to substitute physical travel by teleconferencing or other telecommunications methods, the market might need to be defined as the 'London–Paris meeting market'.

As with industries, there are many ways of defining markets, depending on which buyer characteristics are used to make a clustering. In Figure 4.3, examples of segmentation criteria are given. The first group of segmentation criteria is based on buyer attributes that are frequently thought to be important predictors of actual buying criteria and buyer behaviour. Such customer characteristics are commonly used to group potential clients because this information is objective and easily available. However, the pitfall of segmenting on the basis of buyer attributes is that the causal link between characteristics and actual needs and behaviours

FIGURE 4.2 Alternative industry categorizations

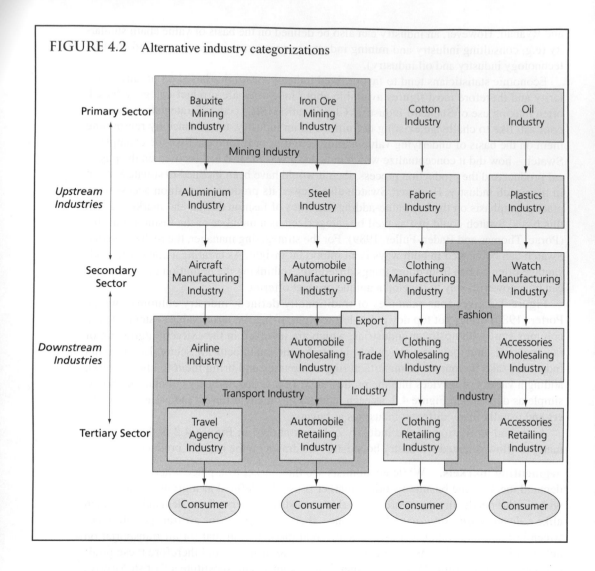

is often rather tenuous – not all Canadians need hockey sticks and not all 3-year-olds nag their parents while shopping. In other words, the market can be segmented on the basis of any demographic characteristic (e.g. income, family composition, employment), but this might not lead to meaningful groups of customers with similar needs and buying behaviour.

Therefore, instead of using buyer attributes as *indirect* – predictive – measures of what clients probably want, segments can also be *directly* defined on the basis of buying criteria employed or buyer behaviours exhibited. The advantage is that segments can then be identified with clearly similar wishes or behaviours. The disadvantage is that it is very difficult to gather and interpret information on what specific people want and how they really act.

For strategists, one of the key challenges is to look at existing categorizations of buyers and to wonder whether a different segmentation would offer new insights and new opportunities for developing a product offering specifically tailored to their needs. As with the redefining of industry boundaries, it is often in the reconceptualization of market segments that a unique approach to the market can be found.

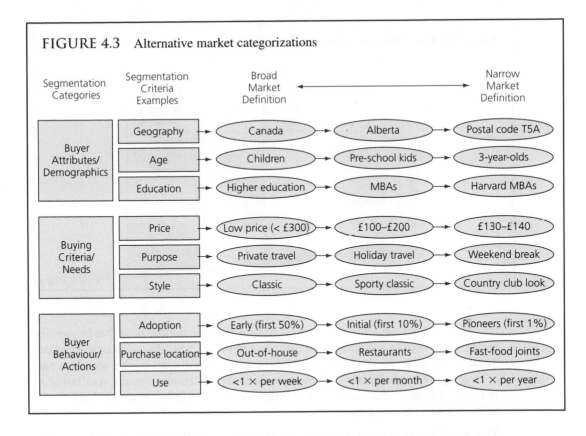

FIGURE 4.3   Alternative market categorizations

Defining and selecting businesses.   A business is a set of related product–market combinations. The term 'business' refers to neither a set of producers nor a group of customers, but to the domain in which the two meet. In other words, a business is a competitive arena in which companies offering similar products serving similar needs compete against one another for the favour of the buyers. Hence, a business is delineated in both industry and market terms (see Figure 4.4). Typically, a business is narrower than the entire industry and the set of markets served is also limited. For instance, within the airline industry the charter business is usually recognized as rather distinct. In the charter business, a subset of the airline services is offered to a number of tourist markets. Cheap flights from London to Jamaica and from London to Barcelona fall within this business, while service levels will be different than in other parts of the airline industry. It should be noted, however, that just as with industries and markets, there is no best way to define the boundaries of a business (Abell, 1980).

As stated earlier, companies cannot afford to be unfocused, operating superficially in a whole range of businesses. They must direct their efforts by focusing in two ways:

1 Selecting a limited number of businesses. The first constraint that companies need to impose on themselves is to choose a limited array of businesses within which they wish to be successful. This essential strategic challenge is referred to as the issue of corporate configuration and will be examined in more detail in Chapter 5 (multi-business level strategy). Here it suffices to say that firms need to analyse the structural characteristics of interesting businesses to be able to judge whether they are attractive enough for the firm, or can be made to be attractive. Porter presents the 'five forces analysis' as a framework for mapping the structure of industries and businesses.

FIGURE 4.4   Industries, markets and businesses

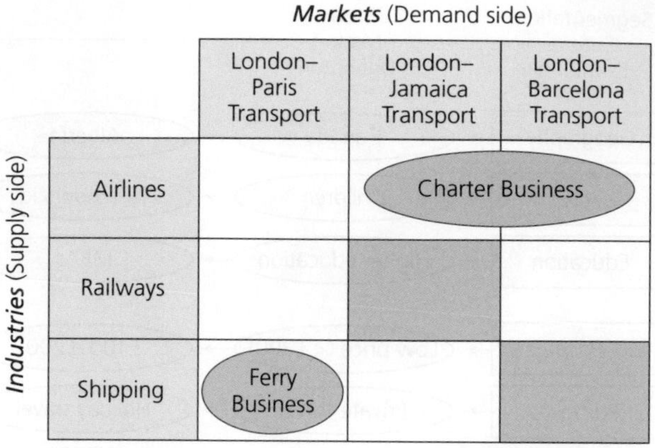

Markets (Demand side)

		London–Paris Transport	London–Jamaica Transport	London–Barcelona Transport
Industries (Supply side)	Airlines		Charter Business	
	Railways			
	Shipping	Ferry Business		

2 Focusing within each selected business. Even within the limited set of businesses se-lected, firms need to determine what they want to be and what they want to leave aside. To be competitive, it is necessary to choose a number of distinct market segments and to target a few special product offerings to meet these customers' needs. As illustrated in Figure 4.1, these specific product offerings in turn need to be aligned with a focused value chain and resource base.

This act of focusing the overall business model to serve the particular needs of a tar-geted group of buyers, in a way that distinguishes the firm vis-á-vis rivals, is called po-sitioning. This positioning of the firm in the business requires a clearly tailored product offering (product positioning), but also a value chain and resource base that closely fit with the demands of the specific group of customers and competitors being targeted.

Positioning within a business.   Positioning is concerned with both the questions of 'where to compete' and 'how to compete' (Porter, 1980). Determining in which product–market combinations within a business a firm wants to be involved is referred to as the issue of competitive scope. Finding a way to beat rivals and win over customers for a product offering is the issue of competitive advantage. The two questions are tightly linked, because firms need to develop a specific advantage to be competitive within a spe-cific product–market domain. If they try to use the same competitive advantage for too many dissimilar products and customers, they run the risk of becoming unfocused.

In selecting a competitive scope, firms can vary anywhere between being widely ori-ented and very tightly focused. Firms with a broad scope compete in a large number of segments within a business, with varied product offerings. Firms with a narrow scope tar-get only one, or just a few, customer segments and have a more limited product line (see Figure 4.5). If there is a small part of the business with very specific demands, requiring a distinct approach, firms can narrowly focus on this niche as their competitive scope. In between these two extremes are firms with a segment focus and firms with a product fo-cus, but in practice many other profiles are also possible.

FIGURE 4.5   Determining competitive scope

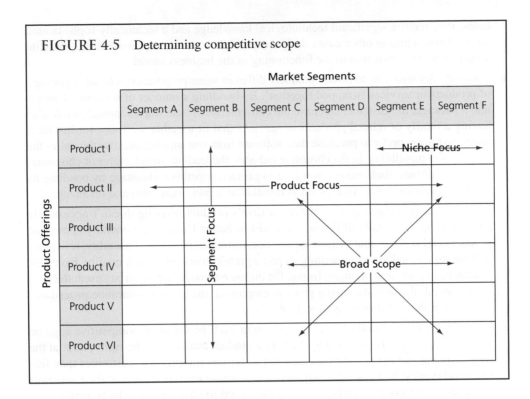

In developing a competitive advantage, firms have many dimensions along which they can attempt to outdo their rivals. Some of the most important bases of competitive advantage are the following:

- Price. The most straightforward advantage a firm can have in a competitive situation is the ability to charge a lower price. All things being equal, buyers generally prefer to pay the lowest amount necessary. Hence, when purchasing a commodity product or service, most customers will be partial to the lowest priced supplier. And even when selecting among differentiated products, many customers will be inclined to buy the cheapest or at least the cheapest within a subgroup of more comparable products. For a firm wanting to compete on price, the essential point is that it should have a *low cost* product offering, value chain and resource base to match the price positioning. After all, in the long run a firm can survive at a lower price level only if it has developed a business model that can sustainably operate at a lower cost level.

- Features. Firms can also distinguish their product offerings by having different intrinsic functional characteristics rather than competing offerings. There are many ways to make a product or service different, for instance by changing its size, smell, taste, colour, functionality, compatibility, content, design or style. An ice cream manufacturer can introduce a new flavour and more chunky texture, a motorcycle producer can design a special low rider model for women, a pay TV company can develop special channels for dog owners and science fiction addicts, and a utility company can offer environmentally friendly electricity. To be able to compete on each of these product features, firms need to command different specialized resources and value chains. In some cases, they require significant technological knowledge and a technically sophisticated value chain, while in other cases design capabilities, marketing prowess or a satellite infrastructure are essential to the functioning of the business model.

■ Bundling. Another way to offer a uniquely different value proposition is to sell a package of products or services 'wrapped together'. By bundling a number of separate elements into a package, the customer can have the convenience of 'one stop shopping', while also having a family of related products or services that fit together well. So, for instance, many customers prefer to purchase their software from one supplier because this raises the chance of compatibility. In the chocolate industry, the leading manufacturer of chocolate-making machines, Rademakers, was able to gain a competitive advantage by bundling its machines with various services, such as installation, repair, spare parts and financing.

■ Quality. When competing with others, a firm's product offering doesn't necessarily have to be fundamentally different, it can just be better. Customers generally appreciate products and services that exhibit superior performance in terms of usability, reliability and durability, and are often willing to pay a premium price for such quality. Excellent quality can be secured on many fronts, for instance through the materials used, the people involved, the manufacturing process employed, the quality assurance procedures followed or the distribution system used.

■ Availability. The method of distribution can in itself be the main competitive edge on which a firm bases its positioning. Having a product available at the right place, at the right moment and in the right way, can be much more important to customers than features and quality. Just ask successful ice cream manufacturers – most of their revenues are from out-of-doors impulse sales, so they need to have their products available in individually wrapped portions at all locations where people have the urge to indulge. In the same way, Avon's cosmetics are not primarily sold because of their uniqueness or low price, but because of the strength of their three million sales force, who can be at the right place at the right time.

■ Image. In the competition for customers' preference, firms can also gain an advantage by having a more appealing image than their rivals. In business-to-consumer markets this is particularly clear when looking at the impact of brands. Consumers often feel attracted to brands that project a certain image of the company or the products it sells. Brands can communicate specific values that consumers want to be associated with (Nike's 'just do it'), or can help to build trust among consumers who have too little information on which to base their product choices (GE's 'we bring good things to life'). But even in business-to-business markets, buyers often suffer from a shortage of information about the available product offerings or lack the time to research all possible suppliers. Therefore, the image of suppliers, mostly in terms of their standing ('a leading global player') and reputation ('high quality service') can be essential to be considered at all (to be 'shortlisted') and to be trusted as a business partner.

■ Relations. Good branding can give customers the impression that they know the supplier, without actually being in direct contact. Yet, having a direct relation with customers can in itself be a potent source of competitive advantage. In general, customers prefer to know their suppliers well, as this gives them more intimate knowledge of the product offering being provided. Having a relationship with a supplier can also give the customer more influence on what is offered. Besides these rational points, customers often value the personal contact, the trust and the convenience of having a longstanding relationship as well. For suppliers this means that they might acquire a competitive edge by managing their customer relationships well. To do so, however, does imply that the value chain and resource base are fit to fulfil this task.

The type of competitive advantage that a firm chooses to pursue will be influenced by what the targeted group of buyers find important. These factors of importance to potential clients are referred to as 'value drivers' – they are the elements responsible for creating value in the eyes of the customer. Which value drivers a firm will want to base its value proposition on is a matter of positioning.

According to Porter (1980) all the specific forms of competitive advantage listed above can be reduced to two broad categories, namely lower cost and differentiation. On the one hand, firms can organize their business models in such a manner that, while their products or services are largely the same as other manufacturers, their overall cost structure is lower, allowing them to compete on price. On the other hand, firms can organize their business models to supply a product or service that has distinctive qualities compared to rival offerings. According to Porter, these two forms of competitive advantage demand fundamentally different types of business model and therefore are next to impossible to combine. Firms that do try to realize both at the same time run the risk of getting 'stuck in the middle' – not being able to do either properly.

Treacy and Wiersema (1995) argue that there are three generic competitive advantages, each requiring a fundamentally different type of business model (they speak of three distinctive 'value disciplines'). They, too, warn firms to develop an internally consistent business model focused on one of these types of competitive advantage, avoiding a 'mix-and-match' approach to business strategy:

- Operational excellence. Firms striving for operational excellence meet the buyers' need for a reliable, low cost product offering. The value chain required to provide such no-frills, standardized, staple products emphasizes a 'lean and mean' approach to production and distribution, with simple service.
- Product leadership. Firms taking the route of product leadership meet the buyers' need for special features and advanced product performance. The value chain required to provide such differentiated, state-of-the-art products emphasizes innovation and the creative collaboration between marketing and R&D.
- Customer intimacy. Firms deciding to focus on customer intimacy meet the buyers' need for a tailored solution to their particular problem. The value chain required to provide such a client-specific, made-to-measure offering emphasizes flexibility and empowerment of the employees close to the customer.

Other strategy researchers, however, argue that there is no such thing as generic competitive strategies that follow from two or three broad categories of competitive advantage (e.g. Baden-Fuller and Stopford, 1992). In their view, there is an endless variety of ways in which companies can develop a competitive advantage, many of which do not fit into the categories outlined by Porter or Treacy and Wiersema – in fact, finding a new type of competitive advantage might be the best way of obtaining a unique position in a business.

Value chain

To be able to actually make what it wants to sell, a firm needs to have a value chain in place. A value chain is an integrated set of value creation processes leading to the supply of product or service offerings. Whether goods are being manufactured or services are being provided, each firm needs to perform a number of activities to successfully satisfy the customers' demands. As these value-adding activities need to be coordinated and linked together, this part of the business model is also frequently referred to as the 'value chain' (Porter, 1985).

Value chains can vary widely from industry to industry. The value chain of a car manufacturer is quite distinct from that of an advertising agency. Yet even within an industry there can be significant differences. Most 'bricks and mortar' bookstores have organized their value chain differently from online book retailers like amazon.com. The value chains of most 'hub-and-spoke' airline companies hardly resemble that of 'no-frills' carriers such as Southwest in the United States and easyJet in Europe.

While these examples point to radically different value chains, even firms that subscribe to the same basic model can apply it in their own particular way. Fast-food restaurants such as McDonald's and Burger King may employ the same basic model, but their actual value chains differ in quite a few ways. The same goes for the PC manufacturers HP and Lenovo, which share a similar type of value chain, but which still differ on many fronts. 'Online mass-customization' PC manufacturer Dell, by the same token, has a different model and consequently a more strongly differing value chain than HP and Lenovo.

Having a distinct value chain often provides the basis for a competitive advantage. A unique value chain allows a firm to offer customers a unique value proposition, by doing things better, faster, cheaper, nicer or more tailored than competing firms. Developing the firm's value chain is therefore just as strategically important as developing new products and services.

Although value chains can differ quite significantly, some attempts have been made to develop a general taxonomy of value-adding activities that could be used as an analytical framework (e.g. Day, 1990; Norman and Ramirez, 1993). By far the most influential framework is Porter's value chain, which distinguishes primary activities and support activities (see Figure 4.6). Primary activities 'are the activities involved in the physical creation of the product and its sale and transfer to the buyer, as well as after-sale assistance' (Porter, 1985, p. 16). Support activities facilitate the primary process, by providing purchased inputs, technology, human resources and various firm-wide functions. The generic categories of primary activities identified by Porter are:

- Inbound logistics. Activities associated with receiving, storing and disseminating inputs, including material handling, warehousing, inventory control, vehicle scheduling and returns to suppliers.

- Operations. Activities associated with transforming inputs into final products, including machining, packaging, assembly, equipment maintenance, testing, printing and facility operations.

- Outbound logistics. Activities associated with collecting, storing and physically distributing products to buyers, including warehousing, material handling, delivery, order processing and scheduling.

- Marketing and sales. Activities associated with providing a means by which buyers can purchase the product and inducing them to do so, including advertising, promotion, sales force, quoting, channel selection, channel relations and pricing.

- Service. Activities associated with providing service to enhance or maintain the value of products, including installation, repair, training, parts supply and product adjustment.

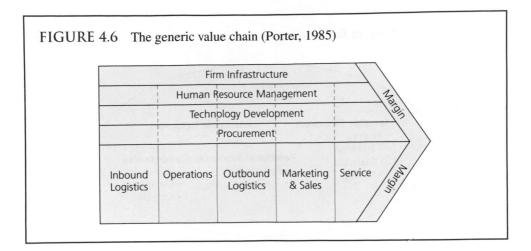

FIGURE 4.6   The generic value chain (Porter, 1985)

For service industries, Porter argues that the specific activities will be different, and might be performed in a different order, but can still be subdivided into these five generic categories. To ensure that the primary activities can be carried out, each firm also needs to organize four types of support activity:

- Procurement. Activities associated with the purchasing of inputs to facilitate all other activities, including vendor selection, negotiations, contracting and invoice administration.

- Technology development. Activities associated with the improvement of technologies throughout the firm, including basic research, product and process design, and procedure development.

- Human resource management. Activities associated with the management of personnel throughout the organization, including recruiting, hiring, training, development and compensation.

- Firm infrastructure. Firm infrastructure consists of all general activities that support the entire value chain, including general management, planning, finance, accounting, legal, government affairs and quality management.

The uniqueness of the value chain and its strength as the source of competitive advantage will usually not depend on only a few specialized activities, but on the extraordinary configuration of the entire value chain. An extraordinary configuration multiplies the distinctness of a particular value chain, while often raising the barrier to imitation (Amit and Zott, 2001; Porter, 1996).

Resource base

To carry out activities and to produce goods and services, firms need resources. A firm's resource base includes all means at the disposal of the organization for the performance of value-adding activities. Other authors prefer the term 'assets', to emphasize that the resources belong to the firm (e.g. Dierickx and Cool, 1989; Itami, 1987).

Under the broad umbrella of 'resource-based view of the firm', there has been much research into the importance of resources for the success and even existence of firms

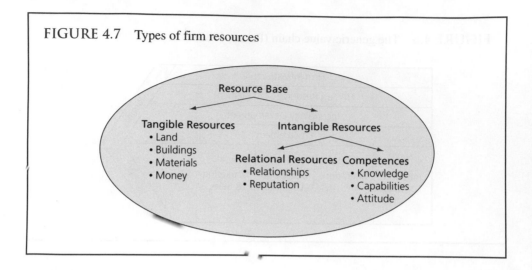

FIGURE 4.7   Types of firm resources

(e.g. Barney, 1991; Penrose, 1959; Wernerfelt, 1984). No generally accepted classification of firm resources has yet emerged in the field of strategic management, however the following major distinctions (see Figure 4.7) are commonly made:

- Tangible vs intangible resources. Tangible resources are all means available to the firm that can physically be observed (touched), such as buildings, machines, materials, land and money. Tangibles can be referred to as the 'hardware' of the organization. Intangibles, by way of contrast, are the 'software' of the organization. Intangible resources cannot be touched, but are largely carried within the people in the organization. In general, tangible resources need to be purchased, while intangibles need to be developed. Therefore, tangible resources are often more readily transferable, easier to price and usually are placed on the balance sheet.

- Relational resources vs competences. Within the category of intangible resources, relational resources and competences can be distinguished. Relational resources are all of the means available to the firm derived from the firm's interaction with its environment (Lowendahl, 1997). The firm can cultivate specific relationships with individuals and organizations in the environment, such as buyers, suppliers, competitors and government agencies, which can be instrumental in achieving the firm's goals. As attested by the old saying, 'it's not what you know, but whom you know', relationships can often be an essential resource (see Chapter 6 for a further discussion). Besides direct relationships, a firm's reputation among other parties in the environment can also be an important resource. Competence, however, refers to the firm's fitness to perform in a particular field. A firm has a competence if it has the knowledge, capabilities and attitude needed to successfully operate in a specific area.

This description of competences is somewhat broad and therefore difficult to employ. However, a distinction between knowledge, capability and attitude (Durand, 1996) can be used to shed more light on the nature of competences:

- Knowledge. Knowledge can be defined as the whole of rules (know-how, know-what, know-where and know-when) and insights (know-why) that can be extracted from, and help make sense of, information. In other words, knowledge flows from, and influences, the interpretation of information (Dretske, 1981). Examples of knowledge that a firm can possess are market insight, competitive intelligence, technological expertise and understanding of political and economic developments.

- Capability. Capability refers to the organization's potential for carrying out a specific activity or set of activities. Sometimes the term 'skill' is used to refer to the ability to carry out a narrow (functional) task or activity, while the term 'capability' is reserved for the quality of combining a number of skills. For instance, a firm's capability base can include narrower abilities, such as market research, advertising and production skills, that if coordinated could result in a capability for new product development (Stalk, Evans and Shulman, 1992).

- Attitude. Attitude refers to the mindset prevalent within an organization. Sometimes the terms 'disposition' and 'will' are used in the same sense, to indicate how an organization views and relates to the world. Although ignored by some writers, every sports coach will acknowledge the importance of attitude as a resource. A healthy body (tangible resource), insight into the game (knowledge), speed and dexterity (capabilities) – all are important, but without the winning mentality a team will not get to the top. Some attitudes may change rapidly within firms, yet others may be entrenched within the cultural fabric of the organization – these in particular can be important resources for the firm. A company's attitude can, for instance, be characterized as quality-driven, internationally oriented, innovation minded or competitively aggressive.

It must be noted that the term 'competences' is used in many different ways, partially due to the ambiguous definition given by its early proponents (Prahalad and Hamel, 1990). It is often used as a synonym for capabilities, while Prahalad and Hamel seem to focus more on technologically oriented capabilities ('how to coordinate diverse production skills and integrate multiple streams of technologies'). Others (e.g. Durand, 1996) have suggested that a firm has a competence in a certain area, when the firm's underlying knowledge base, capabilities and attitude are all aligned. So, Honda's engine competence is built on specific knowledge, development capabilities and the right predisposition. Wal-Mart's inventory control competence depends on specific information technology knowledge, coordination capabilities and a conducive state of mind. Virgin's service competence combines customer knowledge, adaptation capabilities and a customer-oriented attitude.

As in the case of industries, markets and businesses, employing the concepts of tangible and intangible resources is quite difficult in practice. Two problems need to be overcome – resources are difficult to categorize, but worse, are often difficult to recognize. The issue of categorization is a minor one. For some resources it is unclear how they should be classified. Are human resources tangible or intangible? Problematically, both. In humans, hardware and software are intertwined – if an engineer's expertise is required, the physical person usually needs to be hired. Knowledge, capabilities and attitudes need human carriers. Sometimes it is possible to separate hardware and software by making the intangibles more tangible. This is done by 'writing the software down'. In such a manner, knowledge can be codified, for instance in a patent, a capability can be captured in a computer programme and a relationship can be formalized in a contract. Sometimes intangibles become more tangible, as they become attached to physical carriers – for instance, attitude can be embodied by a person or a symbol, while reputation becomes attached to a brand.

More important is the problem of resource identification. One the one hand, tangible resources, by their very nature, are relatively easy to observe. Accountants keep track of the financial resources, production managers usually know the quality of their machinery and stock levels, while the personnel department will have an overview of all people on the payroll. Intangible resources, on the other hand, are far more difficult to identify (e.g. Grant, 2002; Itami, 1987). With whom does the firm have a relationship and what is the state of this relationship? What is the firm's reputation? These relational resources are hard to pin down. Competences are probably even more difficult to determine. How do you know what you know? Even for an individual it is a formidable task to outline areas of expertise, let alone for a more complex organization. Especially the *tacit* (non-articulated) nature of much organizational knowledge makes it difficult to identify the firm's knowledge base (Nonaka and Konno, 1998; Polanyi, 1958). The same is true for a firm's capabilities, which have developed in the form of organizational routines (Nelson and Winter, 1982). Likewise, the firm's attitudes are difficult to discern, because all people sharing the same disposition will tend to consider themselves normal and will tend to believe that their outlook is 'a matter of common sense' (see Chapter 2). Hence, firms intent on identifying their competences find that this is not an easy task.

While an overview of the firm's resource base is important in itself, a strategizing manager will want to compare the firm's resources to other companies to determine their relative strength. In other words, are the firm's resources unique, superior to or inferior to the resources of (potential) competitors? This type of analysis is particularly difficult, as comparison requires insight into other firms' resource bases. The identification of other firms' intangible resources can be especially arduous.

Sustaining competitive advantage

A firm has a competitive advantage when it has the means to edge out rivals when vying for the favour of customers. In the previous subsections, it was argued that competitive advantage is rooted in a unique business model, whereby the resource base, value chain and product–market position are all aligned to provide goods and/or services with a superior fit to customer needs.

A competitive advantage is said to be sustainable if it cannot be copied, substituted or eroded by the actions of rivals, and is not made redundant by developments in the environment (Porter, 1980). In other words, sustainability depends on two main factors, competitive defendability and environmental consonance:

■ Competitive defendability. Some competitive advantages are intrinsically easier to defend than others, either because they are difficult for rivals to imitate, or because rivals find it next to impossible to find an alternative route of attack. In general, a firm's competitive advantage is more vulnerable when it is based on only a limited number of distinct elements (e.g. a different packaging technology, a different delivery system or different product colours). For rivals, imitating or substituting a few elements is comparatively easy. If, however, a firm's business model has an entirely different configuration altogether, the barriers to imitation and substitution are much higher. In such a case, it is said that a firm has a 'distinct business model'. So, for instance, in the airline industry the traditional firms have tried to imitate some parts of the low cost service of Southwest in the United States, and Ryanair and easyJet in Europe, but have been largely unsuccessful because their business model as a whole is based on a different logic. Yet, many strategists note that the best defence is not to build walls around a competitive position to 'keep the barbarians out', but to have the ability to run faster than rivals – to be able to upgrade one's resources, value chain and product offering more rapidly than competitors. In this view, a competitive advantage is sustainable due to a company's capacity to stay one step ahead of rivals, *outpacing* them in a race to stay ahead (e.g. Gilbert and Strebel, 1989; Stalk, Evans and Shulman, 1992).

- Environmental consonance. The sustainability of a firm's competitive advantage is also threatened by developments in the market. Customer needs and wants are in constant flux, distribution channels can change, government regulations can be altered, innovative technologies can be introduced and new entrants can come into the competitive arena. All of these developments can undermine the fit between the firm's competitive advantage and the environment, weakening the firm's position (Rumelt, 1980).

Yet, these two factors for sustaining competitive advantage seem to pose opposite demands on the organization. Building a distinctive business model to fend off competition would suggest, on the one hand, that a firm should remain true to its fundamental *strengths,* especially when it comes to unique resources and activities that it has built up over a prolonged period of time. On the other hand, environmental consonance requires a firm to continually adapt its business model to the demands and new *opportunities* in the marketplace. The tension created by these opposite pressures will be discussed in the following section.

THE PARADOX OF MARKETS AND RESOURCES

Instead of being concerned that you have no office, be concerned to think how you may fit yourself for office. Instead of being concerned that you are not known, seek to be worthy of being known.

Confucius (551–479 BCE), Chinese philosopher

There must be a fit between an organization and its environment. This point is often expressed in terms of the classic SWOT analysis tool, which suggests that a sound strategy should match a firm's strengths (S) and weaknesses (W) to the opportunities (O) and threats (T) encountered in the firm's environment. The key to success is *alignment* of the two sides (further discussed in Chapter 8). Yet, fitting internal strengths and weaknesses to external opportunities and threats is often frustrated by the fact that the two sides pull in opposite directions – the distinctive resource base and value chain of a firm can point in a totally different direction, as compared to the developments in their current markets. Take the example of Bally, in the 1990s the worldwide market leader in pinball machines. Their strength in the manufacturing of electromechanical games was no longer aligned with developments in the market, where young people were turning to video games developed by companies such as Nintendo, Sega and Sony. As sales of pinball machines were quickly deteriorating, it was clear that Bally had to find a new fit with the market to survive. On the one hand, this meant that there was a strong pressure on Bally to adapt to market developments, for instance by upgrading its technology to also produce video games. On the other hand, Bally felt a strong pressure to exploit its current strength in electromechanical manufacturing, instead of building a new competence base from scratch. It was not self-evident for Bally how the demands for market adaptation and resource leveraging could be met simultaneously, as they seemed to be tugging the firm in diametrically opposite directions.

This tension arising from the partially conflicting demands of market adaptation and resource leveraging is referred to as the paradox of markets and resources. In the following subsections, both sides of the paradox will be examined in more detail.

The demand for market adaptation

While adaptation to the environment is a vital requirement for the success of any organization, Bally had been very slow in responding to external developments ever since the introduction of Pac-Man. Bally had not exhibited the ability to shift its product offering to follow changing customer preferences and to respond to new entrants in the gaming market. It had lost its leading position because it no longer fully understood 'the rules of the game' in its own market. As Bally drifted further and further away from developments in the market, the misalignment was threatening the survival of its business. 'Game over' was impending.

To counter this downward trend, Bally needed to identify an attractive market opportunity that it could exploit. Not a short-term sales opportunity, but a market position that could be defended against rival firms and potential new entrants over a longer period. Ideally, this market position would serve buyers willing and able to pay a premium price, and whose loyalty could be won, despite the efforts of the competition. This market position would also need to be largely immune to substitute products and should not make the firm overly dependent on strong suppliers. Once such an opportunity had been identified, it would be essential for Bally to reorganize itself to fully meet the demands of this new positioning.

Adapting to a new market position and subsequently following the many shifts in such factors as customer preferences, competitor moves, government regulations and distribution structures, can have a significant impact on a firm. It requires significant agility in changing the product offering, value chain and resource base to remain in constant alignment with the fluctuating external circumstances. For Bally, adapting to the digital technology and software environment of the current gaming industry would have had far-reaching consequences for its entire business model. Even if Bally decided to stick to electromechanical pinball machines and to target the home market of ageing pinball wizards, the company would need to make significant alterations to its business model, getting to know new distribution channels and developing new marketing competences.

The demand for resource leveraging

Yet, for Bally, it was essential to build on the resource base and value chain that it had already developed. It did not want to write off the investments it had made in building up a distinctive profile – it had taken years of acquiring and nurturing resources and fine-tuning the value chain to reach its level of expertise. Its strength in electromechanical manufacturing and the development of large 'moving parts' games was much too valuable to casually throw away just because video games were currently in fashion.

However, building a new area of competence, it was understood, should not be considered lightly. It would take a considerable amount of time, effort and money to shift the resource base and reconfigure the value chain, while there would be many risks associated with this transformation process as well. And, of course, the danger of attempting to exploit the firm's current resources would be to excel at something of increasing irrelevance. The pinball machine might be joining the buggy whip and the vacuum tube as a museum exhibit, with a real threat that Bally too could become history.

Eventually, the solution found by Bally was to give up on pinball machines altogether and to redirect its existing resources towards a much more attractive market opportunity – slot machines. This move allowed Bally to exploit its electromechanical manufacturing capability and game-making expertise, while building a strong market position in a fast growing market. Even though Bally was able to find a synthesis, reconciling the two conflicting demands, not all companies are as successful. Neither do all managers agree on how the paradox of markets and resources can best be tackled.

EXHIBIT 4.1   SHORT CASE

YAKULT: MESSAGE IN A TINY BOTTLE

The health of the human body is heavily influenced by the food that enters it. Simply eating appropriately can get you quite far, but there seem to be more ways to decrease the risk of getting ill and improve one's body condition. The Japanese pharmaceutical company Yakult first started with the development of functional food, successfully creating a completely new industry segment. It did so in particular by commercializing a certain probiotic milk-like beverage. That size does not matter has been proved well by these 65ml Yakult bottles; they turned out to be filled with blockbuster potential.

When Minoru Shirota finished his medical studies at Kyoto Imperial University in the 1920s, Japan was far from the economic power it is today. Unsanitary conditions caused infectious diseases, which made microorganism research a great opportunity. In his study, Shirota found that certain lactic acid bacteria were useful for improving the state of one's intestines. After he succeeded in culturing and strengthening this *Lactobacillus casei* strain, he decided to capitalize on his discovery in the form of small beverages containing the probiotic preventive medicine.

With the help of volunteers, Shirota managed to manufacture and sell his little drink to the Japanese market from 1935 onwards with the establishment of the Shirota Institute for Research on Protective Bacteria, but it was not until 1955 that he founded Yakult. Although the health condition of Japanese people drastically improved in correlation with Japan's economic rise, Shirota believed that there would still be demand for an illness-preventing beverage. Yet, there was one question that popped up in his mind: How do you sell a 65ml bottle drink to people on a daily basis?

In the hope of providing an appropriate response, the management of Yakult decided to introduce the concept of Yakult Ladies in the 1960s. These women are not your average milkmen, however. In addition to home delivering the small bottles – by bicycle, car, cart, motorbike and on foot – Yakult Ladies are also able to sell the *Lactobacilli*-fermented milk drink on the spot. The concept of women selling the preventive beverage proved to be successful: Who can say no to a sweet lady carrying a few bottles of probiotic drinks? Shirota and his team quickly discovered that their special sales organization carries benefits beyond simple face-to-face marketing.

Since Yakult Ladies are recruited locally, they are able to quickly build an extensive network and thus help Yakult take root into local communities. By being locally active, by paying periodic visits to retirement homes and organizing crime prevention activities for example, Yakult's special sales

▶

women have become familiar in their close environment. As such, Yakult Ladies are able to promote Yakult's products and values more successfully.

Although Yakult makes use of special sales ladies, it primarily remains a pharmaceutical company with a focus on microorganism research. In addition to the 65ml bottles filled with lactic acid bacteria and a wide range of varieties on this beverage, Yakult also concerns itself with other types of edible nourishment. In Japan, the company sells guava leaf tea, recommended for diabetic patients anxious about their sugar intake, but also deals with vitamin and mineral drinks, in addition to vegetable, soy and fruit beverages.

By starting out with microbiological research, Yakult's R&D ends up with other projects as well, such as cosmetic products created as a result of the positive effect lactic acid bacteria have on skin. Furthermore, Yakult is occupied with pharmaceuticals. For example, the company verified that *Lactobacillus casei* YIT 9018 would inherit an anticancer effect, which resulted in the development of *lactobacilli*-based medical drugs. Even though the company is active in over 30 other countries, the Japanese market alone is responsible for the vast majority of these sales. Furthermore, these business segments have not even come close to the level of profitability of Yakult's food and beverages, which contributed 92 per cent of Yakult's net sales in the fiscal year of 2016.

These numbers illustrate the problem Yakult is facing. Whereas the company is dominant in Japan and parts of Asia, Yakult is relatively small in the rest of the world, while the competition is fierce. Outside Japan, only the regular 65ml Yakult bottles and its Light counterpart have reached firm ground. Where the 'one Yakult bottle a day' concept has been integrated into the daily life of many Japanese, the same can hardly be said about the Western market. Especially

Yakult's entrance into the European market was accompanied with issues, since plenty of competitors had already jumped on the functional food bandwagon. In Yakult's case, the French Groupe Danone, owner of Actimel and Activia, is especially active.

Since the late 1980s, the European market for functional food has expanded, but most food products companies have used microorganisms in their products only to expand into the newly created market segment. That these promises of health improvement not necessarily yielded desirable results is highlighted by the European Food Safety Authority (EFSA), which provides scientific advice to the European Commission. Recent legislation demands that promises of health benefits need to be backed up by evidence, as a response to which several companies withdrew their claims precautionarily. Danone Group did so too with its probiotic Actimel and Activia products, while the US division of the corporation even had to pay US$35 million in a lawsuit as a result of making misleading claims. Even though the functional food branch is perceived with increased scepticism, Danone retained its position largely due to expansive marketing.

But how can Yakult convince people that the positive effects claimed by its own beverages do work? Another problem is its relation with competitor Danone Group. Because the corporation signed a strategic alliance with Yakult in 2004 and became its biggest shareholder, allowing for the representation of three members on Yakult's board, it effectively exerts influence over the Japanese firm.

The strategic alliance between Yakult and Danone Group, aimed at strengthening the global position of both companies, was terminated in 2013 due to the latter wanting to boost its stake in Yakult. The Japanese company did not regain managerial freedom, however, as Groupe Danone's members remained on its board. Yet, the clause that ensured Yakult was represented on Danone's board vanished. Although the corporation declared it had no intention of taking over Yakult, with its history of aggressive takeovers of competitors, Danone's loyalty concerning Yakult's independence can at the very least be called doubtful, putting the need for strategic choices on the Japanese company's even further on the front burner.

Does Yakult need to replicate its competitors in order to successfully compete in the European market? Since the image of functional food has been smudged by negative publicity, it demands a grand marketing campaign in order to alter the negative view shared by many. By putting an emphasis on the positive difference between Yakult and its competitors, the differentiation of the little beverages could be exploited.

By the same token, one could say that you cannot put new wine into old bottles, but perhaps Yakult is able to put old wine into new containers. In Japan, Yakult has limited competition, but, in Europe, the situation is quite different. With Yakult's limited assortment in most countries outside of Japan, the expansion of Yakult's probiotic products abroad might be a solution. Yakult's research resulted in a wide range of innovative products, with some of them not having a direct equivalent in the portfolio of competitors, allowing for product differentiation.

Yakult might also emphasize its Yakult Ladies. There are about 80,000 Ladies operating worldwide, but it is a channel from which Europe, where the sales of beverages are limited to stores, is excluded. With Yakult Ladies accounting for 57.2 per cent of the sales of Yakult's dairy products in Japan as of 2015 and the women being able to create long-term loyalty to the company, this channel might be worth expanding, not only towards Europe but also in countries in which Yakult already operates.

With a limited budget and equally narrow elbowroom, Yakult's management faces a difficult decision. Due to fierce competition and the current image of functional food in Europe, the message of Yakult's probiotic products may need aggressive marketing. Alternatively, by replicating the successful business model it has in Japan, Yakult Ladies might tell the probiotics story and sell more products to help swing Yakult on top. Which route will crack the tiny bottle and release Yakult's message?

Co-author: Wester Wagenaar

Sources: www.yakult.co.jp; institute.yakult.co.jp; Yakult Annual Report 2015; Yakult Supplementary Materials for Financial Statements 2005–2016; *Bloomberg*, 15 April 2010 and 26 April 2013; *Business Week*, 25 November 2007; *Financial Times*, 27 November 2013; Heasman and Mellentin (2001); *Wall Street Journal*, 26 April 2013.

PERSPECTIVES ON BUSINESS LEVEL STRATEGY

Always to be best, and to be distinguished above the rest.

The Iliad, Homer (8th century BCE), Greek poet

Firms need to adapt themselves to market developments and need to build on the strengths of their resource bases and value chains. The main question dividing managers is 'who should be fitted to whom' – should an organization adapt itself to its environment or should it attempt to adapt the environment to itself? What should be the dominant factor driving a firm: its strengths or the opportunities? Should managers take the environment as the starting point, choose an advantageous market position and then build the resource base and value chain necessary to implement this choice? Or should managers take the organization's resource base (and possibly also its value chain) as the starting point, selecting and/or adapting an environment to fit with these strengths?

As before, the strategic management literature comes with strongly differing views on how managers should proceed. The variety of opinions among strategy theorists is dauntingly large, posing many incompatible prescriptions. Here the two diametrically opposed positions will be identified and discussed in order to show the richness of differing opinions. On the one side of the spectrum, there are those managers who argue that the market opportunities should be leading, while implying that the organization should adapt itself to the market position envisioned. This point of view is called the 'outside-in perspective'. On the other side of the spectrum, many managers believe that competition eventually revolves around rival resource bases and that firms must focus their strategies on the development of unique resources and value chains. They argue that product–market positioning is a tactical decision that can be taken later. This view is referred to as the 'inside-out perspective'.

The outside-in perspective

 Managers with an outside-in perspective believe that firms should not be self-centred, but should continuously take their environment as the starting point when determining their strategy. Successful companies, it is argued, are externally oriented and market-driven (e.g. Day, 1990; Webster, 1994). They have their sights clearly set on developments in the marketplace and are determined to adapt to the unfolding opportunities and threats encountered. They take their cues from customers and competitors, and use these signals to determine their own game plan (Jaworski and Kohli, 1993). For these successful companies, markets are leading, resources are following.

Therefore, for the outside-in directed manager, developing strategy begins with an analysis of the environment to identify attractive market opportunities. Potential customers must be sought, whose needs can be satisfied more adequately than currently done by other firms. Once these customers have been won over and a market position has been established, the firm must consistently defend or build on this position by adapting itself to changes in the environment. Shifts in customers' demands must be met, challenges from rival firms must be countered, impending market entries by outside firms must be rebuffed and excessive pricing by suppliers must be resisted. In short, to the outside-in manager the game of strategy is about market positioning and understanding, and responding to external developments. For this reason, the outside-in perspective is sometimes also referred to as the 'positioning approach' (Mintzberg, Ahlstrand and Lampel, 1998).

Positioning is not short-term, opportunistic behaviour, but requires a strategic perspective, because superior market positions are difficult to attain. Once conquered, however, it can be the source of sustained profitability. Some proponents of the outside-in perspective argue that in each market a number of different positions can yield sustained profitability. For instance, Porter suggests that companies that focus on a particular niche, and companies that strongly differentiate their product offering, can achieve strong and profitable market positions, even if another company has the lowest cost position (Porter, 1980, 1985). Other authors emphasize that the position of being market leader is particularly important (e.g. Buzzell and Gale, 1987). Companies with a high market share profit more from economies of scale, benefit from risk aversion among customers, have more bargaining power towards buyers and suppliers, and can more easily flex their muscles to prevent new entrants and block competitive attacks.

Unsurprisingly, proponents of the outside-in perspective argue that insight into markets and industries is essential. Not only the general structure of markets and industries needs to be analysed, but also the specific demands, strengths, positions and intentions of all major forces need to be determined. For instance, buyers must be understood with regard to their needs, wants, perceptions, decision-making processes and bargaining chips. The same holds true for suppliers, competitors, potential market and/or industry entrants and providers of substitute products (Porter, 1980, 1985). Once a manager knows 'what makes the market tick' – sometimes referred to as the 'rules of the game' – a position can be identified within the market that could give the firm bargaining power vis-á-vis suppliers and buyers, while keeping competitors at bay. Of course, the wise manager will not only emphasize winning under the current rules with the current players, but will attempt to anticipate market and industry developments, and position the firm to benefit from these. Many outside-in advocates even advise firms to initiate market and industry changes, so that they can be the first to benefit from the altered rules of the game (this issue will be discussed further in Chapters 9 and 10).

Proponents of the outside-in perspective readily acknowledge the importance of firm resources and activities for cashing in on market opportunities the firm has identified. If the firm does not have, or is not able, to develop or obtain the necessary resources to implement a particular strategy, then specific opportunities will be unrealizable. Therefore, managers should always keep the firm's strengths and weaknesses in mind when choosing an external position, to ensure that it remains feasible. Yet, to the outside-in strategist, the firm's current resource base should not be the starting point when determining strategy, but should merely be acknowledged as a potentially limiting condition on the firm's ability to implement the best business strategy.

Actually, firms that are market-driven are often the first ones to realize that new resources and/or activities need to be developed and, therefore, are better positioned to build up a 'first mover advantage' (Lieberman and Montgomery, 1988, 1998). Where the firm does not have the ability to catch up with other firms' superior resources, it can always enter into an alliance with a leading organization, offering its partner a crack at a new market opportunity.

EXHIBIT 4.2 THE OUTSIDE-IN PERSPECTIVE

CHALLENGING CONVENTION: A RIOT IN THE GAMING INDUSTRY

Currently, Riot Gaming's multiplayer online PC game League of Legends is the most played video game across the globe. With more than 100 million active monthly users it draws parallels with social networking services, such as LinkedIn or Pinterest and its 36 million viewers of the 2015 world championship finals vastly exceed those of popular television series, such as *Game of Thrones* or *The Big Bang Theory*. Putting this big bang into practice, League of Legends generated $1.6 billion revenue in fiscal 2015, grossing more than any of its adversaries across all platforms that year. The massive influx of capital might suggest that its success stems from Riot's accumulation of financial resources into some superior hard-to-copy internal resource. Yet, the opposite holds true: League of Legends was developed with limited resources, under a corporate motto of prioritizing player experience over revenues. Rather than taking internal elements of the organization as a vantage point, Riot's strategic focal point is centered around, and embarks on paths paved by understanding gamers' needs.

Although many roads lead to Rome, every road charted by Riot leads to its customers. Founded in the US in 2006, Riot dubbed the crafting process of League of Legends as constituting 'player-focused game development'. This customer-centric rationale was enshrined as the number one cardinal rule in the company manifesto in terms of 'Player Experience First'. Similarly was this notion echoed by Brandon Beck, CEO and co-founder of Riot, who stressed the importance of impeccable alignment with its customers. As League of Legends was the sole game under Riot's development, this meant that synchronizing the game to the needs of the customer went hand in hand with the reconfiguring and co-evolving of the company as a whole. Needless to say, this customer-centric philosophy manifested itself as a fundamental pillar driving Riot's strategic endeavors. Yet, for a small and newly established firm to be audible through the noise of big competitors, words alone are not enough.

One way Riot sought to convert its words into action was by employing a free-to-play business model. When it published League of Legends in 2009, anyone having access to a PC could acquire the game free of charge. By adopting a 'freemium' pricing strategy, the core of the game was offered for free, while players were opted to purchase additional content such as character customizations, in-game currency and other virtual goods. This was not business as usual in gaming land; however, most videogame studios easily charged customers $60 for debut titles, while costs paired with development could rise to hundreds of millions of dollars, let alone publishing. Riot, in sharp contrast to this, had a starting budget of $3 million to accomplish both. Although it might seem odd to create 'value' by offering a game free of charge, what constitutes as value and what not, is all a matter of perspective. Creating 'superior value' might bear connotations with pulling in huge revenues, yet this would flow over in the higher pricing of games, which raises costs for consumers. Instead, by offering League of Legends free of charge, Riot sought to enhance customer value by providing a priceless experience for gamers, literally.

Another instrument deployed by Riot to cater to its customers are its broadcasting channels, through which it airs live events and tournaments of competitive gaming for a live audience, also known as e-sports. At Riot, they take the outside-in approach at word value; not only does it exclusively hire gamers at the company, it applies the same principle by offering gamers contracts to participate in competitive matches. Although the hosting of these events entails more costs than earnings through ticket sales – or price pools numbering to the millions – they contribute in creating and keeping customers. As the community evolving League of Legends keeps growing, so does the ensuing revenue gained from sponsorships and ads. Corporate legends like Coca Cola, Intel, Sony and many others are eager to capitalize on myriad business opportunities as provided by Riot. By building a loyal community of gamers, League of Legends has become a legend itself.

Co-author: Sander Wisman

Sources: www.riotgames.com; www.superdataresearch.com; *Bloomberg*, 15 January 2016; *The Economist*, 10 December 2011 and 25 May 2014; *Fortune*, 27 January 2016; *Harvard Business Review*, 3 June 2014; *Statista*, 2016.

The inside-out perspective

Managers adopting an inside-out perspective believe that strategies should not be built around external opportunities, but around a company's strengths. Successful companies, it is argued, build up a strong resource base over an extended period of time, which offers them access to unfolding market opportunities in the medium and short term. For such companies, the starting point of the strategy formation process is the question of which resource base it wants to have. The fundamental strategic issue is which difficult-to-imitate competences and exclusive assets should be acquired and/or further refined. Creating such a resource platform requires major investments and a long breath, and to a large extent will determine the culture and identity of the organization. Hence, it is of the utmost importance and should be the central tenet of a firm's strategy. Once the long-term direction for the building of the resource infrastructure has been set, attention can be turned to identifying market opportunities where these specific strengths can be exploited. To the inside-out oriented manager, the issue of market positioning is essential, as only a strong competitive position in the market will result in above-average profitability. However, market positioning must take place within the context of the broader resource-based strategy and not contradict the main thrust of the firm – selected market positions must leverage the existing resource base, not ignore it. In other words, market positioning is vital, but tactical, taking place within the boundaries set by the resource-driven strategy. For success, resources should be leading, and markets following.

Many managers taking an inside-out perspective tend to emphasize the importance of a firm's competences over its tangible resources (physical assets). Their way of looking at strategy is referred to as the resource-based view (e.g. Barney, 1991; Wernerfelt, 1984), competence-based view (e.g. Prahalad and Hamel, 1990; Sanchez, Heene and Thomas, 1996) or capabilities-based view (e.g. Stalk, Evans and Shulman, 1992; Teece, Pisano and Shuen, 1997). These managers point out that it is especially the development of unique abilities that is such a strenuous and lengthy process, more so than the acquisition of physical resources such as production facilities and computer systems. Some companies might be able to achieve a competitive advantage based on physical assets, but usually such tangible infrastructure is easily copied or purchased. However, competences are not readily for sale on the open market as 'plug-and-play' components, but need to be painstakingly built up by an organization through hard work and experience. Even where a company takes a shortcut by buying another organization or engaging in an alliance, it takes significant time and effort to internalize the competences in such a way that they can be put to productive use. Hence, having distinctive competences can be a very attractive basis for competitive advantage, as rival firms generally require a long time to catch up (e.g. Barney, 1991; Collis and Montgomery, 1995).

The 'nightmare scenario' for inside-out oriented strategists is where the firm flexibly shifts from one market demand to the next, building up an eclectic collection of unrelated competences, none of which is distinctive compared to competence-focused companies. In this scenario, a firm is fabulously market-driven, adaptively responding to shifts in the environment, but incapable of concentrating itself on forming the distinctive competence base needed for a robust competitive advantage over the longer term.

Most inside-out oriented managers also recognize the 'shadow side' of competences – they are not only difficult to learn, but difficult to unlearn as well. The laborious task of building up competences makes it hard to switch to new competences, even if that is what the market demands (e.g. Christensen, 1997; Rumelt, 1996). Companies far down the route of competence specialization find themselves locked in by the choices made in the past. In the same way as few concert pianists are able (and willing) to switch to playing saxophone when they are out of a job, few companies are able and willing to scrap their competence base just because the market is taking a turn for the worse. Becoming a concert pianist not only costs years of practice but is a way of life, with a specific way of working, network and career path, making it very unattractive to make a mid-career shift towards a more marketable trade. Likewise, companies experience that their core competences can simultaneously be their core rigidities, locking them out of new opportunities (Leonard-Barton, 1995). From an inside-out perspective, both companies and concert pianists should therefore first try to build on their unique competences and attempt to find or create a more suitable market, instead of reactively adapting to the unpredictable whims of the current environment (see Figure 4.8).

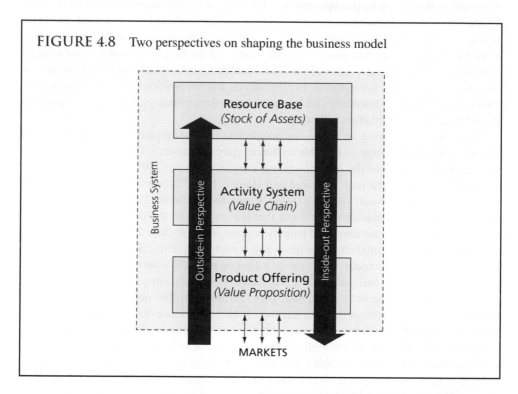

FIGURE 4.8   Two perspectives on shaping the business model

EXHIBIT 4.3   THE INSIDE-OUT PERSPECTIVE

DYSON: BLOWN BY THE WIND

Who could have envisioned that the somewhat strange looking invention of the 'Ballbarrow' resulted in a number of innovating game changers in multiple markets, and made its founding father Britain's most famous engineer and a billionaire? James Dyson's revolutionary vacuum cleaners, hand-dryers, fans and heaters all changed their marketplace – and at a premium price.

It all started in 1971 with James Dyson renovating his property. The wheel of his wheelbarrow got stuck in the mud, the steel body damaged the paintwork, and the bucket got an unwanted cement coating that could not be removed. A few years later James Dyson came up with the 'Ballbarrow', a wheelbarrow with a spherical wheel and a moulded plastic bucket that solved all problems. And while everyone expected the Ballbarrow to flop, it turned into a huge success.

Frustration also triggered the idea for Dyson's next success. When he bought a new Hoover, it got clogged quickly and lost suction over time. The only option was to change the filters and put in a new bag, resulting in exactly the same problems. Inspired by the way sawdust was removed at a local sawmill, he came up with the idea to use air cyclones in vacuum cleaners. Although it took Dyson more than 5 000 prototypes, his invention became a breakthrough in 1993: a cyclonic vacuum cleaner, capable of generating 100,000 G of centrifugal force (around 20,000 times higher than a roller-coaster ride), and spinning the dirt into a high-grade transparent plastic bin. That same year James Dyson started the company Dyson and opened a research centre and a factory in England.

His cyclonic vacuums conquered the world much more quickly than anybody could have imagined. In 2002 the average price of a vacuum in the US was about $125. In that same year Dyson introduced its DC07 upright vacuum cleaner in the US for the astonishing price of $399. Two years later, Dyson conquered almost 15 per cent of the $4 billion dollar US vacuum cleaner market and 40 per cent of the UK market and it is assumed to be the current market leader in many different countries.

Profits have been rising rapidly with Dyson expanding its operations to more countries and adding new inventions to its product range. The Airblade, an innovative hand-dryer that starts with a $1,199 price tag, can be seen in public lavatories worldwide.

It uses a HEPA filter to get rid of bacteria in the bathroom air and it then blows a sheet of air onto your hands to scrape off water like a windshield wiper. Because it only takes about 12 seconds to dry your hands, it is not only a must-have in public toilets; it is also much more energy and cost efficient than paper towels or standard hand-dryers. And then there are Dyson's cooling fans: fans without actual fans. The airflow passes over the curved outer circle of the machines, while air around it is also drawn into the airflow and amplified up to 18 times. This – according to the company – prevents the machine from 'chopping the air before it hits you' like conventional fans do, providing an uninterrupted flow of air instead. The company also invented the first LED light with an effective cooling system, which supposedly performs at least 1.5 times as long as regular LEDs. All these innovations have resulted in Dyson creating revenues of £1.74 billion in 2015, with more than £448 million of profit. The company now employs over 7 000 people worldwide, among which over 2 000 engineers.

What is the secret of this company? What is the key to its success? 'Our success is down to new ideas and the work of teams around the world', James Dyson said. The company relies heavily on resources, entering new markets and coming up with new products. With this perspective, it is very important to keep a steady stream of new ideas. For many years now, Dyson has created the perfect conditions for innovations, resulting in the second highest number of patent applications filed in the UK in 2009, only second to Rolls-Royce. Until now, the inside-out perspective has consistently proved to be the driver of Dyson's success.

Co-author: Jeroen Brinkhuis and Wester Wagenaar

Sources: www.dyson.com; www.mintel.com; *The Guardian*, 26 May 2010 and 21 March 2016; *Newsweek*, 13 January 2011 and 13 August 2013; *New Yorker*, 20 September 2010.

MANAGING THE PARADOX OF MARKETS AND RESOURCES

One does not gain much by mere cleverness.

Marquis de Vauvenargues (1715–1747), French soldier and moralist

So, how can a sustainable competitive advantage be created? Should generals create a sustainable competitive advantage by first selecting a superior position in the environment (e.g. a mountain pass) and then adapt their military resources to this position, or should generals develop armies with unique resources and then try to let the battle take place where these resources can best be employed? Should football coaches first determine how they want the game to be played on the field and then attract and train players to fit this style, or should coaches develop uniquely talented players and then adapt the team's playing style to make the best use of these resources? Should strategizing managers first understand industry dynamics and then develop resources that fit the environment? Or should they focus on developing unique and difficult-to-imitate resources and compete in industries where these resources fit best? Whether a military, sports or business strategist, an approach to creating competitive advantage must be chosen (see Table 4.1).

While no consensus has yet been developed within the field of strategic management on how to manage the paradox of markets and resources, two options have been suggested by scholars. The first option is *parallel processing* and the second *juxtaposing* based on dynamic capabilities (see taxonomy in Chapter 1).

Parallel processing

In parallel processing, the company deals with the paradox of markets and resources by separating demands over different organizational units. Some organizational units focus on market demands only – such as sales managers – and others on resource leveraging – such as R&D managers. For example, the sales department analyses client demands, competitive

TABLE 4.1   Outside-in versus inside-out perspective

	Outside-in perspective	Inside-out perspective
Emphasis on	Markets over resources	Resources over markets
Orientation	Opportunity-driven (external potential)	Strength-driven (internal potential)
Starting point	Market demand and industry structure	Resource base and value chain
Fit through	Adaptation to environment	Adaptation of environment
Strategic focus	Attaining advantageous position	Attaining distinctive resources
Strategic moves	External positioning	Building resource base
Tactical moves	Acquiring necessary resources	External positioning
Competitive weapons	Bargaining power and mobility barriers	Superior resources and imitation barriers

moves and industry dynamics, and then positions the company within the industry environment, while the research and development department leverages company resources to create unique value propositions. In this case, managing the paradox of markets and resources takes place at the next organizational level up. The phenomenon of dual processing companies has also been called 'spatial separation' (see Chapter 1).

Juxtaposing

While some organizational members focus on market demands only – such as sales managers – and others on resource leveraging – such as R&D managers – strategizing managers at different organizational units or with higher hierarchical positions have to juxtapose between both demands, employing dynamic capabilities. Defined as 'the distinct skills, processes, procedures, organizational structures, decision rules and disciplines that form the basis of a company's ability to sensing, seizing and reconfiguring capabilities' (Teece, 2007; Teece, Pisano and Shuen, 1997), dynamic capabilities propel strategists to accommodate both demands at the same time.

Dynamic capabilities enable strategizing managers to manage the paradox of markets and resources by juxtaposing between the demand for market adaptation and the demand for resource leveraging. Juxtaposing is the continuous process of creating and maintaining a dynamic equilibrium in the paradox of markets and resources. The equilibrium is dynamic because companies continuously upgrade their competences to protect them against competitors that imitate the firms' competences and to defend their market position. At the same time, they must also actively develop new capabilities in a changing business environment. The paradox is managed either on a project basis, or within the same organizational unit or at a higher organizational level.

BUSINESS LEVEL STRATEGY IN INTERNATIONAL PERSPECTIVE

Co-authors: Gep Eisenloeffel and Wester Wagenaar

Whoever is winning at the moment will always seem to be invincible.

George Orwell (1903–1950), English novelist

Comparative management research has not reported specific national preferences for an inside-out or an outside-in perspective thus far. This may be due to the fact that there are actually no distinct national inclinations when dealing with this paradox. Another cause may lie in the difficulty of international comparative research, or this lack of research reflects the implicit assumption that theories on strategizing are universally applicable. However, it might also be the case that the late emergence of resource-based theories – starting in the early 1980s – has not yet allowed for cross-national comparisons. Whatever the reason, the bottom line remains that little cross-cultural research has been conducted in the field of strategic management and this is especially true for specific national preferences for an inside-out or outside-in perspective.

Nevertheless, it is possible to provide a better understanding of the international playing field regarding business level strategy. Differences on the societal, industry and personal level can be held responsible for different international preferences across the world.

On the societal level

While cultural differences have not been identified yet by comparative management research, there are elements on the societal level that can have an influence on whether companies within a societal context prefer inside-out or outside-in thinking. National cultures also seem to play a role, but international comparative studies on this topic have not been carried out yet. We thus identify two factors that can influence preferences here: mobility barriers and resource mobility.

In general, industry and market positions will be of more value if there are high mobility barriers within the environment (Porter, 1980). Some of these barriers can be specifically national in origin. Government regulation, in particular can be an important source of mobility barriers. For instance, import quotas and duties, restrictive licensing systems, and fiscal regulations and subsidies, can all – knowingly or unknowingly – result in the protection of incumbent firms. Such government intervention enhances the importance of obtained positions. Other national sources of mobility barriers can be unions' resistance to change and high customer loyalty. In some economies, high mobility barriers might also be imposed by powerful groups or families. Here strategists might have a strong preference to think in terms of market positions first, because these are more difficult to obtain than the necessary resources. The opposite would be true in more dynamic economies, where market positions might easily be challenged by competitors, unless they are based on distinctive and difficult-to-imitate resources.

A second international difference might be found in the types of resources employed across countries. In nations where the dominant industries are populated by firms using relatively simple and abundant resources, market positions are far more important, since acquisition of the necessary resources is much less of an issue. If resources are not rare, are imitable and everybody has access to them, it is hard to make money from them (Peng, 2013). However, if a national economy is composed of industries using complex bundles of resources, requiring many years of painstaking development, there might be a tendency to emphasize the importance of resources over market positions.

On the industry level

Research has not been conclusive as to whether different industries have clear preferences for either an inside-out or an outside-in perspective on strategy. A general rule seems to be that primary sector industries are predominantly controlled through inside-out strategies. Companies operating in the tertiary sector, or the service industry, focus more on positioning themselves to follow the markets.

Some industries do have certain characteristics that make it more logical for them to prefer either one of the perspectives. As the emphasis of the field of marketing lies on communicating with the world outside of a company, marketers are often more familiar with the outside-in perspective. Industries with few marketers can be expected to gravitate more towards an inside-out focus. This is for instance the case for engineering and heavy industries, such as steel. Within business-to-consumer industries, however, preferences for outside-in perspectives can be expected. Here specialized product knowledge and personal networks are considered important and a focus on the environment is a logical consequence.

To the strategist

Independent of where strategists are operating or what nationality they possess, their behaviour is likely to be largely influenced and shaped by the education they received. This is especially true for a preference for inside-out or outside-in thinking and decision-making. A manager primarily schooled in marketing will likely have a preference towards an outside-in perspective. The opposite is true for a strategist with a background in HR (Wright, Snell and Jacobsen, 2004), in addition to someone proficient in the R&D side of businesses. In this case, it is expected they will make strategic decisions through an inside-out perspective, emphasizing internal strengths. Since education lays the foundation on how to perceive business and interpret the world, this is reflected in one of the basic ways to look at business, the paradox between market adaptation and resource leveraging.

Returning to the position of the strategists, for them it is important to take notice of who they are dealing with. Since there have not been any cross-cultural studies into national preferences, it is impossible for a strategist operating on the international stage to base expectations on people's nationalities. Instead, the work experience and academic background can provide an indication towards one of the two perspectives. In addition, international strategists may find their preference stem from mobility barriers or resource mobility. It is also imperative for a strategist to stay aware of his own background to realize the natural preference inherent to him. This inclination might always seem like the most logical option for him, but it is not guaranteed to be the best mode of operation.

5 CORPORATE LEVEL STRATEGY

We are not all capable of everything.
Virgil (70–19 BCE), Roman philosopher

INTRODUCTION

A s firms seek growth, they have a number of directions in which they can expand. The most direct source of increased revenue is to enlarge their market share, selling more of their current product offerings in their current market segments. Besides this growth through focused market penetration, firms can also broaden their scope by extending their product range (product development) or move into neighbouring market segments and geographic areas (market development). All of these growth options can be pursued while staying within the 'boundaries' of a single business (see Figure 5.1). However, firms can broaden their scope even further, venturing into other lines of business, thus becoming multi-business corporations. Some multi-business firms are involved in only two or three businesses, but there are numerous corporations spanning 20, 30 or more business areas.

This chapter deals with the specific strategic questions facing firms as they work on determining their multi-business scope. At this level, strategists must not only consider how to gain a competitive advantage in each line of business the firm has entered, but also which businesses they should be in at all. Corporate level strategy is about selecting an optimal set of businesses and determining how they should be integrated into the corporate whole. This issue of deciding on the best array of businesses and relating them to one another is referred to as the issue of 'corporate configuration'.

THE ISSUE OF CORPORATE CONFIGURATION

All multi-business firms have a particular configuration, either intentionally designed or as the result of emergent formation. Determining the configuration of a corporation can be disentangled into two main questions: (a) What businesses should the corporation be active in? and (b) How should this group of businesses be managed? This first question of deciding on the business areas that will be covered by the company is called the topic of 'corporate composition'. The second question, of deciding on the organizational system necessary to run the cluster of businesses, is labelled as the issue of 'corporate management'. In the following pages, both questions will be explored in more detail.

Corporate composition

A multi-business firm is composed of two or more businesses. When a corporation enters yet another line of business, either by starting up new activities (internal growth) or by buying another firm (acquisition), this is called diversification. There are two general categories of diversification moves, vertical and horizontal. Vertical diversification, usually called vertical integration, is when a firm enters other businesses upstream or downstream within its own industry column (see Chapter 4) – it can strive for backward integration by getting involved in supplier businesses or it can initiate forward integration by entering the businesses of its buyers. The firm can also integrate related businesses at the same tier in the industry column – an example of such horizontal integration is when a newspaper and magazine publisher moves into educational publishing. If a firm expands outside of its current industry, the term 'integration' is no longer employed, and the step is referred to as straightforward (horizontal) diversification (see Figure 5.1).

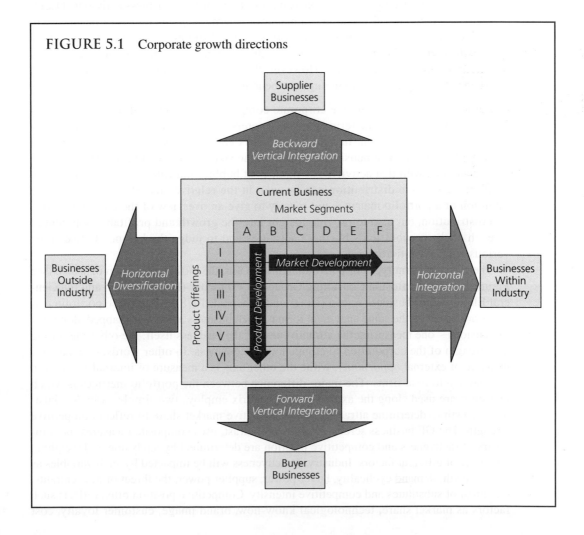

FIGURE 5.1   Corporate growth directions

The issue of corporate composition deals with the question of where the firm wants to have which level of involvement. Corporate level strategists must decide where to allocate resources, build up activities and try to achieve market sales. The issue of corporate composition can be further subdivided into two parts:

- Corporate scope. First, the composition of the corporation depends on the business areas selected. The more 'business components' chosen, the broader the scope of the corporation. Deciding on the corporate scope is not only a matter of choosing from the diversification options depicted in Figure 5.1, but can also work in the opposite direction, as a firm can withdraw from a certain line of business, either by divesting, or closing down, its activities.

- Corporate distribution. The composition of the corporation also depends on the relative size of the activities in each business area covered. The distribution within the corporation is determined by the relative weight of each business component. Some corporations are equally active in all of their selected businesses, while other firms are more asymmetrical, placing more emphasis on just a few of their business activities. Deciding on the corporate distribution is a matter of determining which lines of business will receive more attention than others. Corporate level strategists need to decide which activities will be the focus of further growth and increased weight within the firm, allocating resources accordingly. However, they must also keep in mind that a certain balance within the corporation might be beneficial.

A common way of depicting the corporate composition is to plot all of the businesses in a 'portfolio matrix'. The term 'portfolio' refers to the set of business activities carried out by the corporation. In a portfolio matrix each business activity is represented as a 'bubble' in a two-dimensional grid, with the size of the bubble reflecting the revenue generated with that activity. The number of bubbles indicates the corporate scope, while the corporate distribution can be seen in the relative size of the bubbles. The intention of a portfolio matrix is not merely to give an overview of the corporate scope and distribution, but also to provide insight into the growth and profitability potential of each of the corporation's business activities and to judge the balance between the various business activities.

There are different types of portfolio matrix in use, the most well-known of which (see Figure 5.2) are the Boston Consulting Group (BCG) matrix (Hedley, 1977) and the General Electric (GE) business screen (Hofer and Schendel, 1978). All of these portfolio matrices are based on the same analytical format. Each business activity is mapped along two dimensions – one measuring the attractiveness of the business itself, the other measuring the strength of the corporation to compete in the business. In other words, one axis is a measure of external *opportunity*, while the other axis is a measure of internal *strength* in comparison to rival firms. The major difference between the portfolio matrices is which measures are used along the axes. The BCG matrix employs two simple variables: business growth to determine attractiveness and relative market share to reflect competitive strength. The GE business screen, by way of contrast, uses composite measures: both industry attractiveness and competitive position are determined by analysing and weighing a number of different factors. Industry attractiveness will be impacted by such variables as sales growth, demand cyclicality, buyer power, supplier power, the threat of new entrants, the threat of substitutes and competitive intensity. Competitive position often reflects such factors as market share, technological know-how, brand image, customer loyalty, cost

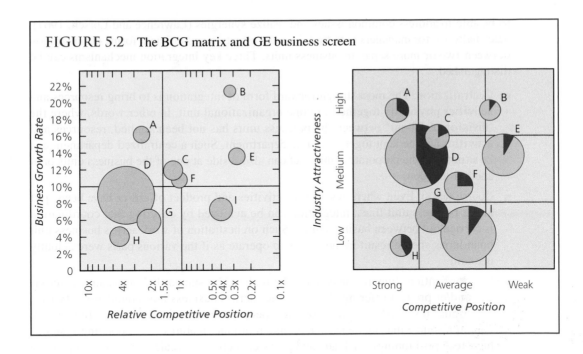

FIGURE 5.2   The BCG matrix and GE business screen

structure and distinctive competences. Another difference between the two matrices is that in the BCG portfolio grid the bubbles represent the company's sales in a line of business, while in the GE business screen the bubbles reflect the total business size, with the pie slices indicating the firm's share of the business.

Deciding which portfolio of businesses to pursue, both in terms of corporate scope and corporate distribution, will depend on how the corporate strategist intends to create value – or as Porter (1987) puts it, how the corporate strategist wants to make 'the corporate whole add up to more than the sum of its business unit parts'. After all, there must be some benefit to having the various business activities together in one corporation, otherwise each business activity could just as easily (and with less overhead) be carried out by autonomous firms. This added value of having two or more business activities under one corporate umbrella is called 'multi-business synergy' and it strongly determines the corporate composition the strategist will prefer. But before turning to the topic of synergy, the counterpart of corporate composition, namely corporate management, needs to be reviewed first.

Corporate management

It has become a widespread policy to organize multi-business firms into strategic business units (SBUs). This organizational structure is often referred to as the M-form (Williamson, 1975). Each strategic business unit is given the responsibility to serve the particular demands of one business area. The business units are labelled 'strategic', because each is driven by its own business level strategy.

This dominant approach to structuring multi-business firms does present managers with the issue of how to bring together the separate parts into a cohesive corporate whole. The corporation can be divided into business units with the intent of focusing each on separate business areas, but this *differentiation* must be offset by a certain degree of *integration* to be able to address common issues and realize synergies (Lawrence and Lorsch, 1967). The challenge for managers is to find the most effective and efficient forms of integration between two or more separate business units. Three key integration mechanisms can be distinguished:

- Centralization. The most straightforward form of integration is to bring resources and activities physically together into one organizational unit. In other words, where the 'division of labour' between the business units has not been applied, resources and activities will be kept together in one department. Such a centralized department can be situated at the corporate centre, but can also reside at one of the business units or at another location.

- Coordination. Even where resources, activities and product offerings have been split along business unit lines, integration can be achieved by ensuring that coordination is carried out between business units. Such orchestration of work across business unit boundaries should result in the ability to operate as if the various parts were actually one unit.

- Standardization. Integration can also be realized by standardizing resources, activities and/or product offering characteristics across business unit boundaries. By having similar resources (e.g. technologies, people), standardized activities (e.g. R&D, human resource management) and common product features (e.g. operating systems, high-tech positioning), such advantages as economies of scale and rapid competence development can be achieved without the need to physically centralize or continuously coordinate.

These three integration mechanisms are the tools available to managers to achieve a certain level of harmonization between the various parts of the corporate whole. Yet often the question is, who should take the initiative to realize integration – where in the management system is the responsibility vested to ensure that centralization, coordination and standardization are considered and carried out? If all business unit managers are looking after their own backyard, who is taking care of the joint issues and cross-business synergies? Basically there are two organizational means available to secure the effective deployment of the integration mechanisms (see Figure 5.3):

- Control. A straightforward way to manage activities that cross the boundaries of an individual business unit is to give someone the formal power to enforce centralization, coordination and standardization. Such a division level or corporate level manager can exert control in many ways. It can be by direct supervision (telling business units what to do), but often it is indirect, by giving business units objectives that must be met and discussing initiatives. The formal authority to secure integration does not always have to be given to a manager at the corporate centre, but can be assigned to a manager within one of the business units as well. There are also various levels of authority that can be defined, ranging from full final decision-making power to 'coordinator' or 'liaison officer', who have only limited formal means at their disposal.

- Cooperation. Centralization, coordination and standardization between business units can also be achieved without the use of hierarchical authority. Business units might be willing to cooperate because it is in their interest to do so, or because they recognize the overall corporate interests. If business units believe in the importance of certain joint activities, this can be a powerful impetus to collaborate. Corporate strategists interested in such integration by mutual adjustment will focus on creating the organizational

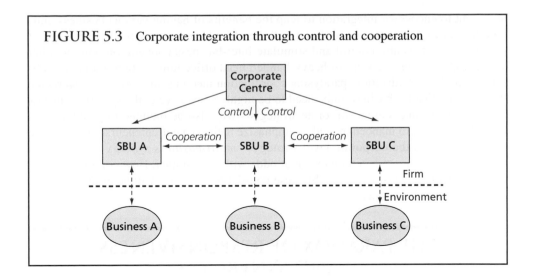

FIGURE 5.3   Corporate integration through control and cooperation

circumstances under which such self-organization can take place. (See Chapter 11 for a further discussion.) For instance, they might strengthen formal and informal ties between the business units in order to enhance mutual understanding and encourage the exchange of ideas and joint initiatives. They may also support cross-business career paths and try to instil a corporation-wide culture, to facilitate the communication between business units (Eisenhardt and Galunic, 2000).

It is the task of the corporate level strategist to determine the mix of control and cooperation needed to manage the corporation. In their seminal research, Goold and Campbell (1987) distinguish three general corporate control styles, each emphasizing different levels of centralization, coordination and standardization:

- Financial control style. In the financial control style the strategic business units are highly autonomous from the corporate centre. Few activities are centralized or standardized (except for the financial reporting system) and the corporate centre does not explicitly attempt to coordinate activities across business unit boundaries. Control is exerted by negotiating, setting and monitoring financial objectives.

- Strategic control style. In the strategic control style the strategic business units have a closer relationship with the corporate centre. A number of central services exist, some systems and activities are standardized and the corporate centre explicitly tries to coordinate activities that reach beyond the boundaries of only one business unit. Control is exerted by negotiating, setting and monitoring strategic objectives.

- Strategic planning style. In the strategic planning style the strategic business units have relatively little autonomy from the corporate centre. Many key activities are centralized or standardized, and the corporate centre is also heavily involved in securing cross-business coordination. Control is exerted by means of direct supervision.

Which corporate management style is adopted depends strongly on what the corporate strategist wishes to achieve. The preferred corporate management style will be determined by the type of multi-business synergies that the corporate strategist envisages, but also on the level of autonomy that the business units require. On the one hand, strategists will want to encourage integration to reap the benefits of having various business units together under one corporate roof and will therefore have a strong motivation to exert strong corporate centre control and stimulate inter-business cooperation. On the other hand, strategists will be wary of heavy-handed head office intervention, blunt centralization, rigid standardization, paralysing coordination meetings and excessive overhead. Recognizing that the business units need to be highly responsive to the specific demands of their own business area, corporate strategists will also be inclined to give business units the freedom to manoeuvre and to emphasize their own entrepreneurship. Yet, these two demands on the corporate level strategy – *multi-business synergy* and *business responsiveness* – are to a certain extent at odds with one another. How corporate strategists deal with the tension created by these conflicting demands will be examined more closely in the following section.

THE PARADOX OF RESPONSIVENESS AND SYNERGY

None ever got ahead of me except the man of one task.

Azariah Rossi (1513–1578), Italian physician

When Cor Boonstra took over as CEO of Philips Electronics in 1996, after a long career at the fast-moving consumer goods company Sara Lee, one of his first remarks to the business press was that Philips reminded him of 'a plate of spaghetti' – the company's more than 60 business units were intertwined in many different ways, sharing technologies, facilities, sales forces and customers, leading to excessive complexity, abundant bureaucracy, turf wars and a lack of accountability. To Boonstra the pursuit of multi-business synergy had spiralled into an overkill of centralization, coordination and standardization, requiring direct rectification. Thus Boonstra set out to restructure Philips into, in his own words, 'a plate of asparagus', with business units neatly lined up, one next to the other. Over a period of five years he disposed of numerous business units and made sure that the others were independent enough 'to hold up their own pants'. The result was a loss of some valuable synergies, but a significant increase in the business units' responsiveness to the demands in their own business. Then, in 2001, Boonstra handed over the reins to a Philips insider, Gerard Kleisterlee, who during one of his first media encounters as new CEO stated that the business units within Philips had become too insular and narrowly focused, thereby missing opportunities to capture important synergies. Therefore, he indicated that it would be his priority to get Philips to work more like a team.

What this example of Philips illustrates is that corporate level strategists constantly struggle with the balance between realizing synergies and defending business unit responsiveness. To achieve synergies, a firm must to some extent integrate the activities carried out in its various business units. The autonomy of the business units must be partially limited, in the interest of concerted action. However, integration comes with a price tag. An extra level of management is often required, more meetings, extra complexity, potential conflicts of interest, additional bureaucracy. Harmonization of operations costs money and diminishes a business unit's ability to precisely tailor its strategy to its specific business environment. Hence, for the corporate strategist the challenge is to realize more *value creation* through multi-business synergies than *value destruction* through the loss of business responsiveness (e.g. Campbell, Goold and Alexander, 1995; Prahalad and Doz, 1987).

This tension arising from the partially conflicting demands of business responsiveness and multi-business synergy is called the paradox of responsiveness and synergy. In the following subsections, both sides of the paradox will be examined in more detail.

The demand for multi-business synergy

Diversification into new business areas can only be economically justified if it leads to value creation. According to Porter (1987), entering into another business (by acquisition or internal growth) can only result in increased shareholder value if three essential tests are passed:

- The attractiveness test. The business 'must be structurally attractive, or capable of being made attractive'. In other words, firms should only enter businesses where there is a possibility to build up a profitable competitive position (see Chapter 4). Each new business area must be judged in terms of its competitive forces and the opportunities available to the firm to sustain a competitive business model.

- The cost-of-entry test. "The cost of entry must not capitalize all the future profits". In other words, firms should only enter new businesses if it is possible to recoup the investments made. This is important for internally generated new business ventures, but even more so for external acquisitions. Many researchers argue that, on average, firms significantly overpay for acquisitions, making it next to impossible to compensate for the value given away during the purchase (e.g. Sirower, 1997).

- The better-off test. 'Either the new unit must gain competitive advantage from its link with the corporation or vice versa'. In other words, firms should only enter new businesses if it is possible to create significant synergies. If not, then the new unit would be better off as an independent firm or with a different parent company, and should be cut loose from the corporation.

It is this last test that reveals one of the key demands of corporate level strategy. Multi-business level firms need to be more than the sum of their parts. They need to create more added value than the extra costs of managing a more complex organization. They need to identify opportunities for synergy between business areas and manage the organization in such a way that the synergies can be realized.

But what are the sources of synergy? For quite some time, strategists have known that potential for synergy has something to do with 'relatedness' (Rumelt, 1974). Diversification moves that were unrelated (or 'conglomerate'), for example a food company's entrance into the bicycle rental business, were deemed to be less profitable, in general, than moves that were related (or 'concentric'), such as a car-maker's diversification into the car rental business (e.g. Chatterjee, 1986; Rumelt, 1982). However, the problem has been to determine the nature of 'relatedness'. Superficial signs of relatedness do not indicate that there is potential for synergy. Drilling for oil and copper mining might seem highly related (both are 'extraction businesses'), but Shell found out the hard way that they were not related, selling the acquired mining company Billiton to Gencor after they were unable to create synergy. Chemicals and pharmaceuticals seem like similar businesses (especially if pharmaceuticals are labelled 'specialty chemicals'), but ICI decided to split itself in two (into ICI and Zeneca), because it could not achieve sufficient synergy between these two business areas.

FIGURE 5.4   Forms of multi-business synergy

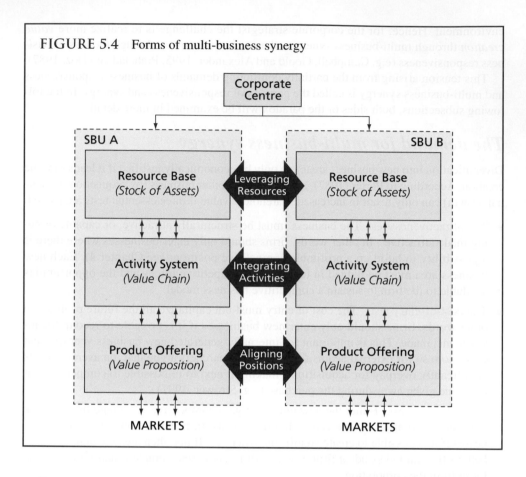

Strategy researchers have therefore attempted to pin down the exact nature of relatedness (e.g. Prahalad and Bettis, 1986; Ramanujam and Varadarajan, 1989). Following the business model framework outlined in Chapter 4, the areas of relatedness that have the potential for creating synergy can be organized into three categories (see Figure 5.4): resource relatedness, product offering relatedness and activity relatedness.

Synergy by leveraging resources.   The first area of relatedness is at the level of the businesses' resource bases. Two or more businesses are related if their resources can be productively shared between them. In principle, all types of resources can be shared, both the tangible and the intangible, although in practice some resources are easier to share than others – for example, it is easier to transfer money than knowledge. Such 'resource leveraging' (Hamel and Prahalad, 1993) can be achieved by physically reallocating resources from one business area to another, or by replicating them so they can be used in a variety of businesses simultaneously:

■ Achieving resource reallocation. Instead of leaving firm resources in the business unit where they happen to be located, a corporation can create synergy by transferring resources to other business units, where better use can be made of them (Helfat and Eisenhardt, 2004). For instance, money and personnel are often shifted between business units, depending on where they are needed and the potential return is highest.

■ Achieving resource replication. While physical resources can only be used in one place at a time, intangible resources can often be copied from one business unit to another, so that the same resource can be used many times over. This happens, for example, when knowledge and capabilities are copied and reused in other business units.

Synergy by aligning positions.   A second area of relatedness is at the level of product offerings. Two or more businesses are related if they can help each other by aligning their positioning in the market. Such coordination between product–market combinations can both improve the businesses' bargaining position vis-á-vis buyers, as well as improve the businesses' competitive position vis-á-vis rival firms:

■ Improving bargaining position. Business units can improve their bargaining power vis-á-vis buyers by offering a broad package of related products or services to specific customer groups. Especially when the products being offered are complementary, share a common brand and have a comparable reputation, they will support one another in the market.

■ Improving competitive position. Coordination of product offerings within one firm can also prevent a number of business units from fighting fiercely among one another, which might have happened if all units were independent companies. Moreover, it is even possible for multiple business units to support each other in attacking a third party, for example by setting a common standard or aggressively pricing selected products. Similarly, business units can team up to protect each other from attacks and create barriers to entry into the industry/ market (Baum and Greve, 2001; Jayachandran, Gimeno and Varadarajan, 1999).

Synergy by integrating value chain activities.   The third area of relatedness is at the level of value chains. Two or more businesses are related if an integration of their value chains is more efficient and/or more effective than if they were totally separated. Such integration of value-creation activities can focus on the sharing of similar activities or the linking up of sequential activities:

■ Sharing value-adding activities. Business units often combine some of their value-adding activities, such as logistics, production or marketing, if this leads to significant scale advantages or quality improvements. It is also common to see that the corporate centre organizes certain support activities centrally. These 'shared services' often include functions such as human resource management, procurement, quality control, legal affairs, research and development, finance and corporate communication.

■ Linking value-adding activities. Business units that are not horizontally but vertically related (see Figure 5.1) can have an internal customer–supplier relationship. Such vertical integration of sequential value-adding activities in one firm can be more efficient than operating independently where supplies need to be highly tailored to a specific type of customer demand.

Much attention in the literature has been paid to this issue of vertical integration of activities. It is also referred to as 'internalization' because firms decide to perform activities inside the firm, instead of dealing with outside suppliers and buyers. In general, companies will strive to integrate upstream or downstream activities where one or more of the following conditions are deemed important (e.g. Harrigan 1985; Mahoney, 1992):

■ Operational coordination. It can be necessary for various parts of the value system to be tightly coordinated or even physically integrated, to ensure that the right components, meeting the right specifications, are available in the right quantities, at the right moment, so that high quality, low cost or timely delivery can be achieved. To realize this level of coordination it can be necessary to gain control over a number of key activities in the value system, instead of trying to get suppliers and buyers to cooperate.

■ Avoidance of transaction costs. Reaching a deal with a supplier or buyer and transferring the goods or services to the required location may be accompanied by significant direct costs. These contracting costs can include the expenses of negotiations, drawing up a contract, financial transfers, packaging, distribution and insurance. Add to these the search costs required to locate and analyse potential new suppliers or buyers, as well as the policing costs which are incurred to check whether the contract is being met according to expectations and to take action against those parties not living up to their contractual responsibilities. If a firm vertically integrates, many of these costs can be avoided, leading to potential savings (Williamson, 1975).

■ Increased bargaining power. If a firm is facing a supplier or buyer with a disproportionately high level of bargaining power (for instance, a monopolist), vertical integration can be used to weaken or neutralize such a party. By fully or partially performing the activities in-house, the firm can lessen its dependence on a strong buyer or supplier. The firm can also strive to acquire the other party, to avoid the bargaining situation altogether.

■ Learning curve advantages. Where vertically linked business units work closely together, exchanging knowledge and personnel, they might also learn more quickly and more efficiently than if the business units were independent. Especially where they initiate joint R&D projects and collaborate on business process improvement efforts, then significant learning curve advantages can be realized.

■ Implementing system-wide changes. Besides continual operational coordination and ongoing learning, there may be a need to coordinate strategic changes throughout the value system. Switching over to new technologies, new production methods and new standards can sometimes only be implemented if there is commitment and a concerted effort in various parts of the value system. Sometimes even neighbouring value systems need to be involved in the changes. Vertical integration and horizontal diversification can give a firm the formal control needed to push through such changes.

Corporate level strategy is about determining the corporate configuration that offers the best opportunities for synergy, and implementing a corporate management system capable of realizing the intended synergies. However, what types of synergy can realistically be achieved without paying a heavier penalty in terms of integration costs? Recognizing the possible benefits of bringing together various businesses under one corporate umbrella is one thing, but developing a corporate management system that does not cost more than it yields is another. Therefore, corporate strategists need to carefully consider the potential downside of resource leveraging, activity integration and position alignment – the loss of business responsiveness.

The demand for business responsiveness

Responsiveness is defined as the ability to respond to the competitive demands of a specific business area in a timely and adequate manner. A business unit is responsive if it has the capability to tightly match its strategic behaviour to the competitive dynamics in its business. If a business unit does not focus its strategy on the conditions in its direct environment and does not organize its value-adding activities and management systems to fit with the business characteristics, it will soon be at a competitive disadvantage compared to more responsive rivals. Business responsiveness is therefore a key demand for successful corporate level strategy.

Yet, in multi-business firms, the responsiveness of the business units is constantly under pressure. Various scope disadvantages limit the ability of the corporation to ensure business responsiveness. The major problems encountered by multi-business firms are the following:

- High governance costs. Coordinating activities within a firm requires managers. Layers of management, and the bureaucratic processes that might entail, can lead to escalating costs.

- Slower decision-making. Business units must usually deal with more layers of management, more meetings for coordination purposes, more participants in meetings, more conflicts of interest and more political infighting. This not only increases governance costs, but also slows down decision-making and action.

- Strategy incongruence. The resource leveraging, activity integration and position alignment envisioned in the corporate strategy can be more suited to the conditions in some businesses than to others. Consequently, some business units might need to compromise, adapting their business strategy to fit with the corporate strategy. However, such internal adaptation might lead to a misfit with the business demands.

- Dysfunctional control. The corporate centre might not have the specific business know-how needed to judge business unit strategies, activities and results. However, the corporate centre might feel the need to exert some control over business units, potentially steering them in an inappropriate direction.

- Dulled incentives. Limited autonomy combined with the aforementioned problems can have a significant negative impact on the motivation to perform optimally. This dulled incentive to be entrepreneurial and to excel can be compounded by poorly delineated responsibilities, a lack of clear accountability and the existence of 'captive' internal customers.

Together, these factors limit the business unit's drive to be responsive.

These threats make clear that multi-business firms must determine their composition and management systems in a way that enables business units to be responsive. Yet, simultaneously, corporate strategists need to strive towards the identification and realization of synergies. The question is how these two conflicting demands can be reconciled – how can corporate level strategists deal with the paradox of responsiveness and synergy?

EXHIBIT 5.1   SHORT CASE

HYUNDAI MOTOR GROUP: DRIVING APART TOGETHER?

Steel, automobiles, construction, finances, logistics, hotels, machine parts, marketing. All of these are businesses in which the Hyundai Motor Group (HMG) is active. HMG's core philosophy is that it aims to provide innovative products able to create a better future for humanity. In other words, it allows itself to be involved in any business it pleases. This has been the way in which Hyundai was formed, and it still remains how HMG approaches industries today. Although old habits die hard, it by no means guarantees that this can be maintained in the upcoming years.

The South-Korean economy started to pick up in the 1960s in what was later called the 'miracle on the Han river', characterized by industrialization, better education, an increase in living standards and technological advancement. South Korea's developmental state model was formed principally during the authoritarian regime of Park Chung-hee, the controversial president who seized power in 1961. In order to expand the exports of South Korea, the government decided to pursue cooperation with corporations. This helped *chaebol* come into existence: giant Korean financial conglomerates run by powerful families. Hyundai became one of them.

Yet, this bright future was not apparent when the company was founded in 1947, with the poor Ju-yung Chung establishing a small construction firm. Profiting from the government's drive to rebuild the country in the wake of the Second World War (1939–1945) and the Korean War (1950–1953), his Hyundai Civil Works Company grew at a rapid pace. Chung had the luck to be at the right place at the perfect time, but fortune does not necessarily have to happen accidentally; it can also be enforced. He actively extorted his luck by entering infant industries, which is how he got involved in manufacturing and selling automobiles.

After establishing the Hyundai Motor Company (HMC) in 1967, Hyundai started with the production of cars. The newly founded company helped out Ford with car manufacturing, and after nine years Hyundai launched its own car: the Hyundai Pony, the first ever mass-produced Korean passenger automobile. This model comprised mostly of parts from overseas partners and Hyundai was still more of an automotive assembler, but there were big plans for the company's future. These were not necessarily Hyundai's, however, it was the South Korean government that wanted to drastically improve the domestic automotive industry from the early 1970s onwards. The government allowed three companies to mass produce cars: Hyundai, Daewoo and Kia. In addition, it issued high protectionist tariff barriers to protect the infant industry, on the condition that the car manufacturers would utilize as many locally produced car parts as possible. Chung had hit the mark again.

Chung accumulated an assortment of companies that could benefit from one another with the steel business functioning as Hyundai's core. For example, he secured a multitude of companies concerned with manufacturing steel, developing of auto parts and producing ships. Chung also entered seemingly unconnected industries by expanding into commercial banking activities, chemicals, life-insurance businesses and electronics, thus diversifying the portfolio of his company intensely. This expansionist attitude seemed to work well though: what started as a small construction firm eventually became South Korea's biggest *chaebol*. In the mid-1990s, Hyundai had 60 subsidiary companies, comprised of 200,000 employees, with total annual revenues of approximately $90 billion. Yet, Chung's luck did not last forever.

His success started to crumble after the 1997 Asian financial crisis. At first this did not seem to impact Hyundai that much. While its *chaebol* competitors LG and Samsung backed down and reorganized, Chung continued to expand. He dropped some assets that did not add much to the corporation, but his take-overs were more abundant: he acquired Kia Motors and a 60 per cent share of chip-maker LG Semicon. He did so under the premise that the government would save the *chaebol* in case things would get out of hand as South Korea could not afford such a loss. Chung guessed wrongly.

Early in the crisis five major *chaebol* went bankrupt, while only a few of the largest 30 conglomerates were seen as financially stable. The impact was devastating; several thousands of Koreans lost their source of income. With the South Korean government recording a deficit of $8.7 billion and in desperate need of a financial bailout, the International Monetary Fund gained the power to act. It decided that South Korea grew too dependent on *chaebol* and put pressure on the South Korean government, which in turn forced the family conglomerates to restructure and focus more on their core businesses. Hyundai, with debts of no less than $10.5 billion, also coping with the death of Chung, was not spared. Since Hyundai had multiple core businesses, it was divided into a multitude of companies with the Hyundai name but without an actual corporate connection to a group. While Chung's empire crumbled, not all was lost.

Chung had played the game well. He had positioned relatives in top positions throughout his conglomerate, and even though his offspring and other family members were fighting for the lucrative parts of the former *chaebol*, the group still lived on – albeit in a disconnected way. The multiple Hyundai companies moved into more businesses and became shareholders of each other, forming complex structures. In this way, even with minority shareholdings the Chung family generally managed to maintain control.

This is illustrated well by Hyundai Motor Group, holding company for many of the Hyundai businesses. Hyundai Motor Company, de facto representative of the group, possesses some 34 per cent of Kia Motors, which holds 17 per cent of parts supplier Hyundai Mobis. In turn, Mobis owns approximately 21 per cent of HMC. Similar structures are found in the connections between HMG's other subsidiaries, such as finance, logistics and railways. Thanks to good relations with the vast network of the diverse Hyundai businesses and with shares in Hyundai Motor Company and Mobis, Mong-koo Chung, chairman and CEO of HMC and son of the late Ju-yung Chung, retains control of the Motor Group.

Yet the holding company is not necessarily built to last. The many Hyundai affiliates are not autonomous companies but depend on one another with cross-shareholding and family-based relationships, while integrating compatible resources and activities is a real challenge with minority shareholdings. Hyundai Motor Company may capture synergies with affiliated steel companies and car parts manufacturers by boasting close relationships and leveraging activities, however these may not justify integrating the corporation.

The alternatives are contradictory though. If Chung would decide to take apart the current structure of the Hyundai Motor Group and reorganize it into a vertical structure of parent and subsidiaries, this would not only cost approximately $9.6 billion according to a research conducted in 2012, but would also result in HMG becoming a true *chaebol* all over again. This would contradict South Korea's contemporary politics, which are particularly concerned with curtailing the power of family conglomerates. Keeping HMG as it is now is risky as well, since cross-shareholdings are also perceived as a problem in South Korea's political discourse. With the third generation of Chung management dawning, it is imperative that HMG does not suffer the same fate as Hyundai did in the early 2000s.

Hyundai, which posted its ninth straight quarterly profit decline in May 2016, needs Mong-koo Chung to make decisions. Should he pick one of the alternative routes, or act on the company's promise: new thinking, new possibilities? Whatever his choice, he will be aware of the situation that Hyundai Motor Group is not driven by only one motor.

Co-author: Wester Wagenaar

Sources: www.hyundaimotorgroup.com; www.imf.org; *Bloomberg*, 8 February 2011 and 21 December 2012; *Business Week*, 13 November 2012; *The Economist*, 4 February 1999 and 25 February 2013; Hyundai Motor Company Audit Report 2016 1Q; *The Korea Times*, 21 February 2010; Lim, Y. (2002) *Journal of East Asian Studies*, Vol. 2, No. 1; Rowley, C. and Paik, Y. (2008) *The Changing Face of South Korean Management*, London: Routledge.

PERSPECTIVES ON CORPORATE LEVEL STRATEGY

We must indeed all hang together, or, most assuredly, we shall all hang separately.

Benjamin Franklin (1706–1790), American politician, inventor and scientist

Corporations need to capture multi-business synergies and they need to ensure each business unit's responsiveness to its competitive environment. In other words, corporations need to be integrated and differentiated at the same time – emphasizing the *whole* and respecting the *part*. Striving towards synergy is a centripetal force, pulling the firm together into an integrated whole, while being responsive to business demands is a centrifugal force, pulling the firm apart into autonomous market-focused units (Ghoshal and Mintzberg, 1994). The main question dividing strategists is whether a corporation should primarily be a collection of parts or an integrated whole. Should corporations be loose federations of business units or tightly knit teams? Should corporations be business groups made up of distinctive parts, where only modest synergies can be realized and business units accorded a large measure of leeway to be responsive to their specific market conditions? Or should corporations actually be unitary organizations, with the parts serving the whole, allowing for significant synergies to be achieved, with the challenge of being responsive enough to varied business demands?

As before, the strategic management literature comes with strongly different views on how strategists should proceed. Here the two diametrically opposed positions will be identified and discussed to show the richness of differing opinions. On the one side of the spectrum, there are those strategists who believe that multi-business firms should be viewed as portfolios of autonomous business units in which the corporation has a financial stake. They argue that business responsiveness is crucial and that only a limited set of financial synergies should be pursued. This point of view is referred to as the 'portfolio organization perspective'. On the other side of the spectrum, there are strategists who believe that corporations should be tightly integrated, with a strong central core of shared resources, activities and/or product offerings keeping the firm together. They argue that corporations built up around these strong synergy opportunities can create significantly more value than is lost through limitations to responsiveness. This point of view is referred to as the 'integrated organization perspective'.

The portfolio organization perspective

In the portfolio organization perspective, responsiveness is strongly emphasized over synergy. Managers taking this perspective usually argue that each business has its own unique characteristics and demands. Firms operating in different businesses must therefore develop a specific strategy for each business and assign the responsibility for each business strategy to a separate strategic business unit. In this manner, the (strategic) business units can be highly responsive to the competitive dynamics in the business, while being a clear unit of accountability towards the corporate centre. High responsiveness, however, requires freedom from corporate centre interference and freedom from cross-business coordination. Hence, a high level of business unit autonomy is required, with the corporate centre's influence limited to arm's-length financial control.

In the portfolio organization perspective, the main reason for a number of highly autonomous business units to be in one firm is to leverage financial resources. The only synergies emphasized are financial synergies (e.g. Lubatkin and Chatterjee, 1994; Trautwein, 1990). Actually, the term 'portfolio' entered the business vocabulary via the financial sector, where it refers to an investor's collection of shareholdings in different companies, purchased to spread investment risks. Transferred to corporate strategy, the portfolio organization perspective views the corporate centre as an active investor with financial stakes in a number of stand-alone business units. The role of the centre is one of selecting a promising portfolio of businesses, keeping tight financial control and allocating available capital – redirecting flows of cash from business units where prospects are dim ('cash cows' or 'dogs'), to other business units where higher returns can be expected ('stars' or 'question marks'). The strategic objective of each business unit is, therefore, also financial in orientation – grow, hold, milk or divest, depending on the business unit's position on the portfolio grid (e.g. Hedley, 1977; Henderson, 1979). A good corporate strategy strives for a balanced portfolio of mature cash producers and high potential ROI cash users, at an acceptable level of overall risk.

The financial synergies can be gained in a number of different ways (e.g. Chatterjee, 1986; Weston, Chung and Hoag, 1990). First, by having various businesses within one firm, the corporate centre can economize on external financing. By internally shifting funds from one business unit to another, the corporation can avoid the transaction costs and taxation associated with external capital markets. Second, the corporation can limit dependence on the whims of external capital providers, who might be less inclined to finance some ventures (e.g. new businesses or high-risk turnarounds) at acceptable levels of capital cost. Third, where the corporation does want to secure external financing, the firm's larger size, debt capacity and creditworthiness can improve its bargaining position in the financial markets. Finally, by having revenue and earning streams from two or more different businesses, the corporation can reduce its exposure to the risk of a single business. This risk balancing, or co-insurance, effect is largest where the portfolio is made up of counter-cyclical businesses. In turn, the stability and predictability of revenue and earning flows enable the corporation to plan and function more effectively and efficiently (e.g. Amit and Livnat, 1988; Seth, 1990).

The business units do not necessarily need to be 'related' in any way other than financially. In practice, the business units can be related, that is, there can be resource leveraging, activity integration and position alignment opportunities that are seized. The portfolio organization perspective does not reject the pursuit of other forms of synergy, but neither does it accommodate such efforts (Haspeslagh, 1982). Responsiveness is not compromised to achieve these synergy opportunities.

New businesses can be entered by means of internal growth, but the portfolio approach to corporate strategy is particularly well suited to diversification through acquisition. In a multi-business firm run on portfolio principles, acquired companies are simple to integrate into the corporation, because they can be largely left as stand-alone units and only need to be linked to corporate financial reporting and control systems. Proponents of the portfolio organization perspective argue that such 'non-synergistic' acquisitions can be highly profitable (Kaplan, 1989; Long and Ravenscraft, 1993). Excess cash can be routed to more attractive investment opportunities than the corporation has internally. Moreover, the acquiring corporation can shake up the management of the acquired company and can function as a strategic sounding board for the new people. In this way, the acquirer can release the untapped value potential of underperforming stand-alone businesses (Anslinger and Copeland, 1996).

The portfolio organization perspective is particularly well-known for the analytical techniques that have been developed to support it. As was mentioned before, a large number of portfolio grids are in widespread use as graphical tools for visualizing corporate composition and for determining the position of each of the business units. These portfolio analysis tools have proven to be popular and much used (Goold and Lansdell, 1997), even among strategists who are not proponents of the portfolio organization perspective.

In conclusion, the basic assumption of the portfolio organization perspective is that business units must be responsible for their own competitive strategy. Business units are the main locus of strategic attention and the corporate centre should understand their limited ability to get involved and stimulate synergy. Corporate centres should be modest in ambition and size, taking heed of the words of the famous 'business philosopher' Groucho Marx that 'The most difficult thing about business is minding your own'.

EXHIBIT 5.2   THE PORTFOLIO ORGANIZATION PERSPECTIVE

CRH: BUILDING A SOLID HOUSE OF BUSINESSES

Although an unfamiliar name to most, CRH has been growing in the past 47 years from serving the small, peripheral Irish construction market to become the third largest building materials firm in the world. While the company name might not ring a bell, the brands kept by this holding surely will. Oldcastle in the United States, Ancon in the UK and Bau King in Germany are all household names that any handyman will relate to producing building materials and selling them in do-it-yourself stores. CRH's impressive growth in a viciously hostile environment, characterized by increased commoditization and ever-decreasing, cyclical demand, has been made possible by its clever acquisition strategy.

In order to overcome industry's challenges, CRH needed to gain a deep understanding of its customers in all businesses and countries in which it is active. This is challenging, as customer demands in this sector are immensely versatile across countries and products. The fact that CRH operates all over Europe and the United States, where it sells hundreds of different products, makes a centralized solution to this challenge unfeasible. Instead, CRH grew tremendously by repeatedly buying up small to medium sized companies, to then exploit their expert knowledge of its products and markets. CRH's headquarters only house 250 people, a relatively small number for a firm pulling in over €23 billion revenue a year, which leaves running the shop to the acquired businesses themselves.

What CRH does provide to their business units is increased efficiency by providing an experienced manager who optimizes the – often inexperienced family – company. Every year the performance of all of its business units is tested against performance and growth benchmarks. By doing so, in the words of former CEO, Myles Lee, they 'earn the right to grow'. Profitable units can expand rapidly due to managerial support and the financial backing CRH will continue to provide. The latter is of paramount importance since a firm the size of CRH has much more favourable credit conditions compared to the much smaller units they maintain.

CRH's approach has proved to be a formula for success. Both the small yet professional central headquarters and the visible, expert brands capitalize on their strengths to create impressive growth. CRH was clever to take this approach as opposed to one of internal growth or larger scale acquisitions, as many small to medium size businesses are struggling and looking for help. Banks maintain increasingly stringent conditions for funding small firms and, especially in the case of family businesses in this sector; growth often leads to new challenges the business does not have the competencies to meet. Through acquisitions, on the other hand, CRH is able to realize its ambition to have a specialized market and product knowledge in all their markets.

Clever and innovative as its approach might be, CRH's profits had slumped in fiscal 2013. This has to do with the fact that the pace of the construction industry is, as a rule of thumb, about half the size of the economic growth of a region. As the United States and Europe are facing either minimal or even negative growth, the building business is not exactly booming. About 90 per cent of today's demand for cement, for example, stems from emerging markets; a trend that is not expected to let up soon. These shifts in the environment prompted CRH to pursue their approach with renewed vigour, as they streamlined their portfolio through a series of divestments and investments, reallocating their capital from lower growth areas into core businesses for growth. Although these events were relatively small in scale, the cascading effects certainly were not, as they preluded the largest acquisitions ever made in the company's history.

In 2015 CRH first acquired cement assets from rivals Holcim and Lafarge for €6.5 billion, which provides a foothold in the Canadian, the Brazilian, and the Philippine markets, while it solidifies CRH's position in the European market. Another large-scale acquisition followed as C.R. Laurence, a US glazing products firm, was purchased for $1.3 billion. Both acquisitions circumvent issues of stagnation and decline in US and European cement markets, as the US glazing market continues to flourish, while cement markets in other regions provide new growth opportunities. Yet challenges still remain, as these large scale acquisitions need to be properly streamlined, while cross-cultural competences will be put to the test. Although CRH has always pursued a small and medium scale acquisition strategy – and still does so until this very day – it was able to act swiftly as it recognized an opportunity. As adaptation, rigour and a good read of their business environment are qualities that have led to their monumental growth in the last 47 years, it will be interesting to see how CRH's future unfolds.

Co-author: Jasper de Vries

Sources: 'CRH issues profit warning after first-half loss of €71m', *Financial Times*, 20 August 2013; 'CRH to acquire €6.5bn in cement assets from Holcim and Lafarge', *Financial Times*, 1 February 2015; CRH Annual Report, 2012–2015; CRH: Still to play its trump card, goodbody stockbrokers, 13 July 2005; CRH Strategy, www.crh.com/ourgroup/strategy/acquisitions, accessed 15 September, 2013.

The integrated organization perspective

The integrated organization perspective is fundamentally at odds with the portfolio organization perspective's minimalist interpretation of corporate level strategy. To proponents of the integrated organization perspective, a multi-business firm should be more than a loose federation of businesses held together by a common investor. Actually, a corporation should be quite the opposite – a tightly knit team of business units grouped around a common core. Having various businesses together in one corporation, it is argued, can only be justified if the corporate centre has a clear conception of how strategically relevant multi-business synergies can be realized. It is not enough to capture a few operational synergies here and there – a compelling logic must lie at the heart of the corporation, creating a significant competitive advantage over rivals who operate on a business-by-business basis. The multi-business synergies generated at the core of the organization should enable the corporation to beat its competitors in a variety of business areas.

As corporate level strategists 'lead from the centre' (Raynor and Bower, 2001) and develop a joint competitive strategy together with business level strategists, they must make very clear which multi-business synergies they intend to foster as the nucleus of the corporation. It is their task to determine what the core of the organization should be and to take the lead in building it. To be successful, it is necessary for them to work closely together with business level managers whose main task it is to apply the core strengths of the corporation to their specific business area. The consequence of this joint strategy development and synergy realization is that all business units are highly interdependent, requiring continual coordination.

Many different multi-business synergies can form the core of the corporation. In the strategic management literature one specific form has received a large amount of attention – the *core competence*-centred corporation (Prahalad and Hamel, 1990). In such an organization a few competences are at the heart of the corporation and are leveraged across various business units. Prahalad and Hamel's metaphor for the corporation is not an investor's portfolio, but a large tree: 'the trunk and major limbs are core products, the smaller branches are business units, the leaves, flowers and fruit are end products; the root system that provides nourishment, sustenance and stability is the core competence'. Business unit branches can be cut off and new ones can grow on, but all spring from the same tree. It is the corporate centre's role to nurture this tree, building up the core competences and ensuring that the firm's competence carriers can easily be redeployed across business unit boundaries. The strategic logic behind leveraging these intangible resources is that high investments in competence development can then be spread over a number of different businesses. Moreover, by using these competences in different business settings they can be further refined, leading to a virtuous circle of rapid learning, profiting the entire corporation. In line with the arguments of the inside-out perspective (see Chapter 4), it is pointed out that in the long run inter-firm rivalries are often won by the corporation who has been able to upgrade its competences fastest – battles in particular markets are only skirmishes in this broader war. From this angle, building the corporation's core competences is strategic, while engaging other corporations in specific business areas is tactical. The corporate centre is therefore at the forefront of competitive strategy, instead of the business units that are literally divisions in the overall campaign (e.g. Kono, 1999; Stalk, Evans and Schulman, 1992).

As all business units should both tap into, and contribute to, the corporation's core competences, the business unit's autonomy is necessarily limited. Unavoidably, the responsiveness to the specific characteristics of each business does suffer from this emphasis on coordination. Yet, to advocates of the core competence model, the loss of business responsiveness is more than compensated for by the strategic benefits gained.

Besides competences as the core of the corporation, other synergies can also be at the heart of a multi-business firm. For instance, corporations can focus on aligning a variety of product offerings for a group of 'core customers'. Many professional service firms, such as PricewaterhouseCoopers and Capgemini, are involved in a broad range of businesses, with the intention of offering an integrated package of services to their selected market segments. Another type of core is where a multi-business firm is built around shared activities. Many of the large airlines, for example, have one 'core process', flying planes, but operate in the very different businesses of passenger travel and cargo transport. Yet another central synergy can be the leveraging of the firm's 'software'. For instance, Disney is such a 'core content' corporation, letting Cinderella work hard selling Disney videos, luring families to Disney theme parks, getting kids to buy Disney merchandise and enticing people to watch the Disney Channel. Whichever synergy is placed centre stage, to the proponents of the integrated organization perspective it should not be trivial, as such minor value-creation efforts do not provide the driving motivation to keep a corporation together. The 'glue' of the corporation must be strong enough to convince all involved that they are much better off as part of the whole than on their own.

The flip side of having a tightly knit group of businesses arranged around a common core is that growth through acquisition is generally much more difficult than in the 'plug-and-play' set-up of a portfolio organization. To make an acquisition fit into the corporate family and to establish all of the necessary links to let the new recruits profit from, and contribute to, the core synergies, can be very challenging. Taking the previous metaphor a step further, the corporate centre will find it quite difficult to graft oak roots and elm branches onto an existing olive tree. Consequently, acquisitions will be infrequent, as the firm will prefer internal growth.

EXHIBIT 5.3   THE INTEGRATED ORGANIZATION PERSPECTIVE

THE NEW EMPEROR IN MEDIA: FOCUSED BUT NOT SMALL

The way tycoons lead their media empires is starting to change drastically. Whereas the generation of Rupert Murdoch has mainly been after wielding influence and power, their successors take a less flamboyant approach. They trade in 'fruit and flower expenses', a well-known metaphor in some businesses for, in the words of News Corp CEO Robert Thomson, *relentless* cost-cutting. The shift in mindset can be observed in two main areas: increased focus on the core business and creating benefits from scale.

To effectively focus on their core business, media tycoons are shedding their non-core assets. Albeit lagging behind the same trend in other industries, this development is greatly appreciated by investors. In 2013 three major spin-offs occurred. The largest involved Rupert Murdoch's News Corporation splitting its profitable TV and film business from the declining newspaper business. This was a much contested decision, as it was the latter with which Murdoch had built his media empire. Equally painful decisions had to be made by Time Warner, spinning off

its magazine unit and Tribune divesting its newspaper business.

The main rationale behind this focus is the increasingly popular notion, held by external constituents, that TV networks, newspapers, film studios and the music business have very little benefit from sharing a parent. Some even argue that their success can be hindered by their proximity as a result of distracting management. As a result most media empires have decided to divest the shrinking publishing business, and either focus on other more promising markets or devote more attention to their main brand. Whatever the reason, the new way of thinking is very different from what we used to see in the media business.

In addition to shedding non-core assets, a second trend in the media business is to benefit from being very large – which happens to be something quite characteristic of the media industry. In 2009, it made up over two-thirds of the value of the S&P 500 index, which comes down to about $200 billion in assets. News Corp, Viacom, Disney and Time Warner deliver double the average S&P return of 6.1 per cent, with the exception of a number of years in which alternative content providers such as Netflix were feared to disrupt the pay TV business model. Combining

▶

the ever-growing scale with the newfound desire to focus activities have led to Time Warner having 80 per cent of its revenues coming from cable TV in 2013, as opposed to just 23 per cent in 2008. Viacom has made a comparable leap, leading to 90 per cent of their revenue coming from this source. This allowed both players to benefit greatly from increased efficiencies and strategic clarity.

Not everyone thinks pleasing the investors by becoming more integrated is the right way forward. Comcast bought NBCUniversal and Disney acquired Lucasfilm, which increasingly diversified their activities. Who made the right decision can only be speculated about, but the success of firms providing an alternative business model to deliver content, like Netflix and Hulu, might be a detrimental factor. For firms relying on cable TV for a predominant portion of their revenues, lack of diversification might become a liability when a real alternative to pay TV is offered.

Whatever the future might look like, investors are thrilled by the new mindset and subsequent actions. Jeff Bewkes, CEO of Time Warner, states:

Time Inc. will benefit from the flexibility and focus of being a stand-alone public company and will now be able to attract a more natural stockholder base.

In addition, he mentioned that being involved in less categories provided both him and the outside world with greater strategic clarity. Although possibly difficult to accept for those who have built their fortunes in the old fashioned media, the industry will start to focus on its profitable businesses, while leaving behind the less performing counterparts. Whether consolidation is a stroke of genius or a fatal mistake can only be told in hindsight. For now, soaring share prices, continuous growth and happy shareholders make sure the end of this trend is not soon in sight.

Co-author: Jasper de Vries

Sources: 'Time Warner to offload magazine unit in third major spin-off', *Bloomberg*, 7 March 2013; 'News Corp. spin-off forces publishing arm to prove growth', *Bloomberg*, 29 June 2013; 'Tribune to spin off newspaper business', *Bloomberg*, 10 July 2013; 'Breaking up is not so very hard to do', *The Economist*, 22 June 2013; 'Cutting the cord', *The Economist*, 16 July 2016.

MANAGING THE PARADOX OF RESPONSIVENESS AND SYNERGY

Consider the little mouse, how sagacious an animal it is which never entrusts its life to one hole only.

Plautus (254–184 BCE), Roman playwright

So, how should the corporate configuration be determined? Should corporate strategists limit themselves to achieving financial synergies, leaving SBU managers to 'mind their own business'? Or should corporate strategists strive to build a multi-business firm around a common core, intricately weaving all business units into a highly integrated whole? As before, the strategic management literature does not offer a clear-cut answer to the question of which corporate level strategies are the most successful (see Table 5.1).

TABLE 5.1   Portfolio organization versus integrated organization perspective

	Portfolio organization perspective	*Integrated organization perspective*
Emphasis on	Responsiveness over synergy	Synergy over responsiveness
Conception of corporation	Collection of business shareholdings	Common core with business applications
Corporate composition	Potentially unrelated (diverse)	Tightly related (focused)
Key success factor	Business unit responsiveness	Multi-business synergy
Focal type of synergy	Cash flow optimization and risk balance	Integrating resources, activities and positions
Corporate management style	Exerting financial control	Joint strategy development
Primary task corporate centre	Capital allocation and performance control	Setting direction and managing synergies
Position of business units	Highly autonomous (independent)	Highly integrated (interdependent)
Coordination between BUs	Low, incidental	High, structural
Growth through acquisitions	Simple to accommodate	Difficult to integrate

In the management field, a number of options have been put forward on how to manage the opposing demands of responsiveness and synergy. Taking the taxonomy in Chapter 1, the following options are at the strategist's disposal.

Navigating

The common means of managing the paradox of multi-business synergy and business responsiveness is to focus on one demand at a time. Strategists in large firms are often involved in contrary company-wide initiatives. One such initiative aims at strengthening the corporation's advantage of having more than one business unit. Managers at corporate, division and business unit levels are brought together in groupings to find potential synergies within the firm. The initiatives usually have an *ad hoc* character, with more or less defined end dates, and jazzy names such as 'one firm' and 'all for one'. The initiatives may include capturing and strengthening the firm's core competences, sharing value chain activities such as establishing a shared services centre and leadership training.

Capturing multi-business synergies usually goes at the expense of market responsiveness. As a result the next corporate initiative will focus on the opposite side of the paradox: improving market responsiveness. Marked with flashy labels such as 'client first' and 'agility', strategizing managers need to find avenues to enhance speed and client orientation in the firm's markets. Examples of such initiatives are visiting key clients to find product improvements, reducing overhead and, again, leadership training. After finishing this *ad hoc* project, the strategizing managers will navigate the firm capturing corporate synergies by 'tacking' to the next initiative.

Balancing

After having navigated the firm to accumulated multi-business synergies or enhanced business responsiveness, the strategists have to manage the new equilibrium. During the phase 'in-between corporate initiatives', managers have to continue balancing demands for multi-business synergies and business responsiveness. SBU managers strive to achieve more business unit autonomy by enhancing responsiveness and reducing 'corporate bureaucracy', while corporate managers seek more multi-business synergies while trying to reduce SBU managers' liberty to act in the interest of separate units only. As the paradox will never be resolved, strategizing managers are destined to permanently deal will with the tension.

Resolving

While dealing with the opposing demand for multi-business synergy and business responsiveness, strategizing managers notice several frictions within the firm. Most common is the friction between corporate strategists, such as the executive board members, and business unit leaders. A key factor in the game between corporate strategists, who are expected to capture synergies, and business unit managers with the main aim to strengthen the business' competitive position, is the firm's reward and compensation scheme. For example, when salaries, bonuses and promotion are related to one demand only, measured by the business unit's revenue and profit, many strategizing managers will not bother too much with corporate level initiatives. This issue is well understood and so rewards and compensation schemes often include stimuli to capture corporate synergies.

By managing the tension, opportunities to combine the best-of-both often come across. For example, many firms have discovered the advantages of client relationship software (CRM), which not only has the potential to strengthen the firm's client relationship (at the business unit level) but also to reveal growth options for other business units. Such opportunities often manifest during a company-wide initiative to capture multi-business synergy.

The tension between multi-business synergy and business responsiveness has resulted in arguably the most effective means to combining advantages of synergy and responsiveness: the franchise. While being regarded as a modern organizational form, the franchise is by no means new. The history goes back to the 1840s when German ale brewers granted rights to a selected number of taverns to market their beer. The first person recognized as a franchiser with actual franchise contracts was Albert Singer, an American. This 'business model innovator' started distributing his Singer sewing machines across a large geographic area. The franchise became especially popular in the 'restaurant' business, with Kentucky Fried Chicken in 1930, Dunkin Donuts in 1950, Burger King in 1954 and McDonald's in 1955. Currently there are franchise formulas in many industries, including hotels, manpower companies and retail.

The most well-known franchise, McDonald's, explicates the franchise formula's strength: being close to the market while capturing synergies. McDonald's provides their franchisees with, for example, a strong brand, purchasing power, training (a Hamburger University), restaurant lay-out designs and corporate-wide values (would 'Ich Bin Ein Hamburger' be an idea?). Franchisees are close to their local or niche customers with some room to adapt, and, while being agile to respond to client needs, they also capitalize on the corporate synergies.

CORPORATE LEVEL STRATEGY IN INTERNATIONAL PERSPECTIVE

Co-authors: Gep Eisenloeffel and Wester Wagenaar

The key to growth is the introduction of higher dimensions of consciousness into our awareness

Laozi (6th–5th century BCE), Chinese philosopher and founder of Taoism

Despite the high media profile of major corporations from different countries and despite researchers' fascination with large companies, little comparative research has been carried out. Yet, it does not seem unlikely that corporate strategy practices and preferences vary across national boundaries. Casual observation of the major corporations around the globe quickly shows that one cannot easily divide the world into portfolio-oriented and integration-oriented countries. In order to discuss to what extent international differences in corporate strategy perspectives exist, several factors will be put forward that might be of influence on how the paradox of responsiveness and synergy is managed in different countries.

On the national level

In the early 1980s, waves of hostile takeovers and overall poor performances in Western conglomerates led to a focus on integration. In most Western countries, most notably in the US, the belief that focused companies are better at increasing shareholder value and that diversification destroys value seems to prevail. Opportunities are generally met with a 'divisionalize or divest' approach; only if there is enough potential for shared value, is a division created. This explains why in recent history many conglomerates in the West, such as McGraw-Hill and General Electric, have been broken up into more focused, 'coherent' bodies (Ramachandran, Manikandan and Pant, 2013).

Germany is a different case, highlighting the importance of heritage. In European countries without colonies that could absorb a huge influx of capital, banks gained prominent positions by investing in promising new enterprises in their home country. Deutsche Bank for instance, founded in 1870 to facilitate foreign trade and investments, was involved in founding steel conglomerate Krupp and chemical giant Bayer. Today, it maintains over 25 per cent of the stocks in car manufacturing powerhouse Daimler-Benz. The result is strong ties between national financial institutions and industrial companies or *das Finanzkapital* (finance capital), as Rudolf Hilferding, economist and former German Finance Minister, described it in 1910.

In Japan, the *keiretsu* structure, conglomerations of businesses linked by cross-shareholdings, puts a similar emphasis on banks. The *keiretsu* are an inheritance from the pre-war family-controlled *zaibatsu*, institutions that proved vital in the development of Japan's modern economy (Morikawa, 1992). Unlike *zaibatsu*, the *keiretsu* is not centred around a family and either has a horizontal (or financial) or vertical (or industrial) structure (Miyashita and Russell, 1994). The horizontal *keiretsu* is set up around a Japanese bank, which supports its affiliated companies with numerous financial services. Japanese law allows banks to be both creditors and equity holders, unlike most Western economies.

These inter-corporate ownerships led the *keiretsu* banks to involve themselves in their partners' corporate governance and strategic decisions with greater regularity. Vertical *keiretsu* are linked through ownership of long-term equity and production activities to suppliers, manufacturers and distributors of one industry. A vertical organizational model is further created to benefit the parent company. This model is divided into different tiers where major suppliers make up the second tier and the third and fourth tiers consist of smaller manufacturers. As a result of the 1991 crash and the subsequent 'lost decades', the lines between the individual *keiretsu* blurred and many of them merged. Since then, *keiretsu* are not as integrated as they used to be, major companies are no longer easily bailed out by their banks and the major corporations generally adopted lower-risk profiles (Suetorsak, 2007). Nevertheless, *keiretsu* like Sumitomo Mitsui Financial Group, Mitsubishi UFJ Financial Group and Mizuho Group still make up an important part of the contemporary Japanese business landscape.

Although the *keiretsu* corporate model is unique to Japan, conglomerates with strong ties, hierarchy and loyalty between members of the inner circle or the family can be observed in many emerging markets or in societies where relational resources are highly valued. Latin America calls family conglomerates *grupos económicos*, in Turkey they are simply known as 'holding companies' and India refers to them as 'business houses'. They are also common in many (emerging) Asian economies, such as China, India, Indonesia, Malaysia and Thailand.

In Asia, South Korea's *chaebol* are among the most well-known institutions. These giant financial conglomerates are run by powerful families, traditionally supported by the South Korean government to expand domestically and internationally. Leading *chaebol* such as the Samsung Group, the LG group and the Hyundai Motor Group, are generally characterized by not sticking to one core business, but by operating in a wide range of businesses. Family conglomerates like these typically profit from various competitive advantages in their country of origin, like government assistance and protection, networks and influence in numerous industries, access to capital and exceptional market knowledge (Cavusgil *et al.*, 2014).

On the industry level

Although different preferences on corporate level strategy on the international differences are apparent, there are also some industries where one of the perspectives of the corporate level paradox is more prevalent. When laws allow it, the common investors in federations of businesses are often banks, as German and Japanese cases show. In the case of both *keiretsu* and *chaebol* banking, insurance, chemicals, manufacturing and steel are common businesses.

When it comes to vertical integration, the most well-known examples are the do-it-all giants of the oil industry, where control 'from the source to the gas station' is common practice. The international computer industry used to be dominated by vertically integrated firms, such as IBM, but then Apple came. In the 1970s, that company assembled a network of independent specialists that managed to manufacture machines far more efficiently. Industries are not black and white though, as Dell found a successful way to be a competitive vertically integrated company in the 1990s. Founder Michael Dell dubbed his creation 'virtual integration', assembling computers from other firm's parts, while having tight bound links between buyer and supplier.

To the strategist

Turning to the position of the strategist, the international dimension can prove quite the predicament. As shown, there are different approaches to the paradox over the world. Companies in the West still tend to swear by integration, but as the increasing competitiveness of conglomerates from Asia and Latin America highlights, the whole of multi-divisional companies does not have to be more valuable than the sum of their parts.

A strategist has not only to deal with the paradox of responsiveness and synergy for his or her own enterprise, he or she also has to understand how to deal with other corporations in the international playing field. For example, when foreign companies try to enter markets dominated by family conglomerates, the many advantages enjoyed by these corporations can be overwhelming (Cavusgil *et al.*, 2014). Strategists also have to decide whether to control as a parent or to cooperate without sharing a parent. If the essence of corporate strategy is about realizing synergies between businesses while retaining some autonomy, is it not possible for these businesses to coordinate with one another and achieve synergies without being a part of the same corporation? In other words, is it necessary to be owned and controlled by the same parent in order to leverage resources, integrate activities and align product offerings? Or could individual businesses band together and work as if they were one company – acting as a 'virtual corporation'?

6 NETWORK LEVEL STRATEGY

When bad men combine, the good must associate; else they will fall, one by one, an unpitied sacrifice in a contemptible struggle.
Edmund Burke (1729–1797), British political writer

INTRODUCTION

A business unit can have a strategy, while a group of business units can also have a strategy together – this joint course of action at the divisional or corporate level was discussed in the previous chapter. What has not been examined yet is whether a group of companies can also have a strategy together. Is it possible that companies do not develop their strategies in 'splendid isolation', but rather coordinate their strategies to operate as a team? And is it a good idea for firms to link up with others for a prolonged period of time to try to achieve shared objectives together?

Where two or more firms move beyond a mere transactional relationship and work jointly towards a common goal, they form an alliance, partnership or network. Their shared strategy is referred to as a network level strategy. In such a case, strategy is not only 'concerned with relating a firm to its environment', as was stated in Chapter 4, but also with relating a network to its broader environment.

The existence of networks does raise a range of questions, not the least of which is whether they make strategic sense or not. Is it beneficial to engage in long-term collaborative relationships with other firms or is it more advantageous for firms to 'keep their distance' and to interact with one another in a more market-like, transactional way? Is it viable to manage a web of partnership relations or is it preferable to keep it simple, by having the firm operate more or less independently? To address these questions is to raise the issue of inter-organizational relationships – what should be the nature of the relationship between a firm and other organizations in its surroundings? This issue will be the focus of further discussion in this chapter.

THE ISSUE OF INTER-ORGANIZATIONAL RELATIONSHIPS

No firm exists that is autarchic. All firms must necessarily interact with other organizations (and individuals) in their environment and therefore they have inter-organizational (or inter-firm) relationships. These relationships can evolve without any clear strategic

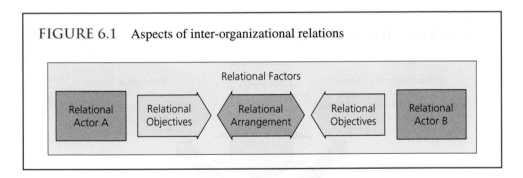

FIGURE 6.1   Aspects of inter-organizational relations

intent or tactical calculation, but most managers agree that actively determining the nature of their external relations is a significant part of what strategizing is about. Even avoiding relations with some external parties can be an important strategic choice.

To gain a better understanding of the interaction between firms, four aspects are of particular importance and will be reviewed here – the who, why, what and how of inter-organizational relationships (see Figure 6.1). The first aspect is the question of who – who are the potential counterparts with whom a firm can actually have a relationship? This is referred to as the topic of 'relational actors'. The second aspect is the question of why – why do the parties want to enter into a relationship with one another? This is referred to as the topic of 'relational objectives'. The third aspect is the question of what – what type of influences determine the nature of the relationship? This is referred to as the topic of 'relational factors'. The fourth aspect is the question of how – how can relationships be structured into a particular organizational form to let them function in the manner intended? This is referred to as the topic of 'relational arrangements'.

Relational actors

In Figure 6.2, an overview is given of the eight major groups of external parties with whom the firm can, or must, interact. A distinction has been made between industry and contextual actors. The industry actors are those individuals and organizations that perform value-adding activities or consume the outputs of these activities. The contextual actors are those parties whose behaviour, intentionally or unintentionally, sets the conditions under which the industry actors must operate. The four main categories of relationships between the firm and other industry parties are the following (e.g. Porter, 1980; Reve, 1990):

- Upstream vertical (supplier) relations. Every company has suppliers of some sort. In a narrow definition, these include the providers of raw materials, parts, machinery and business services. In a broader definition, the providers of all production factors (land, capital, labour, technology, information and entrepreneurship) can be seen as suppliers, if they are not part of the firm itself. All these suppliers can be either the actual producers of the input, or an intermediary (distributor or agent) trading in the product or service. Besides the suppliers with which the firm transacts directly (first-tier suppliers), the firm may also have relationships with suppliers further upstream in the industry. All these relationships are traditionally referred to as upstream vertical relations, because economists commonly draw the industry system as a column.

- Downstream vertical (buyer) relations. On the output side, the firm has relationships with its customers. These clients can be either the actual users of the product or service,

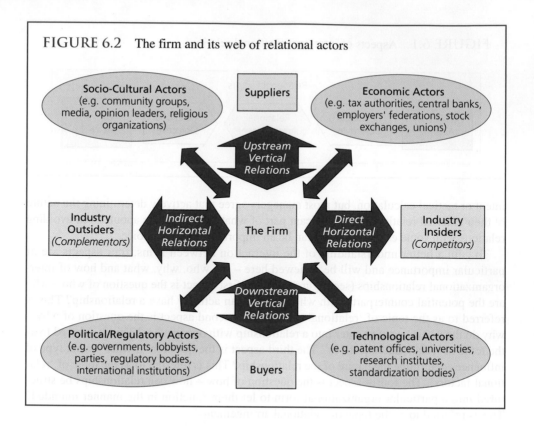

FIGURE 6.2 The firm and its web of relational actors

or intermediaries trading the output. Besides the buyers with which the firm transacts directly, it may also have relationships with parties further downstream in the industry column.

- Direct horizontal (industry insider) relations. This category includes the relations between the firm and other industry incumbents. Because these competitors produce similar goods or services, they are said to be at the same horizontal level in the industry column.

- Indirect horizontal (industry outsider) relations. Where a firm has a relationship with a company outside its industry, this is referred to as an indirect horizontal relation. Commonly, companies will have relationships with the producers of complementary goods and services (e.g. hardware manufacturers with software developers). Such a relationship can develop with the producer of a substitute good or service, either as an adversary or as an ally. A relation can also exist between a firm and a potential industry entrant, whereby the incumbent firm can assist or attempt to block the entry of the industry outsider. Furthermore, a firm can establish a relationship with a firm in another industry, with the intention of diversifying into that, or a third, industry. In reality, where industry boundaries are not clear, the distinction between direct and indirect horizontal relations is equally blurred.

Besides relationships with these industry actors, there can be many contacts with condition-setting parties in the broader environment. Employing the classic SEPTEMBER distinction, the following rough categories of contextual actors can be identified:

- Socio-cultural actors. Individuals or organizations that have a significant impact on societal values, norms, beliefs and behaviours may interact with the firm. These could include the media, community groups, charities, religious organizations and opinion leaders.

- Economic actors. There can also be organizations influencing the general economic state of affairs, with which the firm interacts. Among others, tax authorities, central banks, employers' federations, stock exchanges and unions may be of importance.

- Political/legal actors. The firm may also interact with organizations setting or influencing the regulations under which companies must operate. These could include governments, political parties, special interest groups, regulatory bodies and international institutions.

- Technological actors. There are also many organizations that influence the pace and direction of technological development and the creation of new knowledge. Among others, universities, research institutes, patent offices, government agencies and standardization bodies may be important to deal with.

As Figure 6.2 visualizes, companies can choose, but are often also forced, to interact with a large number of organizations and individuals in the environment. This configuration of external actors with which the organization interacts is referred to as the company's group of 'external stakeholders'.

Relational objectives

How organizations deal with one another is strongly influenced by what they hope to achieve (e.g. Dyer and Singh, 1998; Preece, 1995). Both parties may have clear, open and mutually beneficial objectives, but it is also possible that one or both actors have poorly defined intentions, hidden agendas and/or mutually exclusive goals. Moreover, it is not uncommon that various people within an organization have different, even conflicting, objectives and expectations with regard to an external relationship (e.g. Allison, 1969; Doz and Hamel, 1998).

Where two or more firms seek to work together with one another, they generally do so because they expect some value added – they assume more benefit from the interaction than if they had proceeded on their own. This expectation of value creation as a driver for cooperation was also discussed in Chapter 5, where two or more business units worked together to reap synergies. In fact, the same logic is at play between business units and between companies. In both cases, managers are oriented towards finding sources of added value in a potential relationship with another – either across business unit boundaries or across company boundaries. Hence, the same sources of synergy identified in the discussion on corporate level strategy are just as relevant when examining the objectives for inter-organizational cooperation (see Figure 6.3).

Relations oriented towards leveraging resources. The first area where companies can cooperate is at the level of their resource bases. By sharing resources with one another, companies can improve either the quantity or quality of the resources they have at their disposal. There are two general ways for firms to leverage resources to reap mutual benefit:

- Learning. When the objective is to exchange knowledge and skills, or to engage in the joint pursuit of new know-how, the relationship is said to be learning oriented. Firms can enter into new learning relationships with industry outsiders, but can also team up with industry incumbents, for instance to develop new technologies or standards (e.g. Hamel, Doz and Prahalad, 1989, Reading 6.1; Shapiro and Varian, 1998). However, firms can add a learning objective to an already existing relationship with a buyer or supplier as well.

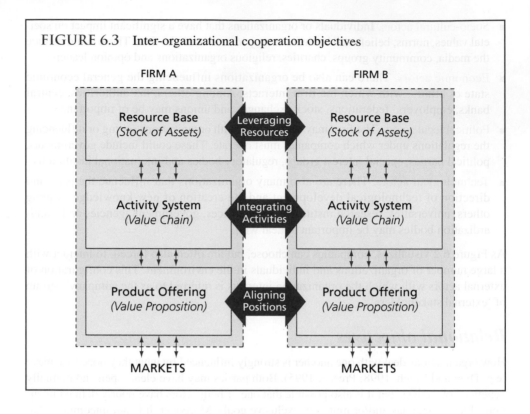

FIGURE 6.3 Inter-organizational cooperation objectives

- Lending. Where one firm owns specific resources that it cannot make full use of, or another firm can make better use of, it can be attractive for both to lend the resource to the other. Lending relationships happen frequently in the areas of technology, copyrights and trademarks, where licensing is commonplace. But physical resources can also be lent, usually in the form of lease contracts. In all cases the benefit to lenders can be financial or they receive other resources in return.

Relations oriented towards integrating activities. The second area where companies can cooperate is at the level of their activity systems. Few companies can span an entire industry column from top to bottom and excel at every type of activity. Usually, by integrating their value chains with other organizations, firms can be much more efficient and effective than if they were totally separated. There are two general ways for firms to integrate their activities with others:

- Linking. The most common type of relationship in business is the vertical link between a buyer and a seller. All relationships in which products or services are exchanged fall into this category. Most firms have many linking relationships, both upstream and downstream, because they want to focus on only a limited number of value-adding activities, but need a variety of inputs, as well as clients to purchase their finished goods.
- Lumping. Where firms bring together their similar activities to gain economies of scale, the relationship is said to be oriented towards lumping. Sharing operations (e.g. airline alliances), sales infrastructure (e.g. software cross-selling deals), logistics systems

(e.g. postal partnerships) or payment facilities (e.g. inter-bank settlement agreements) are examples of where firms can lump their activities together. Because the activities need to be more or less the same to be able to reap scale economies, lumping relationships are usually found between two or more industry insiders.

Relations oriented towards aligning positions.   The third area in which companies can cooperate is at the level of their market positions. Even where companies want to keep their value-adding activities separate, they can coordinate their moves in the environment with the intention of strengthening one another's position. Usually, this type of coalition-building is directed at improving the joint bargaining power of the cooperating parties. These position-enhancing relationships can be further subdivided into two categories:

- Leaning. Where two or more firms get together to improve their bargaining position vis-á-vis other industry actors, it is said that they lean on one another to stand stronger. Leaning can be directed at building up a more powerful negotiation position towards suppliers or to offer a more attractive package of products and services towards buyers. Getting together with other companies to form a consortium to launch a new industry standard can also bolster the position of all companies involved. At the same time, the cooperation can be directed at weakening the position of an alternative group of companies or even heightening the entry barriers for interested industry outsiders.
- Lobbying. Firms can also cooperate with one another with the objective of gaining a stronger position vis-á-vis contextual actors. Such lobbying relationships are often directed at strengthening the firms' voice towards political and regulatory actors, such as governments and regulatory agencies. However, firms can get together to put pressure on various other contextual actors, such as standard-setting bodies, universities, tax authorities and stock exchanges as well.

In practice, cooperative relationships between organizations can involve a number of these objectives simultaneously. Moreover, it is not uncommon for objectives to shift over time and for various participants in the relationship to have different objectives.

Relational factors

How inter-organizational relationships develop is strongly influenced by the objectives pursued by the parties involved. However, a number of other factors also have an impact on how relationships unfold. These relational factors can be grouped into four general categories (e.g. Gulati, 1998; Mitchell, Agle and Wood, 1997):

- Legitimacy. Relationships are highly impacted by what is deemed to be legitimate. Written and unwritten codes of conduct give direction to what is viewed as acceptable behaviour. Which topics are allowed on the agenda, who has a valid claim, how interaction should take place and how conflicts should be resolved, are often decided by what both parties accept as the 'rules of engagement'. There is said to be 'trust', where it is expected that the other organization or individual will adhere to these rules. However, organizations do not always agree on 'appropriate behaviour', while what is viewed as legitimate can shift over time as well. It can also be (seen as) advantageous to act opportunistically by not behaving according to the unwritten rules (e.g. Gambetta, 1988; Williamson, 1991).

- Urgency. Inter-organizational relations are also shaped by the factor of 'timing'. Relationships develop differently when one or both parties are under time pressure to achieve results, as opposed to a situation where both organizations can interact without experiencing a sense of urgency (e.g. James, 1985; Pfeffer and Salancik, 1978).

- Frequency. Inter-organizational relations also depend on the frequency of interaction and the expectation of future interactions. Where parties expect to engage in a one-off transaction, they usually behave differently than when they anticipate a more structural relationship extending over multiple interactions. Moreover, a relationship with a low rate of interaction tends to develop differently than one with a high regularity of interaction (e.g. Axelrod, 1984; Dixit and Nalebuff, 1991).

- Power. Last but not least, relations between organizations are strongly shaped by the power held by both parties. Power is the ability to influence others' behaviour and organizations can have many sources of power. Most importantly for inter-organizational relationships, a firm can derive power from having resources that the other organization requires. In relationships with a very high level of resource dependence, firms tend to behave differently towards each other than when they are interdependent or relatively independent of one another (e.g. Pfeffer and Salancik, 1978; Porter, 1980).

Especially the impact of power differences on inter-organizational relationships is given extensive attention in the strategic management literature. Many authors (e.g. Chandler, 1990; Kay, 1993; Pfeffer and Salancik, 1978; Porter, 1980; Schelling, 1960) stress that for understanding the interaction between firms it is of the utmost importance to gain insight into their relative power positions. One way of measuring relative power in a relationship is portrayed in Figure 6.4, where a distinction is made between the closeness of the relationship (loose vs tight) and the distribution of power between the two parties involved (balanced vs unbalanced). This leads to a categorization of four specific types of inter-firm relationships from the perspective of relative power position. These four categories (adapted from Ruigrok and Van Tulder, 1995) are:

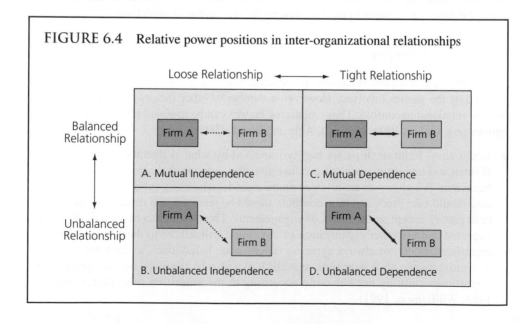

FIGURE 6.4   Relative power positions in inter-organizational relationships

A Mutual independence. Organizations are independent in a relationship if they have full freedom to act according to their own objectives. Independence in an inter-organizational relationship means that organizations will only interact on their own terms and that they have the ability to break off the relationship without any penalty. In a situation of mutual independence, neither organization has significant influence over the other.

B Unbalanced independence. When two organizations work together in a loose relationship, one side (Firm A) can have more power than the other (Firm B). In such a case, it is said that Firm A is more independent than Firm B – Firm A's power gives it more freedom to act, while Firm B can be influenced by the powerful Firm A. This situation is called unbalanced independence, as both sides are independent, but one more so than the other.

C Mutual dependence. Two organizations can have a tight relationship, in which they are mutually dependent, while having an equal amount of sway over their counterpart. This type of situation, where there is a substantial, yet balanced, relationship between two or more parties, is also called interdependence.

D Unbalanced dependence. Where a tight relationship is characterized by asymmetrical dependence, one party will be able to dominate the other. In this situation of unbalanced dependence, the organization with the lower level of dependence will have more freedom to manoeuvre and impose its conditions than its counterpart.

The first category, mutual independence, is what is typically expected of a *market* relationship, although it is not strange to also witness market relationships that fit more in the second category, unbalanced independence. At the other extreme, unbalanced dependence is very close to the situation that would occur if the dominant firm acquired its counterpart. Whether acquired or fully dependent, the dominant firm controls its behaviour. For this reason it is said that in cases of unbalanced dependence the inter-organizational relationship comes close to resembling the *hierarchy-type* relationship found within a firm. Interdependence seems to be somewhere between market and hierarchy-type relationships. What this means for the structuring of these relationships will be examined below.

Relational arrangements

In the classic dichotomy, the firm and its environment are presented as rather distinct entities. Within a firm coordination is achieved by means of direct control, leading transaction cost economists to refer to this organizational form as a 'hierarchy' (Williamson, 1975, 1985). In a hierarchy a central authority governs internal relationships and has the formal power to coordinate strategy and solve inter-departmental disputes. In the environment, relationships between firms are non-hierarchical, as they interact with one another without any explicit coordination or dispute settlement mechanism. This organizational form is referred to as a 'market'.

In Chapter 5, it was argued that there are all types of activity that companies should not want to internalize and run themselves, but should leave up to the marketplace. In many situations, it is much more efficient to buy inputs in the market than to make them yourself – where activities are performed by autonomous parties and outputs are sold in the marketplace, costs will often be lowest. As summarized by Ouchi (1980, p. 130), 'in a market relationship, the transaction takes place between the two parties and is mediated by a price mechanism in which the existence of a competitive market reassures both parties that the terms of exchange are equitable'.

Integration of activities into the firm is only necessary where 'markets do not function properly' – where doing it yourself is cheaper or better. The firm must internalize activities, despite the disadvantages of hierarchy, where the 'invisible hand' of the market cannot be trusted to be equitable and effective. Control over activities by means of formal authority – the 'visible hand' – is needed under these conditions. This is particularly true of all of the synergy advantages mentioned in Chapter 5 that the corporation would not be able to reap if the various business activities were not brought together under one 'corporate roof'.

In reality, however, there are many organizational forms between markets and hierarchies (e.g. Hakansson and Johanson, 1993; Powell, 1990; Thorelli, 1986). These are the networks, partnerships or alliances introduced at the start of this chapter. In networks, strategies are coordinated and disputes resolved, not through formal top-down power, but by mutual adaptation. To extend the above metaphor, networks rely neither on the visible nor invisible hand to guide relationships, but rather employ the 'continuous handshake' (Gerlach, 1992).

The organizations involved in networks can employ different sorts of collaborative arrangement to structure their ties with one another. In Figure 6.5, an overview of a number of common types of collaborative arrangement is presented. Two major distinctions are made in this overview. First, between bilateral arrangements, which only involve two parties, and multilateral arrangements, which involve three or more. Commonly, only the multilateral arrangements are referred to as networks, although here the term is employed to cover all groupings of two or more cooperating firms. The second distinction is between non-contractual, contractual and equity-based arrangements. Non–contractual arrangements are cooperative agreements that are not binding by law, while contractual arrangements do have a clear legal enforceability. Neither, however, involve taking a financial stake in each other or in a new joint venture, while the equity-based arrangements do.

FIGURE 6.5   Relative power positions in inter-organizational relationships

	Non-Contractual Arrangements	Contractual Arrangements	Equity-based Arrangements
Multilateral Arrangements	• Lobbying coalition (e.g. European Roundtable of Industrialists) • Joint standard setting (e.g. Linux coalition) • Learning communities (e.g. Strategic Management Society)	• Research consortium (e.g. Symbian in PDAs) • International marketing alliance (e.g. Star Alliance in airlines) • Export partnership (e.g. Netherlands Export Combination)	• Shared payment system (e.g. Visa) • Construction consortium (e.g. Eurotunnel) • Joint reservation system (e.g. Galileo)
Bilateral Arrangements	• Cross-selling deal (e.g. between pharmaceutical firms) • R&D staff exchange (e.g. between IT firms) • Market information sharing agreement (e.g. between hardware and software makers)	• Licensing agreement (e.g. Disney and Coca-Cola) • Co-development contract (e.g. Disney and Pixar in movies) • Co-branding alliance (e.g. Coca-Cola and McDonald's)	• New product joint venture (e.g. Sony and Ericsson in cellphones) • Cross-border joint venture (e.g. Daimler-Benz and Beijing Automotive) • Local joint venture (e.g. CNN Turk in Turkey)

The intent of these collaborative arrangements is to profit from some of the advantages of vertical and horizontal integration, without incurring their costs. Networks are actually hybrid organizational forms that attempt to combine the benefits of hierarchy with the benefits of the market. The main benefits of hierarchy are those associated with the structural coordination of activities. In non-market relational arrangements, all parties collaborate on a more long-term basis with the intent of realizing a common goal. They will organize procedures, routines and control systems to ensure effective and efficient functioning of their joint activities and a smooth transition at their organizational interfaces. The benefits of the market that these collaborative arrangements retain are flexibility and motivation. By not being entirely locked into a fixed hierarchy, individual firms can flexibly have multiple relationships of varying length and intensity, and can change these relationships more easily where circumstances require adaptation. The market also provides the motivation to be efficient and to optimize the pursuit of the organization's self-interest. This entrepreneurial incentive can be a strong spur for risk-taking, innovation and change.

A significant advantage of collaborative arrangements is that such relationships facilitate the process of 'co-specialization'. Much of humanity's economic progress is based on the principle of specialization by means of a division of labour. As people and firms focus more closely on performing a limited set of value-adding activities, they become more effective and efficient in their work. This division of labour assumes, however, that the value-adding activities that are outsourced by one become the specialization of another, hence co-specialization. Yet, many activities cannot be outsourced to outsiders on the basis of normal market relations, either due to the risk of dependence or because of the need for the structural coordination of activities. Under these conditions, collaborative arrangements can act as a synthesis of hierarchy and market relations, thus catalysing the process of specialization (e.g. Axelsson and Easton, 1992; Best, 1990).

Such co-specialization can progress to such an extent that clusters of firms work together in more or less permanent networks. Such symbiotic groups of collaborating firms can actually function as 'virtual corporations' (e.g. Chesbrough and Teece, 1996; Quinn, 1992). In such networks, the relationships between the participating firms are often very tight and durable, based on a high level of trust and perceived mutual interest. While each organization retains its individual identity, the boundaries between them become fuzzy, blurring the clear distinction between 'the organization' and 'its environment'. When a high level of trust and reciprocity has been achieved, relations can move far beyond simple contractual obligations. The collaborative relations can become more open ended, with objectives, responsibilities, authority and results not fully determined in advance in a written contract, but evolving over time, given all parties' sincere willingness to 'work on their relationship' (e.g. Jarillo, 1988; Kanter, 1994).

While the intention of collaborative arrangements may be to blend the advantages of hierarchy with the qualities of the market, it is also possible that the weaknesses of both are actually combined. The main weakness of hierarchy is bureaucracy – creating red tape, unnecessary coordination activities and dulling the incentive to perform. In reality, collaborative arrangements might be mechanisms for structuring static relationships and dampening entrepreneurial behaviour. A further danger is that the mutual dependence might become skewed, shifting the balance of power to one of the partners. Under such conditions, one or more organizations can become dependent on a dominant party, without much influence (voice) or the possibility to break off the relationship (exit). Such unbalanced dependency relationships (see Figure 6.4) might be a great benefit for the stronger party, but can easily lead to the predominance of its interests over the interests of the weaker partners (e.g. Oliver and Wilkinson, 1988; Ruigrok and Van Tulder, 1995).

Simultaneously, such partnerships are vulnerable to the main disadvantage of the market, namely opportunism. Companies run the risk of opportunism, which is (according to Williamson, 1985, p. 47):

> *Self-interest seeking with guile. This includes but is scarcely limited to more blatant forms, such as lying, stealing and cheating ... More generally, opportunism refers to the incomplete or distorted disclosure of information, especially to calculated efforts to mislead, distort, disguise, obfuscate, or otherwise confuse.*

Such behaviour can be limited by clearly defining objectives, responsibilities, authority and expected results ahead of time, preferably in an explicit contract. Even then collaborative arrangements expose companies to the risk of deception, the abuse of trust and the exploitation of dependence, making their use by no means undisputed.

THE PARADOX OF COMPETITION AND COOPERATION

We have no eternal allies and we have no perpetual enemies. Our interests are eternal and perpetual, and those interests it is our duty to follow.

Lord Palmerston (Henry John Temple) (1784–1865), British prime minister

When former CEO of KLM Royal Dutch Airlines, Pieter Bouw, teamed up with Northwest Airlines in 1989, he was thrilled to have the first major transatlantic strategic alliance in the industry, involving joint flights, marketing and sales activities, catering, ground handling, maintenance and purchasing. Northwest was the fourth largest American carrier at that time, but was in 'Chapter 11', balancing on the verge of bankruptcy and in dire need of cash. To help their new ally, KLM gave a $400 million capital injection, in return for 20 per cent of the shares and the option to increase this to a majority stake within a few years. KLM and Northwest were on their way to becoming a virtual transatlantic company – a marriage 'made in heaven'.

Commercially the deal was a success, but relationally the alliance was a Shakespearean drama. KLM gave up its hopes of an alliance with Swissair, SAS and Delta to remain loyal to Northwest, but as soon as Northwest emerged from Chapter 11, it blocked KLM's efforts to increase its shareholding. In the resulting two-year legal shooting match between 1995 and 1997, relations deteriorated sharply and the goose that laid the golden eggs was almost certain to be killed in the cross fire. Disappointed and dismayed, Bouw decided to give in, selling Northwest back its shares in return for a prolongation of the alliance, after which he immediately resigned. His successor, Leo van Wijk, has managed the alliance since then and it is still 'up in the air', in both senses of the expression. His most important conclusion has been that a collaborative alliance is not only about working together towards a common interest, but equally about being assertive with regard to one's own interests. Alliances are not only *cooperative*, but also have *competitive* aspects.

What this example of KLM and Northwest illustrates is that firms constantly struggle with the tension created by the need to work together with others, while simultaneously needing to pursue their own interests. Firms cannot isolate themselves from their environments, but must actively engage in relationships with suppliers and buyers, while selectively teaming up with other firms inside and outside their industry to attain mutual benefit. But while they are collaborating to create joint value, firms are also each other's rivals when it comes to dividing the benefits. These opposite demands placed on organizations are widely referred to as the pressures for competition and cooperation (e.g. Brandenburger and Nalebuff, 1996; Lado, Boyd and Hanlon, 1997). In the following sections both pressures will be examined in more detail.

The demand for inter-organizational competition

Competition can be defined as the act of working against others, where two or more organizations' goals are mutually exclusive. In other words, competition is the rivalry behaviour exhibited by organizations or individuals where one's win is the other's loss.

Organizations need to be competitive in their relationships with others. As the interests or objectives of different organizations are often mutually exclusive, each organization needs to be determined and assertive in pursuing its own agenda. Each organization needs to be willing to confront others to secure its own interests. Without the will to engage in competitive interaction, the organization will be at the mercy of more aggressive counterparts, e.g. suppliers will charge excessively for products, buyers will express stiff demands for low prices, governments will require special efforts without compensation, and rival firms will poach from among existing customers. Taking a competitive posture towards these external parties means that the organization is determined to assert its own interests and fight where necessary.

The resulting competitive relations can vary between open antagonism and conflict on the one hand, and more subtle forms of friction, tension and strain on the other. Blatant competitive behaviour is often exhibited towards organizations whose objectives are fully in conflict – most clearly other producers of the same goods, attempting to serve the same markets (aptly referred to as 'the competition'). Highly competitive behaviour can also be witnessed where a supplier and a buyer confront each other for dominance in the industry value chain (e.g. Porter, 1980; Van Tulder and Junne, 1988). A more restrained competitive stance can be observed where organization's objectives are less at odds, but assertiveness is still important to protect the organization's interests. Negotiation and bargaining will commonly be employed under these circumstances.

To be competitive an organization must have the power to overcome its rivals and it must have the ability and will to use its power. Many factors shape the power of an organization, but its relative level of resource dependence is one of the most important determining elements. The more independent the organization, and the more others are dependent on it, the more power the organization will wield. In competitive relationships, manoeuvring the other party into a relatively dependent position is a common approach. In general, calculation, bargaining, manoeuvring, building coalitions and outright conflict are all characteristic of the competitive interaction between organizations.

The demand for inter-organizational cooperation

Cooperation can be defined as the act of working together with others, where two or more organizations' goals are mutually beneficial. In other words, cooperation is the collaborative behaviour exhibited by organizations or individuals where both sides need each other to succeed.

Organizations need to be cooperative in their relationships with others. The interests or objectives of different organizations are often complementary and working together can be mutually beneficial. Therefore, organizations must be willing to behave as partners, striving towards their common good. Without the will to engage in cooperative interaction, the organization will miss the opportunity to reap the advantages of joint efforts, e.g. developing new products together with suppliers, creating a better service offering together with buyers, improving the knowledge infrastructure together with government and setting new technical standards together with other firms in the industry. Taking a cooperative posture towards these external parties means that the organization is determined to leverage its abilities through teamwork.

The resulting cooperative relations can vary between occasional alliances on the one hand, to tight-knit, virtual integration on the other. Strongly cooperative behaviour can be witnessed where the long-term interests of all parties are highly intertwined. This type of symbiotic relationship can be found between the producers of complementary goods and services, where success by one organization will positively impact its partners – aptly referred to as the 'network effect' (Arthur, 1994; Shapiro and Varian, 1998). Highly cooperative behaviour can also be observed where suppliers and buyers face a joint challenge (such as government regulation, an innovative technology or a new market entrant) that can only be tackled by significant mutual commitment to a shared objective.

More restrained cooperative behaviour is common where there is potential for a 'positive sum game', but some parties seek to optimize their own returns to the detriment of others. Under such circumstances, exhibiting cooperative behaviour does not mean being naive or weak, but creating conditions under which the long-term shared interests prevail over the short-term temptation by some to cheat their partners. An important ingredient for overcoming the lure of opportunism is to build long-term commitment to one another, not only in words and mentality, but also practically, through a high level of interdependence. Where organizations are closely linked to one another, the pay-off for cooperative behaviour is usually much more enticing than the possibility to profit from the dependence of one's partner. But to be willing to commit to such a high level of interdependence, people on both sides of a relationship need to trust each other's intentions and actions, while there must be coordination and conflict-resolution mechanisms in place to solve evolving issues (e.g. Dyer, Kale and Singh, 2001; Simonin, 1997).

EXHIBIT 6.1   SHORT CASE

ETIHAD: COOPERATING AGAINST ALLIANCES

If a passenger makes an intercontinental flight, chances are high she will end up transferring somewhere in the Gulf area. Instead of international airlines that rely mostly on travellers going to and from their home countries, the Gulf's 'superconnectors' attract passengers from all over the world to change planes at the carriers' hub airports. Thanks to geography and pro-aviation government policies, three giants in the commercial airline industry manage to pull this off. Two of these, Emirates and Qatar Airways, follow similar strategies. With home bases in big cities, Dubai and Doha respectively, the streamlined airlines pursue organic growth by slowly expanding their fleet and destinations. Etihad, the youngest of the Gulf trio, takes the road less travelled.

Set up in 2003 by royal decree, Etihad Airways is the second flag carrier of the United Arab Emirates and is the carrier of Abu Dhabi. But what is a flagship without a decent fleet? An $8 billion order for five Boeing 777s and 24 Airbus aircraft in 2004 was follow by the largest aircraft order in the history of commercial aviation in 2008. A $43 billion order included the effective purchase of 100 aeroplanes. Etihad does not call itself the fastest-growing airline in commercial aviation history for nothing. Today, Abu Dhabi's carrier serves 117 destinations with over 120 aeroplanes, resulting in revenues close to $10 billion.

James Hogan, a bullish Australian who earned his spurs at British Midland International and Gulf Air, can be held responsible for Etihad's reach for the sky. He was personally plucked by Abu Dhabi's government in 2006 to oversee the expansion of Etihad as its CEO. Etihad started decades after its major competitors, so how can it catch up? When airlines from one region are arguably heavily funded by their oil-rich governments and manage to scoop up global traffic, this does not create friends; not among governments abroad or among competing airlines. Europe does not have Open Skies treaties with the United Arab Emirates and there are no plans to sign any. When Etihad tried to join the major global alliances – Star Alliance, Sky Team and OneWorld – it discovered there were no membership options for the airline. Nevertheless, Hogan decided to pursue a partnership strategy – albeit an aggressive one.

Hogan pursues investments in minority stakes in struggling regional carriers operating in key strategic markets. Restrictions on foreign ownership of airlines prevent Etihad from gaining total control, but these partners do serve to create closer bonds and gain benefits. Etihad currently has shares in Virgin Australia, Air Berlin, India's Jet Airways, Air Serbia, Alitalia, Aer Lingus and a stake in a Swiss regional carrier it renamed Etihad Regional. With 'skin in the game', as Etihad calls it, these investments open doors to new network alignment and timetable coordination. They also help Etihad to get more passengers and cargo through its Abu Dhabi hub and to feed them into its long-haul routes. As regulations limit the number of destinations – and flights – per country the Gulf carrier is allowed to serve, these partners can fly from secondary cities and connect them to Abu Dhabi instead. The poorly connected cities served by these partners, such as Leipzig and Florence, can now bring passengers to Etihad's hub, creating a web of Etihad services as a result.

This strategy is not without risks, however. Etihad is not actually able to grab the joystick and control its partners; it is limited to a hands-off approach. As an investor, cash injections are the only incentive to make Etihad's partners change their course. For example, in return for an investment from Etihad, Alitalia agreed to cut 20 per cent of its workforce in 2014. This strategy has an ill-fated precedent. The attempts of Swissair to carry out similar techniques – even though the airline had more control over its stable – resulted in its bankruptcy in 2002.

In addition to his unorthodox endeavours, Hogan also pursues a more conventional strategy concerning industry cooperation, visible in the way he deals with the heavy competition of the big airline alliances. Hogan's rhetoric is that if there is no good access to markets and if it is impossible to join overarching alliances, then you strike partnerships with its members. Etihad managed to establish codeshare partners with 49 airlines, covering over 400 destinations. This allows passengers seats on the planes of other airlines. Code-sharing increases the number of occupied seats and it allows Etihad to offer connecting flights, even to places it does not officially fly to itself. Etihad's own code-sharing collection is small fry compared to the global alliances, but Etihad argues it does provide the airline with a viable alternative to the big alliance trio.

What goes up, can come down and while Etihad is still flying high, there are a number of dangers that can take down the airline. Running an airline as efficient as Etihad is difficult, but factoring in the strategic interests of its partners is a different case altogether. This goes for its own collection of collaborating code-sharing partners, but it is even more pressuring for the partner airlines of which it holds shares. How should Etihad proceed? Throwing money around to change their course does not seem like a viable long-term option, especially if Etihad continues to receive government subsidies. The ensuing backlash of airline competitors and foreign governments might bring about irreversible consequences for Etihad's endeavours. If it does not receive subsidies, the airline can at least publish full accounts like Emirates does. This might open doors to future cooperation with current

competitors. Etihad also needs to realize how it can continue to thrive among fellow regional giants Qatar and Emirates and their respective hub cities. In addition, the rise of Turkish Airlines brings new competition to the skies and the Gulf hubs. With which parties Hogan competes and with which he cooperates, are tricky questions. Should Etihad continue going at it alone, gaining precious market access via stakes in regional airlines? Or should it avoid the territory of the American and European markets dominated and saturated by the global alliances and seek collaboration with others, such as the other Gulf airlines or regional airlines in upcoming economies? Whatever decision Hogan ultimately makes, it is clear that if he can find the right mix of cooperation and competition, he can continue to prove that for Etihad the sky is the limit.

Co-author: Wester Wagenaar

Sources: www.etihad.com; *Economist*, 3 June 2010, 28 June 2014 and 25 April 2015; *Forbes*, 24 August 2015 and 28 June 2016.

PERSPECTIVES ON NETWORK LEVEL STRATEGY

Concordia discors (discordant harmony).

Horace (65–8 BCE), Roman poet

Firms need to be able to engage in competition and cooperation simultaneously, even though these demands are each other's opposites. Firms need to exhibit a strongly cooperative posture to reap the benefits of collaboration, and they need to take a strongly competitive stance to ensure that others do not hamper their interests. Some theorists conclude that what is required is 'co-opetition' (Brandenburger and Nalebuff, 1996). While a catchy word, managers are still left with the difficult question of how to deal with these conflicting demands. To meet the pressure for cooperation, firms must actually become part of a broader 'team', spinning a web of close collaborative relationships. But to meet the pressure for competition, firms must not become too entangled in restrictive relationships, but rather remain free to manoeuvre, bargain and attack, with the intention of securing their own interests. In other words, firms must be *embedded* and *independent* at the same time – embedded in a network of cooperative interactions, while independent enough to wield their power to their own advantage.

The question dividing strategizing managers is whether firms should be more embedded or more independent. Should firms immerse themselves in broader networks to create strong groups, or should they stand on their own? Should firms willingly engage in long-term interdependence relationships or should they strive to remain as independent as possible? Should firms develop network level strategies at all, or should the whole concept of multi-firm strategy-making be directed to the garbage heap?

While strategy writers generally agree about the need to manage the paradox of competition and cooperation, they come to widely differing prescriptions on how to do so. Views within the field of strategic management are strongly at odds with regard to the best approach to inter-organizational relations. As before, here the two diametrically opposed positions will be identified and discussed to show the scope of differing ideas. On one side of the spectrum, there are strategists who believe that it is best for companies to be primarily competitive in their relationships to all outside forces. They argue that firms should remain independent and interact with other companies under market conditions as much as possible. As these strategists emphasize the discrete boundaries separating the firm from its 'competitive environment', this point of view is called the 'discrete organization perspective'. On the other side of the spectrum, there are strategists who believe that companies should strive to build up more long-term cooperative relationships with key organizations in their environment. They argue that firms can reap significant benefits by surrendering a part of their independence and developing close collaborative arrangements with a group of other organizations. This point of view will be referred to as the 'embedded organization perspective'.

The discrete organization perspective

Managers taking the discrete organization perspective view companies as independent entities competing with other organizations in a hostile market environment. In line with neoclassical economics, this perspective commonly emphasizes that individuals, and the organizations they form, are fundamentally motivated by aggressive self-interest and therefore that competition is the natural state of affairs. Suppliers will try to enhance their bargaining power vis-á-vis buyers with the aim of getting a better price, while conversely, buyers will attempt to improve their negotiation position to attain better quality at lower cost. Competing firms will endeavour to gain the upper hand against their rivals if the opportunity arises, while new market entrants and manufacturers of substitute products will consistently strive to displace incumbent firms (e.g. Porter, 1980, 1985).

In such a hostile environment, it is a strategic necessity for companies to strengthen their competitive position in relation to the external forces. The best strategy for each organization is to obtain the market power required to get good price/quality deals, ward off competitive threats, limit government demands and even determine the development of the industry. Effective power requires independence and therefore heavy reliance on specific suppliers, buyers, financiers or public organizations should be avoided.

The label 'discrete organization' given to this perspective refers to the fact that each organization is seen as being detached from its environment, with sharp boundaries demarcating where the outside world begins. The competitive situation is believed to be *atomistic*, that is, each self-interested firm strives to satisfy its own objectives, leading to rivalry and conflict with other organizations. Vertical interactions between firms in the industry column tend to be transactional, with an emphasis on getting the best possible deal. It is generally assumed that under such market conditions the interaction will be of a zero-sum nature, that is, a fight for who gets how much of the pie. The firm with the strongest bargaining power will usually be able to appropriate a larger portion of the 'economic rent' than will the less potent party. Therefore, advocates of the discrete organization perspective emphasize that the key to competitive success is the ability to build a powerful position and to wield this power in a calculated and efficient manner. This might sound Machiavellian to the faint hearted, but it is the reality of the marketplace that is denied at one's own peril.

Essential for organizational power is the avoidance of resource dependence. Where a firm is forced to lean on a handful of suppliers or buyers, this can place the organization in a precariously exposed position. To managers taking a discrete organization perspective, such dependence on a few external parties is extremely risky, as the other firm will be tempted to exploit their position of relative power to their own advantage. Wise firms will therefore not let themselves become overly dependent on any external organization, certainly not for any essential resources. This includes keeping the option open to exit from the relationship at will – with low barriers to exit, the negotiating position of the firm is significantly stronger. Therefore the firm must never become so entangled with outsiders that it cannot rid itself of them at the drop of a hat. The firm must be careful that in a web of relationships, it is the spider, not the fly (e.g. Pfeffer and Salancik, 1978; Ruigrok and Van Tulder, 1995).

Keeping other organizations at arm's length also facilitates clear and business-like interactions. Where goods and services are bought or sold, distinct organizational boundaries help to distinguish tasks, responsibilities, authority and accountability. But as other firms will always seek to do as little as possible for the highest possible price, having clear contracts and a believable threat to enforce them will serve as a method to ensure discipline. Arm's-length relations are equally useful in avoiding the danger of vital information leaking to the party with whom the firm must (re)negotiate.

In their relationships with other firms in the industry, it becomes even clearer that companies' interests are mutually exclusive. More market share for one company must necessarily come at the expense of another. Coalitions are occasionally formed to create power blocks if individual companies are not strong enough to compete on their own. Such tactical alliances bring together weaker firms, not capable of doing things independently. But 'competitive collaboration' is usually short-lived – either the alliance is unsuccessful and collapses, or it is successful against the common enemy, after which the alliance partners become each other's most important rivals.

Proponents of the discrete organization perspective argue that collaborative arrangements are always second best to doing things independently. Under certain conditions, weakness might force a firm to choose an alliance, but it is always a tactical necessity, never a strategic preference. Collaborative arrangements are inherently risky, fraught with the hazard of opportunism. Due to the ultimately competitive nature of relationships, allies will be tempted to serve their own interests to the detriment of the others, by manoeuvring, manipulating or cheating. The collaboration might even be a useful ploy, to cloak the company's aggressive intentions and moves. Collaboration, it is therefore concluded, is merely 'competition in a different form' (Hamel, Doz and Prahalad, 1989, Reading 6.1). Hence, where collaboration between firms really offers long-term advantages, a merger or acquisition is preferable to the uncertainty of an alliance.

Where collaboration is not the tool of the weak, it is often a conspiracy of the strong to inhibit competition. If two or more formidable companies collaborate, chances are that the alliance is actually ganging up on a third party – for instance on buyers. In such cases, the term 'collaboration' is just a euphemism for collusion and not in the interest of the economy at large.

Worse yet, collaboration is usually also bad for a company's long-term health. A highly competitive environment is beneficial for a firm, because it provides the necessary stimulus for companies to continually improve and innovate. Strong adversaries push companies towards competitive fitness. A more benevolent environment, cushioned by competition-inhibiting collaboration, might actually make a firm more content and less eager to implement tough changes. In the long run, this will make firms vulnerable to more aggressive companies, battle hardened by years of rivalry in more competitive environments.

In conclusion, the basic assumption of the discrete organization perspective is that companies should not develop network level strategies, but should strive for 'strategic self-sufficiency'. Collaborative arrangements are a tactical tool, to be selectively employed. The sentiment of this perspective has been clearly summarized by Porter (1990, p. 224): 'alliances are rarely a solution … no firm can depend on another independent firm for skills and assets that are central to its competitive advantage … Alliances tend to ensure mediocrity, not create world leadership'.

EXHIBIT 6.2   THE DISCRETE ORGANIZATION PERSPECTIVE

DANGOTE: WAGING WARS ON THE AFRICAN CONTINENT

Aliko Dangote, born, raised and doing business in Nigeria, was named Africa's richest man for the last six years in a row. His empire was founded over three decades ago when Mr Dangote started trading in commodities, an enterprise he expanded in the early 2000s to a fully fledged production business. His take on producing local, value-added products that meet the needs of the African population, is a rather warlike one. Although the subject matter, ranging from cement to pasta, might seem mundane, Mr Dangote's approach to growing his business certainly is not.

Dealing with competitors and governments can be a tiresome business. Whereas most businessmen and women try diplomacy to deal with such issues, Mr Dangote started a full-fledged war campaign in order to gain market dominance. Doing so didn't leave the ability to make good deals up to chance, good arguments or charisma. Instead, he forced the market to bend to his wishes, making sure that failure was no longer an option. His weapon of choice was to besiege his competitors by undercutting their prices on major

commodities. This forced his adversaries to either give up or sell their goods with negative margins. With a net worth of $75 billion, the Dangote group time and again turned out to have the longest breath, thus taking out many of its rivals and creating a near monopoly in most commodities in Nigeria.

Besides siege tactics, Mr Dangote has developed the ability to make the right allies, but not letting them get too close. Being in good favour with Olugegun Obasanjo by generously funding his presidential campaign would certainly have helped him to take part in the rapid privatization of failing state businesses. Buying these failing businesses cheaply and making them profitable was one of the major early sources of his financial wealth. Another example has to do with the recent collaboration with GE to improve Nigeria's infrastructure. Western companies are anxious to expand into Africa's untapped markets, a dream that Mr Dangote certainly can make reality by using his power, connections and experience in navigating the Nigerian landscape. While GE will make a pretty penny from this building contract, the long-term benefits for Mr Dangote's commodity business and the deal's success depending on his ability to

▶

navigate Nigeria's upper echelons surely makes clear who calls the shots.

Mr Dangote's current-day empire maintains clear similarities with its early beginnings. As a commodity trader, he was dependent on no one and was able to act as he thought best. Although he certainly made friends as his business expanded, the Dangote group never became dependent on any of them but used them as a lever to reach increasingly greater heights. While his competitors that did make alliances had to take each other's interests into account, without strategic partners Mr Dangote is as free in making business decisions as he ever was. Many wars are waged to retain freedom, a practice the Dangote group managed to successfully convey into the business realm.

Co-author: Jasper de Vries

Sources: '5 Machiavellian business lessons from billionaire Aliko Dangote', *Forbes*, 13 July 2011; 'Cementing a fortune: The king of concrete has ambitions beyond Nigeria', *The Economist*, 23 June 2012; 'GE partners Dangote on power, transportation, oil & gas', *The Sun*, 4 February 2013; 'Meet the richest man in Africa – the only black billionaire among the world's 50 richest people', *Business Insider*, 1 February 2016.

The embedded organization perspective

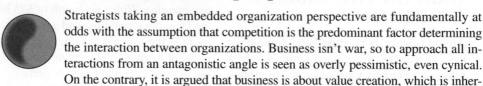 Strategists taking an embedded organization perspective are fundamentally at odds with the assumption that competition is the predominant factor determining the interaction between organizations. Business isn't war, so to approach all interactions from an antagonistic angle is seen as overly pessimistic, even cynical.

On the contrary, it is argued that business is about value creation, which is inherently a positive-sum activity. Creating value brings together organizations towards a common goal, as they can achieve more by working together than by behaving autonomously. In the modern economy, no organization can efficiently perform all activities in-house, as the division of labour has encouraged companies to specialize and outsource as many non-core activities as possible. Companies are necessarily cogs in the larger industrial machine and they can achieve little without working in unison with the other parts of the system. In the embedded organization perspective, atomistic competition is a neoclassical theoretical abstraction that seriously mischaracterizes the nature of relationships between organizations. In reality, cooperation is the predominant factor determining inter-organizational relations. Symbiosis, not aggression, is the fundamental nature of economic functioning (e.g. Jarillo, 1988; Moore, 1996, Reading 6.3).

A company can always find many organizations in its environment with which it shares an interest and whose objectives are largely parallel to its own (Child and Faulkner, 1998). A company might want to develop new products together with its buyers, optimize the logistical system together with its suppliers, expand the industry's potential together with other manufacturers, link technological standards with other industries and improve employment conditions together with the government. In general, most organizations have a stronger interest in increasing the size of the pie, than in deciding who gets what – keeping the focus on making a success of value creation eases the process of finding an equitable solution to the issue of value distribution.

The label 'embedded organization' given to this perspective refers to the fact that firms are becoming increasingly integrated into webs of mutually dependent organizations (e.g. Gnyawali and Madhavan, 2001; Granovetter, 1985). As companies strive to focus on a limited set of core competences and core business processes, they have moved to outsource as many non-core activities as possible. But as firms have attempted to further specialize by outsourcing activities that are close to their core business, they have become more vulnerable to outside suppliers and the need for explicit coordination of activities has often remained high. The outsourcing of such essential and coordination-intensive activities can only take place where the other party can be trusted to closely collaborate with the joint interests in mind. Of course, a company will not quickly move to such dependence on an outside supplier. But as experience and trust build over time, a strategic partnership can develop, where both sides come to accept the value of the close cooperation (e.g. Axelsson and Easton, 1992; Lorenzoni and Baden-Fuller, 1995, Reading 6.2).

For a firm to willingly surrender a part of its independence, it must be certain that its partners are also willing to invest in the relationship and will not behave opportunistically. Ideally, therefore, durable partnerships are based on mutual dependence and reciprocity. Both sides of the relationship must need each other, which gives an important incentive for both to find solutions to the disputes that will inevitably pop up. A balance in the benefits to be gained and the efforts to be exerted will also contribute to the success of a long-term collaborative relationship.

While such close collaborative relationships place a firm in a position of resource dependence, the benefits are well worth it. By specializing in a certain area, the firm can gain scale and experience advantages much faster. Specialization helps the firm to focus on a more limited set of core competences, which can be developed more efficiently and rapidly than if the firm were a 'conglomerate' of activities. At the same time the firm can tap into the complementary resources (Richardson, 1972) developed by its co-specialized partners. These complementary resources will usually be of higher quality and lower price than if the firm had built them up independently.

Specialized firms also use collaborative arrangements to quickly combine their resources with industry outsiders, to create new products and services. As product and business innovation are high paced and usually require the combination of various types of resources, developing everything in isolation is unworkable for most firms. By teaming up with other firms that have complementary resources, a company can make the most of its own resource base, without having to build up other resources from scratch. But again, trust is needed to engage in such a joint venture, as there are significant downside risks that the firm needs to take into account.

So, from the embedded organization perspective, collaboration is not competition in disguise, but a real alternative means of dealing with other organizations (e.g. Contractor and Lorange, 1988; Piore and Sabel, 1984). Successful firms embed themselves in webs of cooperative relationships, developing strategies together with their partners. These networks might compete against other networks (e.g. Gomes-Casseres, 1994; Hamilton and Woolsey Biggart, 1988; Weidenbaum and Hughes, 1996), but even here the relationships need not be fundamentally antagonistic. Proponents of the embedded organization perspective do not believe that firms should become obsessed with 'putting the competition out of business', as this again reduces business to a win-lose, zero-sum game. Firms should be focused on creating value and avoiding direct confrontation with other manufacturers, emphasizing the opportunity for a win-win, positive-sum game (e.g. Kim and Mauborgne, 2004; Moore, 1996, Reading 6.3). With this approach, firms in the same industry will recognize that they often have parallel interests as well. Setting industry standards, lobbying the government, finding solutions to joint environmental problems, improving the image of the industry, investing in fundamental research and negotiating with the unions are just a few of the issues where cooperation can be fruitful.

EXHIBIT 6.3   THE EMBEDDED ORGANIZATION PERSPECTIVE

NIKE: RUNNING NETWORK FOR GOLD

No sporting event in the world attracts more global viewers than the Olympics, with 3.6 billion people worldwide tuning into the 2016 Olympic Games in Rio de Janeiro, Brazil. Old records being broken dominated headlines, like runner Wayde van Niekerk smashing Michael Johnson's 17-year-old record on the 400-meter dash. With all these viewers, the Olympics provide a great opportunity to market products; but becoming an official sponsor requires footing a $100 to $200 million fee. Any non-sponsoring brand that promotes products at the Olympics can expect a visit from the IOC's fierce pack of lawyers, suing anyone who breaks their tight marketing rules.

These strict rules originated 20 years ago at the 1996 Olympics in Atlanta, when Nike pulled off an excellent marketing trick. They offered the Olympic sprinter Michael Johnson, the same who saw his 1999 record broken in Rio, a pair of gold-coloured lightweight racing shoes (worth $30,000) that he used while setting his gold medal-winning time on the 400-meter dash. Millions of people saw the shoes the day of the race and even more people saw them on the cover of *Time* magazine a few days later. Michael Johnson turned out to be a very profitable partner for Nike. What Nike did in 1996, besides prompting the IOC to come up with more stringent marketing guidelines, demonstrates their excellence in marketing. It is their expertise in marketing, as well as in R&D, that makes Nike one of the world's leading footwear and apparel companies. By focusing on just a few core competences, Nike can demonstrate greatness exactly there.

Of course, there is more to Nike's value chain than R&D and marketing; in 2014 Nike moved roughly 900 million units through its manufacturing network. This network partially consists of over 700 factories, yet none of them is owned by Nike. The manufacturing process is outsourced to third parties that specialize in this process, while the raw materials are sourced by independent contractors. The company is considered to be one of the pioneers in manufacturing outsourcing strategy and is currently focusing on new, innovative ways of manufacturing to allow for more customized products. In November 2015 Nike announced a partnership with Flex, a global manufacturer with experience in design, engineering and manufacturing in industries other than footwear and apparel. At the same time, Nike partnered up with NOVA, a company with 3D digital design system experience, enabling Nike to enhance its digital design capabilities. While these two partnerships are intended to give Nike a competitive advantage, another element of Nike's strategy focuses on sustainability. In 2013 Nike opened a water-free dyeing facility at its Taiwan-based manufacturer Far Eastern New Century Corp. It employs dyeing technology from a small Dutch company called DyeCoo, which uses carbon dioxide as a replacement for water to dye polyester.

Part of Nike's vision is to bring advanced innovation to its manufacturing supply chain. This is a prerequisite for meeting ever-changing customer needs, which currently demand customized solutions, quick delivery and products that communicate with each other. Nike has demonstrated that it is very capable of managing relationships with its network partners while specializing on its core competences, but it may be up for a network challenge on a different level. Platform businesses are disrupting the traditional business landscape, so if Nike hopes to fend off this platform disruption it should reevaluate its business model. Instead of focusing on vertical integration with its suppliers or distributors, it should now focus on partnering up with its end user. By offering a platform that creates value for its end consumer, Nike can reinvent its partnership strategy and continue to hold its number one position. Yet speed is of the essence, so a pair of gold-coloured lightweight racing shoes would be more than welcome.

Co-author: Adriaan de Bruijn

Sources: 'How Nike brilliantly ruined Olympic marketing forever', *Adweek*, 10 August 2016; 'Nike's manufacturing revolution accelerated by new partnership with Flex', *news.nike.com*, 14 October 2015; 'An overview of Nike's supply chain and manufacturing strategies', *Marketrealist*, 2 December 2014; 'Nike and Adidas strategic partners for Dyecoo's business model', www.between-us.com; 'Here's how Nike became a platform business', *Fortune*, 10 April 2016.

MANAGING THE PARADOX OF COMPETITION AND COOPERATION

All for one, one for all.

The Three Musketeers, Alexandre Dumas Jr. (1824–1895), French novelist

So, should managers form network level strategies or not? Should firms consciously embed themselves in a web of durable collaborative relationships, emphasizing the value of cooperative inter-organizational interactions for realizing their long-term aims? Or should firms try to remain as independent as possible, emphasizing the value of competitive power in achieving their strategic objectives? Is it 'all for one, one for all' or must the strong truly stand alone? (See Table 6.1.)

TABLE 6.1   Discrete organization versus embedded organization perspective

	Discrete organization perspective	Embedded organization perspective
Emphasis on	Competition over cooperation	Cooperation over competition
Preferred position	Independence	Interdependence
Environment structure	Discrete organizations (atomistic)	Embedded organizations (networked)
Firm boundaries	Distinct and defended	Fuzzy and open
Inter-organizational relations	Arm's-length and transactional	Close and structural
Interaction outcomes	Mainly zero-sum (win-lose)	Mainly positive-sum (win-win)
Interaction based on	Bargaining power and calculation	Trust and reciprocity
Network level strategy	No	Yes
Use of collaboration	Temporary coalitions (tactical alliance)	Durable partnerships (strategic alliance)
Collaborative arrangements	Limited, well-defined, contract-based	Broad, open, relationship-based

The debate on this issue within the field of strategy is far from being concluded. Many perspectives exist on how to reconcile the conflicting demands of competition and cooperation and many 'best practices' have been put forward. Therefore strategists need to determine their own point of view, with a number of suggestions from the literature in mind. From all the discussed strategy issues in this book, the number of available options to manage the paradox of cooperation and competition is highest. Three options have been brought forward: navigating, parallel processing and juxtaposing.

Navigating

By focusing on one contrary element at a time, the paradox is managed by a series of contrary initiatives. In network level strategy, Gary Hamel, Yves Doz and C.K. Prahalad have suggested the route for strategists to cooperate first and compete later in their *HBR* article: 'Collaborate with your competitor and win' (1989, Reading 6.1). They describe how Japanese strategists collaborate with competitors from the West with the explicit intention to learn and then beat them as competitors. In this case, vertical (cooperative supply chain) relations become horizontal (competitive). But also without this specific change of relationship, navigating vertical partnering is an option. For example, in the retail industry it is common practice that suppliers (A Brand manufacturers) cooperate with clients (supermarkets) to jointly develop logistical processes and technologies to enhance efficiency. Both parties benefit, but once the new technology and process are in place, parties start negotiating prices and conditions again. This cycle of cooperating and competing is repeated many times.

Other suggestions have also been made. Under the guidance of the Japanese Ministry of International Trade and Industry (MITI), groups of (Japanese) companies have been brought together to jointly develop new technologies, stimulated with government money. The intention was to cooperate in the 'pre-competitive stage' and once the technology was developed to compete in the marketplace. This industrial policy has been adopted by the European Union with initiatives such as ESPRIT and EUREKA, to promote innovation and to introduce new standards in the telecommunications sector (Gastells, 2006; Van Tulder and Junne, 1988).

Cooperating first and competing later is not an exclusive industrial policy option. Companies have learned that on some occasions it makes strategic sense to join forces with competitors in the early phase of developing technologies and industry standards. Well described in the literature is the case of developing an industry standard for video devices (e.g. Bartlett, Ghoshal and Beamish, 2008). Three competitors had been competing for the world standard, Philips with V2000, Sony with Betamax and Matsushita with VCR. The victor was VCR in this winner-takes-all game (Arthur, 1994); the contestants learned the hard way that competing for standards may be heroic and exciting, but often proves disappointing. For developing a world Wi-Fi standard, several stakeholders have participated in a standardization group; competition started after the new standard had created a level playing field.

Parallel processing

The term co-opetition, an astute portmanteau of cooperation and competition, has become popularized by game theorists (e.g. Brandenburger and Nalebuff, 1996). It is explained as companies interacting with partial congruence of interests. For example, the French car manufacturer PSA Peugeot Citroën and the Japanese firm Toyota share components of city cars, the Peugeot 107, Toyota Aygo and Citroën C1, while competing fiercely for market share. Cooperating to reduce costs while competing for market share are being executed in different organizational units and hence are an example of parallel processing.

Companies can also separate competing and cooperating in different country units. For example, the French company Danone and the Japanese firm Yakult (see also the short case on Yakult in Exhibit 4.1) compete in Europe but cooperate in India. In this case, the arguments in the strategic decision-making process to 'make, buy or cooperate' differ over country units, and therefore the decisions vary. Without an overarching corporate policy, the organizational units have the freedom to choose, and so parallel processing is possible.

Juxtaposing

Simultaneously managing competition and cooperation, even with the same network partners, is a next option for strategists. Lord Palmerston's quote earlier in this chapter articulates the position of a strategizing manager quite well: there are no eternal allies and perpetual enemies. Comparable to a cycling race, rival teams can become allies and then turn rivals again, depending on the situation during the race. Managers also keep their options open; rivals can become allies and rivals again, depending on the situation. For example, in the battle for mobile operating model standards some competing providers have a joint interest to defend the chosen platform and join forces, and after a cooperative meeting start competing again.

Juxtaposing is common in business ecosystems, as Moore (1996, Reading 6.3) points out. Moore argues that the pattern of business co-evolution consists of 'a complex network of choices, which depend, at least in part, on what participants are aware of'. In other words, managers cannot afford to label firms as definite rivals or allies. Positions within the ecosystem can change so fast that allies can turn into rivals within days and vice versa. Ecosystems are often described in innovation contexts, with eroding industry boundaries and companies often unexpectedly finding themselves in fierce competition with the most unlikely of rivals.

NETWORK LEVEL STRATEGY IN INTERNATIONAL PERSPECTIVE

Co-authors: Gep Eisenloeffel and Wester Wagenaar

Do as adversaries in law, strive mightily, but eat and drink as friends.

William Shakespeare (1564–1616), English dramatist and poet

Of all the debates in the field of strategic management, the one on network level strategy has received the most attention from comparative management researchers. Almost all of them have concluded that firms from different countries display widely divergent propensities to compete and cooperate. Many authors suggest there are recognizable national inclinations, even national styles, when it comes to establishing inter-firm relationships (Contractor and Lorange, 1988; Kagono *et al.*, 1985).

Since there can be significant variance within a country, it is difficult to generalize at the national level. Nevertheless it is challenging to debate these observed international dissimilarities. Are there really national inter-organizational relationship styles and what factors might influence their existence? As a stimulus to the international dimension of this debate, a number of country characteristics are put forward as possible influences on how the paradox of competition and cooperation is dealt with in different national settings. In addition to analyses on the societal level, preferences on the industry merit discussion.

On the societal level

It is generally argued that most countries have developed an idiosyncratic economic system – that is, their own brand of capitalism – with a different emphasis on competition and cooperation. One prominent analysis is that of historian Chandler (1986, 1990), who has described the historical development of 'personal capitalism' in the United Kingdom, 'managerial capitalism' in the United States, 'group capitalism' in Japan and 'cooperative capitalism' in Germany from 1850 to 1950. We can also identify other types of institutional environment, such as what can be dubbed 'bureaucratic capitalism' in France and 'familial capitalism' in Italy. The legacy of these separately evolving forms of capitalism is that, to this day, there are significantly different institutional philosophies, roles and behaviour in each of these countries. It goes without saying that not only institutions define general preferences of countries, but that social networks and cultural values also have an influence.

In the English-speaking nations, governments have generally limited their role to the establishment and maintenance of competitive markets (Hampden-Turner and Trompenaars, 1993). A shared belief in the basic tenets of classical economies has led these governments to be suspicious of competition-undermining collusion masquerading under the term 'cooperation'. For instance, in the US, the Sherman Antitrust Act was passed in 1890 and has been applied with vigour since then to guard the functioning of the market. Many companies that would like to cooperate have been discouraged or barred from doing so (Teece, 1992). On the cultural level, Hofstede's research found the US to be the highest scoring nation in the world on the individualism scale, closely followed by the other English-speaking countries. In the socially atomistic Anglo-Saxon nations, individuals are seen as the building blocks of society and each person is inclined to optimize his own interests (Hofstede, 1993; Lessem and Neubauer, 1994). One result is that in the US cooperation tends to only exist 'under a system of formal rules and regulations, which have to be negotiated, agreed to, litigated and enforced, sometimes by coercive means' (Fukuyama, 1995). Not surprisingly, the US has the highest number of corporate lawyers in the world and transaction costs are high.

Japan is generally put at the opposite side of the spectrum, emphasizing group affiliation instead of individualism (Lessem and Neubauer, 1994). In more collectivist societies, a relationship is 'not calculative, but moral: It is based not on self-interest, but on the individual's loyalty toward the clan, organization, or society – which is supposedly the best guarantee of that individual's ultimate interest' (Hofstede, 1993). Japan's 'group capitalism' is characterized by partnerships between business and social institutions to promote mutually beneficial developments. On the multi-company level Japan's collectivist bent manifests itself in the bank-led *keiretsu* system. Firms within a *keiretsu* are familiar with one another through long historical association and have had durable, open-ended relationships, partially cemented by multilateral shareholdings. Collectivism, resulting in different modes of group orientation, correlates with importance adhered to trust-building and social capital, a characteristic also observable in many other countries in Asia (Fukuyama, 1995). In China, for instance, longstanding informal relationships form the basis for the functioning of business networks or *guanxi* in Chinese. Without the proper *guanxi*, doing business is particularly difficult.

The German system and culture are often compared with those of Japan. Lessem and Neubauer argue that both cultures exhibit a holistic worldview, in which 'management and banker, employer and employee, government and industry combine forces rather than engage in adversarial relations', to the benefit of the entire system (1994). In Germany's 'cooperative capitalism', the government has major shareholdings in hundreds of companies outside the public services. The large German banks especially have played an important role in guiding industrial development, promoting cooperation and defusing potentially dangerous conflicts between companies. Since the late 1990s this system has been unravelling, but trade associations and unions, like the German banks, also employ a long-term, cooperative perspective.

Similar to the Germans and the Japanese ones, Italian culture is also characterized by a strong group orientation, but in the 'familial capitalism' of Italy the affiliations valued by Italians tend to be mostly family like. These are based on blood ties, friendships or ideological bonds between individuals. There is strong loyalty and trust within these communities, but distrust prevails towards the outside world, among which are institutions like the central government, tax authorities, bankers and trade unions. Therefore, the role of the government tends to be small and instead trading associations, purchasing cooperatives, educational institutions and cooperative marketing are often created to support a large number of small, specialized firms working together as a loose federation. Family-like cooperation tends to be high within these communities and it is thus unsurprising that Italy is often cited for its high number of networked companies (Piore and Sabel, 1984). Besides the well-known example of Benetton, examples can be found in the textile industry of Prato, the ceramics industry of Sassuolo, the farm machine industry of Reggio Emilia and the motorcycle industry of Bologna.

The 'bureaucratic capitalism' system observable in France focuses strongly on the state as industrial strategist, coordinating many major developments in the economy. It is the planners' job 'to maintain a constant pressure on industry – as part industrial consultant, part banker, part plain bully – to keep it moving in some desired direction' (Lessem and Neubauer, 1994). This was for instance the case in France's state-supported filière policy, supporting the national communication industry in the mid-1980s (Groenewegen and Beije, 1989). The unions, contrariwise, tend to be more antagonistic, particularly in their relationship to the government. On the work floor, however, a more cooperative attitude prevails. There is a strong sense that cooperation in economic affairs is important. Generally, however, there is a preference to impose such cooperation in a top-down manner by integrating companies into efficiently working bureaucracies. Such structuring of the economy usually takes place under the influence, or by direct intervention, of the French government. The extent of this French philosophy is deep: even relationships with firms not absorbed into the hierarchy are of a bureaucratic nature – that is, formal, rational and depersonalized.

On the industry level

The nature of some industries makes inter-organizational competition more likely than cooperation and vice versa. Industries where available projects are limited can be expected to fall in the category with a preference for competition. For example, the construction industry is one of the most highly competitive industries worldwide and 'is characterized by opportunistic behaviour and the lack of vertical cooperation' (Welling and Kamann, 2001). One reason is the competition contractors have to engage in to obtain contracts. Usually, contractors who submit the lowest bids get selected, but even when other methods to find a contractor are employed, the stakes to secure projects remain high. In addition, the specialized nature of some of the tasks in the industry makes diversification outside of construction fairly difficult. The limited options of players in the construction industry and the intense competition to secure contracts generally result in a zero-sum game.

Oligopoly industries are also dominated by a focus on competition. If one company in such a setting changes its organization, strategy or price, this will have a significant impact on its rivals. The aircraft manufacturing industry is arguably the most well-known example of a highly competitive arena controlled by just a few players. Airbus and Boeing practically own the jet airliner market together, but as a result they engage in fierce competition over the limited number of orders. Other global oligopolies are the steel, oil, wholesale beer, photo camera and cellular phone market industries.

Inter-organizational cooperation, on the other hand, can generally be expected in high-technology or knowledge-based industries. Here, collaborative projects are considered fairly commonplace. Examples are the space and biotechnology industries. For instance, since 1990, the EU-US Task Force on Biotechnology Research has shared, cooperated on and promoted biotechnology research. The knowledge gained can then be turned into products (Aguilar, Bochereau and Matthiessen-Guyader, 2008). Higher education can also be considered a cooperative industry: Universities can be found collaborating in order to provide student exchange programmes, share research findings and engage in projects.

Cooperation is at the heart of industries that are – partly or wholly – organized as business ecosystems, such as international sourcing (Alibaba), the music industry (Spotify) and the taxi industry (Uber). Here companies create platforms, establishing partnerships with other companies and individuals. The quality of these platforms generally increases along with a higher number of platform partnerships.

To the strategist

There is a variety of ways to deal with the paradox of cooperation and competition, as showcased by differences in the perceptions of companies, industries and countries. A strategist can and should learn from the ways others around the world and across industries perceive these seemingly opposing concepts, but also has to be aware of international differences when her or his company wishes to reach across borders. Research by Bleeke and Ernst found that only half of the cross-border alliances succeed, fuelling the need for accurately predicting a company's ability to collaborate and having a good understanding of international differences (1991, 1993). Since companies, countries and industries vary widely, there is not one given answer.

STRATEGY PROCESS

Follow the course opposite to custom and you will almost always do well.

Jean-Jacques Rousseau (1712–1778), French philosopher

Given the variety of perspectives on strategy, finding a precise definition with which all people agree is probably impossible. Therefore, in this book we will proceed with a very broad conception of strategy as 'a course of action for achieving an organization's purpose'. In this section, it is the intention to gain a better insight into how such a course of action comes about – how is, and should, strategy be made, analysed, dreamt up, formulated, implemented, changed and controlled; who is involved; and when do the necessary activities take place?

The process by which strategy comes about can be dissected in many ways. Here, the strategy process has been unravelled into three partially overlapping issues, each of which requires managers to make choices, and each of which is (therefore) controversial (see Figure III.1):

- Strategy formation. This issue focuses on the question of how managers should organize their strategizing activities to achieve a successful strategy formation process.
- Strategic change. This issue focuses on the question of how managers should organize their strategizing activities to achieve a successful change process.
- Strategic innovation. This issue focuses on the question of how managers should organize their strategizing activities to achieve a successful strategic innovation process.

The most important term to remember throughout this section is *process*. In each chapter the discussion is not about one-off activities or outcomes – a formed strategy, a strategic change or a strategic innovation – but about the ongoing processes of forming, changing and innovating. These processes need to be organized, structured, stimulated, nurtured and/or facilitated over a prolonged period of time and the question concerns which approach will be successful in the long term, as well as in the short term.

FIGURE III.1   The strategy process chapters

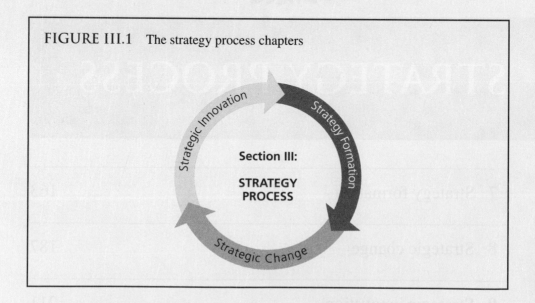

STRATEGY FORMATION

7

Nothing in progression can rest on its original plan. We may as well think of rocking a grown man in the cradle of an infant.

Edmund Burke (1729–1797), Irish-born politician and man of letters

INTRODUCTION

There are many definitions of strategy and many ideas of how strategies should be made. In the introduction to Section III of this book, our definition of strategy was kept basic to encompass the large majority of these different views – 'strategy is a course of action for achieving an organization's purpose'. Taking this definition as a starting point, a major distinction can be observed between people who see strategy as an *intended* course of action and those who regard strategy as a *realized* course of action. Mintzberg and Waters (1985) have remarked that these two views of strategy are not contradictory, but complementary. Intended strategy is what individuals or organizations formulate prior to action (a *pattern of decisions*), while realized strategy refers to the strategic behaviour exhibited in practice (a *pattern of actions*). Of course, not all behaviour is necessarily strategic – if the actions do not follow a pattern directed at achieving the organization's purpose, it does not qualify as strategy.

The process by which an intended strategy is created is called 'strategy formulation'. Normally strategy formulation is followed by strategy implementation. However, intentions sometimes end up not being put into practice – plans can be changed or cancelled along the way. The process by which a realized strategy is formed is called 'strategy formation'. What is realized might be based on an intended strategy, but it can also be the result of unplanned actions as time goes by. In other words, the process of strategy formation encompasses both formulation and action. Strategy formation is the entire process leading to strategic behaviour in practice.

For managers with the responsibility for getting results, it would be too limited to only look at the process of strategy formulation and to worry about implementation later. Managers must ask themselves how the entire process of strategy formation should be managed to get their organizations to act strategically. Who should be involved, what activities need to be undertaken and to what extent can strategy be formulated in advance? In short, for managers, finding a way to realize a strategic pattern of actions is the key issue.

THE ISSUE OF REALIZED STRATEGY

Getting an organization to exhibit strategic behaviour is what all strategists aim to achieve. Preparing detailed analyses, drawing up plans, making extensive slide presentations and holding long meetings might all be necessary means to achieve this end, but ultimately it is the organization's actions directed at the marketplace that count. The key issue facing managers is, therefore, how this strategic behaviour can be attained. How can a successful course of action be realized in practice?

To answer these questions, it is first necessary to gain a deeper understanding of the 'who' and 'what' of strategy formation – 'what type of strategy formation activities need to be carried out?' and 'what type of strategy formation roles need to be filled by whom?' Both questions will be examined in the following sections.

Strategy formation activities

In Chapter 2, it is argued that the process of strategic reasoning could be divided into four general categories of activities – identifying, diagnosing, conceiving and realizing. These strategic problem-solving activities, taking place in the mind of the strategist, are in essence the same as those encountered in organizations at large. Organizations also need to 'solve strategic problems' and achieve a successful pattern of actions. The difference is that the organizational context – involving many more people, with different experiences, perspectives, personalities, interests and values – leads to different requirements for structuring the process. Getting people within an organization to exhibit strategic behaviour necessitates the exchange of information and ideas, decision-making procedures, communication channels, the allocation of resources and the coordination of actions.

When translated to an organizational environment, the four general elements of the strategic reasoning process can be further divided into the eight basic building blocks of the strategy formation process, as illustrated in Figure 7.1.

Strategic issue identification activities.   If a strategy is seen as an answer to a perceived 'problem' or 'issue', managers must have some idea of what the problem is. 'Identifying' refers to all activities contributing to a better understanding of what should be viewed as problematic – what constitutes an important opportunity or threat that must be attended to if the organization's purpose is to be met. The key activities here are:

- Mission setting. What the organization sees as an issue will in part depend on its mission – the enduring set of fundamental principles outlining what purpose the organization wishes to serve, in what domain and under which conditions. A company's mission, encompassing its core values, beliefs, business definition and purpose, forms the basis of the organization's identity and sets the basic conditions under which the organization wishes to function. Where a company has a clearly developed mission, shared by all key players in the organization, this will strongly colour its filtering of strategic issues. The mission does not necessarily have to be formally captured in a mission statement, but can be informally internalized as part of the company culture. The topic of mission has been discussed at more length in Chapter 3.

- Agenda-setting. Besides the organizational mission as a screening mechanism, many other factors can contribute to the focusing of organizational attention on specific

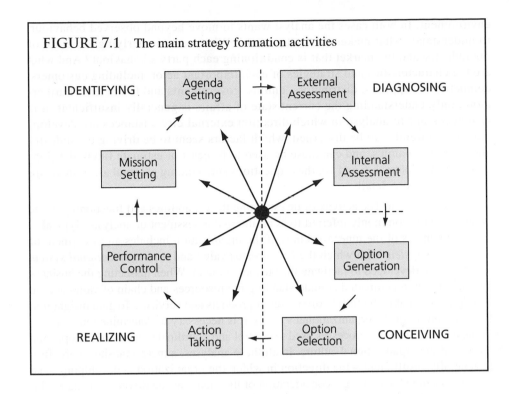

FIGURE 7.1   The main strategy formation activities

strategic issues. For instance, the cognitive map of each strategist will influence which environmental and organizational developments are identified as issues. Furthermore, group culture will have an impact on which issues are discussible, which are off-limits to open debate, and under what conditions discussions should take place. Getting people to sit up and take notice will also depend on each actor's communication and political skills, as well as their sources of power, both formal and informal. Together these attention-focusing factors determine which issues are picked up on the 'organizational radar screen', discussed and looked into further. It is said that these issues make it on to the 'organizational agenda', while all other potential problems receive less or no attention. Many of these organizational factors are discussed more extensively in Chapters 8 and 11.

Strategic issue diagnosis activities.   To come to grips with a 'problem' or 'issue', managers must try to comprehend its structure and its underlying causes. Especially since most strategic issues are not simple and straightforward, but complex and messy, it is very important to gain a deeper understanding of 'what is going on' – which 'variables' are there and how are they interrelated? This part of the strategy formation processes can be divided into the following activities:

■ External assessment. The activity of investigating the structure and dynamics of the environment surrounding the organization is commonly referred to as an external assessment or analysis. Typically, such a diagnosis of the outside world includes both a scan of the direct (market) environment and the broader (contextual) environment. In both cases the analyst wants to move beyond observed behaviour, to understand 'what makes the system tick'. What is the underlying structure of the industry and the market that is conditioning each party's behaviour? And what are the characteristics and strategies of each important actor, including customers, competitors, suppliers, distributors, unions, governments and financiers? Furthermore, only understanding the current state of affairs is generally insufficient; it is also necessary to analyse in which direction external circumstances are developing. Which trends can be discerned, which factors seem to be driving the industry and market dynamics, and can these be used to forecast or estimate future developments? In Chapters 4, 6 and 10, these questions surrounding external assessment are discussed in more detail.

- Internal assessment. The activity of investigating the capabilities and functioning of the organization is commonly referred to as an internal assessment or analysis. Typically, such a diagnosis of the inner workings of the organization includes an assessment of the *business system* with which the firm creates value and the *organizational system* that has been developed to facilitate the business system. When dissecting the business system, attention is directed at understanding the resources and chain of value-adding activities that enable the firm to offer a set of products and services. To gain insight into the functioning of the organizational system, it is necessary to determine the structure of the organization, the processes used to control and coordinate the various people and units, and the organizational culture. In all these analyses, a mere snapshot of the firm is generally insufficient – the direction in which the organization is developing must also be examined, including a consideration of the main change drivers and change inhibitors. Furthermore, for strategy-making it is important to compare how the organization scores on all aforementioned factors compared to rival firms. In Chapters 4 and 8, these topics are investigated in more depth.

Strategy conception activities. To deal with a strategic 'problem' or 'issue', managers must come up with a potential solution. A course of action must be found that will allow the organization to relate itself to the environment in such a way that it will be able to achieve its purpose. 'Conceiving' refers to all activities that contribute to determining which course of action should be pursued. In this part of the strategy formation process, the following categories of activities can be discerned:

- Option generation. Creating potential strategies is what option generation is about. Sometimes managers will immediately jump at one specific course of action, limiting their strategic option generation activities to only one prime candidate. However, many managers will be inclined to explore a number of different avenues for approaching a specific strategic issue, thereby generating multiple strategic options. Each option can range in detail from a general outline of actions to be taken, up to a full-blown strategic plan, specifying goals, actions, tasks, responsibilities, resource allocation, milestones and performance measures. Which questions each strategic option should address is the main focus of discussion in the strategy content section of this book.

- Option selection. The potential 'solutions' formulated by managers must be evaluated to decide whether they should be acted on. It must be weighed whether the strategic option generated will actually lead to the results required and then it must be concluded whether to act accordingly. Especially where two or more strategic options have come forward, managers need to judge which one of them is most attractive to act on. This screening of strategic options is done on the basis of evaluation criteria, for instance perceived risk, anticipated benefits, the organization's capacity to execute, expected competitor reactions and follow-up possibilities. Sometimes a number of the evaluation criteria used are formally articulated, but generally the evaluation will at least be partially based on the experience and judgement of the decision-makers involved. Together, these activities of assessing strategic options and arriving at a selected course of action are also referred to as 'strategic decision-making'.

Strategy realization activities.   A strategic 'problem' or 'issue' can only be resolved if concrete actions are undertaken that achieve results. Managers must make adjustments to their business or organizational system, or initiate actions in the market – they must not only think, talk and decide, but also do, to have a tangible impact. 'Realizing' refers to all these practical actions performed by the organization. If there is a clear pattern to these actions, it can be said that there is a realized strategy. In this part of the strategy formation process, the following activities can be distinguished:

- Action-taking. A potential problem solution must be carried out – intended actions must be implemented to become realized actions. This performing of tangible actions encompasses all aspects of a firm's functioning. All hands-on activities, more commonly referred to as 'work', fall into this category – everything from setting up and operating the business system to getting the organizational system to function on a day-to-day basis.

- Performance control. Managers must also measure whether the actions being taken in the organization are in line with the option selected and whether the results are in line with what was anticipated. This reflection on the actions being undertaken can be informal, and even unconscious, but it can be formally structured into a performance monitoring and measuring system as well. Such performance measurement can be employed to assess how well certain people and organizational units are doing vis-à-vis set objectives. Incentives can be linked to achieving targets and corrective steps can be taken to ensure conformance to an intended course of action. However, deviation from the intended strategy can also be a signal to re-evaluate the original solution or even to re-evaluate the problem definition itself. An important issue when engaging in performance control is to determine which performance indicators will be used – micro-measuring all aspects of the organization's functioning is generally much too unwieldy and time consuming. Some managers prefer a few simple measures, sometimes quantitative (e.g. financial indicators), sometimes qualitative (e.g. are clients satisfied?), while others prefer more extensive and varied measures, such as a balanced scorecard (Kaplan and Norton, 2001; Simons, 1995).

Note that these strategy formation activities have not been labelled 'steps' or 'phases'. While these eight activities have been presented in an order that seems to suggest a logical sequence of steps, it remains to be seen in which order they should be carried out in practice. In Figure 7.1, the outer arrows represent the logical clockwise sequence, similar to the analytic reasoning process discussed in Chapter 2. The inner arrows represent the possibility to jump back and forth between the strategy formation activities, similar to the irregular pattern exhibited in the holistic reasoning process in Chapter 2.

Strategy formation roles

In all strategy formation processes, the activities discussed above need to be carried out. However, there can be significant differences in who carries out which activities. Roles in the strategy formation process can vary as tasks and responsibilities are divided in alternative ways. The main variations are due to a different division of labour along the following dimensions:

- Top vs middle vs bottom roles. Strategy formation activities are rarely the exclusive domain of the CEO. Only in the most extreme cases will a CEO run a 'one-man show', carrying out all activities except realization. Usually some activities will be divided among members of the top management team, while other activities will be pushed further down to divisional managers, business unit managers, and department managers (e.g. Bourgeois and Brodwin, 1983; Floyd and Wooldridge, 2000). Some activities might be delegated or carried out together with people even further down the hierarchy, including employees on the work floor. For activities such as external and internal assessment and option generation it is more common to see participation by people lower in the organization, while top management generally retains the responsibility for selecting, or at least deciding on, which strategic option to follow. The recurrent theme in this question of the vertical division of activities is how far down activities can and should be pushed – how much *empowerment* of middle and lower levels is beneficial for the organization?

- Line vs staff roles. By definition line managers are responsible for realization of strategic options pertaining to the primary process of the organization. Because they are responsible for achieving results, they are often also given the responsibility to participate in conceiving the strategies they will have to realize. Potentially, line managers can carry out all strategy formation activities without staff support. However, many organizations do have staff members involved in the strategy formation process. Important staff input can come from all existing departments, while some organizations institute special strategy departments to take care of strategy formation activities. The responsibilities of such strategy departments can vary from general process facilitation, to process ownership to full responsibility for strategy formulation.

- Internal vs external roles. Strategy formation activities are generally seen as an important part of every manager's portfolio of tasks. Yet, not all activities need to be carried out by members of the organization, but can be 'outsourced' to outsiders (e.g. Robinson, 1982). It is not uncommon for firms to hire external agencies to perform diagnosis activities or to facilitate the strategy formation process in general. Some organizations have external consultants engaged in all aspects of the process, even to the extent that the outside agency has the final responsibility for drawing up the strategic options.

In organizing the strategy formation process, a key question is how formalized the assignment of activities to the various potential process participants should be. The advantage of formalization is that it structures and disciplines the strategy formation process (e.g. Chakravarthy and Lorange, 1991; Hax and Majluf, 1984). Especially in large organizations, where many people are involved, it can be valuable to keep the process tightly organized. Formalization can be achieved by establishing a strategic planning system. In such a system, strategy formation steps can be scheduled, tasks can be specified, responsibilities can be assigned, decision-making authority can be clarified, budgets can be allocated and evaluation mechanisms can be put in place. Generally, having unambiguous responsibilities, clearer accountability and stricter review of performance will lead to a better functioning organization. The added benefit of formalization is that it gives top management more control over the organization, as all major changes must be part of approved plans and the implementation of plans is checked.

Yet, there is a potential danger in using formal planning systems as a means to make strategy. Formalization strongly emphasizes those aspects that can be neatly organized such as meetings, writing reports, giving presentations, making decisions, allocating resources and reviewing progress, while having difficulty with essential strategy-making activities that are difficult to capture in procedures. Important aspects such as creating new insights, learning, innovation, building political support and entrepreneurship can be sidelined or crushed if rote bureaucratic mechanisms are used to produce strategy. Moreover, planning bureaucracies, once established, can come to live a life of their own, creating rules, regulations, procedures, checks, paperwork, schedules, deadlines and double-checks, making the system inflexible, unresponsive, ineffective and demotivating (e.g. Marx, 1991; Mintzberg, 1994a).

THE PARADOX OF DELIBERATENESS AND EMERGENCE

The ability to foretell what is going to happen tomorrow, next week, next month and next year. And to have the ability afterwards to explain why it didn't happen.

Winston Churchill (1874–1965), British prime minister and writer

Strategy has to do with the future. And the future is unknown. This makes strategy a fascinating, yet frustrating, topic. Fascinating because the future can still be shaped and strategy can be used to achieve this aim. Frustrating because the future is unpredictable, undermining the best of intentions, thus demanding flexibility and adaptability. To managers, the idea of creating the future is highly appealing, yet the prospect of sailing for *terra incognita* without a compass is unsettling at best.

This duality of wanting to intentionally design the future, while needing to gradually explore, learn and adapt to an unfolding reality, is the tension central to the topic of strategy formation. It is the conflicting need to figure things out in advance, versus the need to find things out along the way. On the one hand, managers would like to forecast the future and to orchestrate plans to prepare for it. Yet, on the other hand, managers understand that experimentation, learning and flexibility are needed to deal with the fundamental unpredictability of future events.

In their influential article, 'Of strategies: Deliberate and emergent', Mintzberg and Waters (1985) were one of the first to explicitly focus on this tension. They argued that a distinction should be made between deliberate and emergent strategy (see Figure 7.2). Where realized strategies were fully intended, one can speak of 'deliberate strategy'. However, realized strategies can also come about 'despite, or in the absence of, intentions', which Mintzberg and Waters labelled 'emergent strategy'. In their view, few strategies were purely deliberate or emergent, but usually a mix between the two.

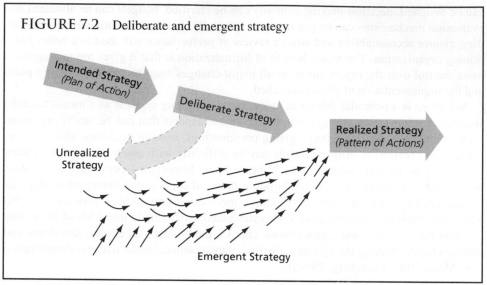

FIGURE 7.2   Deliberate and emergent strategy

Source: Mintzberg and Waters, 1985; reprinted with permission from *Strategic Management Journal*, © 1985 John Wiley and Sons Ltd.

Hence, in realizing strategic behaviour managers need to blend the conflicting demands for deliberate strategizing and strategy emergence. In the following paragraphs, both sides of this paradox of deliberateness and emergence will be examined further.

The demand for deliberate strategizing

Deliberateness refers to the quality of acting intentionally. When people act deliberately, they 'think' before they 'do'. They make a plan and then implement the plan. A plan is an intended course of action, stipulating which measures a person or organization proposes to take. In common usage, plans are assumed to be articulated (made explicit) and documented (written down), although, strictly speaking, this is not necessary to qualify as a plan.

As an intended course of action, a plan is a means towards an end. A plan details which actions will be undertaken to reach a particular objective. In practice, however, plans can exist without explicit objectives. In such cases, the objectives are implicitly wrapped up in the plan – the plan incorporates both ends and means.

All organizations need to plan. At the operational level, most firms will have some degree of production planning, resource planning, manpower planning and financial planning, to name just a few. When it comes to strategic behaviour, there are also a number of prominent advantages that strongly pressure organizations to engage in deliberate strategizing:

- Direction. Plans give organizations a sense of direction. Without objectives and plans, organizations would be adrift. If organizations did not decide where they wanted to go, any direction and any activity would be fine. People in organizations would not know what they were working towards and therefore would not be able to judge what constitutes effective behaviour (e.g. Ansoff, 1965; Chakravarthy and Lorange, 1991).

- Commitment. Plans enable early commitment to a course of action. By setting objectives and drawing up a plan to accomplish them organizations can invest resources, train people, build up production capacity and take a clear position within their environment. Plans allow organizations to mobilize themselves and to dare to take actions that are difficult to reverse and have a long payback period (e.g. Ghemawat, 1991; Marx, 1991).

- Coordination. Plans have the benefit of coordinating all strategic initiatives within an organization into a single cohesive pattern. An organization-wide master plan can ensure that differences of opinion are ironed out and one consistent course of action is followed throughout the entire organization, avoiding overlapping, conflicting and contradictory behaviour (e.g. Ackoff, 1981; Andrews, 1987).

- Optimization. Plans also facilitate optimal resource allocation. Drawing up a plan disciplines strategizing managers to explicitly consider all available information and consciously evaluate all available options. This allows managers to choose the optimal course of action before committing resources. Moreover, documented plans permit corporate level managers to compare the courses of action proposed by their various business units and to allocate scarce resources to the most promising initiatives (e.g. Ansoff and McDonnell, 1990; Bower, 1970).

- Programming. Last, but not least, plans are a means for programming all organizational activities in advance. Having detailed plans allows organizations to be run with the clockwork precision, reliability and efficiency of a machine. Activities that might otherwise be plagued by poor organization, inconsistencies, redundant routines, random behaviour, helter-skelter firefighting and chaos, can be programmed and controlled if plans are drawn up (e.g. Grinyer, Al-Bazzaz and Yasai-Ardekani, 1986; Steiner, 1979).

Given these major advantages, it can come as no surprise that organizations feel the pressure to engage in deliberate strategizing. Deliberateness is a quality that the strategy formation process cannot do without.

The demand for strategy emergence

Emergence is the process of becoming apparent. A strategy emerges when it comes into being along the way. Where there are no plans, or people divert from their plans but their behaviour is still strategic, it can be said that the strategy is emergent – gradually shaped during an iterative process of 'thinking' and 'doing'.

Emergent strategy differs from *ad hoc* behaviour in that a coherent pattern of action does evolve. While managers may have no prior intentions, they can explore, learn and piece together a consistent set of behaviours over time. Such an approach of letting strategy emerge has a number of major advantages that organizations also need to consider:

- Opportunism. As the future is unknown and therefore unpredictable, organizations must retain enough mental freedom to grab unforeseen opportunities as they emerge. Organizations must keep an open mind to sense where positive and negative circumstances are unfolding, so that they can respond rapidly to these new conditions – proactively riding the wave of opportunity, using the momentum in the environment and/or the organization to their advantage. This ability to 'play the field' is an important factor in effective strategy formation (e.g. Quinn, 2002; Stacey, 2001).

- Flexibility. Not only must managers keep an open mind, they must keep their options open as well, by not unnecessarily committing themselves to irreversible actions and investments. Letting strategy emerge means not prematurely locking the organization into a preset course of action, but keeping alternatives open for as long as practically possible. And where commitments must be made, managers need to select 'robust' options, which permit a lot of leeway to shift along with unfolding events. This pressure to remain flexible is also an important demand on strategizing managers (e.g. Beinhocker, 1999; Evans, 1991).

■ Learning. Often, the best way to find out what works is to give it a try – to act before you know. Letting strategy emerge is based on the same principle, that to learn what will be successful in the market must be discovered by experimentation, pilot projects, trial runs and gradual steps. Through the feedback obtained by hands-on 'doing', a rich insight can grow into what really works. As Thomas Alva Edison is well-known for remarking, invention is 5 per cent inspiration and 95 per cent perspiration, and this is probably equally true for 'inventing the corporate future'. Learning is hard work, but it is an essential part of strategy formation (e.g. Mintzberg, 1994b; Pascale, 1984).

■ Entrepreneurship. Building on the previous point, often the best way to find out what works is to let various people give it a try – to tap into the entrepreneurial spirits within the organization. Different people in the organization will have different strategic ideas and many of them will feel passionately about proving that their idea 'can fly'. By providing individuals, teams and/or entire units with a measure of autonomy to pursue innovative initiatives, firms can use the energy of 'intrapreneurs' within the organization, instead of forcing them to conform or start on their own (e.g. Amabile, 1998; Pinchot, 1985). As true incubators, firms can facilitate various divergent projects simultaneously, increasing commitment or closing them down as their potential unfolds (e.g. Burgelman, 1983, 1991; Lyon, Lumpkin and Dess, 2000).

■ Support. A major shift in strategy generally requires a major shift in the political and cultural landscape of an organization – careers will be affected, vested departmental interests will be impacted and cultural values and beliefs will be challenged. Rarely can such shifts be imposed top down by decree. Getting things done in organizations includes building coalitions, blocking rivals, convincing wavering parties, confronting opposing ideas and letting things 'sink in', all with the intention of gradually building enough support to move forward. Yet, finding out where enough support can be mustered to move forward, and where side steps or even reversals are needed, is an ongoing process and cannot be predicted in advance. Hence, strategizing managers must understand the internal political and cultural dynamics of their organizations and pragmatically shape strategy depending on what is feasible, not on what is ideal (e.g. Allison, 1971; Quinn, 1980).

Each of these points seems to be the counterpart to the advantages of deliberate strategizing – while deliberateness creates commitment, emergence allows for flexibility; while deliberateness gives direction, emergence allows for opportunism; while deliberateness facilitates fixed programming, emergence allows for ongoing learning. This places managers in a paradoxical position. While both deliberate strategizing and strategy emergence seem to have advantageous characteristics, they are each other's opposites and are to a certain extent contradictory – a firm cannot be fully committed to detailed and coordinated long-term plans, while simultaneously adapting itself flexibly and opportunistically to unfolding circumstances, ongoing learning and unpredictable political and cultural processes. With two conflicting demands placed on the strategy formation process at the same time, managers need to choose one at the expense of the other, trying to strike the best possible balance between deliberateness and emergence.

EXHIBIT 7.1 SHORT CASE

TOMTOM: NAVIGATING THROUGH UNCHARTED WATERS

Few companies can claim to have navigated clients to exactly the right spot. TomTom can. The Dutch company sold millions of navigation devices and still does so today. This travelled road was hardly evident when CEO Harold Goddijn founded the company in 1991, however. TomTom started out as a small software firm, developing mobile applications for personal digital assistants (PDAs). When more accurate GPS satellite readings became available, the company quickly recognized the potential of this technology and developed its first in-car navigation for PDAs: the TomTom Navigator. Although innovative, the real breakthrough came when the decision was made to put the software in its own box. It was this all-in-one Portable Navigation Device (PND), the TomTom GO that was almost solely responsible for the company's massive sudden growth. In two years, revenues increased from €39 million in 2003 to €720 million in 2005. The TomTom GO quickly managed to pave the road to further success.

Being well aware that neither product nor software has eternal life, CEO Goddijn decided to invest in areas that would broaden the company's revenue base. Goddijn knew that the mobile platform for navigation products is not a stable basis for a sustainable business model. A diversity of platforms and various hardware suppliers, in addition to the threat of piracy, make up a volatile environment indeed. Goddijn was in search of new growth areas to broaden the firm's base.

He did so with a couple of strategic acquisitions. In August 2005 the German telematics company Datafactory AG was acquired, laying the foundation for the business unit 'Telematics', currently Europe's fastest-growing telematics service provider for fleet management. The acquisition of Applied Generics, specializing in using data from mobile networks for advanced routing of vehicles, formed the basis of TomTom's traffic services. As it was expected that within a few years each car would have built-in navigation by default, an automotive engineering team from the Siemens research and development division was attracted in June 2007. They became the core of TomTom's Automotive business unit, geared towards developing these built-in navigation systems.

Since TomTom's core business remained its navigation devices, maps were of utmost importance to the company's activities. In July 2007 TomTom made a bid of €2 billion for digital map developer Tele Atlas. Nokia responded by making an even bigger bid for geographic information provider Navteq, currently known as Here, for $8.1 billion in October 2007. Garmin, TomTom's biggest competitor, felt threatened by this development and offered €2.3 billion for Tele Atlas. TomTom raised its bid to €2.9 billion after which Garmin pulled out. TomTom now consisted of four market-facing business units: consumer (organized around the PND and GPS Sport products), automotive (built-in navigation software, map content and services), licensing (selling map content and services), and telematics (offering fleet management solutions), in addition to two centralized technology units.

The storm had not calmed down for TomTom yet, however. The financial crisis commenced, and Google announced it would be offering Google Maps for free, based on its own content. The combination of crisis and free maps resulted in an immense decline in sales of PNDs, TomTom's main source of revenues. Google's announcement, the firm's largest licensing client, had another effect: the scarcity value of its maps deteriorated and TomTom's stock value made a dive. TomTom went through financial restructuring and had to reduce its workforce by 7 per cent.

▶

Goddijn had to respond to stronger competition in the PND market and the 'free' business models that were shrinking the market. He answered by attracting a new Chief Technology Officer (CTO), Charles Davies. After 20 years of being software director at PDA developer Psion, Davies had been CTO of Symbian, Nokia's mobile operating system. He was expected to not only understand the future need for mapping and navigation technology, but also bring in a more deliberate strategy mode. Although 2010 fared fairly well, the same could not be said for the next year. In 2011 economic decline had weakened the consumer electronics markets, a trend that was expected to last. The European PND market was expected to continue to shrink and in four months' time, TomTom's shares lost half their value.

This new wake-up call gave Goddijn and his fellow board members another impetus to do something to act on this negative trend. TomTom's top management held various meetings. Tough decisions were needed on the group structure, the firm's activities, reporting lines and review processes, as well as on how to achieve the highly needed savings. The process was a top-down one; only a limited number of organizational members were involved. The main outcomes were a new organization structure and savings in support activities. The newly created structure would bring more transparency and accountability, speed up making innovation choices and reduce time to market.

In addition, the company decided to change its internal structure, emphasizing its diversification. Products would continue to be delivered to the market through the existing consumer, automotive, licensing and telematics business units. Furthermore, existing R&D activities would be regrouped into various smaller product units within the technology units maps and location technology products. Each product unit is mandated to invest in ongoing development of a well-defined product category to deliver the best products to TomTom's customers.

In the new structure – still in place today – product units are imposed to develop a business plan based on a standardized strategy template, including coherent actions, a product roadmap and a financial paragraph. Templates were provided by a corporate staff organization, headed by CTO Charles Davies. Every product unit is supposed to follow the ideas of Richard Rumelt's book *Good Strategy/Bad Strategy*, in which good planning is emphasized. Review sessions with the product units are planned three times a year. Furthermore, the business of each business unit and product unit is updated annually and presented to TomTom's management board and CTO.

Clearly, a much more formal strategy approach has been installed. This strategy has proved to navigate TomTom to a renewed state of growth and stability, but that does not mean it will last. After all, the firm's history has proved that the industry is in constant flux. This holds especially true for the next step TomTom is undertaking: delivering products to support autonomous driving. However, this raises some obvious questions. How soon will autonomous driving be taken on the road on a mass scale and what technologies will be used? Who will be the future competitors? Next to existing competitors like Here – nowadays owned by Audi, BMW and Daimler – companies like Nvidea and Mobileye might play a role as well. And what will be the role of Apple, Uber and Google in autonomous driving?

With its future uncertain, it is clear that a good strategy is imperative to navigate through these unchartered waters successfully. Should TomTom continue with its current structured strategy, or should the company prepare for stormy waters and build in an additional emergency response unit?

Co-authors: Claudia Janssen and Wester Wagenaar

Source: Company information.

PERSPECTIVES ON STRATEGY FORMATION

It is impossible for a man to learn what he thinks he already knows.

Epictetus (c. 60–120), Roman philosopher

In Hollywood, most directors do not start shooting a movie until the script and storyboard are entirely completed – the script details each actor's words, expression and gestures, while the storyboard graphically depicts how each scene will look in terms of camera angles, lighting, backgrounds and stage props. Together they form a master plan, representing the initial intentions of the director. However, it frequently happens that a director has a new insight, and changes are made to the script or storyboard 'on the fly'. Yet, on the whole, most 'realized movies' are fairly close to directors' initial intentions.

For some directors, this is madness. They might have a movie idea, but in their mind's eye, they cannot yet picture it in its final form. Some elements might have already crystallized in their thoughts, but other parts of the film can only be worked out once the cameras are rolling and the actors start playing their roles. In this way, directors can let movies emerge without having a detailed script or storyboard in advance to guide them. It can be said that such movies are shaped by gradually blending together a number of small intentional steps over a long period of time, instead of taking one big step of making a master plan and implementing it. This approach of taking many small steps is called 'incrementalism'.

The question is how this works for managers making strategy. Is it best to deliberately draw up a storyboard for the film and trust that the 'actors' are flexible enough to adapt to minor changes in the script as time goes by? Or is the idea of a master plan misplaced, and are the best results achieved by developing a strategy incrementally, emergently responding to opportunities and threats as they unfold along the way? In short, how should strategizing managers strike a balance between deliberateness and emergence?

Unfortunately, the strategic management literature does not offer a clear-cut answer to this question. In both the academic journals and the practitioner-oriented literature, a wide spectrum of views can be observed on how managers should engage in strategy formation. While some writers suggest that there might be different styles in balancing deliberateness and emergence (e.g. Chaffee, 1985; Hart, 1992), most seem intent on offering 'the best way' to approach the issue of strategy formation – which often differs significantly from 'the best way' advised by others.

To come to grips with this variety of views, here the two diametrically opposed pole positions will be identified and discussed. On the basis of these two 'points of departure' the debate on how to deal with the paradox of deliberateness and emergence can be further explored. At one pole we find those managers and theorists who strongly emphasize deliberateness over emergence. They argue that organizations should strive to make strategy in a highly deliberate manner, by first explicitly formulating comprehensive plans, and only then implementing them. In accordance with common usage, this point of view will be referred to as the 'strategic planning perspective'. At the other pole are those who strongly emphasize emergence over deliberateness, arguing that in reality most new strategies emerge over time and that organizations should facilitate this messy, fragmented, piecemeal strategy formation process. This point of view will be referred to as the 'strategic incrementalism perspective'.

The strategic planning perspective

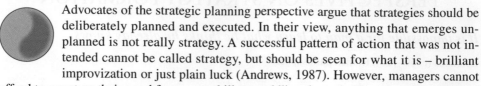

Advocates of the strategic planning perspective argue that strategies should be deliberately planned and executed. In their view, anything that emerges unplanned is not really strategy. A successful pattern of action that was not intended cannot be called strategy, but should be seen for what it is – brilliant improvization or just plain luck (Andrews, 1987). However, managers cannot afford to count on their good fortune or skill at muddling through. They must put time and effort into consciously formulating an explicit plan, making use of all available information and weighing all of the strategic alternatives. Tough decisions need to be made and priorities need to be set, before action is taken. 'Think before you act' is the strategic planning perspective's motto. But once a strategic plan has been adopted, action should be swift, efficient and controlled. Implementation must be secured by detailing the activities to be undertaken, assigning responsibilities to managers and holding them accountable for achieving results (e.g. Ansoff and McDonnell, 1990; Chakravarthy and Lorange, 1991).

Hence, in the strategic planning perspective, strategies are intentionally designed, much as an engineer designs a bridge. Building a bridge requires a long formulation phase, including extensive analysis of the situation, the drawing up of a number of rough designs, evaluation of these alternatives, choice of a preferred design, and further detailing in the form of a blueprint. Only after the design phase has been completed do the construction companies take over and build according to plan. Characteristic of such a planning approach to producing bridges and strategies is that the entire process can be disassembled into a number of distinct steps that need to be carried out in a sequential and orderly way. Only by going through these steps in a conscious and structured manner will the best results be obtained (e.g. Armstrong, 1982; Powell, 1992).

For advocates of the strategic planning perspective, the whole purpose of strategizing is to give organizations direction, instead of letting them drift. Organizations cannot act rationally without intentions – if you do not know where you are going, any behaviour is fine, which soon degenerates into 'muddling through' (e.g. Ansoff, 1991; Steiner, 1979). By first setting a goal and then choosing a strategy to get there, organizations can get 'organized'. Managers can select actions that are efficient and effective within the context of the strategy. A structure can be chosen, tasks can be assigned, responsibilities can be divided, budgets can be allotted and targets can be set. Not unimportantly, a control system can be created to measure results in comparison to the plan, so that corrective action can be taken.

Another advantage of the planning approach to strategy formation is that it allows for the *formalization* and *differentiation* of strategy tasks. Because of its highly structured and sequential nature, strategic planning lends itself well to formalization. The steps of the strategic planning approach can be captured in planning systems (e.g. Kukalis, 1991; Lorange and Vancil, 1977), and procedures can be developed to further enhance and organize the strategy formation process. In such strategic planning systems, not all elements of strategy formation need to be carried out by one and the same person, but can be divided among a number of people. The most important division of labour is often between those formulating the plans and those implementing them. In many large companies, the managers proposing the plans are also the ones implementing them, but deciding on the plans is passed up to a higher level. Often other tasks are spun off as well, or shared with others, such as diagnosis (strategy department or external consultants), implementation (staff departments) and evaluation (corporate planner and controller). Such task differentiation and specialization, it is argued, can lead to a better use of management talent, much as the division of labour has improved the field of production. At the same time, having a formalized system allows for sufficient coordination and mutual adjustment, to ensure that all specialized elements are integrated back into a consistent organization-wide strategy (e.g. Grinyer *et al.*, 1986; Jelinek, 1979).

Last, but not least, an advantage of strategic planning is that it encourages long-term thinking and commitment. 'Muddling through' is short-term oriented, dealing with issues of strategic importance as they come up or as a crisis develops. Strategic planning, by the same token, directs attention to the future. Managers making strategic plans have to take a more long-term view and are stimulated to prepare for, or even create, the future (Ackoff, 1981). Instead of just focusing on small steps, planning challenges managers to define a desirable future and to work towards it. Instead of wavering and opportunism, strategic planning commits the organization to a course of action and allows for investments to be made at the present that may only pay off in the long run (e.g. Ansoff, 1991; Miller and Cardinal, 1994).

One of the difficulties of strategic planning, advocates of this perspective will readily admit, is that plans will always be based on assumptions about how future events will unfold. Plans require forecasts. And as the Danish physicist Niels Bohr once joked, 'prediction is very difficult, especially about the future'. Even enthusiastic planners acknowledge that forecasts will be inaccurate. As Makridakis, the most prolific writer on the topic of forecasting, writes (1990, p. 66), 'the future can be predicted only by extrapolating from the past, yet it is fairly certain that the future will be different from the past'. Consequently, it is clear that rigid long-range plans based on such unreliable forecasts would amount to nothing less than Russian roulette. Most proponents of the strategic planning perspective therefore caution for overly deterministic plans. Some argue in favour of 'contingency planning', whereby a number of alternative plans are held in reserve in case key variables in the environment suddenly change. These contingency plans are commonly based on different future 'scenarios' (Bodwell and Chermack, 2010; Van der Heijden, 1996; Wilson, 2000). Others argue that organizations should stage regular reviews, and realign strategic plans to match the altered circumstances. This is usually accomplished by going through the planning cycle every year and adapting strategic plans to fit with the new forecasts.

The strategic planning perspective shares many of the assumptions underlying the analytic reasoning perspective discussed in Chapter 2. Both perspectives value systematic, orderly, consistent, logical reasoning and assume that humans are capable of forming a fairly good understanding of reality. And both are based on a calculative and optimizing view of strategy-making. It is, therefore, not surprising that many managers who are rationally inclined also exhibit a distinct preference for the strategic planning perspective.

EXHIBIT 7.2   THE STRATEGIC PLANNING PERSPECTIVE

KOOYMAN: BUILDING ISLANDS

For three generations now, Kooyman has been building much of the Caribbean islands. Doing business with big do-it-yourself stores for building materials, hardware and home improvement, the Kooyman family business is the largest player on the islands of Curaçao, Bonaire, Aruba and St. Maarten. It has to cope with unique small island economies where logistics require complex knowledge of supply and demand, and where markets are generally small and very mature. With little growth potential and a thoroughly competitive market, Kooyman fends off the challenges that come with operating in island economies by efficiency and good planning.

The company's planning used to follow a straightforward yearly procedure. Kooyman's board of directors updated their analysis of the current and future situation and changed strategic directions accordingly. The company's middle management then had to carry out a sanity check. This yearly update was subsequently translated by board members and middle management into more practical action plans. There was one problem though: with little public information on island economics available, assumptions on business environments and customers are often not accurate enough, and strategic planning turns out to be less than effective. In order to connect better to the wishes and expectations of Kooyman's customers, the company decided to bring its planning process to a next level.

Because middle management is closer to consumer's needs, Kooyman's CEO Herbert van der Woude has decided to involve them more closely when creating the company's yearly plans. Middle management first outlines its understanding of the current situation, emphasizing Kooyman's strengths and weaknesses, and then proposes its desired future for the company. The inputs are being discussed by the board of directors and related to other available sources, and then consolidated in the strategic plan. In a joint meeting with middle management, the board explains how and why their inputs are being included or not, and what future objectives have been decided on. Since the inputs from the middle management form the basis for the company's assumptions, Kooyman's new planning procedure manages to create more robust strategic plans that are also more widely embraced among the firm's management. One result of this strategy process has been the key finding of middle management – based on customer meetings – that another strategic pillar needs to be developed: customers want Kooyman to engage in e-tailing.

However, the tricky part with e-tailing strategies is that these are extremely hard to plan. In Kooyman's case, this is even more so. Although e-tailing has similarities with the company's core competences, such as logistics, it also requires several as yet underdeveloped internet-related skills. In addition, e-tailing on an island is even more difficult to establish. Since deep market knowledge, complex logistics channels and strategic alliances with suppliers are necessary to operate on Kooyman's islands, Amazon and Ali Baba do not actively operate there. This means that Kooyman possesses a competitive advantage, but also that the firm has few examples to get inspired by.

In order to deal with the difficulty of incorporating e-tailing in its planning, Kooyman decided to push a similar strategy as it did with its corporate strategy: focus on what customers want and expect. The firm therefore decided to create customer panels, divided into key customer segments, and asked them how they experience different aspects of the Kooyman experience. From here the company deduces what is required to improve and expand upon this experience through online means. Kooyman then makes use of its regular strategic planning process to define what has to be carried out exactly and how to do so efficiently.

Kooyman shows the merits of strategic planning in small island economies due to their static nature. In this context it is more difficult to imitate partnerships, logistics channels and the indispensable deep market knowledge. To properly channel this knowhow into appropriate action, the company's middle management got a leading role in the strategy formation process. This leads to planning more in accordance with customers' expectations, ensuring Kooyman can continue to assist islanders building and improving houses for years to come.

Co-authors: Jasper de Vries and Wester Wagenaar

Source: Company information.

The strategic incrementalism perspective

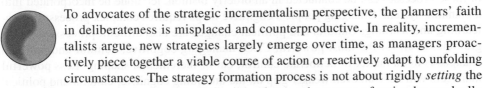

To advocates of the strategic incrementalism perspective, the planners' faith in deliberateness is misplaced and counterproductive. In reality, incrementalists argue, new strategies largely emerge over time, as managers proactively piece together a viable course of action or reactively adapt to unfolding circumstances. The strategy formation process is not about rigidly *setting* the course of action in advance, but about flexibly *shaping* the course of action by gradually blending together initiatives into a coherent pattern of actions. Making strategy involves sense-making, reflecting, learning, envisioning, experimenting and changing the organization, which cannot be neatly organized and programmed. Strategy formation is messy, fragmented and piecemeal – much more like the unstructured and unpredictable processes of exploration and invention than like the orderly processes of design and production (e.g. Mintzberg, 1990; Quinn, 1978).

Yet proponents of the strategic planning perspective prefer to press strategy formation into an orderly, mechanistic straightjacket. Strategies must be intentionally designed and executed. According to strategic incrementalists, this excessive emphasis on deliberateness is due to planners' obsession with rationality and control (e.g. Mintzberg, 1993; Wildavsky, 1979). Planners are often compulsive in their desire for order, predictability and efficiency. It is the intention of strategic planning to predict, analyse, optimize and programme – to deliberately fine-tune and control the organization's future behaviour. For them, 'to manage' is 'to control' and therefore only deliberate patterns of action constitute good strategic management.

Incrementalists do not question the value of planning and control as a means for managing some organizational processes, but point out that strategy formation is not one of them. In general, planning and control are valuable for routine activities that need to be efficiently organized (e.g. production or finance). But planning is less suitable for non-routine activities – that is, for doing new things. Planning is not appropriate for innovation (e.g. Hamel, 1996; Kanter, 2002). Just as R&D departments cannot plan the invention of new products, managers cannot plan the development of new strategies. Innovation, whether in products or strategies, is not a process that can be neatly structured and controlled. Novel insights and creative ideas cannot be generated on demand, but surface at unexpected moments, often in unexpected places. Neither are new ideas born fully grown, ready to be evaluated and implemented. In reality, innovation requires brooding, tinkering, experimentation, testing and patience, as new ideas grow and take shape. Throughout the innovation process it remains unclear which ideas might evolve into blockbuster strategies and which will turn out to be miserable disappointments. No one can objectively determine ahead of time which strategic initiatives will 'fly' and which will 'crash'. Therefore, managers engaged in the formation of new strategies must move incrementally, letting novel ideas crystallize over time, and increasing commitment as ideas gradually prove their viability in practice. This demands that managers behave not as planners, but as 'inventors' – searching, experimenting, learning, doubting and avoiding premature closure and lock-in to one course of action (e.g. Beinhocker, 1999; Stacey, 1993).

Recognizing that strategy formation is essentially an innovation process has more consequences. Innovation is inherently subversive, rebelling against the status quo and challenging those who are emotionally, intellectually or politically wedded to the current state of affairs. Creating new strategies involves confronting people's cognitive maps, questioning the organizational culture, threatening individuals' current interests and disrupting the distribution of power within the organization (e.g. Hamel, 1996; Johnson, 1988). None of these processes can be conducted in an orderly fashion, let alone be incorporated into a planning system. Changing people's cognitive maps requires complex processes of unlearning and learning. Cultural and political changes are also difficult processes to programme. Even for the most powerful CEO, managing cognitive, cultural and political changes is not a matter of deliberate control, but of incremental shaping. Less powerful managers will have an even weaker grip on the unfolding cognitive, cultural and political reality in their organization and therefore will be even less able to plan. In short, managers who understand that strategy formation is essentially a disruptive process of organizational change will move incrementally, gradually moulding the organization into a satisfactory form. This demands that managers behave not as commanders, but as 'organizational developers' – questioning assumptions, challenging ideas, getting points on the strategic agenda, encouraging learning, championing new initiatives, supporting change and building political support.

Incrementalists point out that planning is particularly inappropriate when dealing with wicked problems. While solving tame problems can often be planned and controlled, strategizing managers rarely have the luxury of using generic solutions to fix clearly recognizable strategic problems. Strategic problems are inherently wicked – they are essentially unique, highly complex, linked to other problems, can be defined and interpreted in many ways, and have neither a correct answer nor a delimited set of possible solutions. The planning approach of recognizing the problem, fully analysing the situation, formulating a comprehensive plan and then implementing the solution, is sure to choke on a wicked problem. A number of weaknesses of planning show up when confronted with a wicked problem:

- Problems cannot be simply recognized and analysed, but can be interpreted and defined in many ways, depending on how the manager looks at them. Therefore, half the work of the strategizing manager is *making sense* out of complex problems. Or, as Rittel and Webber (1973) put it, the definition of a wicked problem is the problem! Managers must search for new ways for understanding old problems and must be aware of how others are reinterpreting what they see (e.g. Liedtka, 2000; Smircich and Stubbart, 1985). This inhibits strategic planning and encourages strategic incrementalism.

- A full analysis of a wicked problem is impossible. Due to a wicked problem's complexity and links to other problems, a full analysis would take, literally, forever. And there would always be more ways of interpreting the problem, requiring more analysis. Strategic planning based on the complete understanding of a problem in advance therefore necessarily leads to paralysis by analysis (e.g. Langley, 1995; Lenz and Lyles, 1985). In reality, however, managers move proactively despite their incomplete understanding of a wicked problem, learning as they go along. By acting and thinking at the same time, strategizing managers can focus their analyses on what seems to be important and realistic in practice, gradually shaping their understanding along the way.

- Developing a comprehensive plan to tackle a wicked problem is asking for trouble. Wicked problems are very complex, consisting of many sub-problems. Formulating a master plan to solve all sub-problems in one blow would require a very high level of planning sophistication and an organization with the ability to implement plans in a highly coordinated manner – much like circus performers who can keep 10 plates twirling at the ends of poles at the same time. Such organizations are rare at best, and the risk of a grand strategy failing is huge – once one plate falls, the rest usually come crashing down. This is also known as Knagg's law: the more complex a plan, the larger the chance of failure. Incrementalists therefore argue that it is wiser to tackle sub-problems individually, and gradually blend these solutions into a cohesive pattern of action.

■ Planners who believe that formulation and implementation can be separated underestimate the extent to which wicked problems are interactive. As soon as an organization starts to implement a plan, its actions will induce counteractions. Customers will react, competitors will change behaviour, suppliers will take a different stance, regulatory agencies might come into action, unions will respond, the stock markets will take notice and company employees will draw conclusions. Hence, action by the organization will change the nature of the problem. And since the many counterparties are intelligent players capable of acting strategically, their responses will not be entirely predictable. Planners will not be able to forecast and incorporate other parties' reactions into the plans. Therefore, plans will be outdated as soon as implementation starts. For this reason, incrementalists argue that action must always be swiftly followed by redefinition of the problem and reconsideration of the course of action being pursued. Over time, this iterative process of action–reaction–reconsideration will lead to the emergence of a pattern of action, which is the best possible result given the interactive nature of wicked problems.

■ This last point, on the unpredictability of external and internal reactions to a plan, leads to a weakness of strategic planning that is possibly its most obvious one – strategy has to do with the future and the future is inherently *unknown*. Developments cannot be clearly forecast, future opportunities and threats cannot be predicted, neither can future strengths and weaknesses be accurately foreseen. In such unknown terrain, it is foolhardy to commit oneself to a preset course of action unless absolutely necessary. It makes much more sense in new and unpredictable circumstances to remain flexible and adaptive, postponing fixed commitments for as long as possible. An unknown future requires not the mentality of a train conductor, but of an explorer – curious, probing, venturesome and entrepreneurial, yet moving cautiously, step by step, ready to shift course when needed.

To proponents of the strategic incrementalism perspective, it is a caricature to call such behaviour *ad hoc* or muddling through. Rather, it is behaviour that acknowledges the fact that strategy formation is a process of innovation and organizational development in the face of wicked problems in an unknown future. Under these circumstances, strategies must be allowed to emerge and 'strategic planning' must be seen for what it is – a contradiction in terms.

EXHIBIT 7.3 THE STRATEGIC INCREMENTALISM PERSPECTIVE

PIXAR: 'GOING FROM SUCK TO NON-SUCK'

From its early beginnings with *Toy Story* all the way to its latest movie iteration *Finding Dory*, Pixar has consistently churned out blockbusters. All of its 17 movies to date have been remarkable successes at the box office and most have been highly praised by critics all over the world. One of the key factors contributing to the unblemished record of Pixar's movies is the company's emergent strategy. The assumption that the first ideas on new products are likely to be wrong or incomplete is embedded in the way Pixar approaches its movies. Pixar co-founder and President Ed Catmull refers to this as 'going from suck to non-suck'.

Hollywood generally approaches film productions with deliberate planning. The work begins with a script, after which resources are devoted to the project and studios produce the movie. This can work out fine, but there is also a real possibility it leads to mediocrity or flops. When problems arise while creating the film, usually more money is used to solve it. Pixar's answer? As Andrew Stanton, director of *Finding Nemo* and *WALL-E*, puts it: 'Be wrong as fast as we can, which basically means, we're gonna screw up, let's just admit that. Let's not be afraid of that'.

Pixar thus does not initiate new movies with a script. Instead, ideas start with rough story ideas. Small 'incubation teams' work with directors to find holes in these ideas and to refine them. Then storyboards are made and extensively revised. These get developed and thousands of problems are met and dealt with on the way. As a result, Pixar used an astounding 43,536 storyboards for *Finding Nemo*, 69,562 for *Ratatouille* and 98,173 for *WALL-E*. The storyboards are then converted into story reels, improved storyboards with a voice track. Here feedback and iteration also play a key role. According to Catmull, 'Every time we show a film for the first time, it sucks', but the comments people provide to the director make sure substantial changes are made throughout the moviemaking process. If a project manages to pass through all of Pixar's internal processes, it moves to the costly digital animation phase. This is how the studio can continue to breed original movies that 'would all fail an elevator pitch', but still end up as multimillion blockbusters.

Sometimes this constant struggle for 'non-suck' can result in painful decisions, but even these can end on a happy note. The cancellation of the movie *Newt* is an example of this process. The idea of this film, which was supposed to come out in 2011, did not seem to work and the project was given to someone else to direct. Pete Docter, director of *Up*, took it up but completely turned it around. This ultimately resulted in a completely different film altogether: the critically acclaimed 2015 hit *Inside Out*, Pixar's take on human emotions.

Of course, Pixar's way of operating is slow; creating one movie can easily take more than five years. Even then, as chief creative officer of Pixar John Lasseter states, 'We don't actually finish our films, we release them'. Pixar's successful emergent strategy follows the same idea.

Co-author: Wester Wagenaar

Sources: Ed Catmull, 'Creativity, Inc.: Overcoming the unseen forces that stand in the way of true inspiration', 2014; *Fast Company*, 19 March 2014; *Forbes*, 11 September 2014; *Innoblog*, 6 April 2011.

MANAGING THE PARADOX OF DELIBERATENESS AND EMERGENCE

Those who triumph compute at their headquarters a great number of factors prior to a challenge. Little computation brings defeat. How much more so with no computation at all!

Sun Tzu (5th century BCE), Chinese military strategist

So, how should strategies be formed in practice? Should managers strive to formulate and implement strategic plans, supported by a formalized planning and control system? Or should managers move incrementally, behaving as inventors, organizational developers and explorers? (See Table 7.1).

TABLE 7.1   Strategic planning versus strategic incrementalism perspective

	Strategic planning perspective	Strategic incrementalism perspective
Emphasis on	Deliberateness over emergence	Emergence over deliberateness
Nature of strategy	Intentionally designed	Gradually shaped
Nature of formation	Figuring out	Finding out
View of future	Forecast and anticipate	Partially unknown and unpredictable
Posture towards the future	Make commitments, prepare	Postpone commitments, remain flexible
Formation process	Formally structured and comprehensive	Unstructured and fragmented
Formation process steps	First think, then act	Thinking and acting intertwined
Decision-making	Hierarchical	Dispersed
Decision-making focus	Optimal resource allocation and coordination	Experimentation and parallel initiatives
Implementation focused on	Programming (organizational efficiency)	Learning (organizational development)
Strategic change	Implemented top-down	Requires broad cultural and cognitive shifts

No consensus has yet developed within the field of strategic management on how to manage deliberateness and emergence, which is understandable as it – among other things such as personal and culture differences (see also the next paragraph on the international perspective) – depends on the company's context. For example, strategy formation in hypercompetitive and stable environments will differ significantly. Yet, a number of suggestions have been made by scholars in the strategy and organizational behaviour fields. Taking the taxonomy in Chapter 1, the following options can be considered.

Balancing

In balancing opposite demands, elements of the opposing demands are traded off to find the most appropriate balance. The demand for deliberate strategizing and strategy emergence often differ over departments within the organization; depending on the organizational unit's primary process (see Chapter 4). Within business units, production departments are generally more planning oriented, product development units take a more incremental process and research and development takes a bit of both.

In large organizations, the strategy process not only differs over departments but also between the business units. Strategists of business units that are active in stable industries prefer deliberateness over emergence, while in hypercompetitive industries the reverse occurs. The balance between demands in large firms also depends on the firm's perspective on corporate level strategy: in portfolio organizations more variety of strategy processes can be noticed than in integrated organizations (see Chapter 5).

Balancing the paradox of deliberateness and emergence can also be institutionalized into a formal process. Popular in many organizations is the scenario process. This method, popularized by Royal/Dutch Shell, intentionally combines elements of deliberateness and emergence. It is a formal process, but by developing multiple scenarios and providing opportunity for intuitive and entrepreneurial inputs, it provides a balanced approach to strategy formation.

Juxtaposing

From the perspective of a business level manager the paradox of deliberateness and emergence is managed by balancing the two opposite demands; however, a corporate level manager needs to engage in different strategy formation processes. Apart from participating in the corporate strategy process, the strategizing manager is also involved in formation processes in other corporate units – divisions and business units – and company-wide initiatives, international activities and *ad hoc* projects. Being engaged in such a variety of processes the strategizing manager needs to be juxtaposing, managing opposites or different blends simultaneously. This requires specific dynamic capabilities (Teece, 2007; Teece, Pisano and Shuen, 1997).

In professional firms, the situation for strategists complicates even further. Managing a professional firm is one thing, delivering services is yet another. With multiple clients, professionals need flexibility to juxtapose between clients and their own firm. For example, King (2008) reports that venture capitalists are 'bifurcated strategists', using planning for their portfolio companies, while using emergent strategies on their own behalf.

STRATEGY FORMATION IN INTERNATIONAL PERSPECTIVE

Co-authors: Gep Eisenloeffel and Wester Wagenaar

What we anticipate seldom occurs; what we least expect generally happens.

Benjamin Disraeli (1804–1881), British prime minister and novelist

Whether there are specific national preferences for the strategic planning or the strategic incrementalism perspective seems like a legitimate question, yet it is not often asked. It has generally been assumed that international differences are a non-issue, but the few international comparative studies that have been carried out – albeit not conducted recently – suggest the opposite. There are also studies suggesting international similarities, most notably when it comes to the size of firms. Of course, the position of a strategist is not only bound by the international or industrial playing field and there is variance among individuals as well. Nevertheless, it is important for a strategist to take heed of differences in order to best understand strategy across countries and industries.

On the national level

Among others, international comparative studies show significantly different levels of formal planning across various industrialized countries. Planning was found to be the most common and most formalized in the United States, with other English-speaking countries – Australia, Britain, Canada and New Zealand respectively – also exhibiting a high score

(Steiner and Schollhammer, 1975). The popularity of formal planning systems in these societies seems odd, given their high level of individualism and strong preference for a market economy. One might expect that the English-speaking countries' fondness of unplanned markets would be a reflection of a general dislike of planning. Yet, so concludes Ohmae, strangely 'most large US corporations are run like the Soviet economy' of yesteryear, emphasizing central planning and top-down control (1982, p. 224). One explanation for this behaviour is a strong labour division. Nowhere in the industrialized world, with the exception of France, has there been a stronger development of a distinct managerial class than in the English-speaking countries (Hampden-Turner and Trompenaars, 1993; Lessem and Neubauer, 1994). In the division of labour, managers are the officers who formulate the strategies and the workforce concentrates their efforts on implementing them. The general preference for planning, however, is typically limited to the predictable, not-too-distant future. As such, English-speaking countries belong to the category of short-term oriented cultures (Hofstede, 1993).

At the other extreme, according to the research by Steiner and Schollhammer (1975), are Italy and Japan. Here, very little formal planning was witnessed and, in the case of Japan, the low propensity to engage in formalized strategic planning has been noted by a number of others as well (e.g. Kagono *et al.*, 1985). Hayashi (1978) remarks that Japanese firms 'distrust corporate planning in general', while Ohmae (1982) characterizes Japanese companies as 'less planned, less rigid, but more vision- and mission-driven' than their Western counterparts. Japanese giants Canon, Honda and Komatsu did not commit to long-term plans for global leadership positions, instead prioritizing 'strategic intent' over strategic planning (Hamel and Prahalad, 2005).

Preferences for different *types* of internal control and related organizational models have been discussed above, yet countries can also differ with regard to the *level* of internal control their citizens favour. In some societies, people have a strong desire for order and structure, with clear tasks, responsibilities, power rules and procedures. Ambiguous situations and uncertain outcomes are shunned and therefore management strives to control organizational processes. Management can reduce uncertainty in a number of ways. Structure can be offered by strictly following traditions or by imposing top-down paternalistic rule. Uncertainty can also be reduced by planning (Kagono *et al.*, 1985; Schneider, 1989). By setting direction, coordinating initiatives, committing resources and programming activities, structure can be brought to the organization. In societies that are more tolerant towards ambiguity and uncertainty, one can expect a weaker preference for planning.

It is not only preferences for internal control that can have an impact on inclinations towards certain views on strategy formation; societies also differ with regard to the level of control they wish to have over their environment. At the one extreme are countries in which people strive to manage or even dominate their surroundings. The consequence is that organizations in these nations are drawn to proactive and deliberate strategy-making, under the motto 'plan or be planned for' (Ackoff, 1981). This characteristic is particularly pronounced in Western countries (Trompenaars and Hampden-Turner, 2012). At the other extreme are fatalistic cultures in which most people passively accept their destiny. As people here approach opportunities and threats reactively on a day-to-day basis, this muddling rarely leads to successful emergent strategies but can be characterized more as disjointed, unpatterned action. In between are societies where people accept that events are unpredictable and that the environment cannot be tightly controlled, yet trust that individuals and organizations can proactively seek and pave their own path. This requires firms to 'develop an attitude of receptivity and high adaptability to changing conditions' (Maruyama, 1984).

This way of thinking is particularly pronounced in South-East Asia, and leads towards a stronger inclination towards the strategic incrementalism perspective (Kagono *et al.*, 1985; Schneider, 1989)

On the industry level

Theoretical studies on strategy emergence are plentiful, but empirical data remain scarce. As such, there has been little research confirming industry preferences for strategic incrementalism or strategic planning. Nevertheless, some studies have suggested that generalizations can be made on the impact of the size of firms; the strategy process in smaller companies is mainly emergent (e.g. Harris, Forbes and Fletcher, 2000). In small and medium sized enterprises (SMEs) emergent strategies are particularly important regarding product and market-related decisions (Leitner, 2014). Industries where the majority of incumbents are SMEs can be expected to have a higher tendency towards emergent strategy formation. In contrast, strategic development in large firms has traditionally been described as more planned at the higher echelons, with middle managers functioning more as the facilitators of emergent strategies (e.g. Wooldridge and Floyd, 1990).

To the strategist

As previously highlighted, there is international variance when it comes to the degree to which people aim to regulate the environment, but individual propensities also play a role. Strategy formation is the interplay between two forces: an unstable environment and an organizational operating system seeking to stabilize. The role of leadership is to mediate between the two and enforce a correct strategy (Mintzberg, 1978). Yet, because the understanding of the surroundings is subjectable to perceptions and interpretations, the disposition of a strategist has a significant impact on strategy formation (Schneider, 1989). The strategist should be aware of his own preferences and those of others around him. In the international playing field, such as at an international company with multiple subsidiaries, it is particularly important to be aware of differing international preferences and act accordingly.

STRATEGIC CHANGE

8

Alteration, movement without rest, Flowing through the six empty places, Rising and sinking without fixed law, It is only change that is at work here.

I Ching, *Book of Changes* (3rd to 2nd millennium BCE)

INTRODUCTION

In a world of new technologies, transforming economies, shifting demographics, re-forming governments, fluctuating consumer preferences and dynamic competition, it is not a question of whether firms *should* change, but of where, how and in what direction they *must* change. For 'living' organizations, change is a given. Firms must constantly be aligned with their environments, either by reacting to external events, or by proactively shaping the businesses in which they operate.

While change is pervasive, not all change in firms is strategic in nature. Much of the change witnessed is actually the ongoing operational kind. To remain efficient and effective, firms constantly make 'fine-tuning' alterations, whereby existing procedures are upgraded, activities are improved and people are reassigned. Such operational changes are directed at increasing the performance of the firm within the confines of the existing system – within the current basic set-up used to align the firm with the environment. Strategic changes, on the contrary, are directed at creating a new type of alignment – a new fit between the basic set-up of the firm and the characteristics of the environment. Strategic changes have an impact on the way the firm does business (its 'business model') and on the way the organization has been configured (its 'organizational system').

For managers, the challenge is to implement strategic changes on time, to keep the firm in step with the shifting opportunities and threats in the environment. Some parts of the firm's business model and organizational system can be preserved, while others need to be transformed for the firm to stay up to date and competitive. This process of constantly enacting strategic changes to remain in harmony with external conditions is called 'strategic alignment'. This chapter examines the issue of the series of strategic change steps required in order to bring about a process of ongoing strategic alignment.

THE ISSUE OF STRATEGIC ALIGNMENT

There are many actions that constitute a strategic change – a reorganization, a diversification move, a shift in core technology, a business process redesign and a product portfolio reshuffle, to name a few. Each one of these changes is fascinating in itself. Yet, here the discussion will be broader than just a single strategic change, looking instead at the process of how a series of strategic changes can be used to keep the firm in sync with its surroundings (see Figure 8.1). How can 'a path of strategic changes' be followed to constantly align the firm and avoid a situation whereby the firm 'drifts' too far away from the demands of the environment (Johnson, 1988)?

To come to a deeper understanding of the issue of strategic alignment, the first step that must be taken is to examine what is actually being aligned during a process of strategic change. The areas of strategic alignment have been explored in the previous section. After this initial analysis of 'what' is being changed, a distinction will be made between the magnitude and the pace of change. The magnitude of change refers to the size of the steps being undertaken, whereby the question is whether managers should move in bold and dramatic strides, or in moderate and undramatic ones. The pace of change refers to the relative speed at which the steps are being taken, whereby the question is whether managers should move quickly in a short period of time, or more gradually over a longer time span.

Areas of strategic alignment

Firms are complex systems, consisting of many different elements, each of which can be changed. Therefore, to gain more insight into the various areas of potential change, firms need to be analytically disassembled into a number of component parts. The most fundamental distinction that can be made within a firm is between the business model and the organizational system:

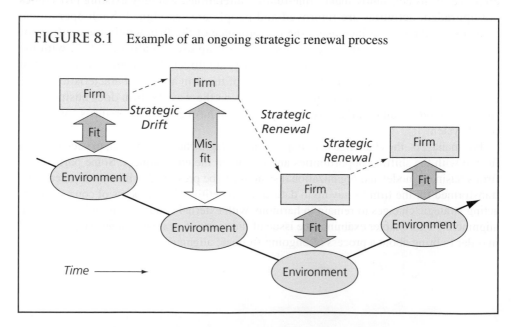

FIGURE 8.1   Example of an ongoing strategic renewal process

■ Business model. The term 'business model' refers to the way a firm conducts its business (for an extensive explanation, see Chapter 4). A simple definition would be 'how a firm makes money'. A more formal definition of a business model is 'the specific configuration of resources, value-adding activities and product/service offerings directed at creating value for customers'. Each firm has its own specific system for taking certain resources as inputs (e.g. materials and know-how), adding value to them in some type of manner (e.g. production and branding) and then selling a particular package of products and/or services as output. As such, a firm's business model (or 'value creation system') is particular to the type of business that the firm is in – an airplane manufacturer conducts its business differently from an airline.

■ Organizational system. The term 'organizational system' refers to the way a firm gets its people to work together to carry out the business. A simple definition would be 'how a firm is organized'. A more formal definition of the organizational system would be 'how the individuals populating a firm have been configured, and relate to one another, with the intention of facilitating the business model'. Every firm needs to determine some type of organizational structure, dividing the tasks and responsibilities among the organizational members, thereby instituting differing functions and units. Firms also require numerous organizational processes to link individual members to each other, to ensure that their separate tasks are coordinated into an integrated whole. Furthermore, firms necessarily have organizational cultures and subcultures, as organizational members interact with one another and build up joint beliefs, values and norms.

In Figure 8.2 the relationship between the business model and the major components of the organizational system is depicted. As this figure illustrates, the business model is 'supported' by the organizational system, with the organizational members 'at its base'. While each firm's business model and organizational system are essentially unique, their general configuration can be fairly similar to that of other firms. Where firms have a comparable business 'formula', it is said that they share the same business model. Likewise, where firms have a similar organizational 'form', they are said to subscribe to the same organizational system.

FIGURE 8.2   General view of the business model and the organizational system

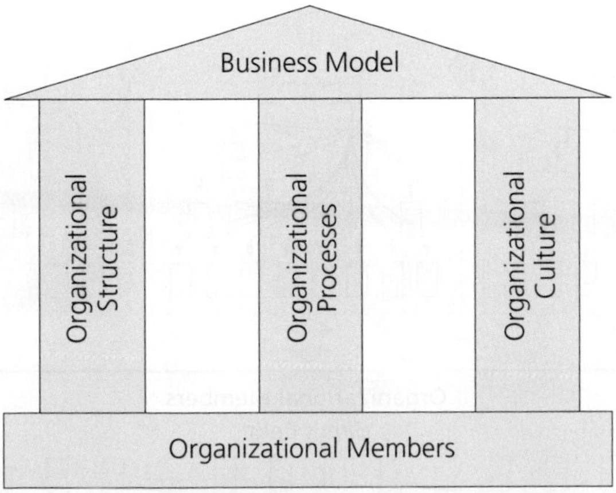

Both the business model and the organizational system can be further disaggregated into component parts and examined in more detail. With this aim in mind, the business model has been at the centre of attention in Chapter 4. In this chapter, the organizational system will be further dissected. Actually, the term 'dissection' conjures up images of the organizational system as 'corporate body', which is a useful metaphor for distinguishing the various components of an organizational system (Morgan, 1986).

Following Bartlett and Ghoshal (1995), the organizational system can be divided into its anatomy (structure), physiology (processes) and psychology (culture). Each of these components, summarized in Figure 8.3, will be examined in the following subsection.

Organizational structure.   Organizational structure refers to the clustering of tasks and people into smaller groups. All organizations need at least some division of labour in order to function efficiently and effectively, requiring them to structure the organization into smaller parts. The main question when determining the organizational structure is which criteria will be used to differentiate tasks and to cluster people into particular units. While there are numerous structuring (or decomposition) criteria, the most common ones are summarized in Figure 8.4. In a simple organization tasks might be divided according to just one criterion, but in most organizations multiple criteria are used (either sequentially or simultaneously).

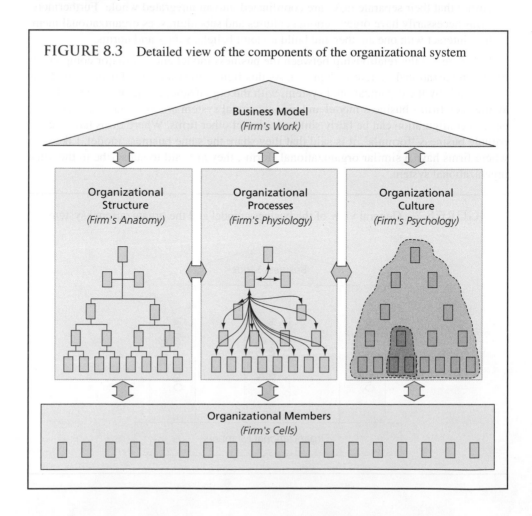

FIGURE 8.3   Detailed view of the components of the organizational system

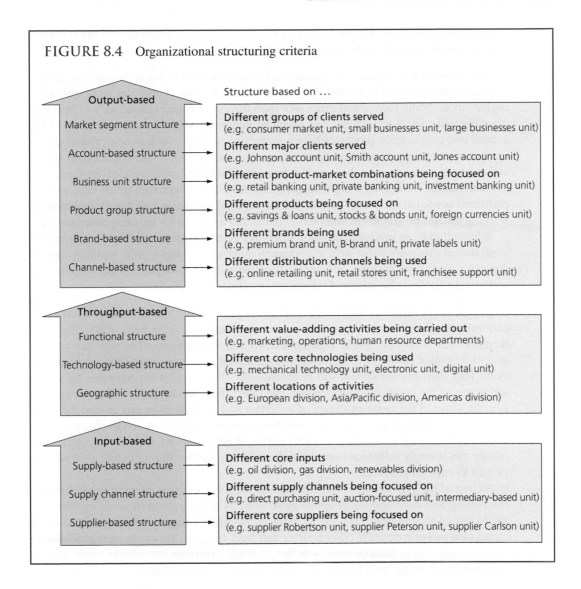

FIGURE 8.4   Organizational structuring criteria

To balance this horizontal differentiation of tasks and responsibilities, all organizations also have integration mechanisms, intended to get the parts to function well within the organizational whole (Lawrence and Lorsch, 1967). While some of these integration mechanisms are found in the categories of organizational processes and culture, the most fundamental mechanism is usually built into the organizational structure – formal authority. In organizations, managers are appointed with the specific task of supervising the activities of various people or units and to report to managers higher up in the hierarchy.

Depending on the span of control of each manager (the number of people or units reporting to her), an organizational structure will consist of one or more layers of management. At the apex of this vertical structure is the board of directors, with the ultimate authority to make decisions or ratify decisions made at lower levels in the hierarchy. The most important questions in this context are the number of management layers needed and the amount of authority delegated to lower levels of management. It should be noted that the organizational charts used to represent the formal structure of an organization (see Figure 8.3) need not be an accurate reflection of the informal organizational structure as it operates in reality.

Organizational processes. Organizational processes refer to the arrangements, procedures and routines used to control and coordinate the various people and units within the organization. Some formalized processes span the entire organization, such as business planning and control procedures, and financial budgeting and reporting processes. Other control and coordination processes have a more limited scope, such as new product development meetings, yearly sales conferences, weekly quality circles, web-based expert panels and quarterly meetings with the board of directors. But not all organizational processes are institutionalized as ongoing integration mechanisms. Often, integration across units and departments is needed for a short period, making it useful to employ task forces, committees, working groups, project teams and even joint lunches as means for ensuring coordination.

While all of these processes are formalized to a certain degree, many more informal organizational processes exist, such as communicating via hallway gossip, building support through personal networking, influencing decision-making through informal negotiations and solving conflicts by means of impromptu meetings.

Organizational culture. Organizational culture refers to the worldview and behavioural patterns shared by the members of the same organization (e.g. Schein, 1985; Trice and Beyer, 1993). As people within a group interact and share experiences with one another over an extended period of time, they construct a joint understanding of the world around them. This shared belief system will be emotionally charged, as it encompasses the values and norms of the organizational members and offers them an interpretive filter with which to make sense of the constant stream of uncertain and ambiguous events around them. As this common ideology grows stronger and becomes more engrained, it will channel members' actions into more narrowly defined patterns of behaviour. As such, the organizational culture can strongly influence everything, from how to behave during meetings to what is viewed as ethical behaviour.

As part of the organizational system, culture can act as a strong integration mechanism, controlling and coordinating people's behaviour, by getting them to abide by 'the way we do things around here'. Having a common 'language', frame of reference and set of values also makes it easier to communicate and work together. However, an organizational culture is not always homogeneous – in fact, strongly divergent subcultures might arise in certain units, creating 'psychological' barriers within the organization.

The magnitude of change

Strategic change is by definition far reaching. We speak of strategic change when fundamental alterations are made to the business model or the organizational system. Adding a lemon-flavoured Coke to the product portfolio was interesting, maybe important, but not a strategic change, while branching out into bottled water was – it was a major departure from Coca-Cola's traditional business model. Hiring a new CEO is also important, but is in itself not a strategic change, while his consequent reorientation towards a new vision is.

Strategic alignment is often even more far-reaching, as a number of strategic changes are executed in a variety of areas to keep the firm aligned with market demands. But while the result of all these strategic changes is far reaching, this says nothing about the size of the steps along the way. The strategic alignment process might consist of a few large change steps or numerous small ones. This distinction is illustrated in Figure 8.5. The total

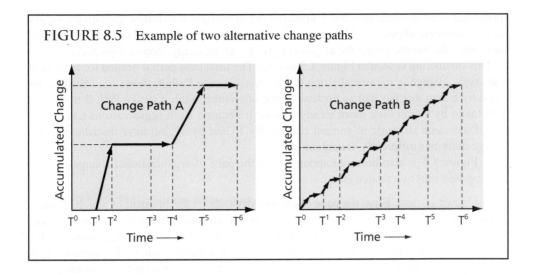

FIGURE 8.5   Example of two alternative change paths

amount of strategic changes envisaged is measured along the Y-axis. Change Path A shows the change path taken by a firm that has implemented all changes in two big steps, while Change Path B shows the change path followed by a firm taking numerous smaller steps. Both organizations have completed the same alignment, but via distinctly different routes.

The size of the change steps is referred to as the magnitude of change. This issue of change magnitude can be divided into two component parts:

- Scope of change. The scope of change in a firm can vary from broad to narrow. Change is broad when many aspects and parts of the firm are aligned at the same time. In the most extreme case the changes might be comprehensive, whereby the business model is entirely revised, and the organizational structure, processes, culture and people are changed in unison. However, change can also be much more narrowly focused on a specific organizational aspect (e.g. new product development processes) or department (e.g. marketing). If many changes are narrowly targeted, the total result will be a more piecemeal change process.

- Amplitude of organizational changes. The amplitude of change in firms can vary from high to low. The amplitude of change is high when the new business model, organizational culture, structure, processes or people are a radical departure from the previous situation. The amplitude of change is low when the step proposed is a moderate adjustment to the previous circumstances.

Where a change is comprehensive and radical, the magnitude of the change step is large. In Figure 8.5, this is represented as a large jump along the Y-axis. Where a change is narrow and moderate, the magnitude of the step is small. However, the above distinction also clarifies that there are two rather different types of medium sized change step – a focused radical change (narrow scope, high amplitude) and a comprehensive moderate change (broad scope, low amplitude). Both changes are 'mid-sized', yet significantly different to manage in practice.

The pace of change

Strategic alignment takes time. Yet, there are a variety of ways by which the strategic alignment process can take place over time. Strategic change measures can be evenly spread out over an extended period, allowing the organization to follow a relatively steady pace of strategic alignment. However, it is also possible to cluster all changes into a few short irregular bursts, giving the alignment process an unsteady, stop-and-go pace.

This distinction is seen in Figure 8.5 as well. The total time period needed for achieving a strategic change is measured along the X-axis. Change Path A shows the change path taken by a firm that has had an unsteady pace of change, while Change Path B tracks the path taken by a firm on a more steady change trajectory. Both organizations have completed the same strategic alignment process by T^3 and by T^6, but have distributed their change activities differently during the period.

In Figure 8.5, it also becomes apparent that the pace of organizational changes can be decomposed into two related parts:

- Timing of change. First, the pace of change depends on the moment at which changes are initiated. The timing of change can vary from intermittent to constant. Where change is intermittent, it is important for a firm to determine the right moment for launching a new initiative (for example, T^1 and T^4 in Change Path A). The need to 'wait for the right timing' is often a reason for spreading change activities unevenly over time. However, change can be constant, so that the exact moment for kicking off any new set of measures is less important, as long as there is no peak at any one moment in time (see Change Path B).

- Speed of change. The pace of change also depends on the time span within which changes take place. The speed of change can vary from high to low. Where a major change needs to be implemented within a short period of time, the speed of change must be high. A short burst of fast action can bring about the intended changes. In Figure 8.5, the speed can be seen by the slope of the arrow (in Change Path A, the speed between T^1 and T^2 is higher than between T^4 and T^5). By contrast, where the change measures are less formidable and the time span for implementation is longer, the speed of change can be lower.

The variables of timing and speed of change, together with the variables of scope and amplitude of change, create a wide range of possible strategic alignment paths. Firms have many different ways of bringing about strategic change. Unavoidably, this raises the question of which route is best. Why should a firm choose one trajectory over another?

THE PARADOX OF REVOLUTION AND EVOLUTION

It is not the strongest of the species that survive, nor the most intelligent, but the one most responsive to change.

Charles Darwin (1809–1882), English naturalist

In selecting an approach to strategic change, most managers struggle with the question of how bold they should be. On the one hand, they usually realize that to fundamentally transform the organization, a break with the past is needed. To achieve strategic alignment, it is essential to turn away from the firm's heritage and to start with a clean slate. On the other hand, they also recognize the value of continuity, building on past experiences, investments and loyalties. To achieve lasting strategic alignment, people in the organization will need time to learn, adapt and grow into a new organizational reality.

This distinction between disruptive change and gradual change has long been recognized in the strategic management and organizational behaviour literature (e.g. Greiner, 1972; Tushman and O'Reilly, 1996). Disruptive change is variably referred to as 'frame-breaking' (e.g. Baden-Fuller and Stopford, 1992; Grinyer, Mayes and McKiernan, 1987), 'radical' (e.g. Greenwood and Hinings, 1996; Stinchcombe, 1965) and 'revolutionary' (e.g. Gersick, 1991; Tushman, Newman and Romanelli, 1986). Gradual change is variably referred to as 'incremental' (e.g. Johnson, 1987; Quinn, 1980) and 'evolutionary' (e.g. Nelson and Winter, 1982; Tushman and O'Reilly, 1996). Here the labels revolutionary and evolutionary change will be used, in keeping with the terminology used by Greiner (1972) in his classic work.

It is widely accepted among researchers that firms need to balance revolutionary and evolutionary change processes. However, most authors see this as a balancing of strategic (revolutionary) change and operational (evolutionary) change. As strategic change is far reaching, it is often automatically equated with radical means, while gradual means are reserved for smaller scale operational changes. Yet, in the previous section it was made clear that a radical result (a strategic change) can be pursued by both revolutionary and evolutionary means (e.g. Hayes, 1985; Krüger, 1996; Nonaka, 1988; Strebel, 1994).

While these two change processes are each other's opposites, and they seem to be at least partially contradictory, both approaches are needed within firms. In practice both change processes have valuable, yet conflicting, qualities. The tension that this creates between revolution and evolution will be explored in the following sections.

The demand for revolutionary change processes

Revolution is a process whereby an abrupt and radical change takes place within a short period of time. Revolutionary change processes are those that do not build on the status quo, but overthrow it. 'Revolutionaries' revolt against the existing business model and organizational system and attempt to push through changes that will reinvent the firm. Thus, revolution leads to a clear break with the past – a discontinuity in the firm's development path.

Such a 'big bang' approach to strategic change is generally needed when organizational rigidity is so deeply rooted that smaller pushes do not bring the firm into movement. If the firm threatens to become paralysed by these inherited rigidities in the business model and organizational system, the only way to get moving can be to radically break with the past. Typical sources of organizational rigidity include:

- Psychological resistance to change. Many people resist change because of the uncertainty and ambiguity that unavoidably accompanies any shift in the old way of doing business (e.g. Argyris, 1990; Pondy, Boland and Thomas, 1988). As people become accustomed to fixed organizational routines and established habits, their ability to learn and gradually adapt invariably recedes. New business methods or job descriptions are not seen as a challenging opportunity to learn, but as an unwelcome interference in the existing system. It can be necessary to break through this psychological resistance to change by imposing a new business model and/or organizational system on people (e.g. Hammer, 1990; Powell, 1991).

- Cultural resistance to change. As discussed in Chapter 2, people can easily become immune to signals that their cognitive maps are outdated, especially if they are surrounded by others with the same flawed belief system. Once an organizational culture develops that perpetuates a number of obsolete assumptions about the market or the organization, it is very difficult for organizational members to challenge and gradually reshape the organizational belief system. It can be necessary to break through this cultural resistance to change by exposing the organization to a shocking crisis or by imposing a new organizational system (e.g. Senge, 1990; Tushman, Newman and Romanelli, 1986).

- Political resistance to change. Change is hardly ever to everyone's advantage. Each organizational change leads to a different constellation of winners and losers. Generally, the potential losers reject a strategic change, although they are likely to think of some seemingly objective reasons for their opposition. Even a situation in which a person or department thinks that it might run the risk of losing power to others can be enough to block a change. Since strategic changes invariably have a significant impact on all people within an organization, there will always be a number of open and hidden opponents. It can be necessary to break through this political resistance by imposing a new business model and reshuffling management positions (e.g. Allison, 1969; Krüger, 1996).

- Investment lock-in. Once a firm has committed a large amount of money and time to a certain product portfolio, activity system or technology, it will find that this fixed investment locks the organization in. Any gradual movement away from the past investment will increase the risk of not earning back the sunk cost. Therefore, it can be necessary to break through the lock-in by radically restructuring or disposing of the investment (e.g. Bower and Christensen, 1995; Ghemawat, 1991).

- Competence lock-in. The better a firm becomes at something, the more a firm becomes focused on becoming even better still – which is also known as the virtuous circle of competence-building. Once a competitive advantage has been built on a particular type of competence, the natural tendency of firms is to favour external opportunities based on these competences. New people are hired that fit the corporate competence profile and R&D spending further hones the firm's skill. But if the firm's competence base threatens to become outdated due to market or technological changes, its former advantage could become its downfall – the firm could become caught in a vicious 'competence trap', unable to gradually shift the organization to an alternative set of competences, because the entire business model and organizational system have been aligned to the old set (e.g. Leonard-Barton, 1995; Teece, Pisano and Shuen, 1997). Changing the core competence of the corporation in a comprehensive and radical manner can be the only way to 'migrate' from one competence profile to another.

- Systems lock-in. Firms can also become locked into an open standard (e.g. sizes in inches, GAAP accounting rules) or a proprietary system (e.g. Windows operating system, SAP enterprise resource planning software). Once the firm has implemented a standard or system, switching to another platform cannot be done gradually or at low cost. Therefore, the lock-in can usually only be overcome by a big bang transition to another platform (e.g. Arthur, 1996; Shapiro and Varian, 1998).

- Stakeholder lock-in. Highly restrictive commitments can also be made towards the firm's stakeholders. Long-term contracts with buyers and suppliers, warranties, commitments to governments and local communities and promises to shareholders can all lock firms into a certain strategic direction. To break through the stakeholders' resistance to change, it can be necessary to court a crisis and aim for a radical restructuring of the firm's external relationships (e.g. Freeman, 1984; Oliver, 1991).

Besides the use of revolutionary change to overcome organizational rigidity, such a radical approach to strategic alignment is often also necessary given the short time span available for a large change. The 'window of opportunity' for achieving a strategic change can be small for a number of reasons. Some of the most common triggers for revolutionary strategic change are:

- Competitive pressure. When a firm is under intense competitive pressure and its market position starts to erode quickly, a rapid and dramatic response might be the only approach possible. Especially when the organization threatens to slip into a downward spiral towards insolvency, a bold turnaround can be the only option left to the firm.

- Regulatory pressure. Firms can also be put under pressure by the government or regulatory agencies to push through major changes within a short period of time. Such externally imposed revolutions can be witnessed among public sector organizations (e.g. hospitals and schools) and highly regulated industries (e.g. banks and utilities), but in other sectors of the economy as well (e.g. antitrust break-ups, public health regulations).

- First mover advantage. A more proactive reason for instigating revolutionary change is to be the first firm to introduce a new product, service or technology and to build up barriers to entry for late movers. Especially for know-how that is dissipation sensitive, or for which the patent period is limited, it can be important to cash in quickly before others arrive on the market (e.g. Kessler and Chakrabarthi, 1996; Lieberman and Montgomery, 1988, 1998).

To some extent all managers recognize that their organizations are prone to inertia, and most will acknowledge that it is often vital to move quickly, either in response to external pressures or to cash in on a potential first mover advantage. It should therefore come as no surprise that most managers would like their organizations to have the ability to successfully pull off revolutionary strategic changes.

The demand for evolutionary change processes

Evolution is a process whereby a constant stream of moderate changes gradually accumulates over a longer period of time. Each change is in itself small, but the cumulative result can be large. Evolutionary change processes take the current firm as a starting point, constantly modifying aspects through extension and adaptation. Some 'mutations' to the firm prove valuable and are retained, while other changes are discarded as dysfunctional. Thus, a new business model and/or organizational system can steadily evolve out of the old, as if the organization were shedding its old skin to grow a new one (e.g. Aldrich, 1999; Kagono *et al.,* 1985).

This 'metamorphosis' approach to strategic change is particularly important where the strategic alignment hinges on widespread organizational learning. Learning is not a process that is easily compressed into a few short bursts of activity (as anyone who has studied knows). Learning is a relatively slow process, whereby know-how is accumulated over an extended period of time. It can take years to learn things, especially if the necessary knowledge is not readily available but must be acquired 'on the job' (e.g. Argyris, 1990; Senge, 1990). This is true for both individuals and firms. When groups of people in a firm need to develop new routines, new competences, new processes, as well as new ways of understanding the world, time is needed to experiment, reflect, discuss, test and internalize. Even in the circumstances where individuals or departments are merely asked to adjust their behaviours to new norms, the learning process is often protracted and difficult (e.g. Nelson and Winter, 1982; Pfeffer and Sutton, 1999).

While the evolutionary nature of learning is a positive factor stimulating gradual change, the organizational reality is often also that power is too dispersed for revolutionary changes to be imposed on the firm. Where no one has enough sway in the organization to push through radical changes, a more evolutionary approach can be the only viable route forward.

To some extent all managers recognize that their firms need to continuously learn and adapt, while most will acknowledge that they do not have the absolute power to impose revolutionary changes at will. For these reasons, managers generally would like their organizations to have the ability to pursue evolutionary changes.

Yet, engaging in evolutionary change is the opposite of revolutionary change. On the one hand, being opposites might make revolution and evolution complementary. Some authors suggest that organizations should be 'ambidextrous', using both revolution and evolution, contingent on internal and external conditions (e.g. Duncan, 1976; Krüger, 1996; Tushman and O'Reilly, 1996). On the other hand, the above discussion makes clear that the two are, to a certain extent, mutually incompatible. Once the one form of change has been chosen, this will seriously limit the ability of the strategist to simultaneously, or even subsequently, use the other. Hence, managers are once again faced with a paradox, between revolution and evolution.

EXHIBIT 8.1   SHORT CASE

CHINA COSCO: CHANGING SHIPS?

Thanks to the rise of the Internet, distance has rapidly decreased and communication has become easier and faster. There are, however, things the Internet is not capable of: sending physical goods. Even now, the primary means of transporting products is still shipping. A lot of goods need to be transported from China in particular, that country being the world's main production site. Large amounts of products, 'made in China', are shipped around the globe. Even though many industries are in flux, there is no alternative for shipping bulk products. This would suggest that shipping is an oasis of stability in a world of change; yet, even giants in seemingly calm waters have no guarantee of stable income. The state-owned China Ocean Shipping Company (COSCO), China's largest corporate group in global shipping, modern logistics and shipbuilding,

has encountered restless waters, which its subsidiary China COSCO in particular has to circumnavigate. For China COSCO, this is the final call to choose the right speed and the correct direction.

Founded in 1961, COSCO was China's first international shipping company. What started out as a passenger transportation company, quickly diversified to container shipping. COSCO gathered steam with purchasing and operating ships, financed by long-term bank loans. By the end of 1975, the company proudly announced that the capacity of its fleet had surpassed five million deadweight tons (DWT); the sum of the weights a ship can safely carry. Yet, COSCO's international activities remained limited and it was only during the 1980s that COSCO really gained momentum.

After the death of Mao Zedong in 1976, his successor, Deng Xiaoping, embarked on a wave of economic reforms and steered China towards trade liberalization and a free market-oriented economy. Also attracted by the country's cheap labour, Western companies started manufacturing products in China, and the demand for shipping started booming. Through government-established special economic zones – coastal areas given more flexible regulation and other preferential treatment – inflow of foreign capital and exports started to grow, along with COSCO's profits. China's economy was only partially opened to the global market and ministries overlooking COSCO cleverly mobilized resources to enhance the company's position. Ample use was made of domestic trade linkages, while the influx of foreign currency and technological know-how through regional and global linkages were utilized for various high value-adding activities, such as the production of technologically advanced ships.

Possessing a large share of the Chinese shipping market, COSCO expanded its overseas activities by establishing partnerships and setting up transnational business operations. The company created its first overseas joint venture in 1980 in Rotterdam, the Netherlands, and set up a wholly owned subsidiary in London in 1988 by purchasing the remaining shares held by its business partner. Although growth continued in the 1990s, COSCO was also forced to respond to an important change in its environment.

In anticipation of China's WTO ascension in 1997, successive waves of state legislation were enacted. State-owned enterprises lost virtually all types of government subsidy, could now go bankrupt, and COSCO's ties with the Chinese government disintegrated further. COSCO now lost its monopoly over China's overseas transport. These upcoming shifts prompted the COSCO's management to readjust their strategy. It decided to pursue a dynamic strategy of investing in core businesses through vertical linkages, while enhancing horizontal linkages to support the former. COSCO severed its ties with partners that relied heavily on global alliances and networks and instead decided to create a network of its own. It turned into the China Ocean Shipping (Group) Company, or COSCO Group for short. The Group's first overseas-listed subsidiary was COSCO Corporation (Singapore), followed by COSCO Hong Kong, COSCO Korea and COSCO Container Lines (Japan), among others. The businesses of COSCO were further expanded by adding modern logistics, the building of vessels and ship maintenance to its activities. Yet, the pursuit of expansion does not necessarily result in better performances, as is highlighted by China COSCO.

This subsidiary, established in 2005, forms the flagship of the COSCO Group, providing core services like dry bulk shipping, terminal operations and the manufacturing, leasing and shipping of containers. As such, the subsidiary basically covers the whole shipping value chain. All seemed to go well for China COSCO, especially profiting from the dry bulk unit that it purchased in 2007 from its parent. With 45 per cent of its 2007 revenues coming from dry bulk shipping, the company's management believed the future was bright. China COSCO's CEO stated in the annual report of 2007 that 'it is expected that the overall dry bulk shipping market supply and demand conditions will remain favourable'. Unfortunately, this was not to be.

In 2008, economies suffered from the global financial crisis and the international shipping industry, a barometer of the global economy, was adversely affected. Still, the COSCO Group was able to keep its head above water, making minor profits during a challenging time for global shipping. However, the same could not be said for China COSCO. In 2009 revenues decreased by 48 per cent, with immense operating losses of 144 per cent. Nevertheless, a turnaround seemed to dawn during the next year. Due to

▶

a modest recovery from the global financial crisis, while also minimizing costs, cancelling new ships and selling a 49 per cent stake in COSCO Logistics to its parent, China COSCO was able to announce an annual profit of $361 million in 2010.

Whereas China COSCO's logistics unit and terminal operations continued to make profits, its dry bulk shipping rebounded to losses. Its chairman ascribed this to rising fuel prices and overcapacity in the sector, but also pointed to 'oversupply in the market, low freight rate, high cost and [an] imbalanced fleet composition'. Although China COSCO's debts racked up – in 2012 alone it had to endure a loss of $1.54 billion – this was the least of the company's worries. China COSCO last recorded annual profit stemmed from 2010, and according to the Shanghai stock exchange rules a company could well be delisted after three consecutive annual losses. The stock exchange regulations could make China COSCO sink, fuelling the necessity for strategic change.

In order to regain profitability in 2013, solutions were sought by following an evolutionary path to carefully reforming the company. For instance, China COSCO had to focus on strengthening coordination among internal departments and centralizing procurement. These measures were backed up by downsizing the company's assets in a prudent fashion: one by one. The lucrative COSCO Logistics was sold to its parent company for $1.1 billion, providing a one-off pre-tax gain of approximately $316 million for 2013. China COSCO also sold its stakes in a container manufacturer and office properties, so that dry bulk shipping – China COSCO's core business – could remain intact. When the 2013 fiscal year ended, it managed to scrape together a minor profit of $37.9 million, sparing the company a disaster.

This bought China COSCO three more years but does not ensure its future; it could very well be a reprieve. The chairman of the group indicated in 2014 that he was not sure how China COSCO could return to profits, since 'there aren't that many ways left to tackle losses through asset disposal'. The chosen answer was to consolidate. A merger of China COSCO and China Shipping Container Lines (CSCL) resulted in China COSCO Shipping, the biggest shipping fleet in the world with over 800 vessels. This is almost three times the number owned by competitor Maersk Line.

The worst downturn of the shipping industry since the financial crisis was met with a merger of two companies in the midst of heavy weather. Yet, is efficiency the right direction to deal with the oversupply and weak demand in the bulk shipping sector or does the group have to sell more of its assets and take other cautious measures? Perhaps bolder actions are necessary. Should the troublesome core business perhaps be discarded, thus giving up the position as the world's largest bulk cargo fleet operator? Time is running out again, and given the difficult situation of the shipping industry the bulk assets are difficult to value, and therefore hard to sell at a reasonable price. Continuing on the evolutionary path or pursuing a revolutionary direction: change is eminent at any rate. China COSCO has to be steered in a direction that would prevent the company from rebounding to losses and would keep the boat afloat.

Co-author: Wester Wagenaar

Sources: en.cosco.co; www.chinacosco.com; China COSCO Annual Reports 2007–2015; *Bloomberg*, 13 March 2013 and 28 March 2013; *Financial Times*, 30 August 2012; William A. Joseph, *Politics in China: An Introduction*, 2014 (2nd ed.); Moore, 2002; Barry J. Naughton, *The Chinese Economy: Transitions and Growth*, 2006; David Pinder and Brian Slack, *Shipping and Ports in the Twenty-first Century*, 2004; *Reuters*, 29 March 2012, 27 March 2014 and 18 February 2016; *Wall Street Journal*, 23 March 2011, 20 May 2013 and 2 July 2013.

PERSPECTIVES ON STRATEGIC CHANGE

Although the demand for both revolutionary and evolutionary change is clear, this does place managers in the difficult position of having to determine how both must be combined and balanced in a process of ongoing strategic alignment. Revolutionary change is necessary to create *discontinuity* in the alignment process – radical and swift breaks with the past. Evolutionary change is necessary to ensure *continuity* in the alignment process – moderate and gradual metamorphosis from one state into another. In finding a balance between these two demands, the question is which of the two must play a leading role and what type of change path this leads to. Does successful strategic alignment hinge on a few infrequent big bangs, with some minor evolutionary changes in the intervening time span, or is successful strategic alignment essentially a gradual process of mutation and selection, where revolutionary changes are used only in case of emergency?

Yet, as in previous chapters, we see that the strategic management literature comes up with a wide variety of answers to this question. Both among business practitioners and strategy researchers, views differ sharply about the best way of dealing with the paradox of revolution and evolution. To gain insight into the major points of disagreement between people on the issue of strategic alignment, we will again outline the two diametrically opposed perspectives here.

At one end of the virtual continuum of views are the strategists who argue that real strategic alignment can only be achieved by radical means. Revolutionary change, although difficult to achieve, is at the heart of alignment, while evolutionary changes can only figure in a supporting role. This point of view will be referred to as the 'discontinuous alignment perspective'. At the other end of the spectrum are the strategists who argue that real strategic alignment is not brought about by an 'axe', but must grow out of the existing firm, in a constant stream of small adjustments. Evolutionary change, although difficult to sustain, is at the heart of alignment, while revolutionary changes are a fallback alternative, if all else fails. This point of view will be referred to as the 'continuous alignment perspective'.

The discontinuous alignment perspective

 According to advocates of the discontinuous alignment perspective, it is a common misconception that firms develop gradually. It is often assumed that organizations move fluidly from one state to the next, encountering minimal friction. In reality, however, strategic change is arduous and encounters significant resistance. Pressure must be exerted, and tension must mount, before a major shift can be accomplished. Movement, therefore, is not steady and constant, as a current in the sea, but abrupt and dramatic, as in an earthquake, where resistance gives way and tension is released in a short shock. In general, the more significant a change is, the more intense the shock will be.

Proponents of this perspective argue that people and organizations exhibit a natural reluctance to change. Humans have a strong preference for stability. Once general policy has been determined, most firms are inclined to settle into a fixed way of working. The organizational structure will solidify, formal processes will be installed, standard operating procedures will be defined, key competence areas will be identified, a distribution of power will emerge and a corporate culture will become established. The stability of an organization will be especially high if all of these elements form a consistent and cohesive configuration (e.g. Mintzberg, 1991; Waterman, Peters and Philips, 1980). Moreover, if a firm experiences a period of success, this usually strongly reinforces the existing way of working (e.g. Markides, 1998; Miller, 1990).

It must be emphasized that stability is not inherently harmful, as it allows people to 'get to work'. A level of stability is required to function efficiently (e.g. March and Simon, 1958; Thompson, 1967). Constant change would only create an organizational mess. There would be prolonged confusion about tasks and authority, poorly structured internal communication and coordination, and a lack of clear standards and routines. The instability brought on by such continuously changing processes and structures would lead to widespread insecurity, political manoeuvring and inter-departmental conflicts.

Advocates of the discontinuous alignment perspective, therefore, argue that long periods of relative stability are necessary for the proper functioning of firms. However, the downside of stability is rigidity – the unwillingness and/or inability to change, even when it is urgently required. To overcome rigidity and get the firm in motion, a series of small nudges will by no means be sufficient. Instead, a big shove will be needed. For strategic changes to really happen, measures must be radical and comprehensive. A coordinated assault is usually required to decisively break through organizational defences and 'shock therapy' is needed to fundamentally change people's cognitive maps. Solving lock-in problems generally also demands a quick, firm-wide switchover to a new system. For instance, business process reengineering must involve all aspects of the value chain at once (e.g. Hammer, 1990; Hammer and Champy, 1993). However, proponents of the discontinuous alignment perspective emphasize that the period of turmoil must not take too long. People cannot be indefinitely confronted with high levels of uncertainty and ambiguity, and a new equilibrium is vital for a new period of efficient operations.

Some proponents of the discontinuous change perspective argue that episodes of revolutionary change are generally not chosen freely, but are triggered by crises. A major environmental jolt can be the reason for a sudden crisis (e.g. Meyer, 1982; Meyer, Brooks and Goes, 1990) – for example, the introduction of a new technology, a major economic recession, new government regulations, a novel market entrant or a dramatic event in international political affairs. However, misalignment between the firm and its environment often grows over a longer period of time, causing a mounting sense of impending crisis (e.g. Johnson, 1988; Strebel, 1992). As tension increases, people in the firm become more receptive to submitting to the painful changes that are necessary. This increased willingness to change under crisis circumstances coincides with the physical law that 'under pressure things become fluid'. As long as the pressure persists, revolutionary change is possible, but as soon as the pressure lets up the firm will resolidify in a new form, inhibiting any further major changes (e.g. Lewin, 1947; Miller and Friesen, 1984). For this reason, managers often feel impelled to heighten and prolong the sense of crisis, to keep organization members receptive to the changes being pushed through. Where a crisis is lacking, some managers will induce one, to create the sense of urgency and determination needed to get people in the change mind-set.

It can be concluded that strategic changes, whether proactive or reactive, require an abrupt break with the status quo. Change management demands strong leadership to rapidly push through stressful, discomforting and risky shifts in the business and organizational system. Battling the sources of rigidity and turning crisis into opportunity are the key qualities needed by managers implementing strategic change. Ultimately, strategizing managers should know when to change and when it is wiser to seek stability – they should know when to trigger an 'earthquake' and when to avoid one.

EXHIBIT 8.2   THE DISCONTINUOUS ALIGNMENT PERSPECTIVE

CHANGE BANKING FOR GOOD

In 2012, with the £133 billion financial crisis still echoing, UK citizens again received surprising news: Banks had manipulated their Libor rates (London Inter-Bank Offered Rate) to appear more creditworthy or to profit from trades. The Houses of Parliament responded by installing a 'Parliamentary Commission on Banking Standards'. The commission was founded to conduct an inquiry into professional standards and culture in the UK banking sector and to formulate recommendations for future legislation. Those expecting minor measures were in shock. If the commission would find support from the UK treasury, top bankers who had enriched themselves during the financial crisis would have faced colossal penalties or even time in jail: The price the industry had to pay to restore trust in banking.

The commission concluded that too many bankers were not personally accountable, taking shelter in collective decision-making, with sanctions being disproportionate to the severity of the consequences of failure. In addition, many bank staff had been paid too much for doing the wrong things:

bonuses provoked short-term personal gain and long-term societal pain. This has led the commission to develop a new framework for individuals working in the industry, the main element being a senior persons regime, which would ensure that the key responsibilities within banks are assigned to specific individuals. The bankers would be made fully and unambiguously aware of their responsibilities and held accountable for carrying them out. Regulators would apply the civil powers of fines, restrictions on responsibilities and a ban from the industry.

The new rigorous regime will restore trust in banking – crucial for the UK's dominant position within the global financial services industry. A reformed banking industry with higher standards has the potential, once again, to be a great asset to the United Kingdom. For good.

Co-author: Adriaan de Bruijn

Sources: *House of Lords, House of Commons Parliamentary Commission on Banking Standards. June 2013. Volume 1: Summary, and Conclusions and recommendations.* www.parliament.uk/business/committees/committees-a-z/joint-select/professional-standards-in-the-banking-industry/news/changingbanking-for-good-report/. *The Economist*, 22 June 2013.

The continuous alignment perspective

According to proponents of the continuous alignment perspective, if firms shift by 'earthquake' it is usually their own 'fault'. The problem with revolution is that it commonly leads to the need for further revolution at a later time – discontinuous change creates its own boom-and-bust cycle. Revolutionary change is generally followed by a strong organizational yearning for stability. The massive, firm-wide efforts to implement agonizing changes can often be sustained for only a short period of time, after which change momentum collapses. Any positive inclination towards change among employees will have totally disappeared by the time the reorganizations are over. Consequently, the firm lapses back into a stable state in which only minor changes occur. This stable situation is maintained until the next round of shock therapy becomes necessary, to jolt the organization out of its ossified state.

To supporters of the continuous alignment perspective, the boom-and-bust approach to strategic change is like running a marathon by sprinting and then standing still to catch one's breath. Yet, marathons are not won by good sprinters, but by runners with endurance and persistence, who can keep a steady pace – runners who are more inspired by the tortoise than by the hare. The same is true for companies in the marathon of competition. Some companies behave like the hare in Aesop's fable, showing off their ability to take great leaps, but burdened by a short span of attention. Other companies behave more like the tortoise, moving gradually and undramatically, but unrelentingly and without interruption, focusing on the long-term goal. In the short run, the hares might dash ahead, suggesting that making big leaps forward is the best way to compete. But, in the long run, the most formidable contenders will be the diligent tortoises, whose ability to maintain a constant speed will help them to win the race.

Therefore, the 'big ideas' and 'quantum leaps' that so mesmerize proponents of the discontinuous alignment perspective are viewed with suspicion by supporters of continuous alignment. Revolution not only causes unnecessary disruption and dysfunctional crises, but also is usually the substitute for diligence. If organizations do not have the stamina to continuously improve themselves, quick fix radical change can be used as a short-term remedy. Where firms do not exhibit the drive to permanently upgrade their capabilities, revolutionary alignment can be used as the short cut to improved competitiveness. In other words, the lure of revolutionary change is that of short-term results. By abruptly and dramatically making major changes, managers hope to rapidly book tangible progress – and instantly win recognition and promotion.

To advocates of the continuous alignment perspective, a preference for revolution usually reflects an unhealthy obsession with the short term. Continuous alignment, on the other hand, is more long-term in orientation. Development is gradual, piecemeal and undramatic, but as it is constantly maintained over a longer period of time, the aggregate level of change can still be significant.

Everyone in the firm must be motivated to continuously learn. People within the organization must constantly update their knowledge base, which not only means acquiring new information, but challenging accepted company wisdom as well. Learning goes hand in hand with unlearning – changing the cognitive maps shared within the organization. In this respect, it is argued that an atmosphere of crisis actually inhibits continuous alignment. In a situation of crisis, it is not a matter of 'under pressure things become fluid', but 'in the cold everything freezes'. Crisis circumstances might lower people's resistance to imposed change, but it also blunts their motivation for experimenting and learning, as they brace themselves for the imminent shock. Crisis encourages people to seek security and to focus on the short term, instead of opening up and working towards long-term development (e.g. Bate, 1994; Senge, 1990).

Everyone in the firm must not only continuously learn, but also be motivated to continuously adapt. Constant adjustment to external change and fluid internal realignment should be pursued. To this end, the organization must actively avoid inertia, by combatting the forces of ossification. Managers should strive to create flexible structures and processes (e.g. Bartlett and Ghoshal, 1995; Eisenhardt and Brown, 1997), to encourage an open and tolerant corporate culture, and to provide sufficient job and career security for employees to accept other forms of ambiguity and uncertainty (e.g. Kagono *et al.*, 1985; Nonaka, 1988).

In an evolutionary firm basically everyone in the organization is involved. Revolutionary change can be initiated by top management, possibly assisted and urged on by a few external consultants, and carried by a handful of change agents or champions (e.g. Day, 1994; Maidique, 1980). Evolutionary change, by way of contrast, requires a firm-wide effort. Leaders cannot learn on behalf of their organizations, neither can they orchestrate all of the small adaptations needed for continuous alignment. Managers must realize that evolution can be led from the top, but not be imposed from the top. For strategizing managers to realize change, hands-on guidance of organizational developments is more important than commanding organizational actions.

EXHIBIT 8.3   CONTINUOUS ALIGNMENT PERSPECTIVE

STORA ENSO: CENTURIES OF CHANGE

Like no other, Stora Enso knows how to adapt. The company not only coped with social and political changes throughout the ages, but also had the foresight to change its business when necessary. Swedish mining company Stora Kopparberg – Swedish for 'big copper mountain' – started operating in the 13th century, its first share dating from 1288. This effectively makes the firm the oldest limited liability company and the oldest still existing corporation in the world.

Stora rose to prominence during the 17th century. For some periods in this age, the company's mine in Falun produced around two-thirds of the world's production of copper. When copper mining gradually lost its importance in the next century, the company decided to purchase an iron ore mine. Its foresight proved successful as it did not take long before iron ore proved more profitable for the company than copper. Another century passed, but towards the end of the 19th century Stora decided to switch its business once again. The company kept operating in the primary sector of the economy, but divested its mining and steel mill businesses and entered paper and pulp production instead. In home country Sweden, where forests are plentiful and the country is thinly populated, Stora quickly accumulated a big chunk of territory of its own and a turnover to match. In 1997 the company owned 1.6 million hectares of forest in Sweden and

0.7 million hectares in Portugal, Canada and Brazil. The next year the company merged with Finnish forest giant Enso Oyj to form Stora Enso. It did not take long before the company needed to shed its skin again.

In an era in which consumers increasingly move from paper to digital media, the demand for paper continues to decline. Stora Enso thus had to scale down its global workforce by about 10 per cent in 2013, most notably in the Nordic region, and restructured by putting the paper and wood products business into one division. As a response to the decline in Western markets, Stora Enso now invests heavily in pulp and packaging production outside of Europe. The company is part of a pulp mill joint venture in Uruguay and owns a cardboard plant in China's Guangxi province.

Stora Enso is well aware this is no viable long-term solution; it honours its history by divesting and exploring once again. Increasing awareness among consumers for the environment and renewable solutions creates growth opportunities, and Stora Enso aims to ride that wave. It reinvigorated its packaging by making it increasingly renewable and is developing alternatives for card board and pulp. One of its projects involves Nutella spread producer Ferrero. This company produces 180 million kilograms of Nutella every year, resulting in an enormous amount of hazelnut shell waste. Stora Enso and Ferrero are now developing EcoPaper, in which hazelnut fibre are used to create an alternative to carton board.

▶

To keep Stora Enso even more relevant, the company is also shifting into biochemistry, biomaterials and green construction products. All of these measures are to prevent Stora Enso from getting beaten to a pulp by a changing environment, and to ensure that the centuries-old company will continue to be the world's oldest firm in the future.

Co-author: Wester Wagenaar

Sources: www.storaenso.com; Stora Enso Financial Report 2015; *The Economist*, 16 December 2004; *Financial Times*, 10 November 2015; *The Guardian*, 21 April 2015; *Wall Street Journal*, 18 June 2013.

MANAGING THE PARADOX OF REVOLUTION AND EVOLUTION

Slow and steady wins the race.

The Hare and the Tortoise, Aesop (c. 620–560 BCE), Greek writer

So, how should managers align their organizations? Should managers strive to align abruptly, by emphasizing radical, comprehensive and dramatic changes? Or should they try to align in a more continuous fashion by learning and adaptation? How can strategists best manage the paradox of revolution and evolution (see Table 8.1)?

No consensus has yet been developed within the field of strategic management on how to balance revolution and evolution. In the end, strategic managers have to make up their mind, taking into consideration their specific situation. Fortunately, some researchers have brought forward their views on how to manage the paradox of revolution and evolution. The starting point is the set of arguments put forward in the taxonomy in Chapter 1.

TABLE 8.1   Discontinuous alignment versus continuous alignment perspective

	Discontinuous alignment perspective	Continuous alignment perspective
Emphasis on	Revolution over evolution	Evolution over revolution
Strategic alignment as	Disruptive turnaround	Uninterrupted improvement
Magnitude of change	Radical, comprehensive and dramatic	Moderate, piecemeal and undramatic
Pace of change	Abrupt, unsteady and intermittent	Gradual, steady and constant
Lasting alignment requires	Sudden break with status quo	Permanent learning and flexibility
Reaction to external jolts	Shock therapy	Continuous adjustment
View of organizational crises	Under pressure things become fluid	In the cold everything freezes
Long-term alignment dynamics	Stable and unstable states alternate	Persistent transient state
Long-term alignment pattern	Punctuated equilibrium	Gradual development

Navigating

Strategizing managers have to deal with technological developments, political changes, economic crises and competitive moves, to mention just a few, that differ in their pace and magnitude. Over the long term, the pattern of environmental change is episodic. Periods of relative stability are interrupted by short and dramatic periods of instability, a pattern of development that has been recognized in a variety of other sciences as well (Gersick, 1991). Following the natural historians Eldredge and Gould, this pattern is often called 'punctuated equilibrium' – stability punctuated by episodes in which many changes take place simultaneously (Tushman and O'Reilly, 1996).

When the environment is in flux, organizations must align. Therefore strategizing managers must possess a variety of options in dealing with environmental change. In periods of relative stability, gradual change is the appropriate alignment pattern, while during discontinuous change more drastic measures are needed (Greiner, 1972). Although the strategic alignment process does not precisely mirror environmental developments, it somehow relates to the pace and magnitude of change. Often with a delay and sometimes overly reacting, strategists aim at catching up with the long-term development of the environment.

Management scholars have been looking into this long-term alignment process (Anderson and Tushman, 1990; Tushman and O'Reilly, 1996; Tushman, Newman and Romanelli, 1986). They argue that to be successful during periods of relative stability, the emphasis should be on evolutionary adaptation to the always changing demands in the market. But during discontinuous changes, firms also need to be able to be revolutionary, adapting to whatever external change comes their way. In other words, comparable with a captain of a ship strategists need to navigate the company during sunny weather and occasionally through stormy waters, with one hand on the wheel and one on the throttle.

STRATEGIC CHANGE IN INTERNATIONAL PERSPECTIVE

Co-author: Gep Eisenloeffel

Wisdom lies neither in fixity nor in change, but in the dialectic between the two.

Octavio Paz (1914–1998), Mexican poet and essayist

Authors from different countries, as well as from similar ones, exhibit divergent perspectives on how to deal with the paradox of revolution and evolution. Why do firms in different countries prefer such significantly different approaches to strategic change? Which factors determine the existence of national strategic change styles? Answers to these questions might assist in defining the most appropriate context for revolutionary change, as opposed to circumstances in which evolutionary change would be more fitting. Understanding international dissimilarities and their roots would clarify whether firms in different countries can borrow practices from one another or are limited by their national context.

As a stimulus to the international dimension in this debate, an overview will be given of the country characteristics mentioned in the literature as the major influencers on how the paradox of revolution and evolution is dealt with in different national settings. It should

be noted, however, that cross-cultural research on this topic has not been extensive. Therefore, the propositions brought forward here should be viewed as tentative explanations,
intended to encourage further discussion and research.

Prevalence of mechanistic organizations

In Chapter 7, the international differences in organizing work were briefly discussed. It
was argued that, in some countries, the machine bureaucracy is a particularly dominant
form of organization, while in other countries organizations can be characterized as more
organic. The machine bureaucracy that is more predominant in English-speaking countries
and France, is characterized by clear hierarchical authority relationships, strict differentiation of tasks, and highly formalized communication, reporting, budgeting, planning and
decision-making processes. In such organizations, there is a relatively clear line separating
the officers (management) from the troops, and internal relationships are depersonalized
and calculative. In more organic forms of organization, management and production activities are not strictly separated, leading to less emphasis on top-down decision-making, and
more on bottom-up initiatives. Job descriptions are less strictly defined and control systems
are less sophisticated. Integration within the organization is not achieved by these formal
systems, but by extensive informal communication and consultation, both horizontally and
vertically, and by a strong common set of beliefs and a shared corporate vision. Internal relationships are based on trust, cooperation and a sense of community, leading Ouchi (1981)
to call such organizations 'clans'. This type of organization is more prevalent in Japan and,
to a lesser extent in, for example, Germany, the Netherlands and the Nordic countries.

Various researchers have suggested that machine bureaucracies exhibit a high level of
inertia (e.g. Kanter, 1989; Mintzberg, 1994). Once formal systems have been created, they
become difficult to change. As soon as particular tasks are specified and assigned to a person or group, it becomes their turf, while all else is 'not their business'. Once created, hierarchical positions, giving status and power, are not easily abolished. The consequence, it
is argued, is that machine bureaucracies are inherently more resistant to change than clan-
like organizations (Kagono *et al.*, 1985). Therefore, revolution is usually the potent mode
of change needed to make any significant alterations. It can be expected that in countries
where organizations are more strongly mechanistic, the preference for the discontinuous
alignment perspective will be more pronounced.

Clan-like organizations, contrariwise, are characterized by a strong capacity for
self-organization – the ability to exhibit organized behaviour without a boss being in
control (Nonaka, 1988; Stacey, 1993). They are better at fluidly and spontaneously reor-
ganizing around new issues because of a lack of rigid structure, the close links between
management and production tasks, the high level of group-oriented information-sharing
and consensual decision-making, and the strong commitment of individuals to the organization, and vice versa. In countries where organizations are more organic in this way, a
stronger preference for continuous alignment can be expected. This issue will be discussed
at greater length in Chapter 11.

Position of employees

This second factor is linked to the first. A mechanistic organization, it could be said, is a
system into which groups of people have been brought, while an organic organization is
a group of people into which some system has been brought. In a machine bureaucracy,

people are human resources *for* the organization, while in a clan, people *are* the organization. These two conceptions of organization represent radically different views on the position and roles of employees within organizations.

In mechanistic organizations, employees are seen as valuable, yet expendable resources utilized by the organization. Salaries are determined by prices on the labour market and the value added by the individual employee. In the contractual relationship between employer and employee, it is a shrewd bargaining tactic for employers to minimize their dependence on employees. Organizational learning should, therefore, be captured in formalized systems and procedures, to avoid the irreplaceability of their people. Employees, however, will, of course, strive to make themselves indispensable for the organization, for instance by not sharing their learning. Furthermore, calculating employees will not tie themselves too strongly to the organization, but will keep their options open to job-hop to a better paying employer. None of these factors contributes to the long-term commitment and receptiveness for ambiguity and uncertainty needed for continuous alignment.

In clan-like organizations the tolerance for ambiguity and uncertainty is higher, because employees' positions within the organization are more secure. Information is more readily shared, as it does not need to be used as a bargaining chip and acceptance within the group demands being a team player. Employers can invest in people instead of systems, since employees are committed and loyal to the organization. These better trained people can consequently be given more decision-making power and more responsibility to organize their own work to fit with changing circumstances. Therefore, clan-like organizations, with their emphasis on employees as permanent co-producers, instead of temporary contractors, are more conducive to evolutionary change.

A number of factors have been brought forward to explain these international differences in the structuring of work and the position of employees. Some authors emphasize cultural aspects, particularly the level of individualism. It is argued that the mechanistic-organic distinction largely coincides with the individualism–collectivism division (e.g. Ouchi, 1981; Pascale and Athos, 1981). In this view, machine bureaucracies are the logical response to calculative individuals, while clans are more predominant in group-oriented cultures. Other authors point to international differences in labour markets (e.g. Calori, Valla and De Woot, 1994; Kagono *et al.*, 1985). High mobility of personnel is thought to coincide with the existence of mechanistic organizations, while low mobility (e.g. lifetime employment) fits with organic forms. Yet others suggest that the abundance of skilled workers is important. Machine bureaucracies are suited to deal with narrowly trained individuals, requiring extensive supervision. Clan-like organizations, however, need skilled, self-managing workers, who can handle a wide variety of tasks with relative autonomy. Kogut (1993, p. 11) reports that the level of workers within a country with these qualifications 'has been found to rest significantly upon the quality of education, the existence of programmes of apprenticeship and worker qualifications, and the elimination of occupational distinctions'.

Role of top management

Various researchers have observed important international differences in leadership styles and the role of top management. In some countries, top management is considered the 'central processing unit' of the company, making the key decisions and commanding the behaviour of the rest of the organizational machine. Visible top-down leadership is the norm, and therefore, strategic change is viewed as a top management responsibility (e.g. Hambrick and Mason, 1984; Hitt *et al.*, 1997). Strategic changes are formulated by top managers and then implemented at lower levels. Top managers are given significant power and discretion to develop bold new initiatives and to overcome organizational resistance to change. If organizational advances are judged to be insufficient or if an organization ends up in a crisis situation, a change of top management is often considered to be a necessary measure to transform or turn around the company (e.g. Boeker, 1992; Fredrickson, Hambrick and Baumrin, 1988). In nations where people exhibit a strong preference for this commander type of leadership, an inclination towards the discontinuous alignment perspective can be expected.

In other countries, top managers are viewed as the captains of the team and leadership is less direct and less visible (e.g. Hofstede, 1993; Kagono *et al.*, 1985). The role of top managers is to facilitate change among the members of the group. Change comes from within the body of the organization, instead of being imposed on it by top management. Therefore, change under this type of leadership will usually be more evolutionary than revolutionary. In nations where people exhibit a strong preference for this servant type of leadership, an inclination towards the continuous alignment perspective is more likely.

Time orientation

Earlier in the text, a distinction was made between cultures that are more oriented towards the past, the present and the future. Obviously, it can be expected that cultural inclination to either past or present will perceive change to be much less favourable than future-oriented cultures. Among these future-minded cultures, a further division can be made between those with a long-term and a short-term orientation.

Various researchers have argued that short-term-oriented cultures exhibit a much stronger preference for fast, radical change than cultures with a longer time horizon. In short-term-oriented cultures, such as most English-speaking countries, there are significant pressures for rapid results, which predispose managers towards revolutionary change. Especially sensitivity to stock prices is often cited as a major factor encouraging firms to focus on short spurts of massive change and pay much less attention to efforts and investments with undramatic long-term benefits. Other contributing factors include short-term-oriented bonus systems, stock option plans and frequent job-hopping (e.g. Calori, Valla and De Woot, 1994; Kagono *et al.*, 1985).

In long-term oriented cultures, such as Japan, China and South Korea, there is far less pressure to achieve short-term results. There is broad awareness that firms are running a competitive marathon and that a high, yet steady, pace of motion is needed. Generally, more emphasis is placed on facilitating long-term change processes, instead of intermittently shifting between one short-term change and another. Frequently mentioned factors contributing to this long-term orientation include long-term employment relationships, the lack of short-term bonus systems and, most importantly, the accent on growth as opposed to profit, as firms' prime objective (e.g. Abegglen and Stalk, 1985; Hitt *et al.*, 1997). This topic is discussed at length in Chapter 3.

STRATEGIC INNOVATION

There is nothing more difficult to take in hand, more perilous to conduct, or more uncertain in its success, than to take the lead in the introduction of a new order of things. Because the innovator has for enemies all those who have done well under the old conditions, and lukewarm defenders in those who may do well under the new.

Niccolò Machiavelli (1469–1527), Florentine statesman and political philosopher

INTRODUCTION

In Chapter 8, the magnitude and pace of strategic change in aligning the business model and organizational system to the external environment were addressed. The distinction was made between operational change that aims at maintaining the current business model and organizational system and strategic changes that are directed at aligning them with the firm's environment. Strategizing managers are particularly concerned with business model changes, as this affects the way the company creates value and competes in the business environment (see also Chapter 4).

Changing a firm's business model to defend and create a sustainable advantage over the competition is referred to as strategic innovation. It relates to all technologies, resources, activities and processes by which new ideas are generated and converted into products and services that increase satisfaction of current customers and attract new customers. Strategists innovate to strengthen the firm's competitive position, a process that is both necessary and unending due to the dynamics of the competitive game. Hence this chapter deals with the enduring, and arguably the most challenging, topic for strategizing managers of strategic innovation.

Although a large and increasing number of studies address the topic of strategic innovation, definitions either differ widely or remain implicit. In this chapter, strategic innovation is defined as renewing the firm's business model to create or sustain a competitive advantage (Amit and Zott, 2001, 2012). Ultimately, strategic innovation aims to achieve a successful long-term corporate life.

THE ISSUE OF STRATEGIC RENEWAL

The idea of eternal life has always appealed to people in many parts of the world, including Europe, China and India. For centuries, people have been searching for the golden formula of an elixir of life that would provide eternal life and eternal youth. Indeed, it is a fascinating thought that by just consuming a drink, even if it would work only at a defined moment, in a specific place and from a certain cup, we would live forever. Because the idea is so appealing, there have been blooming markets of supply – the alchemists – and demand – usually rich and powerful people. It is unlikely that an elixir of life has even been found to be efficacious; however, we are quite sure that people have died after consuming an acclaimed elixir. The British historian Joseph Needham (Needham, Ho and Lu, 1976) compiled a list of Chinese emperors whose death was likely due to elixir poisoning. Chinese interest in alchemy and the elixir of life vanished with the rise of Buddhism, which claimed to have alternative avenues to eternity.

Although the health industry is working hard on lengthening human life through research and technological innovations, eternal life is most likely not achievable. For organizations, the situation is different, albeit not in the sense that they can exist forever. Yet, organizations have the ability to stay young and vital for hundreds of years. In a study, initiated by Royal Dutch/Shell, on large companies older than 100 years and important in their industry, De Geus (1997) found 40 large and dominant companies over 100 years old. The oldest company that De Geus and his team found was the Swedish paper, pulp and chemical manufacturer Stora (that in 1998 merged with the Finnish company Enzo to form the new entity Stora Enzo), which started as a copper mine in central Sweden over 700 years ago. As second oldest company, De Geus nominated the Japanese Sumitomo with origins in a copper casting shop founded by Riemon Soga in the year 1590. Furthermore, De Geus estimated the average life expectancy of multinational Fortune 500 corporations between 40 and 50 years, and speculated that the natural average lifespan of a corporation could be as long as two or three centuries. So firms can potentially become much older than humans, yet the average age of companies turns out to be much lower. The question is thus, why is it so difficult to renew the company?

Characteristics of strategic innovation

Strategic renewal processes are arguably *the* most complex processes to bring to a successful ending, the main reason being that strategic innovation consists of four different processes that are already challenging on their own, and therefore extremely demanding in combination. The following paragraph discusses the constituting elements of strategic innovation: strategizing, entrepreneurial, changing and investing processes (see Figure 9.1).

Strategic innovation as a strategizing process.   In strategic renewal processes, strategizing managers must be aware of the unfolding opportunities and threats in the environment, and the evolving strengths and weaknesses of the organization. They must be able to constantly re-evaluate their views and generate a new understanding of the competitive situation, often against the company's dominant logic. For strategists, a fundamental question in renewal processes is how to avoid getting stuck with an outdated cognitive map

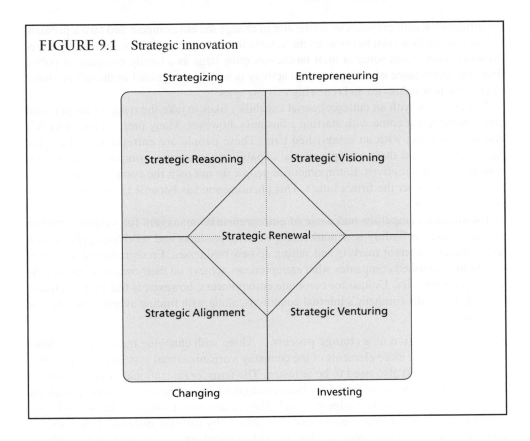

FIGURE 9.1 Strategic innovation

(see also Chapter 2). How can they avoid the danger of building up a flawed picture of their industry, their markets and themselves?

While creative thinking is imperative for generating a new understanding of the current situation, it is at the essence of developing a new business model. Creativity is in every human being, albeit at different levels as not everyone is equally talented and lives a life that pushes their creative talent to the limit. Everyone can learn to paint, but few will find their paintings displayed in a gallery. Likewise the level of creativity that business model innovation requires is quite scarce. Moreover, creativity appears in a variety of modes. While artists have the freedom to choose any kind of material, form and subject with no imposed time constraints, architects are bound by available space, functionality, budget and time. Being engaged in strategic renewal, strategists are like architects, working in a context of 'bounded creativity'. Constrained by, for example, lead time and resource availability, the context of strategic renewal processes is usually framed by more or less articulated input and output criteria.

Strategic innovation as an entrepreneurial process.   Each year, thousands of individuals start a new business, expecting to have identified an opportunity that can be exploited. The backgrounds and basic ideas of these entrepreneurs differ widely. For example, some entrepreneurs may have just graduated, others hold many years of experience in an industry they know well; some build their newly established company on the basis of a new technology, others start serving a group of customers that has been overlooked. With all the differences, entrepreneurs share the aim to change the environment and take a personal risk in starting their own business as the vehicle for their dreams. Many, but not all, entrepreneurs succeed and some of their businesses grow large as a family company or public firm. The importance of entrepreneurial activity is widely recognized as the driving force of creating new industries and renewing existing ones.

Not everyone with an entrepreneurial capability likes to take the risks, or the personal consequences that come with starting a business, however. Many prefer a less risky life and start working with an established firm. These people are entrepreneurial but not entrepreneurs, and their entrepreneurial capabilities become a company resource for entrepreneurial initiatives. Entrepreneurial people do not own the company, but they do take ownership over the firm's future. This phenomenon has become known as corporate entrepreneurship.

Established companies make use of entrepreneurial managers for various strategic activities, such as finding new markets for existing products and services, applying new technologies in current markets and setting up new businesses. Entrepreneurial managers realize in established companies what entrepreneurs achieve on their own account: finding growth opportunities. Unique for corporate entrepreneurs, however, is that they often also have to change the company's internal conditions, along with finding avenues for strategic innovation.

Strategic innovation as a change process.   Along with changing the company's business model, one or more elements of the company's organizational system (see Figure 9.2; see also Chapter 8) also need to be adjusted. The term 'organizational system' refers to how the individuals in the firm have been configured and relate to one another, with the intention of facilitating the business model. The organizational structure divides tasks and responsibilities among the organizational members, by forming different functions and units. The organizational processes link individual members to each other and coordinate their separate tasks into an integrated whole. Furthermore, firms have organizational cultures and subcultures, as organizational members interact with one another and build up joint beliefs, values and norms.

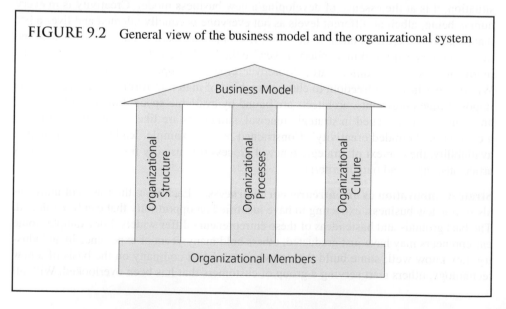

FIGURE 9.2   General view of the business model and the organizational system

Some strategic innovation processes require organizational restructuring, for example when new products combine resources that are located in separate units. Also, organizational processes may need to be redesigned, for example as a result of new product offerings. And finally, a change of the firm's culture may be needed to enable strategists renewing the business model, for example when different units are not inclined to share ideas. (Strategic change is discussed at length in Chapter 8.)

Strategic innovation as an investing process.   Strategic innovation requires resources, such as money, time and management capabilities, and can, therefore, be considered an investment into the company's future. As with all investments, strategic innovation requires a positive return on invested resources. Investments in strategic innovation compete with other investment categories, such as mergers, acquisitions and entering new countries. Consequently, companies engage in decision-making routines to decide whether or not to allocate scarce resources for proposed strategic innovation projects.

Generally, investments that promise to generate returns in the long term are riskier than short-term options and therefore harder to take. The same applies to innovation options. In addition, investing in an enhanced long-term competitive position involves more uncertainty about the expected effects as the company environment changes along the way. So, investing in strategic innovation becomes both riskier and more uncertain as the results are to be expected over a longer term.

Managers with the responsibility for innovation processes cannot afford to develop ideas only. They must think of the entire process, from generating ideas and managing the renewal process up to successfully implementing innovations. Managers must ask themselves upfront how the entire process of strategic innovation should be managed to renew their organizations. Who should be involved, what activities need to be undertaken and to what extent can the results be described in advance? For strategizing managers, strategic innovation encompasses the entire process to arrive at the best possible position to achieve a positive return on the innovation investment.

In sum, strategic innovation is complex for strategizing managers as it combines four processes that separately are, in themselves, challenging to bring to a successful ending: strategizing, entrepreneurial, changing and investing processes. Strategic innovation is equally challenging for management scholars, as the topic crosses and combines several academic disciplines such as organizational behaviour, technology management, marketing, finance and, of course, strategy. The multi-disciplinary character of the topic thwarts researchers in understanding strategic innovation in full, with diverse academic contributions as an understandable result. The diverse research findings point to a number of factors that further complicate strategic innovation.

Inhibitors of strategic innovation

As described above, strategic innovation is a difficult process to manage. Although companies may potentially exist for over 100 years, there are good reasons why only a few companies succeed in surviving for such an extensive period. Some obvious reasons include bad management and unfortunate consequences of wars and natural disasters. But even in the absence of such occasions, strategic renewal is hard to accomplish as strategists face several inhibitors of strategic renewal. The following paragraph discusses such inhibitors of strategic renewal: the effects of innovation results, inertia and bias and feedback.

Effects of innovation results.   The advantage of start-up innovators is a blank cognitive map, as there have not been past innovation successes and failures that influence perceptions on the viability of innovation options. Over time, however, the innovator collects experiences of past projects, both positive and negative. Successes stimulate going forward on this path, while disappointing results lead to reconsidering the choices that have been made. The results influence future innovating behaviour and strategic choices. Innovators continue on routes that lead to success, while changing direction when results prove disappointing. Radical innovations that have paid off in terms of strengthened competitive position, stimulate strategists to replicate bold innovative moves, while disappointing results urge strategists to rethink the choices that have been made. The same applies to incremental improvement successes leading to continued gradual innovation, while disappointing effects on the company's competitive position prompt for evaluating innovation policies.

Established companies do not have the advantage of blank cognitive maps. When considering innovation options, past experiences influence how alternatives are valued and evaluated. Strategists become reluctant to explore alternatives that had been tried before with disappointing pay-offs. They have learned what works and what doesn't; as a result, they develop perceptions and opinions on the viability of certain options. Past experiences lead to following the proven innovation routines in which they become increasingly more effective – a phenomenon that has been commonly termed path dependency (Nelson and Winter, 1982). In other words, positive results of certain innovation routines lead to replicating these routines and building up relevant innovation process competences. Such competences lead to increased chances of success, and ultimately come to define the way the company innovates.

As the organization develops innovation routines and institutionalizes successful practices, the chances of inertia magnify. The organization increasingly comes to rely on patterns of actions it has had sustainable success with in the past (Hannan and Freeman, 1984; Tripsas and Gavetti, 2000), thus becoming less likely to change course (Kelly and Amburgey, 1991). As the organization becomes older, it tends to select innovation routines that have proved to be fruitful (Rahmandad, 2008). Successes lead to bias in evaluating innovation options and outcomes, inertia builds up over time and the organization loses the ability to value different innovation patterns.

The effects of inertia and bias.   Building up inertia and bias over time prohibits organizations from appreciating the potential of innovation options outside the dominant organizational logic and managers' cognitive maps. As a consequence, successful innovations of competitors are hardly noticed, the importance of these innovations is not understood in full and the organization might miss a crucial industry development. For example, the US retailer Sears Roebuck has missed the advent of discount retailers and home centres (Christensen, 1997, 2011).

The effects of inertia and bias apply to all innovation routines. Organizations that continuously improve the current business model have a high chance of missing a breakthrough technology, such as Kodak missing the digital imaging revolution, or a revolutionary new business model, as the Sears Roebuck case illustrates. In contrast, companies focusing on the 'next big thing', concentrating key resources on the new breakthrough innovation, build up a blind spot for continuous improvements of competitors. As a result, they may well end up with products that are too expensive or which, when compared with alternatives, lack differentiation value. For example, by continuously improving products, the Japanese electronics firms have come to dominate the market of television sets in the United States, the country, *par excellence*, of TV.

The effects of feedback.   When innovation results are satisfying according to higher level managers, strategists are not challenged to explore innovations that could be even more promising. Innovations are evaluated according to the current dominant logic and based on existing mental models (see also Chapter 2). As long as the results meet the criteria, there is no compelling reason to change course. The company's absorption of innovations that are 'good enough' is reinforced when the full potential of different innovation options is not fully understood or valued.

Continuous feedback of the innovation portfolio complicates business model renewal processes, especially for innovations with a longer development time. During the innovation period, innovations with an extensive lead time are evaluated in multiple intermediate states. Since in each state disappointing progress might be noted, innovations with a long lead time are vulnerable to be discontinued. For example, promising process improvement initiatives can prematurely be abandoned (Repenning and Sterman, 2002), and product development capability can be compromised by reduced investments in concept design activities (Repenning, 2001). The effect of intermediate evaluations is that innovation projects with a relatively short duration, delivering immediate pay-offs, become dominant (Rahmandad, 2008). Process improvements in manufacturing pay off relatively fast, while it takes some time before the results of business development become visible.

Of course, strategizing managers do not merely focus on the immediate payback of innovations. The expected future value continues to be a significant factor while evaluating innovations with long lead times. The problem is, however, that in allocating resources priorities may change. For example, some resources may be needed in urgent innovation projects with immediate pay-offs and temporal budget cuts may eliminate long-term investments. If intermediate moments of evaluation become more frequent, innovations are, thus, more likely to be abandoned.

The key to bringing long-term investment projects to a successful end is to define milestones with clearly described mid-term targets. However, the end state of long-term innovations can usually not be clearly envisioned, making intermediate states difficult to define. In sum, investment projects with long lead times have the highest chance of being abandoned along the way, especially when intermediate feedback occurs more frequently.

The combination of four challenging processes – strategizing, entrepreneurial, changing and investing – in conjunction with the three main inhibitors may well explain why most companies are unable to approach a century-enduring corporate life, which De Geus' study has proved to be possible. The question is, thus, how can strategizing managers extend corporate life? Is there a magic formula for sustained youth, a corporate elixir from magicians in academia or consulting? While this cannot be fully excluded, a much more likely answer is that companies should master the ability to renew themselves. This would indicate that strategic renewal is the key strategic issue for a company's long-term success.

Business model renewal

Strategizing managers striving for long-term success are well aware that many factors may change the competitive arena. Although strategists cannot predict the future, they know that it will differ from today. Customer needs, competitor's actions and technological advancements are among the many elements that may create a future misfit between the current business model and the company's environment. In order to prepare for a competitive future that is yet unknown, strategizing managers need to renew several elements of the business model. Not only current products and services are to be improved; to create future demands new products and services must also be developed. Strategists are not only *reacting* to changes, they can also *initiate* changes by innovating activities, effectively creating an environmental misfit for competitors.

As strategic innovation is defined as renewing the business model that creates a competitive advantage, the term business model renewal needs to be introduced. Strategists can renew each element of the company's business model. A business model is the configuration of resources (inputs), activities (throughput) and product/service offerings (output) intended to create value for customers – it is the way in which a firm conducts its business (see Chapter 4). The first element in a successful business model (*product offering*) is a superior 'value proposition'. A firm must be able to supply a product or service that has a superior mix of attributes (e.g. price, availability, reliability, technical specifications, image, colour, taste, ease of use, etc.). The second element (*value chain*) is the ability to actually develop and supply the superior product offering. It needs to have the capability to perform the necessary value-adding activities in an effective and efficient manner. These value-adding activities, such as R&D, production, logistics, marketing and sales, are jointly referred to as a firm's value chain. The third element of a business model (*resource base*) consists of the resources required to perform the value-adding activities. Resources such as know-how, patents, facilities, money, brands and relationships make up the stock of assets that can be employed to create the product offering. If these firm-specific assets are distinctive and useful, they can form the basis of a superior value proposition. Strategizing managers can choose between outside-in renewal, inside-out renewal and value chain renewal (see Figure 9.3).

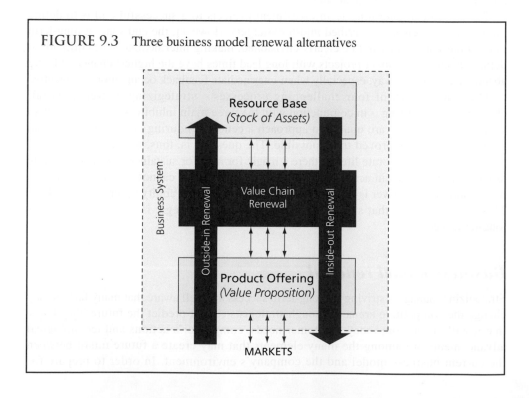

FIGURE 9.3   Three business model renewal alternatives

Outside-in renewal.   Strategizing managers can renew their value proposition to customers by increasing the perceived product and service value, and by lowering prices. Reliability, for example, is highly valued by customers in most industries. By continuously improving the reliability of its products, the Korean car maker Hyundai has become known as a company offering high quality yet affordable products (see also the short case in Chapter 5). Another case of outside-in renewal, usually coined marketing innovation or product offering renewal, has to do with the creation of new markets or market segments with existing products. For example, Unilever created new market demand by offering instant soup to the corporate market and by repositioning ice cream to increase adult consumption.

Inside-out renewal.   By renewing the company's resource base, new products and services can be created and existing ones can be improved. New technologies are often the prime starting point for inside-out renewal. For example, companies like Philips (medical technology, lighting and household appliances), Merck (pharmaceuticals), and Toyota (motorized vehicles) invest heavily in technological research and development. The know-how and patents add to the firm's resource base, and from there new technologies will create and improve new products and services. Other resources can also be renewed. For example, brands can be renewed by an intensive marketing campaign, and the firm's human resources by training.

Value chain renewal.   Along with renewing the firm's value proposition or resource base, strategists can renew some, or even all, elements of the value chain. For example, IKEA has become the world's largest furniture retailer by redesigning the end-to-end value chain, from standardizing production processes to developing flat pack designs and lowering transportation costs. The value chain innovation of Amazon has prompted competitors and firms in other industries to rethink and renew their chain of value-adding activities.

THE PARADOX OF EXPLOITATION AND EXPLORATION

If you realize that all things change, there is nothing you will try to hold on to.
If you are not afraid of dying, there is nothing you cannot achieve.

Lao Tzu (6th century BCE), Chinese philosopher and author

Many management theorists have addressed the tension between exploitation and exploration (March, 1991; Gupta, Smith and Shalley, 2006; Raisch *et al.*, 2009; Tushman and O'Reilly, 1996; Zott and Amit, 2013). The question being addressed is whether the company should renew itself by improving the current organization (exploitation) or by radically rejuvenating the organization through disrupting technologies and processes (exploration). On the one hand, they realize that ongoing improvement of products and services will increase customer satisfaction and therefore strengthens the company's competitive position. When ongoing improvement becomes an organizational routine, the company becomes better and faster, which would, in the long run, wear out competitors. On the other hand, they recognize the effects of changing the competitive rules with radically new products, technologies and novel ways of organizing the company. Rule changers leave competitors in the awkward position of catching up with their rules; a feat at which they often fail.

Researchers agree that companies need both exploitative and explorative processes (March, 1991). The problem is, however, that these renewal processes are each other's opposites and are at least partially contradictory. Improving the current business model starts with defining how the company can become more efficient and effective. Customers are asked how the current products and services may become even better than they are today and what changes would meet their demands even more; employees are invited to come up with ideas on how to streamline production and distribution processes, and how to adapt the sales organization to increase effectiveness. On the basis of these data, the business model is incrementally improved and becomes more efficient and effective. The point of departure for radically rejuvenating firms, however, is not a list of today's possible improvements, but an imagined future of a different industry. It does not start with asking customers what they need, because customers generally do not know if they need something that does not exist yet. The starting point is either a new technology or a radically new idea of how future customers may be served. From this vision, new products, services and business models are being developed, and new customer needs are shaped. Customers need to adapt to the firm's great new offerings, not the other way around. The company *shapes* the future; it *does not build* on the present situation.

Both renewal processes have value, however the problem is that processes to improve current products, services and technologies are very different and often even opposite to processes to explore breakthrough innovations. It requires a different mindset, different people, different processes and a different time horizon. Even the criteria of measuring success differ. Renewal processes aiming at improving current products and services can be measured in terms of realized client value (lower price and higher quality). The success of radical renewal with disrupting technologies and new processes is measured by the extent to which a new industry is created or new customer value is realized. The resulting tension between exploitation and exploration will be explored in the following sections.

The demand for sustained renewal

Sustained renewal refers to the process of permanently improving products and services to strengthen the company's competitive position. It is the never-ending quest for raising quality standards and increasing efficiency, achieving ever better and cheaper value propositions – including after-sales, marketing and sales. Each time a higher standard has been reached, the bar is raised to the next level. Quality standards include not only technologies, materials and other physical inputs into the renewal process, but also people – the human resources. People are also developed at ever higher levels.

Sustained renewal is based on factual information, such as customer feedback and market research as well as on ideas from anyone within and outside of the firm. Anything that may bring the current products and services to a higher level is included in the renewal process. The higher level then becomes the new standard both for the company and for competitors and customers. A company needs to improve, even to maintain its current position, because without engaging in this permanent process of improvement, the firm would lag behind competitors and eventually deteriorate. People do not want to read yesterday's newspaper or buy outdated products, and therefore without sustained renewal there is no long-term future for a company.

Ideas for improvement arrive from different internal and external stakeholders. The areas of improvement can widely vary, yet these are usually based on the current understanding of the business the company is in and what kinds of product and service the company relates to the dominant logic (see also Chapter 2). Thinking within the boundaries of a shared paradigm is generally accepted and people tend to proceed accordingly – that is, they renew to sustain the current business model. The downside of a dominant logic is that it usually locks people into shared paradigms that have been tried and tested, and thus becomes immune to external signals that may not fit. This is where the need for disruptive renewal comes in.

The demand for disrupting renewal

Disrupting renewal refers to a process in which current competitive positions are challenged by introducing new technologies and business models. As described above, when improving products and services, a strategist defines each renewing activity on the basis of facts while following the dominant logic. However, when searching for an innovation that will disrupt the industry, a strategist needs to take leaps of imagination. Disruptive innovations do not follow from the facts, but need to be invented. They are not analysed into existence, but need to be generated if they are to be distinctive and rule changing.

When generating disrupting solutions, creative thinking is not just important, it is the essence. In disrupting creative thinking, the strategist abandons the rules governing sound argumentation and draws a conclusion that is not justified based on prior arguments. In this way, the strategist generates a new understanding, but without objective proof that the new idea 'makes sense'. Creative thinking takes liberty in following thinking rules. One idea might lead to another idea, without formal logic interfering. One variable might be linked to another, without a sound explanation of why a correlation is assumed. Creativity in effect creates a new understanding, with little attention paid to supporting evidence. Often logic is used afterwards to justify an idea that was actually generated by creative means.

Disruptive renewal does not follow from the dominant logic, but is the unexpected outcome that emerges when the dominant logic is challenged. Changing a shared paradigm requires strategists to imagine new ways of understanding the world that do not follow from current beliefs. Strategic thinkers need to be willing and able to break with orthodoxy and make leaps of imagination, to generate novel ways of looking at old problems.

The conclusion must be that sustained renewal and disruptive renewal are not only opposites, but they are partially incompatible as well. They are based on methods that are at odds with one another. Strategizing managers would probably love to exploit and explore at the same time, yet both require such a different mindset and range of cognitive skills that in practice it is very difficult to achieve both simultaneously (March, 1991). The demand for sustained renewal and disruptive renewal is not only contradictory for each individual, but also within teams, departments and the overall firm. While strategizing groups would like to be fully capable of both exploiting and exploring, finding ways of incorporating both into a workable renewal process is extremely challenging. Conflicting styles often lead to mutual misunderstanding and conflicts among people. Therefore, a blend between the two is not that simple. It is for this reason that we speak of the 'paradox of exploitation and exploration' – the two demands on innovating managers seem to be contradictory, yet both are required at the same time. Inspired by Christensen (1997, 2011), this can be called *the innovator's paradox.*

EXHIBIT 9.1   SHORT CASE

3M: IN SEARCH OF RENEWAL

If one organization would represent 20th-century innovations and technological breakthroughs it would likely be 3M. The Minnesota Mining and Manufacturing Company had managed to conquer the world with products such as cellotape and Post-It notes, and had become famous for its innovative culture. Yet, while in 2004 still the world's most innovative company, 3M was no longer listed on the BCG Top 50 of most innovative companies when Inge Thulin took the helm as the new CEO in 2012. Shareholders were happy, however: with a steady growth and expanding sales in emerging markets such as China and Brazil, 3M had gradually climbed the ranks of best performing companies from place 110 to 95. But could this be sustained? 3M was facing tough competition, increased environmental regulations and a versatile global market, while the firm's strong financial performance was largely the result of past innovations – and 3M seemed to have lost its innovation capability. Inge Thulin was wondering how he could keep shareholders satisfied, while also rebuilding the innovation capability that had made 3M famous and had created strong growth.

The Minnesota Mining and Manufacturing Company was founded in 1902 by five entrepreneurs with the initial objective to mine and market a relatively rare mineral known as *corundum* to be sold as an abrasive. When the mine called Crystal Bay proved to contain insufficient amounts of minerals, the founders' focus changed. They had noted customers' great need for better processing materials, and so they developed high quality sandpaper that caused less dust than the hitherto conventional abrasives. From there 3M worked itself to one of the most successful companies it is today, in roughly four phases.

3M's first phase consisted of building an innovation-centred company. The focal point in the first decades of success was CEO William McKnight, an engineer who stood at the base of the first 3M products. He defined 3M's mission as: *solving unsolved problems in innovative ways.* In 1948 he laid the management foundation for 3M's innovative culture:

As our business grows, it becomes increasingly necessary to delegate responsibility and to encourage men and women to exercise their initiative. This requires considerable tolerance. Those men and women, to whom we delegate authority and responsibility, if they are good people, are going to want to do their jobs in their own way.

Mistakes will be made. But if a person is essentially right, the mistakes he or she makes are not as serious in the long run as the mistakes management will make if it undertakes to tell those in authority exactly how they must do their jobs.

Management that is destructively critical when mistakes are made kills initiative. And it's essential that we have many people with initiative if we are to continue to grow.

3M employees gained independence and space to experiment and investigate. Staff was allowed to spend 15 per cent of their working time on self-initiated projects; exploring became part of each employee's job. An endless array of new products and variants thereof were developed. Examples of breakthrough innovations were the cellotape, magnetic tape, and, not to be forgotten, the Post-It note. By combining competences, 3M had entered different industries such as the pharmaceutical sector with new generation patches and electronics where 3M materials allowed for higher resolution flat screens.

The eight divisions had the autonomy to develop new products within their sector and bring them to the market. From 1914 to 1966 – when McKnight acted as CEO – the company's sales exploded from $264,000 to an astonishing $1.15 billion. His internal successors continued this policy: Renewal remained paramount and the bottom-up organization sustained. In the early 1990s, however, 3M seemed to have lost grip on financial and intellectual resources. Costly investments in people and products failed to generate the desired results, while no new breakthrough product had been launched since the Post-It note in 1980. Time to market for new products had been too lengthy, managers were insufficiently challenged, and the company that relied heavily on innovative initiatives had been characterized as reactive. At the end of the 1990s 3M missed focus and was sensitive to all kinds of fads and fashions. Shareholders were muttering. It was time for a change.

As such, the second phase welcomed an increased focus and an accelerated time to market of 3M's products. In early 2000, on the initiative of shareholders, outsider James McNerney was appointed CEO. Unlike his engineering predecessors McNerney had a marketing background, and had previously worked under the leadership of General Electric's CEO Jack Welch where he had gained credits in creating and transforming lean organizations. McNerney's arrival at 3M was the start of a transformation process in search of hidden costs. In a short time period he managed to bring focus to both the manufacturing and R&D departments. Focusing on the mindset of 3M employees he imported the GE Six Sigma programme, a series of management techniques aimed at reducing production errors and increasing efficiency. And not without result: performance at 3M improved significantly.

In parallel, McNerney took some – for 3M – unprecedented steps. He increased competition within the company, while existing plants and research laboratories were downsized and some activities were transferred to low-wage countries. In a short time, the US workforce was reduced by 8,000 employees – over 10 per cent of the total employment. Never before in the existence of the organization had job security of workers of the Minnesota plants been threatened. These events had a negative impact on the open and innovative culture of 3M that had been built on the strong bond between company and employees. In addition, innovation focused on only those R&D projects that promised the highest and safest return. The time from idea to product was shortened, which resulted in an expanded product portfolio in a relatively short time period. Sales increased by 10 per cent annually, delighting the shareholders. In 2005, McNerney decided to leave the company and moved to Boeing.

The third phase of 3M consisted of accelerating growth by acquisitions and the strengthening of new markets. George Buckley, a former engineer from Brunswick Company was appointed CEO at the end of 2005. After a detailed study of the firm he concluded that 3M was a highly scientific engineering and manufacturing company with conservative values, successfully participating in many niche markets. Success, he concluded, was related to collaboration within the company, and therefore sharing and transferring technologies across products and markets became a key ingredient of the company's strategy. Buckley decided to restore the original 3M innovative culture by rehabilitating the 15 per cent rule without restrictions for R&D operations. A technology market architecture was set up, in which nine technology platforms (such as adhesives and non-woven materials) were distinguished as the fundament for 3M's core assets and interconnected with the various markets (such as aerospace and health care) in which 3M was active. This way the gap between research and customers had been narrowed.

Expansion of the product portfolio had mainly been realized by Buckley's choice for an acquisition strategy, focused on booming sectors and emerging markets such as China and Brazil. In 2006 only, 16 acquisitions were being made – representing 24 per cent of the company's annual turnover – and more acquisitions followed suit. When Buckley retired in 2012, he had increased revenues by 40 per cent to $29.6 billion in his CEO term, yet only 3 per cent of the increase had resulted from internal organic growth.

3M's final phase is thus a possible restoration of organic growth. Buckley's successor Inge Thulin joined 3M in 1979, and climbed the ranks through the company's health care business. Thulin was the first company insider after a period of 12 years in which outsiders held sway at 3M. He had run international operations, for which he had expanded sales to almost $20 billion, two-thirds of 3M's $29.6 billion total revenues. When taking the helm in 2012, Thulin had challenging shareholder expectations and inherited his predecessor's ambition of 7 to 8 per cent annual sales growth. Four years later, in 2016, shareholders were happy: 3M had gradually climbed on the Fortune 500 list of best performing companies from position 102 in 2012 to number 93 in 2016.

Not all went well, though. While in 2014 the company had gained position 22 on the BCG top 50 of the world's most innovative companies after many years of re-installing 3M's innovative power, a year later in 2015 it had plummeted again: to position 40. The company that was once the 20th-century champion of innovation, then dropping to position 22 in 2008 and out of BCG's list of the world's most innovative companies in 2010, regaining place 22 in 2014, had dropped again. In his CEO letter, Thulin described his motto as 'finding the balance between a microscope view focusing on the day-to-day challenges and a telescope view focusing on strengthening 3M for the future'. With 5.8 per cent of its sales spent on R&D in 2015, slightly above the industrial average, Thulin seemed not to have found the desired balance between short and long term yet. Future value comes from invention and innovation – even one single idea may create the company's future – while short-term value relates to operational excellence. How should Thulin glue the present to the future? He has one advantage over competitors: There is no shortage of cellotape and Post-It notes.

Co-author: Jeroen van der Velden

Sources: www.3m.com; 3M Annual report 2012; 3M Annual report 2015; 'At 3M, a struggle between efficiency and creativity', *Business Week* 2007; '3M's Thulin to keep Buckley focus on research, emerging markets', *Business Week* 2012; www.bcgperspectives. com (innovative companies 2005–2015); www. fortune500.com; IBS (3M cultivating core competency).

PERSPECTIVES ON STRATEGIC INNOVATION

Innovation opportunities do not come with the tempest but with the rustling of the breeze.

Peter Drucker (1909–2005), Austrian-American writer, management thinker and consultant

The demand for both sustained and disruptive renewal puts strategizing managers in the difficult position of having to determine how these two must be combined and balanced in a process of ongoing renewal. Sustained renewal is necessary to ensure ongoing improvement of the current business model – elevating current products and services to ever higher levels of customer satisfaction. Disruptive renewal is necessary to create new business models – imposing competitors to follow the new rules of the competitive game. The question is how strategizing managers go about the demands of renewing the company.

The strategic management literature comes up with a variety of answers to this question. Both among business practitioners and strategy researchers, views differ sharply about the best way of dealing with the paradox of exploitation and exploration. To gain insight into the major points of disagreement on the issue of strategic renewal, the two diametrically opposed perspectives will be outlined here.

At one end of the virtual continuum of views are the strategists who argue that strategic innovation must be achieved by ongoing renewal of the existing firm. Continuous improvement, although difficult to sustain, is at the heart of strategic innovation. This point of view will be referred to as the *strategic improvement perspective*. At the other end of the spectrum are the strategists who argue that real strategic innovations are radical departures from the current business model, disrupting the industry in which the firm is active. Not minor improvements are the heart of strategic innovation, but, instead, striving for a significant rejuvenation towards a next state. Disrupting renewal, although difficult to achieve, is at the heart of strategic innovation. This point of view will be referred to as the *radical rejuvenation perspective*.

The strategic improvement perspective

Proponents of the strategic improvement perspective advocate that companies should focus on improving their business model. The point of departure is the permanent battle between rivalling companies that fight for the same customer group. With customers having a choice between comparable products and services that may satisfy their needs, competitive success requires offering the best, cheapest and most novel value propositions. Improved products and services attract more customers, increase market share and generate more returns, and therefore are the key success factor in the competitive game.

The attitude that things can always be advanced is important for the strategic improvement perspective. Everyone within the firm should be driven by constructive dissatisfaction with the status quo. Furthermore, all employees within the firm should be committed to improving all elements of the business model. Company leaders are facilitative in the sustained renewal process; their main role is to coordinate several renewal initiatives. They must also be aware of the danger of the 'success trap': 'sustained renewal often leads to early success, which in turn reinforces further renewal along the same trajectory' (Gupta *et al.*, 2006).

Proponents of the strategic improvement perspective agree that game-changing innovations provide a significant competitive advantage for the innovator. They point out, however, that although the benefits of success can be considerable, it is a risky route with a moderate chance of success at best. In order to increase the chance of a successful breakthrough innovation, the company must allocate the best resources, leaving ample capacity for engaging in continuous improvements that generate immediate competitive success. As the chance of breakthrough success is low, all innovation efforts may well be without results, while the company's rivals have progressed to higher standards. The conclusion must be that radical innovation initiatives absorb the most precious resources for corporate renewal while, due to the high chance of failure, the most likely outcome is that the company loses competitive position, or worse gets kicked out of business by rivals (Imai, 1986).

EXHIBIT 9.2   THE STRATEGIC IMPROVEMENT PERSPECTIVE

WEBER-STEPHEN PRODUCTS: HOT FOR GRILLS

In the 1940s, brick-made grills were the norm. Surrounded by low walls with a grill rack in the middle, these open-air grills were a staple of American life. Although hugely popular at the time, these types of grill are far from perfect. They cannot be moved, the grill rusts from constant exposure to the elements, bad weather extinguishes the fire and wind can cause ash to blow up and attach itself to food and the occasional piece of clothing.

This annoyed George Stephen Sr., who was working at Weber Brothers Metal Works in Chicago at the time. So much so that he tried to fix it. George went to his workplace, grabbed a metal half-sphere used to make marine buoys and turned it into a tight-fitting lid for his grill. In order to fuel the fire, a neighbour suggested he poke holes in the kettle. The result was a dome-shaped grill that protects food from the elements, keeps the fire burning and all the while sealing in

that distinct barbeque flavour. Thus the Weber grill was born, a charcoal kettle grill that would bring about a backyard revolution.

The invention caught fire among George Stephen's friends. They raved about his grill and the taste of the dishes his invention helped make. The kettle design also allows heat to circulate around the food evenly and this has a profound effect on the food. The enthusiastic responses made Stephen sell the first ever kettle grills in 1952 and soon did this under his own brand: Weber-Stephen Products. It did not take long before the spherical grill became the most popular grill in the United States and the majority of Americans gave their meat the kettle treat. The company is now the world's largest grill manufacturer and holds about 35 per cent of the US grill market.

Weber-Stephen Products is continuously looking for ways to improve its grill offering. In the 1970s it started producing electric grills and kettles fitted with propane tanks. These did not sell like hotcakes, however, for the kettle shape was associated too strongly with charcoal grilling. Setting his sights on creating a better gas grill, Weber-Stephen launched the Genesis line. These rectangular gas-based grills are fitted with triangular 'Flavorizer' cooking bars, designed to distribute heat more evenly, reduce flare-ups and mimic the sizzling of food on hot coals. The company kept improving its grill assortment, by introducing the Handle Light to illuminate the grilling surface and came up with built-in charcoal buckets for its coal-based grills. More compact grills were also designed for dense urban areas in order to better serve the South-East Asian market.

Resembling General Motors' Chevy-to-Caddy product range, Weber-Stephen offers differently priced grills. As consumers climb the income ladder, they can start off with the miniature Smokey Joe kettle for $30 and keep purchasing better, more expensive grills, such as the $2,000 Genesis gas models. With a wide product range and incessant improvement, Weber-Stephen aims to keep firing up audiences worldwide and let the grilling continue.

Co-author: Wester Wagenaar

Sources: weber.com; weberstephen.nl; *Bloomberg*, 27 June 2013; *Wall Street Journal*, 21 May 2015.

The radical rejuvenation perspective

According to proponents of the radical rejuvenation perspective, companies should focus on breakthrough innovations that change the rules of the competitive game rather than becoming better at playing by the current rules. Game-changing innovations provide innovators with a significant competitive advantage, forcing rivals to follow and play by their rules. The more radical the departure from the industry rules, the more difficult it will be for competitors to follow and the higher the benefits for the innovator are likely to be.

If a firm decides to use a breakthrough technology or a new business model to strengthen its competitive position vis-à-vis rivals, this requires some major changes in a short period of time, as such innovations to the business model are inherently disrupting. Creating novel products and developing a unique business formula require a sharp break with the past. Old ways must be discarded before new methods can be adopted. This is the essence of what Schumpeter (1950) referred to as the process of 'creative destruction', inherent in the capitalist system. This process is not orderly and protracted, but disruptive and intense. Therefore, it is argued, successful firms must learn to master the skill of radical innovation (e.g. D'Aveni, 1994; Hamel, 1996). Rapid implementation of system-wide change is an essential organizational capability.

In the radical rejuvenation perspective, strong company leadership is essential (Leifer, 2000). Break-through renewal is not only disrupting for rivals, but also for the organization itself. The business model needs to be renewed, usually in conjunction with the organizational system. Such dramatic alterations can only be successful when a strong company leader is in a position to get things done. This is even more prominent as a disruptive renewal project usually takes extensive time to be developed from an idea into an actual product, which makes the continuity of the project vulnerable for feedback sessions along the way. It is crucial that the disruptive renewal project will be a success, because in the absence, there is the danger of the 'failure trap': 'failure promotes the search for even newer ideas and thus more exploration' (Gupta *et al.*, 2006).

Proponents of the radical rejuvenation perspective agree that improvements are useful to help companies defending and strengthening their competitive positions, however, they argue that it comes at a high price. Sustained improvement and allocating key company resources on projects that enhance existing products, services and technologies, goes at the expense of strategically more effective game-changing innovations. Focusing on serving current customers with better propositions at lower costs, leads to maximizing short-term return on innovation budgets, and diminishes the capacity to engage in breakthrough innovations to serve customers in the future. Indeed, many well-managed companies that continuously improve on the basis of customer needs fail *exactly because* they are well managed, a phenomenon dubbed by Christensen (1997, 2011) as the innovator's dilemma.

EXHIBIT 9.3   THE RADICAL REJUVENATION PERSPECTIVE

CHOBANI: KEEPING THE YOGHURT MARKET FRESH

Born in Turkey to a Kurdish dairy farmer, Hamdi Ulukaya used his childhood knowledge to build a Greek yoghurt empire that made him a billionaire in just six years. While his original intent of coming to America was to study business and English, he soon got side-tracked by an ad in the paper offering an old dairy plant for sale. He dropped out of his studies, a parallel that might have contributed to his unofficial title, the 'Steve Jobs of yoghurt', to buy the 80-year-old plant that he restored himself. He sold his first container of yoghurt just 18 months later and went on to expand at an impressive pace, today employing over 2,000 people.

Until a decade ago, a very sweet type of yoghurt dominated the American supermarket shelves. The alternative to this popular breakfast item, Greek yoghurt, containing more protein and less fat, had never been available outside specialty shops. Recession-weary and health-conscious shoppers took very warmly to Mr Ulukaya's efforts to extend their breakfast choices with his traditional Greek product, consequently growing Greek yoghurt sales from 1 to 60 per cent of the total yoghurt business.

One might wonder why yoghurt giants Stark or Danone did not act on these trends, as retailers certainly welcomed Mr Ulukaya's products with open arms, right from the start. In fact, the Greek yoghurt invasion was not the first time that food and beverage incumbents were caught by surprise. Plum Organics revolutionized baby food packaging, resulting in 20 per cent of American babies now being fed by squirting food out of a container instead of being spoon fed, while Koppert Cress commoditized decorative foodstuffs to liven up plates in restaurants all over the world; a very profitable niche in which it still maintains a monopoly.

The common practice in the food and beverage industry is that successful start-ups are being acquired by incumbents. Mr Ulukaya, however, has never accepted any of the lucrative offers he got for his Greek yoghurt empire, keeping all shares under his own control. This resulted in his not just disrupting the market once and then being integrated in a large bureaucracy, but allowed him to keep going. After his first success of introducing Greek yoghurt to the American public, he opened a store in Soho, one of New York's most fashionable neighbourhoods, selling the most exquisite combinations of Greek yoghurt with peach, dates and many more. With his unique and healthy snacks – nearly as exclusive and expensive as the neighbouring VIP bars' cocktails – Mr Ulukaya tried to vamp up the image of breakfast items. Other savvy moves, in a similar vein, are a new line of healthy products for children and healthy alternatives to Red Bull or coffee.

Mr Ulukaya is an innovator *par excellence*. He has been able to keep surprising the establishment with new and exciting ways to position his products. Whether he can keep momentum once his company has reached a similar size as the yoghurt giants he is competing with remains to be seen, but based on his passion and continuous streak of awards, we can look forward to many more delicious market disruptions.

Co-author: Jasper de Vries

Sources: 'At Chobani, the Turkish king of Greek yogurt', *Bloomberg*, 31 January 2013; 'Cultural revolution: The Greek-yogurt phenomenon in America left big food firms feeling sour. They are trying to get better at innovation', *The Economist*, 31 August 2013; 'At Chobani, now it's not just the yoghurt that's rich', *New York Times*, 26 April 2016.

MANAGING THE PARADOX OF EXPLOITATION AND EXPLORATION

He that will not apply new remedies must expect new evils, for time is the greatest innovator.

Francis Bacon (1561–1626), English philosopher, statesman, scientist, jurist, orator and author

So, how should managers go about renewing their organizations? Should strategizing managers focus on sustained renewal by ongoing improvement of their current business model? Or should they strive for disruptive renewal by focusing on radical, breakthrough innovations? There is no consensus within the field of strategic management on how to balance exploitation and exploration; however, a number of scholars have discussed different ways of dealing with the arguments put forward in the debate (see Table 9.1). Depending on the situation, strategizing managers can assess the arguments and develop their own way of dealing with the paradox.

While the general notion of strategy paradoxes and competing demands is often not – or not fully – embraced among scholars, it is one of the key research areas in innovation research. Initiated by March's (1991) pioneering article, the paradox of exploitation and exploration has become highly influential in the fields of organizational learning and organizational behaviour, and currently also enjoys the attention from many strategy researchers. As strategic innovation concerns the future of the company, it is at the core of what strategizing managers are actually doing. The question is thus, how can they best manage the paradox of exploitation and exploration? Taken from the taxonomy in Chapter 1 (Figure 1.9), the following options are discussed in the literature.

Parallel processing

Parallel processing involves separating exploitation and exploration processes in different organizational units (differentiation), while integration takes place at a different – usually higher – organizational level. This option has been coined 'spatial separation' – an academic term still used by organization behaviour scholars. Organizations that employ both exploitation – for example, by improving production processes – and exploration – such as technological research and development – as the means of dealing with the paradox of exploitation and exploration are called ambidextrous organizations

TABLE 9.1   Strategic improvement versus strategic rejuvenation perspective

	Strategic improvement perspective	Radical rejuvenation perspective
Emphasis on	Exploitation over exploration	Exploration over exploitation
Strategic innovation as	Sustained improvements	Disruptive rejuvenation
Innovation effects	Undramatic and long-lasting	Dramatic and short-term
Innovation ideas come from	All internal and external company stakeholders	Entrepreneurial company leaders
Innovation investments are	Low-risk, small returns	High-risk, high returns
Main reinforcement mechanism	Success trap	Failure trap
Strategic renewal process	Organic adaptation	Creative destruction
View on the future	Building the future	Shaping the future
Lasting renewal requires	Continuous learning	Radical breakthrough series
Long-term renewal dynamics	Persistent transient state	Stable and unstable states alternate

(Benner and Tushman, 2003). Ambidextrous organizations separate exploitative and explorative processes in different organizational units. The literature has suggested two distinct parallel processing practices.

Parallel processing internally.   One well-known practice is to build a separate research and development (R&D) unit that develops new technologies. The outcomes are then transferred to other organizational units, such as business units or market groups. Some researchers have indicated, however, that differentiating may be easy but integrating often fails. The problems are many, for example when researchers have developed technologies and patents, while managers have difficulties matching the technologies to client demands.

Parallel processing with external partners.   Exploitation and exploration can also be separated by outsourcing one of the processes to an external strategic partner. When exploitation is outsourced, partners take responsibility to adopt the firm's exploitative processes, such as manufacturing products, including the ongoing improvement of current processes and products. In this case, the company is able to focus the key organizational resources on exploration processes, creating the new generation of products and services. Conversely, the firm can also outsource exploration to specialized companies, and stay focused on efficient and effective exploitation. Strategizing managers then integrate the partner's deliverables within the company processes. A main advantage of parallel processing with external partners is that it effectively combines the contradicting core capabilities of two firms; a main pitfall is, however, that the partner's strategic objectives may change and become conflicting.

Navigating

Entrepreneurs often separate exploration and exploitation over time in the early start-up phase. When starting a new business on the basis of a new idea for a new technology (such as a new app) or a novel market proposition, the entrepreneur first explores and then exploits – hence navigates over time, also called temporal separation.

In this case, the start-up entrepreneur is not renewing as there is not yet an organization to be renewed; however, when this initiative is being taken by a corporate entrepreneur or a business development manager, the entrepreneurial activity may well intend to renew the current company. The new activity is then meant to replace or improve established businesses. This process had become known by the famous CEO from General Electric, Jack Welch, who introduced the 'Destroy your business dot com' programme in the year 2000. The general practice then is that the renewing unit stays at a distance from the established company in order to prevent managers from the current business killing the initiative in its infancy. This practice has been advocated by Peters and Waterman (1982), who dubbed these promising corporate start-ups 'skunk works' as the initiative may threaten the current organization and thus 'stinks'.

Balancing

One of the differences between exploitation and exploration is time orientation: sustaining renewal processes (exploitation) has a short-term focus, while disrupting processes (exploration) is long-term oriented. The differences notwithstanding, it is suggested in the literature that the processes may be combined in the same unit. The strategic agenda then consists of both short-term and long-term innovation projects. The balance between the two is not only company specific, but also dynamic as priorities can change. Although balancing exploitation and exploration is more complex than parallel processing, some scholars prefer balancing because, although differentiating is relatively easy and fast, the integrating part is usually a problem (Smith *et al.*, 2016).

When balancing takes place at the individual level, some strategists are expected to fulfil roles in both sustaining and disrupting renewal processes. For example, knowledge workers both build their professional practice at higher levels and also explore radically different ways to serve future clients. Being able to do so requires personal characteristics that not all individuals possess. Smith and Tushman (2005) argue that 'the ability to engage in paradoxical thinking may be vital for effectively managing exploitation and exploration'.

The human factor in balancing the paradox, in particular the composition of the company's leadership team, has been explored by Peter Robertson. In a book provocatively entitled *Always Change a Winning Team* (2005), Robertson combines insights from ethology – a field strongly related to neuroanatomy, ecology and evolution theory – with the dynamics of the well-known S-curve. Robertson argues that the composition of a successful leadership team should differ over the S-curve. In the early phase, the leadership team should mainly be composed of leaders employing visionary feedforward-thinking with a passion to explore the unknown, while in the mature phase, the leadership team should mainly consist of analytic feedback-thinking leaders (see Figure 9.4). Over the S-curve, the composition of the leadership team should be changed in anticipation of the next phase. According to Robertson, the key role in permanently changing the leadership team is a 'chairperson', the CEO, who connects the feedforward and feedback thinkers and who is in charge of continuously rebalancing the 'winning team'. This individual needs to have what Robertson calls high 'complexity maturity', a term that relates to what Smith and Tushman (2005) describe as 'the ability to engage in paradoxical thinking'.

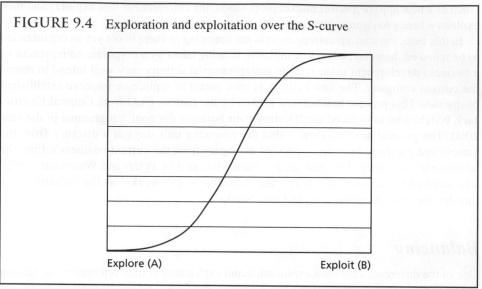

FIGURE 9.4 Exploration and exploitation over the S-curve

Explore (A) Exploit (B)

Source: Robertson, 2005.

STRATEGIC INNOVATION IN INTERNATIONAL PERSPECTIVE

Co-authors: Gep Eisenloeffel and Wester Wagenaar

Imagination is more important than knowledge.

Albert Einstein (1879–1955), German-American physicist

Pronounced international variance on inclinations towards exploitation or exploration is apparent across countries. For what reason do firms in different societies prefer different views on strategic innovation? Are there any country-specific factors that lead to divergent perspectives? Understanding international differences and their causes helps get a better grip on the extent to which companies are able to learn from international practices or are limited by their national context. In addition to national differences, some industries focus more on radical breakthroughs than do others. A strategist can learn from both the national level as well as international industry similarities.

On the national level

Strategic innovation is responsible for turning small firms into industry leaders and for falling giants that fail to successfully renew (Bilton and Cummings, 2010; Utterback, 1994). This is true for the national level as well as for the global scale. Although most agree that innovation is important, preferences on how to innovate differ across societies. Imai (1986) explicitly introduces specific national preferences in his approach to strategic innovation. He argues that 'Japanese companies generally favor the gradualist approach and Western companies the great-leap approach – an approach epitomized by the term innovation'. This general, yet fundamental, distinction is supported by other research, although these studies are relatively old (e.g. Kagono *et al.*, 1985; Ouchi, 1981; Pascale and Athos, 1981). Nevertheless, the common suggestion is that the US and Japan represent two extremes, with most other industrialized countries somewhere in between (e.g. Calori, Valla and De Woot, 1994; Krüger, 1996).

Elucidating the differences in preferences for innovation styles generally boils down to cultural explanations. For example, studies claim a correlation between individualism and innovation (e.g. Goncalo and Staw, 2006; Hampden-Turner and Trompenaars, 2000). Individualistic-minded teams foster internal competition, which improves innovation (Tellis, Prabhu and Chandy, 2009, p. 8). The two countries considered most individualistic, the US and Great Britain, also show tremendous capacity to realize radical frame-breaking innovations. Furthermore, the US leads the world ranking of Nobel Prizes won, in the practical application of scientific principles.

Another cultural explanation can be found in national preferences towards uncertainty avoidance. Because radical innovation inherently yields unexpected and unintended outcomes (Starbuck, 2014), a natural tendency towards feeling threatened by the unknown may limit possibilities. Especially adopting radical changes can be expected to be met with a degree of reluctance in countries scoring high on Hofstede's uncertainty avoidance index (1980).

Culture cannot explain everything, however. Government support and prevailing rules and regulations may also play a decisive role in the transition from one technological platform to another. For instance, since the Second World War, the European Union has been crucial in the transition from coal to an oil- and gas-based energy supply. In China, the government promotes solar power batteries to reduce emissions from two- to four-wheeled motor vehicles.

Traditionally, most recent radical innovations have originated from the West, but a shift seems to be imminent. A good indicator of shifting technological innovations from the traditional industrialized countries in the North West to the upcoming economies in the South East is the number of patents granted per country. This concentration of patents is highly uneven. Between 2000 and 2006, applicants from Japan, the US, the Republic of Korea and Germany received 73 per cent of total patents worldwide. In that same period, the number of patents granted to applicants from China and South Korea grew with an average annual growth rate of 26.5 per cent and 23.2 per cent respectively (WIPO, 2008). China is now the country with the most filed patents per year, although it is in the Republic of Korea that the highest number of patents per unit of GDP are filed. High-income countries in total still account for about 60 per cent of the applications filed. This reflects their high R&D spending (WIPO, 2015). The rapid growth of Chinese patents matches the emergence of this country as the second largest producer of scientific knowledge as revealed by a Thomson Reuters analysis of 10,500 scientific journals worldwide for the period 1981–2008 (Cookson, 2010).

On the industry level

Are there industries with a preference for radical rejuvenation and industries where a focus on strategic improvement can be observed? Every industry follows an S-curve of exploration and exploitation. It depends on the industry how long it takes before a radical innovation changes the game and traditional processes or technologies become outdated. Furthermore, there is not a strict distinction between disruptive and evolutionary industries, because innovation is by nature inter-disciplinary (Story *et al.*, 2014, p. 1272). Nevertheless, some industries do display a stronger focus on exploring possibilities for disruptive innovations, such as the high-tech sector. Capital often proves essential for innovative technological breakthroughs and this is especially true for these high-tech industries. Collaboration or co-opetition is thus a common way to advance promising technological initiatives. Nevertheless, it is important to note that collaboration among those with complementary technology and processes contributes to developing radical innovations, while partners with similar technologies innovate incrementally (Quintana-García and Benavides-Velasco, 2011).

Because of the power of capital to find and develop drastic breakthroughs, it is little surprising that proactive government support is often responsible for radical innovation. One straightforward example is the military industry. The development of aviation, for example, was made possible because of war. Dutch engineer Anthony Fokker, working for the Germans during the First World War, was one of the first great pioneers in the field exploiting opportunities presented as a result of conflict. Many other entrepreneurs, like American Lockheed and French Dassault followed suit. The Cold War is responsible for both the improvement of helicopters and the development of stealth technology. Helicopters were used for the first time in the Korean War and stealth technology was developed in the late 1950s after earlier attempts by the Soviet Union to prevent radar tracking of US spy planes had been unsuccessful. The Defense Advanced Research Projects Agency (DARPA) research teams made computer networking possible, paving the way for the development of the Internet, and present-day drones were primarily invented for war and not for commercial purposes.

Although many of the inventions by the military are adopted by other industries, non-military sectors can also profit directly from government support. For example, Japan's Ministry of International Trade and Industry (MITI) is highly influential in developing industries and the European Commission promotes technological development programmes in the field of information technologies.

To the strategist

Increasingly, the innovator is not merely seen as an individual. He plays a role in a team, organization and network in fostering innovation (Fichter and Beucker, 2012). Nevertheless, the individual strategist still has a powerful role to play in the innovation process. He should not see his context, national and international, as eternally stable, but as in flux and malleable. In order to make the right strategic decisions, he needs to be able to continuously adapt to a changing industry environment. Not only does this mean having the ability to abandon processes, products and services when these prove outdated, the strategist also needs to shift between leadership styles when the need arises. Making radical changes may make some previous commitments and policies obsolete, so a versatile strategist is necessary when dealing with innovation – both during the exploration and in the exploitation phase (Starbuck, 2014).

STRATEGY CONTEXT

Circumstances? I make circumstances!

Napoleon Bonaparte (1769–1821), French emperor

The strategy context is the set of circumstances surrounding strategy-making – the conditions under which both the strategy process and the strategy content are formed. It could be said that strategy context is concerned with the *where* of strategy – where (i.e. in which firm and which environment) the strategy process and strategy content are embedded.

Most strategizing managers have an ambivalent relationship with their strategy context. On the one hand, strategizing is about creating something new, and for this, a healthy level of disregard, or even disrespect, for the present circumstances is required. Much like Napoleon, managers do not want to hear about current conditions limiting their capability to shape the future – they want to create their own circumstances. On the other hand, managers recognize that many contextual limitations are real and that wise strategists must take these circumstances into account. In this section, this fundamental tension between *shaping* the context and *adapting* to it is at the centre of attention.

As depicted in Figure IV.1, the strategy context can be dissected along two different dimensions: industry versus organization, and national versus international. This gives the three key contexts that are explored in Chapters 10, 11 and 12:

- The industry context. The key issue here is how industry development takes place. Can the individual firm influence its industry and to what extent does the industry context dictate particular types of firm behaviour?

- The organizational context. The key issue here is how organizational development takes place. Can strategizing managers influence their own organizational conditions and to what extent does the organizational context determine particular types of firm behaviour?

- The international context. The key issue here is how the international context is developing. Must firms adapt to ongoing global convergence or will international diversity remain a characteristic with which firms will need to cope?

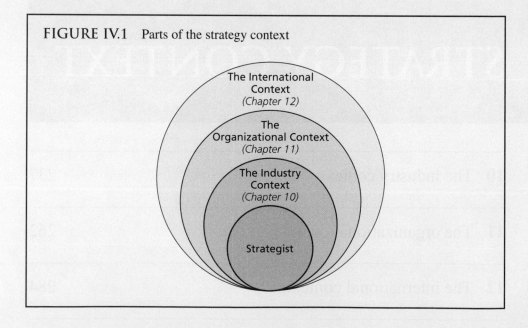

FIGURE IV.1   Parts of the strategy context

THE INDUSTRY CONTEXT

Know the other and know yourself: Triumph without peril.
Know nature and know the situation: Triumph completely.

Sun Tzu (5th century BCE), Chinese military strategist

INTRODUCTION

If strategic management is concerned with relating a firm to its environment, then it is essential to know this environment well. In the previous chapters, the factors and actors that shape the external context of the firm have been thoroughly reviewed. While the entire outside world was taken into consideration, emphasis was placed on the direct environment in which a firm needs to compete – its industry context. It has been concluded that an understanding of competitors, buyers, suppliers, substitutes and potential new entrants, as well as the structural factors that influence their behaviour, is invaluable for determining a successful strategy.

A constant theme in the strategy content and strategy process sections was industry change. Knowing the current industry context, it became clear, is not enough to secure an ongoing alignment between a firm and its environment. Strategizing managers need to recognize in which direction the industry is developing to be able to maintain a healthy fit. However, what was not addressed in these discussions is how industry development actually takes place. Important questions such as 'what are the drivers propelling industry development?' and 'what patterns of development do industries exhibit?' have not yet been examined. Neither has it been established whether industries develop in the same way and at the same speed, and whether change is always accompanied by the same opportunities and threats. In this chapter, these questions surrounding the issue of industry development are at the centre of attention.

For strategizing managers, however, the most important question linked to the issue of industry development is how a firm can move beyond *adapting* to *shaping*. How can a firm, or a group of collaborating firms, modify the structure and competitive dynamics in their industry to gain an advantageous position? How can the industry's evolutionary path be proactively diverted into a particular direction? If a firm would be capable of shaping its industry environment instead of following it, this would give them the potential for creating a strong competitive advantage – they could 'set the rules of the competitive game' instead of having to 'play by the rules' set by others. This topic of industry leadership – shaping events as opposed to following them – will be the key focus throughout this chapter.

THE ISSUE OF INDUSTRY DEVELOPMENT

When strategists look at an industry, they are interested in understanding 'the rules of the game' (e.g. Hamel, 1996; Prahalad and Doz, 1987). The industry rules are the demands dictated to the firm by the industry context, limiting the scope of potential strategic behaviours. In other words, industry rules stipulate what must be done to survive and thrive in any chosen line of business – they determine under what conditions the competitive game will be played. For example, an industry rule could be 'must have significant scale economies', 'must have certain technology' or 'must have strong brand'. Failure to adhere to the rules leads to being selected out.

The industry rules arise from the structure of the industry (e.g. McGahan, 2000; Porter, 1980; Tirole, 1988). All of Porter's five forces can impose constraints on a firm's freedom of action. Where the rules are strict, the degrees of freedom available to the strategist are limited. Strict rules imply that only very specific behaviour is allowed – firms must closely follow the rules of the game or face severe consequences. Where the rules are looser, firms have more room to manoeuvre and exhibit distinctive behaviour – the level of managerial discretion is higher (e.g. Carpenter and Golden, 1997; Hambrick and Abrahamson, 1995).

As industries develop, the rules of competition change – vertical integration becomes necessary, certain competences become vital or having a global presence becomes a basic requirement. To be able to play the competitive game well, strategizing managers need to identify which characteristics in the industry structure and which aspects of competitive interaction are changing. This is the topic of 'dimensions of industry development', which is reviewed in more detail in this chapter. To determine their response, it is also essential to understand the nature of the change. Are the industry rules gradually shifting or is there a major break with the past? Is the industry development more evolutionary or more revolutionary? A process of slow and moderate industry change demands a different strategic reaction than a process of sudden and dramatic disruption of the industry rules. This topic of 'paths of industry development' is also examined more closely.

As strategists generally like to have the option to shape instead of always being shaped, they need to recognize the determinants of industry development as well. What are the factors that cause the industry rules to change? This subject can be divided into two parts. First, the question of what the drivers of industry development are, pushing the industry in a certain direction. Second, the question of what the inhibitors of industry development are, placing a brake on changes. Together, these forces of change and forces for stability will determine the actual path of development that the industry will follow. How these four topics are interrelated is outlined in Figure 10.1.

Dimensions of industry development

Industry development means that the structure of the industry changes. In Chapter 4, the key aspects of the industry structure have already been discussed. Following Porter (1980), five important groups of industry actors were identified (i.e. competitors, buyers, suppliers, new entrants and substitutes) and the underlying factors determining their behaviour were reviewed. Industry development (which Porter calls 'industry evolution'; see also McGahan, 2000) is the result of a change in one or more of these underlying factors.

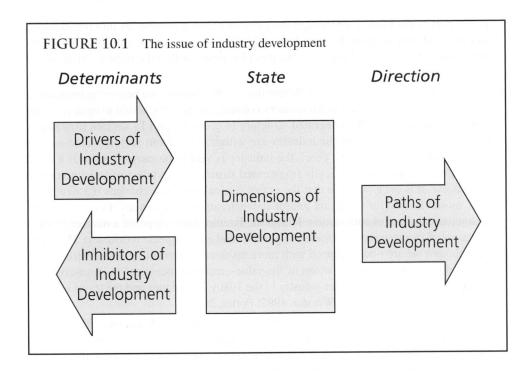

FIGURE 10.1   The issue of industry development

Determinants   **State**   **Direction**

Drivers of Industry Development

Inhibitors of Industry Development

Dimensions of Industry Development

Paths of Industry Development

As Porter has already indicated, the industry structure can be decomposed into dozens of elements, each of which can change, causing a shift in industry rules. Here it is not the intention to go through all of these elements, but to pick out a number of important structural characteristics that require special attention. Each of these structural characteristics represents a dimension along which significant industry developments can take place:

- Convergence–divergence. Where the business models that firms employ increasingly start to resemble each other, the industry is said to be moving towards convergence (e.g. insurance and airline industries). In contrast, where many firms introduce new business models, the industry is said to be developing towards more diversity (e.g. car retailing and restaurant industries). Higher diversity can result from the 'mutation' of existing firms, as they strive to compete on a different basis, or the result of new entrants with their own distinct business model. Convergence is the consequence of adaptation by less successful firms to a 'dominant design' in the industry and the selecting out of un-fit firms incapable of adequate and timely adaptation (e.g. Hannan and Freeman, 1977; Porter, 1980). Generally, patterns of divergence and convergence can be witnessed in all industries, although the amount of mutation and the pressure for convergence can greatly differ, as can the overall cycle time of an 'evolutionary phase' of mutation and selection (e.g. Aldrich, 1999; Baum and Singh, 1994).

- Concentration–fragmentation. Where an increasing share of the market is in the hands of only a few companies, the industry is said to be developing towards a more concentrated structure (e.g. aircraft and food retailing industries). Conversely, where the average market share of the largest companies starts to decrease, the industry is said to be moving towards a more fragmented structure (e.g. airline and telecom services industries). Concentration can be due to mergers and acquisitions, or result from companies exiting the business. Fragmentation can happen when new companies are formed and grab a part of the market, or through the entry of existing companies into the industry. In a concentrated industry it is much more likely that only one or two firms are dominant than in a fragmented industry, but it is also possible that the industry structure is more balanced.

- Vertical integration–fragmentation. Where firms in the industry are becoming involved in more value-adding activities in the industry column, the industry is said to be developing towards a more vertically integrated structure (e.g. media and IT service providers). Conversely, where firms in the industry are withdrawing from various value-adding activities and 'go back to the core', the industry is said to be moving towards a more disintegrated, layered or vertically fragmented structure (e.g. telecom and automotive industries). It is even possible that the entire vertical structure changes if a new business model has major upstream and/or downstream consequences. In recent years, technological changes surrounding IT and the Internet have triggered a number of such instances of industry reconfiguration (e.g. travel and encyclopedia industries). However, even though we are now equipped with more fashionable terms (e.g. 'deconstruction'), such industry-wide transformations of the value-creation process are in themselves not new (e.g. PCs and the computer industry in the 1980s; aeroplanes and the travel industry in the 1950s) (e.g. Evans and Wurster, 1997; Porter, 2001).

- Horizontal integration–fragmentation. Where the boundaries between different businesses in an industry become increasingly fuzzy, the industry is said to be developing towards a more horizontally integrated structure (e.g. consumer electronics and defence industries). Conversely, where firms become more strictly confined to their own business, the industry is said to be moving towards a more segmented or horizontally fragmented structure (e.g. construction and airline industries). Links between businesses can intensify or wane, depending on the mobility barriers and potential cross-business synergies. However, horizontal integration and fragmentation are not limited to the intra-industry domain. Inter-industry integration between two or more industries can also increase, creating a more or less open competitive space (Hamel and Prahalad, 1994) with few mobility barriers (e.g. the digital industries). Inter-industry integration can also occur where the producers of different products and services are complementary or converge on a common standard or platform (e.g. Android and Linux), making them 'complementers' (e.g. Cusumano and Gawer, 2002; Moore, 1996). Yet, the opposite trend is possible as well, whereby an industry becomes more isolated from neighbouring sectors (e.g. accountancy).

- International integration–fragmentation. Where the international boundaries separating various geographic segments of an industry become increasingly less important, the industry is said to be developing towards a more internationally integrated structure (e.g. food retailing and business education industries). Conversely, where the competitive interactions in an industry are increasingly confined to a region (e.g. Europe) or country, the industry is said to be moving towards a more internationally fragmented structure (e.g. satellite television and internet retailing). These developments are more thoroughly examined in Chapter 12, which deals with the international context.

- Expansion–contraction. Industries can also differ with regard to the structural nature of the demand for their products and/or services. Where an industry is experiencing an ongoing increase in demand, the industry is said to be in growth or expansion. Where demand is constantly receding, the industry is said to be in decline or contraction. If periods of expansion are followed by periods of contraction, and vice versa, the industry is said to be cyclical. A prolonged period of expansion is usually linked to the growth phase of the industry life cycle (e.g. McGahan, 2000; Moore, 2000; Porter, 1980), while contraction is linked to the decline phase. Often, however, it is rather difficult to apply the 'life cycle' concept to an entire industry (as opposed to a product or technology). As industry growth (expansion) can easily follow a period of industry decline (contraction), the life cycle model has little descriptive value – what does it mean to be mature? – and even less predictive value.

Paths of industry development

The development of an industry can be mapped along any one of the dimensions listed above. The most popular is to track the pattern of expansion and contraction, to gain some indication of the life cycle phase in which the industry might have arrived. Another frequently analysed characteristic is the level of concentration, commonly using a concentration index to measure the market share of the four or eight largest companies. But it is equally viable to trace the trajectory of vertical, horizontal or international integration. In Figure 10.2, examples of these paths of industry development are given.

In Figure 10.3, one particular element of the convergence–divergence dimension has been selected for further magnification. As discussed above, in the development of an industry a particular business model can become the dominant design around which the rest of the industry converges. A strategically relevant development occurs when the dominant business model is replaced by a new business model that offers customers higher value. In Figure 10.3, four generic patterns of industry development are outlined, each describing a different type of transition from the old dominant model to the new (Burgelman and Grove, 1996; D'Aveni, 1999):

■ Gradual development. In an industry where one business model is dominant for a long period of time and is slowly replaced by an alternative that is a slight improvement, the development process is gradual. The firms adhering to the dominant design will generally have little trouble adapting to the new rules of the game, leading to a situation of relative stability. Competition can be weak or fierce, depending on the circumstances, but will take place on the basis of the shared rules of the game. In this type of environment, companies with an established position have a strong advantage.

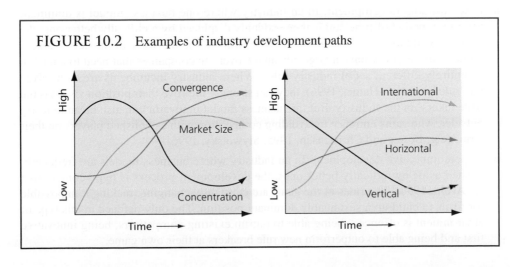

FIGURE 10.2   Examples of industry development paths

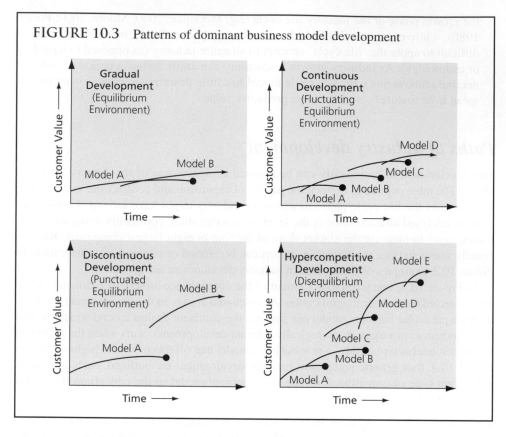

FIGURE 10.3   Patterns of dominant business model development

- Continuous development. In an industry where changes to the dominant business model are more frequent, but still relatively modest in size, the development process is continuous. While firms need not have difficulties adjusting to each individual change to the rules of the game, they can fall behind if they do not keep up with the pace of improvement. In this type of environment, rapid adaptation to developments will strengthen the competitive position of firms vis-à-vis slow movers.

- Discontinuous development. In an industry where one business model is dominant for a long period of time and is then suddenly displaced by a radically better one, the development process is discontinuous. The firms riding the wave of the new business model will generally have a large advantage over the companies that need to adjust to an entirely different set of industry rules. Where industry incumbents are themselves the 'rule breakers' (Hamel, 1996), they can strongly improve their position vis-à-vis the 'rule takers' in the industry. But the business model innovator can also be an industry outsider, who gains entrance by avoiding competition with established players on their terms (e.g. Bower and Christensen, 1995; Slywotsky, 1996).

- Hypercompetitive development. In an industry where business models are frequently pushed aside by radically better ones, the development process is hypercompetitive (D'Aveni, 1994). The rules of the game are constantly changing, making it impossible for firms to build up a sustainably dominant position. The only defence in this type of environment is offence – being able to outrun existing competitors, being innovative first and being able to outperform new rule breakers at their own game.

Drivers of industry development

There is an endless list of factors in the environment that can change and that can influence the direction of industry development. Following the categorization made in Chapter 6, these factors can be divided into change drivers that are external or internal to the industry (see Figure 10.4). The change drivers in the contextual environment can be split roughly into socio-cultural, economic, political/regulatory and technological forces for change. The change drivers in the industry environment can be divided into groups surrounding suppliers, buyers, incumbent rivals, new entrants, and substitutes and complementors.

As the arrows indicate, change in a complex system like an industry does not always start in one discernible part and then reverberate throughout the whole. Rather, change can also be the result of the interplay of various elements in the system, without any clear start or ending point. Yet, for the discussion on shaping industry development it is important to recognize the distinction between industry changes that are largely triggered by an individual firm, as opposed to broader, system-wide changes for which no one actor can claim responsibility. Where one firm is the major driver of industry development, it can claim industry leadership. However, if there is no industry leader and the evolution of the industry is due to the complex interaction of many different change drivers, it is said that the industry dynamics determine the path of industry development.

Inhibitors of industry development

Forces of change do not always go unopposed. In the discussion on strategic change in Chapter 8, the sources of organizational rigidity were reviewed, each of which acts as an inhibitor to organizational change. In the same way, there are many sources of industry rigidity, making the industry rules much more difficult to bend or break. Industry rigidity can be defined as the lack of susceptibility to change. If an industry is rigid, the rules of

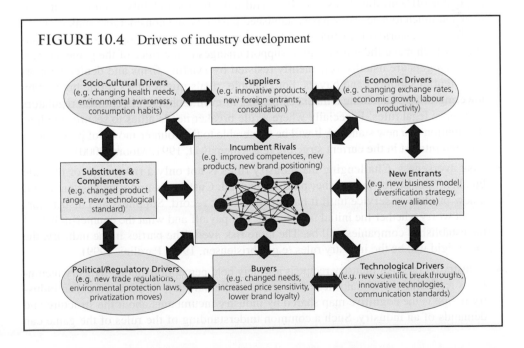

FIGURE 10.4   Drivers of industry development

the game cannot be altered and competitive positions are relatively fixed. The opposite term is industry plasticity – an industry's susceptibility to change.

A large number of factors can contribute to rigidity, thereby inhibiting industry development. Some of the most important ones are the following:

- Underlying conditions. Basically, some rules might be immutable because the underlying industry conditions cannot be changed. In some industries, economies of scale are essential (e.g. aeroplane manufacturing, merchant shipping), while in others economies of scale are not of importance (e.g. wedding services, dentistry services). In some industries, buyers are fragmented (e.g. newspapers, moving services), while in others, they are highly concentrated (e.g. defence systems, harbour construction). In some industries, buyers value product differentiation (e.g. clothing, restaurants), while in others bulk producers must compete on price (e.g. chemicals, general construction). Many of these structural factors are inherent to the industry and defy any attempts to change them (e.g. Bain, 1959; Porter, 1980).

- Industry integration. Besides the limited plasticity of individual aspects of the industry context, it is also important to recognize that some industries are particularly rigid because of the complex linkages between various aspects of the industry. For example, to be a rule-breaking music company not only requires developing new delivery methods via the Internet, but also getting electronics manufacturers to adopt the new standards, finding ways to safeguard copyrights, working together with governments to find new policing methods and, not least, to change consumers' buying behaviour. Such interrelations between various elements of the industry can make it particularly difficult to actually influence the direction of events over time. The industry can become 'locked in' to a specific structure for a long period of time (e.g. Arthur, 1994; Shapiro and Varian, 1998).

- Power structures. The industry rules can also be kept in place by those who feel they are better off with the status quo. Powerful industry incumbents often have little to gain and much to lose. They have established positions and considerable sunk costs, in the form of historical investments in technology, competences, facilities and relationships, which make them reluctant to support changes to the rules of the game. Hence, rule changers are usually vehemently resisted by existing firms and denied support by potential suppliers and buyers. For example, rivals might attack a rule breaker by lowering prices, launching a media campaign, or even lobbying government regulators to impose legal rules. Especially where a rule breaker needs allies to secure supplies, distribution or a new standard, it will be vulnerable to the counter-moves of parties with a vested interest in the current structure (e.g. Ghemawat, 1991; Moore, 2000).

- Risk averseness. Challenging the industry rules is not only a risky step for the rule breaker, but also for many other parties involved. Customers might be hesitant about a new product or service until it has a firmer track record. Suppliers and distributors might worry whether the initial investments will pay off and what the counter-moves of the established companies will be. The more risk averse the parties in the industry, the more rigid will be the industry rules (e.g. Christensen, 1997; Parolini, 1999).

- Industry recipes. An industry recipe is a widely held perception among industry incumbents regarding the actual rules of the game in the industry. In other words, an industry recipe is the cognitive map shared by industry incumbents about the structure and demands of an industry. Such a common understanding of the rules of the game can develop over time through shared experiences and interaction – the longer people are in the industry and converse with each other, the greater the chance that a consensus will grow about 'what makes the industry tick'. Thus, the industry recipe can limit people's openness to rule changers who challenge the industry orthodoxy (e.g. Baden-Fuller and Stopford, 1992; Spender, 1989).

■ Institutional pressures. While the industry recipe is a shared understanding of how the industry actually functions, industry incumbents usually also share norms of what constitutes socially acceptable economic behaviour. Companies experience strong pressures from governments, professional associations, customers, consultants, trade unions, pressure groups and other industry incumbents prescribing permissible strategies and actions, and generally internalize these behavioural standards. Such conformity to institutional pressures gives companies legitimacy, but makes them less willing to question industry conventions, let alone work together with a maverick rule breaker (e.g. Aldrich and Fiol, 1994; Oliver, 1997).

Taken together, these historically determined factors inhibit developments in the industry. It is said that industry evolution is path dependent – the path that the industry has travelled in the past will strongly limit how and in which direction it can develop in the future. In other words, 'history matters', setting bounds on the freedom to shape the future.

THE PARADOX OF COMPLIANCE AND CHOICE

When people are free to do as they please, they usually imitate each other.

Eric Hoffer (1902–1983), American philosopher

Yet, the question is whether firms should attempt to shape their industries at all, given the required effort and apparent risk of failure. There might be attractive rewards if a firm can lead industry developments, but trying to break industry rules that turn out to be immutable can be a quick way to achieve bankruptcy. Being an industry leader might sound very proactive, and even heroic, but it is potentially suicidal if the industry context defies being shaped.

This duality of wanting to change the industry rules that are malleable, while needing to adapt to the industry rules that are fixed, is the tension central to dealing with the industry context. On the one hand, managers must be willing to irreverently transgress widely acknowledged industry rules, going against what they see as the industry recipe. On the other hand, managers must respectfully accept many characteristics of the industry structure and play according to existing rules of the competitive game. Yet, these conflicting demands of being irreverent and respectful towards the industry rules are difficult for strategists to meet at the same time.

Where firms cannot influence the structure of their industry, *compliance* with the rules of the game is the strategic imperative. Under these circumstances, the strategic demand is for managers to adapt the firm to the industry context. Where firms do have the ability to manipulate the industry structure, they should exercise their freedom of *choice* to break the industry rules. In such a case, the strategic demand is for managers to try to change the terms of competition in their own favour.

This tension between compliance and choice has been widely acknowledged in the strategic management literature (e.g. Hrebiniak and Joyce, 1985; McGahan, 2000;

Porter, 1980). The pressure for compliance has usually been presented as a form of environmental determinism, as the industry developments force firms to adapt or be selected out (e.g. Astley and Van der Ven, 1983; Wilson, 1992). The freedom of choice has often been labelled as organizational voluntarism, to convey the notion that industry developments can be the result of the wilful actions of individual organizations (e.g. Bettis and Donaldson, 1990; Child, 1972). In the following sections, both compliance and choice are further examined.

The demand for firm compliance

It goes almost without saying that organizations must, to a large extent, adapt themselves to their environments. No organization has the ability to shape the entire world to fit its needs. Therefore, to be successful, all organizations need to understand the context in which they operate and need to play by most of the rules of the game.

After all, the alternative of ignoring the rules is fraught with danger. Probably the most common cause of 'corporate death' is misalignment between the organization and its environment (discussed in Chapter 8). And misalignment can happen very quickly, as most industries are constantly in flux. Companies can misinterpret the direction of the changes, can fail to take appropriate corrective action or can be plainly self-centred, paying insufficient attention to external developments. Most companies have enough difficulty just staying attuned to the current rules of the competitive game, let alone anticipating how the industry context will change in the future.

To achieve compliance with the industry rules, firms must develop structures, processes and a culture in which listening and adapting to the environment become engrained. Firms must learn to become customer and market oriented, reacting to the 'pull' of the market instead of 'pushing' their standard approach and pet projects at an unwilling audience. Firm compliance means avoiding the pitfall of organizational arrogance – knowing better than the market and imposing an approach that no one desires (e.g. Miller, 1990; Whitley, 1999).

The demand for strategic choice

While compliance with the industry rules can be very beneficial, contradicting them can also be strategically valuable. If firms only play by the current rules, it is generally very difficult to gain a significant competitive advantage over their rivals. After all, adapting to the current industry structure means doing business in more or less the same way as competitors, with few possibilities to distinguish the organization. In other words, 'compliance' might be another way of saying 'a follow me-too strategy'.

To be unique and develop a competitive advantage, firms need to do something different, something that does not fit within the current rules of the game. The more innovative the rule breaker, the larger will be the competitive advantage over rivals stuck with outdated business models. The more radical the departure from the old industry recipe, the more difficult it will be for competitors to imitate and catch up. Where companies are capable of constantly leading industry developments, they will have the benefit of capturing attractive industry positions before less proactive competitors eventually follow. In other words, there is a strong pressure for firms to attempt to shape the industry rules.

To achieve organizational choice, firms must find ways of escaping the pitfall of organizational conformity – the strict adherence to current industry rules. Firms must develop structures, processes and a culture in which the current industry recipe is constantly questioned, challenged and changed. Managers must come to see that in the long run the easy path of following the industry rules will be less productive than the rocky road of innovation and change (e.g. Hamel and Prahalad, 1994; Kim and Mauborgne, 2005).

EXHIBIT 10.1   SHORT CASE

NINTENDO: PRESS START TO CONTINUE

Founded in 1889, Nintendo's journey is one that leads a humble playing card manufacturer to become the most well-known video game company of all time. Producing both hardware and software – video game systems and their games – with a portfolio of multimillion franchises ranging from Mario and Donkey Kong to Pokémon and The Legend of Zelda, the company has repeatedly inspired, innovated and revolutionized the video game industry. The Japanese firm has not done so without its fair share of challenges.

When Nintendo entered the video game market with its first dedicated video game console in 1983 (1985 in the West), it did so with a bang. The Family Computer, known as Nintendo Entertainment System (NES) abroad, was to be the first console with a revolutionary business model. Instead of only producing games for the hardware itself, Nintendo licensed and encouraged external game developers to produce and distribute products for Nintendo's hardware. This authorization process provided Nintendo with its share, increased the platform's software library and provided the company with quality control. It became a standard in the video game industry and it would take years before Nintendo's monopoly position was challenged. The NES managed to achieve lifetime sales of 61.9 million units worldwide.

As hardware improved and competitors started adopting Nintendo's business model, competition grew fiercer. Having proved itself with the NES and a winning streak of

high quality self-published titles such as Super Mario Bros., The Legend of Zelda and Metroid, the Japanese video game company did more of the same in terms of its hardware. Owing mostly to the high quality of its software, Nintendo systems managed to remain relevant. When Sony entered the game with its PlayStation, this new system introduced players to 3D graphics and emphasized more mature games. This proved a lethal combination: It went on to sell more than 102 million units over more than a decade. Its successor, the PlayStation 2 (2000), would become the most successful video game platform in history with a sales record of 155 million units sold. In an effort to challenge Sony's new hegemonic position, Nintendo released the GameCube (2001), technically, a better machine than the second PlayStation, but a system that did nothing new. It performed poorly, ending its run with a measly 21.7 million units sold. Even the new kid, Microsoft's Xbox (2001), which catered towards older consumers and introduced its own well-run Internet service to consoles, exceeded that figure by a couple of million. Competitors played Nintendo's game and started winning.

Thanks to acclaimed software on Nintendo's platforms, the company maintained a share of dedicated fans, but it was not enough to sell sufficient hardware units. Nintendo's only consistent success story proved to be its portable video game devices. The Game Boy (1989) and its improved Color version (1998), sold a combined 118.7 million units. At a time when Nintendo had difficulty appealing to consumers, the follow-up to its blockbuster handheld, the

▶

Game Boy Advance (2001), achieved lifetime sales of 81.5 million units. Nintendo had the means to continue, but playing by the rules of the industry proved not to do Nintendo any favours. It was up to Satoru Iwata, newly crowned CEO of the company, to turn things around.

Iwata needed to change Nintendo's game and he did so with an unprecedented strategy. He would approach radically new demographics. In 2004 Nintendo released the DS, the newest addition to its portable game system portfolio. This piece of hardware features two screens, the lowest one functioning as a touch screen, introducing a whole new way to play. To compare: the iPhone, which introduced touch screens on a big scale to the smartphone market, only came out in 2007. The launch of the Nintendo DS was Iwata's first big product release, but he was not present in Tokyo to promote the system. Instead, he was visiting neuroscientist Ryuta Kawashima. Iwata thought his 'train the brain' exercise books could form the foundations of a game that had the potential to appeal to gamers and non-gamers alike. He guessed right. The resulting *Brain Age: Train Your Brain in Minutes a Day!* – known as *Dr. Kawashima's Brain Training* outside the US – became an industry phenomenon and helped introduce many adults to gaming. Nintendo also captured the previously underestimated girl demographic, releasing successful titles such as Nintendogs, Animal Crossing: Wild World and Super Princess Peach. Iwata soon proved that he could also change the playing field in which Nintendo had struggled the most: the home console market.

The codename for Nintendo's follow-up to the poor performing GameCube was 'Revolution', an apt premonition of what was to come. Instead of just making games look better and better, Nintendo once again wanted to change the way people played. Released as the Nintendo Wii in late 2006, the system did not focus on traditional button-based gameplay, but introduced motion controls. No need to remember tricky button combinations: You swing the remote-shaped controller like a tennis racket and so does the character on screen. The games were social, intuitive and fun. As a result, the barrier between gamers and non-gamers dissolved and the Wii became an instant must-have for families.

Nintendo had truly altered the rules of the game. While most hardware is initially expensive and only gets adopted by the mainstream relatively late in their life cycle, the Wii was sold at a budget price and appealed to everyone from its inception. Gamers wanted to try something new, while consumers new to gaming met an accessible and fun device. The Wii left its technically superior competitors in the dust – by mid-2007, Nintendo's system had sold more units than Sony and Microsoft's newest consoles put together. The me-too products Microsoft and PlayStation, launched as a response to Nintendo's new-found success, never managed to get off the ground.

Nevertheless, smartphones and tablets slowly entered the fray, eating into the handheld console market, Nintendo's safe card. Why buy an expensive gaming handheld with expensive software, when smartphones allow you to play at significantly lower cost? With the successor to the DS, Nintendo tried to offer something not possible on mobiles: stereoscopic 3D. With its Nintendo 3DS it offered an improved DS, with the addition of 'glasses-free 3D'. This seemingly magic feat did not prevent the system from selling poorly at launch. Iwata took personal responsibility. Nintendo's CEO apologized, cut his own salary by 50 per cent and gave early adopters of the handheld 10 Nintendo games for free. Owing to a significant price drop and a steady stream of quality games later in its life cycle, the 3DS luckily turned out to be a slow-burner – as of 2016 the system has been sold almost 59 million times.

The same could not be said for the successor of the Wii. Nintendo was ahead of the curve with the Wii, but its follow-up ended up stuck in the middle. It did not appeal to its existing fans or to the more casual gamers. The confusingly named Wii U followed the tablet trend, a phenomenon introduced to the mass market by Apple and Google. It came with a tablet-like controller with buttons, but Nintendo had a hard time explaining to consumers what actually made the Wii U different. As the reveal to the console was unclear and Wii controllers are compatible with the Wii U, many were under the impression that the new system was a mere upgrade. Nintendo also struggled to make good use of its new hardware as many of the systems' more successful games, such as Mario Kart 8 and Super Smash Bros. for Wii U, did not use the features of the tablet. As a response to the poor results of the Wii U – Nintendo only managed to sell about 13 million units of the system in total compared to more than 100 million Wiis – investors pressed Iwata to lay off employees. He refused to do so, under the philosophy that employees who fear they may get fired are in no state to develop impressive software.

He did, however, listen to a different demand, one that investors had been repeatedly making: Nintendo decided to also start releasing games on smartphones. Iwata had been cautious about separating Nintendo hardware and software, claiming the company would then 'cease to be Nintendo' – its business strategy had thus far consisted of making compelling exclusive software to prompt people to buy hardware. However, Iwata soon declared that the 'era has ended when people play all kinds of games only on dedicated gaming systems'. Nintendo would form partnerships to publish applications and games on smartphones.

Iwata did not live to see the first app released; a tumour in his bile duct took the life of Nintendo's CEO in 2015. This was the same year in which Nintendo finally entered the black again with an operating income of $206 million, after three years of consecutive losses. One of the last ideas for which Iwata can be held responsible helped establish this feat. He envisioned a line of toy figures based on Nintendo characters that can be connected to Nintendo games for in-game bonuses and extra options. In itself the idea was not new; companies such as Activision and Disney had done the same with Skylanders and Disney Infinity respectively. Nintendo's so-called Amiibo figures proved appealing enough to sell over six million units in their first month. By March 2016, the sales of Amiibo exceeded 64 million units. Sometimes a catch-up strategy could be beneficial for Nintendo as well.

This was also true for the first two smartphone apps Nintendo released. While its first application, the social app Miitomo, turned profitable rather quickly, it failed to remain relevant over the long run. The second one, however, became a truly global phenomenon. Pokémon Go, developed by independent American company Niantic, lets people all over the world catch little monsters in the real environment using augmented reality. The game became so popular that Nintendo's market value doubled in a matter of days – from about $20 billion to more than $40 billion – marking the biggest daily turnover in stock ever on the Tokyo Stock Exchange. Nintendo, however, only had about a 13 per cent interest in Pokémon Go and the app would thus ultimately not have a big impact on the company's profits. After Nintendo made a financial statement about this, its shares plunged.

Nevertheless, it did prove a point: So long as it can make good use of its intellectual properties, playing follow-up also has

▶

potential for Nintendo. Its first smartphone endeavours can easily be called successful, and jumping on the so-called 'toys-to-life' market with Amiibo also turned out to be lucrative. The danger of being neither an industry leader nor a good follower, was proved by the Nintendo Wii U, however. Nintendo's newest system, codenamed NX, is set to release in 2017 and much is riding on the success of the console. It is thus necessary for Nintendo to decide: What now? Can Nintendo find ways to shape the video game industry once again or can it find a way to play by the rules of others? Will the NX manage to put Nintendo alongside Sony and Microsoft again? And how long can the 3DS and similar future products remain relevant in a smartphone dominated environment? If Nintendo can make the right decisions, it will not reach 'game over' any time soon.

Co-author: Wester Wagenaar

Sources: nintendo.co.jp; nintendo.com; Nintendo Annual Report 2015; *Bloomberg*, 19 July 2016 and 25 July 2016; *Fortune*, 5 December 2014; *Gamesindustry. biz*, 15 July 2016; *Gamespot*, 25 July 2016; *Games Radar*, 29 April 2016; *Guardian*, 13 July 2015; *Japan Times*, 16 July 2016; David Sheff, 'Game over: How Nintendo conquered the world', 1994.

PERSPECTIVES ON THE INDUSTRY CONTEXT

A wise man will make more opportunity than he finds.

Francis Bacon (1561–1624), Lord Chancellor of England

Once again the strategizing manager seems 'stuck between a rock and a hard place'. The pressures for both compliance and choice are clear, but as opposites they are at least partially incompatible. Developing an organizational culture, structure and processes attuned to compliance will to some extent be at odds with the culture, structure and processes needed to shape an industry. An organization well-rehearsed in the art of adaptation and skilful imitation is usually quite different from one geared towards business innovation and contrarian behaviour. How should managers actually deal with the issue of industry development – should they lead or follow?

In the strategic management literature, many answers to this question are given – unfortunately, many contradictory ones. The views among management theorists differ sharply, as they emphasize a different balance between the need to comply and the need to choose. To gain a better overview of the range of conflicting opinions, the two diametrically opposed positions will be identified and discussed. On the one hand, there are strategists who argue that industry development is an autonomous process, which individual firms can hardly hope to shape. They believe that compliance to shifting industry characteristics is mandatory – adjust or risk being selected out. This point of view is referred to as the 'industry dynamics perspective'. On the other hand, many strategists believe that the industry context can be shaped in an infinite variety of ways by innovative firms. Therefore, industry development can be driven by firms willing and able to take a leading role. This point of view is referred to as the 'industry leadership perspective'.

The industry dynamics perspective

 To those taking an industry dynamics perspective, the popular notion that individual firms have the power to shape their industry is an understandable, but quite misplaced, belief. Of course, the illusion of control is tempting – most people, especially strategists, would like to control their own destiny. Most individuals assume they have a free will and can decide their own future. Many governments suppose that they can shape society and many cultures assume that they control nature. In the same way, it is seductive to believe that the individual firm can matter by influencing the development of its industry.

Unfortunately, this belief is largely a fallacy, brought on by a poor understanding of the underlying industry dynamics. In reality, according to advocates of the industry dynamics perspective, industries are complex systems, with a large number of forces interacting simultaneously, none of which can significantly direct the long-term development of the whole. Firms are relatively small players in a very large game – their behaviours may have some impact on industry development, but none can fundamentally shape the direction of changes. On the contrary, as industries evolve, all firms that do not meet the changing demands of the environment are weeded out. Firms not suited to the new circumstances die, while firms complying with the changing rules prosper. Hence, through selection the industry context determines the group of industry survivors, and through the pressures for adaptation, the behaviour of the remaining firms is determined. In short, the industry shapes the firm, not the other way around.

The industry dynamics perspective is often also referred to as the industry evolution perspective, due to the strong parallel with biological evolution. Both evolutionary processes, it is argued, share a number of basic characteristics. In nature, as in business, the survival and growth of entities depends on their fit with the environment. Within each environment variations on a successful theme might come about. These new individuals will thrive, as long as they suit the existing circumstances, but as the environment changes, only those that meet the new demands will perish. Hence, Darwin's well-known principle of 'survival of the fittest' is based on a cycle of variation and environmental selection. Many proponents of the industry dynamics perspective believe that this biological view of evolution is a good model for what happens in industries – new organizations arise as mutations and only the fittest mutations survive. However, it is usually pointed out that in a business environment, organizations do not vary 'at random', but purposefully, and they possess the ability to adapt to selection pressures during the evolution process (e.g. Baum and Singh, 1994; Nelson and Winter, 1982). Therefore, organizations have much more flexibility to evolve along with the unfolding industry dynamics than lifeforms generally do. This process of mutual adaptation and development between entities in the system is called 'co-evolution' (e.g. Aldrich, 1999; Moore, 1996). To proponents of the industry dynamics perspective, the objective of a firm should be to co-evolve with its environment, instead of trying to conquer it.

Supporters of the industry dynamics perspective do not deny that every once in a while a rule breaker comes along, turning an industry upside down and spawning dozens of case studies by admiring business professors and hours of television interviews. But these successes must be put into perspective, just as a lottery winner should not encourage everyone to invest their life savings into buying lottery tickets. Yes, some business innovators are successful, but we have no idea how many challengers were weeded out along the way – only the most spectacular failures make it into the media, but most go unreported. This is called the 'survivor's bias', and the emphasis on case-based reasoning in the field of strategy makes theorists and practitioners equally susceptible to fall into this trap. But even where a firm has been able to pull off a major industry change once, this does not make it the industry leader of the future. It might have been the right company in the right place at the right time, able to push the industry in a certain direction once, but to assume that it will 'win the lottery twice' is not particularly realistic.

The conclusion drawn by advocates of the industry dynamics perspective is that 'winning big' by changing the rules of the game sounds easy, fast and spectacular – but isn't. If one thing has been learnt from the Internet bubble, it is that changing the rules of the game is extremely difficult, slow and hazardous, and should be left up to those 'high rollers' willing to play for 'high stakes' with only a low chance of success (i.e. venture capitalists and entrepreneurs). For regular companies, such an approach cannot be the mainstay of their strategy. Their basic approach must be to stick closely to the shifting currents in their industry, which is challenging enough in most cases. Competitive advantage can be sought, but requires hard work within the rules of the game.

The bad news is that this leaves limited freedom to manoeuvre and that the general level of profitability that a firm can achieve is largely predetermined. Once in a poor industry, a firm's growth and profit potential are significantly limited (Porter, 1980). The good news is that this still leaves plenty of room for a firm to score above the industry average, by positioning better than competitors, but also by adapting better to the ongoing industry changes, or even anticipating changes more skilfully and reacting appropriately.

EXHIBIT 10.2 THE INDUSTRY DYNAMICS PERSPECTIVE

AB-INBEV: DOWNSTREAM GLOBAL BEER

One of the biggest beer conglomerates of the 21st century once had to sell ice cream to keep its brewing business afloat. Anheuser-Busch – renowned for its Budweiser label – was no ordinary company to begin with: It had co-evolved better with shifts in the beer industry than virtually any of its adversaries. Established in the mid-1800s in St. Louis, founders Adolphus Busch and Eberhard Anheuser employed a lager style of beer, brought to the US through the influx of fellow German immigrants. This type of beer has a smoother aftertaste than traditional beers in US society and became a local hit across multiple cities. Meanwhile, the Industrial Age brought marvels of its own. The advent of motor, railroad and pasteurization technology allowed for beer to be transported over vast distances without spoiling. These factors combined contributed to the proliferation of bottled beer – rather than barrel-aged beer – both at home and abroad. Not just Anheuser-Busch, but many other big names such as Miller, Pabst, Schlitz and Coors hopped on these trend bandwagons in order to expand their local businesses across the nation. Ample use was made of economies of scale stemming from technological progress, increasing the firm size of manufacturers as they increased their scale of production and scope of distribution. A total of 750,000 barrels were produced in 1850 by breweries in the US, while in 1910 this amounted to 59.6 million barrels. This rise in production was not solely reflected in a growing population, but it was also mirrored by a rise in beer consumption per capita, as it soared from approximately 3.5 gallons in 1850 to 21 gallons in 1910. These shifts would foreshadow the dawning of the US domestic beer industry and at the turn of the 20th century many had bright prospects for its unfolding future.

Beer history took a turn, however. In 1920 a 'war on alcohol' commenced under the banner of Prohibition – a constitutional ban on the manufacturing, sales and distribution of alcoholic beverages across the nation. Armed with mandates of Prohibition, one state after the other ratified the convention, obliterating breweries by the thousands. Yet, there were some who endured. A select few cheated corporate death by producing 'near beer' products – low percentage alcoholic content often used for culinary purposes. Other breweries such as Anheuser-Busch reinvented themselves as soft drink or ice cream manufacturers. Once Prohibition's reign ended after repeal in 1933, these newly gained experiences paved the way for mass consumption. Brewers had acquired expertise to produce canned beer, craft new beer recipes and to diversify their businesses. Although only 45 survivors were left standing in the aftermath of Prohibition, in ensuing years new breweries spawned on an unprecedented scale, able to thrive throughout the decades as the industry had found peace in the wake of war. Nevertheless, this live and let live principle which dominated until the 1950s was not meant to last; it soon converted into a live and let die policy adopted by the bigger firms, as they charted a course of mergers and acquisitions. Anheuser-Busch, Miller, Pabst, Schlitz, Coors and other beer giants that had lasted through Prohibition, grew ever bigger as they swallowed smaller companies, while they utilized the economies of scale at their disposal for aggressive marketing strategies. In 1950 the top 10 producers controlled 38 per cent of beer sales in the US, while in 1980 this number had risen to 93 per cent.

These 10 giants had in common that they were founded in the 1800s and had lived through Prohibition. Yet, several decades later none of these companies exist any more as a separate entity.

Similar to the evolving patterns of the US market, its West European counterpart also became increasingly consolidated and matured, as regional champions such as Heineken (Holland), Interbrew (Belgium) and Carlsberg (Denmark) had engaged in a series of mergers, acquisitions and joint ventures. Prompted by the descent of the Iron Curtain and the rise of China, local and regional practices increasingly turned global, as giant beer conglomerates were eager to capitalize on opportunities provided by new markets in emerging economies. Heineken and Carlsberg reinvigorated their acquisition strategies by deploying divide and conquer tactics where both parties partially swallow other big conglomerates, in order to sway antitrust legislators across regions. The Belgian champion Interbrew and the regional champion of Latin America AmBev added momentum to their international endeavours, by establishing InBev after a mega-merger in 2004. Brewing legends Miller and Coors combined their efforts in order to repel foreign takeovers, yet got swallowed by South African Breweries (SAB) nonetheless. In 2004, after 15 years of accelerated mergers and acquisitions, it was none other than Anheuser-Busch that was in global leadership position, as it commanded an 8.5 per cent global market share by volume. The beer giant was not new to all-out warfare, as its road to dominance was paved by the acquisition of past companies. Yet even for giants this cut-throat competition was hard to swallow, as Anheuser-Busch fell prey to InBev through a hostile takeover of $52 billion in 2008 – forming AB-InBev. Even though Anheuser-Busch had survived throughout Prohibition and both world wars, it could not

▶

last in the hypercompetitive environment triggered by globalization. Within their regions, giants could be relatively safe of a dominant position in consolidated markets, yet their stability was rendered obsolete through the advent of globalization, as the global market still remained highly splintered.

Consolidating the global market continued with a wave of mergers, acquisitions and joint ventures, similar to what had occurred earlier in the US and Western Europe on a more regional scale. In 2005, 10 companies controlled 48.4 per cent of the global market by volume, with InBev (10.8 per cent), Anheuser-Busch (9.4 per cent), SAB-Miller (7.3 per cent), Heineken (5.7 per cent), and Carlsberg (2.9 per cent) claiming the top five positions. In 2012, after Anheuser-Busch and InBev had megamerged into AB-InBev, four global beer goliaths remained, accounting for approximately 50 per cent of beer sales in volume, reeling in 70 per cent of the revenues. In 2016 AB-InBev swallowed SABMiller, then the world's second largest, consolidating its global leadership position with a portfolio of blockbuster brands such as Stella Artois, Budweiser, Brahma, Skol, Harbin, Hoegaarden, and many more.

No time to chill, however. Japanese breweries Asahi and Kirin are climbing the ladder and so too are Chinese breweries China Resources Enterprise and Tsingtao. Especially the latter is growing at an unprecedented pace after Snow and Tsingtao replaced AB-InBev's Budweiser brands as top-selling beers in the world. Additionally, SABMiller had to sell 49 per cent of its stake in Snow to China Resources Enterprise, paving the way for enormous revenues for the colossal Chinese brewer. As opposed to the US and European markets, China's domestic market remains largely untapped, providing novel ways to generate profits in China's flourishing economy.

Co-author: Sander Wisman

Sources: www.ab-inbev.com; www.sabmiller.com; www.heineken.com; AB-InBev Annual 334 Reports 2009–2015; AB-InBev Second Quarter and Half Year 2016 Results; *Bloomberg*, 29 July 2016; James Brock, 'The structure of American industry', 2013; Carlsberg Annual Report 2008; *The Economist*, 19 September 2015 and 17 October 2015; *Financial Times*, 10 February 2016; Yuantao Guo, 'Global big business and the Chinese brewing industry', 2006; Martin Scott, *The SAGE Encyclopedia of Alcohol: Social, Cultural, and Historical Perspectives*, 2014; Mark W. Patterson and Nancy Hoalst, 'The geography of beer: Regions, environment and societies', 2014; SABMiller plc Annual Report 2012; *Reuters*, 2 March 2016, 6 July 2016 and 21 July 2016.

The industry leadership perspective

Strategists taking an industry leadership perspective fundamentally disagree with the determinism inherent in the industry dynamics perspective. Even in biology, breeders and genetic engineers consistently attempt to shape the natural world. Of course, in industries, as in biology, some rules are immutable. Certain economic, technological, social and political factors have to be accepted as hardly changeable. But the remaining environmental factors can be manipulated to leave strategists with an enormous scope for moulding the industry of the future. This belief is reflected in the remark by the Dutch poet Jules Deelder that 'even within the limits of the possible, the possibilities are limitless'. It is up to the strategist to identify which rules of the game must be respected and which can be ignored in the search for new strategic options. The strategist must recognize both the limits of the possible and the limitless possibilities.

Advocates of the industry leadership perspective do not deny that in many industries the developments are largely an evolutionary result of industry dynamics. For an understanding of the development paths of these 'leaderless' industries, the industry dynamics perspective offers a powerful explanatory 'lens' – many industries do evolve without a clear industry leader. However, these industries have only followed this path because no firm was creative and powerful enough to actively shape the direction of change. A lack of leadership is not the 'natural state of affairs', but simply weakness on behalf of the industry incumbents. Industry developments can be shaped, yet do require innovative companies willing to take on the leadership role (e.g. Baden-Fuller and Stopford, 1992; Hamel and Prahalad, 1994).

A leadership role, supporters of this perspective argue, starts with envisioning what the industry of tomorrow might look like. The firm's strategists must be capable of challenging the existing industry recipe and building a new conception of how the industry could function in the future. They must test their own assumptions about which industry rules can be changed and must, in fact, think of ways of 'destroying their current business'. Hamel and Prahalad (1994) refer to this as intellectual leadership, noting that smart strategists also develop 'industry foresight', anticipating which trends are likely to emerge, so that they can be used to the firm's advantage.

Not only must a firm have the intellectual ability to envision the industry's future, but it must also be able to communicate this vision in a manner that other firms and individuals are willing to buy into. If a vision of the industry of tomorrow is compelling enough, people inside and outside the company will start to anticipate, and will become committed to, that future, making it a self-fulfilling prophecy. This 'inevitability' of an industry vision can be important in overcoming risk averseness and resistance from industry incumbents (e.g. Levenhagen, Porac and Thomas, 1993; Moore, 2000).

To actually change the rules of the competitive game in an industry, a firm must move beyond a compelling vision and work out a new competitive business model. If this new business model is put into operation and seems to offer a competitive advantage, this can attract sufficient customers and support to gain 'critical mass' and break through as a viable alternative to the older business models. To shape the industry, the firm will also need to develop new competences and standards required to make the new business model function properly. The better the firm is at building new competences and setting new standards, alone or in cooperation with others, the more power it will have to determine the direction of industry development (e.g. D'Aveni, 1999; Hamel, 1996).

All of the above points together add up to quite a considerable task. But then, industry leadership is not easy and changing the industry rules rarely happens overnight. Rather, it can take years, figuring out which rules can be broken and which cannot. It can be a marathon, trying to get the business model right, while building competences and support. Therefore, organizations require perseverance and commitment if they are to be successful industry shapers (Hamel and Prahalad, 1994).

EXHIBIT 10.3   THE INDUSTRY LEADERSHIP PERSPECTIVE

SPOTIFY: WHO PAYS THE PIPER CALLS THE TUNE

Revenues have been declining in the music industry for many years, a trend that started when the illegal download site Napster entered the scene in 1999. At first glance, iTunes was hailed as the solution, but this changed people's buying behaviour from purchasing entire albums to simply buying single songs. Revenues continued to drop, and it became clear that a revolution was needed to save the music industry. Daniel Ek came up with the solution: Give it away for free.

In 1999 the music industry was shocked when Napster reached 80 million users in only two years, all of whom had access to free (illegal) music. This fascinated Daniel Ek, who found his two favourite bands on the website: the Beatles and Led Zeppelin. Daniel wanted to find a way to let music inspire people, just as it inspired him. The new status quo was characterized by illegal downloads, but could there be a legal approach to serving freely available music while making people willing to pay for it again?

In 2008 Daniel Ek came up with an innovative *freemium* business model for the music industry in Sweden. With fellow entrepreneur Martin Lorentzon, he launched the music service Spotify, containing a large catalogue of songs, which grew to over 30 million in 2015. The service and its music itself is offered for free, but ads are inserted between songs to fund the 'free music'. Paying subscribers experience higher quality music without ads and paying a monthly fee also allows them to download songs of choice to be played back offline.

Daniel Ek started with Spotify in Sweden and quickly started to conquer the world. Spotify is a game changer; a new industry leader with new ideas and new innovations. This is supported by the fact that others – such as Apple Music, Google Play and Amazon's Prime Music in addition to private companies like Deezer – quickly tried to follow in Spotify's tracks. Although there are some minor differences these initiatives are all trying to find their way into this new era of experiencing music.

Spotify remains the undisputed industry leader, however. The company is valued at $8.4 billion and it entertains a paid user base surpassing 30 million subscribers. An additional 70 million make use of the ad-based free version of the service. Meanwhile its biggest competitor, Apple Music, is only half as big as the Swedish streaming giant, having accumulated 15 million paid subscriptions.

Spotify is set to keep expanding as long as musicians continue to cooperate with the service. That is also where it sometimes goes wrong. Some artists, such as Taylor Swift and Radiohead's Thom Yorke, have removed their songs from the service, as they consider the business model to unfairly compensate artists, producers and writers. One problem is that Spotify pays artists based on their 'market share' or the number of streams for an artist's songs relative to the service's total number of streams. This comes down to Spotify paying as little as $0.006 to $0.008 per stream on average. Another issue is that revenues go to the publishers – about 70 per cent of its turnover – who then distribute to their musicians on their own terms.

Nevertheless, Spotify could well have established a more sustainable business model for the previously dying music industry. The firm fits perfectly in this age's spirit: offering free streaming music to the masses. Since it can never outspend Apple or Google, it has to stay on its toes, however. If Spotify manages to keep ahead of its competitors, it might well set the tone of the music industry for years to come.

Co-author: Jeroen Brinkhuis and Wester Wagenaar

Sources: Spotify.com; *The Economist*, 5 May 2016 and 27 May 2016; *Forbes*, 16 January 2012 and 21 July 2013; *The Guardian,* 16 January 2013; *Pocket-lint*, 16 May 2013; *TechRadar*, 20 November 2015.

MANAGING THE PARADOX OF COMPLIANCE AND CHOICE

The reasonable man adapts himself to the world; the unreasonable one persists in trying to adapt the world to himself. Therefore, all progress depends on the unreasonable man.

George Bernard Shaw (1856–1950), Irish playwright and critic

So, how should managers deal with the industry context? Should they concentrate on adapting to the dynamics in the industry, honing their ability to respond to changing demands and to adjust their business model to meet new requirements? Or should they take a more proactive role in shaping the future of the industry, changing the rules of the competitive game to suit their own needs? Within the field of strategic management, the views are far apart and no consensus seems to be emerging on how to manage the paradox of compliance and choice (see Table 10.1 for the main arguments).

With so many competing opinions on the nature of the industry context, readers may now want to 'select the fittest one'. Or maybe readers conclude that one view has rewritten the rules of competition in the strategy industry. In the international context especially, a much more strategizing stance would be to challenge one's own cognitive map, as perspectives on the industry context are closely related to the well-described and culturally skewed voluntarism versus determinism debate.

TABLE 10.1   Industry dynamics versus industry leadership perspective

	Industry dynamics perspective	Industry leadership perspective
Emphasis on	Compliance over choice	Choice over compliance
Industry development	Uncontrollable evolutionary process	Controllable creation process
Change dynamics	Environment selects fit firms	Firm creates fitting environment
Firm success due to	Fitness to industry demands	Manipulation of industry demands
Ability to shape industry	Low, slow	High, fast
Normative implication	Play by the rules (adapt)	Change the rules (innovate)
Development path	Convergence towards dominant design	Divergence, create new design
Firm profitability	Largely industry dependent	Largely firm dependent

Balancing

Even rule-breaking companies cannot make or break all industry rules. Some industry rules – such as the importance of brands in consumer markets and economies of scale in capital-intensive industries – are not to be moulded. Strategists then need to follow some rules while trying to change others. The balancing act is common, while the balance itself is industry specific. In other words, larger firms that are active in multiple businesses are also multi-balancing.

Parallel processing

While business unit managers have to play by the industry rules as they have little influence on the company's context, corporate strategists of large firms are often engaged in initiatives that may well change the industry context. For example, as members of national and supra-national (e.g. European) industrial policy boards, corporate strategists are involved in government initiatives to formulate policy priorities which would lead to innovation funds and subsidies for particular technologies. By influencing governments, corporate strategists change the industry rules, while business managers have to play by the rules.

Juxtaposing

As described in this chapter, industry characteristics determine which industry rules are malleable by strategists' actions. Attempts to break particular industry rules – such as scale advantages in the steel industry – are outright dangerous, while others may well be successful. Even when the large majority of industry rules cannot be broken, the important attribute of corporate strategists is to know which ones can. So from the perspective of the strategizing manager, the industry dynamics perspective is applicable in some occasions while the industry leadership perspective is preferred in others. The proportion of compliance and choice differs between both perspectives, yet independent from perspectives strategists need to juxtapose between firm compliance and strategic choice.

In the international context, managing the paradox of compliance and choice becomes even more challenging. Not only does the strategist need to find the right combination of rules that need to be followed and can be moulded, the combination often also differs over countries. As will be further explained in the next section, in many businesses, the industry context is country specific. For example, industrial policies may influence industry forces, and local or national networks determine the strategic window of opportunities. Hence, the conclusion must be that strategists not only need to juxtapose; in international firms they need to 'country specifically' juxtapose between demands for firm compliance and strategic choice.

It goes without saying that it takes special capabilities of strategizing managers to juxtapose the paradox. In Chapter 4 on business level strategy it was discussed that strategists need *dynamic capabilities* (Teece, 2007; Teece, Pisano and Shuen, 1997) to juxtapose between demands for firm compliance and strategic choice, which would 'higher level' dynamic capabilities. In the international human resources field the scarcity of such strategists is well-known. In most cases, firms choose to manage the paradox by appointing local managers or expatriates who know the local culture very well.

THE INDUSTRY CONTEXT IN INTERNATIONAL PERSPECTIVE

Co-authors: Gep Eisenloeffel and Wester Wagenaar

When I hear any man talk of an unalterable law, the only effect it produces on me is to convince me that he is an unalterable fool.

Sydney Smith (1771–1845), English writer and Anglican cleric

In the field of strategy, views differ sharply on whether the industry context can be shaped or not. These differences of opinion usually remain implicit – few practising managers or strategy theorists make a point of expounding their assumptions about the nature of the environment. For this reason, it is difficult to identify whether there are national preferences when it comes to industry context perspectives. Yet, it seems not unlikely that strategists in different countries have different inclinations regarding this issue. Strategists in some nations gravitate more towards an industry leadership perspective than they do in others. Interestingly, there are distinct differences in preferences within industries as well.

On the national level

Culture researchers have tried to understand differences in how people perceive the power of individuals to shape their environment. In some cultures, the view prevails that the individual is at the mercy of external forces, while in other cultures, there is a strong belief in the freedom of individuals to act independently of the environment and even to create their own circumstances (Hampden-Turner and Trompenaars, 2000). Psychologists refer to this as the perceived 'locus of control' (e.g. Miller, Kets de Vries and Toulouse, 1982). People with an internal locus of control believe they mostly are in control of their own fate. Their efforts will shape their circumstances – success is earned and failure is one's own fault. People with an external locus of control, by the same token, believe their fate is largely the result of circumstances beyond their control. Any effort to improve one's position, if at all possible, should be directed towards complying with external demands – fortune favours those who go with the flow. In countries with a culture that is more inclined towards an internal locus of control, such as the United States, the industry leadership perspective is more widespread. In cultures in which people exhibit a strong emphasis for an external locus of control, like in most Asian countries, the industry dynamics perspective is likely to be more predominant.

The role that governments can play in encouraging the shaping of industries also differs internationally. In some countries the predominant view is that governments should facilitate industry development by creating supportive business circumstances and then staying out of the way of company initiatives. Governments are needed to set basic rules of business conduct, but firms should not be impeded by other governmental intervention in the functioning of industries and markets. Individual companies are seen as the primary drivers of industry development and if companies are given enough leeway, game-changing firms can shake the industry context. Such economic liberalism is particularly strong in the English-speaking nations, where governments facilitate the industry-shaping efforts of companies.

In other nations, the predominant view is that Adam Smith's free market ideal often proves to be dysfunctional. A fully liberal market, it is believed, can lead to short-termism, negative social consequences, mutually destructive competition and an inability to implement industry-wide changes. Governments must therefore adopt a more proactive role. They must protect weaker parties, such as workers and the environment, against the negative side of the market system, and actively create a shared infrastructure for all companies. Furthermore, the government can develop an industrial policy to encourage the development of new industries, force companies to work together where this is more effective and push through industry-wide changes, otherwise a stalemate would occur. This 'managed competition' view has been prevalent in Japan and France, and to a lesser extent in Germany (e.g. Hampden-Turner and Trompenaars, 1993; Lessem and Neubauer, 1994). In these countries, the industry leadership perspective is not as strongly held as in the English-speaking nations – industries can be shaped, but few companies have the power to do so without a good industrial policy and government backing.

In countries where the discrete organization perspective (Chapter 6) is predominant, companies often strive to retain their independence and power position vis-à-vis other companies. As these firms are not embedded in complex networks but operate free from constraining relationships, they are more at liberty to challenge the existing rules of the game. In other words, where firms are not entangled in a web of long-term relationships, they are better positioned for rule-breaking behaviour – every firm can make a difference. In these countries an industry leadership perspective is more prevalent. However, in nations where firms are more inclined to operate in networks, each individual firm surrenders a part of its freedom in exchange for long-term relationships. Even though a group of firms, once in agreement, is often more powerful than each individual firm, it is difficult to get network partners to agree. As all changes must be negotiated with partners, the ability to shape an industry declines.

On the industry level

In some countries, an inclination towards the industry leadership or the industry dynamics perspective is apparent, but are there industries for which the same can be said? Many industries develop along evolutionary paths and here there are no leaders who have managed to bend the rules of the game – or at least not yet. Incumbents in a 'leaderless' industry adapt to the changing environment, but do not attempt to drastically alter the context of the industry themselves. There are a variety of reasons why an industry can have more or less strategists aiming to change the rules and win big.

Industries are complex systems, but some are more complex than others. The heterogeneity and concentration within an industry provide challenges in the information process to come to the right strategy. When many stakeholders are involved in an industry, this further constrains strategic decisions. The more complex the industry, the more rigid its players. The industry context can also be more rigid because of regulations. Some industries, such as the pharmaceutical industry, are constrained and the rules of the game are strongly enforced.

Business model innovation hardly originates from established big companies; their common response is to imitate (Markides, 2013). As such, the more difficult it is to enter an industry – for example because of high sums of venture capital required to play along – the industry dynamics are most prevalent. Entrepreneurs and venture capitalists, who are willing to play a high stakes game in the hope of winning big, have a hard time participating in an industry which they can only enter with the utmost difficulty.

To the strategist

The individual strategist can also have different opinions on the strategic paradox of the industry context. The individual disposition of a leader and supposed preferable character traits that go along with it have received much attention (e.g. Bass and Steidlmeier, 1999; Bennis, 1989; Cromie, 2000; Olson-Buchanan, Bryan and Thompson, 2013). Not every strategist is able to develop proper 'industry foresight' (Hamel and Prahalad, 1994) and not every individual is necessarily out there to change the rules of the game.

Regardless of the individual disposition of a strategist, it is also simply difficult to mitigate the industry context paradox internationally. An international firm has to analyse the demands for firm compliance and choice on a country-by-country basis and found his strategy on that. Becoming an industry leader on a global scale through juxtaposing nation-specific requirements is a tough cookie to bake.

11 THE ORGANIZATIONAL CONTEXT

We shape our environments, then our environments shape us.
Winston Churchill (1874–1965), British statesman and writer

INTRODUCTION

In organizations, just as in families, each new generation does not start from scratch but inherits properties of its predecessors. In families, a part of this inheritance is in the form of genetic properties, but other attributes are also passed down such as family traditions, myths, habits, connections, feuds, titles and possessions. People might think of themselves as unique individuals, but, to some degree, they are an extension of the family line and their behaviour is influenced by this inheritance. In firms, the same phenomenon is observable. New top managers may arrive on the scene, but they inherit a great deal from the previous generation. They inherit traditions and myths in the form of an organizational culture. Habits are passed along in the form of established organizational processes, while internal and external relationships and rivalries shape the political constellation in which new managers must function. They are also handed the family jewels – brands, competences and other key resources.

In Chapter 8, it is pointed out that such inheritance is often the source of organizational rigidity and inertia (e.g. Hannan and Freeman, 1977; Rumelt, 1995). Inheritance limits 'organizational plasticity' – the capacity of the organization to change shape. As such, organizational inheritance can partially predetermine a firm's future path of development – which is referred to as path dependency, or sometimes simply summed up as 'history matters' (e.g. Aldrich, 1999; Nelson and Winter, 1982). Therefore, it was concluded that for strategic alignment to take place, some inherited characteristics could be preserved, but others needed to be changed, by either evolutionary or revolutionary means.

What is not discussed in Chapter 8 is *who* should trigger the required strategic changes. Who should initiate adaptations to the firm's business model and who should take steps to reshape the organizational system? Typically, managers have some role to play in all developments in the organizational context, but the question is what role? It is unlikely that any manager will have complete influence over all organizational developments or would even want to exert absolute control. Inheritance and other organizational factors limit 'organizational malleability' – the capacity of the organization to be shaped by someone. As such, managers need to determine what power they have and where this power should be applied to achieve the best results. At the same time, managers will generally also look for opportunities to tap into the capabilities of other people in the firm to contribute to ongoing organizational adaptation.

So, the question can be summarized as: 'What is the role of managers in achieving a new alignment with the environment and what input can be garnered from other organizational members?' This question is also referred to as the issue of organizational development and is the central topic of further discussion in this chapter.

THE ISSUE OF ORGANIZATIONAL DEVELOPMENT

When it comes to realizing organizational development, managers generally acknowledge that they have some type of leadership role to play. Leadership refers to the act of influencing the views and behaviours of organizational members with the intention of accomplishing a particular organizational aim (e.g. Bass, 1990; Selznick, 1957). Stated differently, leadership is the act of getting organizational members to follow. From this definition it can be concluded that not all managers are necessarily leaders and not all leaders are necessarily managers. Managers are individuals with a formal position in the organizational hierarchy, with associated authority and responsibilities. Leaders are individuals who have the ability to sway other people in the organization to get something done.

To be able to lead organizational developments, managers need power: the capability to influence. They also need to know how to get power and how and where to exert it. In the following sections, these three topics are examined in more detail. First, the sources of leadership influence are described, followed by the levers of leadership influence. Finally, the arenas of leadership influence are explored.

Sources of leadership influence

To lead means to use power to influence others. Leaders can derive their potential influence from two general sources – their position and their person (Etzioni, 1961). 'Position power' comes from a leader's formal function in the organization. 'Personal power' is rooted in the specific character, knowledge, skills and relationships of the leader. Managers always have some level of position power, but they do not necessarily have the personal power needed to get organizational members to follow them. These two main types of power can be further subdivided into the following categories (French and Raven, 1959):

- Legitimate power. Legitimate power exists when a person has the formal authority to determine certain organizational behaviours and other employees agree to comply with this situation. Examples of legitimate power are the authority to assign work, spend money and demand information.

- Coercive power. People have coercive power when they have the capability to punish or withhold rewards to achieve compliance. Examples of coercive power include giving a poor performance review, withholding a bonus and dismissing employees.

- Reward power. Reward power is derived from the ability to offer something of value to a person in return for compliance. Examples of reward power include giving praise, awarding wage raises and promoting employees.

- Expert power. Expert power exists when organizational members are willing to comply because of a person's superior knowledge or skills in an important area. Such expert power can be based on specific knowledge of functional areas (e.g. marketing, finance), technologies (e.g. pharmaceuticals, information technology), geographic areas (e.g. South-East Asia, Florida) or businesses (e.g. mining, automotive).

- Referent power. When organizational members let themselves be influenced by a person's charismatic appeal, this is called referent power. This personal attraction can be based on many attributes, such as likeableness, forcefulness, persuasiveness, visionary qualities and image of success.

The first three types of power are largely determined by the organizational position of leaders and their willingness to exert them – coercive and reward capabilities without the credibility of use are not a viable source of power. The last two sources of power, expert and referent power, are largely personal in nature and therefore more subjective. Whether someone is seen as an expert, and therefore accorded a certain level of respect and influence, depends strongly on the perceptions of the people being led. Expert power can be made more tangible by wearing a white lab coat, putting three pens in your breast pocket or writing a book, but perceived expertise will still be in the eyes of the beholder. The same is true for referent power, as people do not find the same characteristics equally charismatic. What is forceful to one follower might seem pushy to someone else; what is visionary to one person might sound like the murmurings of a madman to others (e.g. Klein and House, 1998; Waldman and Yammarino, 1999).

In practice, leaders will employ a mix of all five types of power to achieve the influence they desire. However, leadership styles can differ greatly depending on the relative weight placed on the various sources of power within the mix.

Levers of leadership influence

The sources of power available to the leader need to be used to have influence. There are three generic ways for leaders to seek influence, each focused on a different point in the activities of the people being influenced. These levers of leadership influence are:

- Throughput control. Leaders can focus their attention directly at the actions being taken by others in the organization. Throughput control implies getting involved hands on in the activities of others, either by suggesting ways of working, engaging in a discussion on how things should be done, leading by example or simply by telling others what to do. This form of direct influence does require sufficiently detailed knowledge about the activities of others to be able to point out what should be done.

- Output control. Instead of directly supervising how things should be done, leaders can set objectives that should be met. Output control implies reaching agreement on certain performance targets and then monitoring how well they are being lived up to. The targets can be quantitative or qualitative, financial or strategic, simple or complex, realistic or stretch oriented. And they can be arrived at by mutual consent or imposed by the leader. The very act of setting objectives can have an important influence on people in the organization, but the ability to check ongoing performance and to link results with punishment and rewards can further improve a person's impact.

■ Input control. Leaders can also choose to influence the general conditions under which activities are carried out. Input control implies shaping the circumstances preceding and surrounding the actual work. Before activities start a leader can influence who is assigned to a task, which teams are formed, who is hired, where they will work and in what type of environment. During the execution of activities the leader can supply physical and financial resources, mobilize relationships and provide support. Not unimportantly, the leader can also be a source of enthusiasm, inspiration, ambition, vision and mission.

Of these three, throughput control is the most direct in its impact and input control the least. However, throughput control offers the lowest leverage and input control the highest, allowing a leader to influence many people over a longer period of time, while leaving more room for organizational members to take on their own responsibilities as well. In practice, leaders can combine elements of all three of the above, although leadership styles differ greatly with regard to the specific mix.

Arenas of leadership influence

As leaders attempt to guide organizational development, there are three main organizational arenas in which they need to direct their influence to achieve strategic changes. These three overlapping arenas are the parts in the organization most resistant to change – they are the subsystems of the firm in which organizational inheritance creates its own momentum, resisting a shift into another direction (e.g. Miller and Friesen, 1980; Tushman, Newman and Romanelli, 1986):

■ The political arena. While most top managers have considerable position power with which they can try to influence the strategic decision-making process within their organization, very few top managers can impose their strategic agenda on the organization without building widespread political support. Even the most autocratic CEO will need to gain the commitment and compliance of key figures within the organization to be able to successfully push through significant changes. In practice, however, there are not many organizations where the 'officers and the troops' unquestioningly follow the general into battle. Usually, power is more dispersed throughout organizations, with different people and units having different ideas and interests, as well as the assertiveness to pursue their own agenda. Ironically, the more leaders that are developed throughout the organization, the more complex it becomes for any one leader to get the entire organization to follow – broad leadership can easily become fragmented leadership, with a host of strong people all pointing in different directions. For top management to gain control of the organization, they must build coalitions of supporters, not only to get favourable strategic decisions made, but also to ensure acceptance and compliance during the period of implementation. Otherwise strategic plans will be half-heartedly executed, opposed or silently sabotaged. However, gaining the necessary political support in the organization can be very difficult if the strategic views and interests of powerful individuals and departments differ significantly. Cultural and personality clashes can add to the complexity. Yet, top managers cannot recoil from the political arena, for it is here that new strategic directions are set (e.g. Allison, 1969; Pfeffer, 1992).

- The cultural arena. Intertwined with the process of gaining political influence in the organization, there is the process of gaining cultural influence. After all, to be able to change the organization, a leader must be able to change people's beliefs and associated behavioural patterns. Yet, affecting cultural change is far from simple. A leader must be capable of questioning the shared values, ideas and habits prevalent in the organization, even though the leader has usually been immersed in the very same culture for years. Leaders must also offer an alternative worldview and set of behaviours to supersede the old. All of this requires exceptional skills as visionary – to develop a new image of a desired future state for the firm – and as missionary – to develop a new set of beliefs and values to guide the firm. Furthermore, the leader needs to be an excellent teacher to engage the organizational members in a learning process to adapt their beliefs, values and norms to the new circumstances. In practice, this means that leaders often have to 'sell' their view of the new culture, using a mix of rational persuasion, inspirational appeal, symbolic actions, motivational incentives and subtle pressure (e.g. Ireland and Hitt, 1999; Senge, 1990).

- The psychological arena. While leaders need to influence the political process and the cultural identity of the organization, attention also needs to be paid to the psychological needs of individuals. To affect organizational change, leaders must win both the hearts and minds of the members of the organization. People must be willing to, literally, 'follow the leader' – preferably not passively, but actively, with commitment, courage and even passion (e.g. Bennis and Nanus, 1985; Kelley, 1988). To achieve such 'follower-ship', leaders must gain the respect and trust of their colleagues. Another important factor in winning people over is the ability to meet their emotional need for certainty, clarity and continuity, to offset the uncertainties, ambiguities and discontinuities surrounding them (e.g. Argyris, 1990; Pfeffer and Sutton, 1999).

Even where political, cultural and psychological processes make the organization difficult to lead, managers might still be able to gain a certain level of control over their organizations. Yet there will always remain aspects of the organizational system that managers cannot control and should not even want to control, which are discussed in the following section.

THE PARADOX OF CONTROL AND CHAOS

Of all men's miseries the bitterest is this, to know so much and to have control over nothing.

Herodotus (5th century BCE), Greek historian

In general, managers like to be in control. Managers like to be able to shape their own future, and by extension, to shape the future of their firm. Managers do not shy away from power – they build their power base to be able to influence events and steer the development of their organization. In short, to be a manager is to have the desire to be in charge.

Yet, at the same time, most managers understand that their firms do not resemble machines, where one person can sit at the control panel and steer the entire system.

Organizations are complex social systems, populated by numerous self-thinking human beings, each with her own feelings, ideas and interests. These people need to decide and act for themselves on a daily basis, without the direct intervention of the manager. They must be empowered to weigh situations, take initiatives, solve problems and grab opportunities. They must be given a certain measure of autonomy to experiment, do things differently and even constructively disagree with the manager. In other words, managers must also be willing to 'let go' of some control for the organization to function at its best.

Moreover, managers must accept that in a complex system, like an organization, trying to control everything would be a futile endeavour. With so many people and so many interactions going on in a firm, any attempt to run the entire system top down would be an impossible task. Therefore, letting go of some control is a pure necessity for normal organizational functioning.

This duality of wanting to control the development of the organization, while understanding that letting go of control is often beneficial, is the key strategic tension when dealing with the organizational context. On the one hand, managers must be willing to act as benevolent 'philosopher kings', autocratically imposing on the company what they consider to be best. On the other hand, managers must be willing to act as constitutional monarchs, democratically empowering organizational citizens to take their own responsibilities and behave more like entrepreneurs. The strategic paradox arises from the fact that the need for top-down *imposition* and bottom-up *initiative* are conflicting demands that are difficult for managers to meet at the same time.

On one side of this strategy paradox is 'control', which can be defined as the power to direct and impose order. On the other side of the paradox is the need for 'chaos', which can be defined as disorder or the lack of fixed organization. The paradox of control and chaos is a recurrent theme in the literature on strategy, organization, leadership and governance.

In most writings, the need for control is presented as a pressure for a directive leadership style or an autocratic governance system (e.g. Tannenbaum and Schmidt, 1958; Vroom and Jago, 1988). The need for chaos is presented as a pressure for a participative leadership style and/or a democratic governance system (e.g. Ackoff, 1980; Stacey, 1992). In the following subsections, both control and chaos are further examined.

The demand for top management control

As Herodotus remarked, it would be bitter indeed to have control over nothing. Not only would it be a misery for the frustrated managers, who would be little more than mere administrators or caretakers, it would also be a misery for their organizations, which would need to constantly adjust course without a helmsman to guide the ship. Managers cannot afford to let their organizations drift on the existing momentum. It is a manager's task and responsibility to ensure that the organization changes in accordance with the environment, so that the organizational purpose can still be achieved.

Top management cannot realize this objective without some level of control. They need to be able to direct developments in the organization. They need to have the power to make the necessary changes in the organizational structure, processes and culture, to realign the organization with the demands of the environment. This power, whether positional or personal, needs to be applied towards gaining sufficient support in the political arena, challenging existing beliefs and behaviours in the cultural arena, and winning the hearts and minds of the organizational members in the psychological arena.

The control that top management needs is different from the day-to-day control built in to the organizational structure and processes – they need *strategic control* as opposed to *operational control*. While operational control gives managers influence over activities within the current organizational system, strategic control gives managers influence over changes to the organizational system itself (e.g. Goold and Quinn, 1990; Simons, 1994). It is this power that managers require to be able to steer the development of their organization.

The demand for organizational chaos

To managers, the term 'chaos' sounds quite menacing – it carries connotations of rampant anarchy, total pandemonium and a hopeless mess. Yet, chaos only means disorder, coming from the Greek term for the unformed original state of the universe. In the organizational context, chaos refers to situations of disorder, where phenomena have not yet been organized, or where parts of an organizational system have become 'unfrozen'. In other words, something is chaotic if it is unformed or has become 'disorganized'.

While this still does not sound particularly appealing to most managers, it should, because a period of disorganization is often a prerequisite for strategic renewal. Unfreezing existing structures, processes, routines and beliefs, and opening people up to different possibilities might be inefficient in the short run, as well as making people feel uncomfortable, but it is usually necessary to provoke creativity and to invent new ways of seeing and doing things. By allowing experimentation, skunk works, pilot projects and out-of-the-ordinary initiatives, managers accept a certain amount of disorder in the organization, which they hope will pay off in terms of organizational innovations.

But the most appealing effect of chaos is that it encourages 'self-organization'. To illustrate this phenomenon, one should first think back to the old Soviet 'command economy', which was based on the principle of control. It was believed that a rational, centrally planned economic system, with strong top-down leadership, would be the most efficient and effective way to organize industrial development. In the West, by way of contrast, the 'market economy' was chaotic – no one was in control or could impose order. Everyone could go ahead and start a company. They could set their own production levels and even set their own prices! As entrepreneurs made use of the freedom offered to them, the economy 'self-organized' bottom up. Instead of the 'visible hand' of the central planner controlling and regulating the economy, it was the 'invisible hand' of the market that created relative order out of chaos.

As the market economy example illustrates, chaos does not necessarily lead to pandemonium, but can result in a self-regulating interplay of forces. A lack of top-down control frees the way for a rich diversity of bottom-up ventures. Managers who also want to release the energy, creativity and entrepreneurial potential pent up in their organizations must therefore be willing to let go and allow some chaos to exist. In this context, the role of top management is comparable to that of governments in market economies – creating suitable conditions, encouraging activities and enforcing basic rules.

EXHIBIT 11.1 SHORT CASE

GAZPROM: BUILT TO DREAM

Although the slogan *mechty sbyvayutsya* or 'dreams come true' will probably not be familiar to most, the owner of the motto most likely is. The open joint stock company Gazprom is Russia's national champion and one of the world's largest energy companies. It has over 270,000 employees, its latest shareholder count exceeds 4,616,000 and with a total of 1,712,000 kilometres of pipelines in Russia alone it could wrap the globe more than four times. Its core business consists of geological exploration, production, transportation and storage processing of hydrocarbons, as well as generating heat and electric power. Gazprom equals big business, with the company accounting for about 8 per cent of Russia's GDP and generating about one-fifth of the Russian government's revenues. In others words: if Gazprom suffers, Russia does as well.

Gazprom was an offshoot of the Soviet Gas Ministry, created by Viktor Chernomyrdin, the last Soviet Minister of Gas Industry, in 1989. This young professional made an enterprise association that was granted special privileges, such as favourable taxes and a full monopoly over the foreign trade in piped gas. For years the state corporate enterprise enjoyed sky-high gas prices with a net profit of $25 billion in 2007. No matter what difficulties came across the company's path, it could always, as Natalia Volchkova of the New Economic School in Moscow phrased it, 'drown it with money'. In May 2008 Gazprom's market capitalization peaked at $350 billion, making it the third most valuable company in the world. Investment banks and energy consultants foresaw a dazzling future and its officials predicted

that the giant would become the biggest in the world, worth $1 trillion.

Unfortunately for Gazprom, all good things eventually come to an end. The global financial crisis hit oil prices in 2009, which resulted in Gazprom's production plummeting by about 16 per cent. The company not only suffered a decline in revenues, structural management problems also showed their face. With financial crises demonstrated to bring structural weaknesses to light, Russia's national champion seemed no exception to the rule.

Because of recent events, Gazprom faces several challenges, with its reliability as a supplier being one of them. Whereas Gazprom considers itself a trustworthy gas supplier to Russia and foreign countries, its purchasers tend to see this differently. Few need to be reminded of the trick it pulled with Ukraine by cutting off gas in 2006, leaving 16 other European countries in the cold. The conflict in eastern Ukraine from 2014 effectively reduced Gazprom's exports to Ukraine from 36 billion cubic metres in 2010 to zero on 1 July 2015. The energy blockade against Kiev ultimately failed, but it pushed European customers into further diversifying their energy imports. The unreliable gas supply makes Gazprom's consumers eager for alternative routes to meet their demands.

And these exist. Normally a warned man counts for two, but CEO Alexei Miller clearly underestimated the development of shale gas in North America by calling it a 'myth' and 'shale fever' in 2010. Shale gas production in Europe is off to a slow start; nevertheless, it offers an affordable alternative to Russian gas. Furthermore, Norway manages to further exploit its oil reserves. In fact, in the winter of 2014 Norway overtook Russia as Western Europe's top gas supplier. In addition, Gazprom not only has to deal

▶

with more pressure in the European market, it is challenged by fierce competition in the domestic market as well. Unlike Gazprom, independent producers are now capable of selling gas volumes with high profits.

Gazprom is not only losing ground, but faces more problems with less money at the same time. If it wants to remain a global player, drowning obstacles with money will not be an option any more. An answer seems to lie in one particular area: Gazprom's management. During the last couple of years, its corporate governance has been criticized for being incompetent, bureaucratic, inert and mismanaged. Bearing Russia's history in mind, this summary does not come as a total surprise. During the Soviet regime, Joseph Stalin introduced the concept of the 'command economy', with planned and centralized production replacing a free market. The corporate governance of the current Gazprom illustrates that shaking off the past is easier said than done.

When looking at the enterprise's structure, one might say it resembles an authoritarian system. Gazprom's holding group is comprised of the parent company OAO Gazprom and its seven subsidiaries engaged in gas processing, oil, transmission, power industry, ancillary activities, marketing and gas exploration, exploitation and distribution. The Chairman of Gazprom Group forms the broad policy for the CEO and his directors to execute. The CEO is next in line of command, followed by the board of directors that execute the chairman's policy by passing this through to the company's various departments. The responsibility of managers is to ensure the observance of the decisions taken by the board of directors, who can thus be called foot soldiers, rather than leaders.

For Alexei Miller, Gazprom's current head, there was no need to choose between the two top positions; he became Gazprom's chairman as well as its CEO. Although decision-making within Gazprom is controlled and centralized by top-down focused management, he is not in total control of the company. The Russian government owns over 50 per cent of Gazprom's shares, making it the most powerful shareholder and thus allowing it to exert pressure while also ensuring a certain degree of command.

Whether Miller is actually in control, is becoming an increasingly poignant question, however. Gazprom seems to increasingly be one of Putin's most favoured geopolitical instruments. In 2015, the Kremlin decided to block energy to Ukraine during the conflict in the eastern part of that country, effectively reducing Gazprom's exports to Ukraine from 36 billion cubic metres in 2010 to zero on 1 July 2015. While the energy blockade against Kiev ultimately failed, it did cost Gazprom about $6 billion in lost revenues. In addition, the Putin administration pushed the company into purchasing major media outlets, sponsoring the expensive Sochi Olympic Games and embarking on big projects.

One of these is the grand Power of Siberia project, a 4,000 km pipeline through East Siberia to the Russian Pacific Coast. Although a project accompanied by a $46 billion bill can be called rather pricey, even for a company the size of Gazprom, government support makes it feasible. Power of Siberia is able to create a valuable opportunity for the company as it could lessen the dependence of Gazprom on European markets, especially with talks on connecting the project with the extensive Chinese market in the pipeline. In this case, Gazprom might actually profit from its bureaucratic, state-centred position, since no commercial company would ever attempt or accomplish something like this.

Nevertheless, the idea that a rational and centralized system would be the most efficient and effective way to organize Gazprom has not fully proved itself. The Gazprom management did not truly understand the severity of recent economic changes, with it calling the decline in gas demand a 'temporary inconvenience'. Therefore, the top-down leadership within Gazprom seems unfit at adapting to changes on the global stage. Perhaps when managers, as opposed to external shareholders, are given more control, they can allow for more internal organizational freedom to stimulate self-regulating departments.

By way of contrast: Is it advisable for Gazprom to adapt to the industry and is it realistic to expect Gazprom's customers' stance to change in the upcoming years even if Miller changes his management? Although his top-down focused organization has proved to inherit flaws, one can argue that Gazprom is actually in need of strict control in order to successfully compete in the oil and gas industry, especially in Russia. In order to best preserve its monopoly, playing it hard seems like a logical option, something that can best be accomplished with a more autocratic company.

With a changing oil and gas industry, decreasing revenues and increasing competition, something needs to change. Disorganizing the extremely organized company and disconnecting it more from the Russian state might help accomplish strategic renewal and herewith better adapt itself to the industry. Yet, keeping management control exclusive to the top provides Gazprom with merits as well, with a large company demanding a certain level of control. And that is without even considering the difficulty tinkering with Gazprom's management would bring. While both options embody disadvantages as well, making the right decision is definitely challenging. It is up to Miller to decide, but what choice can ultimately make Gazprom's dreams come true?

Co-authors: Larissa Kalle and Wester Wagenaar

Sources: www.gazprom.com; Åslund (2010); *The Economist*, 23 March 2013; *EurasiaNet*, 3 August 2015; *Financial Times*, 5 June 2013 and 17 June 2013; *Forbes*, 2 June 2005.

PERSPECTIVES ON THE ORGANIZATIONAL CONTEXT

I claim not to have controlled events, but confess plainly that events have controlled me.

Abraham Lincoln (1809–1865), American President

While the pressures for both control and chaos are clear, this does leave managers with the challenging question of how they must reconcile two opposite, and at least partially incompatible, demands. Gaining a considerable level of top management control over the development of the organization will to some extent be at odds with a policy of accepting, or even encouraging, organizational chaos. To control or not to control, that is the question.

And yet again managers should not hope to find widespread consensus in the strategic management literature on what the optimal answer is for dealing with these two conflicting pressures. For among strategy academics and business practitioners alike, opinions differ strongly with regard to the best balance between control and chaos. Although many writers do indicate that there may be different styles in dealing with the paradox and that these different styles might be more effective under different circumstances (e.g. Strebel, 1994; Vroom and Jago, 1988), most authors still exhibit a strong preference for a particular approach – which is duly called the 'modern' or 'new' style, or better yet, '21st Century practices' (Ireland and Hitt, 1999).

Following the dialectical enquiry method used in previous chapters, here the two diametrically opposed positions are identified and discussed. On the one hand, there are those who argue that top managers should lead from the front. Top managers should dare to take on the responsibility of imposing a new strategic agenda on the organization and should be at the forefront in breaking away from organizational inheritance where necessary. This point of view, with its strong emphasis on control and leading top down, is referred to as the 'organizational leadership perspective'. This view is also known as the strategic leadership perspective (e.g. Cannella and Monroe, 1997; Rowe, 2001), but to avoid confusion with the industry leadership perspective discussed in Chapter 10, here the prefix 'organizational' is preferred. On the other hand, there are people who believe that managers rarely have the ability to shape their organizations at will, but rather that organizations develop according to their own dynamics. These strategists argue that in most organizations no one is really in control and that managers should not focus their energy on attempting to impose developments top down, but rather focus on facilitating processes of self-organization. This point of view, with its strong emphasis on chaos and facilitating bottom-up processes, is referred to as the 'organizational dynamics perspective'.

The organizational leadership perspective

To proponents of the organizational leadership perspective, top management can – and should – take charge of the organization. In their view, organizational inertia and a growing misfit between the organization and its environment are not an inevitable state of affairs, but result from a failure of leadership.

Bureaucracy, organizational fiefdoms, hostile relationships, inflexible corporate cultures, rigid competences and resistance to change – all of these organizational diseases exist, but they are not unavoidable facts of organizational life. 'Healthy' organizations guard against falling prey to such degenerative illnesses, and when symptoms do arise it is a task of the leader to address them. If organizations do go 'out of control', it is because weak leadership has failed to deal with a creeping ailment. The fact that there are many sick, poorly controlled companies does not mean that sickness should be accepted as the natural condition.

At the basis of the organizational leadership perspective lies the belief that if people in organizations are left to 'sort things out' by themselves, this will inevitably degenerate into a situation of strategic drift (see Chapter 8). Without somebody to quell political infighting, set a clear strategic direction, force through tough decisions and supervise disciplined implementation, the organization will get bogged down in protracted internal bickering. Without somebody to champion a new vision, rally the troops and lead from the front, the organization will never get its heavy mass in motion. Without somebody who radiates confidence and cajoles people into action, the organization will not be able to overcome its risk averseness and conservatism. In short, leaders are needed to counteract the inherent inertia characteristic of human organization.

As organizational order and direction do not happen spontaneously, the 'visible hand' of management is indispensable for the proper functioning of the organization (e.g. Child, 1972; Cyert, 1990). And this hand must be firm. Managers cannot afford to take a *laissez-faire* attitude towards their task as leader – to lead means to get the organizational members to follow and this is usually plain hard work (e.g. Bennis and Nanus, 1985; Kelley, 1988). To convince people in the organization to let themselves be led, managers cannot simply fall back on their position power. To be able to steer organizational developments managers need considerable personal power. To be successful, managers must be trusted, admired and respected. The forcefulness of their personality and the persuasiveness of their vision must be capable of capturing people's attention and commitment. And as leaders, managers must also be politically agile, able to build coalitions where necessary to get their way.

Of course, not all managers have the qualities needed to be effective leaders – either by nature or nurture. Some theorists emphasize the importance of 'nature', arguing that managers require specific personality traits to be successful leaders (e.g. House and Aditya, 1997; Tucker, 1968). Yet, other theorists place more emphasis on 'nurture', arguing that most effective leadership behaviour can be learned if enough effort is exerted (e.g. Kotter, 1990; Nanus, 1992). Either way, the importance of having good leadership makes finding and developing new leaders one of the highest priorities of the existing top management team.

To proponents of the organizational leadership perspective, being a leader does not mean engaging in simple top-down, command-and-control management. There are circumstances where the CEO or the top management team design strategies in isolation and then impose them on the rest of the organization. This type of direct control is sometimes necessary to push through reorganizations or to make major acquisitions. In other circumstances, however, the top managers can control organizational behaviour more indirectly. Proposals can be allowed to emerge bottom up, as long as top management retains its power to approve or terminate projects as soon as they become serious plans (e.g. Bourgeois and Brodwin, 1983; Quinn, 1980). Some authors suggest that top management might even delegate some decision-making powers to lower level managers, but still control outcomes by setting clear goals, developing a conducive incentive system and fostering a particular culture (e.g. Senge, 1990; Tichy and Cohen, 1997).

What leaders should not do, however, is relinquish control over the direction of the organization. The strategies do not have to be their own ideas, neither do they have to carry out everything themselves. But they should take on themselves the responsibility for leading the organization in a certain direction and achieving results. If leaders let go of the helm, organizations will be set adrift and will be carried by the prevailing winds and currents in directions unknown. Someone has to be in control of the organization, otherwise its behaviour will be erratic. Leadership is needed to ensure that the best strategy is followed.

In conclusion, the organizational leadership perspective holds that the upper echelons of management can, and should, control the strategy process and by extension the strategy content. The CEO, or the top management team (e.g. Finkelstein and Hambrick, 1996; Hambrick and Mason, 1984), should have a grip on the organization's process of strategy formation and should be able to impose their will on the organization. Leaders should strive to overcome organizational inertia and adapt the organization to the strategic direction they intend. This type of controlled strategic behaviour is what Chandler (1962) had in mind when he coined the aphorism 'structure follows strategy' – the organizational structure should be adapted to the strategy intended by the decision-maker. In the organizational leadership perspective, it would be more fitting to expand Chandler's maxim to 'organization follows strategy' – all aspects of the company should be matched to the strategist's intentions.

EXHIBIT 11.2   THE ORGANIZATIONAL LEADERSHIP PERSPECTIVE

LEADING BY ITALIAN EXAMPLE AT CHRYSLER

One of the most talked about change makers in the automobile industry is Sergio Marchionne, who miraculously saved the left-for-dead Fiat – with Alfa Romeo, Maserati and Ferrari a distinctive Italian car maker – in just a couple of years after taking control in 2004. Then, Mr Marchionne aimed at applying his tried and tested method at Chrysler in which Fiat gained a 20 per cent stake at close to no cost. With Chrysler he chose not the easiest of challenges as the German firm Daimler – the parent company of Mercedes-Benz – had failed in the same job only a couple of years earlier.

Central to the approach employed by Fiat's saviour is a monumental turnaround in leadership. Management should control the strategy process, focusing on dealing quickly with the volatile yet hardly growing industry. To do so, overhead must be cut quickly and old managers that hold on to top-down management need to be replaced by younger executives. This creates an accountable, open, quickly communicating and less politics-ridden ecosystem at the top, capable of steering a firm through the industry's testing challenges.

Mr Marchionne's 60-day 'killing spree', which he initiated after taking over at Chrysler, is a good illustration of the new leadership style. Just as he did with Fiat, he redefined the structure and replaced people himself to become more responsive. This left many of the upper echelons of management being startled with new opportunities or, alternatively, anxiously looking for different jobs. Having forward thinking and flexible leaders at the helm of an organization in an industry as pressured as the car industry is no excessive luxury. The market is expected to become increasingly volatile and the benefits of scale, although necessary for mutual survival, bring about a new class of challenges. For this reason, a sudden jolt given by renewing the upper echelons of management is not enough. Instead, to be able to continuously benefit from its newfound boons, Mr Marchionne is visibly leading his senior staff, who, in turn, need to be visible to the rest of the organization. Only by continuously displaying the right behaviour can a sustainable competitive advantage be maintained.

Leading by example and being visible is surely something Marchionne does not shy away from. In June 2013, he visited Fiat and Chrysler's headquarters in Turin and Auburn Hills in addition to visiting half a dozen other places around the world. While there he was far from enjoying the tourist locations, but instead visibly busying himself with quenching labour union issues, boosting productivity in Italy as well as his stake in Chrysler and setting up cooperative ventures in China.

According to Marchionne, faulty leadership is underlying a firm's immediate problems, which one should not hesitate to replace. Saving hundreds of thousands of jobs worldwide surely weighs up to getting rid of a handful of senior executives that are partly responsible for creating the problems in the first place. His second stroke of genius, to make abundantly visible the upper ranks of managers including himself while showing the desired behaviour, might have been even more impressive. Not fearing structure changes and replacing people while being consistent and visible is what sets him apart. Will Mr Marchionne succeed where even the renowned carmaker Daimler couldn't? Consecutive years of profits and growing car sales suggest that this Italian pilot has successfully tuned up Chrysler's economic engine.

Co-author: Jasper de Vries

Sources: 'The Italian solution: Fiat chief executive, Sergio Marchionne, has gone merger mad', *The Economist*, 7 May 2009; 'Sergio Marchionne's high-wire act at Fiat-Chrysler', *CNN Money*, 12 July 2013; 'Lessons from Chrysler: How to rev up a purpose-driven corporate culture', *The Guardian*, 31 July 2014; FCA Annual Report, 2013–2015.

The organizational dynamics perspective

To proponents of the organizational dynamics perspective, such a heroic depiction of leadership is understandable, but usually more myth than reality. There might be a few great, wise, charismatic managers that rise to the apex of organizations, but unfortunately, all other organizations have to settle for regular mortals. Strong leaders are an exception, not the norm and even their ability to mould the organization at will is highly exaggerated – good stories for best-selling autobiographies, but legend nevertheless (e.g. Chen and Meindl, 1991; Kets de Vries, 1994). Yet, the belief in the power of leadership is quite popular, among managers and the managed alike (e.g. Meindl, Ehrlich and Dukerich, 1985; Pfeffer, 1977). Managers like the idea that as leaders of an organization or organizational unit, they can make a difference. To most, 'being in control' is what management is all about. They have a penchant for attributing organizational results to their own efforts (e.g. Hayward, Rindova and Pollock, 2004; Sims and Lorenzi, 1992). As for 'the managed', they too often ascribe organizational success or failure to the figurehead leader, whatever that person's real influence has been – after all, they too like the idea that somebody is in control. In fact, both parties are subscribing to a seductively simple 'great person model' of how organizations work. The implicit assumption is that an individual leader, by the strength of personality, can steer large groups of people, like a present-day Alexander the Great.

However seductive, this view of organizational functioning is rarely satisfactory. A top manager does not resemble a commander leading the troops into battle, but rather a diplomat trying to negotiate peace. The top manager is not like a jockey riding a thoroughbred horse, but more like a cowboy herding mules. Organizations are complex social systems, made up of many 'stubborn individuals' with their own ideas, interests and agendas (e.g. Greenwood and Hinings, 1996; Stacey, 1993). Strategy formation is therefore an inherently political process that leaders can only influence depending on their power base. The more dispersed the political power, the more difficult it is for a leader to control the organization's behaviour. Even if leaders are granted, or acquire, significant political power to push through their favoured measures, there may still be considerable resistance and guerrilla activities. Political processes within organizations do not signify the derailment of strategic decision-making – politics is the normal state of affairs and few leaders have real control over these political dynamics.

Besides such political limitations, a top manager's ability to control the direction of a company is also severely constrained by the organization's culture. Social norms will have evolved, relationships will have been formed, aspirations will have taken root and cognitive maps will have been shaped. A leader cannot ignore the cultural legacy of the organization's history, as this will be deeply etched into the minds of the organization's members. Any top manager attempting to radically alter the direction of a company will find out that changing the underlying values, perceptions, beliefs and expectations is extremely difficult, if not next to impossible. As Weick (1979) puts it, an organization does not have a culture, it *is* a culture – shared values and norms are what make an organization. And just as it is difficult to change someone's identity, it is difficult to change an organization's culture (e.g. Schein, 1993; Smircich and Stubbart, 1985). Moreover, as most top managers rise through the ranks to the upper echelons, they themselves are a product of the existing organizational culture. Changing your own culture is like pulling yourself up by your own bootstraps – a great trick, too bad that nobody can do it.

In Chapters 4 and 5, a related argument was put forward, as part of the resource-based view of the firm. One of the basic assumptions of the resource-based view is that building up competences is an arduous task, requiring a relatively long period of time. Learning is a slow process under the best of circumstances, but even more difficult if learning one thing means unlearning something else. The stronger the existing cognitive maps (knowledge), routines (capabilities) and disposition (attitude), the more challenging it is to 'teach an old dog new tricks'. The leader's power to direct and speed up such processes, it was argued, is quite limited (e.g. Barney, 1991; Leonard-Barton, 1995).

Taken together, the political, cultural and learning dynamics leave top managers with relatively little direct power over the system they want to steer. Generally, they can react to this limited ability to control in one of two basic ways – they can squeeze tighter or let go. Many managers follow the first route, desperately trying to acquire more power, to gain a tighter grip on the organization, in the vain attempt to become the heroic leader of popular legend. Such a move to accumulate more power commonly results in actions to assert control, including stricter reporting structures, more disciplined accountability, harsher punishment for non-conformists and a shakeout among managers. In this manner, control comes to mean restriction, subordination or even subjugation. Yet, such a step towards authoritarian management will still not bring managers very much further towards having a lasting impact on organizational development.

The alternative route is for managers to accept that they cannot, but also should not try to, tightly control the organization. As they cannot really control organizational dynamics, all heavy-handed control approaches will have little more result than making the organization an unpleasant and oppressive place to work. If managers emphasize control, all they will do is run the risk of killing the organization's ability to innovate and learn. Innovation and learning are very difficult to control, especially the business innovation and learning happening outside R&D labs. Much of this innovation and learning is sparked by organizational members, out in the markets or on the work floor, questioning the status quo. New ideas often start 'in the margins' of the organization and grow due to the room granted to offbeat opinions. Fragile new initiatives often need to be championed by their owners lower down in the hierarchy and only survive if there is a tolerance for unintended 'misfits' in the organization's portfolio of activities. Only if employees have a certain measure of freedom and are willing to act as intrapreneurs, will learning and innovation be an integral part of the organization's functioning (e.g. Amabile, 1998; Quinn, 1985).

In other words, if managers move beyond their instinctive desire for control and recognize the creative and entrepreneurial potential of self-organization, they will not bemoan their lack of control. They will see that a certain level of organizational chaos can create the conditions for development (e.g. Levy, 1994; Stacey, 1993). According to the organizational dynamics perspective, the task for managers is to use their limited powers to facilitate self-organization (e.g. Beinhocker, 1999; Wheatley and Kellner-Rogers, 1996). Managers can encourage empowerment, stimulate learning and innovation, bring people together, take away bureaucratic hurdles – all very much like the approach by most governments in market economies, who try to establish conditions conducive to entrepreneurial behaviour instead of trying to control economic activity. Managers' most important task is to ensure that the 'invisible hand of self-organization' functions properly and does not lead to 'out-of-hand disorganization'.

So, does the manager matter? Yes, but in a different sense than is usually assumed. The manager cannot shape the organization – it shapes itself. Organizational developments are the result of complex internal dynamics, which can be summarized as strategy follows organization, instead of the other way around. Managers can facilitate processes of self-organization and thus indirectly influence the direction of development, but at the same time managers are also shaped by the organization they are in.

EXHIBIT 11.3   ORGANIZATIONAL DYNAMICS PERSPECTIVE

MIGROS: BY AND FOR THE PEOPLE

It is 1925, Zurich, Switzerland. Money is scarce, and healthy yet affordable groceries are hard to find in what has currently become the economic centre of a wealthy country. It was at that time when Gottlieb Duttweiler, a man with a vision and a kind heart, founded Migros, a firm that would later leave a mark on the Swiss retailing industry, as well as on Swiss society. His objective was to meet the demand for low-priced basic food by cutting out the middleman. He would sell a few basic products to households that didn't have easy access to markets, but as demand for his services grew, so did the company. This led to a dilemma for Mr Duttweiler: Should he keep control of the growing company and ownership of its potential profits, or become a company 'by and for the people'? In 1941 Mr Duttweiler decided

to put the customers in charge and transfer the branches into regional cooperatives.

The Migros community organizes itself bounded by a very society-oriented way of doing business. There is still a board as well as a Federation of Migros Cooperatives heading the different enterprises, but this governance structure takes more of a facilitating or coordinating form. The two million strong customer base, amounting to over one-quarter of the Swiss population, effectively run the firm, meaning that it is owned by the same people that it serves. Every two years, 100 members of the cooperative are elected to take a seat in the Assembly of Delegates. The powers of the Assembly of Delegates include defining and amending the statutes, electing or dismissing board members and defining and amending business policy.

One of the collectively taken decisions is to refrain from selling alcoholic beverages

▶

in the Migros flagship supermarkets. Offering products at the lowest price possible has always been a major objective, but when applying this policy to potentially harmful products, the well-being of individuals could be compromised. While a profitability-focused firm may perceive this as an acceptable consequence, for the consumer-operated Migros it is not.

In 1996 Migros initiated the M-Budget brand, aimed at individuals with a lower income, which follows tradition. In 2015 the M-Budget brand was voted Switzerland's second favourite brand, close behind the Migros brand itself, which came in first. As it turns out, the idealistic philosophy behind this M-Budget initiative resulted in these items not only appealing to those living on a budget, but also to trendy shoppers who share this philosophy. Migros followed up on this development by initiating M-budget parties where people were challenged to cook high-end, gastronomic meals using only M-budget products. Naturally, the beverages served at those parties were non-alcoholic.

Co-author: Adriaan de Bruijn

Sources: Migros Annual Report 2012, report.migros. ch/2015/en/; Peter Gloor and Scott Cooper, 'The new principles of a swarm business', *Sloan Management Review*, April 2007.

MANAGING THE PARADOX OF CONTROL AND CHAOS

Chaos often breeds life, when order breeds habit.

Henry Brooks Adams (1838–1919), American writer and historian

So, how should organizational development be encouraged? Can the top management of a firm shape the organization to fit with their intended strategy or does the organizational context determine the strategy that is actually followed? And should top management strive to have a tight grip on the organization, or should they leave plenty of room for self-organization? (See Table 11.1.)

As before, views differ strongly, both in business practice and in academia; not only in the field of strategy, but also in neighbouring fields such as organizational behaviour, human resource management and innovation management, and more broadly in the humanities, including sociology, economics, political science and psychology. The economic sociologist Duesenberry once remarked that 'economics is all about how people make choices; sociology is all about how they don't have any choices to make'. Although half in jest, his comment does have a ring of truth to it. Much of the literature within the field of economics assumes that people in organizations can freely make choices and have the power to shape their strategy, while possible restraints on their freedom usually come from the environment. Sociological literature, but also psychological and political science work, often features the limitations on individual's freedom. These different disciplinary inclinations are not absolute, but can be clearly recognized in the debate.

TABLE 11.1   Organizational leadership versus organizational dynamics perspective

	Organizational leadership perspective	Organizational dynamics perspective
Emphasis on	Control over chaos	Chaos over control
Organizational development	Controllable creation process	Uncontrollable evolutionary process
Development metaphor	The visible hand	The invisible hand
Development direction	Top-down, imposed organization	Bottom-up, self-organization
Decision-making	Authoritarian (rule of the few)	Democratic (rule of the many)
Change process	Leader shapes new behaviour	New behaviour emerges from interactions
Change determinants	Leader's vision and skill	Political, cultural and learning dynamics
Organizational malleability	High, fast	Low, slow
Development driver	Organization follows strategy	Strategy follows organization
Normative implication	Strategize, then organize	Organize, then strategize

With so many conflicting views and incompatible prescriptions on the issue of organizational development, the question is how to manage the paradox of control and chaos. Following the taxonomy in Chapter 1, strategizing managers have the following options at their disposal.

Balancing

Depending on the organization, strategists blend elements of opposite demands for top management control and organizational chaos into a balance. As has been discussed in Chapter 7 on strategy formation, the primary process of the firm or organizational unit is a key factor. For example, the demand for top management control is higher in production units than in a professional services firm, while the demand for organizational chaos prevails in business development units.

Organizational culture is another factor influencing the blend of opposite demands. For example, the founder's leadership style and the firm's native country are among the factors that create an organization-specific culture (further discussed in the next section on the international perspective on the organizational context).

Juxtaposing

Within the organization, strategists are leading many groups, projects and corporate initiatives. The larger the organization the more variety of organizational processes strategizing leaders participate in. For example, a manager may be heading a product innovation project, a cost-cutting operation and an acquisition process at the same time. These activities require different organizational leadership styles, and thus the strategizing manager needs to juxtapose between different opposites or blends simultaneously. This requires high flexibility and leadership styles of specific dynamic capabilities (Teece, Pisano and Shuen, 1997).

Embracing

The tension between the demand for top management control and organizational chaos can also be exploited at the leadership team level, by intentionally bringing together opposite individuals. Diverse leadership teams, bringing together different disciplines and cultures for example, are not the easiest of organizational configurations. Yet, tensions can be exploited as sources of creativity and opportunity.

One specific manifestation of an intentionally designed tension is the phenomenon of 'dynamic duos' who have built large firms such as Hewlett and Packard, and Walt and Roy Disney. Actually some authors argue that a large number of new ventures are successful *exactly because* of the combination of two contrary individuals forming the leadership team. They argue that while the attention of academics and journalists is directed to the more outgoing member of the leadership team, the correct level of analysis should be the duo, the yin and yang of success.

One such author was the late David Thomson (2006) who analysed the 387 high growth companies that have IPO'd since 1980 and concluded that success often depends on dynamic duos, one of them being the external part and the other the internal half of the effort. Together, they are able to combine change and stability.

THE ORGANIZATIONAL CONTEXT IN INTERNATIONAL PERSPECTIVE

Co-authors: Gep Eisenloeffel and Wester Wagenaar

So long as men worship the Caesars and Napoleons, Caesars and Napoleons will duly arise and make them miserable.

Aldous Huxley (1894–1963), English novelist

Views on the nature of the organizational context are diverse and research indicates divergent national preferences. A variety of factors can be held responsible for inclinations on how the paradox of control and chaos is viewed in different countries. When discussing the international perspective of the organizational context, dealing with national preferences is self-evident. Yet, not every perceptional difference should be attributed to international differences; preferences in industries taken on a global scale and individual dispositions should not be ignored.

On the national level

In large scale fieldwork carried out by researchers at Cranfield Business School in the United Kingdom (Myers *et al.*, 1995), significantly different leadership styles were recognized among European executives. The research notes that the predominant approach in Sweden and Finland can be typified as the 'consensus' style – with low power distance and low masculinity. This finding can be generalized for all of the Nordic countries, where cooperation and consensus are often valued over individualistic decision-making (Goldsmith and Larsen, 2004). Executives in Germany and Austria have a style labelled 'working towards a common goal', where specialists work together within a rule-bound structure. In France, the most popular style is 'managing from a distance' where planning is emphasized in a hierarchic setting. Executives from the United Kingdom, Ireland and Spain prefer 'leading from the front'. According to the researchers, this last style of leadership relies on the belief that it is the skills and charisma of particular individuals at the top that are responsible for the success or failure of an organization. This suggests that the organizational leadership perspective is more popular in these three countries as well as in other Anglo-Saxon and Latin cultures, than in the rest of Europe. Other cross-cultural theorists support this supposition (e.g. Hampden-Turner and Trompenaars, 1993; Lessem and Neubauer, 1994).

The perceived locus of control can also explain international preferential differences. People with an internal locus of control believe that they can shape events and have an impact on their environment, while those with an external locus of control believe they are caught up in events they can hardly influence. In countries where the culture is more inclined towards an internal locus of control, it is reasonable to expect that the organizational leadership perspective will be more widespread. Managers in such societies will be more strongly predisposed to believe that they can shape organizational circumstances. In cultures that are characterized by a predominantly external locus of control, more support for the organizational dynamics perspective can be expected.

A cultural characteristic related to perceived loci of control is the preference for order and structure that prevails in some countries. Hofstede (1993) refers to this issue as uncertainty avoidance. In some cultures, there is a low tolerance for unstructured situations, poorly defined tasks and responsibilities, ambiguous relationships and unclear rules. People in these nations exhibit a distinct preference for predictability – they need to feel they are in control. In other cultures however, people are less nervous about uncertain settings. The tolerance for situations that are unorganized or self-organizing is much higher – even in relatively chaotic circumstances, the call for 'law and order' will not be particularly strong. It can be expected that there will be a more pronounced preference for the organizational leadership perspective in countries that score high on uncertainty avoidance, than in nations with a low score on this cultural dimension.

Another distinction that can be made is between two types of organization. In the mechanistic view, organizations exist as systems that are staffed with people, while in the organic view organizations exist as groups of people into which some system has been brought. Taking the former perspective, leaders will be regarded as mechanics – the organizational system can be redesigned, re-engineered and restructured to pursue another course of action where necessary. In countries where the mechanistic view of organizations is more predominant, an inclination towards the organizational leadership can be expected. The organic view, however, sees the leader as the head of the clan – bound by tradition and loyalty, but able to count on the emotional commitment of the members. Important in reorienting and rejuvenating the organization is the leader's ability to challenge orthodox ideas, motivate people and manage the political processes. Countries where this view is more predominant will likely lean towards the organizational dynamics perspective.

Closely related to the distinction between mechanistic and organic organizations, is the level of formalization of a firm. If companies aim to govern the activities and behaviours of employees through imposing extensive rules and procedures, an organizational leadership perspective is taken. When little formalization is in place and employees are encouraged to self-organize, this indicates the organizational dynamics perspective. Some countries show distinct differences in the level of formalization. For example, Japanese firms are quite formalized, while companies in the Nordic countries are often less so (Dobbin and Boychuk, 1999; Horváth *et al.*, 1976).

On the industry level

Although the average level of formalization of companies correlates with country-specific preferences, it is a common rule that the bigger the firm, the more formalized it becomes. This is true regardless of the country of origin of the company. Only big companies can develop and produce trains, airplanes, spacecraft, national defence systems and oil platforms for instance. Industries requiring a large scale to properly operate can thus be expected to have an inclination towards the organizational leadership perspective.

Reluctant to call it chaos, most researchers do agree organizations need a decent degree of disorder to foster the flow of innovative ideas. As such, many companies in the creative sector try to refrain from imposing authoritarian control and instead see the value of self-organization.

To the strategist

It is not just culture that plays a role in the organizational context; research has suggested behaviours of leaders to be gender stereotypic. The heroic, individualized depiction of leadership is an association particularly strong among men. Leadership styles have traditionally been grouped as a dichotomy between task orientation as opposed to relations orientation; men are commonly associated with task-oriented leadership and women with the interpersonally-oriented style (e.g. Eagly and Johannesen-Schmidt, 2001; Eagly and Johnson, 1990; Gevedon, 1992; Gibson, 1995; Oshagbemi and Gill, 2003; Rigg and Sparrow, 1994; Taleb, 2010). The country of origin of a leader does not appear to influence this gendered perception much, as these gender preferences have been confirmed across a variety of countries – even in more 'feminine', less patriarchal societies (e.g. Bellou, 2011; Gibson, 1995; Oshagbemi and Gill, 2003; Taleb, 2010).

Another individual characteristic that can influence a preference for either the organizational dynamics or the organizational leadership perspective is the leader's age. Studies in the UK, US and India suggest that the higher the manager's age, the more participative he is, preferring collective decision-making over the authoritarian kind. This in contrast to younger managers who take decisions that may not necessarily be popular among the majority of the workers (e.g. Kotur and Anbazhagan, 2014; Mitchell, 2000; Oshagbemi, 2004, 2008).

A strategist has to be aware of his own disposition and what the environmental demands are. Does a strategist need to adapt to internal or external needs and is a bit of chaos then beneficial to the development of the firm? Or is it the vision and skill of the leader that needs to guide the organization? Operating on the international level brings along more difficulties, for employees from different countries are likely to have divergent opinions on what behaviour the organizational context is supposed to encourage and facilitate.

CHAPTER

12 THE INTERNATIONAL CONTEXT

There never were, since the creation of the world, two cases exactly parallel.

Philip Dormer Stanhope (1694–1773), English secretary of state

INTRODUCTION

As firms move out of their domestic market on to the international stage, they are faced with differing business arenas. The nations they expand to can vary with regard to consumer behaviour, language, legal system, technological infrastructure, business culture, educational system, labour relations, political ideology, distribution structures and fiscal regime, to name just a few. At face value, the plurality of the international context can seem daunting. Yet, the question is how important the international differences are for firms operating across borders. Do firms need to adapt to the international diversity encountered, or can they find ways of overcoming the constraints imposed by distinct national systems, structures and behaviours? This matter of understanding and dealing with international variety is one of the key topics for managers operating across borders.

A second question with regard to the international context is that of international linkages. To what extent do events in one country have an impact on what happens in other countries? When a number of nations are tightly linked to one another in a particular area, this is referred to as a case of international integration. If, contrariwise, there are very weak links between developments in one country and developments elsewhere, this is referred to as a situation of international fragmentation. The question for managers is how tightly linked nations around the world actually are. Countries might be quite different, yet developments in one nation might significantly influence developments elsewhere. For instance, if interest rates rise in the United States, central bankers in most other countries cannot ignore this. If the price of oil goes down on the spot market in Rotterdam, this will have a 'spillover effect' towards most other nations. And if a breakthrough chip technology is developed in Taiwan, this will send a shockwave through the computer industry around the world. If nations are highly integrated, the manager must view all countries as part of the same system – as squares on a chessboard, not to be judged in isolation.

When looking at the subjects of international variety and linkages, it is also important to know in which direction they have been moving, and will develop further, over time. Where a development towards lower international variety and tighter international linkages on a worldwide scale can be witnessed, a process of globalization is at play. Where a movement towards more international variety and a loosening of international linkages is apparent, a process of localization is taking place.

For managers operating in more than one nation, it is vital to understand the nature of the international context. Have their businesses been globalizing or localizing, and what can be expected in the future? Answers to these questions should guide strategizing managers in choosing which countries to be active in and how to manage their activities across borders. Taken together, these international context questions constitute the issue of international configuration, and are the focus of the further discussion in this chapter.

THE ISSUE OF INTERNATIONAL CONFIGURATION

How a firm configures its activities across borders is largely dependent on how it deals with the fundamental tension between the opposite demands of globalization and localization. To understand these forces, pulling the organization in contrary directions, it is first necessary to further define them. Globalization and localization are terms used by many, but explained by few. This lack of uniform definition often leads to an unfocused debate, as different people employ the same terms, but actually refer to different phenomena. Therefore, this discussion starts with a clarification of the concepts of globalization and localization. Subsequently, attention will turn to the two central questions facing the international manager: Which countries should the firm be active in and how should this array of international activities be managed? This first question, of deciding in which geographic areas the organization should be involved, is the issue of international composition. The second question, of deciding on the organizational structure and systems needed to run the multi-country activities, is the issue of international management.

Dimensions of globalization

Clearly, globalization refers to the process of becoming more global. But what is global? Although there is no agreement on a single definition, most writers use the term to refer to one or more of the following elements (see Figure 12.1):

- Worldwide scope. 'Global' can simply be used as a geographic term. A firm with operations around the world can be labelled a global company, to distinguish it from firms that are local (not international) or regional in scope. In such a case, the term 'global' is primarily intended to describe the spatial dimension – the broadest possible international scope is to be global. When this definition of global is employed, globalization is the process of international expansion on a worldwide scale (e.g. Patel and Pavitt, 1991).

- Worldwide similarity. 'Global' can also refer to homogeneity around the world. For instance, if a company decides to sell the same product in all of its international markets, it is often referred to as a global product, as opposed to a locally tailored product. In such a case, the term 'global' is primarily intended to describe the variance dimension – the ultimate level of worldwide similarity is to be global. When this definition

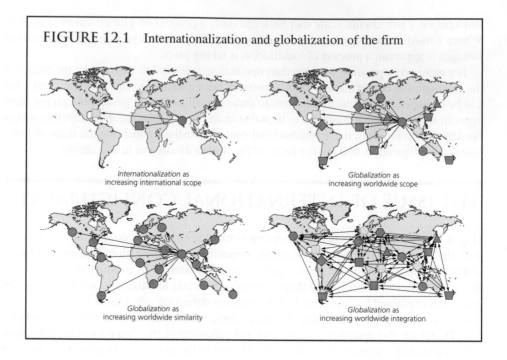

FIGURE 12.1   Internationalization and globalization of the firm

Internationalization as
increasing international scope

Globalization as
increasing worldwide scope

Globalization as
increasing worldwide similarity

Globalization as
increasing worldwide integration

of global is employed, globalization is the process of declining international variety (e.g. Levitt, 1983).

■ Worldwide integration. 'Global' can also refer to the world as one tightly linked system. For instance, a global market can be said to exist if events in one country are significantly impacted by events in other geographic markets. This contrasts with local markets, where price levels, competition, demand and fashions are hardly influenced by developments in other nations. In such a case, the term 'global' is primarily intended to describe the linkages dimension – the ultimate level of worldwide integration is to be global. When this definition of global is employed, globalization is the process of increasing international interconnectedness (e.g. Porter, 1986).

So, for example, is McDonald's a global company? That depends along which of the above three dimensions the company is measured. When judging the international scope of McDonald's, it can be seen that the company is globalizing, but is far from being global. The company operates in approximately half the countries in the world, but in many of these only in one or a few large cities. Of McDonald's worldwide revenues, more than half is still earned in the United States. This predominance of the home country is even stronger if the composition of the company's top management is looked at (Ruigrok and Van Tulder, 1995). However, when judging McDonald's along the dimension of international similarity, it is simple to observe that the company is relatively global, as it takes a highly standardized approach to most markets around the world. Although, it should be noted that on some aspects such as menu and interior design, there is leeway for local adaptation. Finally, when judging McDonald's along the dimension of international integration, the company is only slightly global, as it is not very tightly linked around the world. Some activities are centralized or coordinated, but in general there is relatively little need for concerted action.

As for localization – the opposite of the process of globalization – it is characterized by decreasing international scope, similarity and integration. From the angle of international strategy, the most extreme form of localness is when firms operate in one country and there is no similarity or integration between countries (e.g. the hairdressing and driving school businesses). However, this equates local with national, while firms and businesses can be even more local, all the way down to the state/province/department/district and municipal playing fields.

Levels of globalization

The second factor complicating a clear understanding of the concept of globalization is that it is applied to a variety of subjects, while the differences are often not made explicit. Some people discuss globalization as a development in the economy at large, while others debate globalization as something happening to industries, markets, products, technologies, fashions, production, competition and organizations. In general, debates on globalization tend to concentrate on one of three levels of analysis:

- Globalization of companies. Some authors focus on the micro level, debating whether individual companies are becoming more global. Issues are the extent to which firms have a global strategy, structure, culture, workforce, management team and resource base. In more detail, the globalization of specific products and value-adding activities is often discussed. Here it is of particular importance to acknowledge that the globalization of one product or activity (e.g. marketing) does not necessarily entail the globalization of all others (e.g. Bartlett and Ghoshal, 1987; Prahalad and Doz, 1987).

- Globalization of businesses. Other authors are more concerned with the meso level, debating whether particular businesses are becoming more global. Here it is important to distinguish those who emphasize the globalization of markets, as opposed to those accentuating the globalization of industries (see Chapter 4 for this distinction). The issue of globalizing markets has to do with the growing similarity of worldwide customer demand and the growing ease of worldwide product flows (e.g. Douglas and Wind, 1987; Levitt, 1983). For example, the crude oil and foreign currency markets are truly global – the same commodities are traded at the same rates around the world. The markets for accountancy and garbage collection services, by way of contrast, are very local – demand differs significantly, there is little cross-border trade and consequently prices vary sharply. The globalization of industries is quite a different issue, as it has to do with the emergence of a set of producers that compete with one another on a worldwide scale (e.g. Porter, 1990a, 1990b; Prahalad and Doz, 1987). So, for instance, the automobile and consumer electronics industries are quite global – the major players in most countries belong to the same set of companies that compete against each other all around the world. The accountancy industry is relatively global, even though the markets for accountancy services are very local. However, the hairdressing and retail banking industries are very local – the competitive scene in each country is relatively uninfluenced by competitive developments elsewhere.

- Globalization of economies. Yet other authors take a macro level of analysis, arguing whether or not the world's economies in general are experiencing a convergence trend. Many authors are interested in the macroeconomic dynamics of international integration and its consequences in terms of growth, employment, inflation, productivity, trade and foreign direct investment (e.g. Kay, 1989; Krugman, 1990). Others focus more on the political realities constraining and encouraging globalization (e.g. Klein, 2000; McGrew and Lewis, 1992). Yet others are interested in the underlying dynamics of technological, institutional and organizational convergence (e.g. Dunning, 1986; Kogut, 1993).

Ultimately, the question in this chapter is not only whether economies, businesses and companies are actually globalizing, but also whether these developments are a matter of choice. In other words, is global convergence or continued international diversity an uncontrollable evolutionary development with which firms (and governments) must comply, or can managers actively influence the globalization or localization of their environment?

International composition

An international firm operates in two or more countries. When a firm starts up value-adding activities in yet another country, this process is called internationalization. In Figure 12.2, an overview is presented of the most common forms of internationalization. One of the earliest international growth moves undertaken by firms is to sell their products to foreign buyers, either directly (Internet or telephone sales), through a travelling sales-person, or via a local agent or distributor. Such types of export activity are generally less taxing for the organization than the establishment of a foreign sales subsidiary (or sales unit). Serving a foreign market by means of a sales subsidiary often requires a higher level of investment in terms of marketing expenditures, sales force development and after-sales

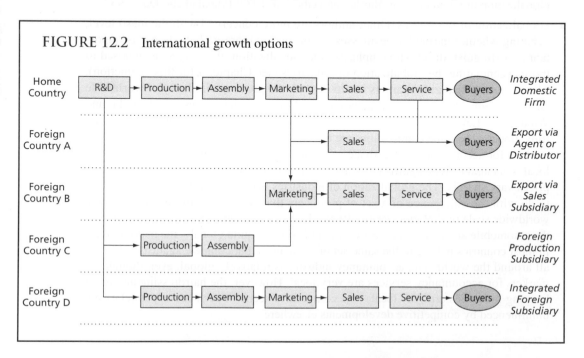

FIGURE 12.2   International growth options

service provision. A firm can also set up a foreign production subsidiary (or 'off-shore' production unit), whose activities are focused on manufacturing goods to be exported back to the firm's other markets. Alternatively, a firm can begin an integrated foreign subsidiary that is responsible for a full range of value-adding activities, including production and sales. In practice, there are many variations to these basic forms of internationalization, depending on the specific value-adding activities carried out in different countries. For example, some subsidiaries have R&D, assembly and marketing their portfolio of activities, while others do not (Birkinshaw and Hood, 1998).

When establishing a foreign subsidiary, the firm must decide whether to purchase an existing local company (entry by acquisition) or to start from scratch (greenfield entry). In both cases the firm can work independently or by means of a joint venture with a local player or foreign partner. It is also possible to dispense with the establishment of a subsidiary at all, by networking with local manufacturers, assemblers, sales agents and distributors (as discussed in Chapter 6).

The issue of international composition deals with the question of where the firm wants to have a certain level of involvement. The firm's strategists must decide where to allocate resources, build up activities and try to achieve results. The issue of international composition can be further subdivided into two parts:

- International scope. The international composition of the firm depends first of all on the countries selected to do business in. The geographic spectrum covered by the firm is referred to as its international scope. The firm's strategists must decide how many countries they want to be active in, and which countries these should be.

- International distribution. The international composition of the firm also depends on how it has distributed its value-adding activities across the countries selected. In some firms, all national subsidiaries carry out similar activities and are of comparable size. However, in many firms, activities are distributed less symmetrically, with, for example, production, R&D and marketing concentrated in only a few countries (Porter, 1986). Commonly, some countries will also contribute much more revenue and profits than others, but these might not be the countries where new investments can best be made. It is the task of the firm's strategists to determine how activities can best be distributed and how resources can best be allocated across the various countries.

Just as a corporation's portfolio of businesses could be visualized by means of a portfolio grid, so too can a business's portfolio of foreign sales markets be displayed using such a matrix. In Figure 12.3, a fictitious example is given of a firm's international sales portfolio using the GE business screen as analysis tool. Instead of industry attractiveness along the vertical axis, country attractiveness is used, calculating items such as market growth, competitive intensity, buyer power, customer loyalty, government regulation and operating costs. Following a similar logic, firms can also evaluate their international portfolios of, for instance, production locations and R&D facilities.

Deciding which portfolio of countries to be active in, both in terms of international scope and distribution, will largely depend on the strategic motives that have stimulated the firm to enter the international arena in the first place. After all, there must be some good reasons why a firm is willing to disregard the growth opportunities in its home market and to enter into uncertain foreign adventures. There must be some advantages to being international that offset the disadvantages of foreignness and distance. These advantages

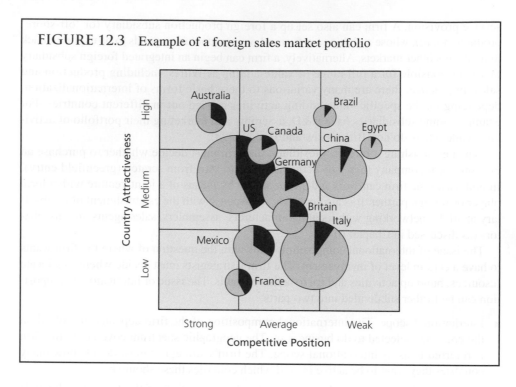

FIGURE 12.3 Example of a foreign sales market portfolio

of having activities in two or more countries – cross-border synergies – are discussed in more detail, after an account of the second international configuration question, the issue of international management.

International management

A firm operating in two or more countries needs to find some way of organizing itself to deal with its border-spanning nature. As managing across borders is difficult and costly, the simplest solution would be to organize all operations on a country-by-country basis, and to leave all country units as autonomous as possible. Yet, internationalization is only economically rational if 'the international whole is more than the sum of the country parts' (see Chapter 5). In other words, internationalization only makes sense if enough cross-border synergies can be reaped to offset the extra cost of foreignness and distance.

Therefore, the firm needs to have international integration mechanisms to facilitate the realization of cross-border synergies. The three most important integration mechanisms used in international management are:

■ Standardization. An easy way to reap cross-border synergies is to do the same thing in each country, without any costly adaptation. Such standardization can be applied to all aspects of the business model (see Chapter 4) – the product offerings, value-adding activities and resources employed. Standardization is particularly important for achieving economies of scale (e.g. Hout, Porter and Rudden, 1982; Levitt, 1983), but can be equally valuable for serving border-crossing clients who want to encounter a predictable offering (e.g. Hamel and Prahalad, 1985; Yip, 1993).

- Coordination. Instead of standardizing products or activities, international firms can align their varied activities in different countries by means of cross-border coordination. Getting the activities in the various countries aligned is often inspired by the need to serve border-crossing clients in a coordinated manner (e.g. global service level agreements), or to counter these clients' policy of playing off the firm's subsidiaries against one another (e.g. cross-border price shopping). International coordination can be valuable when responding to, or attacking, competitors as well. A coordinated assault on a few markets, financed by the profits from many markets (i.e. cross-subsidization), can sometimes lead to competitive success (Prahalad and Doz, 1987).

- Centralization. Of course, activities within the firm can also be integrated at one central location, either in the firm's home country or elsewhere. Such centralization is often motivated by the drive for economies of scale (e.g. Buckley and Casson, 1985; Dunning, 1981), but might be due to the competitive advantage of a particular country as well. For example, production costs might be much lower, or quality much higher, in a certain part of the world, making it a logical location for centralized production. Centralization of knowledge-intensive activities is sometimes also needed, to guard quality or to ensure faster learning than could be attained with decentralized activities (e.g. Dunning, 1993; Porter, 1990b).

It is up to the firm's strategists to determine the most appropriate level of standardization, coordination and centralization needed to function efficiently and effectively in an international context. The level chosen for each of these three characteristics will largely determine the organizational model adopted by the international firm.

In their seminal research, Bartlett and Ghoshal (1989) distinguish four generic organizational models for international firms, each with its own mix of standardization, coordination and centralization (see Figure 12.4):

- Decentralized federation. In a decentralized federation, the firm is organized along geographic lines, with each full-scale country subsidiary largely self-sufficient and autonomous from international headquarters in the home country. Few activities are centralized and little is coordinated across borders. The level of standardization is also low, as the country unit is free to adapt itself to the specific circumstances in its national environment. Bartlett and Ghoshal refer to this organizational model as 'multinational'. Another common label is 'multi-domestic' (e.g. Prahalad and Doz, 1987; Stopford and Wells, 1972).

- Coordinated federation. In a coordinated federation, the firm is also organized along geographic lines, but the country subsidiaries have a closer relationship with the international headquarters in the home country. Most of the core competences, technologies, processes and products are developed centrally, while other activities are carried out locally. As a consequence, there is some standardization and coordination, requiring some formalized control systems (i.e. planning, budgeting, administration). Another name employed by Bartlett and Ghoshal to refer to this organizational model is 'international'.

- Centralized hub. In a centralized hub, national units are relatively unimportant, as all main activities are carried out in the home country. Generally, a highly standardized approach is used towards all foreign markets. As centralization and standardization are high,

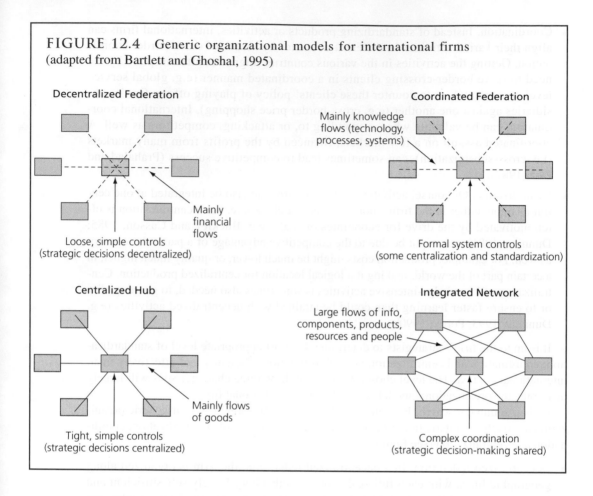

FIGURE 12.4 Generic organizational models for international firms (adapted from Bartlett and Ghoshal, 1995)

foreign subsidiaries are limited to implementing headquarters' policies in the local markets. Coordination of activities across countries is made easy by the dominance of headquarters. Bartlett and Ghoshal use the term 'global' to describe this organizational model.

■ Integrated network. In an integrated network, the country subsidiaries have a close relationship with international headquarters, just as in the coordinated federation, but also have a close relationship with each other. Very little is centralized at the international headquarters in the home country, but each national unit can become the worldwide centre for a particular competence, technology, process or product. Thus subsidiaries need to coordinate the flow of components, products, knowledge and people between one other. Such a networked organization requires a certain level of standardization to function effectively. Another name used by Bartlett and Ghoshal for this organizational model is 'transnational'.

Which international organizational model is adopted depends strongly on what the corporate strategist wishes to achieve. The preferred international management structure will be largely determined by the type of cross-border synergies that the strategists envisage. This topic of multi-country synergies is examined more closely in the following section.

THE PARADOX OF GLOBALIZATION AND LOCALIZATION

The axis of the earth sticks out visibly through the center of each and every town or city.

Oliver Wendell Holmes (1809–1894), American physician, poet and essayist

It requires almost no argumentation that internationally operating companies are faced with a tension between treating the world as one market and acknowledging national differences. During the last few decades, achieving a balance between international uniformity and meeting local demands has been the dominant theme in the literature on international management. All researchers have recognized the tension between international standardization and local adaptation. The key question has been whether international firms have the *liberty* to standardize or face the *pressure* to adapt.

However, since the mid-1980s, this standardization–adaptation discussion has progressed significantly as strategy researchers have moved beyond the organizational design question, seeking the underlying strategic motives for standardization and adaptation (e.g. Bartlett and Ghoshal, 1987; Porter, 1986; Prahalad and Doz, 1987). It has been acknowledged that international standardization is not a matter of organizational convenience that companies naturally revert to when the market does not demand local adaptation. Rather, international standardization is a means for achieving cross-border synergies. A firm can achieve cross-border synergies by leveraging resources, integrating activities and aligning product offerings across two or more countries. Creating additional value in this way is the very *raison d'etre* of the international firm. If internationalizing companies would fully adapt to local conditions, without leveraging a homegrown quality, they would have no advantage over local firms, while they would be burdened by the extra costs of international business (e.g. overcoming distance and foreignness). Therefore, international companies need to realize at least enough cross-border synergies to compensate for the additional expenses of operating in multiple countries.

Much of the theoretical discourse has focused on the question of which cross-border synergies can be achieved on the ultimate, global scale. Most researchers identify various potential opportunities for worldwide synergy, yet recognize the simultaneous demands to meet the specific conditions in each local market (e.g. Dicken, 1992; Yip, 1993). These possibilities for reaping global synergy will be examined first, followed by the countervailing pressures for local responsiveness.

The demand for global synergy

Striving for cross-border synergies on as large a scale as possible can be an opportunity for an international firm to enhance its competitive advantage. However, realizing global synergies is often less an opportunity than a competitive demand. If rival firms have already successfully implemented a global strategy, there can be a severe pressure to also reap the benefits of globalization through standardization, coordination or centralization.

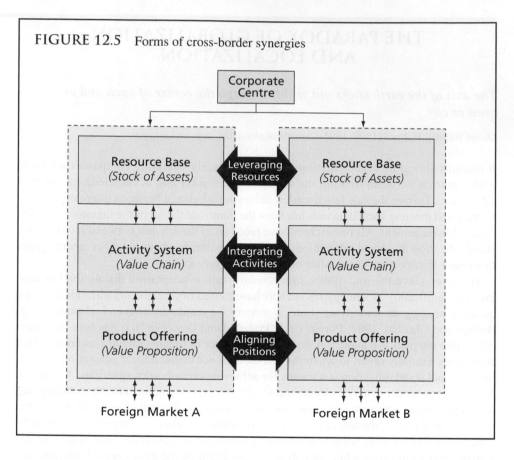

FIGURE 12.5 Forms of cross-border synergies

There are many different types of cross-border synergy. In accordance with the business model framework described in Chapter 4, these synergies can be organized into three categories: aligning product offerings, integrating activities and leveraging resources (see Figure 12.5).

Synergy by aligning positions. The first way to create cross-border synergies is to align market positions in the various countries in which the firm operates. Taking a coordinated approach to different national markets can be necessary under two circumstances – namely to provide a concerted cross-border product offering to customers and to stage a concerted cross-border attack on competitors:

- Dealing with cross-border customers. An international firm is ideally placed to offer border-crossing customers an internationally coordinated product or service offering. Whether it is for a tourist who wants to have the same hotel arrangements around the world, or for an advertiser who wants to stage a globally coordinated new product introduction, it can be important to have a standardized and coordinated offering across various nations. It might be equally necessary to counter the tactics of customers shopping around various national subsidiaries for the best deals, or to meet the customer's demand to aggregate all global buying via one central account.

- Dealing with cross-border competition. An international firm is also in an ideal position to successfully attack locally oriented rivals if it does not spread its resources too thinly around the world, but rather focuses on only a few countries at a time. By coordinating its competitive efforts and bringing its global power to bear on a few national markets, an international firm can push back or even defeat local rivals country by country. Of course, an international company must also have the capability of defending itself against such a globally coordinated attack by a rival international firm.

Synergy by integrating activities.   Cross-border synergies can also be achieved by linking the activity systems of the firm in its various national markets. Integrating the value-creation processes across borders can be useful to realize economies of scale and to make use of the specific competitive advantages of each nation:

■ Reaping scale advantages. Instead of organizing the international firm's activity system on a country-by-country basis, certain activities can be pooled to reap economies of scale. Commonly this means that activities must be centralized at one or a few locations, and that a certain level of product and/or process standardization must be accepted. Economies of scale can be realized for many activities, most notably production, logistics, procurement and R&D. However, scale advantages might be possible for all activities of the firm. Although scale advantages are often pursued by means of centralization, it is often possible to achieve economies by standardizing and coordinating activities across borders (e.g. joint procurement, joint marketing campaigns).

■ Reaping location advantages. For some activities certain locations are much more suited than others, making it attractive to centralize these activities in the countries that possess a particular competitive advantage. A national competitive advantage can consist of inexpensive or specialist local inputs, such as raw materials, energy, physical infrastructure or human resources, but can also be due to the presence of attractive buyers and related industries (Porter, 1990a).

Synergy by leveraging resources.   A third manner in which cross-border synergies can be realized is by sharing resources across national markets. Such resource leveraging can be achieved by physically reallocating resources to other countries where they can be used more productively, or by replicating them so they can be used in many national markets simultaneously:

■ Achieving resource reallocation. Instead of leaving resources in countries where they happen to be, international firms have the opportunity to transfer resources to other locations, where they can be used to more benefit. For example, money, machinery and people can be reallocated out of countries where the return on these resources is low, into countries where they can reap a higher return. Managers specializing in market development might be sent to new subsidiaries, while older machinery might be transferred to less advanced markets (Buckley and Casson, 1976; Vernon, 1966).

■ Achieving resource replication. While leveraging tangible resources requires physical reallocation or sharing (see reaping scale advantages), intangible resources can be leveraged by means of replication. Intangibles such as knowledge and capabilities can be copied across borders and reused in another country. This allows international companies to leverage their know-how with regard to such aspects as technology, production, marketing, logistics and sales (Kogut and Zander, 1993; Liebeskind, 1996).

For all of these cross-border synergies it holds that the wider the geographic scope, the greater the potential benefit. Where possible, realizing these synergies on a global scale would result in the highest level of value creation.

These opportunities for global synergy represent a strong demand on all companies, both international and domestic. If a company can reap these synergies more quickly and successfully than its competitors, this could result in a strong offensive advantage. If other companies have a head start in capturing these global synergies, the firm must move quickly to catch up. Either way, there is a pressure on companies to seek out opportunities for global synergy and to turn them to their advantage.

The demand for local responsiveness

Yet the pressure to pursue global synergies is only half the equation. Simultaneously, companies must remain attuned to the specific demands of each national market and retain the ability to respond to these particular characteristics in a timely and adequate manner. In other words, firms must have the capability to be responsive to local conditions. If they lose touch with the distinct competitive dynamics in each of their national markets, they might find themselves at a competitive disadvantage compared to more responsive rivals.

While business responsiveness is always important, it becomes all the more pressing when the differences between various national markets are large. The more dissimilar the national markets, the more pressure on the international firm to be attuned to these distinct characteristics. The most important differences between countries include:

- Differences in market structure. Countries can differ significantly with regard to their competitive landscape. For example, in some national markets there are strong local competitors, requiring the international firm to respond differently than in countries where it encounters its 'regular' international rivals. Another difference is that in some countries there are only a few market parties, while in other countries the market is highly fragmented among numerous competitors. There can also be large differences from country to country in the background of competitors – in some countries, conglomerates dominate the business scene, while in other countries, single business competitors are more frequent.

- Differences in customer needs. Customers in each national market can have needs that are significantly different than the needs exhibited in other countries. The nature of these customer differences can vary from divergent cultural expectations and use circumstances, to incompatible technical systems and languages employed.

- Differences in buying behaviour. Not only can the customers' needs differ across countries, but so, too, can their buying behaviour. For example, customers can be different with regard to the way they structure buying decisions, the types of information they consider and the relationship they wish to have with their suppliers.

- Differences in substitutes. National markets can also differ with regard to the types of indirect competition that needs to be faced. In some countries, for instance, beer brewers have to deal with wine as an important rival product, while in other markets tea or soft drinks might be the most threatening substitutes.

- Differences in distribution channels. Countries can exhibit remarkable differences in the way their distribution channels work. For example, countries can vary with regard to the kinds of distribution channels available, the number of layers in the distribution structure, their level of sophistication, their degree of concentration and the negotiating power of each player.

- Differences in media structure. National markets can have very different media channels available for marketing communication purposes. In the area of television, for instance, countries vary widely with regard to the number of stations on the air (or on the cable), the types of regulation imposed, the amount of commercial time available, and its cost and effectiveness. In the same way, all other media channels may differ.

- Differences in infrastructure. Many products and services are heavily dependent on the type of infrastructure available in a country. For example, some products rely on a digital telephone system, high speed motorways, 24-hour convenience stores, or a national healthcare system. Some services require an efficient postal service, poor public transport, electronic banking or cable television.

- Differences in supply structure. If a company has local operations, the differences between countries with regard to their supply structures can also force the company to be more locally responsive. Not only can the availability, quality and price of raw materials and components vary widely between countries, but the same is true for other inputs such as labour, management, capital, facilities, machinery, research, information and services.

- Differences in government regulations. As most government regulations are made on a country-by-country basis, they can differ significantly. Government regulations can affect almost every aspect of a company's operations, as they range from antitrust and product liability legislation, to labour laws and taxation rules.

Responsiveness to these local differences is not only a matter of adaptation. Simple adaptation can be reactive and slow. Being responsive means that the firm has to have the ability to be proactive and fast. As each market develops in a different way and at a different pace, the international firm needs to be able to respond quickly and adequately to remain in tune.

It is clear that international managers cannot afford to neglect being responsive to local conditions. Yet, at the same time, they need to realize cross-border synergies to create additional value. Unfortunately for managers, these two key demands placed on the international firm are, at least to some extent, in conflict with one another. Striving for cross-border synergies on a global scale will interfere with being locally responsive and vice versa. Therefore, the question is how these two conflicting demands can be reconciled – how can the international manager deal with the paradox of globalization and localization?

EXHIBIT 12.1 SHORT CASE

NESPRESSO IN CHINA: WHERE ELSE?

Ever since the Swiss company Nestlé created a new market segment by developing an innovative system for premium portioned coffee under the Nespresso brand, it has seen remarkable growth in the global coffee market. Nespresso launched its products on the international market in 1991 and is currently operating in 64 countries worldwide. In pursuit of new growth markets, the company's focus has recently shifted towards the huge upcoming Chinese market. This seems an obvious choice, but how to become successful is not an easy question. While coffee is gaining popularity as a hot beverage in China, consumption is still very low

▶

and the age-old tradition of tea consumption in China is deeply imbedded in the national culture. The company's question, expressed in several commercials by actor George Clooney: 'Nespresso: What else?' is easily answered in China.

Nespresso's journey started in 1976 when one of Nestlé's employees, Eric Favre, developed and patented the Nespresso System. During the following years, the system went through several improvements and the company started selling different varieties of coffee flavour and machine model to the business sector in Switzerland, Japan and Italy. Due to low sales in the early years, the company was forced to reposition Nespresso as a premium quality brand targeted at households, with an emphasis on individuals with high incomes. A new and successful business model was born, based on three important elements: individually portioned aluminium coffee capsules, specially designed coffee machines that are exclusively compatible with the Nespresso capsules and unique customer service through the Nespresso Club and Nespresso Boutiques. Nespresso products still cannot be purchased in ordinary stores or supermarkets; the company uses its own distribution channels (webshop, email, telephone) and transport service to sell and deliver its products with an emphasis on personal attention for the customer. Since 2000, the company has opened over 450 Nespresso Boutiques around the world, situated at carefully selected locations to give consumers the opportunity to 'experience the brand with all their senses'. After purchasing Nespresso products, consumers automatically become members of the Nespresso Club. Club members receive information and advice on all grand cru coffees, technical problems, special offers and new machine models. With the Nespresso Club, the company aims at building stronger brand loyalty, encouraging repeat purchasing among its consumers. The company's

decision to reposition Nespresso has resulted in a period of rapid expansion and can be marked as the beginning of developing a strong global brand. Nowadays, Nespresso is the market leader in the single serve portioned coffee market and has seen an average double digit annual profit growth between 2000 and 2010 with revenues exceeding $2.5 billion. Challenges also arise: In recent years Nespresso's growth has slowed down as dozens of rivals offer coffee pods that fit into its machines.

Aware of the growth potential in China, Nespresso decided to enter the Chinese market in 2007. Six Nespresso Boutiques have been established since then, in the cities of Shanghai, Beijing and Chengdu. Country manager of Nespresso China, Alfonso Troisi, is convinced of the huge possibilities for Nespresso in China, as coffee consumption in China is expected to rise by 18 per cent between 2014 and 2019. However, the choice is not as obvious as it seems, considering the strong preference for tea as both a hot and cold beverage in China's domestic market. Tea symbolizes an important cultural element in Chinese society and has been enjoyed by the Chinese for thousands of years. Originally tea was mainly appreciated for its medical effects, in particular, because it helps to digest food. Nowadays, the Chinese drink tea at almost any time of the day, especially during and after every meal. Besides, the majority of the Chinese are not used to the bitter taste of pure coffee. Of 1.28 billion kilograms of hot drinks consumed in 2014, hot tea holds a share of approximately 82 per cent. Coffee accounts for only 5.7 per cent, but it is estimated that coffee will gain a market share of 8.4 per cent in 2019.

American coffee house Starbucks entered the Chinese market in 1998 as one of the first coffee companies, successfully introducing high-end premium coffee to Chinese consumers, and making them more familiar with drinking and appreciating coffee. The consumption of regular and quality coffee is gaining popularity in China, in accordance with the rising living standards of the growing urban middle class who get increasingly accustomed to Western standards and ways of living. This growing middle class is looking for quality brands and a variety of flavours. But still, Chinese consumers only drink an average of five cups of coffee per person per year, compared to, for example, the Americans or Swiss who drink respectively 400 and 1,117 cups of coffee annually. In the big cities of Shanghai and Beijing, only 20 to 30 per cent of the consumers drink coffee and, as there is a general lack of knowledge on how to prepare coffee, drinking instant coffee at home and ready-to-drink coffee at coffee houses is much more common in China. Instant coffee accounts for 84 per cent of the Chinese coffee market, with 3-1 instant coffee (coffee powder, milk, sugar) as the most popular beverage of choice, while preparing ground coffee at home is a rare habit.

Nespresso's country manager Alfonso Troisi is facing a difficult challenge in China. Should Nespresso maintain its way of doing business as the company does in other countries? Nespresso has developed itself as one of the most famous brands for premium coffee, with an important focus on its global status, brand image and exclusive customer service. The company's business model and marketing strategy are homogeneous worldwide, which is manifested in, for example, the Nespresso Club and Boutiques. This uniform strategy proved to be a successful formula in Europe and the United States. In addition, the Chinese upcoming urban middle class consumers increasingly attach importance to popular Western brands to boost their image and enhance their social position. The exclusivity and premium quality of the Nespresso brand could contribute to this image. Should Nespresso maintain its winning global formula?

Contrariwise, it could also be a sagacious move for Nespresso to adapt its comprehensive business model to the Chinese market, since the market is not that familiar with Nespresso's core product: high quality ground coffee for individual households. Chinese consumers have specific preferences compared to other consumers in the global marketplace. Former Nespresso Marketing Director South-East Asia, greater China and Korea, Mark Leenders, already acknowledged the difficulty of selling pricey coffee machines and coffee capsules in a country with an entrenched tea culture. Should Nespresso adjust its products to meet, for example, the dislike of the bitter taste of pure coffee by Chinese consumers? Or should it change its marketing strategy and focus its attention on providing more information about brewing coffee for its Chinese customers?

In attempting to create a higher brand loyalty among its Chinese customers and generate a greater demand for its coffee products, Nespresso has a number of coffee beans to crack. Should the company put effort into making Chinese consumers more accustomed to drinking high quality, pure ground coffee and keep its homogeneous business model? Or should the company offer new varieties of coffee flavours and machine designs, especially developed for Chinese consumer preferences? For example, in 2012 Nespresso collaborated with the Hong Kong-based company Shanghai Tang to develop a red coffee machine with a dragon integrated in the design to adapt to the Chinese taste. Red is a very important colour in Chinese culture and is associated with prosperity, while the dragon is the zodiac sign of the year 2012 and symbolizes good fortune. It could also be an interesting option for Nespresso to target another market, namely, the business sector. For example, in 2016, Nespresso launched a new coffee machine model in China, which is specially designed for restaurants, hotels and bars, in order to offer their customers high-end quality coffee with the least amount of effort. Will it be useful for Nespresso to target the business-to-business sector as well or should the company stick to the market of individual households?

Alfonso Troisi needs to decide which road the company has to follow and how to position in the Chinese market. The Chinese market has a huge potential in several ways and it is definitely worth the try. Whether he decides to stick to Nespresso's homogeneous business model and brand image, adapt to local differences, or even decide to deviate from its core product and focus on tea instead, each decision will have important implications for the company's future position in the Chinese market.

Co-authors: Laura Kamsma and Maria Hu

Sources: www.nestle-nespresso.com; Lu Chang, 'Pod people', *China Daily*, 1 October 2012; *Marketing Channels*, Cengage, 2012; Analysis of the China coffee market, SPR coffee, 2009; Mintel Global Market Navigator, *Coffee in China*, Mintel 2012; Xu Junqian, 'Chinese have got drinking coffee down to a tee', *The Telegraph*, 27 January 2016; Lucy Craymer, 'Chinese changing taste offer upside for coffee', *Wall Street Journal*, 16 September 2015; 'Tea is still most consumed hot drink in China; but coffee making inroads', *Canadean*, 17 August 2015; Corinne Gretler, 'Nestle's coffee business is competing with itself', *Bloomberg*, 28 June 2016.

PERSPECTIVES ON THE INTERNATIONAL CONTEXT

You may say I'm a dreamer, but I'm not the only one; I hope some day you'll join us, and the world will live as one.

John Lennon (1940–1980), British musician and songwriter

When doing business in an international context, it is generally accepted that the challenge for firms is to strive for cross-border synergies, while simultaneously being responsive to the local conditions. It is acknowledged that international managers need to weigh the specific characteristics of their business when reconciling the paradox of globalization and localization – some businesses are currently more suited for a global approach than others. Where opinions start to diverge is on the question of which businesses will become more global, or can be made more global, in the near future. It is evident to some managers that countries are rapidly becoming increasingly similar and more closely interrelated. To them, globalization is already far advanced and will continue into the future, wiping out the importance of nations as it progresses. Therefore, they argue that it is wise to anticipate, and even encourage, a 'nationless' world, by focusing on global synergies over local responsiveness. Other managers, however, are more sceptical about the speed and impact of globalization. In their view, much so-called globalization is quite superficial, while at a deeper level, important international differences are not quickly changing and cross-border integration is moving very slowly. They also note that there are significant counter-currents creating more international variety, with the potential of loosening international linkages. Therefore, wise managers should remain highly responsive to the complex variety and fragmentation that characterizes our world, while only carefully seeking out selected cross-border synergy opportunities.

These differing opinions among international strategists are reflected in differing views in the strategic management literature. While there is a wide spectrum of positions on the question of how the international context will develop, here the two opposite poles in the debate will be identified and discussed. On the one side of the spectrum there are the managers who believe that globalization is bringing Lennon's dream of the 'world living as one' closer and closer. This point of view is called the 'global convergence perspective'. At the other end of the spectrum are the managers who believe that deep-rooted local differences will continue to force firms to 'do in Rome as the Romans do'. This point of view is referred to as the 'international diversity perspective'.

The global convergence perspective

 According to proponents of the global convergence perspective, the growing similarity and integration of the world can be argued by pointing to extensive economic statistics showing significant rises in foreign direct investment and international trade. Yet, it is simpler to observe things directly around you.

For instance, are you wearing clothing unique to your country or could you mingle in an international crowd without standing out? Is the television you watch, the vehicle you drive, the telephone you use and the timepiece you wear specific to your nation or based on the same technology and even produced by the same companies as those in other countries? Is the music you listen to made by local bands, unknown outside your country, or is this music equally popular abroad? Is the food you eat unique to your region or is even this served in other countries? Now compare your answers with what your parents would have answered 30 years ago – the difference is due to global convergence.

Global convergence, it is argued, is largely driven by the ease, low cost and frequency of international communication, transport and travel. This has diminished the importance of distance. In the past world of large distances, interactions between countries were few and international differences could develop in relative isolation. But the victory of technology over distance has created a 'global village', in which goods, services and ideas are easily exchanged, new developments spread quickly and the 'best practices' of one nation are rapidly copied in others. Once individuals and organizations interact with one another as if no geographic distances exist, an unstoppable process towards cultural, political, technological and economic convergence is set in motion   countries will become more closely linked to one another and local differences will be superseded by new global norms.

Of course, in the short run there will still be international differences and nations will not be fully integrated into a 'world without borders'. Managers taking a global convergence perspective acknowledge that such fundamental and wide-ranging changes take time. There are numerous sources of inertia, e.g. vested interests, commitment to existing systems, emotional attachment to current habits and fear of change. The same type of change inhibitors could be witnessed during the Industrial Revolution, as well. Yet, these change inhibitors can only slow the pace of global convergence, not reverse its direction the momentum caused by the shrinking of distance can only be braked, but not stopped. Therefore, firms thinking further than the short term should not let themselves be guided too much by current international diversity, but rather by the emerging global reality (Ohmae, 1990).

For individual firms, global convergence is changing the rules of the competitive game. While in the past most countries had their own distinct characteristics, pressuring firms to be locally responsive, now growing similarity offers enormous opportunities for leveraging resources and sharing activities across borders, e.g. production can be standardized to save costs, new product development can be carried out on an international scale to reduce the total investments required, and marketing knowledge can easily be exchanged to avoid reinventing the wheel in each country. Simultaneously, international integration has made it much easier to centralize production in large scale facilities at the most attractive locations and to supply world markets from there, unrestrained by international borders. In the same manner, all types of activities, such as R&D, marketing, sales and procurement, can be centralized to profit from worldwide economies of scale.

An equally important aspect of international integration is that suppliers, buyers and competitors can also increasingly operate as if there were no borders. The ability of buyers to shop around internationally makes the world one global market, in which global bargaining power is very important. The ability of suppliers and competitors to reap global economies of scale and sell everywhere around the world creates global industries in which competition takes place on a worldwide stage, instead of in each nation separately. To deal with such global industries and global markets, the firm must be able to align its market activities across nations.

These demands of standardization, centralization and coordination require a global firm, with a strong centre responsible for the global strategy, instead of a federation of autonomous national subsidiaries focused on being responsive to their local circumstances. According to proponents of the global convergence perspective, such global organizations, or 'centralized hubs' (Bartlett and Ghoshal, 1995), will become increasingly predominant over time. And as more companies switch to a global strategy and a global organizational form, this will in turn speed up the general process of globalization. By operating in a global fashion, these firms will actually contribute to a further decrease of international variety and fragmentation. In other words, globalizing companies are both the consequence and a major driver of further global convergence.

EXHIBIT 12.2 GLOBAL CONVERGENCE PERSPECTIVE

UNILEVER: ONE FOR ALL AND ALL FOR ONE

Unilever is currently the world's third largest consumer products company, pulling in over €50 billion in annual revenue. Seven out of every 10 households across the world contain at least one Unilever product, while two billion people use Unilever's products on a daily basis. Its global brands include 13 'billion dollar brands' such as Dove, Knorr, Lipton, Magnum, Omo, Axe and Sunsilk. From the bustling city of São Paulo to the rural plains of northern Vietnam,

people can spill Knorr soup on their shirts, wash them with Omo detergent, use Axe or Dove products to freshen themselves up and celebrate tidiness with Magnum ice cream.

Unilever was formed on 2 September 1929 with one of the largest mergers at that time between Margarine Unie from the Netherlands and Lever Brothers from the UK. Margarine Unie was established by the two Dutch family businesses of butter merchants Van den Bergh and Jurgens who picked up the new product 'margarine' made from beef fat and milk that promised to replace butter – their core business. Lever

Brothers, by way of contrast, was a British family wholesale grocery that produced a new kind of soap that replaced animal fats with copra and pine kernel oil. The merger was formed to stop producing the same kind of products and combine forces in international expansion.

Growing the diverse portfolio internationally paid off for the newly formed multinational, as joint production saved costs and the joint internationalization leveraged investments. When the world economy expanded, Unilever followed suit. It developed new products, entered new markets and countries, and ran an ambitious acquisition programme. The corporate basis was also strengthened. Higher R&D spending enhanced product quality and enabled continuous product innovations, while the new and improved products were introduced faster and more effectively by professionalizing the sales and marketing functions. Unilever's bargaining power vis-à-vis its customers – shops and supermarkets – increased with the company's growing scale and product portfolio, and as a result its products were better positioned in the supermarkets.

Unilever's scale was also beneficial in other areas. As it became one of the world's largest buyers of raw materials, increased buying power reduced the costs of these inbound resources. Palm oil in particular was used in almost all of Unilever's products in food, detergents and beauty products. The higher margins were invested in sales and marketing campaigns, which increased the value of Unilever's brands and – again – the products' positioning in outlets. The high spending on marketing campaigns made Unilever the second biggest spender on ads in the world at around $9 billion annually. Global presence in products and product categories not only reduced relative marketing costs but also increased marketing quality. The strong competitive position of Unilever

products increased further, particularly vis-à-vis local brands.

Not all of Unilever's products were global brands, however. While most customer needs are comparable throughout the globe, local preferences in smell and taste restricted the company's potential of global synergy advantages in many products. Hard economic conditions and high inflation in the 1970s drove the company into a rationalization programme in which the performance of Unilever's product portfolio was analysed. While thriving on 'global jewels', the majority of the products appeared to be 'local brands', and thus it was decided to sell or withdraw most of the non-core brands. The newly adopted 'compass strategy' imbued principles of 'winning with brands and innovation' and 'winning with the people'. These notions were reinforced by Unilever's R&D development throughout nations in every continent of the world. To date, Unilever operates in over 190 countries with a range of 400 different brands.

Selling consumer products globally makes a company vulnerable to global developments, however. Especially the unfolding importance of sustainability could well be threatening Unilever's position, being one the world's largest users of palm oil. This crop plays a significant role in deforestation, as tropical forests are often cleared illegally to make way for palm-oil plantations. Unilever's 'Polman Plan', a 'sustainable living plan' named after its CEO, aims to 'help a billion people to take steps to improve their health and well-being, halve the environmental impact of its products; and source all its agricultural raw materials sustainably, meaning that they should meet requirements covering everything from forest protection to pest control' by 2020. These are not mere words, as contracts with IOI, a Malaysian palm oil company that supplies palm oil to more than 300 companies, have been cancelled. IOI has been accused of nearly all

▶

elements of the Polman Plan, including the destruction of orangutan habitat, the wrecking of peatland forest and serious labour issues on its Malaysian plantations. While being a global citizen capturing global synergies, Unilever is taking care of us all. Profits must be protected by saving people and planet.

Co-author: Sander Wisman

Sources: www.unilever.com; Unilever sustainable palm oil sourcing policy, 2016; Full Year Results 2013–2015; K. Taufik, 'Unilever palm oil supplier must suspend all plantation expansion to save reputation', *The Guardian*, 9 April 2016; 'In search of the good business', *The Economist*, 9 August, 2014; L. O'Reilly, 'Almost a quarter of Unilever's $8 billion ad budget is now spent on digital', *Business Insider UK*, 28 January 2016.

The international diversity perspective

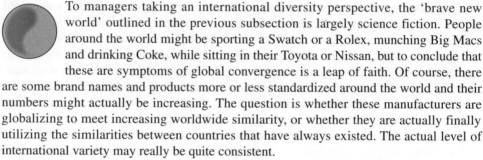

To managers taking an international diversity perspective, the 'brave new world' outlined in the previous subsection is largely science fiction. People around the world might be sporting a Swatch or a Rolex, munching Big Macs and drinking Coke, while sitting in their Toyota or Nissan, but to conclude that these are symptoms of global convergence is a leap of faith. Of course, there are some brand names and products more or less standardized around the world and their numbers might actually be increasing. The question is whether these manufacturers are globalizing to meet increasing worldwide similarity, or whether they are actually finally utilizing the similarities between countries that have always existed. The actual level of international variety may really be quite consistent.

It is particularly important to recognize in which respects countries remain different. For instance, the world might be drinking the same soft drinks, but they are probably doing it in different places, at different times, under different circumstances and for different reasons in each country. The product might be standardized worldwide, but the cultural norms and values that influence its purchase and use remain diverse across countries. According to proponents of the international diversity perspective, it is precisely these fundamental aspects of culture that turn out to be extremely stable over time – habits change slowly, but cultural norms and values are outright rigid. Producers might be lucky to find one product that fits in with such cultural diversity, but it would be foolish to interpret this as worldwide cultural convergence.

Other national differences are equally resilient against the tides of globalization. No countries have recently given up their national language in favour of Esperanto or English. On the contrary, there has been renewed emphasis on the local language in many countries (e.g. Ireland and the Baltic countries) and regions (e.g. Catalonia and Quebec). In the same way, political systems have remained internationally diverse, with plenty of examples of localization, even within nations. For instance, in Russia and the United States, the shift of power to regional governments has increased policy diversity within the country. Similar arguments can be put forward for legal systems, fiscal regimes, educational systems and technological infrastructure – each is extremely difficult to change due to the lock-in effects, vested interests, psychological commitment and complex decision-making processes.

For each example of increasing similarity, a counter-example of local initiatives and growing diversity could be given. Some proponents of the international diversity perspective argue that it is exactly this interplay of divergence and convergence forces that creates a dynamic balance preserving diversity. While technologies, organizing principles, political trends and social habits disperse across borders, resulting in global convergence, new developments and novel systems in each nation arise causing international divergence (Dosi and Kogut, 1993). Convergence trends are usually easier to spot than divergence – international dispersion can be more simply witnessed than new localized developments. To the casual observer, this might suggest that convergence trends have the upper hand, but after more thorough analysis, this conclusion must be cast aside.

Now add to this enduring international diversity the reality of international economic relations. Since the Second World War, attempts have been made to facilitate the integration of national economies. There have been some regional successes (e.g. the North American Free Trade Association and the European Union) and some advances have been made on a worldwide scale (e.g. the World Trade Organization). However, progress has been slow and important political barriers remain.

The continued existence of international diversity and political obstacles, it is argued, will limit the extent to which nations can become fully integrated into one borderless world. International differences and barriers to trade and investment will frustrate firms' attempts to standardize and centralize, and will place a premium on firms' abilities to adapt and decentralize. Of course, there will be some activities for which global economies of scale can be achieved and for which international coordination is needed, but this will not become true for all activities. Empowering national managers to be responsive to specific local conditions will remain an important ingredient for international success. Balancing globalization and localization of the firm's activities will continue to be a requirement in the future international context.

Ideally, the internationally operating company should neither deny nor regret the existence of international diversity, but regard it as an opportunity that can be exploited. Each country's unique circumstances will pose different challenges, requiring the development of different competences. Different national 'climates' will create opportunities for different innovations. If a company can tap into each country's opportunities and leverage the acquired competences and innovations to other countries, this could offer the company an important source of competitive advantage. Naturally, these locally leveraged competences and innovations would subsequently need to be adapted to the specific circumstances in other countries. This balancing act would require an organization that combined strong local responsiveness with the ability to exchange and coordinate internationally, even on a worldwide scale. International organizations blending these two elements are called 'transnational' (Bartlett and Ghoshal, 1995), or 'heterarchical' (Hedlund, 1986). However, in some businesses the international differences will remain so large that an even more locally responsive organizational form might be necessary, operating on a federative basis.

EXHIBIT 12.3 THE INTERNATIONAL DIVERSITY PERSPECTIVE

WALKING DOWN SESAME STREET IN AFGHANISTAN

Ever since its creation, *Sesame Street* educates children with colourful puppets. The TV show is broadcast in over 140 countries, yet it is not the same everywhere. Because Sesame Workshop specifically adapts its formula to the countries in which it operates, its expansion has been especially successful. In 2011, the non-profit organization started with a new group production, this time aimed towards Afghanistan. With around 45 per cent of the population under

15 and less than two-thirds of Afghan children enrolled in primary school, teaching children numbers, letters and messages of love, tolerance and equal treatment seems like a logical step.

The series, known locally as *Baghch-e-Simsim*, is a co-production between Sesame Workshop and Moby Media, an Afghan company operating some of the leading television channels in Afghanistan as well as possessing some of the biggest brands in the country. This partner is responsible for making *Sesame Street* palatable to the local audience by picking shots from the vast amount of already puppeteered videos from other international *Sesame Street* productions, which are then dubbed over. The rest consists of locally recorded mini-documentaries, aimed at delivering educational messages.

Due to the probability of cultural misunderstandings, some important changes are made to the *Sesame Street* formula. For example, the Afghan script writers feared parents might frown on encouraging their young viewers to dance in front of the television, since such activity is often perceived as something sexual in Afghanistan. Instead, children are invited to 'exercise'.

The producers of *Baghch-e-Simsim* have a certain degree of freedom when deciding what is acceptable, most noticeably with picking the puppet videos with the likes of Bert, Ernie, Elmo and Grover. For example, after testing an episode in which Ernie is barking like a dog and getting Bert to copy this, the producers found out that this could encourage indecent behaviour, since a dog is considered to be an unclean animal by many Afghans. Moby Media is also able to leave out characters that are deemed inappropriate altogether. In this regard, the Count has been omitted, since Afghans were thought not to understand why the vampire figure bears fangs, according to Tania Farzana, the Afghan-American executive producer of the show.

It is not just the local producers of Moby Media deciding what is okay and what is not however, since the Sesame Workshop aims to maintain a tight watch on how its international partners handle its show. When trying to film a scene on a building site, the producers struggled with finding one where workers wore clothes in accordance with the health and safety norms Sesame Workshop was accustomed to. Another shot that had to be dropped involved a car ride, because no one in it was actually wearing a seatbelt.

However, some locals might argue that the series still consists of inappropriate scenes. As is quite common for *Sesame Street*, the Afghan edition also occasionally borders on the line of controversy with the messages it tries to convey. When showing the experience of a first day at school, the producers picked a little girl as the main character – a role model – instead of a boy. In a country in which females attending school is still relatively rare, this can be considered quite daring. Furthermore, in 2016 *Bagch-e-Simsim* welcomed Zari, the series' first Afghan Muppet. This 6-year-old female puppet focuses on girls' health and empowerment. Still, as Lilith Dollard, content specialist for the US *Sesame Street*, explains: 'We don't want to overload the programme with messages – we want it to be fun'.

Since November 2011, the series is broadcast on TOLO and LEMAR television stations. In order to best fit with the country's cultural diversity, the series is shown in both the Dari and Pashto languages.

Co-author: Wester Wagenaar

Sources: www.mobygroup.com; www.sesameworkshop.org; *AFP*, 29 March 2013; *The Guardian*, 30 November 2011; *Huffington Post*, 8 December 2011; *New York Times*, 11 April 2016; *Reuters*, 30 November 2011.

MANAGING THE PARADOX OF GLOBALIZATION AND LOCALIZATION

When I am in Milan, I do as they do in Milan; but when I go to Rome, I do as Rome does.

St. Augustine (354–430), Roman theologian and philosopher

So, what does the paradox of global synergy and local responsiveness mean for the international configuration of firms? Should managers anticipate and encourage global convergence by emphasizing global standardization, centralization and coordination? They would choose to place more emphasis on realizing value creation by means of global synergies, accepting some value destruction due to a loss of local responsiveness. Or should managers acknowledge international diversity by emphasizing local adaptation, decentralization and autonomy? They would then focus on being locally responsive, accepting that this will frustrate the realization of cross-border synergies. (See Table 12.1 for the main differences.)

Again, the strategic management literature does not provide a uniform answer to the question of which international strategy firms can best pursue, however four suggestions have been brought forward to manage the paradox of globalization and localization: balancing, navigating, resolving and embracing.

Balancing

The Coca-Cola example illustrates well the paradox of globalization and localization: it had to give up advantages of global scale and worldwide standardization to become more

TABLE 12.1   Global convergence versus international diversity perspective

	Global convergence perspective	International diversity perspective
Emphasis on	Globalization over localization	Localization over globalization
International variety	Growing similarity	Remaining diverse
International linkages	Growing integration	Remaining fragmented
Major drivers	Technology and communication	Cultural and institutional identity
Diversity and fragmentation	Costly, convergence can be encouraged	Reality, can be exploited
Strategic focus	Global-scale synergies	Local responsiveness
Organizational preference	Standardize/centralize	Adapt/decentralize
Innovation process	Centre-for-global	Locally leveraged
Organizational structure	Global (centralized hub)	Transnational (integrated network)

locally adapted. There are, of course, many different possibilities to be attuned to local conditions, but they are all achieved at the expense of global advantages. In other words, companies have to trade off their demands for global synergy and local responsiveness to find a balance. However, the tension remains when companies have found a balance, and so strategizing managers will continue to search for a more favourable balance.

It should be kept in mind that while companies are trading off global synergy and local responsiveness, international firms do capture the advantages of global operations in local markets. Market presence in many countries leads to economies of scale in production and higher R&D and branding budgets, as the Unilever example illustrates (Exhibit 12.2). So while firms have to trade off global synergy and local responsiveness, they reap the benefits of global presence, which is being used as a source of competitive advantage in local markets.

Navigating

In Chapter 5, it was discussed that companies manage the paradox of multi-business synergy and business responsiveness by means of a series of corporate initiatives that sequentially focus on capturing synergy, responsiveness and then synergy again. In the same vein, international strategists navigate multinational companies with international initiatives. Actually, successfully managing the tension of global synergy and local responsiveness is more difficult, as local differences – such as cultural and institutional varieties – come on top of the complexity of managing the corporate level paradox.

Resolving

If one would be satisfied with a fast resolution for the paradox of globalization and localization, the term *glocalization*, widely used by academics, consultants and journalists, would do well. It would suggest that the paradox can be resolved with a synthesis. After taking a closer look at how the term is usually explained, however, a more likely conclusion would be that the solution is not only fast but also rather superficial: going global while adapting to local conditions. With examples such as Coca-Cola that had to adapt to local circumstances as its globally standardized strategy had run its course and McDonald's introducing local products such as Veggie McNuggets in India and McLobster in Canada, the term glocalization is used for companies going global while to some extent adapting locally. Yet, it is hard if not impossible to find a global company that does not need any local adaptations and so the new term is close to empty.

Glocalization, the semantic compilation of the words globalization and localization, originates from the Japanese word *dochakuka*, which means global localization and originally referred to adapting farming techniques to local conditions. In the strategy field, the term has been picked up from one of many Japanese presenters in the 1980s on Japanese management techniques and globalization. These were two hot topics, particularly in the United States, for two reasons. First, Japanese companies had become extremely successful overseas from the 1970s with for example cars and electronic products, and American companies and scholars wanted to understand Japanese success. And since demand creates supply, Japanese writers were invited to share some valuable insights. Second, globalization was a popular subject as new technological innovations changed the firm's understanding of international expansion dramatically (further explained in the next section). The Japanese McKinsey consultant Kenichi Ohmae contributed to this topic with his book *Triad of Economic Power* (1985). Humans need language to exchange and discuss ideas; however, the words' connotations are not always understood, including the Japanese word *dochakuka*, which had to be understood as yin yang balancing and not as a quick solution.

Still, companies can capture the advantages of both global synergies and local responsiveness. In Chapter 5, on corporate level strategy, one prominent synthesis between business responsiveness and multi-business synergy was discussed: the franchise. Franchises can also be – and actually often are – internationally organized, such as Pizza Hut, McDonald's and Kentucky Fried Chicken. Franchises are even more advantageous in the international context, as many complicating issues can be handled in an elegant way, such as specific local characteristics in the local food culture – for example with the above mentioned Veggie McNuggets in India – and import restrictions.

Embracing

Tensions between global synergy and local responsiveness are felt by the employees of the international firms. Not only frictions between head office and business units (see also Chapter 5), but also between people from different countries within the country unit often lead to misunderstandings, while some culture-related values are hardly compatible. For example, while drinking coffee is irrelevant for some, it is crucial for others (never install the company's standard English coffee machine at an Italian branch!). Most international firms provide culture trainings to prepare managers for emerging culture issues to manage the cultural tensions.

Yet, international operations create not only tensions, they can also be exploited. In the next section, 'The international context in international perspective', the so-called *New International Division of Labour* (Fröbel, Heinrichs and Kreye, 1980) is discussed. This paradigm claims that labour intensive production will be concentrated in countries with an abundance of cheap labour, while R&D will be concentrated in countries with superior levels of education, income and infrastructure. For example, the Japanese Uniqlo produces labour-intensive cashmere clothes in China while developing high-tech garments in Japan. This new division of labour includes much more than just production and research. International firms settle in Silicon Valley to become part of the next technological revolution, have designer teams in Italy, software engineers in India, media innovators in South Korea, lawyers in London and production facilities in Germany.

The importance of the global division of labour is that companies are not searching for one global standard, but instead combine countries' relative advantages. By blending country-specific differences, the tensions that arise from the paradox of global synergy and local responsiveness are seen as an opportunity (Beech *et al.*, 2004).

THE INTERNATIONAL CONTEXT IN INTERNATIONAL PERSPECTIVE

Co-authors: Gep Eisenloeffel and Wester Wagenaar

A truth on this side of the Pyrenees, a falsehood on the other.

Michel Eyquem de Montaigne (1533–1592), French philosopher, statesman and essayist

'The international context in international perspective': What a curious title one might think. Is not this a case of the snake biting itself in its own tail? The answer is no. An international angle can be used to view the debate between proponents of the global convergence perspective and those of the international diversity perspective. In other words, are there countries where a focus on attaining global synergies is more prevalent, while in others answering the demand for local responsiveness is more widespread?

For a long time it was mostly companies from industrialized countries that operated on a global scale, utilizing cheap labour from other countries. Knowledge and capital are the crucial inputs in the early stages of product manufacturing; labour intensity dominates in the later ones. This has a large effect on the location of industries as the comparative advantage in production shifts across countries. After the Second World War, foreign direct investment (FDI) accelerated at an unprecedented rate, eventually outpacing the growth of international trade (Dicken, 2015). Now a global shift is occurring.

Most notably after the turn of the century a profound change in the balance of economic power came about. Labour-intensive production found its way from the first generation of newly industrializing countries – Singapore, Hong Kong, Taiwan and South Korea – to second and third tier locations like Indonesia, Thailand, Malaysia and Bangladesh. In addition, new economic powerhouses, such as China, India, Russia, Turkey and Brazil made their presence felt. These awakening giants attracted FDI because of cheap labour, but as the middle class in countries like China rose, they also became interesting markets for Western consumer products. Rising income levels and technological developments in these countries changed locational conditions while markets matured. Now regions within China, like greater Beijing or Shanghai, attract not just cheap labour but also high-end production geared for both export and their own home market. Companies from the developing countries have not only risen, they have done so quickly. For example, between 2006 and 2015 the number of enterprises from the four major developing countries – Brazil, Russia, India and China, or the BRIC countries – has increased from 20 to 61 on the Financial Times Global 500 list (*Financial Times*, 2006, 2015). As it stands, more and more internationalizing firms from developing countries are starting to operate on a global scale. Economic interdependencies have only increased in the last 30 years.

It is important to note that much of the global trade is still limited to the United States, Europe and East Asia. This triad of economic power as the main markets for the influx of FDI makes clear that the much-used term globalization should be put into perspective. Many companies do not make a distinct trade-off between the international and the local level; FDI still mainly takes place in a relatively small number of countries and only a minority of MNEs have an equal share of their production and sales in all countries of the triad (Ghemawat, 2005; Rugman, 2005). Many multinational enterprises do not truly operate globally, but often stick to a region. Moreover, the more strategic the assets, the less global the activities: R&D, headquarter location and stock ownership are mainly concentrated in the MNEs' home countries (Rugman, 2005; Ruigrok and Van Tulder, 1995).

On the national level

History matters in terms of which countries historically had the resources to operate globally, but preferences as to how to deal with international strategy have not been discussed. Which nation-specific factors determine international differences when it comes to preferences for the global convergence or the international diversity perspective? If the proponents of the global convergence perspective are right, history and other factors will play a less and less important role as countries grow more similar. However, if international diversity remains a characteristic of our world, the way strategy paradoxes are dealt with differently in each country will continue to be an important issue to discuss.

One nation-specific factor that plays a role in strategies on the international context is the level of nationalism. In some countries, the belief is widespread that the country's ability to decide its own fate is being compromised. Foreign values, norms, habits and behaviours are being imposed, undermining the national culture. This leads many to argue that global convergence should be, and will be, curtailed. In other countries, such nationalism is far less pronounced and the advantages of globalization are more widely accepted. In general, it can be expected that strategists from countries with a strong streak of nationalism will gravitate more towards the international diversity perspective, while strategists from less nationalist countries will be more inclined towards the global convergence perspective.

The size of a country can also have an impact on national inclinations towards either one of the perspectives on the international context paradox. In general, smaller countries are more exposed to the international context than larger countries. Smaller countries commonly export more of their gross domestic product than larger countries, and import more as well. Hence, their companies are more used to dealing with, and adapting to, a high number of foreign suppliers, customers and competitors. Moreover, companies from smaller countries, confronted with a limited home market, are forced to seek growth in foreign markets earlier than their counterparts in larger countries. During this early internationalization, these companies do not have the benefit of scale economies in the home market and therefore are usually more inclined to adapt themselves to the demands of foreign markets. Companies in larger markets normally grow to a significant size at home, thereby achieving certain economies of scale through national standardization, while also establishing a domestically oriented management style. When they do move abroad, as a more mature company, their international activities will tend to be modest compared to domestic operations and therefore they will be less inclined to be locally adaptive. It stands to reason that this difference in exposure to the international context has an influence on how strategists from different countries perceive developments in the international context. Generally, strategists from smaller countries, to whom adaptation to international variety has become second nature, will favour the view that international diversity will remain. Strategists from larger countries will be more inclined to emphasize the growing similarities and to seek opportunities for international standardization.

Technology and a well-functioning IT infrastructure also play an important role. Some propose that internationalization is an incremental process that unfolds over time as a company shifts from an established domestic market to the international (Johanson and Vahlne, 1977). This so-called Uppsala model is now challenged by a new phenomenon. Entrepreneurial ventures, labelled 'born globals' (BGs), start out more or less globally from their inception, seizing opportunities offered by an increasingly interconnected and integrated global economy (Dicken, 2015; Mathews and Zander, 2007). Born globals are typically companies that take advantage of the global IT infrastructure, such as Airbnb and Alibaba. They tend to be endowed with distinguishing intangible capabilities and superior technological and relational resources (Hennart, 2014; Knight and Liesch, 2016). Most of the software or Internet-focused companies are capturing global synergies in the tech industry, such as social media platforms and firms offering mobile entertainment. Yet the phenomenon is not exclusive to those industries. Logitech, HTC and Zara are all examples of successful companies that went global almost right away. Born globals are emerging all over the world and as time progresses many more across a variety of industries can be expected.

On the industry level

Some industries naturally operate more globally than others. This was already hinted at when discussing born globals, where for instance Internet-focused firms can easily provide a similar product internationally. Some companies have a hard time going global, even if they would want to. Jean-François Hennart argues that the reason why born globals are able to go internationally fast is that their business model allows them to do so. They often 'sell niche products at low information, transportation, and adaptation costs to expert customers dispersed throughout the world'. When Logitech transitioned from a niche to a mass market, a significant amount of time was needed to increase foreign sales, as the Uppsala model predicts (2014).

Whether an industry has a preference for the global convergence perspective over the international diversity perspective largely has to do with culture. Whether a company needs to adapt or not, mostly has to do with national cultures and tastes. European consumers prefer cars with good engines, while Americans tend to pick large and comfortable ones. In Japan, smaller cars are the norm. Local adaptation is a prerequisite and, as such, some products are more suitable for unaltered global distribution than others.

A similar case can be made for the pharmaceutical industry, although here barriers prevent companies from employing a truly global strategy. Here regulation plays a key role. Local and regional rules can have a big impact on a firm's possibilities. The pharmaceutical industry, for instance, is heavily regulated by regional and national governments. Differences in the drug approval process, liability for damage and price controls complicates international sales of pharmaceuticals (Rugman, 2005). Nevertheless, the pharmaceutical industry does aim for global, or at least regional, synergies. Since pharmaceutical products hardly have to be adapted for each geographic market and since the large pharmaceutical companies own the rights to brand-name drugs, the firms can sell their products basically anywhere – so long as regulations do not stop them.

To the strategist

Whether a strategist opts to standardize or adapt on the international level is not always a personal choice. It is also influenced by external factors such as local pressure to adapt to local demand and regulations. The pressure to locally adapt is something strategists who operate internationally should take heed of. Nevertheless, even if a firm decides to remain operating locally it will still have to compete with others who might gain competitive advantages through international synergies. A strategist can then choose to offer more localized products and services and pursue a more responsive strategy.

REFERENCES

Abegglen, J.C. and Stalk, G. (1985) *Kaisha, The Japanese Corporation*, New York: Basic Books.

Abell, D. (1980) *Defining the Business: The Starting Point of Strategic Planning*, Englewood Cliffs, NJ: Prentice Hall.

Abernathy, C.M. and Hamm, R.M. (1995) *Surgical Intuition: What it is and How to Get it*, Philadelphia, PA: Hanley & Belfus.

Abernathy, W.J. and Clark, K. (1985) 'Innovation: Mapping the winds of creative destruction', *Research Policy*, 14, pp. 3–22.

Abernathy, W.J. and Utterback, J.M. (1978) 'Patterns of industrial innovation', *Technological Review*, 80(7), pp. 40–47.

Ackermann, R.W. and Bauer, R.A. (1976) *Corporate Social Performance: The Modern Dilemma*, Reston, VA: Reston.

Ackoff, R.L. (1974) *Redesigning the Future*, New York: Wiley.

Ackoff, R.L. (1980) *Creating the Corporate Future*, Chichester: Wiley.

Ackoff, R.L. (1981) *Creating the Corporate Future*, Chichester: Wiley.

Adler, N.J. and Gundersen, A. (2007) *International Dimensions of Organizational Behavior*, Mason, OH: Thomson South-Western (5th ed.).

Adler, P.S., Goldoftas, B. and Levine, D.I. (1999) 'Flexibility versus efficiency? A case study of model changeovers in the Toyota production system', *Organization Science*, 10(1), pp. 43–68.

Adner, R. and Helfat, C. (2003) 'Dynamic managerial capabilities and corporate effects', *Strategic Management Journal*, 24(10), pp. 1011–1027.

Agor, W.A. (1986) 'The logic of intuition: How top executives make important decisions', *Organizational Dynamics*, 14(3): pp. 5–18.

Agor, W.A. (1989) *Intuition in Organizations: Leading and Managing Productively*, Newbury Park, CA: Sage.

Aguilar, A., Bochereau, L. and Matthiessen-Guyader, L. (2008) 'Biotechnology and sustainability: The role of transatlantic cooperation in research and innovation', *Trends in Biotechnology*, 26(4), pp. 163–165.

Aguilar, F.J., Hamermesh, R.G. and Brainard, C.E. (1993) *General Electric Co.: 1984, Case 385315*, Boston, MA: Harvard Business School Press.

Ala, M. and Cordeiro, W.P. (1999) 'Can we learn management techniques from the Japanese ringi process?', *Business Forum*, 24(1/2), pp. 22 –24.

Albert, M. (1991) *Capitalisme contre Capitalisme*, Paris: Seuil.

Albert, M. (1993) *Capitalism Against Capitalism*, London: Whurr Publishers.

Aldrich, H.E. (1999) *Organizations Evolving*, London: Sage.

Aldrich, H.E. and Fiol, C.M. (1994) 'Fools rush in the institutional context of industry creation', *Academy of Management Review*, 19(4), pp. 645–670.

Ali, A.J. (1995) 'Cultural discontinuity and Arab management thought', *International Studies of Management & Organization*, 25(3), pp. 7–30.

Alkhafaji, A.F. (1989) *A Stakeholder Approach to Corporate Governance: Managing a Dynamic Environment*, Westport, CT: Quorum.

Allaire, Y. and Firsirotu, M. (1990) 'Strategic plans as contracts', *Long Range Planning*, 23(1), pp. 102–115.

Allison, G.T. (1969) 'Conceptual models and the Cuban missile crisis', *American Political Science Review*, 3, September, pp. 689–718.

Allison, G.T. (1971) *The Essence of Decision: Explaining the Cuban Missile Crisis*, Boston, MA: Little Brown.

Alvarez, S.A. and Busenitz, L.W. (2001) 'The entrepreneurship of resource-based theory', *Journal of Management*, 27, pp. 755–775.

Amabile, T.M. (1996) *Creativity in Context*, Boulder, CO: Westview Press.

Amabile, T.M. (1998) 'How to kill creativity', *Harvard Business Review*, 76(5), pp. 76–87.

Amable, B. (2003) *The Diversity of Modern Capitalism*, Oxford: Oxford University Press.

American Productivity and Quality Center (1996) *Reinventing Strategic Planning for a Dynamic Environment*, Houston, TX: APQC's International Benchmarking Clearinghouse.

Amit, R. and Livnat, J. (1988) 'Diversification and the risk–return trade-off', *Academy of Management Journal*, 31(1), pp. 154–165.

Amit, R. and Schoemaker, P.J.H. (1993) 'Strategic assets and organization rent', *Strategic Management Journal*, 14(1), pp. 33–46.

Amit, R. and Zott, C. (2001) 'Value creation in e-business', *Strategic Management Journal*, 22(6–7), pp. 493–520.

Amit, R. and Zott, C. (2012) 'Creating value through business model innovation', *Sloan Management Review*, 53, Spring, pp. 41–49.

Amodio, D.M. (2008) 'The social neuroscience of intergroup relations', *European Review of Social Psychology*, 19, pp. 1–54.

Ancona, D.G. and Nadler, D.A. (1989) 'Top hats and executive tales: Designing the senior team', *Sloan Management Review*, 31(1), pp. 19–28.

Anderson, J.R. (1983) *The Architecture of Cognition*, Cambridge, MA: Harvard University Press.

Anderson, P. (1999) 'Complexity theory and organizational science', *Organization Science*, 10, pp. 216–232.

Anderson, P. and Tushman, M. (1990) 'Technological discontinuities and dominant designs: A cyclical model of technological change', *Administrative Science Quarterly*, 35, pp. 604–633.

Andrews, K.R. (1987) *The Concept of Corporate Strategy*, Homewood, IL: Irwin (3rd ed.).

Ang, J.S. and Chua, J.H. (1979) 'Long-range planning in large United States corporations: A survey', *Long Range Planning*, 12-(April), pp. 99–102.

Anslinger, P.L. and Copeland, T.E. (1996) 'Growth through acquisitions: A fresh look', *Harvard Business Review*, 74(1), pp. 126–135.

Ansoff, H.I. (1965) *Corporate Strategy: An Analytic Approach to Business Policy for Growth and Expansion*, New York: McGraw-Hill.

Ansoff, H.I. (1991) 'Critique of Henry Mintzberg's the "Design School": Reconsidering the basic premises of strategic management', *Strategic Management Journal*, September, pp. 449–461.

Ansoff, H.I. and McDonnell, E. (1990) *Implanting Strategic Management*, New York: Prentice Hall (2nd ed.).

Anthony, W.P., Bennett, R.H., Maddox, E.N. and Wheatley, W.J. (1993) 'Picturing the future: Using mental imagery to enrich strategic environmental assessment', *Academy of Management Executive*, 7(2), pp. 43–56.

Aoki, M. (1990) 'The participatory generation of information rents and the theory of the firm', in: M. Aoki, B. Gustafsson and O.E. Williamson (eds.) *The Firm as a Nexus of Treaties*, London: Sage, pp. 26–52.

Argyres, N. (1995) 'Technology strategy, governance structure and interdivisional coordination', *Journal of Economic Behavior and Organization*, 28, pp. 337–358.

Argyris, C. (1990) *Overcoming Organizational Defenses: Facilitating Organizational Learning*, Needham, MA: Allyn & Bacon.

Argyris, C. and Schon, D. (1978) *Organizational Learning: A Theory of Action Approach*, Reading, MA: Addison-Wesley.

Armour, H. and Teece, D.J. (1978) 'Organizational structure and economic performance: A test of the multidivisional hypothesis', *Bell Journal of Economics*, 9(2), pp. 106–122.

Armstrong, J.S. (1982) 'The value of formal planning for strategic decisions: Review of empirical research', *Strategic Management Journal*, 3, pp. 197–211.

Arrow, K. (1969) 'The organization of economic activity: Issues pertinent to the choice of market vs. nonmarket allocation', in: *The Analysis and Evaluation of Public Expenditures: The PPB System, 1*, US Joint Economic Committee, 91st Session, US Government Printing Office, Washington, DC, pp. 59–73.

Arrow, K. (1996) 'Technical information and industrial structure', *Industrial and Corporate Change*, 5(2), pp. 645–652.

Arthur, W.B. (1983) 'Competing technologies and lock-in by historical events: The dynamics of allocation under increasing returns', working paper WP-83-90, International Institute for Applied Systems Analysis, Laxenburg, Austria.

Arthur, W.B. (1994) *Increasing Returns and Path Dependence in the Economy*, Ann Arbor, MI: University of Michigan Press.

Arthur, W.B. (1996) 'Increasing returns and the new world of business', *Harvard Business Review*, 74(4), pp. 100–109.

Arthur, W.B., Ermoliev, Y.M. and Kaniovsky, Y.M. (1987) 'Path dependent processes and the emergence of macro structure', *European Journal of Operations Research*, 30, pp. 294–303.

Ashby, F.G., Isen, A.M. and Turken, U. (1999) 'A neuropsychological theory of positive affect and its influence on cognition', *Psychological Review*, 106, pp. 529–550.

Ashby, W.R. (1960) *Design for a Brain*, New York: Wiley (2nd ed.).

Astley, W.G. and van der Ven, A.H. (1983) 'Central perspectives and debates in organization theory', *Administrative Science Quarterly*, 28(2), pp. 245–273.

Augier, M. and Teece, D.J. (2009) 'Dynamic capabilities and the role of managers in business strategy and economic performance', *Organization Science*, 20, pp. 410–421.

Axelrod, R. (1976) *The Structure of Decision: The Cognitive Maps of Political Elites*, Princeton, NJ: Princeton University Press.

Axelrod, R. (1984) *The Evolution of Cooperation*, New York: Basic Books.

Axelsson, B. and Easton, G. (1992) *Industrial Networks: A New View of Reality*, New York: Wiley.

Badaracco, J.L. (1991) *The Knowledge Link: How Firms Compete Through Strategic Alliances*, Boston, MA: Harvard Business School Press.

Baden-Fuller, C.W.F. and Stopford, J.M. (1992) *Rejuvenating the Mature Business*, London: Routledge.

Baden-Fuller, C.W.F. and Stopford, J.M. (1994) *Rejuvenating the Mature Business: The Competitive Challenge*, Boston, MA: Harvard Business School Press.

Bain, J.S. (1956) *Barriers to New Competition: Their Character and Consequences in Manufacturing*, Boston, MA: Harvard University Press.

Bain, J.S. (1959) *Industrial Organizations*, New York: Wiley.

Barber, H., Freeland, G. and Brownell, D. (2002) 'A survivor's guide to organization redesign', in: M.S. Deimler (ed.) *The Boston Consulting Group on Strategy: Classic Concepts and New Perspectives*, pp. 302–309 (2nd ed.).

Bargh, J.A. (1996) 'Principles of automaticity', in: E.T. Higgins and A. Kruglanski (eds.) *Social Psychology: Handbook of Basic Principles*, New York: Guilford Press, pp. 169–183.

Bargh, J.A. and Chartrand, T.L. (1999) 'The unbearable automaticity of being', *American Psychologist*, 54(7), pp. 462–479.

Bargh, J.A. and Ferguson, M.J. (2000) 'Beyond behaviorism: On the automaticity of higher mental processes', *Psychological Bulletin*, 126(6), pp. 925–945.

Barnard, C.I. (1938) *The Functions of the Executive*, Cambridge, MA: Harvard University Press.

Barnard, C.I. (1968) *The Functions of the Executive*, Cambridge, MA: Harvard University Press (Vol. 11).

Barney, J.B. (1986a) 'Strategic factor markets: Expectations, luck and business strategy', *Management Science*, 32(10), pp. 1231–1241.

Barney, J.B. (1986b) 'Organizational culture: Can it be a source of sustained competitive advantage?', *Academy of Management Review*, 11, pp. 656–665.

Barney, J.B. (1991) 'Firm resources and sustained competitive advantage', *Journal of Management*, 17(1), pp. 99–120.

Barr, P.S, Stimpert, J.L. and Huff, A.S. (1992) 'Cognitive change, strategic action, and organizational renewal', *Strategic Management Journal*, Summer Special Issue 13, pp. 15–36.

Barrett, D. (1998) *The Paradox Process: Creative Business Solutions Where You Least Expect to Find Them*, New York: Amacom.

Bartlett, C.A. and Ghoshal, S. (1987) 'Managing across borders: New organizational responses', *Sloan Management Review*, 29(1), pp. 43–53.

Bartlett, C.A. and Ghoshal, S. (1988) 'Organizing for worldwide effectiveness: The transnational solution', *California Management Review*, 31, pp. 54–74.

Bartlett, C.A. and Ghoshal, S. (1989) *Managing Across Borders: The Transnational Solution*, New York: Harvard Business School Press.

Bartlett, C.A. and Ghoshal, S. (1993) 'Beyond the M-form: Toward a managerial theory of the enterprise', *Strategic Management Journal*, Winter Special Issue 14, pp. 23–46.

Bartlett, C.A. and Ghoshal, S. (1994) 'Changing the role of top management: Beyond strategy to purpose', *Harvard Business Review*, November–December, pp. 79–88.

Bartlett, C.A. and Ghoshal, S. (1995) *Transnational Management: Text, Cases, and Readings in Cross-Border Management*, Homewood, IL: Irwin (2nd ed.).

Bartlett, C.A. and Ghoshal, S. (2003) 'What is a global manager?', *Harvard Business Review*, 81(8), pp. 101–108.

Bartlett, C.A., Ghoshal, S. and Beamish, P. (2008) *Transnational Management: Text, Cases and Readings in Cross Border Management*, Burr Ridge, IL: McGraw-Hill/Irwin (5th ed.).

Bass, B.M. (1990) *Bass and Stogdill's Handbook of Leadership*, New York: Free Press (3rd ed.).

Bass, B.M. and Steidlmeier, P. (1999) Ethics, character, and authentic transformational leadership behavior, *Leadership Quarterly*, 10(2), pp. 181–217.

Bastick, T. (1982) *Intuition: How We Think and Act*, New York: Wiley.

Bate, P. (1994) *Strategies for Cultural Change*, Oxford: Butterworth-Heinemann.

Bateman, T.S. and Zeithaml, C.P. (1989) 'The psychological context of strategic decisions: A model and convergent experimental findings', *Strategic Management Journal*, 10(1), pp. 59–74.

Bateson, G. (1979) *Mind and Nature: A Necessary Unity*, New York: Dutton.

Baum, A.C. and Singh, J.V. (eds.) (1994) *Evolutionary Dynamics of Organizations*, New York: Oxford University Press.

Baum, J.A.C. and Greve, H.R. (eds.) (2001) *Multiunit Organization and Multimarket Strategy*, Stamford, CT: JAI Press (Vol. 18).

Baumol, W. (2006) 'Entrepreneurship and invention: Toward restoration into microeconomic value theory', working paper, Ringberg Castle Presentation, Germany.

Baumol, W., Panzar, J. and Willig, R. (1982) *Contestable Markets and the Theory of Industry Structure*, New York: Harcourt Brace Jovanovich.

Bavelas, A. (1964) 'Leadership: Man and function', in: H.H. Leavitt and L.R. Pondy (eds.) *Readings in Managerial Psychology*, Chicago, IL: University of Chicago Press.

Baylor, A.L. (2001) 'A U-shaped model for the development of intuition by level of expertise', *New Ideas in Psychology*, 19: pp. 237–244.

Baysinger, B.D. and Hoskisson, R.E. (1990) 'The composition of boards of directors and strategic control: Effects of corporate strategy', *Academy of Management Review*, 15(1), pp. 72–81.

Bazerman, M.H. (1986) *Judgment in Managerial Decision Making*, New York: Wiley.

Bazerman, M.H. (1990) *Judgment in Managerial Decision Making*, New York: Wiley (2nd ed.).

Bazerman, M.H. (1998) *Judgment in Managerial Decision Making*, New York: Wiley (4th ed.).

Bazerman, M.H. and Watkins, M.D. (2004) *Predictable Surprises: The Disasters You Should Have Seen Coming, and How to Avoid Them*, Boston, MA: Harvard Business School Press.

Bechara, A., Damasio, H. and Damasio, A.R. (2000) 'Emotion, decision making, and the orbitofrontal cortex', *Cerebral Cortex*, 10(3), pp. 295–307. Bechara, A., Damasio, H., Tranel, D. and Damasio, A.R. (1997) 'Deciding advantageously before knowing the advantageous strategy', *Science*, 275, pp. 1293–1295.

Beech, N., Burns, H., de Caestecker, L., Mackintosh, R. and MacLean, D. (2004) 'Paradox as invitation to act in problematic change situations', *Human Relations*, 57, pp. 1313–1332.

Behling, O. and Eckel, N.L. (1991) 'Making sense out of intuition', *Academy of Management Executive*, 5(1), pp. 46–54.

Beinhocker, E.D. (1999a) 'Robust adaptive strategies', *Sloan Management Review*, 40(3), pp. 95–106.

Beinhocker, E.D. (1999b) 'Strategy at the edge of chaos', *McKinsey Quarterly*, 1, pp. 24–39.

Bellou, V. (2011) 'Do women followers prefer a different leadership style than men?', *International Journal of Human Resource Management*, 22(13), pp. 2818–2833.

Benner, M.J. and Tushman, M.L. (2002) 'Process management and technological innovation: A longitudinal study of the photography and paint industries', *Administrative Science Quarterly*, 47(4), 676–707.

Benner, M.J. and Tushman, M.L. (2003) 'Exploitation, exploration, and process management: The productivity dilemma revisited', *Academy of Management Review*, 2, pp. 238–256.

Bennis, W. (1989). *On Becoming a Leader*. New York: Addison-Wesley.

Bennis, W. and Nanus, B. (1985) *Leaders: The Strategies for Taking Charge*, New York: Harper & Row.

Berle, A.A. and Means, G.C. (1932) *The Modern Corporation and Private Property*, New York: Transaction Publishers/Macmillan.

Bernheim, B.D. and Rangel, A. (2004) 'Addiction and cue triggered decision processes', *American Economic Review*, 94(5), pp. 1558–1590.

Best, M.H. (1990) *The New Competition: Institutions of Industrial Restructuring*, Cambridge: Polity.

Betsch, C. and Kunz, J.J. (2008) 'Individual strategy preferences and decisional fit', *Journal of Behavioral Decision Making*, 21(5), 532–555.

Bettis, R.A. and Donaldson, L. (1990) 'Market discipline and the discipline of management', *Academy of Management Review*, 15(3), pp. 367–368.

Bilton, C. and Cummings, S. (2010). *Creative Strategy: Reconnecting Business and Innovation*, Chichester: Wiley.

Birkinshaw, J. and Hood, N. (1998) *Multinational Corporate Evolution and Subsidiary Development*, London: Macmillan.

Birnbaum, R. (1988) *How Colleges Work: The Cybernetics of Academic Organization and Leadership*, San Francisco, CA: Jossey-Bass.

Blair, M. (1995) *Ownership and Control: Rethinking Corporate Governance for the Twenty-First Century*, Washington, DC: Brookings Institution.

Blattberg, R.C. and Hoch, S.J. (1990) 'Database models and managerial intuition: 50% model 50% manager', *Management Science*, 36, pp. 887–899.

Bleeke, J. and Ernst, D. (1991) 'The way to win in cross border alliances', *Harvard Business Review*, 69(6), pp. 127–135.

Bleeke, J. and Ernst, D. (1993) *Collaborating to Compete: Using Strategic Alliances and Acquisitions in the Global Marketplace*, New York: Wiley.

Bless, H., Bohner, G., Schwarz, N. and Strack, F. (1990) 'Mood and persuasion: A cognitive response analysis', *Personality and Social Psychology Bulletin*, 16, pp. 331–345.

Bodenhausen, G.V. (1990) 'Stereotypes as judgmental heuristics: Evidence of circadian variations in discrimination', *Psychological Science*, 1, pp. 319–322.

Bodwell, W. and Chermack, T.J. (2010) 'Organizational ambidexterity: Integrating deliberate and emergent strategy with scenario planning', *Technological Forecasting & Social Change*, 77, pp.193–202.

Boeker, W. (1992) 'Power and managerial dismissal: Scapegoating at the top', *Administrative Science Quarterly*, 37(4), pp. 538–547.

Boorstin, D.J. (1973) *The Americans: The Democratic Experience*, New York: Random House.

Bossidy, L. and Charan, R. with Burck, C. (2002) *Execution: The Discipline of Getting Things Done*, New York: Crown Business.

Bouchikhi, H. and Kimberly, J.R. (2003) 'Escaping the identity trap', *Sloan Management Review*, 44(3), pp. 20–26.

Bouchikhi, H. and Kimberly, J.R. (2008) *The Soul of the Corporation: How to Manage the Identity of Your Company*, Upper Saddle River, NJ: Wharton School Publishing.

Bourgeois, L.J. (1980) Strategy and the environment: A conceptual integration, *Academy of Management Review*, 5, pp. 25–39.

Bourgeois, L.J. and Brodwin, D.R. (1983) 'Putting your strategy into action', *Strategic Management Planning*, March–May.

Bower, J.L. (1970) *Managing the Resource Allocation Process*, Boston, MA: Harvard Business School Press.

Bower, J.L. and Christensen, C.M. (1995) 'Disruptive technologies: Catching the wave', *Harvard Business Review*, 73(1), pp. 43–53.

Bowers, K.S., Regehr, G., Balthazard, C. and Parker, K. (1990) 'Intuition in the context of discovery', *Cognitive Psychology*, 22, pp. 72–110.

Boyd, B.K. (1991) 'Strategic planning and financial performance: A meta-analysis', *Journal of Management Studies*, 28, pp. 353–374.

Boyd, B.K. and Reuning-Elliot, E. (1998) 'A measurement model of strategic planning', *Strategic Management Journal*, 19(2), pp. 181–192.

Bradley, F. (2005) *International Marketing Strategy*, London: Pearson.

Brandenburger, A.M. and Nalebuff, B.J. (1996) *Co-opetition*, New York: Doubleday.

Braudel, F. (1949) *The Mediterranean and the Mediterranean World in the Age of Philip II*, Scranton, PA: HarperCollins.

Brews, P.J. and Hunt, M. (1999) 'Learning to plan and planning to learn: Resolving the planning school/ learning school debate', *Strategic Management Journal*, 20(10), pp. 889–914.

Briggs, K.C. and Myers, I.B. (1976) *Myers-Briggs Type Indicator*, Palo Alto, CA: Consulting Psychologists Press.

Brittain, J. and Freeman, J. (1980) 'Organizational proliferation and density-dependent selection', in: J.R. Kimberly and R. Miles (eds.) *The Organizational Life Cycle*, San Francisco, CA: Jossey-Bass, pp. 291–338.

Brocas, I. and Carrillo, J.D. (2008) 'The brain as a hierarchical organization', *American Economic Review*, 98(4), pp. 1312–1346.

Brooks, D. (2012) *The Social Animal*, New York: Random House.

Brown, S. and Eisenhardt, K.M. (1997) 'The art of continuous change: Linking complexity theory and time-paced evolution in relentlessly shifting organizations', *Administrative Science Quarterly*, 42(1), pp. 1–34.

Bruner, J.S. (1962) *On Knowing*, Cambridge, MA: Harvard University Press.

Bucholz, R.A. (1986) *Business Environment and Public Policy*, Englewood Cliffs, NJ: Prentice Hall.

Buckley, P.J. and Casson, M.C. (1976) *The Future of the Multinational Enterprise*, London: Macmillan.

Buckley, P.J. and Casson, M.C. (1985) *The Economic Theory of the Multinational Enterprise*, London: Macmillan.

Bunderson, J.S. (2003) 'Team member functional background and involvement in management teams: Direct effects and the moderating role of power centralization', *Academy of Management Journal*, 46(4), pp. 458–474.

Bunderson, J.S. and Sutcliffe, K.M. (2002) 'Why some teams emphasize learning more than others: Evidence from business unit management teams', in: H. Sondak (ed.) *Towards Phenomenology of Groups and Group Membership*, Oxford: Elsevier Science (Vol. 4), pp. 49–84.

Bunderson, J.S. and Sutcliffe, K.M. (2003) 'Management team learning orientation and business unit performance', *Journal of Applied Psychology*, 88(3), pp. 552–560.

Bungay, S. and Goold, M. (1991) 'Creating a strategic control system', *Long Range Planning*, 24(6), pp. 32–39.

Buono, A.F. and Nichols, L.T. (1985) *Corporate Policy, Values and Social Responsibility*, New York: Praeger.

Burgelman, R.A. (1983) 'Corporate entrepreneurship and strategic management: Insights from a process study', *Management Science*, 29(12), pp. 1349–1364.

Burgelman, R.A. (1991) 'Intraorganizational ecology of strategy making and organizational adaptation: Theory and field research', *Organization Science*, 2(3), pp. 239–262.

Burgelman, R.A. (1994) 'Fading memories: A process theory of strategic business exit in dynamic environments', *Administrative Science Quarterly*, 39, pp. 24–36.

Burgelman, R.A. (1996) 'A process model of strategic business exit: Implications of an evolutionary perspective on strategy', *Strategic Management Journal*, Summer Special Issue 17, pp. 193–214.

Burgelman, R.A. (2002) 'Strategy as vector and the inertia of coevolutionary lock-in', *Administrative Science Quarterly*, 47, pp. 325–357.

Burgelman, R.A. and Grove, A.S. (1996) 'Strategic dissonance', *California Management Review*, 38(2), pp. 8–28.

Burke, L.A. and Miller, M.K. (1999) 'Taking the mystery out of intuitive decision making', *Academy of Management Executive*, 13(4), pp. 91–99.

Burt, G. and Van der Heijden, K. (2003) 'First steps: Towards purposeful activities in scenario thinking and future studies', *Futures*, 35(10), pp. 1011–1026.

Business Week (1996) 'Strategic planning', 26 August, pp. 45–52.

Buzzell, R.D. and Gale, B.T. (1987) *The PIMS Principles: Linking Strategy to Performance*, New York: Free Press.

Calori, R. and de Woot, P. (eds.) (1994) *A European Management Model: Beyond Diversity*, Hemel Hempstead: Prentice Hall.

Calori, R., Valla, J.-P. and De Woot, P. (1994) 'Common characteristics: The ingredients of European management', in: R. Calori and P. De Woot (eds.) *A European Management Model: Beyond Diversity*, Hemel Hempstead: Prentice Hall.

Cameron, K.S. and Quinn, R.E. (1988) 'Organizational paradox and transformation', in: R.E. Quinn and K.S. Cameron, *Paradox and Transformation: Towards a Theory of Change in Organization and Management*, Cambridge, MA: Ballinger.

Camp, R. (1989) *Benchmarking: The Search for Industry Best Practices that Lead to Superior Performance*, Milwaukee, WI: Quality Press.

Campbell, A. and Goold, M. (1998) *Synergy: Why Links Between Business Units Often Fail and How to Make Them Work*, Oxford: Capstone Publishing.

Campbell, A. and Tawadey, K. (1990) *Mission and Business Philosophy*, Oxford: Butterworth-Heinemann.

Campbell, A. and Yeung, S. (1991) 'Creating a sense of mission', *Long Range Planning*, 24(4), pp. 10–20.

Campbell, A., Goold, M. and Alexander, M. (1995) 'The value of the parent company', *California Management Review*, 38(1), pp. 79–97.

Cannella, A.A. and Monroe, M.J. (1997) 'Contrasting perspectives on strategic leaders: Toward a more realistic view of top managers', *Journal of Management*, 23(3), pp. 213–237.

Cannon, T. (1992) *Corporate Responsibility*, London: Pitman.

Cantwell, J. (1989) *Technological Innovations in Multinational Corporations*, Oxford: Basil Blackwell.

Capon, N., Farley, J.U. and Hulbert, J.M. (1987) *Corporate Strategic Planning*, New York: Columbia University Press.

Capron, L., Dussauge, P. and Mitchell, W. (1998) 'Resource redeployment following horizontal mergers and acquisitions in Europe and North America, 1988–1992', *Strategic Management Journal*, 19(7), pp. 631–661.

Carlson, R.A. and Dulany, D.E. (1985) 'Conscious attention and abstraction in concept learning', *Journal of Experimental Psychology: Learning, Memory, and Cognition*, 11: pp. 45–58.

Carpenter, M.A. and Golden, B.R. (1997) 'Perceived managerial discretion: A study of cause and effect', *Strategic Management Journal*, 18(3), pp. 187–206.

Carroll, A.B. (1993) *Business and Society: Ethics and Stakeholder Management*, Cincinnati, OH: South-Western.

Casson, M. (1997) *Information and Organization: A New Perspective on the Theory of the Enterprise*, New York: Oxford University Press.

Castells, M. (1996) *The Rise of the Network Society*, Oxford: Basil Blackwell.

Caves, R.E. (1971) 'International corporations: The industrial economics of foreign investment', *Economica*, 38(149), pp. 1–27.

Caves, R.E. and Porter, M.E. (1977) 'From entry barriers to mobility barriers: Conjectural decisions and contrived deterrence to new competition', *Quarterly Journal of Economics*, 91, pp. 241–262.

Cavusgil, S.T., Knight, G., Riesenberger, J.R., Rammal, H.G. and Rose, E.L. (2014) *International Business: The New Realities,*. Melbourne: Pearson Australia (2nd ed.).

Cernat, L. (2004) 'The emerging European corporate governance model: Anglo-Saxon, Continental, or still the century of diversity?', *Journal of European Public Policy*, 11(1), pp. 147–166.

Chaffee, E.E. (1985) 'Three models of strategy', *Academy of Management Review*, 10(1), pp. 89–98.

Chakravarthy, B.S. and Lorange, P. (1991) *Managing the Strategy Process: A Framework for a Multi-business Firm*, Englewood Cliffs, NJ: Prentice Hall.

Chandler, A.D. (1962) *Strategy and Structure: Chapters in the History of the American Industrial Enterprise,* Cambridge, MA: Harvard University Press.

Chandler, A.D. (1977) *The Visible Hand: The Managerial Revolution in American Business*, Cambridge, MA: Harvard University Press.

Chandler, A.D. (1986) 'The evolution of modern global competition', in: M.E. Porter (ed.) *Competition in Global Industries*, Boston, MA: Harvard Business School Press, pp. 405–448.

Chandler, A.D. (1990a) *Scale and Scope: The Dynamics of Industrial Capitalism*, Cambridge, MA: Harvard University Press.

Chandler, A.D (1990b) 'The enduring logic of industrial success', *Harvard Business Review*, 68(2), pp. 130–140.

Charkham, J. (1994) *Keeping Good Company: A Study of Corporate Governance in Five Countries*, Oxford: Oxford University Press.

Chatterjee, S. (1986) 'Types of synergy and economic value: The impact of acquisitions on merging and rival firms', *Strategic Management Journal*, 7(2), pp. 119–139.

Chen, C.C. and Lee Y.T. (eds.) (2008) *Leadership and Management in China*, Cambridge: Cambridge University Press.

Chen, C.C. and Meindl, J.R. (1991) 'The construction of leadership images in the popular press: The case of Donald Burr and People Express', *Administrative Science Quarterly*, 36(4), pp. 521–551.

Chen, S. and Chaiken, S. (1999) 'The heuristic-systematic model in its broader context', in: S. Chaiken and Y. Trope (eds.) *Dual-Process Theories in Social Psychology*, New York: Guilford Press, pp. 73–96.

Chermack, T.J. (2007) 'Assessing the quality of scenarios in scenario planning', *Futures Research Quarterly*, 22(4), pp. 23–35.

Chesbrough, H. (2003) *Open Innovation: The New Imperative for Creating and Profiting from Technology*, Boston, MA: Harvard Business School Press.

Chesbrough, H. and Rosenbloom, R.S. (2002) 'The role of the business model in capturing value from innovation: Evidence from Xerox Corporation's technology', *Industrial and Corporate Change*, 11(3), pp. 529–555.

Chesbrough, H.W. and Teece, D.J. (1996) 'Organizing for vinnovation: When is Virtual virtuous?', *Harvard Business Review*, 74(1), pp. 65–73.

Chesnais, F. (1984) 'Marx's crisis theory today', in: C. Freeman (ed.) *Design, Innovation and Long Cycles in Economic Development*, London: Pinter.

Chi, M.T.H., Glaser, R. and Farr, M.J. (1998) *The Nature of Expertise*, Hillsdale, NJ: Erlbaum.

Child, J. (1972) 'Organizational structure, environment, and performance: The role of strategic choice', *Sociology*, January, pp. 2–22.

Child, J. and Faulkner, D. (1998) *Strategies for Cooperation: Managing Alliances, Networks, and Joint Ventures*, Oxford: Oxford University Press.

Christensen, C.M. (1997, 2011) *The Innovator's Dilemma, When New Technologies Cause Great Firms to Fail*, New York: HarperBusiness.

Cibin, R. and Grant, R.M. (1996) 'Restructuring among the world's leading oil companies', *British Journal of Management*, 7, pp. 283–307.

Clark, K. and Fujimoto, T. (1991) *Product Development Performance: Strategy, Organization and Management in the World Auto Industries*, Cambridge, MA: Harvard Business School Press.

Clarke, T. (1998) 'The stakeholder corporation: A business philosophy for the information age', *Long Range Planning*, 31(2), pp. 182–194.

Clarkson, M.B.E. (1995) 'A stakeholder framework for analyzing and evaluating corporate social performance', *Academy of Management Review*, 20(1), pp. 92–117.

Claxton, G. (1998) 'Knowing without knowing why', *Psychologist*, 11(5), pp. 217–220.

Cleland, D.I. (1976) *The Origin and Development of a Philosophy of Long-Range Planning in American Business*, Arno Press: New York.

Coase, R. (1937) 'The nature of the firm', *Economica*, 4, pp. 386–405.

Cochran, P.L. and Wartick, S.L. (1994) 'Corporate governance: A review of the literature', in: R.I. Tricker (ed.) *International Corporate Governance: Text, Readings and Cases*, Singapore: Prentice Hall.

Coe, N., Kelly, P. and Yeung, H.W.C. (2012) *Economic Geography: A Contemporary Introduction*, Wiley (2nd ed.).

Cohen, E.G. (1986) 'Artificial intelligence and the dynamic performance of organizational designs', in: J.G. March and R. Weissinger-Baylon (eds.) *Ambiguity and Command: Organizational Perspectives on Military Decision Making*, Boston, MA: Ballinger.

Collins, H.M. (1982) 'The replication of experiments in physics', in: B. Barnes and D. Edge (eds.) *Science in Context*, Cambridge, MA: MIT Press, pp. 94–116.

Collins, J.C. and Porras, J. (1994) *Built To Last: Successful Habits of Visionary Companies*, London: Random House.

Collins, J.C. and Porras, J. (1996) 'Building your company's vision', *Harvard Business Review*, 75(5), pp. 65–77.

Collis, D.J. and Montgomery, C.A. (1995) 'Competing on resources: Strategy in the 1990s', *Harvard Business Review*, 73(4), pp. 118–128.

Compton, R.J. (2003) 'The interface between emotion and attention: A review of evidence from psychology and neuroscience', *Behavioral and Cognitive Neuroscience Reviews*, 2(2), pp. 115–129.

Contractor, F.J. and Lorange, P. (1988) *Cooperative Strategies in International Business*, Lexington, MA: Lexington Books.

Cookson, C. (2010) 'China set for global lead in scientific research', *Financial Times*, 26 January.

Cool, K. and Schendel, D. (1988) 'Performance differences among strategic group members', *Strategic Management Journal*, 9(3), pp. 207–223.

Cox, D. and Harris, R. (1985) 'Trade liberalization and industrial organization: Some estimates for Canada', *Journal of Political Economy*, 93, pp. 115–145.

Coxe D.O., Ganot, I., Keller G. and McGahan, A.M. (1996) 'Passion for Learning', HBS 9-796-057.

Cromie, S. (2000) 'Assessing entrepreneurial inclinations: Some approaches and empirical evidence', *European Journal of Work and Organizational Psychology*, 9(1), pp. 7–30.

Cummings, S. (1993) 'Brief case: The first strategists', *Long Range Planning*, 26(3), pp.

Cummings, S. and Davies, J. (1994) 'Mission, vision, fusion', *Long Range Planning*, 27(6), pp. 147–150.

Cusumano, M.A. and Gawer, A. (2002) 'The elements of platform leadership', *Sloan Management Review*, 43(3), pp. 51–58.

Cyert, R.M. (1990) 'Defining leadership and explicating the process', *Non-Profit Management and Leadership*, 1(1), pp. 29–38.

Cyert, R.M. and March, J.G. (1963) *A Behavioral Theory of the Firm*, Englewood Cliffs, NJ: Prentice Hall.

D'Aveni, R.A. (1994) *Hypercompetition: Managing the Dynamics of Strategic Maneuvering*, New York: Free Press.

D'Aveni, R.A. (1999) 'Strategic supremacy through disruption and dominance', *Sloan Management Review*, 40(3), pp. 127–135.

D'Iribarne, P. (1990) *La Logique d'Honneur*, Paris: Editions du Seuil.

D'Iribarne, P. (1996) 'The usefulness of an ethnographic approach to the international comparison of organizations', *International Studies of Management & Organization*, 26(4), pp. 30–47.

Daft, R.L. and Weick, K.E. (1984) 'Toward a model of organizations as interpretation systems', *Academy of Management Review*, 9(2), pp. 284–295.

Damasio, A.R. (1994) *Descartes' Error: Emotion, Reason, and the Human Brain*, New York: Putnam.

Dane, E. and Pratt, M.G. (2007) 'Exploring intuition and its role in managerial decision making', *Academy of Management Review*, 32(1), pp. 33–54.

David, F.R. (1989) 'How companies define their mission', *Long Range Planning*, 22(1), pp. 90–97.

David, H.A. (1981) *Order Statistics*, New York: Wiley (2nd ed.).

David, P.A. (1985) 'Clio and the economics of QWERTY', *American Economic Review*, 75(2), pp. 332–337.

David, P.A. (1990) 'The hero and the herd in technological history: Reflections on Thomas Edison and the battle of the systems', in: P. Higgonet and H. Rosovski (eds.) *Economic Development Past and Present: Opportunities and Constraints*, Cambridge, MA: Harvard University Press.

David, P.A. (1992) 'Heroes, herds and hysteresis in technological history: Thomas Edison and the battle of the system reconsidered', *Industrial and Corporate Change*, 1(1), pp. 129–180.

David, P.A. and Bunn, J.A. (1988) 'The economics of gateway technologies and network evolution: Lessons from electricity supply history', *Information Economics and Policy*, 3(2), pp. 165–202.

Davidow, W. and Malone, M. (1992) *The Virtual Corporation*, New York: HarperBusiness.

Dawes, R.M., Faust, D. and Meehl, P.E. (1989) 'Clinical versus actuarial judgment', *Science*, 31, pp. 1668–1674.

Day, D.L. (1994) 'Raising radicals: Different processes for championing innovative corporate ventures', *Organization Science*, 5(2), pp. 148–172.

Day, D.V. and Lord, R.G. (1992) 'Expertise and problem categorization: The role of expert processing in organizational sense-making', *Journal of Management Studies*, 29, pp. 35–47.

Day, G. and Moorman, C. (2010) *Strategy from the Outside in: Profiting from Customer Value*, New York: McGraw-Hill Professional.

Day, G.S. (1990) *Market Driven Strategy, Processes for Creating Value*, New York: Free Press.

Day, G.S. and Schoemaker, P.J.H. (2006) *Peripheral Vision: Detecting the Weak Signals That Will Make or Break Your Company*, Boston, MA: Harvard Business School Press.

Day, R.H. (1967) 'Profits, learning and the convergence of satisficing to marginalism', *Quarterly Journal of Economics*, 81, pp. 302–311.

De Geus, A. (1988) 'Planning as learning', *Harvard Business Review*, 66(2), pp. 70–74.

De Geus, A. (1997) *The Living Company*, Boston, MA: Harvard Business School Press.

Deal, T.E. and Kennedy, A.A. (1982) *Corporate Cultures: The Rites and Rituals of Organizational Life*, New York: Addison-Wesley.

DeDreu, C.K.W. (2003) 'Time pressure and closing of the mind in negotiation', *Organizational Behavior and Human Decision Processes*, 91, pp. 280–295.

Demb, A. and Neubauer, F.F. (1992) *The Corporate Board: Confronting the Paradoxes*, Oxford: Oxford University Press.

Denes-Raj, V. and Epstein, S. (1994) 'Conflict between intuitive and rational processing: When people behave against their better judgment', *Journal of Personality and Social Psychology*, 66, pp. 819–829.

Denison, D., Hooijberg, R. and Quinn, R.E. (1995) 'Paradox and performance: Toward a theory of behavioral complexity in managerial leadership', *Organization Science*, 6(5), pp. 524–540.

Denning, B.W. and Lehr, M.E. (1971) 'The extent and nature of long-range planning in the United Kingdom', *Journal of Management Studies*, 8, pp. 145–161.

Derks, B., Inzlicht M. and Kang, S. (2008) 'The neuroscience of stigma and stereotype threat', *Group Processes and Intergroup Relations*, 11(2), pp. 163–181.

Deutsch, M. (1973) *The Resolution of Conflict*, New Haven, CT: Yale University Press.

Diamond, J.M. (1997) *Guns, Germs and Steel: The Fates of Human Societies*, New York: W.W. Norton.

Dicken, P. (1986) *Global Shift: Industrial Change in a Turbulent World*, London: Harper & Row.

Dicken, P. (1992) *Global Shift: The Internationalisation of Economic Activity*, London: Chapman.

Dicken, P. (2003) *Global Shift: Reshaping the Global Economic Map in the 21st Century*, London: Sage.

Dicken, P. (2011) *Mapping the Changing Contours of the World Economy*, New York: Guilford Press (2nd ed.).

Dicken, P. (2015) *Global Shift: Mapping the Changing Contours of the World Economy*, New York: Guilford Press (7th ed.).

Dierickx, I. and Cool, K. (1989) 'Asset stock accumulation and sustainability of competitive advantage', *Management Science*, 35(12), pp. 1504–1511.

Dill, W.R. (1975) 'Public participation in corporate planning: Strategic management in a kibitzer's world', *Long Range Planning*, 8(1), pp. 57–63.

DiMaggio, P. and Powell, W.W. (1983) 'The iron cage revisited: Institutional isomorphism and collective rationality in organizational fields', *American Sociological Review*, 48, pp. 147–160.

Dixit, A.K. (1980) 'The role of investment in entry deterrence', *Economic Journal*, 90, pp. 95–106.

Dixit, A.K. and Nalebuff, B.J. (1991) *Thinking Strategically: The Competitive Edge in Business, Politics, and Everyday Life*, New York: W.W. Norton.

Dobbin, F. and Boychuk, T. (1999) 'National employment systems and job autonomy: Why job autonomy is high in the Nordic countries and low in the United States, Canada, and Australia', *Organization Studies*, 20(2), pp. 257–291.

Donaldson, L. and Davis, J.H. (1995) 'Boards and company performance: Research challenges the conventional wisdom', *Corporate Governance*, 2, pp. 151–160.

Donaldson, T. (2003) Editor's comments: 'Taking ethics seriously – A mission now more possible', *Academy of Management Review*, 28, pp. 363–366.

Donaldson, T. and Preston, L.E. (1995) 'The stakeholder theory of the corporation: Concepts, evidence, and implications', *Academy of Management Review*, 20(1), pp. 65–91.

Dosi, G. (1984) *Technical Change and Industrial Transformation*, London, Macmillan.

Dosi, G. and Kogut, B. (1993) 'National specificities and the context of change: The co-evolution of organization and technology', in: B. Kogut (ed.) *Country Competitiveness: Technology and the Organizing of Work*, Oxford: Oxford University Press.

Douglas, S.P. and Wind, Y. (1987) 'The myth of globalization', *Columbia Journal of World Business*, 22, Winter, pp. 19–29.

Dovidio, J.F., Pearson, A.R. and Orr, P. (2008) 'Social psychology and neuroscience: Strange bedfellows or a healthy marriage? ', *Group Processes and Intergroup Relations*, 11(2), pp. 247–263.

Doz, Y. and Hamel, G. (1998) *The Alliance Advantage: The Art of Creating Value Through Partnering*, Boston, MA: Harvard Business School Press.

Doz, Y. and Prahalad, C.K. (1984) 'Patterns of strategic control within multinational corporations', *Journal of International Business Studies*, 15(2), pp. 55–72.

Doz, Y. and Shuen, A. (1990) 'From intent to outcome: A process framework for partnerships', INSEAD working paper.

Doz, Y. and Kosonen, M. (2008) *Fast Strategy: How Strategic Agility Will Help You Stay Ahead of the Game*, Harlow: Pearson.

Dretske, F. (1981) *Knowledge and the Flow of Information*, Cambridge, MA: MIT Press.

Dreyfus, H.L. and Dreyfus, S.E. (1986) *Mind over Machine: The Power of Human Intuition and Expertise in the Era of the Computer*, New York: Free Press.

Drucker, P.F. (1984) 'The new meaning of corporate social responsibility', *California Management Review*, 26(2), pp. 53–63.

Drummond, H. (2001) *The Art of Decision Making: Mirrors of Imagination, Masks of Fate*, Chichester: Wiley.

Duncan, R. (1976) 'The ambidextrous organization: Designing dual structures for innovation', in: R.H. Killman, L.R. Pondy and D. Sleven (eds.) *The Management of Organization*, New York: North-Holland, pp. 167–188.

Duncan, R.B. (1976) 'The ambidextrous organization: Designing dual structures for innovation', in: R.H. Kilman, L.R. Pondy and D.P. Slevin (eds.), *The Management of Organizational Design*, New York: Elsevier North-Holland, pp. 167–188.

Dunning, J.H. (1958) *American Investment in British Manufacturing Industry*, London: George Allen & Unwin.

Dunning, J.H. (1980) 'Toward an eclectic theory of international production: Some empirical tests', *Journal of International Business Studies*, 11(1), pp. 9–31.

Dunning, J.H. (1981) *International Production and the Multinational Enterprise*, London: Allen & Unwin.

Dunning, J.H. (1986) *Japanese Participation in British Industry: Trojan Horse or Catalyst for Growth?* Dover, NH: Croom Helm.

Dunning, J.H. (1988) *Explaining International Production*, London: Unwin Hyman.

Dunning, J.H. (1993) *The Globalization of Business*, London: Routledge.

Dunning, J.H. (1998) 'Location and the multinational enterprise: A neglected factor?', *Journal of International Business Studies*, 29(1), pp. 45–66.

Dunning, J.H. (2000) 'The eclectic paradigm as an envelope for economic and business theories of MNE activity', *International Business Review*, 9(2), pp.163–190.

Dunning, J.H. (2001) 'The key literature on IB activities: 1960–2000', in: A.M. Rugman and T.L. Brewer, *The Oxford Handbook of International Business*, Oxford: Oxford University Press, pp. 36–68.

Durand, T. (1996) 'Revisiting key dimensions of competence', paper presented to the SMS Conference, Phoenix.

Dutton, J.E. (1988) 'Understanding strategies agenda building and its implications for managing change', in: L.R. Pondy, R.J. Boland, Jr. and H. Thomas (eds.) *Managing Ambiguity and Change*, Chichester: Wiley.

Dutton, J.E. (1993) 'Interpretations on automatic: A different view of strategic issue diagnosis', *Journal of Management Studies*, 30(3), pp. 339–357.

Dutton, J.E. and Ashford, S.J. (1993) 'Selling issues to top management', *Academy of Management Review*, 18(3), pp. 397–428.

Dutton, J.E. and Jackson, S.E. (1987) 'Categorizing strategic issues: Links to organizational action', *Academy of Management Review*, 12(1), pp. 76–90.

Dyer, J.H. and Ouchi, W.G. (1993) 'Japanese-style partnerships: Giving companies a competitive edge', *Sloan Management Review*, Fall, pp. 51–63.

Dyer, J.H. and Singh, H. (1998) 'The relational view: Cooperative strategy and sources of inter-organizational competitive advantage', *Academy of Management Review*, 23(4), pp. 660–679.

Dyer, J.H., Kale, P. and Singh, H. (2001) 'How to make strategic alliances work', *Sloan Management Review*, 42(4), pp. 37–43.

Eagly, A.H. and Johannesen-Schmidt, M.C. (2001) 'The leadership styles of women and men', *Journal of Social Issues*, 57(4), pp. 781–797.

Eagly, A.H. and Johnson, B.T. (1990) 'Gender and leadership style: A meta-analysis', *Psychological Bulletin*, 108(2), p. 233.

Eden, C. (1989) 'Using cognitive mapping for strategic options development and analysis (SODA)', in: J. Rosenhead (ed.) *Rational Analysis in a Problematic World*, London: Wiley.

Eden, C. and Ackermann, F. (1998) *Making Strategy: The Journey of Strategic Management*, London: Sage.

Edland, A. and Svenson, O. (1993) 'Judgment and decision making under time pressure', in: O. Svenson and A. J. Maule (eds.) *Time Pressure and Stress in Human Judgment and Decision making*, New York: Plenum Press, pp. 27–40.

Edmondson, A. (1999) 'Psychological safety and learning behavior in work teams', *Administrative Science Quarterly*, 44(2), pp. 350–383.

Edmondson, A.C., Roberto, M.A. and Watkins, M.D. (2003) 'A dynamic model of top management team effectiveness: Managing unstructured task streams', *Administrative Science Quarterly*, 14(3), pp. 297–325.

Eisenhardt, K.M. (1985) 'Control: Organizational and economic approaches', *Management Science*, 31, pp. 134–149.

Eisenhardt, K.M. (1989a) 'Agency theory: An assessment and review', *Academy of Management Review*, 14(1), pp. 57–74.

Eisenhardt, K.M. (1989b) 'Making fast strategic decisions in high-velocity environments', *Academy of Management Journal*, 32, pp. 543–559.

Eisenhardt, K.M. (2000) 'Paradox, spirals, ambivalence: The new language of change and pluralism', *Academy of Management Review*, 25(4), pp. 703–705.

Eisenhardt, K.M. and Brown, S.L. (1997) 'The art of continuous change: Linking complexity theory and time-paced evolution in relentlessly shifting organizations', *Administrative Science Quarterly*, 42(1), pp. 1–34.

Eisenhardt, K.M. and Brown, S.L. (1998) 'Time pacing: Competing in markets that won't stand still', *Harvard Business Review*, 76(2), p. 59.

Eisenhardt, K.M. and Galunic, D.C. (2000) 'Coevolving: At last, a way to make synergies work', *Harvard Business Review*, 78(1), pp. 91–101.

Eisenhardt, K.M. and Martin, J.A. (2000) 'Dynamic capabilities: What are they?', *Strategic Management Journal*, 21, pp. 1105–1121.

Eisenhardt, K.M. and Sull, D.N. (2001) 'Strategy as simple rules', *Harvard Business Review*, 79(1), pp. 107–116.

Eisenhardt, K.M. and Westcott, B.J. (1988) 'Paradoxical demands and the creation of excellence: The case of just-in-time manufacturing', in: R. Quinn and K. Cameron (eds.) *Paradox and Transformation: Towards a Theory of Change in Organization and Management*, Cambridge, MA: Ballinger, pp. 169–194.

Eisenhardt, K.M. and Zbaracki, M.J. (1992) 'Strategic decision making', *Strategic Management Journal*, 13(S2), pp. 17–37.

Eisenhardt, K.M., Kahwajy, J.L. and Bourgeois L.J. (1997) 'Conflict and strategic choice: How top management teams disagree', *California Management Review*, 39(2), pp. 42–62.

Elkington, J. (1980) *The Ecology of Tomorrow's World*, London: Associated Press.

Elkington, J. (1997) *Cannibals with Forks: The Triple Bottom Line of 21st Century Business*, Oxford: Capstone Publishing.

Elkington, J. and Burke, T. (1987) *The Green Capitalists: Industry's Search for Environmental Excellence*, London: Victor Gollancz.

Elsbach, K.D. and Barr, P.S. (1999) 'The effects of mood on individuals' use of structured decision protocols', *Organization Science*, 10(2), pp. 181–198.

Elsbach, K.D. and Kramer, R.M. (1996) 'Members' responses to organizational identity threats: Encountering and countering the *Business Week* rankings', *Administrative Science Quarterly*, 41(3), pp. 442–476.

Elster, J. (1999) *Alchemies of the Mind: Rationality and the Emotions*, Cambridge: Cambridge University Press.

Emerson, J. (2003) 'The blended value proposition: Integrating social and financial returns', *California Management Review*, Summer.

Emery, F.E. and Trist, E.L. (1965) 'The causal texture of organizational environments', *Human Relations*, 18, pp. 21–32.

Epstein, E.M. (1987) 'The corporate social policy process: Beyond business ethics, corporate social responsibility, and corporate social responsiveness', *California Management Review*, 29(3), pp. 99–114.

Epstein, S. (1990) 'Cognitive-experiential self-theory', in: L. Pervin (ed.) *Handbook of Personality: Theory and Research*, New York: Guilford Press, pp. 165–192.

Epstein, S. (1994) 'Integration of the cognitive and psychodynamic unconscious', *American Psychologist*, 49, pp. 709–724.

Epstein, S. (2002) 'Cognitive-experiential self-theory of personality', in: T. Millon and M. J. Lerner (eds.) *Comprehensive Handbook of psychology. Volume 5: Personality and Social Psychology*, Hoboken, NJ: Wiley, pp. 159–184.

Epstein, S. and Pacini, R. (1999) 'Some basic issues regarding dual-process theories from the perspective of cognitive experiential self-theory', in: S. Chaiken and Y. Trope (eds.) *Dual-Process Theories in Social Psychology*, New York: Guilford Press, pp. 462–482.

Epstein, S., Pacini, R., Denes-Raj, V. and Heier, H. (1996) 'Individual differences in intuitive-experiential and analytical rational thinking styles', *Journal of Personality and Social Psychology*, 71, pp. 390–405.

Ericsson, K.A. and Charness, N. (1994) 'Expert performance: Its structures and acquisition', *American Psychologist*, 49, pp. 725–747.

Ericsson, K.A. and Lehmann, A.C. (1996) 'Experts and exceptional performance: Evidence of maximal adaptation to task constraints', *Annual Review of Psychology*, 47, pp. 273– 305.

Ericsson, K.A. and Smith, J. (1991) 'Prospects and limits of the empirical study of expertise: An introduction', in: K.A. Ericsson and J. Smith (eds.) *Toward a General Theory of Expertise*, New York: Cambridge University Press, pp. 1–38.

Ericsson, K.A., Krampe, R.T. and Tesch-Römer, C. (1993) 'The role of deliberate practice in the acquisition of expert performance', *Psychological Review*, 100, pp. 363–406.

Ettlie, J.E. and Pavlou, P.A. (2006) 'Technology-based new product development partnerships', *Decision Sciences*, 37(2), pp. 117–147.

Etzioni, A. (1961) *A Comparative Analysis of Complex Organizations*, New York: Free Press.

Evans, J.S. (1991) 'Strategic flexibility for high technology manoeuvres: A conceptual framework', *Journal of Management Studies*, 28, January, pp. 69–89.

Evans, P.B. and Wurster, T.S. (1997) 'Strategy and the new economics of information', *Harvard Business Review*, 76(5), pp. 71–82.

Ewing, D.W. (1956) 'Looking around: Long-range business planning', *Harvard Business Review*, 56(4), pp. 135–146.

Falsey, T.A. (1989) *Corporate Philosophies and Mission Statements*, New York: Quorum.

Fama, E.F. (1980) 'Agency problems and the theory of the firm', *Journal of Political Economy*, 88, pp. 288–307.

Fayerweather, J. (1969) 'International business management', *The International Executive*, 11(1), pp. 10–11.

Fayol, H. (1916/1949) *General and Industrial Management*, London: Pitman. February, pp. 3–17.

Ferguson, G. (1999) *Cracking the Intuition Code*, Chicago, IL: Contemporary Books.

Fichter, K. and Beucker, S. (2012) *Innovation Communities: Teamworking of Key Persons – A Success Factor in Radical Innovation*, Amsterdam: Springer-Verlag.

Fieldhouse, D.K. (1978) *Unilever Overseas: The Anatomy of a Multinational 1895–1965*, London: Croom Helm.

Financial Times Global 50 (2015) *Financial Times*, 19 June.

Financial Times Global 500 (2006) *Financial Times*, 9 June.

Finkelstein, S. and Hambrick, D.C. (1996) *Strategic leadership: Top Executives and Their Effect on Organizations*, St. Paul, MN: West.

Finkelstein, S., Whitehead, J. and Campbell, A. (2008) *Think Again: Why Good Leaders Make Bad Decisions and How to Keep it From Happening to You*, Boston, MA: Harvard Business School Press.

Finucane, M.L., Alhakami, A., Slovic, P. and Johnson, S.M. (2000) 'The affect heuristic in judgments of risks and benefits', *Journal of Behavioral Decision Making*, 13(1), pp. 1–17.

Fischhoff, B. (1982) 'Debiasing', in: Kahneman, D., Slovic, P. and Tversky, A. (eds.) *Judgment Under Uncertainty: Heuristics and Biases*, Cambridge: Cambridge University Press, pp. 422–444.

Fiske, S.T. and Taylor, S.E. (1991) *Social Cognition*, New York: McGraw-Hill (2nd ed.).

Fletcher, J.L. and Olwyler, K. (1997) *Paradoxical Thinking: How to Profit from Your Contradictions*, San Francisco, CA: Berrett-Koehler.

Floyd, S.W. and Wooldridge, B. (2000) *Building Strategy from the Middle Reconceptualizing Strategy Process*, Thousand Oaks, CA: Sage.

Flynn, F.J. and Chatman, J.A. (2001) 'Strong cultures and innovation: Oxymoron and opportunity?', in: C. Cooper, S. Cartwright and C. Early (eds.) *International Handbook of Organizational Culture and Climate*, Chichester: Wiley, pp. 263–287.

Follett, M.P. (1925/1996) 'Constructive conflict', in: P. Graham (ed.) *Mary Parker Follett: Prophet of Management*, Boston, MA: Harvard Business School Press.

Ford, J.D. and Backoff, R.W. (1988) 'Organizational change in and out of dualities and paradox', in: R. Quinn and K. Cameron (eds.) *Paradox and Transformation*, Cambridge, MA: Ballinger, pp. 81–121.

Forrester, J.W. (2003) 'Dynamic models of economic systems and industrial organizations', *System Dynamics Review*, 19(4), pp. 329–345.

Foster, R. (1986) *Innovation: The Attacker's Advantage*, New York: Summit Books.

Frank, A.G. (1966) *The Development of Underdevelopment*, New York: Monthly Review Press.

Frankel, V. (1960) 'Paradoxical intention', *American Journal of Psychotherapy*, 14, pp.

Franquemont, S. (1999) *You Already Know What to Do*, New York: Jeremy P. Tarcher/Putnam.

Fredrickson, B.L. and Branigan, C. (2005) 'Positive emotions broaden the scope of attention and thought action repertoires', *Cognition and Emotion*, 19, pp. 313–332.

Fredrickson, J.W., Hambrick, D.C. and Baumrin, S. (1988) 'A model of CEO dismissal', *Academy of Management Review*, 13(2), pp. 255–270.

Freeman, C. (1974) *The Economics of Industrial Innovation*, Harmondsworth: Penguin.

Freeman, C. and Perez, C. (1988) 'Structural crises of adjustment, business cycles and investment behavior', in: G. Dosi, C. Freeman, R. Nelson, G. Silverberg and L. Soete (eds.) *Technical Change And Economic Theory*, London and New York: Pinter.

Freeman, R.E. (1984) *Strategic Management: A Stakeholder Approach*, Boston, MA: Pitman/Ballinger.

Freeman, R.E. and Gilbert Jr., D.R. (1988) *Corporate Strategy and the Search for Ethics*, Englewood Cliffs, NJ: Prentice Hall.

Freeman, R.E. and Liedtka, J. (1991) 'Corporate social responsibility: A critical approach', *Business Horizons*, July–August.

Freeman, R.E. and Reed, D.L. (1983) 'Stockholders and stakeholders: A new perspective on corporate governance', *California Management Review*, 25(3), pp. 88–106.

French, J. and Raven, B.H. (1959) 'The bases of social power', in: D. Cartwright (ed.) *Studies of Social Power*, Ann Arbor, MI: Institute for Social Research.

Friedman, M. (1962) *Capitalism and Freedom*, Chicago, IL: University of Chicago Press.

Friedman, M. (1970) 'The social responsibility of business is to increase its profits', *New York Times Magazine*, September 13–13.

Friedman, T.L. (2005) *The World is Flat: A Brief History of the Twenty-first Century*, New York: Farrar, Straus & Giroux.

Fröbel, F., Heinrichs, J. and Kreye, O. (1980) *The Tendency Towards a New International Division of Labor: The Utilization of a World-Wide Labor Force for Manufacturing Oriented to the World Market*, Cambridge: Cambridge University Press.

Fukayama, F. (1992) *The End of History and the Last Man*, New York: Free Press.

Fukuyama, F. (1995) *Trust: Social Virtues and the Creation of Prosperity*, New York: Free Press.

Fukayama, F. (2004) *State-Building: Governance and World Order in the 21st Century*, Ithaca, NY: Cornell University Press.

Fukayama, F. (2011) *The Origins of Political Order*, London: Profile Books.

Gambetta, D. (ed.) (1988) *Trust: Making and Breaking Cooperative Relations*, New York: Blackwell.

Garvin, D. (1988) *Managing Quality*, New York: Free Press.

Gastells, M. (2006) *The Rise of The Network Society*, Oxford: Basil Blackwell.

Gavetti, G. (2005) 'Cognition and hierarchy: rethinking the microfoundations of capabilities development', *Organization Science*, 16(6), pp. 599–617.

Gavetti, G. and Levinthal, D.A. (2000) 'Looking forward and looking backward: Cognitive and experiential search', *Administrative Science Quarterly*, 45(1), pp. 113–137.

Gavetti, G., Levinthal, D.A. and Ocasio, W. (2007) 'Neo-Carnegie: The Carnegie School's past, present, and reconstructing for the future', *Organization Science*, 18(3), pp. 523–

Gell-Mann, M. (1994) *The Quark and the Jaguar*, New York: Freeman.

Gerlach, M. (1992) *Alliance Capitalism: The Social Organization of Japanese Business*, Berkeley, CA: University of California Press.

Gersick, C.J.G. (1991) 'Revolutionary change theories: A multilevel exploration of the punctuated equilibrium paradigm', *Academy of Management Review*, 17(1), pp. 10–36.

Gevedon, S.L. (1992) 'Leadership behaviors of deans of top-ranked schools of nursing', *Journal of Nursing Education*, 31(5), pp. 221–224.

Ghemawat, P. (1991) *Commitment: The Dynamic of Strategy*, New York: Free Press.

Ghemawat, P. (2002) 'Competition and business strategy in historical perspective', *Business History Review*, 76(1), pp. 37–74.

Ghemawat, P. (2005) 'Regional strategies for global leadership', *Harvard Business Review*, 83(12), p. 98.

Ghemawat, P. (2007) *Redefining Global Strategy*, Boston, MA: Harvard Business School Press.

Ghoshal, S. and Mintzberg, H. (1994) 'Diversification and diversifact', *California Management Review*, 37(1), pp. 8–27.

Gibson, C.B. (1995) 'An investigation of gender differences in leadership across four countries', *Journal of International Business Studies*, pp. 255–279.

Gibson, C.B. and Birkinshaw, J. (2004) 'The antecedents, consequences, and mediating role of organizational ambidexterity', *Academy of Management Journal*, 47(2), pp. 209–226.

Gilbert, C.G. (2005) 'Unbundling the structure of inertia: Resource versus routine rigidity', *Academy of Management Journal*, 48(5), pp. 741–763.

Gilbert, R.J. and Newbery, D.M. (1982) 'Preemptive patenting and the persistence of monopoly', *American Economic Review*, 72, pp. 514–526.

Gilbert, X. and Lorange, P. (1995) 'National approaches to strategic management: A resource-based perspective', *International Business Review*, 3(4), pp. 411–423.

Gilbert, X. and Strebel, P. (1989) 'From innovation to outpacing', *Business Quarterly*, Summer, pp. 19–22.

Gilovich, T., Griffin, D. and Kahneman, D. (eds.) (2002) *Heuristics and Biases: The Psychology of Intuitive Judgment*, New York: Cambridge University Press.

Gioia, D.A. and Chittipeddi, K. (1991) 'Sensemaking and sensegiving in strategic change intuition', *Strategic Management Journal*, 12, pp. 433–448.

Gioia, D.A., Schultz, M. and Corley, K.G. (2000) 'Organizational identity, image, and adaptive instability', *Academy of Management Review*, 25(1), pp. 63–81.

Gladwell, M. (2007) *Blink: The Power of Thinking Without Thinking*, New York: Back Bay Books (1st ed.).

Glassman, R.M. (1986) 'Manufactured charisma and legitimacy', in: R.M. Glassman and W.H. Swatos, Jr. (eds.) *Charisma, History, and Social Structure*, New York: Glenwood Press.

Glynn, M.A. (2000) 'When cymbals become symbols: Conflict over organizational identity within a symphony orchestra', *Organization Science*, 11(3), pp. 285–298.

Gnyawali, D.R. and Madhavan, R. (2001) 'Cooperative networks and competitive dynamics: A structural embeddedness perspective', *Academy of Management Review*, 26(3), pp. 431–445.

Goldsmith, M. and Larsen, H. (2004) 'Local political leadership: Nordic style', *International Journal of Urban and Regional Research*, 28(1), pp. 121–133.

Gollwitzer, P. and Bayer, U. (1999) 'Deliberative versus implemental mindsets in the control of action', in: S. Chaiken and Y. Trope (eds.) *Dual-Process Theories in Social Psychology*, New York: Guilford Press, pp. 403–422.

Gomes-Casseres, B. (1994) 'Group versus group: How alliance networks compete', *Harvard Business Review*, 72(4), pp. 62–74.

Goncalo, J.A. and Staw, B.M. (2006) 'Individualism–collectivism and group creativity', *Organizational Behavior and Human Decision Processes*, 100(1), pp. 96–109.

Goold, M. (1992) 'Design, learning and planning: A further observation on the design school debate', *Strategic Management Journal*, 13(2), pp. 169–170.

Goold, M. and Quinn, J.J. (1990a) 'The paradox of strategic controls', *Strategic Management Journal*, 11, pp. 43–57.

Goold, M. and Quinn, J.J. (1990b) *Strategic Control: Milestones for Long-Term Performance*, London: Hutchinson.

Goold, M. and Campbell, A. (1987) *Strategies and Styles: The Role of the Centre in Managing Diverse Corporations*, Oxford: Basil Blackwell.

Goold, M. and Lansdell, S. (1997) *Survey of Corporate Strategy Objectives, Concepts and Tools*, London: Ashridge Strategic Management Centre.

Goold, M., Campbell, A. and Alexander, M. (1994) *Corporate-Level Strategy: Creating Value in the Multibusiness Company*, New York: Wiley.

Gottschalg, O. and Zollo M. (2007) 'Interest alignment and competitive advantage', *Academy of Management Review*, 32(2), pp. 418–437.

Gramsci, A. (1934) 'Americanism and Fordism', in: A. Gramsci, *The Prison Notebooks*, New York: Columbia University Press.

Granovetter, M.S. (1985) 'Economic action and social structure: The problem of embeddedness', *American Journal of Sociology*, 91, pp. 481–501.

Grant, R.M. (1996) 'Prospering in dynamically-competitive environments: Organizational capability as knowledge integration', *Organization Science*, 7(4), pp. 375–387.

Grant, R.M. (2002) *Contemporary Strategy Analysis: Concepts, Techniques, Applications*, Oxford: Blackwell (4th ed.).

Grant, R.M. and Cibin, R. (1996) 'Strategy, structure and market turbulence: The international oil majors, 1970–91', *Scandinavian Journal of Management*, 12, pp. 165–188.

Grayson, L.E. (1987) *Who and How in Planning for Large Companies: Generalizations from the Experiences of Oil Companies*, New York: St. Martin's Press.

Greenhalgh, L. (2001) *Managing Strategic Relationships*, New York: Free Press.

Greenleaf, R.K. (1977) *Servant Leadership: A Journey into the Nature of Legitimate Power and Greatness*, New York: Paulist Press.

Greenwood, R. and Hinings, C.R. (1996) 'Understanding radical organizational change: Bringing together the old and the new institutionalism', *Academy of Management Review*, 21(4), pp. 1022–1054.

Greider, (1997) *One World, Ready or Not: The Manic Logic of Global Capitalism*, San Francisco, CA: Jossey-Bass.

Greiner, L.E. (1972) 'Evolution and revolution as organizations grow', *Harvard Business Review*, 50(4), pp. 37–46.

Grinyer, P.H. and Norburn, D. (1975) 'Strategic planning in 21 UK companies', *Long Range Planning*, 7, August, pp. 80–88.

Grinyer, P.H., Al-Bazzaz, S. and Yasai-Ardekani, M. (1986) 'Towards a contingency theory of corporate planning: Findings in 48 UK companies', *Strategic Management Journal*, 7, pp. 3–28.

Grinyer, P.H., Mayes, D. and McKiernan, P. (1987) *Sharpbenders: The Secrets of Unleashing Corporate Potential*, Oxford: Blackwell.

Groenewegen, J. and Beije, P.R. (1989) 'The French communication industry defined and analyzed through the social fabric matrix, the filière approach, and network analysis', *Journal of Economic Issues*, 23(4), pp. 1059–1074.

Groves, K.S., Vance, C.M., Choi, D.Y. and Mendez, J.L. (2008) 'An examination of the nonlinear thinking style profile stereotype of successful entrepreneurs', *Journal of Enterprising Culture*, 16(02), 133–159.

Guenther, H.V. (1958) 'The levels of understanding in Buddhism', *Journal of the American Oriental Society*, 78, pp. 19–28.

Guillén, M. (2001) *The Limits of Convergence: Globalization and Organizational Change in Argentina, South Korea and Spain*, Princeton, NJ: Princeton University Press.

Gulati, R. (1998) 'Alliances and networks', *Strategic Management Journal*, 19(4), pp. 293–317.

Gupta, A.K., Smith, K.G. and Shalley, C.E. (2006) 'The interplay between exploration and exploitation', *Academy of Management Journal*, 49(4), pp. 693–706.

Guthrie, J. and Turnbull, S. (1994) 'Audit committees: Is there a role for corporate senates and/or stakeholder councils?', *Corporate Governance*, 3, pp. 78–89.

Hackman, J.R. (2002) *Leading Teams: Setting the Stage for Great Performances*, Boston, MA: Harvard Business School Press.

Haidt, J. (2001) 'The emotional dog and its rational tail: A social intuitionist approach to moral judgment', *Psychological Review*, 108, pp. 814–834.

Hakansson, H. and Johanson, J. (1993) 'The network as a governance structure: Interfirm cooperation beyond markets and hierarchies', in: G. Grabner (ed.) *The Embedded Firm: On the Socioeconomics of Industrial Networks*, London: Routledge, pp. 35–51.

Hall, E.T. (1976) *Beyond Culture*, New York: Knopf Doubleday Publishing Group.

Hall, P.A. and Soskice D. (eds.) (2001) *Varieties of Capitalism: The Institutional Foundations of Comparative Advantage*, New York: Oxford University Press.

Hambrick, D.C. (1987) 'Top management teams: Key to strategic success', *California Management Review*, 30, pp. 88–108.

Hambrick, D.C. (1994) 'Top management groups: A conceptual integration and reconsideration of the "team" label', in: B.M. Staw and L. Cummings (eds.) *Research in Organizational Behavior*, Greenwich, CT: JAI Press.

Hambrick, D.C. and Abrahamson, E. (1995) 'Assessing the amount of managerial discretion in different industries: A multi-method approach', *Academy of Management Journal*, 38(5), pp. 1427–1441.

Hambrick, D.C. and Mason, P.A. (1984) 'Upper echelons: The organization as a reflection of its top managers', *Academy of Management Review*, 9(2), pp. 193–206.

Hambrick, D.C., Geletkanycz, M.A. and Fredrickson, J.W. (1993) 'Top executive commitment to the status quo: Some tests of its determinants', *Strategic Management Journal*, 14(6), pp. 401–418.

Hamel, G. (1991) 'Competition for competence and inter-partner learning within international strategic alliances', *Strategic Management Journal*, 12, Special Issue, Summer, pp. 83–103.

Hamel, G. (1996) 'Strategy as revolution', *Harvard Business Review*, 74(4), pp. 69–82.

Hamel, G. (2000) *Leading the Revolution*, Boston, MA: Harvard Business School Press.

Hamel, G. and Prahalad, C.K. (1985) 'Do you really have a global strategy?', *Harvard Business Review*, 63(4), pp. 139–148.

Hamel, G. and Prahalad, C.K. (1989, 2005) 'Strategic intent', *Harvard Business Review*, 83(7), pp. 148–161.

Hamel, G. and Prahalad, C.K. (1993) 'Strategy as stretch and leverage', *Harvard Business Review*, 71(2), pp. 75–84.

Hamel, G. and Prahalad, C.K. (1994) *Competing for the Future: Breakthrough Strategies for Seizing Control of Your Industry and Creating the Markets of Tomorrow*, Boston, MA: Harvard Business School Press.

Hamel, G., Doz, Y.L. and Prahalad, C.K. (1989) 'Collaborate with your competitors – and win', *Harvard Business Review*, 67(1), pp. 133–139.

Hamilton, G.G. and Woolsey Biggart, N. (1988) 'Market, culture and authority: A comparative analysis of management and organization in the Far East', *American Journal of Sociology*, 94, p. 52.

Hammer, M. (1990) 'Reengineering work: Don't automate, obliterate', *Harvard Business Review*, 68(4), pp. 104–111.

Hammer, M. and Champy, J. (1993) *Reengineering the Corporation: A Manifesto for Business Revolution*, New York: HarperCollins.

Hammer, M., Leonard, D. and Davenport, T. (2004) 'Why don't we know more about knowledge?', *MIT Sloan Management Review*, 45(4), pp. 14–18.

Hammond, K.R., Hamm, R.M., Grassia, J. and Pearson, T. (1987) 'Direct comparison of the efficacy of intuitive and analytical cognition in expert judgment', *IEEE Transactions on Systems, Man, and Cybernetics*, 17, pp. 753–770.

Hampden-Turner, C. and Trompenaars, A. (1993) *The Seven Cultures of Capitalism: Value Systems for Creating Wealth in the United States, Japan, Germany, France, Britain, Sweden and the Netherlands*, New York: Doubleday.

Hampden-Turner, C. and Trompenaars, F. (2000) *Building Cross-cultural Competence: How to Create Wealth from Conflicting Values*, New Haven, CT: Yale University Press.

Handy, C. (1990) *The Age of Unreason*, Boston, MA: Harvard Business School Press.

Hannan, M.T. and Freeman, J. (1977) 'The population ecology of organizations', *American Journal of Sociology*, 82(5), pp. 929–964.

Hannan, M.T. and Freeman, J. (1984) 'Structural inertia and organizational change', *American Sociological Review*, 49(2), pp. 149–164.

Hannan, M.T. and Freeman, J. (1987) 'The ecology of organizational foundings: American labor unions, 1836–1985', *American Journal of Sociology*, 92, pp. 910–943.

Hannan, M.T. and Freeman, J. (1989) *Organizational Ecology*, Cambridge, MA: Harvard University Press.

Hanoch, Y., Johnson, J.G. and Wilke, A. (2006) 'Domain specificity in experimental measures and participant recruitment: An application to risk-taking behavior', *Psychological Science*, 17(4), 300–304.

Hansen, G.S. and Wernerfelt, B. (1989) 'Determinants of firm performance: The relative importance of economic and organizational factors', *Strategic Management Journal*, 10(5), pp. 399–411.

Harper, S.C. (1989) 'Intuition: What separates executives from managers', in: W.H. Agor (ed.) *Intuition in Organizations: Leading and Managing Productively*, Newbury Park, CA: Sage, pp. 111–124.

Harrigan, K.R. (1985) 'Vertical integration and corporate strategy', *Academy of Management Journal*, 28(2), pp. 397–425.

Harris, S., Forbes, T. and Fletcher, M. (2000) 'Taught and enacted strategic approaches in young enterprises', *International Journal of Entrepreneurial Behavior & Research*, 6(3), pp. 125–145

Hart, O.D. (1995) *Firms, Contracts and Financial Structure*, Oxford: Clarendon Press.

Hart, S.L. (1992) 'An integrative framework for strategy-making processes', *Academy of Management Review*, 17(2), pp. 327–351.

Haslam, S.A., Eggins, R.A. and Reynolds, K.J. (2003) 'The ASPIRe model: Actualizing social and personal identity resources to enhance organizational outcomes', *Journal of Occupational and Organizational Psychology*, 76, pp. 83–113.

Haspeslagh, P. (1982) 'Portfolio planning: Uses and limits', *Harvard Business Review*, 60(1), pp. 58–73.

Hax, A.C. (1990) 'Redefining the concept of strategy and the strategy formation process', *Planning Review*, May–June, pp. 34–40.

Hax, A.C. and Majluf, N.S. (1984) *Strategic Management: An Integrative Approach*, Englewood Cliffs, NJ: Prentice Hall.

Hayashi, A.M. (2001) 'When to trust your gut', *Harvard Business Review*, 79(2), pp. 59–65.

Hayashi, K. (1978) 'Corporate planning practices in Japanese multinationals', *Academy of Management Journal*, 21(2), pp. 211–226.

Hayes, R. (1985) 'Strategic planning: Forward in reverse', *Harvard Business Review*, 63(6), pp. 111–119.

Hayes, R. and Abernathy, W. (1980) 'Managing our way to economic decline', *Harvard Business Review*, 58(4), pp. 66–77.

Hayes, R., Wheelwright, S. and Clark, K. (1988) *Dynamic Manufacturing: Creating the Learning Organization*, New York: Free Press.

Hayes, R.H. (1985) 'Strategic planning: Forward in reverse?', *Harvard Business Review*, 63(6), pp. 111–119.

Hayward, M.L.A., Rindova, V.P. and Pollock, T.G. (2004) 'Believing one's own press: The causes and consequences of CEO celebrity', *Strategic Management Journal*, 25(7), pp. 637–653.

He, Z.L. and Wong, P.K. (2004) 'Exploration vs. exploitation: An empirical test of the ambidexterity hypothesis', *Organization Science*, 15(4), pp. 481–494.

Healey, M.P. and Hodgkinson, G.P. (2008) 'Troubling futures: Scenarios and scenario planning for organizational decision making', in: G.P. Hodgkinson and W.H. Starbuck (eds.) *The Oxford Handbook of Organizational Decision Making*, Oxford: Oxford University Press, pp. 565–585.

Heasman, M. and Mellentin, J. (2001) The Functional Foods Revolution: Healthy People, Healthy Profits?, London: Earthscan Publications.

Heath, C. (2010) 'Making the emotional case for change', *McKinsey Quarterly*, March, pp. 88–97.

Hedley, B. (1977) 'Strategy and the "business portfolio"', *Long Range Planning*, 10(1), pp. 9–15.

Hedlund, G. (1986) 'The hypermodern MNC – a heterarchy?', *Human Resource Management*, 25, pp. 9–35.

Heenan, D.A. and Bennis, W.G. (1999) *Co-leaders: The Power of Great Partnerships*, New York: Wiley.

Helfat, C.E. and Eisenhardt, K.M. (2004) 'Inter-temporal economies of scope, organizational modularity, and the dynamics of diversification', *Strategic Management Journal*, 25(13), pp. 1217–1296.

Helfat, C.E. and Peteraf, M. (2003) 'The dynamic resource-based view: Capability lifecycles', *Strategic Management Journal*, October, Special Issue 24, pp. 997–1010.

Hemp, P. and Stewart, T.A. (2004) 'Leading change when business is good: An interview with Sam Palmisano', *Harvard Business Review*, 82(12), pp. 60–71.

Henderson, B.D. (1979) *On Corporate Strategy*, Cambridge, MA: Abt Books.

Henderson, M.D., Gollwitzer, P.M. and Oettingen, G. (2007) 'Implementation intentions and disengagement from a failing course of action', *Journal of Behavioral Decision Making*, 20(1), pp. 81–102.

Henderson, R.M. and Clark, K.B. (1990) 'Architectural innovation: The reconfiguration of existing product technologies and the failure of established firms', *Administrative Science Quarterly*, 35(1), pp. 9–30.

Hennart, J.F. (1977) 'A theory of foreign direct investment', PhD dissertation, University of Maryland.

Hennart, J.-F. (2014) 'The accidental internationalists: A theory of born globals', *Entrepreneurship Theory and Practice*, 38(1), pp. 117–135.

Henry, H.W. (1967) *Long-Range Planning Practices in 45 Industrial Companies*, Englewood Cliffs, NJ: Prentice Hall.

Henry, J. (2003) *Understanding Japanese Society*, London: Routledge.

Herriott, S.R., Levinthal, D.A. and March, J.G. (1985) 'Learning from experience in organizations', *American Economic Review*, 75(2), pp. 298–302.

Hey, J.D. (1982) 'Search for rules for search', *Journal of Economic Behavior and Organization*, 3(1), pp. 65–81.

Hitt, M.A., Dacin, M.T., Tyler, B.B. and Park, D. (1997) 'Understanding the differences in Korean and US executives' strategic orientations', *Strategic Management Journal*, 18, pp. 159–167.

Hitt, M.A., Keats, B. and DeMarie, S.M. (1998) 'Navigating in the new competitive landscape: Building strategic flexibility and competitive advantage in the 21st century', *Academy of Management Executive*, 12(4), pp. 22–42.

Hodgkinson, G.P. (1997) 'Cognitive inertia in a turbulent market: the case of UK residential estate agents', *Journal of Management Studies*, 34, pp. 921–945.

Hodgkinson, G.P. and Clarke, I. (2007) 'Exploring the cognitive significance of organizational strategizing: A dual process framework and research agenda', *Human Relations*, 60(1), pp. 243–255.

Hodgkinson, G.P. and Healey, M.P. (2008) 'Cognition in organizations', *Annual Review of Psychology*, 59, pp. 387–417.

Hodgkinson, G.P. and Healey, M.P. (2011) 'Psychological foundations of dynamic capabilities: Reflexion and reflection in strategic management', *Strategic Management Journal*, 32(13), pp. 1500–1516.

Hodgkinson, G.P. and Sadler-Smith, E. (2003) 'Complex or unitary? A critique and empirical reassessment of the Allinson-Hayes Cognitive Style Index', *Journal of Occupational and Organizational Psychology*, 76, pp. 243–268.

Hodgkinson, G.P. and Wright, G. (2002) 'Confronting strategic inertia in a top management team: Learning from failure', *Organization Studies*, 23, pp. 949–977.

Hodgkinson, G.P., Bown, N.J., Maule, A.J., Glaister, K.W. and Pearman, A.D. (1999) 'Breaking the frame: An analysis of strategic cognition and decision making under uncertainty', *Strategic Management Journal*, 20(10), pp. 977–985.

Hodgkinson, G.P., Langan-Fox, J. and Sadler-Smith, E. (2008) 'Intuition: A fundamental bridging construct in the behavioral sciences', *British Journal of Psychology*, 99(1), pp. 1–27.

Hodgkinson, G.P., Maule, A.J. and Bown, N.J. (2004) 'Causal cognitive mapping in the organizational strategy field: A comparison of alternative elicitation procedures', *Organizational Research Methods*, 7(1), pp. 3–26.

Hodgkinson, G.P., Maule, A.J., Bown, N.J., Pearman, A.D. and Glaister, K.W. (2002) 'Further reflections on the elimination of framing bias in strategic decision making', *Strategic Management Journal*, 23(11), pp. 1069–1076.

Hodgkinson, G.P., Sadler-Smith, G., Burke, L.A., Claxton, G. and Sparrow, P.R. (2009) 'Intuition in organizations: Implications for strategic management', *Long Range Planning*, 42, pp. 277–297.

Hofer, C.W. and Schendel, D. (1978) *Strategy Formulation: Analytical Concepts*, St. Paul, MN: West.

Hoffman, W.M. (1989) 'The cost of a corporate conscience', *Business and Society Review*, 94, pp. 46–47.

Hofstede, G. (1980) *Culture's Consequences: International Differences in Work Related Values*, Beverly Hills, CA: Sage.

Hofstede, G. (1993) 'Cultural constraints in management theories', *Academy of Management Executive*, 7(1), pp. 81–94.

Hofstede, G. (1996) 'Riding the waves of commerce: A test of Trompenaars' "model" of national culture differences', *International Journal of Intercultural Relations*, 20(2), pp. 189–198.

Hofstede, G. (2001) *Culture's Consequences*, Thousand Oaks, CA: Sage, (2nd ed.).

Hogarth, R.M. (1980) *Judgement and Choice: The Psychology of Decision*, Chichester: Wiley.

Hogarth, R.M. (2001) *Educating Intuition*, Chicago, IL: University of Chicago Press.

Hogg, M.A. and Terry, D.J. (2000) 'Social identity and self-categorization processes in organizational contexts', *Academy of Management Review*, 25(1), pp. 121–140.

Holden, N.J. (2002) *Cross-Cultural Management: A Knowledge Management Perspective*, London: Financial Times/Prentice Hall.

Holland, J.H. (1995) *Adaptation in Natural and Artificial Systems*, Ann Arbor, MI: University of Michigan Press.

Holland, J.H. (1998) *Emergence. From Chaos to Order*, Reading, MA: Perseus Books.

Horváth, D., McMillan, C.J., Azumi, K. and Hickson, D.J. (1976) 'The cultural context of organizational control: An international comparison', *International Studies of Management & Organization*, 6(3), pp. 60–86.

House, R.J. and Aditya, R.N. (1997) 'The social science study of leadership: Quo vadis?', *Journal of Management*, 23(3), pp. 409–474.

House, R.J., Hanges, P.J., Javidan, M., Dorfman, P.W. and Gupta, V. (2004) *Culture, Leadership, and Organizations*, London: Sage.

Hout, T.M., Porter, M.E. and Rudden, E. (1982) 'How global companies win out', *Harvard Business Review*, 60(5), pp. 98–108.

Hrebiniak, L.G. and Joyce, W.F. (1985) 'Organizational adaptation: Strategic choice and environmental determinism', *Administrative Science Quarterly*, 30(3), pp. 336–349.

Huff, A.S. (ed.) (1990) *Mapping Strategic Thought*, Chichester, UK: Wiley.

Huff, A.S. (1997) 'A current and future agenda for cognitive research in organizations', *Journal of Management Studies*, 34(6), pp. 947–952.

Huy, Q.N. (1999) 'Emotional capability, emotional intelligence, and radical change', *Academy of Management Review*, 24(2), pp. 325–345.

Huy, Q.N. (2002) 'Emotional balancing of organizational continuity and radical change: The contribution of middle managers', *Administrative Science Quarterly*, 47, pp. 31–69.

Hymer, S (1960) 'The international operations of national firms: A study of direct investment', PhD dissertation, Cambridge, MA: MIT Press.

Imai, M. (1986) *Kaizen: The Key to Japan's Competitive Success*, New York: McGraw-Hill

Ireland, R.D. and Hitt, M.A. (1999) 'Achieving and maintaining strategic competitiveness in the 21st century: The role of strategic leadership', *Academy of Management Executive*, 13(1), pp. 43–57.

Isaack, T.S. (1978) 'Intuition: An ignored dimension of management', *Academy of Management Review*, 3, pp. 917–922.

Isen, A.M., Means, B., Patrick, R. and Nowicki, G. (1982) 'Some factors influencing decision-making strategy and risk taking', in: M.S. Clarke and S.T. Fiske (eds.) *Affect and Cognition*, Hillsdale, NJ: Erlbaum, pp. 243–261.

Isenberg, D.J. (1984) 'How senior managers think', *Harvard Business Review*, 63(6), pp. 81–90.

Itami, H. (with Roehl, T.W.) (1987) *Mobilizing Invisible Assets*, Cambridge: Harvard University Press.

Ito, T.A., Larsen, J.T., Smith, N.K. and Cacioppo, J.T. (1998) 'Negative information weighs more heavily on the brain: The negativity bias in evaluative categorizations', *Journal of Personality and Social Psychology*, 75(4), pp. 887–900.

Jackson, S.E. and Dutton, J.E. (1988) 'Discerning threats and opportunities', *Administrative Science Quarterly*, 33(3), pp. 370–387.

Jacobson, R. (1988) 'The persistence of abnormal returns', *Strategic Management Journal*, 9(5), pp. 415–430.

Jacoby, L.L., Lindsay, D.S. and Toth, J.P. (1992) 'Unconscious influences revealed', *American Psychologist*, 47, pp. 802–809.

James, B.G. (1985) *Business Wargames*, Harmondsworth: Penguin.

Janis, I.L. (1989) *Crucial Decisions: Leadership in Policymaking and Crisis Management*, New York: Free Press.

Janis, I.L. and Mann, L. (1977) *Decision Making: A Psychological Analysis of Conflict, Choice, and Commitment*, New York: Free Press.

Jantunen, A. (2005) 'New HRM practices and knowledge utilization', in: *Proceedings of the 5th International Workshop on Human Resource Management*, Seville, Spain. January-February, pp. 3–9.

Jarillo, J.C. (1988) 'On strategic networks', *Strategic Management Journal*, 9(1), pp. 31–41.

Javidan, M. (1984) 'The impact of environmental uncertainty on long-range planning practices of the U.S. savings and loan industry', *Strategic Management Journal*, 5(4), pp. 381–392.

Jaworski, B. and Kohli, A.K. (1993) 'Market orientation: Antecedents and consequences', *Journal of Marketing*, 57(3), pp. 53–70.

Jay, J. (2013) 'Navigating paradox as a mechanism of change and innovation in hybrid organizations', *Academy of Management Journal*, 56(1), pp. 137–

Jayachandran, S., Gimeno, J. and Varadarajan, P.R. (1999) 'Theory of multimarket competition: A synthesis and implications for marketing strategy', *Journal of Marketing*, 63(3), pp. 49–66.

Jelinek, M. (1979) *Institutionalizing Innovation*, New York: Praeger.

Jennings, D. (2000) 'PowerGen: The development of corporate planning in a privatized utility', *Long Range Planning*, 33(2), pp. 201–218.

Jensen, M.C. and Meckling, W.H. (1976) 'Theory of the firm, managerial behavior, agency costs, and ownership structure', *Journal of Financial Economics*, 3(4), pp. 305–360.

Jett, Q.R. and George, J.M. (2005) 'Emergent strategies and their consequences: A process study of competition and complex decision making', *Advanced Strategic Management*, 22, pp. 387–411.

Johanson, J. and Mattson, L.G. (1992) 'Network position and strategic action: An analytical framework', in: B. Axelsson and G. Easton (eds.) *Industrial Networks: A New View of Reality*, London: Routledge.

Johanson, J. and Vahlne, J.-E. (1977) 'The internationalization process of the firm: A model of knowledge development and increasing foreign market commitments', *Journal of International Business Studies*, 8, pp. 23–32.

Johnson, B. (1996) *Polarity Management*, Amherst, MA: HRD Press Inc.

Johnson, G. (1987) *Strategic Change and the Management Process*, Oxford: Basil Blackwell.

Johnson, G. (1988) 'Rethinking incrementalism', *Strategic Management Journal*, 9(1), pp. 75–91.

Jolls, C., Sunstein, C.R. and Thaler, R. (1998) 'A behavioral approach to law and economics', *Stanford Law Review*, 50(5), pp. 1471–1550.

Jones, T.M. (1995) 'Instrumental stakeholder theory: A synthesis of ethics and economics', *Academy of Management Review*, 20(2), pp. 404–437.

Jung, C.G. (1933) *Psychological Types*, New York: Harcourt, Brace, & Company (first published in 1921).

Kaempf, G.L., Klein, G., Thordsen, M.L. and Wolf, S. (1996) 'Decision making in complex naval command-and-control environments', *Human Factors*, 38, pp. 220–231.

Kagono, T., Nonaka, I., Sakakibara, K. and Okumura, A. (1985) *Strategic vs. Evolutionary Management: A US–Japan Comparison of Strategy and Organization*, Amsterdam: North-Holland.

Kahn, H. and Wiener, A.J. (1967) 'The next thirty-three years: A framework for speculation', *Daedalus*, 96(3), pp. 705–732.

Kahneman, D. (2003) 'A perspective on judgment and choice', *American Psychologist*, 58, pp. 697–720.

Kahneman, D. (2011) *Thinking, Fast and Slow*, New York: Farrar, Straus & Giroux.

Kahneman, D. and Klein, G. (2009) 'Conditions for intuitive expertise: A failure to disagree', *American Psychologist*, 64(6), pp. 515–526.

Kahneman, D. and Klein, G. (2010) 'When can you trust your gut?', *McKinsey Quarterly*, March, pp. 58–67.

Kahneman, D. and Lovallo, D. (1993) 'Timid choices and bold forecasts: A cognitive perspective on risk-taking', *Management Science*, 39(1), pp. 17–31.

Kahneman, D. and Tversky, A. (1979) 'Prospect theory: Analysis of decision under risk', *Econometrica*, 47(2), pp. 263–291.

Kahneman, D. and Tversky, A. (2000) *Choices, Values, and Frames*, Cambridge: Cambridge University Press.

Kahneman, D., Ritov, I. and Schkade, D. (1999) 'Economic preferences or attitude expressions? An analysis of dollar responses to public issues', *Journal of Risk and Uncertainty*, 19, pp. 203–235.

Kahneman, D., Slovic, P. and Tversky, A. (1982) *Judgment Under Uncertainty: Heuristics and Biases*, Cambridge: Cambridge University Press.

Kakabadse, A., Myers, A., McMahon, T. and Spony, G. (1995) 'Top management styles in Europe: Implications for business and cross-national teams', *European Business Journal*, 7(1), pp. 17–27.

Kanter, R.M. (1989) *When Giants Learn to Dance*, New York: Simon & Schuster.

Kanter, R.M. (1994) 'Collaborative advantage: The art of alliances', *Harvard Business Review*, 72(4), pp. 96–108.

Kanter, R.M. (2002) 'Strategy as improvisational theater', *Sloan Management Review*, 43(2), pp. 76–81.

Kaplan, M.F., Wanshula, L.T. and Zanna, M.P. (1993) 'Time pressure and information integration in social judgment', in: O. Svenson and A. J. Maule (eds.) *Time Pressure and Stress in Human Judgment and Decision Making*, New York: Plenum Press, pp. 255–267.

Kaplan, R.S. and Norton, D.P. (2001) *The Strategy-Focused Organization: How Balanced Scorecard Thrive in the New Business Environment*, Boston, MA: Harvard Business School Press.

Kaplan, S. (1989) 'The effects of management buyouts on operating performance and value', *Journal of Financial Economics*, 24(2), pp. 217–254.

Kaplan, S. (2003) 'Framing contests: Strategy-making during a technological discontinuity', working paper, Philadelphia, PA: Wharton School, University of Pennsylvania.

Kaplan, S. (2008) 'Cognition, capabilities, and incentives: Assessing firm response to the fiber-optic revolution', *Academy of Management Journal*, 51(4), pp. 672–695.

Kaplan S., Murray, A. and Henderson, R. (2003) 'Discontinuities and senior management: Assessing the role of recognition in pharmaceutical firm response to biotechnology', *Industrial Corporate Change*, 12(4), pp. 203–233.

Karlsson, N., Loewenstein, G. and Seppi, D. (2009) 'The ostrich effect: Selective attention to information', *Journal of Risk and Uncertainty*, 38, pp. 95–115.

Katz, M.L. and Shapiro, C. (1985) 'Network externalities, competition, and compatibility', *American Economic Review*, 75(3), pp. 424–440.

Katz, M.L. and Shapiro, C. (1986) 'Technology adoption in the presence of network externalities', *Journal of Political Economy*, 9, pp. 822–841.

Kay, J. (1989) 'Myths and realities', in: E. Davis (ed.) *1992: Myths and Realities*, London: Centre for Business Strategy.

Kay, J. (1993) *Foundations of Corporate Success: How Business Strategies Add Value*, Oxford: Oxford University Press.

Keasey, K., Thompson, S. and Wright, M. (eds.) (1997) *Corporate Governance: Economic, Management, and Financial Issues*, Oxford: Oxford University Press.

Keegan, W.J. (1983) 'Strategic market planning: The Japanese approach', *International Marketing Review*, 1, pp. 5–15.

Kelley, R.E. (1988) 'In praise of followers', *Harvard Business Review*, 66(6), p. 142.

Kelly, D. and Amburgey, T. (1991) 'Organizational inertia and momentum: A dynamic model of strategic change', *Academy of Management Journal*, 34(3), pp. 591–612.

Kerr, S. (1975) 'On the folly of rewarding A, while hoping for B', *Academy of Management Journal*, 18(4), pp. 769–782.

Kessel, M. (2014) 'Restoring the pharmaceutical industry's reputation', *Nature Biotechnology*, 32(10), pp. 983–990.

Kessler, E.H. and Chakrabarthi, A.K. (1996) 'Innovation speed: A conceptual model of context, antecedents, and outcomes', *Academy of Management Review*, 21(4), pp. 1143–1191.

Ketchen, D.J., Thomas, J.B. and McDaniel, R.R. (1996) 'Process, content and context: synergistic effects on organizational performance', *Journal of Management*, 22, pp. 231–257.

Kets de Vries, M.F.R. (1994) 'The leadership mystique', *Academy of Management Executive*, 8(3), pp. 73–92.

Khatri, N. and Ng, H.A. (2000) 'The role of intuition in strategic decision making', *Human Relations*, 53, pp. 57–86.

Kihlstrom, J.F. (1987) 'The cognitive unconscious', *Science*, 237, pp. 1445–1452.

Kihlstrom, J.F., Barnhardt, T.M. and Tataryn, D.T. (1992) 'The psychological unconscious', *American Psychologist*, 47, pp. 788–791.

Kim, N.K., Sengupta, S. and Kim, D. (2009) ,How can non-chaebol companies thrive in the chaebol economy?', *Journal of Global Academy of Marketing Science*, 19(3), pp. 28–36.

Kim, W.C. and Mauborgne, R. (2004) 'Blue ocean strategy', *Harvard Business Review*, October, pp. 2–11.

Kim, W.C. and Mauborgne, R. (2005) 'Blue ocean strategy: From theory to practice', *California Management Review*, 47(3), pp. 105–121.

Kindleberger, A. (1962) *Foreign Trade and the National Economy*, New Haven, CT: Yale University Press.

Kindleberger, C.P. (1973) *The World in Depression: 1929–1939*, London: Allen Lane.

King, B.L. (2008) 'Strategizing at leading venture capital firms: Of planning, opportunism and deliberate emergence', *Long Range Planning*, 41, pp. 345–366.

Kirzner, I. (1973) *Competition and Entrepreneurship*, Chicago, IL: University of Chicago Press.

Klein, G. (1998) *Sources of Power: How People Make Decisions*, Cambridge, MA: MIT Press.

Klein, G.A. (2003) *Intuition at Work*, New York: Doubleday.

Klein, K.J. and House, R.J. (1998) 'Further thoughts on fire: Charismatic leadership and levels of analysis', in: F. Dansereauand and F.J. Yammarino (eds.) *Leadership: The Multi-Level Approaches*, Stamford, CT: JAI Press, pp. 45–52 (Vol. 2).

Klein, N. (2000) *No Logo, Taking Aim at the Brand Bullies,* London: Flamingo.

Klein, S.B., Rozendal, K. and Cosmides, L. (2002) 'A socialcognitive neuroscience analysis of the self', *Social Cognition*, 20(2), pp. 105–135.

Klemm, M., Sanderson, S. and Luffman, G. (1991) 'Mission statements', *Long Range Planning*, 24(3), pp. 73–78.

Klimoski, R. and Mohammed, S. (1994) 'Team mental model: Construct or metaphor', *Journal of Management*, 20, pp. 403–437.

Kluckhohn, F.R. and Strodtbeck, F.L. (1961) *Variations in Value Orientations*, New York: Row, Peterson & Company.

Knight, D., Pearce, C.L., Smith, K.G., Olian, J.D., Sims, H.P, Smith, K.A. and Flood, P. (1999) 'Top management team diversity, group process, and strategic cConsensus', *Strategic Management Journal*, 20, pp. 445–465.

Knight, G.A. and Liesch, P.W. (2016) 'Internationalization: From incremental to born global', *Journal of World Business*, 51(1), pp. 93–102.

Koen, C. (2005) *Comparative International Management*, Abingdon: McGraw-Hill.

Kogut, B. (ed.) (1993) *Country Competitiveness: Technology and the Organizing of Work*, Oxford: Oxford University Press.

Kogut, B. and Zander, U. (1992) 'Knowledge of the enterprise, combinative capabilities and the replication of technology', *Organizational Science*, 3(3), pp. 383–397.

Kogut, B. and Zander, U. (1993) 'Knowledge of the firm and the evolutionary theory of the mul', *Journal of International Business Studies*, 24(4), pp. 625–645.

Kono, T. (1999) 'A strong head office makes a strong company', *Long Range Planning*, 32(2), pp. 225–236.

Korte, R.F. (2008) 'Applying scenario planning across multiple levels of analysis', *Advanced Developmental Human Resources*, 10(2), pp.179–197.

Kotler, P. (1967) *Marketing Management: Analysis, Planning and Control*, Englewood Cliffs, NJ: Prentice Hall.

Kotter, J.P. (1990) 'What leaders really do', *Harvard Business Review*, 68(3), p. 103.

Kotur, B.R. and Anbazhagan, S. (2014) ,The influence of age and gender on the leadership styles', *Journal of Business and Management*, 16(1), pp. 30–36.

Kreps, D.M. and Wilson, R. (1982a) 'Reputation and imperfect information', *Journal of Economic Theory*, 27(2), pp. 253–279.

Kreps, D.M. and Wilson, R. (1982b) 'Sequential equilibria', *Econometrica: Journal of the Econometric Society*, 50(4), pp. 863–894.

Kruger, J. and Dunning, D. (1999) 'Unskilled and unaware of it: How difficulties in recognizing one's own incompetence lead to inflated self-assessments', *Journal of Personality and Social Psychology*, 77, pp. 1121–1134.

Krüger, W. (1996) 'Implementation: The core task of change management', *CEMS Business Review*, 1, pp. 77–96.

Kruglanski, A.W. and Freund, T. (1983) 'The freezing and unfreezing of lay-inference: Effects on impressional primacy, ethnic stereotyping, and numerical anchoring', *Journal of Experimental Social Psychology*, 19, pp. 448–468.

Krugman, P. (1980) 'Scale economies, product differentiation, and the pattern of trade', *American Economic Review*, 70(5), pp. 950–959.

Krugman, P. (1985) 'International debt strategies in an uncertain World', in: G. Smith and J. Cuddington (eds.) *International Debt and the Developing Countries*, Washington, DC: World Bank.

Krugman, P. (1990) *Rethinking International Trade*, Cambridge, MA: MIT Press.

Ku, G. (2008) 'Learning to de-escalate: The effects of regret in escalation of commitment', *Organizational Behavior and Human Decision Processes*, 105(2), pp. 221–232.

Kuhn, T.S. (1970) *The Structure of Scientific Revolutions*, Chicago, IL: University of Chicago Press.

Kukalis, S. (1991) 'Determinants of strategic planning systems in large organizations: A contingency approach', *Journal of Management Studies*, 28, pp. 143–160.

Kuran, T. (1998) 'The tenacious past: Theories of personal and collective conservatism', *Journal of Economic Behavior and Organization*, 10, pp. 143–171.

Lado, A.A., Boyd, N.G. and Hanlon, S.C. (1997) 'Competition, cooperation and the search for economic rents: A syncretic model', *Academy of Management Review*, 22(1), pp. 110–141.

Lane, P.J., Koka, B.R. and Pathak, S. (2006) 'The reification of absorptive capacity: A critical review and rejuvenation of the construct', *Academy of Management Review*, 31(4), pp. 833–863.

Langer, E. (1989) *Mindfulness*, Boston, MA: Addison-Wesley.

Langley, A. (1995) 'Between "paralysis and analysis" and "extinction by instinct"', *Sloan Management Review*, 36(3), pp. 63–76.

Langlois, R. (1994) 'Cognition and capabilities: Opportunities seized and missed in the history of the history of the computer industry', working paper, University of Connecticut. Presented at the conference on Technological Oversights and Foresights, Stern School of Business, New York University, 11–12 March 1994.

Langtry, B. (1994) 'Stakeholders and the moral responsibilities of business', *Business Ethics Quarterly*, 4, pp. 431–443.

Latham, G.P. and Locke, E.A. (eds.) (1995) *Goal Setting: A Motivational Technique That Works*, Englewood Cliffs, NJ: Prentice Hall (2nd ed.).

Laughlin, P. (1980) 'Social combination processes of cooperative problem-solving groups on verbal intellective tasks', in: M. Fishbein (ed.), *Progress in Social Psychology*, Hillsdale, NJ: Erlbaum (Vol. 1), pp. 127–155.

Laughlin, P.R. and Ellis, A.L. (1986) 'Demonstrability and social combination processes on mathematical intellective tasks', *Journal of Experimental Social Psychology*, 22, pp. 177–189.

Lawrence, P.R. and Lorsch, J.W. (1967) *Organization and Environment: Managing Differentiation and Integration*, Boston, MA: Harvard University Press.

Lax, D.A. and Sebenius, J.K. (1986) *The Manager as Negotiator: Bargaining for Cooperative and Competitive Gain*, New York: Free Press.

Lazonick, W. (2005) 'The innovative firm', in: J. Fagerberg, D. Mowery and R.R.

Learned, E., Christensen, C., Andrews, K. and Guth, W. (1969) *Business Policy: Text and Cases*, Homewood, IL: Irwin.

LeDoux, J.E. (2000) 'Emotion circuits in the brain', *Annual Review of Neuroscience*, 23, pp. 155–184.

Lee, C.C.K. (2010) *Thought and Governance of East Asia: Confucian Humanism, Human Rights and Business Ethics*, Seoul: PerDream.

Leifer, M. (2000) *The Political and Security Outlook for Southeast Asia*, Institute of Southeast Asian Studies.

Leitner, K.-H. (2014) 'Strategy formation in the innovation and market domain: Emergent or deliberate?', *Journal of Strategy and Management*, 7(4), pp. 354–375.

Lenz, R.T. and Lyles, M. (1985) 'Paralysis by analysis: Is your planning system becoming too rational?', *Long Range Planning*, 18(4), pp. 64–72.

Leonard-Barton, D. (1992) 'Core capabilities and core rigidities: A paradox in managing new product development', *Strategic Management Journal*, 13(S1), pp. 111–125.

Leonard-Barton, D. (1995) *Well-Springs of Knowledge: Building and Sustaining the Sources of Innovation*, Boston, MA: Harvard Business School Press.

Lessem, R. and Neubauer, F.F. (1994) *European Management Systems*, London: McGraw-Hill.

Levenhagen, M., Porac, J.F. and Thomas, H. (1993) 'Emergent industry leadership and the selling of technological visions: A social constructionist view', in: J. Hendry, G. Johnson and J. Newton (eds.) *Strategic Thinking: Leadership and the Management of Change*, Chichester: Wiley.

Levinthal, D.A. and March, J.G. (1981) 'A model of adaptive organizational search', *Journal of Economic Behavior & Organization*, 2(4), pp. 307–333.

Levinthal, D.A. and March, J.G. (1993) 'The myopia of learning', *Strategic Management Journal*, 14(S2), pp. 95–112.

Levinthal, D.A. and Rerup, C. (2006) 'Crossing an apparent chasm: Bridging mindful and less-mindful perspectives on organizational learning', *Organization Science*, 17, pp. 502–513.

Levitt, B. and March, J.G. (1988) 'Organizational learning', *Annual Review of Sociology*, 14, pp. 319–340.

Levitt, T. (1960) 'Marketing myopia', *Harvard Business Review*, 38, July–August, pp. 45–56.

Levitt, T. (1983) 'The globalization of markets', *Harvard Business Review*, 61(3), pp. 92–102.

Levy, D. (1994) 'Chaos theory and strategy: Theory, application, and managerial implications', *Strategic Management Journal*, 15, pp. 167–178.

Lewicki, P., Hill, T. and Bizot, E. (1988) 'Acquisition of procedural knowledge about a pattern of stimuli that cannot be articulated', *Cognitive Psychology*, 20, pp. 24–37.

Lewin, K. (1947) 'Frontiers in group dynamics: Social equilibria and social change', *Human Relations*, 1, pp. 5–41.

Lewis, M. (2000) 'Exploring paradox: toward a more comprehensive guide', *Academy of Management Review*, 25(4), pp. 760–776.

Lewis, R.D. (2003) *The Cultural Imperative: Global Trends in the 21st Century*, London: Nicholas Brealey Publishing.

Lieberman, M.B. and Montgomery, D.B. (1988) 'First mover advantages', *Strategic Management Journal*, 9(1), pp. 41–58.

Lieberman, M.B. and Montgomery, D.B. (1998) 'First-mover (dis)advantages: Retrospective and link with the resource-based view', *Strategic Management Journal*, 19(12), pp. 1111–1126.

Lieberman, M.D. (2000) 'Intuition: A social cognitive neuroscience approach', *Psychological Bulletin*, 126(1), pp. 109–137.

Lieberman, M.D. (2007) 'Social cognitive neuroscience: A review of core processes', *Annual Review of Psychology*, 58, pp. 259–289.

Lieberman, M.D. and Eisenberger, N.I. (2009) 'The pains and pleasures of social life', *Science*, 323, pp. 890–891.

Lieberman, M.D., Gaunt, R., Gilbert, D.T. and Trope, Y. (2002) 'Reflexion and reflection: A social cognitive neuroscience approach to attributional inference', in: *Advances in Experimental Social Psychology* San Diego, CA: Academic Press (Vol. 34), pp. 199–249.

Lieberman, M.D., Ochsner, K.N., Gilbert, D.T. and Schacter, D.L. (2001) 'Do amnesiacs exhibit cognitive dissonance reduction? The role of explicit memory and attention in attitude change', *Psychological Science*, 12(2), pp. 135–140.

Liebeskind, J. (1996) 'Knowledge, strategy and the theory of the firm', *Strategic Management Journal*, 17, Special Issue, Winter, pp. 93–107.

Liedtka, J. (2000) 'In defense of strategy as design', *California Management Review*, 42(3), pp. 8–30.

Lindblom, C.E. (1959) 'The science of "muddling through"', *Public Administration Review*, 19(2), pp. 79–88.

Lindsay, W.M. and Rue, L.W. (1980) 'Impact of organization environment on the long-range planning process: A contingency view', *Academy of Management Journal*, 23, pp. 385–404.

Linehan, M. (1993) *Cognitive-Behavioral Treatment of Borderline Personality Disorder*, New York: Guilford Press.

Lippman, S. and Rumelt, R. (1992) 'Demand uncertainty and investment in industry-specific capital', *Industrial and Corporate Change*, 1(1), pp. 235–262.

Loewenstein, G. (1996) 'Out of control: Visceral influences on behavior', *Organizational Behavior and Human Decision Processes*, 65, pp. 272–292.

Loewenstein, G. and Small, D.A. (2007) 'The Scarecrow and the Tin Man: The vicissitudes of human sympathy and caring', *Review of General Psychology*, 11(2), pp. 112–126.

Loewenstein, G., Rick, S. and Cohen, J.D. (2008) 'Neuroeconomics', *Annual Review of Psychology*, 59, pp. 647–672.

Loewenstein, G., Weber, E.U., Hsee, C.K. and Welch, N. (2001) 'Risk as feelings', *Psychological Bulletin*, 127(2), pp. 267–286.

Long, W.F. and Ravenscraft, D.J. (1993) 'Decade of debt: Lessons from LBOs in the 1980s', in: M.M. Blair (ed.) *The Deal Decade: What Takeovers and Leveraged Buyouts Mean for Corporate Governance*, Washington, DC: Brookings Institution.

Lorange, P. (1980) *Corporate Planning: An Executive Viewpoint*, Englewood Cliffs, NJ: Prentice Hall.

Lorange, P. and Vancil, R.F. (1977) *Strategic Planning Systems*, Englewood Cliffs, NJ: Prentice Hall.

Lord, R.G., Diefendorff, J.M., Schmidt, A.M. and Hall, R.J. (2010) 'Self-regulation at work', *Annual Review of Psychology*, 61, pp. 543–568.

Lorenzoni, G. and Baden-Fuller, C. (1995) 'Creating a strategic center to manage a web of partners', *California Management Review*, 37(3), pp. 146–163.

Lorsch, J.W. and Tierney, T.J. (2002) *Aligning the Stars: How to Succeed When Professionals Drive Results*, Boston, MA: Harvard Business School Press.

Louis, M.R. and Sutton, R.I. (1991) 'Switching cognitive gears: From habits of mind to active thinking', *Human Relations*, 44(1), pp. 55–76.

Lounamaa, P.H. and March, J.G. (1987) 'Adaptive coordination of a learning team', *Management Science*, 33(1), pp. 107–123.

Lovallo, D. and Sibony, O. (2010) 'The case for behavioral strategy', *McKinsey Quarterly*, March, pp. 30–43.

Lovett, M.C. (2002) 'Problem solving', in: H. Pashler and D. Medin (eds.) *Stevens' Handbook of Experimental Psychology. Volume 2: Memory and Cognitive Processes*, New York: Wiley, pp. 317–362.

Lowendahl, B.R. (1997) *Strategic Management of Professional Business Service Firms*, Copenhagen: Copenhagen Business School Press.

Lubatkin, M. and Chatterjee, S. (1994) 'Extending modern portfolio theory into the domain of corporate diversification: Does it apply?', *Academy of Management Journal*, 37(1), pp. 109–136.

Lyles, M.A. and Schwenk, C.R. (1992) 'Top management, strategy and organizational knowledge structures', *Journal of Management Studies*, 29, pp. 155–174.

Lyon, D.W., Lumpkin, G.T. and Dess, G.G. (2000) 'Enhancing entrepreneurial orientation research: Operationalizing and measuring a key strategic decision making process', *Journal of Management*, 26, pp. 1055–1085.

MacGregor, D., Lichtenstein, S. and Slovic, P. (1988) 'Structuring knowledge retrieval: An analysis of decomposed quantitative judgments', *Organizational Behavior and Human Decision Processes*, 42, pp. 303–323.

Mahoney, J.T. (1992) 'The choice of organizational form: Vertical financial ownership versus other methods of vertical integration', *Strategic Management Journal*, 13(8), pp. 559–584.

Maidique, M.A. (1980) 'Entrepreneurs, champions, and technological innovation', *Sloan Management Review*, 21, pp. 18–31.

Makridakis, S. (1990) *Forecasting, Planning and Strategy for the 21st Century*, New York: Free Press.

Mansfield, E., Rapoport, J., Schnee, J., Wagner, S. and Hamburger, M. (1971) *Research and Innovation in the Modern Corporation*, New York: W.W. Norton.

March, J.G. (1988) 'Variable risk preferences and adaptive aspirations', *Journal of Economic Behavior and Organization*, 9, pp. 5–24.

March, J.G. (1991) 'Exploitation and exploration in organizational learning', *Organization Science*, 2(1), pp. 71–87.

March, J.G. and Simon, H.A. (1958) *Organizations*, New York: Wiley.

March, J.G. and Simon, H.A. (1993) *Organizations*, Cambridge, MA: Blackwell (2nd ed.).

Marginson, D. and McAulay, L. (2008) 'Exploring the debate on short-termism: A theoretical and empirical analysis', *Strategic Management Journal*, 29, pp. 273–292.

Margolis, J.D. and Walsh, J.P. (2003) 'Misery loves companies: Rethinking social initiatives by business', *Administrative Science Quarterly*, 48(2), pp. 268–305.

Markides, C. (1998) 'Strategic innovation in established companies', *Sloan Management Review*, 39(3), pp. 31–42.

Markides, C. (1999) *All the Right Moves: a Guide to Crafting Breakthrough Strategy*, Boston, MA: Harvard Business School Press.

Markides, C.C. (2013) *Game-Changing Strategies: How to Create New Market Space in Established Industries by Breaking the Rules*, New York: Wiley.

Markowitz, H.M. (1959) *Portfolio Selection: Efficient Diversification of Investments*, New York: Wiley.

Martin, J. (1992) *Cultures in Organizations: Three Perspectives*, Oxford: Oxford University Press.

Martin, R. (2007) *The Opposable Mind: How Successful Leaders Win through Integrative Thinking*, Cambridge, MA: Harvard Business School Book Press.

Martin, R. (2010) 'The age of customer capitalism', *Harvard Business Review*,

Maruyama, M. (1984) 'Alternative concepts of management: Insights from Asia and Africa', *Asia Pacific Journal of Management*, 1, January, pp. 100–111.

Marx, T.G. (1991) 'Removing the obstacles to effective strategic planning', *Long Range Planning*, 24(4), pp. 21–28.

Mason, E. (1949) 'The current state of the monopoly problem in the US', *Harvard Law Review*, 62, pp. 1265–1285.

Mason, R.O. and Mitroff, I.I. (1981) *Challenging Strategic Planning Assumptions*, New York: Wiley.

Mathews, J.A. and Zander, I. (2007) 'The international entrepreneurial dynamics of accelerated internationalisation', *Journal of International Business Studies*, pp. 1–17.

Matusik, S.F. and Hill, C.W.L. (1998) 'The utilization of contingent work, knowledge creation, and competitive advantage', *Academy of Management Review*, 23, pp. 680–697.

Maule, A.J., Hockey, G.R.J. and Bdzola, L. (2000) 'Effects of time-pressure on decision-making under uncertainty: Changes in affective state and information processing strategy', *Acta Psychologica*, 104, pp. 283–301.

McCarthy, B. (2003a) 'Strategy is personality-driven, strategy is crisis-driven: Insights from entrepreneurial firms', *Management Decision*, 41(4), pp. 327–339.

McCarthy, B. (2003b) 'The impact of the entrepreneur's personality on the strategy-formation and planning process in SMEs', *Irish Journal of Management*, 24(1), pp. 154–172.

McCaskey, M.B. (1982) *The Executive Challenge: Managing Change and Ambiguity*, Boston, MA: Pitman.

McCoy, C.S. (1985) *Management of Values*, Cambridge, MA: Ballinger.

McGahan, A. (2000) 'How industries evolve', *Business Strategy Review*, 11(3), pp. 1–16.

McGahan, A. and Porter, M.E. (1997) 'How much does industry matter, really?', *Strategic Management Journal*, 18(S1), pp. 15–30.

McGrath, J.E. (1984) *Groups: Interaction and Performance*, Englewood Cliffs, NJ: Prentice Hall.

McGrath, R.G. (2013) *The End of Competitive Advantage: How to Keep Your Strategy Moving as Fast as Your Business*, Boston, MA: Harvard Business Review Press.

McGrew, A.G. and Lewis, P.G. (eds.) (1992) *Global Politics: Globalisation and the Nation-State*, Cambridge: Polity Press.

McLuhan, M. (1964) *Understanding Media: The Extensions of Man*, New York: McGraw-Hill.

McMackin, J. and Slovic, P. (2000) 'When does explicit justification impair decision making?', *Applied Cognitive Psychology*, 14, pp. 527–541.

Meehl, P.E. (1954) *Clinical Versus Statistical Prediction*, Minneapolis, MN: University of Minnesota Press.

Meindl, J.R., Ehrlich, S.B. and Dukerich, J.M. (1985) 'The romance of leadership', *Administrative Science Quarterly*, 30(1), pp. 78–102.

Meyer, A., Brooks, G. and Goes, J. (1990) 'Environmental jolts and industry revolutions: Organizational responses to discontinuous change', *Strategic Management Journal*, 11(2), pp. 93–110.

Meyer, A.D. (1982) 'Adapting to environmental jolts', *Administrative Science Quarterly*, 27(4), pp. 515–537.

Meyer, E. (2014) *The Culture Map: Decoding How People Think, Lead, and Get Things Done Across Cultures*, New York: Public Affairs.

Meyer, K.E., Mudambi, R. and Narula, R. (2011) 'Multinational enterprises and local contexts: The opportunities and challenges of multiple embeddedness', *Journal of Management Studies*, 48(2), pp. 235–252.

Miles, R.E. and Snow, C.C., (1978) *Organizational Strategy, Structure, and Process*, New York: McGraw-Hill.

Milgrom, P. and Roberts, J. (1982a) 'Limit pricing and entry under incomplete information: An equilibrium analysis', *Econometrica: Journal of the Econometric Society*, 50, pp. 443–459.

Milgrom, P. and Roberts, J. (1982b) 'Predation, reputation and entry deterrence', *Journal of Economic Theory*, 27, pp. 280–312.

Miller, C.C. and Cardinal, L.B. (1994) 'Strategic planning and firm performance: A synthesis of more than two decades of research', *Academy of Management Journal*, 37(6), pp. 1649–1665.

Miller, D. (1990) *The Icarus Paradox: How Excellent Companies Bring About Their Own Downfall*, New York: HarperBusiness.

Miller, D. and Friesen, P.H. (1980) 'Momentum and revolution in organizational adaptation', *Academy of Management Journal*, 23(4), pp. 591–614.

Miller, D. and Friesen, P.H. (1984) *Organizations: A Quantum View*, Englewood Cliffs, NJ: Prentice Hall.

Miller, D., Eisenstat, R. and Foote, N. (2002) 'Strategy from the inside-out: Building capability-creating organizations', *California Management Review*, 44(3), pp. 37–54.

Miller, D., Kets de Vries, M. and Toulouse, J.M. (1982) 'Top executive locus of control and its relationship to strategy-making, structure and environment', *Academy of Management Journal*, 25, pp. 237–253.

Mintzberg, H. (1978) 'Patterns in strategy formation', *Management Science*, 24(9), pp. 934–948.

Mintzberg, H. (1979) *The Structuring of Organizations: A Synthesis of the Research*, Englewood Cliffs, NJ: Prentice Hall.

Mintzberg, H. (1982) 'If you're not serving Bill and Barbara, then you're not serving leadership', in: J.G. Hunt, U. Sekaran, and C.A. Schreisheim (eds.) *Leadership: Beyond Establishment Views*, Carbondale, IL: Southern Illinois University.

Mintzberg, H. (1984) 'Who should control the corporation?', *California Management Review*, 27(1), pp. 90–115.

Mintzberg, H. (1989) *Mintzberg on Management*, New York: Free Press.

Mintzberg, H. (1990) 'The design school: Reconsidering the basic premises of strategic management', *Strategic Management Journal*, 11, pp. 171–195.

Mintzberg, H. (1991a) 'Learning 1, planning 0: reply to Igor Ansoff', *Strategic Management Journal*, 12(6), pp. 463–466.

Mintzberg, H. (1991b) 'The effective organization: Forces and forms', *Sloan Management Review*, 32(2), pp. 54–67.

Mintzberg, H. (1993) 'The pitfalls of strategic planning', *California Management Review*, 36(1), pp. 32–45.

Mintzberg, H. (1994a) 'The fall and rise of strategic planning', *Harvard Business Review*, 73(1),.

Mintzberg, H. (1994b) *The Rise and Fall of Strategic Planning*, Englewood Cliffs, NJ: Prentice Hall.

Mintzberg, H. (2005) *Managers not MBAs: A Hard Look at the Soft Practice of Managing and Management Practice*, San Francisco, CA: Berrett-Koehler.

Mintzberg, H. and McHugh, A. (1985) 'Strategy formulation in an adhocracy', *Administrative Science Quarterly*, 30, pp. 160–197.

Mintzberg, H. and Norman, R.A. (2001) *Reframing Business: When the Map Changes the Landscape*, New York: Wiley.

Mintzberg, H. and Waters, J.A. (1982) 'Tracking strategy in an entrepreneurial firm', *Academy of Management Journal*, 15, pp. 465–499.

Mintzberg, H. and Waters, J.A. (1985) 'Of strategy: Deliberate and emergent', *Strategic Management Journal*, 6(3), pp. 257–272.

Mintzberg, H., Ahlstrand, B. and Lampel, J. (1998) *Strategy Safari: A Guided Tour through the Wilds of Strategic Management*, New York: Free Press.

Mintzberg, H., Brunet, P. and Waters, J. (1986) 'Does planning impede strategic thinking? Tracking the strategies of Air Canada from 1937 to 1976', in: R.B. Lamb and P. Shivastava (eds.) *Advances in Strategic Management*, Greenwich, CT: JAI Press, pp. 3–41 (Vol. 4).

Misumi, J. (1985) *The Behavioral Science of Leadership*, Ann Arbor, MI: University of Michigan Press.

Mitchell, R.K., Agle, B.R. and Wood, D.J. (1997) 'Toward a theory of stakeholder identification and salience: Defining the principle of who and what really counts', *Academy of Management Review*, 22(4), pp. 853–886.

Mitchell, S. (2000) *American Generations: Who They Are, How They Live, What They Think*, Ithaca, NY: New Strategists (3rd ed.).

Mitchell, W. (1989) 'Whether and when? Probability and timing of incumbents' entry into emerging industrial subfields', *Administrative Science Quarterly*, 34, pp. 208–230.

Mitchell, W. (1991) 'Dual clocks: Entry order influences on industry incumbent and newcomer market share and survival when specialized assets retain their value', *Strategic Management Journal*, 12(2), pp. 85–100.

Miwa, Y. and Ramseyer, J.M. (1996) *The Fable of the Keiretsu*, Chicago, IL: Chicago University Press.

Miyashita, K. and Russell, D. (1994) *Keiretsu: Inside the Hidden Japanese Conglomerates*, New York: McGraw-Hill, pp. 21–33.

Mody, A. (1993) 'Learning through alliances', *Journal of Economic Behavior and Organization*, 20(2), pp. 151–170.

Moncrieff, J. (1999) 'Is strategy making a difference?' *Long Range Planning*, 32(2), pp.

Moore, G.A. (2000) *Living on the Fault Line: Managing for Shareholder Value in the Age of the Internet*, New York: HarperBusiness.

Moore, J.F. (1996) *The Death of Competition: Leadership and Strategy in the Age of Business Ecosystems*, New York: HarperBusiness.

Morgan, G. (1986) *Images of Organization*, London: Sage.

Morikawa, H. (1992) *Zaibatsu: The Rise and Fall of Family Enterprise Groups in Japan*, Tokyo: University of Tokyo Press.

Morris, I. (2010) *Why The West Rules – For Now: The Patterns of History and What They Reveal About the Future*, London and New York: Profile Books /Farrar, Straus & Giroux.

Mudambi, R. and Navarra, P. (2004) 'Is knowledge power? Knowledge flows, subsidiary power and rentseeking within MNCs', *Journal of International Business Studies*, 35(5), pp. 385–406.

Mukherjee, K. (2010) 'A dual system model of preferences under risk', *Psychological Review*, 117(1), 243.

Murnighan, J.K. and Conlon, D.E. (1991) 'The dynamics of intense work groups: A study of British string quartets', *Administrative Science Quarterly*, 36, pp. 165–186.

Myers, A., Kakabadse, A., McMahon, T. and Spony, G. (1995) 'Top management styles in Europe: Implications for business and cross-national teams', *European Business Journal*, 7(1), pp. 17–27.

Myers, D.G. (2002) *Intuition: Its Powers and Perils*, New Haven, CT: Yale University Press.

Nadler, D.A. and Tushman, M.L. (1992) 'Designing organizations that have good fit: A framework for understanding new architectures', in: D. Nadler (ed.), *Organizational Architecture*, San Francisco, CA: Jossey-Bass.

Nadler, D.A. and Tushman, M.L. (1996) *Competing By Design: The Power of Organizational Architecture*, New York: Oxford University Press.

Nag, R., Corley, K.G. and Gioia, D.A. (2007) 'The intersection of organizational identity, knowledge, and practice: Attempting strategic change via knowledge grafting', *Academy of Management Journal*, 50(4), pp. 821–847.

Nag, R., Hambrick, D.C. and Chen, M.J. (2007) 'What is strategic management, really? Inductive derivation of a consensus definition of the field', *Strategic Management Journal*, 28, pp. 935–955.

Nalebuff, B.J. and Brandenburger, A.M. (1995) 'The right game: Use game theory to shape strategy', *Harvard Business Review*, 73(4), pp. 57–71.

Nalebuff, B.J. and Brandenburger, A.M. (1996) *Co-opetition*, New York: HarperBusiness.

Nanus, B. (1992) *Visionary Leadership: Creating a Compelling Sense of Direction for Your Organization*, San Francisco, CA: Jossey-Bass.

Needham, J., Ho, P.Y. and Lu, G.D. (1976) *Science and Civilisation in China*, London: Cambridge University Press (Vol. V).

Nelson, R.R. (1996) 'The evolution of competitive or comparative advantage: A preliminary report on a study', working paper 96-21, International Institute for Applied Systems Analysis, Laxemberg, Austria.

Nelson, R.R. (2005) *Technology, Institutions, and Economic Growth*, Cambridge, MA: Harvard University Press.

Nelson, R.R. (eds.) (2006) *The Oxford Handbook of Innovation*, New York: Oxford University

Nelson, R.R. and Winter, S.G. (1982) *An Evolutionary Theory of Economic Change*, Cambridge, MA: Harvard University Press.

Nelson, R.R. and Winter, S.G. (2002) 'Evolutionary theorizing in economics', *Journal of Economic Perspectives*, 16(2), pp. 23–46.

Nelson, T.O. (1996) 'Consciousness and metacognition', *American Psychologist*, 51(2), pp. 102–116.

Nemeth, C.J. and Wachtler, J. (1983) 'Creative problem solving as a result of majority vs minority influence', *European Journal of Social Psychology*, 13(1), pp. 45–55.

Nisbett, R.E., Peng, K., Choi, I. and Norenzayan, A. (2001) 'Culture and systems of thought: Holistic versus analytic cognition', *Psychological Review*, 108(2), 291–310.

Nissen, M.J. and Bullemer, P. (1987) 'Attentional requirements of learning: Evidence from performance measures', *Cognitive Psychology*, 19, pp. 1–32.

Nonaka, I. (1988) 'Creating organizational order out of chaos: Self-renewal in Japanese firms', *California Management Review*, 30(3), pp. 9–18.

Nonaka, I. (1991) 'The knowledge-creating company', *Harvard Business Review*, 69(6), pp. 96–104.

Nonaka, I. and Johansson, J.K. (1985) 'Japanese management: What about "hard" skills?' *Academy of Management Review*, 10(2), pp. 181–191.

Nonaka, I. and Konno, N. (1998) 'The concept of ba: Building a foundation for knowledge creation', *California Management Review*, 40(3), pp. 40–54.

Nonaka, I. and Takeuchi, H. (1995) *The Knowledge Creating Company*, New York: Oxford University Press.

Nonaka, I. and Toyama, R. (2002) 'A firm as a dialectical being: towards a dynamic theory of a firm', *Industrial and Corporate Change*, 11(5), pp. 995–1009.

Nonaka, I. and Toyama, R. (2007) 'Strategic management as distributed practical wisdom (phronesis)', *Industrial and Corporate Change*, 16(3), pp. 371–394.

Noorderhaven, N.G. (1995) *Strategic Decision Making*, Wokingham: Addison-Wesley.

Norenzayan, A., Smith, E.E., Kim, B.J. and Nisbett, R.E. (2002) 'Cultural preferences for formal versus intuitive reasoning', *Cognitive Science*, 26(5), 653–684.

Norman, R. and Ramirez, R. (1993) 'From value chain to value constellation: Designing interactive strategy', *Harvard Business Review*, July–August, pp. 65–77.

O'Neill, J. (2001) 'Building better global economic BRICs', Global Economics Paper No. 66, Goldman Sachs & Co.

Ocasio, W. (1997) 'Towards an attention-based view of the firm', *Strategic Management Journal*, 18, Special Issue, July, pp. 187–206.

Ochsner, K.N. and Lieberman, M.D. (2001) 'The emergence of social cognitive neuroscience', *American Psychologist*, 56(9), pp. 717–734.

Ochsner, K.N., Bunge, S.A., Gross, J.J. and Gabrieli, J.D.E. (2002) 'Rethinking feelings: An MRI study of the cognitive regulation of emotion', *Journal of Cognitive Neuroscience*, 14(8), pp. 1215–1229.

Ohmae, K. (1982) *The Mind of the Strategist*, New York: McGraw-Hill.

Ohmae, K. (1985) *Triad Power: The Coming Shape of Global Competition*, New York: Free Press.

Ohmae, K. (1989) 'Managing in a borderless world', *Harvard Business Review*, 67(3), pp. 152–161.

Ohmae, K. (1990) *The Borderless World: Power and Strategy in the Interlinked Economy*, London: Fontana.

Oliver, C. (1991) 'Strategic responses to institutional processes', *Academy of Management Review*, 16(1), pp. 145–179.

Oliver, C. (1997) 'Sustainable competitive advantage: Combining institutional and resource-based views', *Strategic Management Journal*, 18(9), pp. 697–713.

Oliver, N. and Wilkinson, B. (1988) *The Japanization of British Industry*, London: Basil Blackwell.

Olson, E.E. and Eoyang, G.H. (2001) *Facilitating Organization Change. Lessons from Complexity Science*, San Francisco, CA: Jossey-Bass.

Olson-Buchanan, J.B., Bryan, L.L.K. and Thompson, L.F. (2013) *Using Industrial-Organizational Psychology for the Greater Good: Helping Those Who Help Others*, London: Routledge.

Osbeck, L.M. (1999) 'Conceptual problems in the development of a psychological notion of "intuition"', *Journal for the Theory of Social Behaviour*, 29, pp. 229–250.

Osbeck, L.M. (2001) 'Direct apprehension and social construction: Revisiting the concept of intuition', *Journal of Theoretical and Philosophical Psychology*, 21, pp. 118–131.

Oshagbemi, T. (2004) 'Age influences on the leadership styles and behaviour of managers', *Employee Relations*, 26(1), pp. 14–29.

Oshagbemi, T. (2008) 'The impact of personal and organizational variables on the leadership styles of managers', *International Journal of Human Resource Management*, 19(10), pp. 1896–1910.

Oshagbemi, T. and Gill, R. (2003) 'Gender differences and similarities in the leadership styles and behaviour of UK managers', *Women in Management Review*, 18(6), pp. 288–298.

Osterloh, M. and Frey, B. (2000) 'Motivation, knowledge transfer, and organizational forms', *Organization Science*, 11, 538–550.

Ostrom, E. (1990) *Governing the Commons: The Evolution of Institutions for Collective Action*, Cambridge University Press.

Ouchi, W. (1979) 'A conceptual framework for design of organizational control mechanisms', *Management Science*, 25, pp. 833–848.

Ouchi, W. (1981) *Theory Z: How American Business Can Meet the Japanese Challenge*, Reading, MA: Addison-Wesley.

Ouchi, W.G. (1980) 'Markets, bureaucracies, and clans', *Administrative Science Quarterly*, 25(1), pp. 129–142.

Pachur, T. and Spaar, M. (2015) 'Domain-specific preferences for intuition and deliberation in decision-making', *Journal of Applied Research in Memory and Cognition*, 4(3), 303–311.

Pacini, R. and Epstein, S. (1999) 'The relation of rational and experiential information processing styles to personality, basic beliefs, and the ratio-bias problem', *Journal of Personality and Social Psychology*, 76, pp. 972–987.

Packard, D. (1995) *The HP Way: How Bill Hewlett and I Built Our Company*, New York: HarperCollins.

Paine, L.S. (2003) *Value Shift: Why Companies Must Merge Social and Financial Imperatives to Achieve Superior Performance*, New York: McGraw-Hill.

Parolini, C. (1999) *The Value Net*, Chichester: Wiley.

Pascale, R.T. (1984) 'Perspectives on strategy: The real story behind Honda's success', *California Management Review*, 26(3), pp. 47–72.

Pascale, R.T. (1999) 'Surfing the edge of chaos', *Sloan Management Review*, Spring: pp. 83–94.

Pascale, R.T. and Athos, A.G. (1981) *The Art of Japanese Management*, New York: Simon & Schuster.

Patel, P. and Pavitt, K. (1991) 'Large firms in the production of the world's technology: An important case of "non-globalisation"', *Journal of International Business Studies*, 22(1), pp. 1–21.

Payne, B. (1957) 'Steps in long-range planning', *Harvard Business Review*, 35(2), pp. 95–101.

Pearce, J.A. (1982) 'The company mission as a strategic tool', *Sloan Management Review*, Spring, pp. 15–24.

Peng, M. W. (2013) *Global Strategy*, Mason, OH: Cengage Learning (3rd ed.).

Penrose, E.T. (1959) *The Theory of the Growth of the Firm*, New York: Wiley.

Perlmutter, H.V. (1969) 'The tortuous evolution of multi-national enterprises', *Columbia Journal of World Business*, 1, pp. 9–18.

Perlow, L.A., Gittell, J.H. and Katz, N. (2004) 'Contextualizing patterns of work group interaction: Toward a nested theory of structuration', *Organization Science*, 15(5), pp. 520–536.

Perlow, L.A., Okhuysen, G.A. and Repenning, N.P. (2002) 'The speed trap: Exploring the relationship between decision making and temporal context', *Academy of Management Journal*, 45, pp. 931–955.

Peteraf, M. and Shanley, M. (1997) 'Getting to know you: A theory of strategic group identity', *Strategic Management Journal*, Summer, Special Issue 18, pp. 165–186.

Peters, J.T., Hammond, K.R. and Summers, D.A. (1974) 'A note on intuitive vs. analytic thinking', *Organizational Behavior and Human Performance*, 12, pp. 125–131.

Peters, T.J. and Waterman, R.H. (1982) *In Search of Excellence*, New York: Harper & Row.

Pettigrew, A.M. (1988) *The Management of Strategic Change*, Oxford: Basil Blackwell.

Pettigrew, A.M. (1992) 'The character and significance of strategy process research', *Strategic Management Journal*, 13, pp. 5–16.

Pettigrew, A.M. and Whipp, R. (1991) *Managing Change for Competitive Success*, Oxford: Basil Blackwell.

Pfeffer, J. (1977) 'The ambiguity of leadership', *Academy of Management Review*, 2(1), pp. 104–112.

Pfeffer, J. (1982) *Organizations and Organization Theory*, Boston, MA: Pitman.

Pfeffer, J. (1992) *Managing With Power: Politics and Influence in Organizations*, Boston, MA: Harvard Business School Press.

Pfeffer, J. and Salancik, G. (1978) *The External Control of Organizations: A Resource Dependency Perspective*, New York: Harper & Row.

Pfeffer, J. and Sutton, R.I. (1999a) 'Knowing "what" to do is not enough: Turning knowledge into action', *California Management Review*, 42(1), pp. 83–108.

Pfeffer, J. and Sutton, R.I. (1999b) *The Knowing–Doing Gap: How Smart Companies Turn Knowledge Into Action*, Boston, MA: Harvard Business School Press.

Piercy, N.F. and Morgan, N.A. (1994) 'Mission analysis: An operational approach', *Journal of General Management*, 19(3), pp. 1–16.

Pinchot, G., III (1985) *Intrapreneuring: Why You Don't Have to Leave the Company to Become an Entrepreneur*, New York: Harper & Row.

Pinkley, R.L. (1990) 'Dimensions of conflict frame: Disputant interpretations of conflict', *Journal of Applied Psychology*, 75(2), pp. 117–126.

Piore, M. and Sabel, C.F (1984) *The Second Industrial Divide*, New York: Basic Books.

Pirsig, R.M. (1974) *Zen and the Art of Motorcycle Maintenance: An Inquiry into Values*, New York: Morrow.

Pizarro, D.A. and Bloom, P. (2003) 'The intelligence of the moral intuitions: Comment on Haidt (2001)', *Psychological Review*, 110, pp. 193–196.

Platt, W.J. and Maines, N.R. (1959) 'Pretest your long-range plans', *Harvard Business Review*, 37(1), pp.119–127.

Poincaré, H. (1969) 'Intuition and logic mathematics', *Mathematics Teacher*, 62, pp. 205–212.

Polanyi, M. (1958) *Personal Knowledge*, Chicago, IL: University of Chicago Press.

Polanyi, M. (1963) 'The potential theory of adsorption: Authority in science has its uses and its sangers', *Science*, 141, pp. 1010–1013.

Polanyi, M. (1966) *The Tacit Dimension*, London: Routledge & Kegan Paul.

Policastro, E. (1999), 'Intuition', in: M.A. Runco and S.R. Pritzker (eds.) *Encyclopedia of Creativity*, San Diego, CA: Academic Press (Vol. 2), pp. 89–93.

Pondy, L.R., Boland, J.R. and Thomas, H. (eds.) (1988) *Managing Ambiguity and Change*, New York: Wiley.

Poole, M.S. and Van de Ven, A.H. (1989) 'Using paradox to build management and organization theories', *Academy of Management Review*, 14(4), pp. 562–578.

Porac, J.F., Thomas, H. and Baden-Fuller, C. (1989) 'Competitive groups as cognitive communities: The case of Scottish knitwear manufacturers', *Journal of Management Studies*, 26, pp. 397–416.

Porac, J.F., Thomas, H., Wilson, F., Paton, D. and Kanfer, A. (1995) 'Rivalry and the industry model of Scottish knitwear producers', *Administrative Science Quarterly*, 40(2), pp. 203–227.

Porras, J.I. and Collins, J.C. (1997) *Built to Last: Successful Habits of Visionary Companies*, New York: HarperBusiness.

Porter, M.E. (1980) *Competitive Strategy: Techniques for Analyzing Industries and Competitors*, New York: Free Press.

Porter, M.E. (1985) *Competitive Advantage: Creating and Sustaining Superior Performance*, New York: Free Press.

Porter, M.E. (ed.) (1986) *Competition in Global Industries*, Cambridge, MA: Harvard Business Press.

Porter, M.E. (1987) 'From competitive advantage to corporate strategy', *Harvard Business Review*, 65(3), pp. 43–59.

Porter, M.E. (1990a) *The Competitive Advantage of Nations*, London: Macmillan.

Porter, M.E. (1990b) 'New global strategies for competitive advantage', *Planning Review*, 18(3), pp. 4–14.

Porter, M.E. (1996) 'What is strategy?', *Harvard Business Review*, 74(6), pp. 61–78.

Porter, M.E. (1998) 'Clusters and the new economics of competition', *Harvard Business Review*, November–December.

Porter, M.E. (2001) 'Strategy and the internet', *Harvard Business Review*, 80(3), pp. 62–78.

Porter, M.E. and Kramer, M.A. (2006) 'Strategy and society: The link between competitive advantage and corporate social responsibility', *Harvard Business Review*, December.

Porter, M.E. and Kramer, M.A. (2011) 'Creating shared value: How to reinvent capitalism and unleash a wave of innovation and growth', *Harvard Business Review*, January–February, pp. 3–17.

Porter, R. (1980) *Presidential Decision Making: The Economic Policy Board*, Cambridge: Cambridge University Press.

Powell, T.C. (1992) 'Strategic planning as competitive advantage', *Strategic Management Journal*, 13, pp. 551–558.

Powell, W. (1990) 'Neither market nor hierarchy: Network forms of organization', *Research in Organizational Behavior*, 12, pp. 295–336.

Powell, W.W. (1991) 'Expanding the scope of institutional analysis', in: W.W. Powell and P.J. DiMaggio (eds.) *The New Institutionalism in Organizational Analysis*, Chicago, IL: University of Chicago Press, pp. 183–123.

Prahalad, C.K. (2004a) 'The blinders of dominant logic', *Long Range Planning*, 37, pp. 171–179.

Prahalad, C.K. (2004b) *The Fortune at the Bottom of the Pyramid*, Philadelphia, PA: Wharton School Publishing.

Prahalad, C.K. and Bettis, R.A. (1986) 'The dominant logic: A new linkage between diversity and performance', *Strategic Management Journal*, 7(6), pp. 485–601.

Prahalad, C.K. and Doz, Y. (1987) *The Multinational Mission: Balancing Local Demands and Global Vision*, New York: Free Press.

Prahalad, C.K. and Hamel, G. (1990) 'The core competence of the corporation', *Harvard Business Review*, 68(3), pp. 79–91.

Prahalad, C.K. and Hart, S.L. (2002) 'The fortune at the bottom of the pyramid', *Strategy+Business*, First quarter(26), pp. 1–14–26.

Prebisch, R. (1950), *The Economic Development of Latin America and Its Principal Problems*, New York: United Nations.

Preece, S.B. (1995) 'Incorporating international strategic alliances into overall firm strategy: A typology of six managerial objectives', *International Executive*, 37(3), pp. 261–277.

Prietula, M.J. and Simon, H.A. (1989) 'The experts in your midst', *Harvard Business Review*, 67(1), pp. 120–124.

Quinn, J.B. (1961) 'Long-range planning of industrial research', *Harvard Business Review*, 39(4), pp. 88–102.

Quinn, J.B. (1978) 'Strategic change: "Logical incrementalism"', *Sloan Management Review*, Fall, pp. 7–21.

Quinn, J.B. (1980a) 'Managing strategic change', *Sloan Management Review*, Summer, pp. 3–20.

Quinn, J.B. (1980b) *Strategies for Change*, Homewood, IL: Irwin.

Quinn, J.B. (1985) 'Managing innovation: Controlled chaos', *Harvard Business Review*, 63(3), pp. 73–84.

Quinn, J.B. (1992) *The Intelligent Enterprise: A Knowledge and Service Based Paradigm for Industry*, New York: Free Press.

Quinn, J.B. (2002) 'Strategy, science and management', *Sloan Management Review*, 43(4).

Quinn, R.E. (1984) 'Applying the competing values approach to leadership: Towards an integrative model', in: J.G. Hunt, R. Steward, C. Schriesheim and D. Hosking (eds.) *Leaders and Managers: International perspectives on Managerial Behavior and Leadership*, New York: Paragon, pp. 10–27.

Quinn, R.E. (1988) *Beyond Rational Management: Mastering the Paradoxes and Competing Demands of High Performance*, San Francisco, CA: Jossey-Bass.

Quintana-García, C., and Benavides-Velasco, C.A. (2011). Knowledge organisation in R&D alliances: its impact on product innovation. *Technology Analysis & Strategic Management*, 23(10), pp. 1047–1061.

Radner, R. and Rothschild, M. (1975) 'On the allocation of effort', *Journal of Economic Theory*, 10(3), pp. 358–376.

Rahmandad, H. (2008) 'Effects of delays on complexity of organizational learning', *Management Science*, 54(7), pp. 1297–1312.

Raidl, M.H. and Lubart, T.I. (2000-2001) 'An empirical study of intuition and creativity', *Imagination, Cognition and Personality*, 20, pp. 217–230.

Raiffa, H. (1968) *Decision Analysis: Introductory Lectures on Choices Under Uncertainty*, Reading, MA: Addison-Wesley.

Raisch, S., Birkinshaw, J., Probst, G. and Tushman, M.L. (2009) 'Organizational ambidexterity: Balancing exploitation and exploration for sustained performance', *Organization Science*, 20(4), pp. 685–695.

Ramachandran, J., Manikandan, K.S. and Pant, A. (2013) 'Why conglomerates thrive (outside the U.S.)', *Harvard Business Review*, 91(12), pp. 110–119.

Ramanujam, V. and Varadarajan, P. (1989) 'Research on corporate diversification: A synthesis', *Strategic Management Journal*, 10(6), pp. 523–551.

Ramanujam, V., Ramanujam, N. and Camillus, J.C. (1986) 'Multi-objective assessment of effectiveness of strategic planning: A discriminant analysis approach', *Academy of Management Journal*, 29(2), pp. 347–472.

Rappaport, A. (1986) *Creating Shareholder Value: The New Standard for Business Performance*, New York: Free Press.

Raynor, M.E. and Bower, J.L. (2001) 'Lead from the center: How to manage diverse businesses', *Harvard Business Review*, 80(5), pp. 93–100.

Reber, A.S. (1976) 'Implicit learning of synthetic languages: The role of instructional set', *Journal of Experimental Psychology: Human Learning and Memory*, 2, pp. 88–94.

Reber, A.S. (1989) 'Implicit learning and tacit knowledge', *Journal of Experimental Psychology: General*, 118, pp. 219–235.

Reber, A.S. (1992) 'An evolutionary context for the cognitive unconscious', *Philosophical Psychology*, 5, pp. 33–51.

Reber, A.S., Kassin, S.M., Lewis, S. and Cantor, G. (1980) 'On the relationship between implicit and explicit modes in learning of complex rule structure', *Journal of Experimental Psychology: Human Learning and Memory*, 6, pp. 492–502.

Reber, A.S., Walkenfeld, F.F. and Hernstadt, R. (1991) 'Implicit and explicit learning: Individual differences and IQ', *Journal of Experimental Psychology: Learning, Memory, and Cognition*, 17, pp. 888–896.

Redding, S.G. (1980) 'Cognition as an aspect of culture and its relationship to management processes: An exploratory view of the Chinese case', *Journal of Management Studies*, 17, May, pp. 127–148.

Reger, R.K. and Palmer, T.B. (1996) 'Managerial categorization of competitors: Using old maps to navigate new environments', *Organization Science*, 7(1), pp. 22–39.

Reich, R. and Mankin, E. (1986) 'Joint ventures with Japan give away our future', *Harvard Business Review*, 64(2), pp. 78–86.

Repenning, N.P. (2001) 'Understanding firefighting in new product development', *Journal of Product Innovation Management*, 18, pp. 285–300.

Repenning, N.P. (2002) 'A simulation-based approach to understanding the dynamics of innovation implementation', *Organization Science*, 13(2), pp. 109–127.

Repenning, N.P. and Sterman, J.D. (2002) 'Capability traps and self-confirming attribution errors in the dynamics of process improvement', *ASQ*, 47, pp. 265–295.

Reve, T. (1990) 'The firm as a nexus of internal and external contracts', in: M. Aoki, B. Gustafsson and O.E. Williamson (eds.) *The Firm as a Nexus of Treaties*, London: Sage.

Ricardo, D. (1817) *On the Principles of Political Economy and Taxation*, London: John Murray.

Richardson, G. (1972) 'The organization of industry', *Economic Journal*, 82, pp. 833–896.

Rigby, D. (1999) *Management Tools and Techniques*, Boston, MA: Bain.

Rigg, C. and Sparrow, J. (1994) 'Gender, diversity and working styles', *Women in Management Review*, 9(1), pp. 9–16.

Rittel, H. (1972) 'On the planning crisis: Systems analysis of the "first and second generations"', *Bedriftsokonomen*, 8, pp. 390–396.

Rittel, H.W. and Webber, M.M. (1973) 'Dilemmas in a general theory of planning', *Policy Sciences*, 4, pp. 155–169.

Rivkin, J.W. and Siggelkow, N. (2003) 'Balancing search and stability: Interdependencies among elements of organizational design', *Management Science*, 49(3), pp. 290–311.

Robertson, P. (2005) *Always Change a Winning Team, Why Reinvention and Change Are Prerequisite for Business Success,* Singapore: Marshall Cavendish Business.

Robinson, R.B. (1982) 'The Importance of Outsider in Small Firm Strategic Planning', *Academic Management Journal*, 25(2), 80–93.

Rorty, R. (1967) 'Intuition', in: P. Edwards (ed.) *Encyclopedia of Philosophy*, New York: Macmillan pp. 204–212.

Rosenberg, N. (1982) *Inside the Black Box: Technology and Economics*, Cambridge, MA. Cambridge University Press.

Rosenkopf, L. and Nerkar, A. (2001) 'Beyond local search: Boundary-spanning, exploration, and impact in the optical disk industry', *Strategic Management Journal*, 22(4), pp. 287–306.

Rothenberg, A. (1979) *The Emerging Goddess: The Creative Process in Art, Science, and Other Fields*, Chicago, IL: University of Chicago Press.

Rothermael, F.T. (2001) 'Incumbent's advantage through exploiting complementary assets via interfirm cooperation', *Strategic Management Journal*, 22(6–7), pp. 687–699.

Rottenstreich, Y. and Hsee, C.K. (2001) 'Money, kisses, and electric shocks: On the affective psychology of risk', *Psychological Science*, 12(3), pp. 185–190.

Rowan, R. (1989) 'What it is', in: W.H. Agor (ed.) *Intuition in Organizations: Leading and Managing Productively*, Newbury Park, CA: Sage, pp. 78–88.

Rowe, W.G. (2001) 'Creating wealth in organizations: The role of strategic leadership', *Academy of Management Executive*, 15(1), pp. 81–94.

Ruder, M. and Bless, H. (2003) 'Mood and the reliance on the ease of retrieval heuristic', *Journal of Personality and Social Psychology*, 85, pp. 20–32.

Rugman, A.M. (2005) *The Regional Multinational: MNEs and 'Global' Strategic Management*, Cambridge: Cambridge University Press.

Rugman, A.M. and Verbeke, A. (1993) 'The double diamond model of international competitiveness: The Canadian experience', *Management International Review*, Special Issue, 33, pp. 17–39.

Rugman, A.M. and Verbeke, A. (2001) 'Location, competitiveness and the multinational enterprise', in: A.M. Rugman and T.L. Brewer, *The Oxford Handbook of International Business*, Oxford: Oxford University Press, pp. 150–177.

Ruigrok, W. and Van Tulder, R. (1995) *The Logic of International Restructuring*, London: Routledge.

Rumelt, R.P. (1974) *Strategy, Structure, and Economic Performance*, Cambridge, MA: Harvard University Press.

Rumelt, R.P. (1980) 'The evaluation of business strategy', in: W.F. Glueck (ed.) *Business Policy and Strategic Management*, New York: McGraw-Hill (3rd ed.).

Rumelt, R.P. (1982) 'Diversification strategy and profitability', *Strategic Management Journal*, 3(4), pp. 359–369.

Rumelt, R.P. (1984) 'Towards a strategic theory of the firm', in: R.B. Lamb (ed.) *Competitive Strategic Management*, Englewood Cliffs, NJ: Prentice Hall, pp. 556–570.

Rumelt, R.P. (1991) 'How much does industry matter?', *Strategic Management Journal*, 12(3), pp. 167–186.

Rumelt, R.P. (1995) 'Inertia and transformation', in: C.A. Montgomery (ed.) *Resource-based and Evolutionary Theories of the Firm: Towards a Synthesis*, Boston, MA: Kluwer Academic, pp. 101–132.

Rumelt, R.P. (1996) 'Inertia and transformation', in: C.A. Montgomery (ed.) *Resource-based and Evolutionary Theories of the Firm: Towards a Synthesis*, Boston, MA: Kluwer Academic, pp. 101–132.

Russo, J.E. and Schoemaker, P.J.H. (1989) *Decision Traps*, New York: Doubleday.

Sabri, H. (2008) 'Jordanian managers' leadership styles in comparison with the International Air Transport Association (IATA) and prospects for knowledge management in Jordan', *International Journal of Commerce and Management*, 17(1/2), pp. 56–72.

Sadler-Smith, E. (2004) 'Cognitive style and the management of small and medium-sized enterprises', *Organization Studies*, 25(2), pp. 155–181.

Sadler-Smith, E. (2010) *The Intuitive Mind: Profiting From the Power of Your Sixth Sense*, Chichester: Wiley.

Sanchez, R., Heene, A. and Thomas, H. (eds.) (1996) *Dynamics of Competence-Based Competition*, London: Elsevier.

Sanfey, A.G., Rilling, J.K., Aronson, J.A., Nystrom, L.E. and Cohen, J.D. (2003) 'The neural basis of economic decision-making in the ultimatum game', *Science*, 300(5626), pp. 1755–1758.

Sarkar, J. and Sarkar, S. (2000) 'Large shareholder activism in corporate governance in developing countries: Evidence from India', *International Review of Finance*, 1(3), pp. 161–194.

Sashkin, M. and Burke, W.W. (1990) 'Organization development in the 1980s', *Journal of Management*, 13(2), pp. 393–417.

Scheepers, D. and Ellemers, N. (2005) 'When the pressure is up: The assessment of social identity threat in low and high status groups', *Journal of Experimental Social Psychology*, 41(2), pp. 192–200.

Schein, E.H. (1985) *Organizational Culture and Leadership*, San Francisco, CA: Jossey-Bass.

Schein, E.H. (1993) 'On dialogue, culture, and organizational learning', *Organizational Dynamics*, 22(2), pp. 40–51.

Schein, E.H. (1995) *Organizational Culture*, Frankfurt/New York: Campus Verlag.

Schein, E.H. (2004) *Organizational Culture and Leadership*, San Francisco, CA: Wiley.

Schelling, T. (1960) *The Strategy of Conflict*, Cambridge, MA: Harvard University Press.

Schmalensee, R. (1983) 'Advertising and entry deterrence: An exploratory model', *Journal of Political Economy*, 91(4), pp. 636–653.

Schneider, S. and Barsoux, J. (1999) *Managing Across Cultures*, London: Pearson.

Schneider, S. and Barsoux, J. (2003) *Managing Across Cultures*, London: Pearson (2nd ed.).

Schneider, S.C. (1989) 'Strategy formulation: The impact of national culture', *Organization Studies*, 10(2), pp. 149–168.

Schneider, W. and Shiffrin, R.M. (1977) 'Controlled and automatic human information processing: 1. Detection, search, and attention', *Psychological Review*, 84(1), pp. 1–66.

Schoemaker, P.J.H. (1993) 'Multiple scenario development: Its conceptual and behavioral basis', *Strategic Management Journal*, 14(3), pp. 193–213.

Schoemaker, P.J.H. (1995) 'Scenario planning: A tool for strategic thinking', *Sloan Management Review*, 23(2), pp. 25–34.

Schoemaker, P.J.H. and Russo, J.E. (1993) 'A pyramid of decision Approaches', *California Management Review*, 36(1), pp. 9–32.

Schumpeter, J.A. (1934) *Theory of Economic Development*, Cambridge, MA: Harvard University Press.

Schumpeter, J.A. (1942) *Capitalism, Socialism, and Democracy*, New York: Harper.

Schumpeter, J.A. (1950) *Capitalism, Socialism and Democracy*, New York: Harper & Brothers (3rd ed.).

Schwartz, S.H. (1999) 'A theory of cultural values and some implications for work', *Applied Psychology*, 48(1), pp. 23–47.

Schwarz, N., Bless, H. and Bohner, G. (1991) 'Mood and persuasion: Affective states influence the processing of persuasive communications', *Advances in Experimental Social Psychology*, 24, pp. 161–199.

Schwenk, C.R. (1984) 'Cognitive simplification processes in strategic decision-making', *Strategic Management Journal*, 5(2), pp. 111–128.

Schwenk, C.R. (1986) 'Information, cognitive biases, and commitment to a course of action', *Academy of Management Review*, 11(2), pp. 298–310.

Schwenk, C.R. (1988) *The Essence of Strategic Decision Making*, Lexington, MA: Lexington Books.

Seger, C.A. (1994) 'Implicit learning', *Psychological Bulletin*, 115, pp. 163–196.

Selznick, P. (1957) *Leadership in Administration: A Sociological Interpretation*, New York: Harper & Row.

Senge, P.M. (1990a) 'The leader's new work: Building learning organizations', *Sloan Management Review*, 32(1), pp. 7–23.

Senge, P.M. (1990b) *The Fifth Discipline: The Art and Practice of the Learning Organization*, New York: Doubleday/Currency.

Servan-Schreiber, J.J. (1967) *Le Defi Americain*, Paris: Denoel.

Seth, A. (1990) 'Value creation in acquisitions: A re-examination of performance issues', *Strategic Management Journal*, 11(2), pp. 99–115.

Shane, S. (2003) *A General Theory of Entrepreneurship*, Northampton, MA: Edward Elgar.

Shanteau, J. and Stewart, T.R. (1992) 'Why study expert decision making? Some historical perspectives and comments', *Organizational Behavior and Human Decision Processes*, 53, pp. 95–106.

Shapiro, C. (1989) 'The theory of business strategy', *RAND Journal of Economics*, 20(1), pp. 125–137.

Shapiro, C. and Varian, H. (1998) *Information Rules: A Strategic Guide to the Network Economy*, Cambridge, MA: Harvard Business School Press.

Shapiro, S. and Spence, M. T. (1997) 'Managerial intuition: A conceptual and operational framework', *Business Horizons*, 40(1), pp. 63–68.

Sherif, M. (1971) 'Superordinate goals in the reduction of intergroup conflict', in: B.L. Hinton and H.J. Reits (eds.) *Groups and Organizations*, Belmonte, CA: Wadsworth.

Shirley, D.A. and Langan-Fox, J. (1996) 'Intuition: A review of the literature', *Psychological Reports*, 79, pp. 563–584.

Shuen, A. (1994) 'Technology sourcing and learning strategies in the semiconductor industry', unpublished PhD dissertation, University of California, Berkeley.

Siggelkow, N. and Levinthal, D.A. (2003) 'Temporarily divide to conquer: Centralized, decentralized, and reintegrated organizational approaches to exploration and adaptation', *Organization Science*, 14(6), pp. 650–669.

Simon, H.A. (1955) 'A behavioral model of rational choice', *Quarterly Journal of Economics*, 69(1), pp. 99–118.

Simon, H.A. (1957) *Models of Man*, New York: Wiley.

Simon, H.A. (1969) *The Sciences of the Artificial*, Cambridge, MA: MIT Press.

Simon, H.A. (1972) 'Theories of bounded rationality', in: C. McGuire and R. Radner (eds.) *Decision and Organization*, Amsterdam: North-Holland, pp. 161–176.

Simon, H.A. (1987) 'Making management decisions: The role of intuition and emotion', *Academy of Management Executive*, 1(1), pp. 57–64.

Simon, H.A. (1992) 'What is an "explanation" of behavior?', *Psychological Science*, 3, pp. 150–161.

Simon, H.A. (1993) 'Altruism and economics', *American Economic Review*, 83(2), pp. 156–161.

Simon, H.A. (1996) *The Sciences of the Artificial*, Cambridge, MA: MIT Press, (3rd ed.).

Simon, H.A. and Chase, W.G. (1973) 'Skill in chess', *American Scientist*, 61, pp. 394–403.

Simonin, B. (1997) 'The importance of collaborative know-how', *Academy of Management Journal*, 40(5), pp. 1150–1174.

Simons, R. (1994) 'How new top managers use control systems as levers of strategic renewal', *Strategic Management Journal*, 15(3), pp. 169–189.

Simons, R. (1995) *Levers of Control: How Managers Use Innovative Control Systems to Drive Strategic Renewal*, Boston, MA: HBS Press.

Simons, R.L. and Weston, H.A. (1990) *MCI Communications Corp.: planning for the 1990s, Case number 1–90136*, Boston, MA: Harvard Business School.

Sims, H.P. and Lorenzi, P. (1992) *The New Leadership Paradigm: Social Learning and Cognition in Organizations*, London: Sage.

Sinclair, M., Ashkanasy, N.M., Chattopadhyay, P. and Boyle, M.V. (2002) 'Determinants of intuitive decision-making in management: The moderating role of affect', in: N.M. Ashkanasy, W. Zerbe and C.E.J. Härtel (eds.) *Managing Emotions in the Workplace*, Armonk, NY: M.E. Sharpe, pp. 143–163.

Sinha, D.K. (1990) 'The contribution of formal planning to decisions', *Strategic Management Journal*, 11(6), pp. 479–492.

Sirower, M.L. (1997) *The Synergy Trap: How Companies Lose the Acquisition Game*, New York: Free Press.

Sivanathan, N., Molden, D.C., Galinsky, A.D. and Ku, G. (2008) 'The promise and peril of self-affirmation in de-escalation of commitment', *Organizational Behavior and Human Decision Processes*, 107(1), pp. 1–14.

Slater, R. (1999) *Jack Welch and the GE Way*, New York: McGraw-Hill.

Sloman, S.A. (1996) 'The empirical case for two systems of reasoning', *Psychological Bulletin*, 119, 3–22.

Slovic, P., Finucane, M.L., Peters, E. and MacGregor, D.G. (2004) 'Risk as analysis and risk as feelings: Some thoughts about affect, reason, risk, and rationality', *Risk Analysis*, 24(2), pp. 311–322.

Slywotsky, A.J. (1996) *Value Migration*, Boston, MA: Harvard Business School Press.

Smircich, L. and Stubbart, C. (1985) 'Strategic management in an enacted world', *Academy of Management Review*, 10(4), pp. 724–736.

Smith, A. (1776) *An Inquiry into the Nature and Causes of the Wealth of Nations*, London: printed for W. Strahan and T. Cadell, in the Strand.

Smith, A. and Venables, J. (1988) 'Completing the internal market in the European Community: Some industry simulations', *European Economic Review*, 32(7), pp. 1501–1525.

Smith, K. and Lewis, M.W. (2011) 'Toward a theory of paradox: A dynamic equilibrium model of organizing', *Academy of Management Review*, 36(2), pp. 381–403.

Smith, K.K. and Berg, D.N. (1987) *Paradoxes of Group Life*, San Francisco, CA: Jossey-Bass.

Smith, W.K. (2009), 'A dynamic approach to managing contradictions', *Industrial and Organizational Psychology: Perspectives on Science and Practice*, 2, pp. 338–343.

Smith, W.K. and Tushman, M.L. (2005) 'Managing strategic contradictions: A top management model for managing innovation streams', *Organization Science*, 16(5), pp. 522–536.

Smith, W.K., Lewis, M.W. and Tushman, M.L. (2016), 'Both/and leadership', *Harvard Business Review*, May, pp. 62–70.

Solomon, R.C. (1992) *Ethics and Excellence: Cooperation and Integrity in Business*, New York: Oxford University Press.

Sorrell, M., Komisar, R. and Mulcahy, A. (2010) 'How we do it: Three executives reflect on strategic decision making', *McKinsey Quarterly*, 2, pp. 46–57.

Spencer, A. (1983) *On the Edge of the Organization: The Role of the Outside Director*, New York: Wiley.

Spender, J.C. (1989) *Industry Recipe: An Enquiry into the Nature and Sources of Managerial Judgement*, New York: Basil Blackwell.

Stacey, R.D. (1992) *Managing Chaos: Dynamic Business Strategies in an Unpredictable World*, London: Kogan Page.

Stacey, R.D. (1993) 'Strategy as corder emerging from Chaos', *Long Range Planning*, 26(1), pp. 10–17.

Stacey, R.D. (2001) *Complex Responsive Processes in Organizations: Learning and Knowledge Creation*, London: Routledge.

Stadler, M.A. and Frensch, P.A. (1998) *Handbook of Implicit Learning*, Thousand Oaks, CA: Sage.

Stalk, G., Evans, P. and Schulman, L.E. (1992) 'Competing on capabilities: The new rules of corporate strategy', *Harvard Business Review*, 70(2), pp. 57–69.

Stanovich, K.E. and West, R.F. (2000) 'Individual differences in reasoning: Implications for the rationality debate?', *Behavioral and Brain Sciences*, 23, pp. 645–665.

Starbuck, W. and Milliken, F. (1988) 'Challenger: Fine-Tuning the odds until something breaks', *Journal of Management Studies*, 25(4), pp. 319–340.

Starbuck, W.H. (2014). Five stories that illustrate three generalizations about radical innovations. *Industrial Marketing Management*, *43*(8), pp. 1278–1283.

Staw, B.M. (1976) 'Knee-deep in the big muddy: A study of escalating commitment to a chosen course of action', *Organizational Behavior and Human Performance*, 16(1), pp. 27–44.

Staw, B.M. and Ross, J. (1987) 'Behavior in escalation situations: Antecedents, prototypes, and solutions', *Research in Organizational Behavior*, 9, pp. 39–78.

Staw, B.M., Sandelands, L.E. and Dutton, J.E. (1981) 'Threat rigidity effects in organizational behavior: A multilevel analysis', *Administrative Science Quarterly*, 26, pp. 501–524.

Steers, R.M., Shin, Y.K. and Ungson, G.R. (1991) *The Chaebol: Korea's New Industrial Might*, New York: HarperCollins.

Steiner, G.A. (1979) *Strategic Planning: What Every Manager Must Know*, New York: Free Press.

Steiner, G.A. and Schollhammer, H. (1975) 'Pitfalls in multi-national long-range planning', *Long Range Planning*, 8(2), pp. 2–12.

Steiner, I. (1972) *Group Processes and Productivity*, New York: Academic Press.

Sternberg, R.J. and Davidson, J.E. (1995) *The Nature of Insight*, Cambridge, MA: MIT Press.

Stinchcombe, A.L. (1965) 'Social structure and organizations', in: J.G. March (ed.) *Handbook of Organizations*, Chicago, IL: Rand McNally, pp. 142–193.

Stone, C.D. (1975) *Where the Law Ends*, New York: Harper & Row.

Stopford, J.M. and Wells, L.T. (1972) *Strategy and Structure of Multinational Enterprise*, New York: Basic Books.

Story, V.M., Daniels, K., Zolkiewski, J., and Dainty, A.R.J. (2014). The barriers and consequences of radical innovations: Introduction to the issue. *Industrial Marketing Management*, *43*, pp. 1271–1277.

Strebel, P. (1992) *Breakpoints: How Managers Exploit Radical Business Change*, Boston, MA: Harvard Business School Press.

Strebel, P. (1994) 'Choosing the right change path', *California Management Review*, 36(2), pp. 29–51.

Suedfeld, P., Tetlock, T. and Streufert, S (1992) 'Conceptual/integrative complexity', in: C. Smith, J. Atkinson, D. McClelland and J. Verof (eds.) *Motivation and Personality: Handbook of Thematic Content Analysis*, Cambridge: Cambridge University Press, pp. 393–400.

Suetorsak, R. (2007) 'Keiretsu and risk: An examination of the risk exposure of keiretsu banks in Japan', *Journal of Economics and Finance*, 31(2), pp. 268–282.

Sull, D.N. (1999) 'The dynamics of standing still: Firestone tire & rubber and the radial revolution', *Business History Review*, 73(3), pp. 430–464.

Sull, D.N., Tedlow, R.S. and Rosenbloom, R.S. (1997) 'Managerial commitments and technological change in the US tire industry', *Industrial and Corporate Change*, 6(2), pp. 461–500.

Sun Tzu (1983) *The Art of War*, New York: Delacorte Press.

Sundaramurthy, C. and Lewis, M. (2003) 'Control and collaboration: Paradoxes of governance', *Academy of Management Review*, 28(3), pp. 397–415.

Suri, R. and Monroe, K.B. (2003) 'The effects of time constraints on consumers' judgments of prices and products', *Journal of Consumer Research*, 30, pp. 92–104.

Sutcliffe, K.M. and Huber, G.P. (1998) 'Firm and industry determinants of executive perceptions of the environment', *Strategic Management Journal*, 19, pp. 793–807.

Sutton, J. (1992) 'Implementing game theoretical models in industrial economics', in: A. Del Monte (ed.) *Recent Developments in the Theory of Industrial Organization*, Ann Arbor, MI: University of Michigan Press, pp. 19–33.

Sutton, R. (2002) *Weird Ideas that Work: 11½ Practices for Promoting, Managing, and Sustaining Innovation*, New York: Free Press.

Sykes, A. (1994) 'Proposals for internationally competitive corporate governance in Britain and America', *Corporate Governance*, 2(4), pp. 187–195.

Taleb, H.M. (2010) 'Gender and leadership styles in single-sex academic institutions', *International Journal of Educational Management*, 24(4), pp. 287–302.

Tannenbaum, R. and Schmidt, W.H. (1958) 'How to choose a leadership pattern', *Harvard Business Review*, 36(2), pp. 95–101.

Taylor, F.W (1903) *Shop Management*, New York: Harper.

Taylor, F.W. (1911) *The Principles of Scientific Management*, New York: Harper.

Teece, D.J. (1976) *The Multinational Corporation and the Resource Cost of International Technology Transfer*, Cambridge, MA: Ballinger.

Teece, D.J. (1977) 'Technology transfer by multinational enterprises: The resource cost of transferring technological know-how', *Economic Journal*, 87, June, pp. 242–261.

Teece, D.J. (1980) 'Economies of scope and the scope of the enterprise', *Journal of Economic Behavior and Organization*, 1(3), pp. 223–247.

Teece, D.J. (1981a) 'Internal organization and economic performance: An empirical analysis of the profitability of principal enterprises', *Journal of Industrial Economics*, 30(2), pp. 173–199.

Teece, D.J. (1981b) 'The market for know-how and the efficient international transfer of technology', *Annals of the Academy of Political and Social Science*, 458, pp. 81–96.

Teece, D.J. (1982) 'Towards an economic theory of the multiproduct firm', *Journal of Economic Behavior and Organization*, 3, pp. 39–63.

Teece, D.J. (1984) 'Economic analysis and strategic management', *California Management Review*, 26(3), pp. 87–110.

Teece, D.J. (1986a) 'Transaction cost economics and the multinational enterprise', *Journal of Economic Behavior and Organization*, 7, pp. 21–45.

Teece, D.J. (1986b) 'Profiting from technological innovation', *Research Policy*, 15(6), pp. 285–305.

Teece, D.J. (1988) 'Technological change and the nature of the firm', in: G. Dosi, C. Freeman, R. Nelson, G. Silverberg L. and Soete (eds.) *Technical Change and Economic Policy*, New York: Pinter, pp. 256–281.

Teece, D.J. (1992) 'Competition, cooperation, and innovation: Organizational arrangements for regimes of rapid technological progress', *Journal of Economic Behavior and Organization*, 18, pp. 1–25.

Teece, D.J. (1996) 'Firm organization, industrial structure, and technological innovation', *Journal of Economic Behavior and Organization*, 31, pp. 193–224.

Teece, D.J. (2000) *Managing Intellectual Capital: Organizational, Strategic, and Policy Dimensions*, Oxford: Oxford University Press.

Teece, D.J. (2003) 'Expert talent and the design of (professional services) enterprises', *Industrial and Corporate Change*, 12(4), pp. 895–916.

Teece, D.J. (2007) 'Explicating dynamic capabilities: The nature and microfoundations of (sustainable) enterprise performance', *Strategic Management Journal*, 28(13), pp. 1319–1350.

Teece, D.J. and Pisano, G. (1994) 'The dynamic capabilities of enterprises: An introduction', *Industrial and Corporate Change*, 3(3), pp. 537–556.

Teece, D.J., Pisano, G. and Shuen, A. (1990a) 'Enterprise capabilities, resources and the concept of strategy', Consortium on Competitiveness and Cooperation, Working Paper CCC 90-8, Berkeley, CA: Institute of Management, Innovation and Organization, University of California.

Teece, D.J., Pisano, G. and Shuen, A. (1990b) 'Firm capabilities, resources and the concept of strategy', Economic Analysis and Policy Working Paper EAP-38, Berkeley, CA: Institute of Management, Innovation and Organization, University of California.

Teece, D.J., Pisano, G, and Shuen, A. (1997) 'Dynamic capabilities and strategic management', *Strategic Management Journal*, 18(7), pp. 509–533.

Teece, D.J., Rumelt, R., Dosi, G. and Winter, S. (1994) 'Understanding corporate coherence: Theory and evidence', *Journal of Economic Behavior and Organization*, 23, pp. 1–20.

Tellis, G.J. (2013) *Unrelenting Innovation: How to Build a Culture for Market Dominance*, San Francisco, CA: Jossey-Bass.

Tellis, G.J., Prabhu, J. C., and Chandy, R.K. (2009). Radical Innovation Across Nations: The Preeminence of Corporate Culture. *Journal of Marketing*, 73(1), pp. 3–23.

Teranishi, J. (1994) 'Loan syndication in war time Japan and the origins of the main bank system', in: N. Aoki H. and Patrick (eds.) *The Japanese Main Bank System*, Oxford: Clarendon Press.

Tetlock, P.E., McGraw, A.P. and Kristel, O.V. (2004) 'Proscribed forms of social cognition: Taboo trade-offs, blocked exchanges, forbidden base rates, and heretical counterfactuals', in: N. Haslam (ed.) *Relational Models Theory: A Contemporary Overview*, Mahwah, NJ: Erlbaum, pp. 247–262.

Thompson, J.D. (1967) *Organizations in Action: Social Science Bases of Administrative Theory*, New York: McGraw-Hill.

Thomson, D.G. (2006) *Blueprint to a Billion: 7 Essentials to Achieve Exponential Growth*, Hoboken, NJ: Wiley.

Thorelli, H.B. (1986) 'Networks: Between markets and hierarchies', *Strategic Management Journal*, 7(1), pp. 37–51.

Thurbin, P.J. (1998) *The Influential Strategist: Using the Power of Paradox in Strategic Thinking*, London: Financial Times.

Thurow, L. (1991) *Head to Head*, Cambridge, MA: MIT Press.

Tichy, N. and Cohen, E. (1997) *The Leadership Engine: How Winning Companies Build Leaders at Every Level*, New York: HarperCollins.

Tidd, J., Bessant, J. and Pavitt, K. (1997) *Managing Innovation: Integrating Technological, Market and Organizational Change*, Chichester: Wiley.

Tiedens, L. and Linton, S. (2001) 'Judgment under emotional certainty and uncertainty: The effects of specific emotions on information processing', *Journal of Personality and Social Psychology*, 81, pp. 1–16.

Tirole, J. (1988) *The Theory of Industrial Organization*, Cambridge, MA: MIT Press.

Trautwein, F. (1990) 'Merger motives and merger prescriptions', *Strategic Management Journal*, 11(4), pp. 283–295.

Treacy, M. and Wiersema, F. (1995) *The Discipline of Market Leaders*, Reading, MA: Addison-Wesley.

Trice, H.M. and Beyer, J.M. (1993) *The Cultures of Work Organizations*, Englewood Cliffs, NJ: Prentice Hall.

Tricker, R.I. (ed.) (1994) *International Corporate Governance: Text, Readings and Cases*, Singapore: Prentice Hall.

Tripsas, M. and Gavetti, G. (2000) 'Capabilities, cognition, and inertia: Evidence from digital imaging', *Strategic Management Journal*, 21(10/11), Special Issue, pp. 1147–1161.

Trompenaars, A. (1993) *Riding the Waves of Culture: Understanding Cultural Diversity in Business*, London: Economist Books.

Trompenaars, A. (2003) *Did the Pedestrian Die: Insights from the World's Greatest Culture Guru*, Oxford: Capstone Publishing

Trompenaars, A. and Hampden-Turner, C. (2000) *Building Cross-Cultural Competence*, New Haven, CT: Yale University Press.

Trompenaars, A. and Hampden-Turner, C. (2012) *Riding the Waves of Culture: Understanding Diversity in Global Business,* London: Hodder & Stoughton General Division.

Tucker, R.C. (1968) 'The theory of charismatic leadership', *Daedalus*, 97(3), pp. 731–756.

Tuna, C. (2009) 'Pendulum is swinging back on "scenario planning"', *Wall Street Journal*, 6 July.

Tushman, M.L and Anderson, P. (1986) 'Technological discontinuities and organizational environments', *Administration Science Quarterly*, 31, pp. 439–465.

Tushman, M.L. and O'Reilly III, C.A. (1996) 'Ambidextrous organizations: Managing evolutionary and revolutionary change', *California Management Review*, 38(4), pp. 8–30.

Tushman, M.L. and O'Reilly III, C.A. (1997) *Winning Through Innovation: A Practical Guide to Leading Organizational Change and Renewal*, Boston, MA: Harvard Business School.

Tushman, M.L., Newman, W.H. and Romanelli, E. (1986) 'Convergence and upheaval: Managing the unsteady pace of organizational evolution', *California Management Review*, 29(1), pp. 29–44.

Tushman, M.L, Smith, W., Wood, R., Westerman, G. and O'Reilly, C. (2003) 'Innovation streams and ambidextrous organizational forms', working paper, Boston, MA: Harvard Business School Press.

Tversky, A. and Kahneman, D. (1974) 'Judgment under uncertainty: Heuristics and biases', *Science*, 185, pp. 1124–1131.

Tversky, A. and Kahneman, D. (1983) 'Extensional versus intuitive reasoning: The conjunction fallacy in probability judgment', *Psychological Review*, 90, pp. 293–315.

Tversky, A. and Kahneman, D. (1986) 'Rational choice and the framing of decisions', *Journal of Business*, 59(4), pp. 251–278.

Tyre, M.J. and Von Hippel, E. (1997) 'The situated nature of adaptive learning in organizations', *Organization Science*, 8(1), pp. 71–83.

UNCTAD (2010) World Investment Report.

US House of Representatives, Committee on Science and Technology (1976) *Long Range Planning*, Washington, DC: U.S. Government Printing Office.

Utterback, J. (1994) *Mastering the Dynamics of Innovation*, Boston, MA: Harvard Business School Press.

Van de Ven, A.D., Poley, D.E., Garud, R. and Venkataraman, S. (1999) *The Innovation Journey*, New York: Oxford University Press.

Van der Heijden K. (1993) 'Strategic vision at work: Discussing strategic vision in management teams', in: J. Hendry, G. Johnson and J. Newton (eds.) *Strategic Thinking: Leadership and the Management of Change*, New York: Wiley, pp. 137–150.

Van der Heijden, K. (1996) *Scenarios: The Art of Strategic Conversation*, New York: Wiley.

Van der Heijden, K. (1997) *Scenarios: Strategies and the Strategy Process*, Amsterdam: Nyenrode University Press.

Van der Heijden, K. (2004) 'Can internally generated futures accelerate organizational learning?', *Futures*, 36, pp.145–159.

Van Maanen, J. (1973) 'Observation of the making of policemen', *Human Relations*, 32, pp. 407–418.

Van Tulder, R. and Junne, G. (1988) *European Multinationals and Core Technologies*, London: Wiley.

Vaughan, F.E. (1979) *Awakening Intuition*, New York: Doubleday.

Veliyath, R. (1992) 'Strategic planning: Balancing short-run performance and longer term prospects', *Long Range Planning*, 25(3), pp. 86–97.

Verluyten, S.P. (2000) *Intercultural Communication in Business and Organisations*, Leuven: Acco.

Verluyten, S.P. (2010) *Intercultural Skills for Business and International Relations: A Practical Introduction with Exercises*, Leuven: Acco.

Vernon, R. (1966) 'International investment and international trade in the product life cycle', *Quarterly Journal of Economics*, 80(2), pp. 190–207.

Vernon, R. (1977) *Storm Over The Multinationals: The Real Issues*, Cambridge, MA: Harvard University Press.

Virany, B., Tushman, M.L. and Romanelli, E. (1992) 'Executive succession and organization outcomes in turbulent environments: An organization learning approach', *Organization Science*, 3(1), pp. 72–91.

Von Winterfeldt, D. and Edwards, W. (1986) *Decision Analysis and Behavioural Research*, Cambridge: Cambridge University Press.

Voorhees, B. (1986) 'Towards duality theory', *General Systems Bulletin*, 16(2), pp. 58–61.

Vroom, V.H., and Jago, A.G. (1988) *The New Leadership: Managing Participation in Organizations*, Englewood Cliffs, NJ: Prentice Hall.

Wack, P. (1985a) 'Scenarios: Unchartered waters ahead', *Harvard Business Review*, 64(5), pp. 73–89.

Wack, P. (1985b) 'Scenarios: Shooting the rapids', *Harvard Business Review*, 64(6), pp. 139–150.

Wageman, R. (2001) 'How leaders foster self-managing team effectiveness: Design choices versus hands-on coaching', *Organization Science*, 12(5), pp. 559–577.

Waldman, D.A. and Yammarino, F.H. (1999) 'CEO charismatic leadership: Levels-of-management and levels-of-analysis effects', *Academy of Management Review*, 24(2), pp. 266–285.

Wallerstein, I. (1974) *The Modern World-System, Vol. I: Capitalist Agriculture and the Origins of the European World-Economy in the Sixteenth Century*, New York/London: Academic Press.

Walsh, J.P. (1995) 'Managerial and organizational cognition: Notes from a trip down memory lane', *Organization Science*, 6(3), pp. 280–321.

Walton, R.E. and McKersie, R.B. (eds.) (1965) *A Behavioral Theory of Labor Negotiations: An Analysis of a Social Interaction System*, New York: McGraw-Hill.

Wartick, S.L. and Wood, D.J. (1998) *International Business and Society*, Oxford: Blackwell.

Waterman, R.H., Peters, T.J. and Phillips, J.R. (1980) 'Structure is not organization', *Business Horizons*, 23, June, pp. 14–26.

Webster, F. (1994) *Market Driven Management: Using the New Marketing Concept to Create a Customer-oriented Company*, New York: Wiley.

Wegner, D. (1986) 'Transactive memory: A contemporary analysis of group mind', in: B. Mullen and G.R. Goethals (eds.) *Theories of Group Behavior*, New York: Springer-Verlag, pp. 185–208.

Weick, K. (1979) *The Social Psychology of Organizing*, Reading, MA: Addison-Wesley (2nd ed.).

Weick, K. (1995) *Sensemaking in Organizations*, Thousand Oaks, CA: Sage.

Weick, K.E. and Bourgnon, M.G. (1986) 'Organizations as cognitive maps', in: H.P Sims Jr. and D.A. Gioia (eds.) *The Thinking Organization*, San Francisco, CA: Jossey-Bass.

Weick, K.E. and Roberts, K.H. (1993) 'Collective mind in organizations: Heedful interrelating on flight decks', *Administrative Science Quarterly*, 38(3), pp. 357–381.

Weick, K.E., Sutcliffe, D. and Obstfeld, D. (1999) 'Organizing for high reliability: Processes of collective mindfulness', in: R.I. Sutton and B.M. Staw (eds.) *Research in Organizational Behavior*, Stamford, CT: JAI Press, pp. 81–123.

Weidenbaum, M. and Hughes, S. (1996) *The Bamboo Network: How Expatriate Chinese Entrepreneurs Are Creating a New Economic Superpower in Asia*, New York: Free Press.

Weiss, H.M. and Cropanzano, R. (1996) 'Affective events theory: A theoretical discussion of the structure, causes and consequences of affective experiences at work', *Research in Organizational Behavior*, 18, pp. 1–74.

Weiss, J.W. (2014) *Business Ethics: A Stakeholder and Issues Management Approach*, San Francisco, CA: Berrett-Koehler (6th ed.).

Welch, J. and Byrne, J.A. (2001) *Jack: Straight from the Gut*, New York: Warner Books.

Welling, D.T. and Kamann, D.-J.F. (2001) 'Vertical cooperation in the construction industry: Size does matter', *Journal of Supply Chain Management*, 37(3), pp. 28–33.

Wernerfelt, B. (1984) 'A resource-based view of the firm', *Strategic Management Journal*, 5(2), pp. 171–180.

Wernerfelt, B. and Montgomery, C. (1988) 'Tobin's Q and the importance of focus in firm performance', *American Economic Review*, 78(1), pp. 246–250.

Westcott, M.R. and Ranzoni, J.H. (1963) 'Correlates of intuitive thinking', *Psychological Reports*, 12, pp. 595–613.

Weston, J.F., Chung, K.S. and Hoag, S.E. (1990) *Mergers, Restructuring, and Corporate Control*, Englewood Cliffs, NJ: Prentice Hall.

Wheatley, M.J. and Kellner-Rogers, M. (1996) 'Self-organization: The irresistible future of organizing', *Strategy, and Leadership*, 24(4), pp. 18–25.

Whitley, R.D. (1999) *Divergent Capitalisms: The Social Structuring and Change of Business Systems*, Oxford: Oxford University Press.

Whittington, R. (1993) *What is Strategy and Does it Matter?*, London: Routledge.

Whyte, W.H. Jr. (1957) *The Organization Man*, Garden City, NY: Doubleday.

Wild, K.W. (1938) *Intuition*, Cambridge: Cambridge University Press.

Wildavsky, A. (1979) *Speaking Truth to Power: The Art and Craft of Policy Analysis,* Toronto: Little, Brown & Co.

Wilkins, M. (2003) 'The history of the international enterprise', in: A.L. Rugman, and T.L. Brewer, *The Oxford Handbook of International Business*, Oxford: Oxford University Press.

Williamson, O.E. (1975) *Markets and Hierarchies: Analysis and Antitrust Implications*, New York: Free Press.

Williamson, O.E. (1985) *The Economic Institutions of Capitalism*, New York: Free Press.

Williamson, O.E. (1991) 'Strategizing, economizing, and economic organization', *Strategic Management Journal*, 12, Special Issue, pp. 75–94.

Wilson, D.C. (1992) *A Strategy of Change*, London: Routledge.

Wilson, I. (1994) 'Strategic planning isn't dead—it changed', *Long Range Planning*, 27(4), pp. 12–24.

Wilson, I. (2000) 'From scenario thinking to strategic action', *Technological Forecasting and Social Change*, 65(1), pp. 23–29.

Wilson, I. and Ralston, W. (2006) *Scenario Planning Handbook: Developing Strategies in Uncertain Times,* Belmont, CA: South-Western Educational Publishers.

Wilson, T.D. and Schooler, J. W. (1991) 'Thinking too much: Introspection can reduce the quality of preferences and decisions', *Journal of Personality and Social Psychology*, 60, pp. 181–192.

Wing, R.L. (1988) *The Art of Strategy: A New Translation of Sun Tzu's Classic 'The Art of War'*, New York: Doubleday.

WIPO (2008) *World Patent Report: A Statistical Review*, World Intellectual Property Organization.

WIPO (2015) *World Intellectual Property Indicators 2015*, World Intellectual Property Organization.

Womack, J.P., Jones, D.T. and Roos, D. (1990) *The Machine that Changed the World*, New York: Harper Perennial.

Wonder, J. and Blake, J. (1992) 'Creativity east and west: Intuition vs. logic', *Journal of Creative Behavior*, 26(3), pp. 172–185.

Wong, K.F.E., Kwong, J.Y.Y. and Ng, C.K. (2008) 'When thinking rationally increases biases: The role of rational thinking style in escalation of commitment', *Applied Psychology: An International Review*, 57(2), pp. 246–271.

Wong, K.F.E., Yik, M. and Kwong, J.Y.Y. (2006) 'Understanding the emotional aspects of escalation of commitment: The role of negative affect', *Journal of Applied Psychology*, 91(2), pp. 282–297.

Wooldridge, B. and Floyd, S.W. (1990) The strategy process, middle management involvement, and organizational performance, *Strategic Management Journal*, 11(3): pp. 231–241.

Woolhouse, L.S. and Bayne, R. (2000) 'Personality and the use of intuition: Individual differences in strategy and performance on an implicit learning task', *European Journal of Personality*, 14, pp. 157–169.

Wrap, H.E. (1957) 'Organization for long-range planning', *Harvard Business Review*, 35(1), pp. 37–47.

Wright, G. and Goodwin, P. (2002) 'Eliminating a framing bias by using simple instructions to "think harder" and respondents with managerial experience: Comment on "breaking the frame"', *Strategic Management Journal*, 23(11), pp. 1059–1067.

Wright, P.M., Snell, S.A. and Jacobsen, P.H. (2004) 'Current approaches to HR strategies: Inside-out versus outside-in', *People and Strategy*, 27(4), 36.

Yergin, D. (2011) *The Quest. Energy, Security and the Remaking of the Modern World*, New York: Penguin Books.

Yip, G.S. (1993) *Total Global Strategy: Managing for Worldwide Competitive Advantage*, London: Prentice Hall.

Yoshimori, M. (1995) 'Whose company is it? The concept of the corporation in Japan and the west', *Long Range Planning*, 28, pp. 33–45.

Zahra, S.A. and Pearce, J.A. (1989) 'Boards of directors and corporate financial performance: A review and integrative model', *Journal of Management*, 15, pp. 291–334.

Zajonc, R.B. (1980) 'Preferences need no inferences', *American Psychologist*, 35, pp. 151–175.

Zalesnik, A. (1977) 'Managers and leaders: Are they different?' *Harvard Business Review*, 55(3), pp. 67–78.

Zander, U. and Kogut, B. (1995) 'Knowledge and the speed of the transfer and imitation of organizational capabilities: An empirical test', *Organization Science*, 6(1), pp. 76–92.

Zhang, L.Q. and Baumeister, R.F. (2006) 'Your money or your self-esteem: Threatened egotism promotes costly entrapment in losing endeavors', *Personality and Social Psychology Bulletin*, 32(7), pp. 881–893.

Zollo, M. and Winter, S.G. (2002) 'Deliberate learning and the evolution of dynamic capabilities', *Organization Science*, 13(3), pp. 339–351.

Zott, C. and Amit, R. (2013) 'The business model: A theoretically anchored robust construct for strategic analysis', *Strategic Organization*, 11, pp. 403–411.

INDEX